COMMAND REFERENCE (m-z)

UNIX SVR4.2

Edited by Lynda Feng

UNIX
Press

Published by Prentice-Hall, Inc.
A Simon & Schuster Company
Englewood Cliffs, New Jersey 07632

IMPORTANT NOTE TO USERS

While every effort has been made to ensure the accuracy and completeness of all information in this document, USL assumes no liability to any party for any loss or damage caused by errors or omissions or by statements of any kind in this document, its updates, supplements, or special editions, whether such errors, omissions, or statements result from negligence, accident, or any other cause. USL further assumes no liability arising out of the application or use of any product or system described herein; nor any liability for incidental or consequential damages arising from the use of this document. **USL disclaims all warranties regarding the information contained herein, whether expressed, implied or statutory, including implied warranties of merchantability or fitness for a particular purpose.** USL makes no representation that the interconnection of products in the manner described herein will not infringe on existing or future patent rights, nor do the descriptions contained herein imply the granting of any license to make, use or sell equipment constructed in accordance with this description.

USL reserves the right to make changes to any products herein without further notice.

Certain pages contained in this document, which bear a notice that they are derived from material which is copyright (c) 1990 the Massachusetts Institute of Technology, are based on information contained in MIT's X Windows documentation. The following paragraph applies to those pages in their original form as provided by M.I.T.:

> "Permission to use, copy, modify, and distribute this documentation (*i.e., the original MIT and DEC material*) for any purpose and without fee is hereby granted, provided that the above copyright notice appears in all copies and that both that copyright notice and this permission notice appear in supporting documentation, and that the name of MIT or Digital not be used in advertising or publicity pertaining to distribution of the software without specific, written prior permission. MIT and Digital make no representation about the suitability of the software described herein for any purpose. It is provided 'as is' without expressed or implied warranty."

TRADEMARKS

UNIX is a registered trademark of UNIX System Laboratories, Inc. in the USA and other countries.
WE is a registered trademark of AT&T.
XENIX is a registered trademark of Microsoft Corporation.

10 9 8 7 6 5 4 3 2 1

ISBN 0-13-042607-5

P R E N T I C E   H A L L

ORDERING INFORMATION

UNIX® SYSTEM V RELEASE 4.2 DOCUMENTATION

To order single copies of UNIX® SYSTEM V Release 4.2 documentation, please call (515) 284-6761.

ATTENTION DOCUMENTATION MANAGERS AND TRAINING DIRECTORS:

For bulk purchases in excess of 30 copies, please write to:

Corporate Sales Department
PTR Prentice Hall
113 Sylvan Avenue
Englewood Cliffs, N.J. 07632

or

Phone: (201) 592-2863
FAX: (201) 592-2249

ATTENTION GOVERNMENT CUSTOMERS:

For GSA and other pricing information, please call (201) 461-7107.

Prentice-Hall International (UK) Limited, *London*
Prentice-Hall of Australia Pty. Limited, *Sydney*
Prentice-Hall Canada Inc., *Toronto*
Prentice-Hall Hispanoamericana, S.A., *Mexico*
Prentice-Hall of India Private Limited, *New Delhi*
Prentice-Hall of Japan, Inc., *Tokyo*
Simon & Schuster Asia Pte. Ltd., *Singapore*
Editora Prentice-Hall do Brasil, Ltda., *Rio de Janeiro*

Command Reference - Volume I

Introduction

Commands a - l

ld(1) .... (BSD) link editor, dynamic link editor
ldd(1) .... list dynamic dependencies
ldsysdump(1M) .... load system dump from floppy diskettes or cartridge tape
lex(1) .... generate programs for simple lexical tasks
lidload(1M) .... load distributed file system security database
line(1) .... read one line
link, unlink(1M) .... link and unlink files and directories
lint(1) .... a C program checker
listdgrp(1M) .... lists members of a device group
listen(1M) .... network listener port monitor
listusers(1) .... list user login information
ln(1) .... (BSD) make hard or symbolic links to files
ln(1) .... link files
loadpci(1M) .... starts the PC-Interface map server and connection server
localmail(1M) .... look up local mail names
lockd(1M) .... network lock daemon
logger(1) .... (BSD) add entries to the system log
login(1) .... sign on
logins(1M) .... list user and system login information
logname(1) .... get login name
look(1) .... (BSD) find words in the system dictionary or lines in a sorted list
lookbib(1) .... (BSD) find references in a bibliographic database
lorder(1) .... find ordering relation for an object library
lp, cancel(1) .... send/cancel print requests
lpadmin(1M) .... configure the LP print service
lpc(1M) .... (BSD) line printer control program
lpfilter(1M) .... administer filters used with the LP print service
lpforms(1M) .... administer forms used with the LP print service
lpmove(1M) .... move print requests
lpq(1) .... (BSD) display the queue of printer jobs
lpr(1) .... (BSD) send a job to the printer
lprm(1) .... (BSD) remove jobs from the printer queue
lprof(1) .... display line-by-line execution count profile data
lpsched, lpshut(1M) .... start/stop the LP print service
lpstat(1) .... print information about the status of the LP print service
lpsystem(1M) .... register remote systems with the print service
lptest(1) .... (BSD) generate lineprinter ripple pattern
lpusers(1M) .... set printing queue priorities
ls, lc(1) .... list contents of directory
ls(1) .... (BSD) list the contents of a directory

Permuted Index

Command Reference - Volume II

Introduction

Commands m - z

Permuted Index

Introduction

The UNIX System is widely praised for its broad set of flexible commands that give ordinary users far more power than other operating systems. This two-volume book contains a description of every UNIX System command in alphabetical order by command name, including the BSD® and XENIX® System variants. The Command Reference is part of a comprehensive reference set produced by the makers of UNIX System V Release 4 software. The set contains a manual page for every UNIX system interface.

Experienced UNIX system users will find the Command Reference indispensable. Readers who are familiar with another operating system, or any programming language, can rely upon the Command Reference to quickly become conversant with UNIX system commands. Those who are not familiar with any command interfaces should use the Command Reference in conjunction with some introductory tutorial material.

The Command Reference describes the superset of commands available on a fully loaded UNIX system. The most commonly used commands are available on all UNIX systems, but more specialized commands may be part of optionally installable software packages. If you cannot execute a command, first look in the directories where most commands reside to see if it is installed on your system. If you find it, try to execute it by typing the command's full pathname. If you still cannot execute it, verify that you have sufficient privileges to run it.

INTRODUCTION

Finding the Right Page

Reference books are handy when you know what command you are looking for, but less useful when you don't known what particular command to use. In such cases, the index (at the back of the book) can be helpful. Its middle column lists keywords and the manual pages on which they appear. Before you use the index, read the explanation that precedes it.

The SEE ALSO line at the bottom of each manual page cross-references related material, including manual pages in other books in the reference set. The Command Reference only contains commands — as opposed to system calls, file descriptions and so on. All commands are designated by a section number beginning with (1), such as (1), (1M), (1C), and (1F). System calls are designated with (2), libraries with (3), files with (4), miscellaneous pages with a (5), and special files with (7). The table on the inner front cover of this book lists the categories denoted by different section numbers, along with the books in which they are found.

The section 1 commands are further broken down into: (1), (1C), (1F), and (1M). The alphabetic appendages provide a clue about a command's purpose: (1) are general user's commands, (1C) are a subset of the networking commands, (1M) are system administration commands, and (1F) are Forms and Menu Language Interface commands.

When looking for a manual page, you will sometimes encounter multiple manual pages for a single command. For example, two manual pages are required when a UNIX system variant, such as XENIX or BSD, has a like-named command that behaves differently than its UNIX System V Release 4 counterpart. The behavior of such commands on your system depends on whether the XENIX or BSD compatibility software is installed.

Similarly, you may find two or more like-named manual pages for commands that function differently on different file system types. The UNIX system supports several types of file systems, including Veritas, UFS, and S5. (File systems are just methods of organizing data on a disk.) File system commands (such as `df`(1M)) may have some options that are valid for all file system types and other options that are only valid for a particular file system type. In such cases, a generic manual page describes the options that apply to all file system types, and a separate manual page describes options that apply to a particular file system.

In cases where there is more than one manual page for a single command, a top center header on the page indicates the distinction among the like-name pages.

Manual Page Format

All manual page entries use a common format, not all of whose parts always appear:

- The **NAME** section gives the name(s) of the entry and briefly states its purpose.
- The **SYNOPSIS** section summarizes the use of the command, program or function. A few conventions are used:
  - `Constant width typeface` strings are literals and are to be typed just as they appear.
  - *Italic* strings usually represent substitutable argument prototypes and functions.
  - Square brackets [ ] around an argument prototype indicate that the argument is optional. When an argument prototype is given as *name* or *file*, it typically refers to a file name.

- Ellipses . . . are used to show that the previous argument prototype may be repeated.
- For commands, an argument beginning with a minus – or plus + sign is often taken to be a flag argument, even if it appears in a position where a file name could appear. Therefore, it is unwise to have files whose names begin with – or +.

- The **DESCRIPTION** section describes the utility.
- The **EXAMPLE** section gives example(s) of usage, where appropriate.
- The **FILES** section gives the file names that are built into the program.
- The **SEE ALSO** section gives pointers to related information. Reference to manual pages with section numbers other than those in this book can be found in other reference manuals, as listed above.
- The **DIAGNOSTICS** section discusses the diagnostic indications that may be produced. Messages that are intended to be self-explanatory are not listed.
- The **NOTES** section gives generally helpful hints about the use of the utility.

NAME

`intro` – introduction to commands and application programs

DESCRIPTION

This section describes, in alphabetical order, commands, including user commands, programming commands and administrative commands.

There are several instances of multiple manual pages with the same name. For example, there are eight manual pages called **mount**(1M). In each such case the first of the multiple pages describes the syntax and options of the generic command, that is, those options applicable to all FSTypes (file system types). The succeeding pages describe the functionality of the FSType-specific modules of the command. These pages all display the name of the FSType to which they pertain centered and in parentheses at the top of the page. You should not attempt to call these modules directly - the generic command provides a common interface to all of them. Thus the FSType-specific manual pages should not be viewed as describing distinct commands, but rather as detailing those aspects of a command that are specific to a particular FSType.

Manual Page Command Syntax

Unless otherwise noted, commands described in the **SYNOPSIS** section of a manual page accept options and other arguments according to the following syntax and should be interpreted as explained below.

name [-*option*...] [*cmdarg*...]
where:

[ ]	Surround an *option* or *cmdarg* that is not required.
. . .	Indicates multiple occurrences of the *option* or *cmdarg*.
name	The name of an executable file.
option	(Always preceded by a "-".) *noargletter*... or, *argletter optarg*[**,**...]
noargletter	A single letter representing an option without an option-argument. Note that more than one *noargletter* option can be grouped after one "-" (Rule 5, below).
argletter	A single letter representing an option requiring an option-argument.
optarg	An option-argument (character string) satisfying a preceding *argletter*. Note that groups of *optargs* following an *argletter* must be separated by commas, or separated by white space and quoted (Rule 8, below).
cmdarg	Path name (or other command argument) *not* beginning with "-", or "-" by itself indicating the standard input.

Command Syntax Standard: Rules

These command syntax rules are not followed by all current commands, but all new commands will obey them. **getopts**(1) should be used by all shell procedures to parse positional parameters and to check for legal options. It supports Rules 3-10 below. The enforcement of the other rules must be done by the command itself.

1. Command names (*name* above) must be between two and nine characters long.
2. Command names must include only lower-case letters and digits.
3. Option names (*option* above) must be one character long.
4. All options must be preceded by "–".
5. Options with no arguments may be grouped after a single "–".
6. The first option-argument (*optarg* above) following an option must be preceded by white space.
7. Option-arguments cannot be optional.
8. Groups of option-arguments following an option must either be separated by commas or separated by white space and quoted (for example, `-o xxx,z,yy` or `-o "xxx z yy"`).
9. All options must precede operands (*cmdarg* above) on the command line.
10. "--" may be used to indicate the end of the options.
11. The order of the options relative to one another should not matter.
12. The relative order of the operands (*cmdarg* above) may affect their significance in ways determined by the command with which they appear.
13. "–" preceded and followed by white space should only be used to mean standard input.

DIAGNOSTICS

Upon termination, each command returns two bytes of status, one supplied by the system and giving the cause for termination, and (in the case of "normal" termination) one supplied by the program [see **wait**(2) and **exit**(2)]. The former byte is 0 for normal termination; the latter is customarily 0 for successful execution and non-zero to indicate troubles such as erroneous parameters, or bad or inaccessible data. It is called variously "exit code", "exit status", or "return code", and is described only where special conventions are involved.

NAME

m4 – macro processor

SYNOPSIS

m4 [*options*] [*files*]

DESCRIPTION

The **m4** command is a macro processor intended as a front end for C, assembler, and other languages. Each of the argument files is processed in order; if there are no files, or if a file name is –, the standard input is read. The processed text is written on the standard output.

The options and their effects are as follows:

-e Operate interactively. Interrupts are ignored and the output is unbuffered.

-s Enable line sync output for the C preprocessor (#line ...)

-B*int* Change the size of the push-back and argument collection buffers from the default of 4,096.

-H*int* Change the size of the symbol table hash array from the default of 199. The size should be prime.

-S*int* Change the size of the call stack from the default of 100 slots. Macros take three slots, and non-macro arguments take one.

-T*int* Change the size of the token buffer from the default of 512 bytes.

To be effective, the above flags must appear before any file names and before any **-D** or **-U** flags:

-D*name*[=*val*] Defines *name* to *val* or to null in *val*'s absence.

-U*name* undefines *name*.

Macro calls have the form:

name(*arg1*,*arg2*, ..., *argn*)

The (must immediately follow the name of the macro. If the name of a defined macro is not followed by a (, it is deemed to be a call of that macro with no arguments. Potential macro names consist of alphanumeric characters and underscore (_), where the first character is not a digit.

Leading unquoted blanks, tabs, and new-lines are ignored while collecting arguments. Left and right single quotes are used to quote strings. The value of a quoted string is the string stripped of the quotes.

When a macro name is recognized, its arguments are collected by searching for a matching right parenthesis. If fewer arguments are supplied than are in the macro definition, the trailing arguments are taken to be null. Macro evaluation proceeds normally during the collection of the arguments, and any commas or right parentheses that happen to turn up within the value of a nested call are as effective as those in the original input text. After argument collection, the value of the macro is pushed back onto the input stream and rescanned.

m4 makes available the following built-in macros. These macros may be redefined, but once this is done the original meaning is lost. Their values are null unless otherwise stated.

define the second argument is installed as the value of the macro whose name is the first argument. Each occurrence of **$***n* in the replacement text, where *n* is a digit, is replaced by the *n*-th argument. Argument 0 is the name of the macro; missing arguments are replaced by the null string; **$#** is replaced by the number of arguments; **$*** is replaced by a list of all the arguments separated by commas; **$@** is like **$***, but each argument is quoted (with the current quotes).

undefine removes the definition of the macro named in its argument.

defn returns the quoted definition of its argument(s). It is useful for renaming macros, especially built-ins.

pushdef like **define**, but saves any previous definition.

popdef removes current definition of its argument(s), exposing the previous one, if any.

ifdef if the first argument is defined, the value is the second argument, otherwise the third. If there is no third argument, the value is null. The word **unix** is predefined.

shift returns all but its first argument. The other arguments are quoted and pushed back with commas in between. The quoting nullifies the effect of the extra scan that will subsequently be performed.

changequote change quote symbols to the first and second arguments. The symbols may be up to five characters long. **changequote** without arguments restores the original values (that is,).

changecom change left and right comment markers from the default **#** and new-line. With no arguments, the comment mechanism is effectively disabled. With one argument, the left marker becomes the argument and the right marker becomes new-line. With two arguments, both markers are affected. Comment markers may be up to five characters long.

divert **m4** maintains 10 output streams, numbered 0-9. The final output is the concatenation of the streams in numerical order; initially stream 0 is the current stream. The **divert** macro changes the current output stream to its (digit-string) argument. Output diverted to a stream other than 0 through 9 is discarded.

undivert causes immediate output of text from diversions named as arguments, or all diversions if no argument. Text may be undiverted into another diversion. Undiverting discards the diverted text.

divnum returns the value of the current output stream.

dnl reads and discards characters up to and including the next new-line.

ifelse has three or more arguments. If the first argument is the same string as the second, then the value is the third argument. If not, and if there are more than four arguments, the process is repeated with arguments 4, 5, 6 and 7. Otherwise, the value is either the fourth string, or, if it is not present, null.

incr returns the value of its argument incremented by 1. The value of the argument is calculated by interpreting an initial digit-string as a decimal number.

decr returns the value of its argument decremented by 1.

eval evaluates its argument as an arithmetic expression, using 32-bit arithmetic. Operators include **+**, **-**, *, **/**, **%**, ** (exponentiation), bitwise **&**, |, ^, and ~; relationals; parentheses. Octal and hex numbers may be specified as in C. The second argument specifies the radix for the result; the default is 10. The third argument may be used to specify the minimum number of digits in the result.

len returns the number of characters in its argument.

index returns the position in its first argument where the second argument begins (zero origin), or –1 if the second argument does not occur.

substr returns a substring of its first argument. The second argument is a zero origin number selecting the first character; the third argument indicates the length of the substring. A missing third argument is taken to be large enough to extend to the end of the first string.

translit transliterates the characters in its first argument from the set given by the second argument to the set given by the third. No abbreviations are permitted.

include returns the contents of the file named in the argument.

sinclude is identical to **include**, except that it says nothing if the file is inaccessible.

syscmd executes the UNIX System command given in the first argument. No value is returned.

sysval is the return code from the last call to **syscmd**.

maketemp fills in a string of **XXXXX** in its argument with the current process ID.

m4exit causes immediate exit from **m4**. Argument 1, if given, is the exit code; the default is 0.

m4wrap argument 1 will be pushed back at final EOF; example: **m4wrap(cleanup( ))**

errprint prints its argument on the diagnostic output file.

dumpdef prints current names and definitions, for the named items, or for all if no arguments are given.

traceon with no arguments, turns on tracing for all macros (including built-ins). Otherwise, turns on tracing for named macros.

traceoff turns off trace globally and for any macros specified. Macros specifically traced by **traceon** can be untraced only by specific calls to **traceoff**.

SEE ALSO

as(1), **cc**(1)

NAME

mach – (BSD) display the processor type of the current host

SYNOPSIS

/usr/ucb/mach

DESCRIPTION

The mach command displays the processor-type of the current host.

SEE ALSO

arch(1), sysinfo(2), uname(1), uname(2)

NAME

mail, **rmail** – read mail or send mail to users

SYNOPSIS

Sending mail:

mail [**-tw**] [**-m** *message_type*] *recipient . . .*

rmail [**-tw**] [**-m** *message_type*] *recipient . . .*

Reading mail:

mail [**-ehpPqr**] [**-f** *file*]

Forwarding mail:

mail -F *recipient . . .*

Debugging:

mail [**-d**] [**-#**] [**-x***debug_level*] [*other_mail_options*] [*recipient . . .*]

mail -T *mailsurr_file recipient . . .*

DESCRIPTION

A *recipient* is usually a user name recognized by **login**(1). When *recipients* are named, **mail** assumes a message is being sent (except in the case of the **-F** option). It reads from the standard input up to an end-of-file (CTRL-d) or, if reading from a terminal device, until it reads a line consisting of just a period. When either of those indicators is received, **mail** adds the *letter* to the *mailfile* for each *recipient*.

A *letter* is composed of some *header lines* followed by a blank line followed by the *message content*. The *header lines* section of the letter consists of one or more UNIX postmarks followed by one or more standardized message header lines. The first UNIX postmark has the form:

> **From** *sender date_and_time* [**remote from** *remote_system_name*]

Any subsequent UNIX postmarks have the form:

> **>From** *sender date_and_time* [**remote from** *remote_system_name*]

Some older UNIX Systems may also generate postmarks of the form:

> **>From** *sender date_and_time* [**forwarded by** *user_name*]

The standardized message header lines have the form:

> *keyword-name***:** [*printable text*]

where *keyword-name* is comprised of any printable, non-whitespace, characters other than colon (':'). If there is text after the *keyword-name*, the colon must be followed by whitespace. A **Content-Length:** header line, indicating the number of bytes in the *message content* will always be present. A **Content-Type:** header line that describes the type of the *message content* (such as text, binary, multipart, etc.) will always be present unless the letter consists of only header lines with no message content. Header lines may be continued on the following line if that line starts with white space. **mail** processes supplementary code set characters according to the locale specified in the **LC_CTYPE** environment variable [see **LANG** on **environ**(5)].

The return address for a mail message is constructed by concatenating all of the *remote_system_names* found in the UNIX postmarks, top to bottom and separated with exclamation points, and then concatenating the *sender* found on the last UNIX postmark.

Sending mail:

The following command-line arguments affect sending mail:

- **-m** causes a **Message-Type:** line to be added to the message header with the value of *message_type*.
- **-t** causes a **To:** line to be added to the message header for each of the intended recipients.
- **-w** causes a letter to be sent to a recipient without waiting for the completion of the delivery.

If a letter is found to be undeliverable, it is returned to the sender with diagnostics that indicate the location and nature of the failure. The return address used will be the first domain-style address found on the **Sender:**, **From:** or **Errors-to:** headers. If no domain-style addresses are found, the return path generated from the UNIX postmark headers will be used.

If **mail** is interrupted during input, the message is saved in the file **dead.letter** to allow editing and resending. **dead.letter** is always appended to, thus preserving any previous contents. The initial attempt to append to (or create) **dead.letter** will be in the current directory. If this fails, **dead.letter** will be appended to (or created in) the user's login directory. If the second attempt also fails, no **dead.letter** processing will be done.

rmail only permits the sending of mail; **uucp**(1C) uses **rmail** as a security precaution. Any application programs that generate mail messages should be sure to invoke **rmail** rather than **mail** for message transport and/or delivery. **rmail** permits a mail message to begin with UNIX postmarks; **mail** does not. Both **rmail** and **mail** prepend a new UNIX postmark indicating the user who ran the command, as determined by the effective user ID.

If the local system has the Basic Networking Utilities installed, mail may be sent to a recipient on a remote system. There are numerous ways to address mail to recipients on remote systems depending on the transport mechanisms available to the local system. The two most prevalent addressing schemes are UUCP-style and Domain-style. With UUCP-style addressing, remote recipients are specified by prefixing the recipient name with the remote system name and an exclamation point (such as **sysa!user**). A series of system names separated by exclamation points can be used to direct a letter through an extended network (such as **sysa!sysb!sysc!user**). With Domain-style addressing, remote recipients are specified by appending an '**@**' and domain (and possibly sub-domain) information to the recipient name (such as **user@sf.att.com**). (The local System Administrator should be consulted for details on which addressing conventions are available on the local system.)

Reading Mail:

The following command-line arguments affect reading mail:

-e causes mail not to be printed. An exit value of 0 is returned if the user has mail; otherwise, an exit value of 1 is returned.

-h causes a window of headers to be initially displayed rather than the latest message. The display is followed by the '**?**' prompt.

-p causes all messages to be printed without prompting for disposition.

-P causes all messages to be printed with *all* header lines displayed, rather than the default selective header line display.

-q causes **mail** to terminate after interrupts. Normally an interrupt causes only the termination of the message being printed.

-r causes messages to be printed in first-in, first-out order.

-f *file* causes **mail** to use *file* (such as **$HOME/mbox**) instead of the default *mailfile*.

mail, unless otherwise influenced by command-line arguments, prints a user's mail messages in last-in, first-out order. The default mode for printing messages is to display only those header lines of immediate interest. These include, but are not limited to, the UNIX **From** and **>From** postmarks, **From:**, **Date:**, **Subject:**, and **Content-Length:** header lines, and any recipient header lines such as **To:**, **Cc:**, **Bcc:**, etc. After the header lines have been displayed, **mail** will display the contents (body) of the message only if it contains no unprintable characters. Otherwise, **mail** will issue a warning statement about the message having binary content and **not** display the content. (This may be overridden via the **p** command. See below.)

Only one invocation of **mail** is permitted to modify the mailbox at a time; other invocations are permitted to read the mail but will not update the mailbox.

For each message, the user is prompted with a **?**, and a line is read from the standard input. The following commands are available to determine the disposition of the message:

#	Print the number of the current message.
-	Print previous message.
<new-line>, **+**, or **n**	Print the next message.
!*command*	Escape to the shell to do *command*.
a	Print message that arrived during the **mail** session.
d, or **dp**	Delete the current message and print the next message.
d *n*	Delete message number *n*. Do not go on to next message.
dq	Delete message and quit **mail**.
h	Display a window of headers around current message.
h *n*	Display a window of headers around message number *n*.
h a	Display headers of all messages in the user's *mailfile*.
h d	Display headers of messages scheduled for deletion.
m *persons*	Mail (and delete) the current message to the named *person*(*s*).

M *persons*	Send mail to the named *person*(*s*), attaching a copy of the current message, then delete the current message.
n	Print message number *n*.
p	Print current message again, overriding any indications of binary (that is, unprintable) content.
P	Override default brief mode and print current message again, displaying all header lines.
q, or CTRL-d	Put undeleted mail back in the *mailfile* and quit **mail**.
r [*users*]	Reply to the sender, and other *user(s)*, then delete the message. The return address used will be the first domain-style address found on the **Reply-to:**, **From:** or **Sender:** headers. If no domain-style addresses are found, the return path generated from the UNIX postmark headers will be used.
R [*users*]	Reply to the sender, and other *user(s)*, attaching a copy of the current message, then delete the message. The return address used will be the first domain-style address found on the **Reply-to:**, **From:** or **Sender:** headers. If no domain-style addresses are found, the return path generated from the UNIX postmark headers will be used.
s [*files*]	Save message in the named *file*(*s*) (**$HOME/mbox** is default) and delete the message.
u [*n*]	Undelete message number *n* (default is last read).
w [*files*]	Save message contents, without any header lines, in the named *files* (**$HOME/mbox** is default) and delete the message.
x	Put all mail back in the *mailfile* unchanged and exit **mail**.
y [*files*]	Same as save.
?	Print a command summary.

When a user logs in, the presence of mail, if any, is usually indicated. Also, notification is made if new mail arrives while using **mail**.

The permissions of *mailfile* may be manipulated using **chmod** in two ways to alter the function of **mail**. The other permissions of the file may be read-write (0666), read-only (0664), or neither read nor write (0660) to allow different levels of privacy. If changed to other than the default (mode 0660), the file will be preserved even when empty to perpetuate the desired permissions. (The administrator may override this file preservation using the **DEL_EMPTY_MAILFILE** option of **mailcnfg**.)

The group id of the mailfile must be **mail** to allow new messages to be delivered, and the mailfile must be writable by group **mail**.

Forwarding mail:

The following command-line argument affects forwarding of mail:

-F *"recipients"*
Causes all incoming mail to be forwarded to *recipients*.

The **-F** option causes the file **/var/mail/:forward/***user* to contain a first line of:

Forward to *recipient...*

Thereafter, all mail sent to the owner of the *mailfile* will be forwarded to each *recipient*.

An **Auto-Forwarded-From: ...** line will be added to the forwarded message's header. This is especially useful in a multi-machine environment to forward all of a person's mail to a single machine, and to keep the recipient informed if the mail has been forwarded.

Installation and removal of forwarding is done with the **-F** invocation option. To forward all your mail to **systema!user** enter:

```
mail -F systema!user
```

To forward to more than one recipient enter:

```
mail -F 'user1, user2@xyz.com, systemc!systemd!user3'
```

Note that when more than one recipient is specified, the entire list should be enclosed in quotes so that it may all be interpreted as the operand of the **-F** option. The list can be up to 1024 bytes; either commas or white space can be used to separate users.

If the first character of any forwarded-to recipient name is the pipe symbol ('|'), the remainder of the line will be interpreted as a command to pipe the current mail message to. The command, known as a *Personal Surrogate*, will be executed in the environment of the recipient of the message (that is, basename of the *mailfile*). For example, if the mailfile is **/var/mail/foo**, **foo** will be looked up in **/etc/passwd** to determine the correct userID, groupID, and **HOME** directory. The command's environment will be set to contain only **HOME**, **LOGNAME**, **TZ**, **PATH** (= **/usr/bin:**), and **SHELL** (= **/usr/bin/sh**), and the command will execute in the recipient's **HOME** directory. If the message recipient cannot be found in **/etc/passwd**, the command will not be executed and a non-delivery notification with appropriate diagnostics will be sent to the message's originator.

After the pipe symbol, double quotes should be used to have strings with embedded whitespace be considered as single arguments to the command being executed. Backslashes (\) may be used to escape a double quote from being treated as such. No shell syntax or metacharacters may be used unless the command specified is **/usr/bin/sh**. For example,

```
mail -F '|/usr/bin/sh -c "shell_command_line"'
```

The user's mail box is locked while the personal surrogate is being executed, thus guaranteeing that only one personal surrogate command can execute at a time. It also means that any attempts to send mail to the user within the personal surrogate will fail.

Certain %keyletters are allowed within the piped-to command specification and will be textually substituted before the command line is executed.

%R Return path to the message originator.
%c Value of the **Content-Type:** header line if present.
%S Value of the **Subject:** header line if present.

If the command being piped to exits with any non-zero value, **mail** will assume that message delivery failed and will generate a non-delivery notification to the message's originator. It is allowable to forward mail to other recipients **and** pipe it to a command, as in

```
mail -F 'carol, joe, |myvacationprog %R'
```

If the first two characters of any forwarded-to recipient name are '>|', the remainder of the line will be interpreted as a personal surrogate, just as above, but the mail message will additionally be appended to the user's mailfile and the exit value from the program will be ignored. This is known as a *Post-processed Personal Surrogate.*

It is possible to control exactly how **mail** will treat different exit codes from the personal surrogate command. Following the | may be placed an exit code specification list which determines which exit codes are to be treated as indicating successful message delivery, which exit codes are to be treated as failed message delivery, and which exit codes are to indicate that mail should continue on and append the message to the user's mailfile. An exit code specification looks like **S=***ec***;C=***ec***;F=***ec***;**. In each case, *ec* is a list of numbers or ranges of numbers, separated by commas, or the wild card *. For example, the personal surrogate | **S=1-5,99;C=0,12;F=*;** *mysurrogate* **%R** will run the command, treating exit codes of 1 through 5 and 99 as a successful message delivery, exit codes of 0 and 12 as indicating continuing with local delivery, and all other exit codes indicating a failed message delivery.

If no exit code specification is given, the default for | is **S=0;F=*;** and the default for >| is **C=*;**.

Two UNIX System facilities that use the forwarding of messages to commands are **notify**(1), which causes asynchronous notification of new mail, and **vacation**(1), which provides an auto-answer capability for messages when the recipient will be unavailable for an extended period of time.

To remove forwarding enter:

```
mail -F ""
```

The pair of double quotes is mandatory to set a NULL argument for the –F option.

In order for forwarding to work properly the *mailfile* should have **mail** as group ID, and the group permission should be read-write.

mail will exit with a return code of **0** if forwarding was successfully installed or removed.

Debugging:

The following command-line arguments cause **mail** to provide debugging information:

-d *recipients . . .*
-# *recipients . . .*
The **-d** and **-#** options provide a trace, causing **mail** to display how a recipient name will be handled when delivering mail. The **-d** option shows how the mail to each mail recipient is treated, reflecting all address translations, while sending mail. The **-#** option does not send mail, but reports instead how the mail would be sent: the sender, the next machine to handle the mail, and the recipient's address relative to that machine. The report reflects address translation but does not follow any forwarded mail addresses.

-T *mailsurr_file* causes **mail** to display how it will parse and interpret the **mailsurr** file.

-x *debug_level* causes **mail** to create a trace file containing debugging information.

The **-T** option requires an argument that will be taken as the pathname of a test **mailsurr** file. If NULL (as in **-T ""**), the system **mailsurr** file will be used. To use, type '**mail -T** *test_file recipient*' and some trivial message (like "testing"), followed by a line with either just a dot ('.') or a CTRL-d. The result of using the **-T** option will be displayed on standard output and show the inputs and resulting transformations as **mailsurr** is processed by the **mail** command for the indicated recipient. Mail messages will never actually be sent or delivered when the **-T** option is used.

The **-x** option causes **mail** to create a file named **/tmp/MLDBG***process_id* that contains debugging information relating to how **mail** processed the current message. The absolute value of *debug_level* controls the verboseness of the debug information. Zero implies no debugging. If *debug_level* is greater than zero, the debug file will be retained **only** if **mail** encountered some problem while processing the message. If *debug_level* is less than zero the debug file will always be retained. The *debug_level* specified via **-x** overrides any specification of **DEBUG** in **/etc/mail/mailcnfg**. The information provided by the **-x** option is esoteric and is probably only useful to System Administrators. The output produced by the **-x** option is a superset of that provided by the **-T** option.

Delivery Notification

Several forms of notification are available for mail by including one of the following lines in the message header.

Default-Options: [*/options*]
Transport-Options: [*/options*]
>To: *recipient* [*/options*]

Where the "*/options*" may be one or more of the following:

/delivery Inform the sender that the message was successfully delivered to the *recipient*'s mailbox.

/nodelivery	Do not inform the sender of successful deliveries.
/ignore	Do not inform the sender of **un**successful deliveries.
/return	Inform the sender if mail delivery fails. Return the failed message to the sender.
/report	Same as **/return** except that the original message is not returned.

The default is **/nodelivery/return**. If contradictory options are used, the first will be recognized and later, conflicting, terms will be ignored. The **>To:** options have precedence over the **Transport-Options:** options, which in turn have precedence over the **Default-Options:** options. The default for mail coming from the user IDs **postmaster**, **mailer-daemon**, **mailer-demon**, **uucp** and **mmdf** is **/nodeliver/ignore**.

$HOME/mbox

The default file for saving mail is **$HOME/mbox**. If **$HOME/mbox** is a directory, then the file **$HOME/mbox/mbox** will be used instead. This permits **$HOME/mbox** to be a Multi-Level Directory, which is necessary if the Enhanced Security Utilities are installed. Consequently, multiple versions of **$HOME/mbox** will be maintained automatically, one for each security level at which mail is saved.

FILES

dead.letter	unmailable text
/etc/passwd	to identify sender and locate recipients
/etc/mail/mailsurr	routing and name translation information
/etc/mail/mailcnfg	initialization information
$HOME/mbox	saved mail
$MAIL	variable containing path name of *mailfile*
/tmp/ma*	temporary file
/tmp/MLDBG*	debug trace file
/var/mail/*.lock	lock for mail directory
/var/mail/:saved	directory for holding temp files to prevent loss of data in the event of a system crash.
/var/mail/:forward	directory for holding mail forwarding information.
/var/mail/:readlocks	directory for locks while reading mail.
/var/mail/*user*	incoming mail for *user*; that is, the *mailfile*
/usr/lib/locale/*locale***/LC_MESSAGES/uxemail**	language-specific message file [See **LANG** on **environ**(5).]

SEE ALSO

chmod(1), **login**(1), **mailcheck**(1), **mailcnfg**(4), **mail_pipe**(1M), **mailsurr**(4), **mailx**(1), **notify**(1), **vacation**(1), **write**(1)

NOTES

The "Forward to recipient" feature may result in a loop. Local loops (messages sent to **usera**, which are forwarded to **userb**, which are forwarded to **usera**) will be detected immediately. Remote loops (mail sent to **sys1!usera**1 which is forwarded to **sys2!userb**, which is forwarded to **sys1!usera**) will also be detected, but only after the message has exceeded the built-in hop count limit of 20. Both cases of forwarding loops will result in a non-delivery notification being sent to the message originator.

As a security precaution, the equivalent of a **chmod u+s** is performed on the forwarding file whenever forwarding is activated via the **-F** option. If the setUID mode bit is not set when **mail** attempts to forward an incoming message to a command, the operation will fail and a non-delivery report with appropriate diagnostics will be sent to the message's originator.

The interpretation and resulting action taken because of the header lines described in the Delivery Notifications section above will only occur if this version of **mail** is installed on the system where the delivery (or failure) happens. Earlier versions of **mail** may not support any types of delivery notification.

Conditions sometimes result in a failure to remove a lock file.

After an interrupt, the next message may not be printed; printing may be forced by typing a **p**.

NAME

mailalias – translate mail alias names

SYNOPSIS

mailalias [**-s**] [**-p**] [**-r**] [**-l**] [**-R**] [**-d**] [**-v**] *name* . . .

DESCRIPTION

mailalias is called by **mail** when delivering mail addressed to a local user name. Note that aliases affect all local mail delivered to the system. **mailalias** places on its standard output a list of mail addresses corresponding to *name*. The mail addresses are found by performing the following steps:

1. Look for a match in the user's local alias file **$HOME/lib/names**. If a line is found beginning with the word *name*, print the rest of the line on standard output and exit.

2. Look for a match in the system-wide alias files and directories, which are listed in the master path file **/etc/mail/namefiles**. For each file listed, if a line is found beginning with the word *name*, print the rest of the line on standard output and exit. Before searching in the file, **mailalias** looks for a hashed version of the file, which will be named the same thing as the file name with a **.s** appended to the end. If **mailalias** is being run from **mail**, and the hashed version is not found or is out of date, the hashed file will be recreated.

   If an alias file name is found to be a directory name, *dir*, then use the file *dir*/*name*. By default, **mailalias** looks for lines which begin with *name*; if the **-d** option is used, the entire file contents will be output.

   By default, the file **/etc/mail/namefiles** lists the alias file **/etc/mail/names** and the alias directory **/etc/mail/lists**.

3. Otherwise print *name* and exit.

The alias files may contain comments (lines beginning with **#**) and information lines of the form:

> *name list-of-addresses*

Tokens on these lines are separated by white-space. Lines may be continued by placing a backslash (\) at the end of the line.

When multiple names are being translated, each line of output will normally be prefixed with the name being translated. If the **-s** option is specified, the names being translated will never be prefixed with the name being translated. If the **-p** option is specified, each line of output will always be prefixed with the name being translated, even if only one name is being translated.

The **-r** option causes **mailalias** to recursively expand each name to its fullest extent.

The **-l** option causes **mailalias** to always use a linear search, ignoring any sorted files.

If the **-R** option is specified, **mailalias** will not attempt to recreate any sorted files. Sorted files which are out of date will be ignored.

The **-v** option causes debugging information to be written.

FILES

`$HOME/lib/names`	private aliases
`/etc/mail/namefiles`	list of files to search
`/etc/mail/names`	standard alias file to search
`/etc/mail/list`	standard alias directory to search

SEE ALSO

`mail`(1), **smtp**(1M), **smtpd**(1M), **smtpqer**(1M), **smtpsched**(1M), **uucp**(1C)

NAME

mailcheck – check for mail

SYNOPSIS

mailcheck [**-Z**]

DESCRIPTION

mailcheck checks for the existence of mail. Whenever it finds some, it prints a message on standard output:

```
You have mail
```

If the Enhanced Security Utilities are installed, **mailcheck** checks for mail at all security levels dominated by the user's current security level. For example, if you were logged in at *TopSecret*, you might see the message:

```
You have mail at level: TopSecret
You have mail at level: Unclassified
```

However, if you were logged in at *Unclassified* , you would only see the message:

```
You have mail at level: Unclassified
```

If there is no mail, it prints on standard error

```
No mail
```

By default, when the Enhanced Security Utilities are installed, **mailcheck** prints the level alias of the fully qualified levels dominated by the level at which the user is currently logged in. The **-Z** option forces **mailcheck** to print the fully qualified level instead of the alias. The **-Z** option is valid only when the Enhanced Security Utilities are installed.

mailcheck is commonly used in a person's **$HOME/.profile** as follows:

```
mailcheck 2>/dev/null
```

This prints a message when there is mail, and is otherwise silent.

EXIT CODES

0	mail exists at some level
1	no mail at any checked level
2	some error occurred

FILES

/var/mail	location of mail

SEE ALSO

mail(1)
User's Guide

mailinfo (1M)

NAME

mailinfo – extract mail configuration information

SYNOPSIS

mailinfo -d | **-n** | **-s** | **-u** | *configuration-parameter . . .*

DESCRIPTION

/usr/lib/mail/surrcmd/mailinfo provides access to mail configuration information. It recognizes the following options:

-d Print the domain name. The domain name may be set in the mail configuration file as **DOMAIN**, or come from the files **/etc/resolv.conf**, **/etc/inet/named.boot** or **/etc/named.boot**, or via the **sysinfo**(2) system call.

-n Print the full system name, which is the concatenation of the system name and the domain name.

-s Print the system name used by **mail**. This is the same as the **CLUSTER** mail configuration value, if set, else the **uname** network name.

-u Print the **uname** network name.

Any other argument is looked up in the mail configuration file.

FILES

/etc/mail/mailcnfg configuration information

SEE ALSO

mail(1), **sysinfo**(2), **uname**(2), **mailcnfg**(4)

NAME

maillog – standard mail logger

SYNOPSIS

maillog [**-f** *date_format*] [**-m** *mode*] [**-O** *original_recipient*] [**-o** *output_file*]
return_path recipient [*other_info* . . .] [— . . .]

DESCRIPTION

/usr/lib/mail/surrcmd/maillog is a standard mail logger that may be used within the surrogate file as a standard mail post processor. For example:

```
'.+'  '.+'  '> W=1;B=*; maillog -o /var/mail/:log'
        '-O %O %R %n %l --'
'.+'  '.+'  'Errors W=1;B=*; maillog -o /var/mail/:errors'
        '-O %O %R %n %l --'
```

maillog is approximately equivalent to

```
echo "'date' $1 -> $2  ($3 ...)" >> /var/mail/:log
```

maillog recognizes the following options:

-f Specify an alternate format to use for the date. *date_format* uses the format specifiers for **strftime**(3C).

-m Specify the mode of the *output_file*; the mode is modified to include group write permission to permit group **mail** to write to the file. (The mode used also does not include execute permission.)

-o Specify a filename to which to append the output. Otherwise the output is written to the standard output.

If the *output_file* does not exist, it will be created with mode 0660.

-O If *original_recipient* is specified and is different from the recipient name, it is recorded after the recipient name.

If an argument of -- is given, subsequent arguments are used as another recipient, complete with new options.

If the Enhanced Security Utilities are installed and running, **/var/mail** is a Multi-Level Directory; a separate log file is created for each Mandatory Access Control level at which mail is delivered.

SEE ALSO

mail(1), **strftime**(3C), **mailsurr**(4)

NAME

mailstats – (BSD) print statistics collected by sendmail

SYNOPSIS

/usr/ucb/mailstats [*filename*]

DESCRIPTION

mailstats prints out the statistics collected by the **sendmail** program on mailer usage. These statistics are collected if the file indicated by the **S** configuration option of **sendmail** exists. **mailstats** first prints the time that the statistics file was created and the last time it was modified. It will then print a table with one row for each mailer specified in the configuration file. The first column is the mailer number, followed by the symbolic name of the mailer. The next two columns refer to the number of messages received by *sendmail,* and the last two columns refer to messages sent by *sendmail.* The number of messages and their total size (in 1024 byte units) is given. No numbers are printed if no messages were sent (or received) for any mailer.

You might want to add an entry to **/var/spool/cron/crontab/root** to reinitialize the statistics file once a night. Copy **/dev/null** into the statistics file or otherwise truncate it to reset the counters.

FILES

/var/spool/cron/crontab/root
/dev/null

SEE ALSO

sendmail(1M)

NOTES

mailstats should read the configuration file instead of having a hard-wired table mapping mailer numbers to names.

NAME

mailx – interactive message processing system

SYNOPSIS

mailx [*options*] [*name* . . .]

DESCRIPTION

The command **mailx** provides a comfortable, flexible environment for sending and receiving messages electronically. When reading mail, **mailx** provides commands to facilitate saving, deleting, and responding to messages. When sending mail, **mailx** allows editing, reviewing and other modification of the message as it is entered. **mailx** processes supplementary code set characters according to the locale specified in the **LC_CTYPE** environment variable [see **LANG** on **environ**(5)].

Many of the remote features of **mailx** work only if the Basic Networking Utilities are installed on your system.

Incoming mail is stored in a standard file for each user, called the **mailbox** for that user. When **mailx** is called to read messages, the **mailbox** is the default place to find them. As messages are read, they are marked to be moved to a secondary file for storage, unless specific action is taken, so that the messages need not be seen again. This secondary file is called the **mbox** and is normally located in the user's **HOME** directory [see **MBOX** (ENVIRONMENT VARIABLES) for a description of this file]. Messages can be saved in other secondary files named by the user. Messages remain in a secondary file until forcibly removed.

The user can access a secondary file by using the **-f** option of the **mailx** command. Messages in the secondary file can then be read or otherwise processed using the same COMMANDS as in the primary **mailbox**. This gives rise to the notion of a current **mailbox**.

On the command line, *options* start with a dash (–) and any other arguments are taken to be destinations (recipients). If no recipients are specified, **mailx** attempts to read messages from the **mailbox**. Command-line options are:

-B	Unbuffer both input and output.
-d	Turn on debugging output.
-e	Test for presence of mail. **mailx** prints nothing and exits with a successful return code if there is mail to read.
-f [*filename*]	Read messages from *filename* instead of **mailbox**. If no *filename* is specified, the **mbox** is used.
-F	Record the message in a file named after the first recipient. Overrides the **record** variable, if set (see ENVIRONMENT VARIABLES).
-h *number*	The number of network "hops" made so far. This is provided for network software to avoid infinite delivery loops. This option and its argument is passed to the delivery program.
-H	Print header summary only.
-i	Ignore interrupts. See also **ignore** (ENVIRONMENT VARIABLES).

`-I`	Include the newsgroup and article-id header lines when printing mail messages. This option requires the **-f** option to be specified.
`-n`	Do not initialize from the system default *mailx.rc* file.
`-N`	Do not print initial header summary.
`-r` *address*	Use *address* as the return address when invoking the delivery program. All tilde commands are disabled. This option and its argument is passed to the delivery program.
`-s` *subject*	Set the Subject header field to *subject*.
`-T` *file*	Message-id and article-id header lines are recorded in *file* after the message is read. This option will also set the **-I** option.
`-t`	Read the **To:**, **Cc:** and **Bcc:** headers found on standard input to determine the list of recipients.
`-u` *user*	Read *user*'s **mailbox**. This is only effective if *user*'s **mailbox** is not read protected.
`-U`	Convert **uucp** style addresses to internet standards. Overrides the **conv** environment variable.
`-V`	Print the **mailx** version number and exit.
`-~`	Enable tilde escape commands when input is not coming from a terminal.

When reading mail, **mailx** is in *command mode*. A header summary of the first several messages is displayed, followed by a prompt indicating **mailx** can accept regular commands (see COMMANDS below). When sending mail, **mailx** is in *input mode*. If no subject is specified on the command line, a prompt for the subject is printed. As the message is typed, **mailx** reads the message and store it in a temporary file. When input is coming from a terminal (or the **-~** option has been used), commands may be entered by beginning a line with the tilde (~) escape character followed by a single command letter and optional arguments. See TILDE ESCAPES for a summary of these commands.

Only one invocation of **mailx** is permitted to modify the mailbox at a time; other invocations are permitted to read the mail but will not update the mailbox.

At any time, the behavior of **mailx** is governed by a set of *environment variables*. These are flags and valued parameters which are set and cleared via the **set** and **unset** commands. See ENVIRONMENT VARIABLES below for a summary of these parameters.

Recipients listed on the command line may be of three types: login names, shell commands, or alias groups. Login names may be any network address, including mixed network addressing. If mail is found to be undeliverable, an attempt is made to return it to the sender's *mailbox*.

If the recipient name begins with a pipe symbol (|), the rest of the name is taken to be a shell command to pipe the message through. This provides an automatic interface with any program that reads the standard input, such as **lp**(1) for recording outgoing mail on paper. Alias groups are set by the **alias** command (see COMMANDS below) and are lists of recipients of any type.

Regular commands are of the form

[*command*] [*msglist*] [*arguments*]

If no command is specified in *command mode*, **next** is assumed. In *input mode*, commands are recognized by the escape character, and lines not treated as commands are taken as input for the message.

Each message is assigned a sequential number, and there is at any time the notion of a current message, marked by a right angle bracket (>) in the header summary. Many commands take an optional list of messages (*msglist*) to operate on. The default for *msglist* is the current message. A *msglist* is a list of message identifiers separated by spaces, which may include:

`n`	Message number `n`.
`.`	The current message.
`^`	The first undeleted message.
`$`	The last message.
`*`	All messages.
`n-m`	An inclusive range of message numbers.
`user`	All messages from `user`.
`/string`	All messages with **`string`** in the subject line (case ignored).
`:`*c*	All messages of type *c*, where *c* is one of:

- `d` deleted messages
- `n` new messages
- `o` old messages
- `r` read messages
- `s` saved messages
- `u` unread messages

Note that the context of the command determines whether this type of message specification makes sense.

Other arguments are usually arbitrary strings whose usage depends on the command involved. File names, where expected, are expanded via the normal shell conventions [see **sh**(1)]. Special characters are recognized by certain commands and are documented with the commands below.

At start-up time, **mailx** tries to execute commands from the optional system-wide file (**/etc/mail/mailx.rc**) to initialize certain parameters, then from a private start-up file (**$HOME/.mailrc**) for personalized variables. With the exceptions noted below, regular commands are legal inside start-up files. The most common use of a start-up file is to set up initial display options and alias lists. The following commands are not legal in the start-up file: **!**, **be**dit, **bv**isual, **C**opy, **e**dit, **fo**llowup, **F**ollowup, **ho**ld, **m**ail, **pre**serve, **r**eply, **R**eply, **sh**ell, and **v**isual. An error in the start-up file causes the remaining lines in the file to be ignored. The **.mailrc** file is optional, and must be constructed locally.

COMMANDS

The following is a complete list of **mailx** commands:

comment
: Null command (comment). This may be useful in **.mailrc** files.

= Print the current message number.

? Prints a summary of commands, paged through the command specified by the **PAGER** variable. The default command is **pg -e**(1) (see ENVIRONMENT VARIABLES).

alias *alias name ...*
group *alias name ...*
: Declare an alias for the given names. The names are substituted when *alias* is used as a recipient. Useful in the **.mailrc** file. See also the **unalias** command.

alternates *name ...*
: Declares a list of alternate names for your login. When responding to a message, these names are removed from the list of recipients for the response. With no arguments, **alternates** prints the current list of alternate names. See also **allnet** (ENVIRONMENT VARIABLES).

Bprint [*msglist*]
: Equivalent to Print, except that non-text content may also be printed.

bprint [*msglist*]
: Equivalent to print, except that non-text content may also be printed.

btop [*msglist*]
: Equivalent to top, except that non-text content may also be printed.

bedit [*msglist*]
: Equivalent to edit, except that non-text content may also be edited.

bvisual [*msglist*]
: Equivalent to visual, except that non-text content may also be edited.

cd [*directory*]
chdir [*directory*]
: Change directory. If *directory* is not specified, **$HOME** is used.

copy [*filename*]
copy [*msglist*] *filename*
: Copy messages to the file without marking the messages as saved. Otherwise equivalent to the save command.

Copy [*msglist*]
: Save the specified messages in a file whose name is derived from the author of the message to be saved, without marking the messages as saved. Otherwise equivalent to the Save command.

delete [*msglist*]
Delete messages from the **mailbox**. If **autoprint** is set, the next message after the last one deleted is printed (see ENVIRONMENT VARIABLES).

discard [*header-field* ...]
ignore [*header-field* ...]
Note: **ignore/discard** has been superseded by **retain**; if both a retained header list and an ignored header list exist, the ignored header list will be ignored. Suppresses printing of the specified header fields when displaying messages on the screen. Examples of header fields to ignore are **status** and **cc**. The fields are included when the message is saved. The **P**rint and **T**ype commands override this command. If no header is specified, the current list of header fields being ignored will be printed. See also the **undi**scard and **unig**nore commands.

dp [*msglist*]
dt [*msglist*]
Delete the specified messages from the **mailbox** and print the next message after the last one deleted. Roughly equivalent to a **d**elete command followed by a **p**rint command.

echo *string* ...
Echo the given strings [like **echo**(1)].

edit [*msglist*]
Edit the given messages. The messages are placed in a temporary file and the **EDITOR** variable is used to get the name of the editor (see ENVIRONMENT VARIABLES). Default editor is **ed**(1).

exit
xit
Exit from **mailx**, without changing the **mailbox**. No messages are saved in the **mbox** (see also **q**uit).

file [*filename*]
folder [*filename*]
Quit from the current file of messages and read in the specified file. Several special characters are recognized when used as file names, with the following substitutions:

%	the current **mailbox**.
%*user*	the **mailbox** for *user*.
#	the previous file.
&	the current **mbox**.

Default file is the current **mailbox**.
If no file is specified, the current file name is printed.

folders
Print the names of the files in the directory set by the **folder** variable (see ENVIRONMENT VARIABLES).

followup [*message*]
followupall [*message*]
Respond to a message, recording the response in a file whose name is derived from the author of the message. Overrides the **record** variable, if set. The **followupall** command is not affected by the **flipf** variable (see ENVIRONMENT VARIABLES). See also the **Followup**, **Save**, and **Copy** commands and **outfolder** (ENVIRONMENT VARIABLES).

Followup [*msglist*]
Followupall [*message*]
Respond to the first message in the *msglist*, sending the message to the author of each message in the *msglist*. The subject line is taken from the first message and the response is recorded in a file whose name is derived from the author of the first message. The **Followupall** command is not affected by the **flipf** variable (see ENVIRONMENT VARIABLES). See also the **followup**, **Save**, and **Copy** commands and **outfolder** (ENVIRONMENT VARIABLES).

forward [*msglist*] [*name*]
Forward [*msglist*] [*name* ...]
Forward a message to the specified users. The message is treated as if it were read. If no message list is given, the current message is forwarded. With **forward**, the subject line is taken from the first message. The forwarded message is surrounded with the **forwardbegin**, **forwardprefix** and **forwardend** strings (or their defaults).

from [*msglist*]
Prints the header summary for the specified messages.

group *alias name ...*
alias *alias name ...*
Declare an alias for the given names. The names are substituted when *alias* is used as a recipient. Useful in the **.mailrc** file. See also the **unalias** command.

headers [*message*]
Prints the page of headers which includes the message specified. The **screen** variable sets the number of headers per page (see ENVIRONMENT VARIABLES). See also the **z** command.

Headers [*message*]
Prints the headers which would be printed by the **headers** command, printing one line per header field. This command is typically used by other programs, not a user.

help Prints a summary of commands.

hold [*msglist*]
preserve [*msglist*]
Holds the specified messages in the **mailbox**.

if *s* | *r*
mail-commands
else
mail-commands
endif Conditional execution, where *s* executes following *mail-commands*, up to an **el**se or **en**dif, if the program is in *send* mode, and *r* causes the *mail-commands* to be executed only in *receive* mode. Useful in the **.mailrc** file.

ignore [*header-field* ...]
discard [*header-field* ...]

Note: **ignore/discard** has been superseded by **retain**; if both a retained header list and an ignored header list exist, the ignored header list will be ignored. Suppresses printing of the specified header fields when displaying messages on the screen. Examples of header fields to ignore are **status** and **cc**. All fields are included when the message is saved. The **P**rint and **T**ype commands override this command. If no header is specified, the current list of header fields being ignored will be printed. See also the **undi**scard and **unig**nore commands.

inc
newmail

Incorporate new mail messages that arrive while you are reading the system mailbox. The new messages are added to the message list in the current *mail* session. This command does not commit changes made during the session, and prior messages are not renumbered. If **newmail** (ENVIRONMENT VARIABLES) is specified, new mail will be looked for before each prompt.

list Prints all commands available. No explanation is given.

mail *name* ...
mailall *name* ...

Mail a message to the specified users. The **maila**ll command is not affected by the **flipm** variable (see ENVIRONMENT VARIABLES).

Mail *name*
Mailrecord *name*

Mail a message to the specified user and record a copy of it in a file named after that user. The **Mailr**ecord command is not affected by the **flipm** variable (see ENVIRONMENT VARIABLES).

mbox [*msglist*]

Arrange for the given messages to end up in the standard **mbox** save file when **mailx** terminates normally. See **MBOX** (ENVIRONMENT VARIABLES) for a description of this file. See also the **ex**it and **q**uit commands.

New[*msglist*]
Unread [*msglist*]
unread [*msglist*]

Mark each message as not having been read. Each message in *msglist* will be treated as if it had never been seen before.

newmail
inc Incorporate new mail messages that arrive while you are reading the system mailbox. The new messages are added to the message list in the current *mail* session. This command does not commit changes made during the session, and prior messages are not renumbered. If **newmail** (ENVIRONMENT VARIABLES) is specified, new mail will be looked for before each prompt.

next [*message*]
Go to next message matching *message*. A *msglist* may be specified, but in this case the first valid message in the list is the only one used. This is useful for jumping to the next message from a specific user, since the name would be taken as a command in the absence of a real command. See the discussion of *msglists* above for a description of possible message specifications.

Pipe [*msglist*] [*shell-command*]
Pipe the message through the given *shell-command*, suppressing the fields specified by the **ig**nore command. The message is treated as if it were read. If no arguments are given, the current message is piped through the command specified by the value of the **cmd** variable. If the **page** variable is set, a form feed character is inserted after each message (see ENVIRONMENT VARIABLES).

pipe [*msglist*] [*shell-command*]
| [*msglist*] [*shell-command*]
Pipe the message through the given *shell-command*. The message is treated as if it were read. If no arguments are given, the current message is piped through the command specified by the value of the **cmd** variable. If the **page** variable is set, a form feed character is inserted after each message (see ENVIRONMENT VARIABLES).

preserve [*msglist*]
hold [*msglist*]
Preserve the specified messages in the **mailbox**.

Print [*msglist*]
Type [*msglist*]
Print the specified messages on the screen, including all header fields. Overrides suppression of fields by the **ig**nore command.

print [*msglist*]
type [*msglist*]
bprint [*msglist*]
Print the specified messages. If **crt** is set, the messages longer than the number of lines specified by the **crt** variable are paged through the command specified by the **PAGER** variable. The default command is **pg -e**(1) (see ENVIRONMENT VARIABLES). Unless it is suppressed by the **ig**nore command, the pseudo-header field **Message:** is printed before each message.

quit Exit from **mailx**, storing messages that were read in **mbox** and unread messages in the **mailbox**. Messages that have been explicitly saved in a file are deleted.

Reply [*msglist*]
Respond [*msglist*]
replysender [*message*]
Send a response to the author of each message in the *msglist*. The subject line is taken from the first message. If **record** is set to a file name, the response is saved at the end of that file (see ENVIRONMENT VARIABLES). The **Replysender** command is not affected by the **flipr** variable (see ENVIRONMENT VARIABLES).

reply [*message*]
respond [*message*]
replyall [*message*]
respondall [*message*]
Reply to the specified message, including all other recipients of the message. If **record** is set to a file name, the response is saved at the end of that file (see ENVIRONMENT VARIABLES). The **replyall/respondall** command is not affected by the **flipr** variable (see ENVIRONMENT VARIABLES).

retain *header-field ...*
Add the list of header fields named to the *retained list*. Only the header fields in the retain list are shown on your terminal when you print a message. All other header fields are suppressed. Examples of header fields to retain are **from, to, cc, bcc** and **subject**. The **Type** and **Print** commands can be used to print a message in its entirety. If **retain** is executed with no arguments, it lists the current set of retained fields. See also the **unretain** command.

Save [*msglist*]
Save the specified messages in a file whose name is derived from the author of the first message. The name of the file is taken to be the author's name with all network addressing stripped off. See also the **Copy**, **followup**, and **Followup** commands and **outfolder** (ENVIRONMENT VARIABLES).

save [*filename*]
save [*msglist*] *filename*
Save the specified messages in the given file. The file is created if it does not exist. The file defaults to **mbox**. The message is deleted from the **mailbox** when **mailx** terminates unless **keepsave** is set (see also ENVIRONMENT VARIABLES and the **exit** and **quit** commands).

set
set *name*
set *name=string*
set *name=number*
Define a variable called *name*. The variable may be given a null, string, or numeric value. **Set** by itself prints all defined variables and their values.

See ENVIRONMENT VARIABLES for detailed descriptions of the **mailx** variables.

shell [*shell-command*]
! [*shell-command*]
Escape to the shell. If no command is specified, invoke an interactive shell [see also **SHELL** (ENVIRONMENT VARIABLES)]. See **SHELL** (ENVIRONMENT VARIABLES).

showheaders [*msglist*] *header* ...
Show the given headers for the given message list. If no message list is given, the current message is examined. This command is typically used by other programs, not a user.

size [*msglist*]
Print the size in characters of the specified messages.

source *filename*
Read commands from the given file and return to command mode.

top [*msglist*]
Print the top few lines of the specified messages. If the **toplines** variable is set, it is taken as the number of lines to print (see ENVIRONMENT VARIABLES). The default is 5.

touch [*msglist*]
Touch the specified messages. If any message in *msglist* is not specifically saved in a file, it is placed in the **mbox**, or the file specified in the **MBOX** environment variable, upon normal termination. See **ex**it and **q**uit.

Type [*msglist*]
Print [*msglist*]
Print the specified messages on the screen, including all header fields. Overrides suppression of fields by the **ig**nore command.

type [*msglist*]
print [*msglist*]
Print the specified messages. If **crt** is set, the messages longer than the number of lines specified by the **crt** variable are paged through the command specified by the **PAGER** variable. The default command is **pg -e**(1) (see ENVIRONMENT VARIABLES).

unalias *alias* ...
Remove an alias for the given names (see **alias**). Takes a list of names defined by **alias** commands and discards the remembered groups of users. The group names no longer have any significance.

undelete [*msglist*]
Restore the specified deleted messages. Will only restore messages deleted in the current mail session. If **autoprint** is set, the last message of those restored is printed (see ENVIRONMENT VARIABLES).

undiscard *header-field ...*
unignore *header-field ...*
Remove the specified header fields from the list being ignored (see **ignore**).

Unread [*msglist*]
unread [*msglist*]
New[*msglist*]
Mark each message as not having been read. Each message in *msglist* will be treated as if it had never been seen before.

unretain *header-field ...*
Remove the specified header fields from the list being retained (see **retain**).

unset *name ...*
Causes the specified variables to be erased. If the variable was imported from the execution environment (i.e., a shell variable) then it cannot be erased.

version
Prints the current version.

visual [*msglist*]
Edit the given messages with a screen editor. The messages are placed in a temporary file and the **VISUAL** variable is used to get the name of the editor (see ENVIRONMENT VARIABLES).

write [*msglist*] *filename*
Write the given messages on the specified file, minus the header and trailing blank line. Otherwise equivalent to the **s**ave command.

xit
exit Exit from **mailx**, without changing the **mailbox**. No messages are saved in the **mbox** (see also **q**uit).

z[+ | –]
Scroll the header display forward or backward one screen–full. The number of headers displayed is set by the **screen** variable (see ENVIRONMENT VARIABLES).

TILDE ESCAPES

The following commands may be entered only from *input mode* when standard input is coming from a terminal, by beginning a line with the tilde escape character (~). See **escape** (ENVIRONMENT VARIABLES) for changing this special character.

~ **!** *shell-command*
Escape to the shell.

~ **.** Simulate end of file (terminate message input).

~ **:** *mail-command*
~_ *mail-command*
Perform the command-level request.

~? Print a summary of tilde escapes, paged through the command specified by the **PAGER** variable. The default command is **pg -e**(1) (see ENVIRONMENT VARIABLES).

~A Insert the autograph string **Sign** into the message (see ENVIRONMENT VARIABLES).

~a Insert the autograph string **sign** into the message (see ENVIRONMENT VARIABLES).

~b *names* ...
Add the *names* to the blind carbon copy (Bcc) list. This is like the carbon copy (Cc) list, except that the names in the Bcc list are not shown in the header of the mail message.

~c *names* ...
Add the *names* to the carbon copy (Cc) list.

~d Read in the **dead.letter** file. See **DEAD** (ENVIRONMENT VARIABLES) for a description of this file.

~e Invoke the editor on the partial message. See also **EDITOR** (ENVIRONMENT VARIABLES).

~f [*msglist*]
Forward the specified messages, or the current message being read if no *msglist* is given. Valid only when sending a message while reading mail. The messages are inserted into the message without alteration, as opposed to the **~m** escape. This command escape will insert message headers into the message with field selection affected by the **discard**, **ignore** and **retain** commands. See also **forwardbracket**, **forwardprefix**, **forwardbegin** and **forwardend** (ENVIRONMENT VARIABLES).

~F [*msglist*]
This will be the equivalent of the **~f** command, except that all headers will be included in the message, regardless of previous **discard**, **ignore** and **retain** commands. Valid only when sending a message while reading mail.

~h Prompt for the message header lines: Subject, To, Cc, and Bcc lists. If the field is displayed with an initial value, you may edit the text as if you had just typed it by backspacing over it and retyping.

~i *string*
Insert the value of the named variable into the text of the message. For example, **~A** is equivalent to "**~i Sign**." Environment variables set and exported in the shell are also accessible by **~i**.

~m [*msglist*]
Insert the specified messages, or the current message being read if no *msglist* is given, into the letter, shifting the new text to the right one tab stop. If **indentprefix** (ENVIRONMENT VARIABLES) is specified, that string will be used instead of a single tab stop. Valid only when sending a message while reading mail. This command escape will insert message headers into the

message with field selection affected by the **discard**, **ignore** and **retain** commands.

~M [*msglist*]
This will be the equivalent of the **~m** command, except that all headers will be included in the message, regardless of previous **discard**, **ignore** and **retain** commands. Valid only when sending a message while reading mail.

~p Print the message being entered. If **crt** is set, the message is paged through the command specified by the **PAGER** variable. The default command is **pg -e**(1) (see ENVIRONMENT VARIABLES).

~q
~Q Quit from input mode by simulating an interrupt. If the body of the message is not empty, the partial message is saved in **dead.letter**. See **DEAD** (ENVIRONMENT VARIABLES) for a description of this file.

~R Mark the message for return receipt. This inserts a **Default-Options** header with the */receipt* value. If the recipient system supports this option, a return receipt will be received.

~r *filename*
~< *filename*
~< !*shell-command*
Read in the specified file. If the argument begins with an exclamation point (!), the rest of the string is taken as an arbitrary shell command and is executed, with the standard output inserted into the message.

~s *string* ...
Set the subject line to *string*.

~t *names* ...
Add the given *names* to the To list.

~v Invoke a screen editor on the partial message. The name of the editor is specified by **VISUAL** (ENVIRONMENT VARIABLES).

~w *filename*
Write the message text into the given file, without the header.

~x Exit as with **~q**, but do not save the message in the **dead.letter** file.

~| *shell-command*
~^ *shell-command*
Pipe the body of the message through the given *shell-command*. If the *shell-command* returns a successful exit status, the output of the command replaces the message.

ENVIRONMENT VARIABLES

The following are environment variables taken from the execution environment and are not alterable within **mailx**.

HOME=*directory*
The user's home directory.

MAIL=*filename*
The name of the initial mailbox file to read. The default is the standard system mailbox **/var/mail/***username*.

MAILRC=*filename*
The name of the start-up file. Default is **$HOME/.mailrc**.

The following variables are internal **mailx** variables. They may be imported from the execution environment or set via the **set** command at any time. The **unset** command may be used to erase variables.

allnet
All network names whose user name component (login name) match are treated as identical. This will be the last component of a bang-style address, or the first component of a domain-style address. This causes the *msglist* message specifications to behave similarly. If **allnet** is set to **uucp**, then the system name must match as well. Default is **noallnet**. See also the **alternates** command and the **metoo** variable.

append
Upon termination, append messages to the end of the **mbox** file instead of prepending them. Default is **noappend.**

askatend
If set, the prompts for Cc and Bcc lists will be performed after the message has been entered instead of after the Subject is entered. See also **askcc** and **askbcc**.

askcc Prompt for the Cc list after the Subject is entered. Default is **noaskcc**. See also **askatend**.

askbcc
Prompt for the Bcc list after the Subject is entered. Default is **noaskbcc**. See also **askatend**.

asksub
Prompt for subject if it is not specified on the command line with the **-s** option. Enabled by default.

autoedit
Automatically edit a message, as in **~e**, after prompting for the subject, To list, Cc list and Bcc list. The variable **autoedit** is looked for after the variable **autovedit**. Default is **noautoedit**.

autoprint
Enable automatic printing of messages after **d**elete and **u**ndelete commands. Default is **noautoprint**.

autosign=*string*
The specified signature string is automatically appended to the body of each message that is sent. The value is echoed to the screen as it is appended. No default [see also **~i** (TILDE ESCAPES)].

autoSign=*string*
The specified signature string is automatically appended to the body of each message that is sent. No default. The variable inserted into the text of a message when the **~A** command is given. No default [see also **~i** (TILDE ESCAPES)].

autovedit
Automatically edit a message, as in **~v**, after prompting for the subject, To list, Cc list and Bcc list. The variable **autovedit** is looked for before the variable **autoedit**. Default is **noautovedit**.

bang Enable the special-casing of exclamation points (!) in shell escape command lines as in **vi**(1). Default is **nobang**.

cmd=*shell-command*
Set the default command for the **pipe** command. No default value.

conv=*conversion*
Convert uucp addresses to the address style specified by conversion, which can be either of the following:

internet
uucp(1C) address paths (bang-style) are converted into domain-style. For example, the address **mach1!mach2!user** becomes **user@mach2.UUCP**. This requires a mail delivery program conforming to the RFC822 standard for electronic mail addressing. The default **/bin/mail** is such a program. This is optional because some information is necessarily lost (e.g. the route it got here via) and if the host in not in the routing tables, the mail cannot be delivered.

optimize
Remove cycles and loops in **uucp**(1C) address paths (typically generated by the reply command). For example, the address **mach1!mach2!mach1!user** becomes **mach1!user** and **mach1!mach1!user** becomes **mach1!user**. No rerouting is performed as **mailx** has no knowledge of UUCP routes or connections.

Conversion is disabled by default. See also the **-U** command-line option.

crt=*number*
Pipe messages having more than *number* lines through the command specified by the value of the **PAGER** variable [**pg -e**(1) by default]. Disabled by default. If *number* is left off, it will default to *0*, meaning that all messages will be passed through the pager.

DEAD=*filename*
The name of the file in which to save partial letters in case of untimely interrupt. Default is **$HOME/dead.letter**.

debug Enable verbose diagnostics for debugging. Messages are not delivered. Default is **nodebug**.

dot Take a period on a line by itself during input from a terminal as end-of-file. Default is **nodot**.

editheaders
Include message headers in the text to be edited by the **~e** and **~v** commands. Enabled by default.

EDITOR=*shell-command*
The command to run when the **be**dit , **e**dit or **~e** command is used. Default is **ed**(1).

escape=*c*
Substitute *c* for the ~ escape character. Takes effect with next message sent.

flipf Swap the meanings of the **F**ollowup and the **f**ollowup commands.

flipm Swap the meanings of the **M**ail and the **m**ail commands.

flipr Swap the meanings of the **R**eply (**R**espond) and the **r**eply (**r**espond) commands.

folder=*directory*
The directory for saving standard mail files. User-specified file names beginning with a plus (+) are expanded by preceding the file name with this directory name to obtain the real file name. If *directory* does not start with a slash (/), **$HOME** is prepended to it. In order to use the plus (+) construct on a **mailx** command line, **folder** must be an exported **sh** environment variable. There is no default for the **folder** variable. See also **outfolder** below.

forwardbegin=string
Use the specified string above the text of forwarding messages. See the **forward** and **Forward** commands. Default is "**---- begin forwarded message ----**".

forwardbracket=
Use the **forwardbegin**, **forwardprefix** and **forwardend** strings (or their defaults) with the **~f** and **~F** commands as well as the **forward** and **Forward** commands.

forwardend=string
Use the specified string after the text of forwarded messages. See the **forward** and **Forward** commands. Default is "**---- end of forwarded message ----**".

forwardprefix=string
Use the specified string instead of the two characters "**>** " when forwarding messages. See the **forward** and **Forward** commands.

from A **From:** header is created on all outgoing messages, and the **Reply-To:** or **From:** headers will be examined to determine the return address when replying to a message. (These headers will only be treated as valid if they contain a domain-style address.) Enabled by default.

header
Enable printing of the header summary when entering **mailx**. Enabled by default.

hold Preserve all messages that are read in the **mailbox** instead of putting them in the standard **mbox** save file. Default is **nohold**.

ignore
Ignore interrupts while entering messages. Handy for noisy dial-up lines. Default is **noignore**.

ignoreeof
Ignore end-of-file during message input. Input must be terminated by a period (.) on a line by itself (if **dot** is enabled) or by the **~.** command. Default is **noignoreeof**. See also **dot** above.

indentprefix=string
Use the specified string instead of a single tab character when inserting messages into a letter. See the **~m** command.

iprompt=string
While in input mode, the specified string is displayed as a prompt for each line of input.

keep When the **mailbox** is empty, truncate it to zero length instead of removing it. Disabled by default.

keepsave
Keep messages that have been saved in other files in the **mailbox** instead of deleting them. Default is **nokeepsave**.

LISTER=*shell-command*
The command (and options) to use when listing the contents of the **folder** directory. The default is **ls**(1).

MAILX_HEAD=string
The specified string is included at the beginning of the body of each message that is sent.

MAILX_TAIL=string
The specified string is included at the end of the body of each message that is sent.

MBOX=*filename*
The name of the file to save messages which have been read. The **xit** command overrides this function, as does saving the message explicitly in another file. Default is **$HOME/mbox**. If **$HOME/mbox** is a directory, then **$HOME/mbox/mbox** will be used instead. This permits **$HOME/mbox** to be a Multi-Level Directory, which is useful if the Enhanced Security Utilities are installed. Consequently, multiple versions of **mbox** will be maintained automatically, one for each security level at which mail is saved.

metoo If your login appears as a recipient when responding or when doing alias expansion of more than one name, do not delete it from the list. Default is **nometoo**.

mprefix=string
Use the specified string instead of a single tab character when inserting messages into a letter. (Note: This variable is being replaced by the **indentprefix** string.)

mustbang
All mail addresses are forced into bang format.

netprecedence
When compares addresses for **allnet** and **metoo** processing, as well as removing duplicates, the addresses are normalized into an internal format before comparison. In order to do this, the relative precedences of the various networking characters must be taken into consideration. The **netprecedence** variable consists of a list of networking characters, each followed by the letter *l* or *r*, depending on if that networking character is left associative or right associative, respectively. The default is "**@r!l%r**".

newmail
Look for new mail before each prompt. Enabled by default.

no When used as a prefix to a variable name, has the effect of unsetting the variable, just like using the **unset** command.

onehop
When responding to a message that was originally sent to several recipients, the other recipient addresses are normally forced to be relative to the originating author's machine for the response. This flag disables alteration of the recipients' addresses, improving efficiency in a network where all machines can send directly to all other machines (i.e., one hop away).

outfolder
Causes the files used to record outgoing messages to be located in the directory specified by the **folder** variable unless the path name is absolute. Default is **nooutfolder**. See **folder** above, **record** below, and the **Save**, **Copy**, **followup**, and **Followup** commands.

page Used with the **pipe** command to insert a form feed after each message sent through the pipe. Default is **nopage**.

PAGER=*shell-command*
The command to use as a filter for paginating output. This can also be used to specify the options to be used. If not set, the default is **pg -e**(1). If set to an empty string, the default is **cat**(1).

postmark=string
The specified string is included in the comment field of the **From:** header of messages that you send. The string is usually set to your name. See **from** and **translate**. If the string includes an **@**, it will be used for the entire **From:** header.

`prompt`=*string*
Set the *command mode* prompt to *string*. Default is "`?` ".

`quiet` Refrain from printing the opening message and version when entering `mailx`. Default is `noquiet`.

`record`=*filename*
Record all outgoing mail in *filename*. Disabled by default. See also `outfolder` above. If you have the `record` and `outfolder` variables set but the `folder` variable not set, messages are saved in *+filename* instead of *filename*.

`save` Enable saving of messages in `dead.letter` on interrupt or delivery error. See `DEAD` for a description of this file. Enabled by default.

`screen`=*number*
Sets the number of lines in a screen–full of headers for the `headers` command. It must be a positive number.

`sendmail`=*shell-command*
Alternate command for delivering messages. Default is `/usr/bin/rmail`.

`sendwait`
Wait for background mailer to finish before returning. Default is `nosendwait`.

`SHELL`=*shell-command*
The name of a preferred command interpreter. Typically inherited from the environment, the shell is normally the one you always use. Otherwise defaults to `sh`(1).

`showto`
When displaying the header summary and the message is from you, print the recipient's name instead of the author's name.

`sign`=*string*
The string inserted into the text of a message when the `~a` (autograph) command is given. No default [see also `~i` (TILDE ESCAPES)].

`Sign`=*string*
The string inserted into the text of a message when the `~A` command is given. No default [see also `~i` (TILDE ESCAPES)].

`toplines`=*number*
The number of lines of header to print with the `top` command. Default is 5.

`translate`=*shell-command*
The name of a command used to translate mail addresses. The program will receive mail addresses as arguments. The program should produce, on standard output, lines containing the following data, in this order:

The postmark for the sender (see the `postmark`).

Translated mail addresses, one per line, corresponding to the program's arguments. Each translated address will replace the corresponding address in the mail message being sent.

A line containing only *y* or *n* . If the line contains *y* , the user will be asked to confirm that the message should be sent.

The translate program will be invoked for each mail message sent. If the program exists with a non-zero exit status, or fails to produce enough output, the message will not be sent.

VISUAL=*shell-command*
The name of a preferred screen editor. Default is **vi**(1).

FILES

$HOME/.mailrc	personal start-up file
$HOME/mbox	secondary storage file
$HOME/dead.letter	undeliverable messages file
/var/mail/*	post office directory
/usr/share/lib/mailx/*locale***/mailx.help***	help message files
/etc/mail/mailx.rc	optional global start-up file
/tmp/R[emqsx]*	temporary files
/usr/lib/locale/*locale***/LC_MESSAGES/uxemail**	language-specific message file [See **LANG** on **environ**(5).]
/var/mail/:readlocks	directory for locks while reading mail.

SEE ALSO

ed(1), **ls**(1), **mail**(1), **pg**(1), **vacation**(1), **vi**(1)

NOTES

The **-h** and **-r** options can be used only if **mailx** is using a delivery program other than **/usr/bin/rmail**.

Where *shell-command* is shown as valid, arguments are not always allowed. Experimentation is recommended.

Internal variables imported from the execution environment cannot be **unset**.

NAME

mail_pipe – invoke recipient command for incoming mail

SYNOPSIS

mail_pipe [**-x** *debug_level*] **-r** *recipient* **-R** *path_to_sender* **-c** *content_type* **-S** *subject*

DESCRIPTION

When a new mail message arrives, the **mail** command first checks the recipient's forwarding file, **/var/mail/:forward/***user*, to see if the message is to be forwarded elsewhere (to some other recipient or as the input to some command). If the message is to be piped into a recipient-specified command, **mail** invokes **mail_pipe** to do some validation and then execute the command in the context of the recipient.

Command-line arguments are:

-x *debug_level*	Turn on debugging for this invocation. See the description of the **-x** option for the **mail** command for details.
-r *recipient*	The recipient's login id.
-R *path_to_sender*	The return address to the message's originator.
-c *content_type*	The value of the **Content-Type:** header line in the message.
-S *subject*	The value of the **Subject:** header line in the message if present.

mail_pipe is installed as a privileged process thus enabling itself to change it's user and group ids to that of the recipient as necessary.

When invoked, **mail_pipe** performs the following steps (if a step fails, the exit code is noted as [*N*]):

- Validate invocation arguments [1].
- Verify that recipient name is ≤ 14 characters long [2].
- Verify that the setuid flag for the recipient mailbox is set and that the file is owned by the recipient [3].
- Open **/var/mail/***recipient* [4].
- Verify that recipient's mailbox starts with the string **Forward to** [5].
- Find command string (prefaced with either '|' or '>|') in the forwarding file [6].
- Find entry for recipient in **/etc/passwd** [7].
- Set gid to recipient's gid [8].
- Set uid to recipient's uid [9].
- Change current directory to recipient's login directory [10].
- Allocate space to hold newly **exec**'ed environment for recipient command [11].
- Parse the recipient command, performing any *%keyletter* expansions required. See the 'Forwarding mail' section of **mail**(1), for more information regarding *%keyletter* substitutions [12].
- Execute recipient command [13 if **exec** fails, otherwise exit code from recipient command itself].

FILES

/etc/passwd	to identify sender and locate recipients
/var/mail/:forward/*recipient*	forwarding information for *recipient*

`/var/mail/`*recipient*	incoming mail for *recipient*; that is, the mail file
`/tmp/MLDBG*`	debug trace file
`/usr/lib/mail/mail_pipe`	mail_pipe program

SEE ALSO

mail(1), **notify**(1), **vacation**(1)

NAME

make – maintain, update, and regenerate groups of programs

SYNOPSIS

make [**-f** *makefile*] [**-eiknpPqrstuw**] [*names*]

DESCRIPTION

make allows the programmer to maintain, update, and regenerate groups of computer programs. **make** executes commands in *makefile* to update one or more target *names* (*names* are typically programs). If the **-f** option is not present, then **makefile**, **Makefile**, and the Source Code Control System (SCCS) files **s.makefile**, and **s.Makefile** are tried in order. If *makefile* is **-**, the standard input is taken. More than one **-f** *makefile* argument pair may appear.

make updates a target only if its dependents are newer than the target. All prerequisite files of a target are added recursively to the list of targets. Missing files are deemed to be outdated.

The following list of directives can be included in makefiles to modify the behavior of **make**. They are used in makefiles as if they were targets:

.DEFAULT: If a file must be made but there are no explicit commands or relevant built-in rules, the commands associated with the name **.DEFAULT** are used if it exists.

.IGNORE: Same effect as the **-i** option.

.MUTEX: Serialize the updating of specified targets (see the "Parallel make" subsection, below).

.PRECIOUS:
Dependents of the **.PRECIOUS** entry will not be removed when quit or interrupt are pressed.

.SILENT: Same effect as the **-s** option.

The options for **make** are listed below:

-e Environment variables override assignments within makefiles.

-f *makefile* Description filename (*makefile* is assumed to be the name of a description file).

-i Ignore error codes returned by invoked commands.

-k Abandon work on the current entry if it fails, but continue on other branches that do not depend on that entry.

-n No execute mode. Print commands, but do not execute them. Even command lines beginning with an **@** are printed.

-p Print out the complete set of macro definitions and target descriptions.

-P Update in parallel more than one target at a time. The number of targets updated concurrently is determined by the environment variable **PARALLEL** and the presence of **.MUTEX** directives in makefiles.

`-q` Question. **make** returns a zero or non-zero status code depending on whether or not the target file has been updated.

`-r` Do not use the built-in rules.

`-s` Silent mode. Do not print command lines before executing.

`-t` Touch the target files (causing them to be updated) rather than issue the usual commands.

`-u` Unconditionally **make** the target, ignoring all timestamps.

`-w` Suppress warning messages. Fatal messages will not be affected.

Creating the makefile

The makefile invoked with the `-f` option (or accessed by default) is a carefully structured file of explicit instructions for updating and regenerating programs, and contains a sequence of entries that specify dependencies. The first line of an entry is a blank-separated, non-null list of targets, then a `:`, then a (possibly null) list of prerequisite files or dependencies. Text following a `;` and all following lines that begin with a tab are shell commands to be executed to update the target. The first non-empty line that does not begin with a tab or `#` begins a new dependency or macro definition. Shell commands may be continued across lines with a backslash-new-line (\ new-line) sequence. Everything printed by make (except the initial tab) is passed directly to the shell as is. Thus,

```
echo a\
b
```

will produce

```
ab
```

exactly the same as the shell would.

Sharp (`#`) and new-line surround comments including contained \ new-line sequences.

The following makefile says that **pgm** depends on two files **a.o** and **b.o**, and that they in turn depend on their corresponding source files (**a.c** and **b.c**) and a common file **incl.h**:

```
pgm: a.o b.o
     cc a.o b.o -o pgm
a.o: incl.h a.c
     cc -c a.c
b.o: incl.h b.c
     cc -c b.c
```

Command lines are executed one at a time, each by its own shell. The **SHELL** environment variable can be used to specify which shell **make** should use to execute commands. The default is **/usr/bin/sh**. The first one or two characters in a command can be the following: `@`, `-`, `@-`, or `-@`. If `@` is present, printing of the command is suppressed. If `-` is present, **make** ignores an error. A line is printed when it is executed unless the `-s` option is present, or the entry **.SILENT:** is included in the makefile, or unless the initial character sequence contains a `@`. The `-n` option specifies printing without execution; however, if the command line has the string **$(MAKE)** in it, the line is always executed (see the discussion of the **MAKEFLAGS** macro in the "Environment" section below). The -t (touch) option updates the modified date of a file without executing any commands.

Commands returning non-zero status normally terminate **make**. If the -i option is present, if the entry .IGNORE: is included in the makefile, or if the initial character sequence of the command contains -, the error is ignored. If the -k option is present, work is abandoned on the current entry, but continues on other branches that do not depend on that entry.

Interrupt and quit cause the target to be deleted unless the target is a dependent of the directive .PRECIOUS.

Parallel make

If **make** is invoked with the -P option, it tries to build more than one target at a time, in parallel. (This is done by using the standard UNIX system process mechanism which enables multiple processes to run simultaneously.) For the makefile shown in the example in the previous section, it would create processes to build a.o and b.o in parallel. After these processes were complete, it would build pgm.

The number of targets **make** will try to build in parallel is determined by the value of the environment variable PARALLEL. If -P is invoked, but PARALLEL is not set, then **make** will try to build no more than two targets in parallel.

You can use the .MUTEX directive to serialize the updating of some specified targets. This is useful when two or more targets modify a common output file, such as when inserting modules into an archive or when creating an intermediate file with the same name, as is done by **lex** and **yacc**. If the makefile in the previous section contained a .MUTEX directive of the form

```
.MUTEX: a.o b.o
```

it would prevent **make** from building a.o and b.o in parallel.

Environment

The environment is read by **make**. All variables are assumed to be macro definitions and are processed as such. The environment variables are processed before any makefile and after the internal rules; thus, macro assignments in a makefile override environment variables. The -e option causes the environment to override the macro assignments in a makefile. Suffixes and their associated rules in the makefile will override any identical suffixes in the built-in rules.

The MAKEFLAGS environment variable is processed by **make** as containing any legal input option (except -f, -p and -r) defined for the command line. Further, upon invocation, **make** "invents" the variable if it is not in the environment, puts the current options into it, and passes it on to invocations of commands. Thus, MAKEFLAGS always contains the current input options. This feature proves very useful for "super-makes". In fact, as noted above, when the -n option is used, the command $(MAKE) is executed anyway; hence, one can perform a **make -n** recursively on a whole software system to see what would have been executed. This result is possible because the -n is put in MAKEFLAGS and passed to further invocations of $(MAKE). This usage is one way of debugging all of the makefiles for a software project without actually doing anything.

Include Files

If the string **include** appears as the first seven letters of a line in a makefile, and is followed by a blank or a tab, the rest of the line is assumed to be a filename and will be read by the current invocation, after substituting for any macros.

Macros

Entries of the form *string1* = *string2* are macro definitions. *string2* is defined as all characters up to a comment character or an unescaped new-line. Subsequent appearances of $(*string1*[:*subst1*=[*subst2*]]) are replaced by *string2*. The parentheses are optional if a single-character macro name is used and there is no substitute sequence. The optional :*subst1*=*subst2* is a substitute sequence. If it is specified, all non-overlapping occurrences of *subst1* in the named macro are replaced by *subst2*. Strings (for the purposes of this type of substitution) are delimited by blanks, tabs, new-line characters, and beginnings of lines. An example of the use of the substitute sequence is shown in the "Libraries" section below.

Internal Macros

There are five internally maintained macros that are useful for writing rules for building targets.

$*** The macro **$* stands for the filename part of the current dependent with the suffix deleted. It is evaluated only for inference rules.

$@** The **$@ macro stands for the full target name of the current target. It is evaluated only for explicitly named dependencies.

$<** The **$< macro is only evaluated for inference rules or the **.DEFAULT** rule. It is the module that is outdated with respect to the target (the "manufactured" dependent file name). Thus, in the **.c.o** rule, the **$<** macro would evaluate to the **.c** file. An example for making optimized **.o** files from **.c** files is:

```
.c.o:
        cc -c -O $*.c
```

or:

```
.c.o:
        cc -c -O $<
```

$?** The **$? macro is evaluated when explicit rules from the makefile are evaluated. It is the list of prerequisites that are outdated with respect to the target, and essentially those modules that must be rebuilt.

$% The **$%** macro is only evaluated when the target is an archive library member of the form **lib(file.o)**. In this case, **$@** evaluates to **lib** and **$%** evaluates to the library member, **file.o**.

Four of the five macros can have alternative forms. When an upper case **D** or **F** is appended to any of the four macros, the meaning is changed to "directory part" for **D** and "file part" for **F**. Thus, **$(@D)** refers to the directory part of the string **$@**. If there is no directory part, **./** is generated. The only macro excluded from this alternative form is **$?**.

Suffixes

Certain names (for instance, those ending with **.o**) have inferable prerequisites such as **.c**, **.s**, and so on. If no update commands for such a file appear in the makefile, and if an inferable prerequisite exists, that prerequisite is compiled to make the target. In this case, **make** has inference rules that allow building files from other files by examining the suffixes and determining an appropriate inference rule to use. The current default inference rules are:

.c	.c~	.f	.f~	.s	.s~	.sh	.sh~	.C	.C~
.c.a	.c.o	.c~.a	.c~.c	.c~.o	.f.a	.f.o	.f~.a	.f~.f	.f~.o
.h~.h	.l.c	.l.o	.l~.c	.l~.l	.l~.o	.s.a	.s.o	.s~.a	.s~.o
.s~.s	.sh~.sh	.y.c	.y.o	.y~.c	.y~.o	.y~.y	.C.a	.C.o	.C~.a
.C~.C	.C~.o	.L.C	.L.o	.L~.C	.L~.L	.L~.o	.Y.C	.Y.o	.Y~.C
.Y~.o	.Y~.Y								

The internal rules for **make** are contained in the source file `rules.c` for the **make** program. These rules can be locally modified. To print out the rules compiled into the **make** on any machine in a form suitable for recompilation, the following command is used:

```
make -pf - 2>/dev/null </dev/null
```

A tilde in the above rules refers to an SCCS file [see **sccsfile**(4)]. Thus, the rule `.c~.o` would transform an SCCS C source file into an object file (`.o`). Because the `s.` of the SCCS files is a prefix, it is incompatible with the **make** suffix point of view. Hence, the tilde is a way of changing any file reference into an SCCS file reference.

A rule with only one suffix (for example, `.c:`) is the definition of how to build *x* from *x*`.c`. In effect, the other suffix is null. This feature is useful for building targets from only one source file, for example, shell procedures and simple C programs.

Additional suffixes are given as the dependency list for **.SUFFIXES**. Order is significant: the first possible name for which both a file and a rule exist is inferred as a prerequisite. The default list is:

```
.SUFFIXES: .o .c .c~ .y .y~ .l .l~ .s .s~ .sh .sh~ .h .h~ .f .f~ .C
.C~ .Y .Y~ .L .L~
```

Here again, the above command for printing the internal rules will display the list of suffixes implemented on the current machine. Multiple suffix lists accumulate; **.SUFFIXES:** with no dependencies clears the list of suffixes.

Inference Rules

The first example can be done more briefly.

```
pgm: a.o b.o
        cc a.o b.o -o pgm
a.o b.o: incl.h
```

This abbreviation is possible because **make** has a set of internal rules for building files. The user may add rules to this list by simply putting them in the makefile.

Certain macros are used by the default inference rules to permit the inclusion of optional matter in any resulting commands. For example, **CFLAGS**, **LFLAGS**, and **YFLAGS** are used for compiler options to **cc**(1), **lex**(1), and **yacc**(1), respectively. Again, the previous method for examining the current rules is recommended.

The inference of prerequisites can be controlled. The rule to create a file with suffix **.o** from a file with suffix **.c** is specified as an entry with **.c.o:** as the target and no dependents. Shell commands associated with the target define the rule for making a **.o** file from a **.c** file. Any target that has no slashes in it and starts with a dot is identified as a rule and not a true target.

Libraries

If a target or dependency name contains parentheses, it is assumed to be an archive library, the string within parentheses referring to a member within the library. Thus, **lib(file.o)** and **$(LIB)(file.o)** both refer to an archive library that contains **file.o**. (This example assumes the **LIB** macro has been previously defined.)The expression **$(LIB)(file1.o file2.o)** is not legal. Rules pertaining to archive libraries have the form **.*XX*.a** where the *XX* is the suffix from which the archive member is to be made. An unfortunate by-product of the current implementation requires the *XX* to be different from the suffix of the archive member. Thus, one cannot have **lib(file.o)** depend upon **file.o** explicitly. The most common use of the archive interface follows. Here, we assume the source files are all C type source:

```
lib:     lib(file1.o) lib(file2.o) lib(file3.o)
         @echo lib is now up-to-date
.c.a:
         $(CC) -c $(CFLAGS) $<
         $(AR) $(ARFLAGS) $@ $(<F:.c=.o)
         rm -f $(<F:.c=.o)
```

In fact, the **.c.a** rule listed above is built into **make** and is unnecessary in this example. A more interesting, but more limited example of an archive library maintenance construction follows:

```
lib:     lib(file1.o) lib(file2.o) lib(file3.o)
         $(CC) -c $(CFLAGS) $(?:.o=.c)
         $(AR) $(ARFLAGS) lib $?
         rm $?
         @echo lib is now up-to-date
.c.a:;
```

Here the substitution mode of the macro expansions is used. The **$?** list is defined to be the set of object filenames (inside **lib**) whose C source files are outdated. The substitution mode translates the **.o** to **.c**. (Unfortunately, one cannot as yet transform to **.c~**; however, this transformation may become possible in the future.) Also note the disabling of the **.c.a:** rule, which would have created each object file, one by one. This particular construct speeds up archive library maintenance considerably. This type of construct becomes very cumbersome if the archive library contains a mix of assembly programs and C programs.

FILES

[Mm]akefile and **s.[Mm]akefile**
/usr/bin/sh

SEE ALSO

cc(1), cd(1), lex(1), printf(3S), sccsfile(4), sh(1), yacc(1)

NOTES

Some commands return non-zero status inappropriately; use -i or the - command line prefix to overcome the difficulty.

Filenames with the characters = : @ will not work. Commands that are directly executed by the shell, notably cd(1), are ineffectual across new-lines in make. The syntax lib(file1.o file2.o file3.o) is illegal. You cannot build lib(file.o) from file.o.

makedbm (1M)

NAME

makedbm – make a Network Information Service (NIS) dbm file

SYNOPSIS

/usr/sbin/makedbm [**-l**] [**-s**] [**-i** *yp_input_file*] [**-o** *yp_output_name*]
[**-d** *yp_domain_name*] [**-m** *yp_master_name*] *infile outfile*

makedbm [**-u** *dbmfilename*]

DESCRIPTION

The **makedbm** command takes *infile* and converts it to a pair of files in **dbm**(3) format, namely *outfile*.**pag** and *outfile*.**dir**. Each line of the input file is converted to a single **dbm** record. All characters up to the first TAB or SPACE form the key, and the rest of the line is the data. If a line ends with '\', then the data for that record is continued on to the next line. It is left for NIS clients to interpret '**#**'; **makedbm** does not itself treat it as a comment character. *infile* can be '–', in which case the standard input is read.

makedbm is meant to be used in generating **dbm** files for NIS and it generates a special entry with the key *yp_last_modified*, which is the date of *infile* (or the current time, if *infile* is '–').

The following options are available:

-l Lowercase. Convert the keys of the given map to lower case, so that host name matches, for example, can work independent of upper or lower case distinctions.

-s Secure map. Accept connections from secure NIS networks only.

-i *yp_input_file*
Create a special entry with the key *yp_input_file*.

-o *yp_output_name*
Create a special entry with the key *yp_output_name*.

-d *yp_domain_name*
Create a special entry with the key *yp_domain_name*.

-m *yp_master_name*
Create a special entry with the key *yp_master_name*. If no master host name is specified, *yp_master_name* will be set to the local host name.

-u *dbmfilename*
Undo a **dbm** file. That is, print out a **dbm** file one entry per line, with a single space separating keys from values.

SEE ALSO

dbm(3)

NAME

makekey – generate encryption key

SYNOPSIS

/usr/lib/makekey

DESCRIPTION

makekey improves the usefulness of encryption schemes depending on a key by increasing the amount of time required to search the key space. It attempts to read eight bytes for its *key* (the first eight input bytes), then it attempts to read two bytes for its *salt* (the last two input bytes). The output depends on the input in a way intended to be difficult to compute (that is, to require a substantial fraction of a second).

The first eight input bytes (the *input key*) can be arbitrary ASCII characters. The last two (the *salt*) are best chosen from the set of digits, **.**, **/**, and upper- and lower-case letters. The salt characters are repeated as the first two characters of the output. The remaining 11 output characters are chosen from the same set as the salt and constitute the *output key*.

The transformation performed is essentially the following: the salt is used to select one of 4,096 cryptographic machines all based on the National Bureau of Standards DES algorithm, but broken in 4,096 different ways. Using the *input key* as key, a constant string is fed into the machine and recirculated a number of times. The 64 bits that come out are distributed into the 66 *output key* bits in the result.

makekey is intended for programs that perform encryption. Usually, its input and output will be pipes.

SEE ALSO

crypt(1), **ed**(1), **passwd**(4), **vi**(1)

NOTES

makekey can produce different results depending upon whether the input is typed at the terminal or redirected from a file.

This command is provided with the Encryption Utilities, which is only available in the United States.

make-owner (1M)

NAME

`make-owner` - add, remove, or change ID of a privileged user

SYNOPSIS

make-owner *new-owner*

make-owner *old-owner new-owner*

make-owner - *old-owner*

DESCRIPTION

The **make-owner** command adds, removes, or transfers owner permissions and adds and removes entrys from the TFM database. It is normally invoked through the UNIX Desktop User Setup window.

make-owner *new-owner*
: add *new-owner* to the database

make-owner *old-owner new-owner*
: transfer owner permissions from *old-owner* to *new-owner*

make-owner - *old-owner*
: removes *old-owner* from the database

Only an owner is allowed to add or remove user accounts, grant privileges to other user accounts, and backup and restore all files on the system.

Files

/etc/security/tfm/users/*user*
/usr/X/desktop/LoginMgr/PrivTable read only
/usr/X/desktop/LoginMgr/Users/*user*

USAGE

make-owner resides in **/usr/X/adm**. Since the **PATH** environment variable does not normally include that path, either specify the full pathname or add **/usr/X/adm** to the **PATH** variable.

Examples

SEE ALSO

adminuser(1M), **dtadduser**(1M), **dtdeluser**(1M), **tfadmin**(1M)

NAME

man – (BSD) display reference manual pages; find reference pages by keyword

SYNOPSIS

/usr/ucb/man [**–**] [**–t**] [**–M** *path*] [**–T** *macro-package*] [[*section*] *title* . . .] *title* . . .
/usr/ucb/man [**–M** *path*] **–k** *keyword* . . .
/usr/ucb/man [**–M** *path*] **–f** *file* . . .

DESCRIPTION

The **man** command displays information from the reference manuals. It can display complete manual pages that you select by *title*, or one-line summaries selected either by *keyword* (**–k**), or by the name of an associated file (**–f**).

A *section*, when given, applies to the *titles* that follow it on the command line (up to the next *section*, if any). **man** looks in the indicated section of the manual for those *title*s. *section* is either a digit (perhaps followed by a single letter indicating the type of manual page), or one of the words **new**, **local**, **old**, or **public**. If *section* is omitted, **man** searches all reference sections (giving preference to commands over functions) and prints the first manual page it finds. If no manual page is located, **man** prints an error message.

The reference page sources are typically located in the **/usr/share/man/man?** directories. Since these directories are optionally installed, they may not reside on your host; you may have to mount **/usr/share/man** from a host on which they do reside. If there are preformatted, up-to-date versions in corresponding **cat?** or **fmt?** directories, **man** simply displays or prints those versions. If the preformatted version of interest is out of date or missing, **man** reformats it prior to display. If directories for the preformatted versions are not provided, **man** reformats a page whenever it is requested; it uses a temporary file to store the formatted text during display.

If the standard output is not a terminal, or if the **–** flag is given, **man** pipes its output through **cat**. Otherwise, **man** pipes its output through **more** to handle paging and underlining on the screen.

The following options are available:

–t **man** arranges for the specified manual pages to be **troff**ed to a suitable raster output device (see **troff**). If both the **–** and **–t** flags are given, **man** updates the **troff**ed versions of each named *title* (if necessary), but does not display them.

–M *path* Change the search path for manual pages. *path* is a colon-separated list of directories that contain manual page directory subtrees. When used with the **–k** or **–f** options, the **–M** option must appear first. Each directory in the *path* is assumed to contain subdirectories of the form **man[1-81-p]**.

–T *macro-package*
man uses *macro-package* rather than the standard **–man** macros defined in **/usr/ucblib/doctools/tmac/an** for formatting manual pages.

When specifying the **–T** option to **/usr/ucb/man**, the full path must be given. For example:

```
/usr/ucb/man -T /usr/ucblib/doctools/tmac/bib ls.
```

-k *keyword* . . .

man prints out one-line summaries from the **whatis** database (table of contents) that contain any of the given *keywords*.

-f *file* . . .

man attempts to locate manual pages related to any of the given *files*. It strips the leading pathname components from each *file*, and then prints one-line summaries containing the resulting basename or names.

MANUAL PAGES

Manual pages are **troff** or **nroff** source files prepared with the **-man** macro package.

When formatting a manual page, **man** examines the first line to determine whether it requires special processing.

Preprocessing Manual Pages

If the first line is a string of the form:

´\" *X*

where *X* is separated from the the '"' by a single SPACE and consists of any combination of characters in the following list, **man** pipes its input to **troff** or **nroff** through the corresponding preprocessors.

e	**eqn**, or **neqn** for **nroff**
r	**refer**
t	**tbl**, and **col** for **nroff**

If **eqn** or **neqn** is invoked, it will automatically read the file **/usr/ucblib/pub/eqnchar** [see **eqnchar**(5)].

ENVIRONMENT

MANPATH If set, its value overrides **/usr/share/man** as the default search path. The **-M** flag, in turn, overrides this value.

PAGER A program to use for interactively delivering **man**'s output to the screen. If not set, '**more -s**' (see **more**) is used.

TCAT The name of the program to use to display **troff**ed manual pages. If not set, '**lp -Ttroff**' (see **lp**) is used.

TROFF The name of the formatter to use when the **-t** flag is given. If not set, **troff** is used.

FILES

/usr/share/man	root of the standard manual page directory subtree
/usr/share/man/man?/*	unformatted manual entries
/usr/share/man/cat?/*	**nroff**ed manual entries
/usr/share/man/fmt?/*	**troff**ed manual entries
/usr/share/man/whatis	table of contents and keyword database
/usr/ucblib/doctools/tmac/an	standard **-man** macro package
/usr/ucblib/pub/eqnchar	

SEE ALSO

apropos(1), **cat**(1), **catman**(1M), **col**(1), **eqn**(1), **eqnchar**(5), **lp**(1), **more**(1), **nroff**(1), **refer**(1), **tbl**(1), **troff**(1), **whatis**(1)

NOTES

The manual is supposed to be reproducible either on a phototypesetter or on an ASCII terminal. However, on a terminal some information (indicated by font changes, for instance) is necessarily lost.

Some dumb terminals cannot process the vertical motions produced by the **e** (**eqn**(1)) preprocessing flag. To prevent garbled output on these terminals, when you use **e** also use **t**, to invoke **col**(1) implicitly. This workaround has the disadvantage of eliminating superscripts and subscripts — even on those terminals that can display them. CTRL-Q will clear a terminal that gets confused by **eqn**(1) output.

mapchan (1M)

NAME

mapchan – Configure tty device mapping.

SYNOPSIS

mapchan [-**ans**] [-**f** *mapfile*] [*channels . . .*]
mapchan [-o] [-**d**] [*channel*]

DESCRIPTION

mapchan configures the mapping of information input and output of the UNIX system. The **mapchan** utility is intended for users of applications that employ languages other than English (character sets other than 7 bit ASCII).

mapchan translates codes sent by peripheral devices, such as terminals, to the internal character set used by the UNIX system. **mapchan** can also map codes in the internal character set to other codes for output to peripheral devices (such as terminals, printers, console screen, etc.). Note that PC keyboard configuration is accomplished through the **mapkey**(1M) utility.

mapchan has several uses: to map a *channel* (-**a** or -**s**); to unmap a *channel* (–**n** and optionally -**a**); or to display the map on a *channel* (optionally -**o**,-**d**, *channels*).

mapchan with no options displays the map on the user's *channel*. The map displayed is suitable as input for **mapchan**.

The options are :

-a When used alone, sets all *channels* given in the default file (**/etc/default/mapchan**) with the specified map. When used with -**n**, it refers to all *channels* given in the default file. Superuser maps or unmaps all *channels*, other users map only *channels* they own. The -**a** option can not be used with the -**d**, -**o**, or -**s** options.

-d Causes the mapping table currently in use on the given device, *channel*, to be displayed in decimal instead of the default hexadecimal. An ASCII version is displayed on standard output. This output is suitable as an input file to **mapchan** for another *channel*. Mapped values are displayed. Identical pairs are not output. The -**d** option can not be used with -**a**, -**f**, -**n**, -**o** or -**s** options.

-f Causes the current *channel* or list of channels to be mapped with *mapfile*. The -**f** option can not be used with -**d**, -**n**, -**s**, or -**o** options.

-n Causes null mapping to be performed. All codes are input and output as received. Mapping is turned off for the user's *channel* or for other *channels*, if given. -**a** used with -**n** will turn mapping off for all *channels* given in the default file. This is the default mapping for all *channels* unless otherwise configured. The -**n** option can not be used with -**d**, -**f**, -**o**, or -**s** options.

-o Causes the mapping table currently in use on the given device, *channel*, to be displayed in octal instead of the default hexadecimal. An ASCII version is displayed on standard output. This output is suitable as an input file to **mapchan** for another port. Mapped values are displayed. Identical pairs are not output. The -**o** option can not be used with -**a**, -**d**, -**f**, -**n**, or -**s** options.

-s Sets the user's current *channel* with the *mapfile* given in the default file. The **-s** option can not be used with any other option.

The user must own the *channel* in order to map it. The super-user can map any channel. Read or write permission is required to display the map on a *channel*.

Each tty device *channel* (display adapter and video monitor on computer, parallel port, serial port, etc.) can have a different map. When the UNIX system boots, mapping is off for all *channels*.

mapchan is usually invoked in the **/etc/rc2** file. This file is executed when the system enters the multiuser mode and sets up the default mapping for the system. Users can invoke **mapchan** when they log in by including a **mapchan** command line in their **.profile** or **.login** file. In addition, users can remap their *channel* at any time by invoking **mapchan** from the command line. *channels* not listed in the default file are not automatically mapped. *channels* are not changed on logout. Whatever mapping was in place for the last user remains in effect for the next user, unless they modify their **.profile** or **.login** file.

For example, the default file **/etc/default/mapchan** can obtain:

```
tty1
tty2   ibm
tty3   wy60.ger
lp     ibm
```

The default directory containing *mapfiles* is **/usr/lib/mapchan**. The default directory containing *channel* files is **/dev**. Full pathnames may be used for *channels* or *mapfiles*. If a *channel* has no entry, or the entry field is blank, no mapping is enabled on that *channel*. Additional *channels* added to the system (for example, adding a serial or parallel port), are not automatically entered in the **mapchan** default file. If mapping is required, the system administrator must make the entries. The format of the *mapfiles* is documented in the **mapchan**(4) manual page.

Using a Mapped channel

The input information is assumed to be 7-or 8-bit codes sent by the peripheral device. The device may make use of dead or compose keys to produce the codes. If the device does not have dead or compose keys, these keys can be simulated using **mapchan**.

One to one mapped characters are displayed when the key is pressed and the mapped value is passed to the kernel.

Certain keys are designated as dead keys in the *mapfile*. Dead key sequences are two keystrokes that produce a single mapped value that is passed to the kernel. The dead key is usually a diacritical character, the second key is usually the letter being modified. For example, the sequence **'e** could be mapped to the ASCII value 0xE9, and displayed as **e'**.

One key is designated as the compose key in the *mapfile*. Compose key sequences are composed of three keystrokes that produce a single mapped value that is passed to the kernel. The compose key is usually a seldom used character or CTRL-*letter* combination. The second key is usually the letter being modified. The third key may be another character being combined, or a diacritical character.

For example, if `@` is the compose key, the sequence `@ c O` could be mapped to the ASCII value 0xA9, and displayed as ©.

Characters are not echoed to the screen during a dead or compose sequence. The mapped character is echoed and passed to the kernel once the sequence is correctly completed.

Characters are always put through the input map, even when part of dead or compose sequences. The character is then checked for the internal value. The value may also be mapped on output. This should be kept mind when preparing map files.

The following conditions will cause an error during input:

1. non-recognized (not defined in the *mapfile*) dead or compose sequence.
2. restarting a compose sequence before completion by pressing the compose key in the middle of a dead or compose sequence (this is an error, but a new compose sequence is initiated).

If the *mapfile* contains the keyword **beep**, a bell sounds when either of the above conditions occurs. In either case, the characters are not echoed to the screen, or passed to the kernel.

In order to allow for character sequences sent to control the terminal (move the cursor, and so on) rather than to print characters on the screen, **mapchan** allows characters sequences to be specified as special sequences which are not passed through the normal mapping procedure. Two sections may be specified, one for each of the input (keyboard) and output (screen) controls.

Character Sets

The internal character set used is defined by the *mapfiles* used. By default, this is the ISO 8859/1 character set which is also known as dpANS X3.4.2 and ISO/TC97/SC2. It supports most of the Latin alphabet and can represent most European languages.

Several partial map files are provided as examples. They must be modified for use with specific peripheral devices. Consult your hardware manual for the codes needed to display the desired characters. Two map files are provided for use with the console device: **/usr/lib/mapchan/ibm** for systems with a standard PC character set ROM, and **/usr/lib/mapchan/iso** for systems with an optional ISO 8859/1 character set ROM.

Care should be taken that the **stty** settings [see **stty**(1)] are correct for 8-bit terminals. The **/etc/gettydefs** file may require modifications to allow logging with the correct settings.

7-bit U.S ASCII (ANSI X3.4) should be used if no mapping is enabled on the *channel*.

FILES

/etc/default/mapchan
/usr/lib/mapchan/*

NOTES

Some non-U.S keyboards and display devices do not support characters commonly used by command shells and the C programming language. It is not recommended that these devices be used for system administration tasks.

Printers can be mapped, output only, and can either be sent 8-bit codes or one-to-many character strings using **mapchan**. Line printer spooler interface scripts can be used (**setuid root**) to change the output map on the printer when different maps are required (as in changing print wheels to display a different character set). See **lpadmin**(1M) and **lp**(7) for information on installing and administering interface scripts.

Not all terminals or printers can display all the characters that can be represented using this utility. Refer to the device's hardware manual for information on the capabilities of the peripheral device.

Use of *mapfiles* that specify a different internal character set per channel, or a set other than the 8-bit ISO 8859 set supplied by default can cause strange side effects. It is especially important to retain the 7-bit ASCII portion of the character set [see **ascii**(5)]. System utilities and many applications assume these values.

Media transported between machines with different internal code set mappings may not be portable as no mapping is performed on block devices, such as tape and floppy drives. However, **trchan** with an appropriate *mapfile* can be used to translate from one internal character set to another.

Do not set **ISTRIP** [see **stty**(1)] when using **mapchan**. This option causes the eighth bit to be stripped before mapping occurs.

SEE ALSO

ascii(5), **keyboard**(7), **lp**(7), **lpadmin**(1M), **mapchan**(4), **mapkey**(1M), **stty**(1)

mapkey (1M)

NAME

mapkey, **mapscrn**, **mapstr** – configure monitor screen mapping

SYNOPSIS

mapkey [**-doxV**] [*datafile*]
mapscrn [**-dg**] [*datafile*]
mapstr [**-dg**] [*datafile*]

DESCRIPTION

mapscrn configures the output mapping of the virtual terminal screen on which it is invoked. **mapkey** and **mapstr** configure the mapping of the keyboard and string keys (for example, function keys) of the virtual terminal. **mapkey** can only be run by the privileged user.

mapscrn and **mapstr** function on a per-virtual terminal (VT) basis. Mapping on one VT does not affect any other VT. Setting the default for every VT can be done using the **-g** option. The **-g** option may be used only by the privileged user.

The mapscrn command sets up a one-to-one character mapping on output. This is also known as the "screen mapping" capability. A screen map is an array of 256 bytes (eight-bit characters). If a character is written to a VT on which screen mapping is enabled, the character actually drawn on the screen is going to be the character in the array at the index value given by the original character.

For example, **char foo[256]** is the screen map. **foo[a]** is set to the value **p**. If the screen map **foo** is enabled on the VT, every time the character **a** is written to the terminal, **p** will be displayed.

If a file name is given on the argument line, the respective mapping table is configured from the contents of the input file. If no file is given, the default files in **/usr/lib/keyboard** and **/usr/lib/console** are used. The **-d** option causes the mapping table to be read from the kernel instead of written and an ASCII version to be displayed on the standard output. The format of the output is suitable for use as input files to **mapscrn**, **mapkey**, or **mapstr**.

The sum of the characters in the strings for **mapstr** (in the **/usr/lib/keyboard/strings** file) can be a maximum of 512.

mapkey, when downloading a mapping table, overwrites the default mapping table for all VTs (thus affecting all VTs using the default mapping table) unless the **-V** option is specified. In this case, only the VT in which **mapkey -V** was invoked is affected, and the VT will revert to using the default mapping table when it is closed or the user logs out.

When **mapkey** displays the mapping table being used, it is the default mapping table unless the **-V** option is specified. In this case, **mapkey** displays the mapping table in use on the VT in which **mapkey -V** was invoked.

Non-superusers can run **mapkey** and **mapstr** when the **-d** option is given.

With the **-o** or **-x** options, **mapkey** displays the mapping table in octal or hexadecimal, respectively.

FILES

`/usr/lib/keyboard/*`
`/usr/lib/console/*`

NOTES

There is no way to specify that the map utilities read their configuration tables from standard input.

SEE ALSO

display(7), **keyboard**(7)

NAME

maplocale – (XENIX) convert Release 4 locale information to different format

SYNOPSIS

maplocale -f *new_format* [**-t** *territory*] [**-c** *codeset*] *SVR4_locale_name*

DESCRIPTION

maplocale converts Release 4 locale information into a format suitable for use with applications that require a different locale format. Currently, only conversion to SCO UNIX/XENIX format is supported, therefore, *new_format* must be **XENIX**.

The *SVR4_locale_name* must be the name of a valid locale, which will be the name of one of the sub-directories in the **/usr/lib/locale** directory.

Release 4 locale names use the form *language*[_*territory*[.*codeset*]]. If the locale name does not have the optional *codeset* or *territory* parts the **-t** and **-c** options must be used to specify the territory and code set for the locale.

SCO Specific Information

The converted data files will be placed in the directory:

/usr/lib/lang/*language***/***territory***/***codeset*.

If an abbreviated Release 4 locale name is used, the file **/etc/default/lang** will be updated and a line of the following form added to it:

LANG=*language_territory.codeset*

EXAMPLE

To convert the Spanish locale which is stored in the ISO 8859-1 code set, use the command:

```
maplocale -fXENIX -tES -c88591 es
```

DIAGNOSTICS

All error messages should be self explanatory.

FILES

/usr/lib/locale
/usr/lib/lang
/etc/default/lang

NAME

mconnect – (BSD) connect to SMTP mail server socket

SYNOPSIS

/usr/ucb/mconnect [**-p** *port*] [**-r**] [*hostname*]

DESCRIPTION

mconnect opens a connection to the mail server on a given host, so that it can be tested independently of all other mail software. If no host is given, the connection is made to the local host. Servers expect to speak the Simple Mail Transfer Protocol (SMTP) on this connection. Exit by typing the **quit** command. Typing EOF sends an end of file to the server. An interrupt closes the connection immediately and exits.

OPTIONS

-p *port* Specify the port number instead of the default SMTP port (number 25) as the next argument.

-r "Raw" mode: disable the default line buffering and input handling. This gives you a similar effect as **telnet** to port number 25, not very useful.

FILES

/usr/ucblib/sendmail.hf help file for SMTP commands

SEE ALSO

sendmail(1M)

Postel, Jonathan B *Simple Mail Transfer Protocol*, RFC821 August 1982, SRI Network Information Center

NAME

mcs – manipulate the comment section of an object file

SYNOPSIS

mcs [**-a** *string*] [**-c**] [**-d**] [**-n** *name*] [**-p**] [**-V**] *file* . . .

DESCRIPTION

The **mcs** command is used to manipulate a section, by default the **.comment** section, in an ELF object file. It is used to add to, delete, print, and compress the contents of a section in an ELF object file, and only print the contents of a section in a COFF object file. **mcs** must be given one or more of the options described below. It applies each of the options in order to each file.

The following options are available.

-a *string* Append *string* to the comment section of the ELF object files. If *string* contains embedded blanks, it must be enclosed in quotation marks.

-c Compress the contents of the comment section of the ELF object files. All duplicate entries are removed. The ordering of the remaining entries is not disturbed.

-d Delete the contents of the comment section from the ELF object files. The section header for the comment section is also removed.

-n *name* Specify the name of the comment section to access if other than **.comment**. By default, **mcs** deals with the section named **.comment**. This option can be used to specify another section.

-p Print the contents of the comment section on the standard output. Each section printed is tagged by the name of the file from which it was extracted, using the format *filename*[*member_name*]**:** for archive files; and *filename***:** for other files.

-V Print, on standard error, the version number of **mcs**.

If the input file is an archive [see **ar**(4)], the archive is treated as a set of individual files. For example, if the **-a** option is specified, the string is appended to the comment section of each ELF object file in the archive; if the archive member is not an ELF object file, then it is left unchanged.

If **mcs** is executed on an archive file the archive symbol table will be removed, unless only the **-p** option has been specified. The archive symbol table must be restored by executing the **ar** command with the **-s** option before the archive can be linked by the **ld** command. **mcs** will produce appropriate warning messages when this situation arises.

International Functions

Characters from supplementary code sets can be used in *object-files*. Comments using characters from supplementary code sets can be specified with the **-a** option.

EXAMPLES

```
mcs -p file          # Print file's comment section

mcs -a string file   # Append string to file's comment section
```

FILES

TMPDIR/**mcs***	temporary files
TMPDIR	usually **/var/tmp** but can be redefined by setting the environment variable **TMPDIR** [see **tempnam** in **tmpnam**(3S)].

SEE ALSO

a.out(4), **ar**(1), **ar**(4), **as**(1), **cc**(1), **ld**(1), **tmpnam**(3S)

NOTES

mcs cannot add to, delete or compress the contents of a section that is contained within a segment.

The section name specified in *name* with the **-n** option must contain ASCII characters only.

menu(1)

NAME

menu - menu/form generator

SYNOPSIS

menu [-r] [-c] -f *form-description-file* **-o** *output-file*

DESCRIPTION

menu is a menu and form generator that creates file-driven, full-screen forms and menus for accepting user input and displaying information. The form or menu to be displayed is specified in a form description file that allows text, lists, input fields, contents of files, and output from commands to be displayed. The **menu** command is equipped with a two-level help facility, with help for the menu or form specified in the form description file, and help on how to use **menu** itself provided in a support file installed with the operating system.

For purposes of internationalization, any text that is displayed by the menu is contained in a file external to the menu binary. This allows the menus and forms to be translated to other languages without changes to the menu command itself.

The options available are:

-c This option clears the screen. No other option is read if **-c** is specified on the command line. It is useful if a form created with the **-r** option is displayed on the screen (see **-r** below).

-r This option retains the form on the screen after input processing is complete, and displays a flashing **Working...** flag at the bottom of the screen. If no input is required (that is, the screen is simply displaying information), the form is displayed initially with a flashing **Working...** flag at the bottom of the screen.

-f *form-description-file*
This file contains the description of the form to be displayed by **menu**. It contains all the text that will appear on the screen. With the exception of error messages sent to **stdout**, no text is generated from within **menu**. This is for ease of internationalization. Unless the **-c** option is specified, **menu** will fail if this option is not specified. Additionally, **menu** will fail if the file specified is not readable.

-o *output-file*
This file contains the output from the menu, which consists of shell statements of the form **VARIABLE="value"**. This output file can be later read in by the shell script that called **menu**. Unless the **-c** option is specified, **menu** will fail if this option is not specified. Additionally, **menu** will fail if the file specified is not writable.

SEE ALSO

menu(4), **menu_colors.sh**(1)

NAME

menu_colors.sh – **menu**(1) tool environment variables

SYNOPSIS

. /etc/inst/locale/${LANG}/menus/menu_colors.sh

DESCRIPTION

The shell file **menu_colors.sh** is used to set up environment variables to manage colors for the **menu**(1) command. (See **menu**(1).)

menu_colors.sh(1), when sourced into the current shell, defines a function **menu_colors()** in the current shell environment that takes an argument. That argument determines the colors or attributes that will be displayed the next time the menu tool is invoked. Valid arguments are:

regular the color scheme is the one defined for regular screens (default white text on blue background, or white text on black background for monochrome displays).

warn the color scheme is the one defined for warning screens (default white text on magenta background, or black text on white background for monochrome displays).

error the color scheme is the one defined for error screens (default white text on red background, or black text on white background for monochrome displays).

These attributes are configurable by editing the file **menu_colors.sh**.

EXAMPLE

To display a warning screen, enter:

```
# This will set up the environment to have the menu_colors()
# function defined.  This should only be done once in a shell
# script.
menu_colors warn
menu -f form_description_file -o output_file
```

SEE ALSO

menu(1), **menu**(4)

mesg (1)

NAME

mesg – permit or deny messages

SYNOPSIS

mesg [-n] [-y]

DESCRIPTION

mesg with argument **-n** forbids messages via **write**(1) by revoking non-user write permission on the user's terminal. **mesg** with argument **-y** reinstates permission. All by itself, **mesg** reports the current state without changing it.

FILES

/dev/tty*

/usr/lib/locale/*locale***/LC_MESSAGES/uxcore**
language-specific message file [See **LANG** on **environ**(5).]

SEE ALSO

write(1)

DIAGNOSTICS

Exit status is 0 if messages are receivable, 1 if not, 2 on error.

NAME

message – put arguments on FMLI message line

SYNOPSIS

message [**-t**] [**-b** [*num*]] [**-o**] [**-w**] [*string*]
message [**-f**] [**-b** [*num*]] [**-o**] [**-w**] [*string*]
message [**-p**] [**-b** [*num*]] [**-o**] [**-w**] [*string*]

DESCRIPTION

The **message** command puts *string* out on the FMLI message line. If there is no string, the *stdin* input to **message** will be used. The output of **message** has a duration (length of time it remains on the message line). The default duration is "transient": it or one of two other durations can be requested with the following mutually-exclusive options:

-t explicitly defines a message to have transient duration. Transient messages remain on the message line only until the user presses another key or a **CHECKWORLD** occurs. The descriptors **itemmsg**, **fieldmsg**, **invalidmsg**, **choicemsg**, the default-if-not-defined value of **oninterrupt**, and FMLI generated error messages (for example, from syntax errors) also output transient duration messages. Transient messages take precedence over both frame messages and permanent messages.

-f defines a message to have "frame" duration. Frame messages remain on the message line as long as the frame in which they are defined is current. The descriptor **framemsg** also outputs a frame duration message. Frame messages take precedence over permanent messages.

-p defines a message to have "permanent" duration. Permanent messages remain on the message line for the length of the FMLI session, unless explicitly replaced by another permanent message or temporarily superseded by a transient message or frame message. A permanent message is not affected by navigating away from, or by closing, the frame which generated the permanent message. The descriptor **permanentmsg** also outputs a permanent duration message.

Messages displayed with **message -p** will replace (change the value of) any message currently displayed or stored via use of the **permanentmsg** descriptor. Likewise, **message -f** will replace any message currently displayed or stored via use of the **framemsg** descriptor. If more than one message in a frame definition file is specified with the **-p** option, the last one specified will be the permanent duration message.

The *string* argument should always be the last argument. Other options available with **message** are the following:

-b [*num*] rings the terminal bell *num* times, where *num* is an integer from 1 to 10. The default value is 1. If the terminal has no bell, the screen will flash *num* times instead, if possible.

`-o` forces **message** to duplicate its message to *stdout*.

`-w` turns on the working indicator.

EXAMPLES

When a value entered in a field is invalid, ring the bell 3 times and then display **Invalid Entry: Try again!** on the message line:

```
invalidmsg=`message -b 3 "Invalid Entry: Try again!"`
```

Display a message that tells the user what is being done:

```
done=`message EDITOR has been set in your environment` close
```

Display a message on the message line and *stdout* for each field in a form (a pseudo-"field duration" message).

```
fieldmsg="`message -o -f "Enter a filename."`"
```

Display a blank transient message (effect is to "remove" a permanent or frame duration message).

```
done=`message  ""` nop
```

NOTES

If **message** is coded more than once on a single line, it may appear that only the right-most instance is interpreted and displayed. Use **sleep**(1) between uses of **message** in this case, to display multiple messages.

message -f should not be used in a stand-alone backquoted expression or with the **init** descriptor because the frame is not yet current when these are evaluated.

In cases where **`message -f "***string*"` is part of a stand-alone backquoted expression, the context for evaluation of the expression is the previously current frame. The previously current frame can be the frame that issued the **open** command for the frame containing the backquoted expression, or it can be a frame given as an argument when **fmli** was invoked. That is, the previously current frame is the one whose frame message will be modified.

Permanent duration messages are displayed when the user navigates to the command line.

SEE ALSO

sleep(1)

NAME

mkdev – make special device files for SCSI peripheral devices

SYNOPSIS

/etc/scsi/mkdev [-d *tcindexfile*]

DESCRIPTION

The **mkdev** utility examines the configuration of equipped SCSI devices and creates special device files if any are needed. New device files are needed when peripherals are added to the SCSI bus or when the bus is reconfigured. The utility is normally run as a step in the system initialization sequence, but it may also be invoked manually.

The naming convention for each type of device is specified in a template file. The **mkdev** utility reads the location of each template file from a target controller index file – a file that is normally located in **/etc/scsi/tc.index**. An alternate path may be specified:

-d *tcindexfile*

On creation, device special files are assigned an owner of **root**, group of **sys**, and permissions of **600**.

If the Mandatory Access Control (MAC) Level Translation Database (LTDB) exists (that is, the files **/etc/security/mac/ltf.*** exist), the level of a newly-created device special file is set to **SYS_PRIVATE**; if the LTDB is not present, then the level of the file **/etc/shadow** (which is expected to be **SYS_PRIVATE**) is used on newly-created device special files; otherwise, no level is set. MAC is installed by the Enhanced Security Utilities.

FILES

/etc/scsi/tc.index
/etc/scsi/mkdev
/etc/scsi/mkdev.d/disk1
/etc/scsi/mkdev.d/9track1
/etc/scsi/mkdev.d/9track2
/etc/scsi/mkdev.d/qtape1
/etc/scsi/mkdev.d/qtape2

SEE ALSO

mkdev(4)

NAME

mkdir – make directories

SYNOPSIS

mkdir [-m *mode*] **[-p]** *dirname* . . .

DESCRIPTION

mkdir creates the specified directories in mode 777 [possibly altered by **umask**(1)].

Standard entries in a directory, **.**, for the directory itself, and **..**, for its parent are made automatically. **mkdir** cannot create these entries by name. Creation of a directory requires write permission in the parent directory.

The owner ID and group ID of the new directories are set to the process's real user ID and group ID, respectively.

The **mkdir** command has the following options:

-m specifies the *mode* to be used for new directories. Choices for *mode* can be found in **chmod**(1).

-p creates all the non-existing parent directories first.

EXAMPLE

To create the subdirectory structure **ltr/jd/jan**, type:

```
mkdir -p ltr/jd/jan
```

FILES

/usr/lib/locale/*locale***/LC_MESSAGES/uxcore.abi**
language-specific message file [See **LANG** on **environ** (5).]

SEE ALSO

intro(2), **mkdir**(2), **rm**(1), **sh**(1), **umask**(1)

DIAGNOSTICS

mkdir returns exit code 0 if all directories given in the command line were made successfully. Otherwise, it prints a diagnostic and returns non-zero.

NAME

mkfifo – make FIFO special file

SYNOPSIS

mkfifo path . . .

DESCRIPTION

mkfifo creates the FIFO special files named by its argument list. The arguments are taken sequentially, in the order specified; and each FIFO special file is either created completely or, in the case of an error or signal, not created at all.

For each *path* argument, the **mkfifo** command behaves as if the function **mkfifo** [see **mkfifo**(3C)] was called with the argument *path* set to *path* and the *mode* set to the bitwise inclusive OR of **S_IRUSR**, **S_IWUSR**, **S_IRGRP**, **S_IWGRP**, **S_IROTH** and **S_IWOTH**.

If errors are encountered in creating one of the special files, **mkfifo** writes a diagnostic message to the standard error and continues with the remaining arguments, if any.

SEE ALSO

mkfifo(3C)

DIAGNOSTICS

mkfifo returns exit code 0 if all FIFO special files were created normally; otherwise it prints a diagnostic and returns a value greater than 0.

mklost+found (1M)

NAME

mklost+found – create a lost+found directory

SYNOPSIS

mklost+found *directory number*

DESCRIPTION

mklost+found creates a **lost+found** directory in which orphan files (allocated but unreferenced) are placed by **fsck**. **mklost+found** creates room for 32 orphans for each increment of *number*. For example, to create a **lost+found** directory in **/tmp** that can hold up to 320 orphans, type:

mklost+found /tmp *10*

mklost+found is executed by **diskadd**, and sometimes by **mkfs**. It is not normally executed directly at the shell prompt.

NOTE

mklost+found is obsolescent.

REFERENCES

fsck(1M

NAME

mkfontdir – create **fonts.dir** file from directory of font files

SYNOPSIS

mkfontdir [*directory-names*]

DESCRIPTION

The **mkfontdir** command searches for properties named "FONT", or the name of the file stripped of its suffix, in all font files in all *directory-names*, and writes them to the **fonts.dir** file in the directory along with the name of the font file.

The types of font files read varies based on configuration, but typically includes SNF (suffixed **.snf**), compressed SNF (suffixed **.snf.Z**), BDF (suffixed **.bdf**), and compressed BDF (suffixed **.bdf.Z**). If a font has multiple formats, the most efficient format is used.

If the specified directory contains PostScript Type 1 outline fonts or other outline (scalable) fonts, the **mkfontdir** command simply copies the **fonts.scale** file to the **fonts.dir** file. The **fonts.scale** file is created by the **mkfontscale** command for Type 1 fonts; for other scalable fonts (such as F3 fonts for the TypeScaler renderer), the **fonts.scale** file needs to be created manually.

Font Name Aliases

The **fonts.alias** file is used to map new names to existing fonts. When a font alias is used, the name it references is searched for in the normal manner, so that aliases need not mention fonts in the alias file's directory. The file should be edited by hand and can be in any directory of the font-path.

Each line of the file lists an alias and font-name patterns. (Use regular expression rules to embed white space or other special characters in aliases and font-name patterns.)

```
"special-alias with spaces"     "\"font\name\" with quotes"
fixed -misc-fixed-medium-r-semicondensed--13-120-75-75-c-80-iso8859-1
```

A line with only the string **FILE_NAMES_ALIASES** causes all file-names in the directory to be stripped of the **.snf** suffix and used as an alias for that font.

USAGE

Xserver looks for both **fonts.dir** and **fonts.alias** in each directory in the font path each time it is set [see **xset**].

SEE ALSO

mkfontscale(1), **X**(1)

NOTES

Portions of this page are derived from material which is copyright Massachusetts Institute of Technology.

mkfontscale (1)

NAME

mkfontscale – enable PostScript Type 1 outline font use for XWIN and **lp**

SYNOPSIS

mkfontscale [*directory*] [. . .]

DESCRIPTION

The **mkfontscale** command allows Type 1 outline fonts installed on the system to be used for both display and printing: by both XWIN (the X Window System) and the **lp** subsystem. For display, **mkfontscale** allows the X Window System, when the Adobe Type Manager™ package is installed, to use the Type 1 outline fonts by mapping the PostScript font name information to the XLFD name required by XWIN. For printing, **mkfontscale** allows the **lp** command to download installed Type 1 fonts to a PostScript printer via the **download** utility, by mapping the PostScript font name to the file name of the installed Type 1 font.

If no arguments are given, **mkfontscale** works with the Type 1 outline font files in the current directory; otherwise, it processes the fonts in each directory given as arguments. For each directory, it reads all Type 1 font files in the directory and maps the font naming information contained therein to XLFD names in the file **fonts.scale**, which it creates or updates as necessary, in the same directory; the **mkfontdir** command uses **fonts.scale** as input and creates the file **fonts.dir**, which X uses directly on startup. In addition, **mkfontscale** updates the file **/usr/share/lib/hostfontdir/map** to associate PostScript font names with the file in which they are located, to allow **download** to download them to PostScript printers.

The Type 1 font files must be the ASCII form of Type 1 fonts and are recognized by **mkfontscale** only if their names have one of the following suffixes: **.PFA**, **.pfa**, **.PS**, or **.ps**. Binary Type 1 files (typically with suffixes of **.PFB** or **.pfb**) are not recognized, though the binary files can be translated to their ASCII equivalents using the **pfb2pfa** command [see **pfb2pfa**(1)]. The suffix **.pfa** is the one used for Type 1 fonts installed by the Font Setup application of the desktop. Files whose names have any other suffix are ignored by **mkfontscale**.

XLFD Mapping: Family Name and Style

There are five XLFD fields for font name and style. They are mapped as follows from the PostScript names (literals) in the Type 1 font file:

XLFD Field	Type 1 PostScript name used
FAMILY_NAME	Set directly from the value of the **/FamilyName** literal.
WEIGHT_NAME	Set directly from the value of the **/Weight** literal.
SLANT	Set to **i** if the pattern **[Ii]ta** appears in the literal **/FontName**; set to **o** if the pattern **[Oo]bl** appears in the literal **/FontName**; set to **r** otherwise.

XLFD Field	Type 1 PostScript name used
SETWIDTH_NAME	Set from the /FullName literal as follows: if the pattern [Cc]ond appears, set to Condensed; if the pattern [Cc]omp appears, set to Compressed; if the pattern [Nn]arr appears, set to Narrow; if the pattern [Tt]hin appears, set to Thin; if the pattern [Uu]lt appears, Ultra added as prefix; if the pattern [Ee]xt appears, Extra added as prefix.
ADD_STYLE_NAME	Set from the /FullName literal: if any of a series of qualifying names appear as part of the FullName, they are placed in the ADD_STYLE_NAME field. These include Capitals, Expert, Alternate, and Old Style.

XLFD Mapping: Character Set Registries and Encodings

If the Type 1 font contains the literal definition /Encoding StandardEncoding, then two XLFD names are created for the font, one with a CHARSET_ENCODING of 1 and the other with a CHARSET_ENCODING of adobe; the CHARSET_REGISTRY is set to iso8859 in both cases. Otherwise, a single XLFD name is created for the font, with a CHARSET_ENCODING of fontspecific and a CHARSET_REGISTRY of adobe.

XLFD Mapping: Other XLFD Fields

There are seven other XLFD fields, set as follows:

XLFD Field	manner set from Type 1 PostScript information
FOUNDRY	Set to a limited number of well-known digital font foundries (Adobe, Bitstream, IBM, Linotype, Monotype), based on the presence of their name in the /Notice literal.
PIXEL_SIZE	Set to 0, per X11R5 XLFD conventions.
POINT_SIZE	Set to 0, per X11R5 XLFD conventions.
RESOLUTION_X	Set to 0, per X11R5 XLFD conventions.
RESOLUTION_Y	Set to 0, per X11R5 XLFD conventions.
SPACING	Set to m if the literal /isFixedPitch is set to true; otherwise set to p.
AVERAGE_WIDTH	Set to 0, per X11R5 XLFD conventions.

XLFD Creation: Derived Instance Pointsizes

To allow pre-X11R5 applications to take limited advantage of outline fonts, XLFD names that have a specific size in the POINT_SIZE field may be created for outline fonts. By doing this for sizes 10 and 12, for example, an X11R4 application, can be informed by X that the font Hobo (from the Adobe Type Set™ 2 collection) is available in pointsizes 10 and 12; the X11R4 application assumes the fonts are bitmapped, but the X server just renders the outlines at the sizes available via these "derived" XLFD names. This is a limited capability: sizes of the font other than 10 and 12 are not available to the pre-X11R5 application, since it does not know how to request an outline to be scaled to any size. Nonetheless, it is a mechanism by which some use of outline fonts may be made by older X applications.

The pointsizes for which this is desired are specified as a comma-separated list in the environment variable **DERIVED_INSTANCE_PS** when **mkfontscale** is executed. An XLFD name for each size specified is generated for each character set encoding of each font in the directory; a scalable name, with a POINT_SIZE field of 0, is of course also generated for each encoding of each Type 1 font file.

Note that when the Integrity Check selection on the Actions menu button of the Font Setup application in the UNIX Desktop causes **mkfontscale** to run, the **DERIVED_INSTANCE_PS** environment variable is set to the value of the **derived-instance-pointsizes** option in the X server font configuration file **/usr/X/defaults/Xwinfont**.

lp Mapping

The first column of the file **/usr/share/lib/hostfontdir/map** is the font name as given in the **/FontName** literal in the Type 1 program. This is the name of the font that must be specified in the **%%DocumentFonts:** comment of PostScript output files from applications if the font is to be downloaded to a PostScript printer. It is the name of the font dictionary created in the PostScript interpreter in the printer when that font is used. Note that an application must obtain the PostScript font name (as coded in the **/FontName** literal in the Type 1 font file) from a font structure in the X server, when the font is open, to be able to place it in the **%%DocumentFonts:** comment in a generated PostScript output file [see **download**(1)].

If the "Fonts Disk" of the DOS retail package for Adobe Type Manager is installed, the 13 base fonts there are not placed into the **hostfontdir/map** file, since it is assumed that all PostScript printers have at least these 13 fonts. If this assumption is untrue, the **map** file must be updated manually [see **download**(1)].

Files

/usr/X/defaults/Xwinfont
/usr/X/lib/fonts/type1/fonts.scale
/usr/X/lib/fonts/mitType1/fonts.scale
/usr/share/lib/hostfontdir/map
/etc/lp/printers/*printer***/residentfonts**

Environment Variables

XWINHOME
specifies where the X libraries are located; if not set, it defaults to **/usr/X**.

DERIVED_INSTANCE_PS
is a comma-separated list of point sizes for which individual XLFD font names are to be generated for each character encoding of each Type 1 font.

LD_LIBRARY_PATH
specifies where the X dynamic shared libraries are located; must be set to **/usr/X/lib** for **mkfontscale** to run (this is usually done in a UNIX Desktop user's environment, but it may not be set for **root** or when the UNIX Desktop is not running)

USAGE

Examples

The file **CP31A___.pfa** on the fonts diskette from the Adobe TypeSet™ 2 package contains the following PostScript literals:

```
/Notice (Copyright (c) 1989, 1990 Adobe Systems Incorporated.\
```

```
   All Rights Reserved.)
/FullName (Copperplate Gothic 31AB)
/FamilyName (Copperplate Gothic)
/Weight (Bold)
/ItalicAngle 0
/FontName /Copperplate-ThirtyOneAB
```

This is mapped to the following two scalable XLFD names in the **fonts.scale** file:

```
CP31A___.pfa -adobe-Copperplate Gothic-Bold-r-normal--0-0-0-0-p-0-iso8859-1
CP31A___.pfa -adobe-Copperplate Gothic-Bold-r-normal--0-0-0-0-p-0-iso8859-adobe
```

The PostScript font name **Copperplate-ThirtyOneAB** would be placed into the **map** file for use for downloaded fonts.

The file **SNOWTHIN.pfa** from another font vendor contains the following PostScript font literals:

```
/Notice (Copyright (c) 1989, Acme Fonts Inc.)
/FullName (Acme Snow-Thin)
/FamilyName (Snow Thin)
/Weight (Thin)
/ItalicAngle 0
/FontName /SnowThin
```

This is mapped to the following scalable XLFD name in the **fonts.scale** file:

```
SNOWTHIN.pfa -unknown-Snow Thin-Thin-r-normal--0-0-0-0-p-0-iso8859-1
```

Note that "Thin" is used in both the FamilyName literal and the Weight literal, and so is used twice in the XLFD name. This means that the word will appear twice in the Font Setup application, once under Family Name and once under Style. This is due to a lack of regularized font naming conventions in the industry.

NOTES

XLFD is the acronym for the X Logical Font Description and more information on it can be obtained from the MIT X Consortium document *X11R5: X Logical Font Description Conventions, Version 1.4.*

The **mkfontscale** command is run automatically by the Font Setup application of the desktop whenever Type 1 fonts are installed from diskette. It is also run when the Integrity Check option of the Actions button of the Font Setup application is used.

SEE ALSO

desktop(1), **download**(1), **lp**(1), **mkfontdir**(1), **pfb2pfa**(1), **Xwinfont**(4)

NAME

mkfs (generic) – construct a file system

SYNOPSIS

mkfs [**-F** *FSType*] [**-V**] [**-m**] [*current_options*] [**-o** *specific_options*] *special* [*operands*]

DESCRIPTION

mkfs constructs a file system by writing on the *special* file; *special* must be the first argument. The file system is created based on the *FSType, specific_options* and *operands* specified on the command line. **mkfs** waits 10 seconds before starting to construct the file system. During this time the command can be aborted by entering a delete (DEL).

operands are *FSType*-specific and the *FSType* specific manual page of **mkfs** should be consulted for a detailed description.

current_options are options supported by the **s5**-specific module of **mkfs**. Other *FSTypes* do not necessarily support these options. *specific_options* indicate suboptions specified in a comma-separated list of suboptions and/or keyword-attribute pairs for interpretation by the *FSType*-specific module of the command.

The options are:

-F Specify the *FSType* to be constructed. The *FSType* should either be specified here or be determinable from **/etc/vfstab** by matching the *special* with an entry in the table.

-V Echo the complete command line, but do not execute the command. The command line is generated by using the options and arguments provided by the user and adding to them information derived from **/etc/vfstab**. This option should be used to verify and validate the command line.

-m Return the command line which was used to create the file system. The file system must already exist. This option provides a means of determining the command used in constructing the file system. It cannot be used with *current_options, specific_options,* or *operands.* It must be invoked by itself.

-o Specify *FSType*-specific options.

NOTES

This command may not be supported for all *FSTypes.*

FILES

/etc/vfstab list of default parameters for each file system

SEE ALSO

bfs-specific **mkfs**(1M), **s5**-specific **mkfs**(1M), **sfs**-specific **mkfs**(1M), **ufs**-specific **mkfs**(1M), **vxfs**-specific **mkfs**(1M), **prtvtoc**(1M), **vfstab**(4)

NAME

mkfs (bfs) – construct a boot file system

SYNOPSIS

mkfs [–F bfs] *special blocks* [*inodes*]

DESCRIPTION

mkfs is used to create a boot file system, which is a contiguous flat file system, to hold the bootable programs and data files necessary for the boot procedure.

The argument *special* is the device special file that refers to the partition on which the file system is to be created. The *blocks* argument is used to specify the size of the file system. The block size is automatically 512 bytes.

The *inodes* argument specifies the number of files that the file system will hold.

NOTES

This file system is intended to hold the bootable files and data files for the boot procedure. Use as a general purpose file system is not recommended.

NAME

mkfs (s5) – construct an **s5** file system

SYNOPSIS

mkfs [**-F s5**] [*generic_options*] *special*
mkfs [**-F s5**] [*generic_options*] [**-b** *block_size*] *special blocks*[*:i-nodes*] [*gap blocks/cyl*]
mkfs [**-F s5**] [*generic_options*] [**-b** *block_size*] *special proto* [*gap blocks/cyl*]

DESCRIPTION

generic_options are options supported by the generic **mkfs** command.

mkfs constructs an **s5** file system by writing on the *special* file using the values found in the remaining arguments of the command line. **mkfs** builds a file system with a **root** directory and a **lost+found** directory. **mkfs** expands the **lost+found** directory to be as large as possible, while still fitting in one disk block.

The options are:

-F s5 Specifies an **s5**-FSType.

-b *blocksize* Specifies the logical block size for the file system. The logical block size is the number of bytes read or written by the operating system in a single I/O operation. Valid values for *blocksize* are 512, 1024, and 2048. The default is 1024.

If the second argument to **mkfs** is a string of digits, the size of the file system is the value of *blocks* interpreted as a decimal number. This is the number of *physical* (512 byte) disk blocks the file system will occupy. If the number of i-nodes is not given, the default is approximately the number of *logical* blocks divided by 4. **mkfs** builds a file system with a single empty directory on it. The boot program block (block zero) is left uninitialized.

If the second argument is the name of a file that can be opened, **mkfs** assumes it to be a prototype file *proto*, and will take its directions from that file. The prototype file contains tokens separated by spaces or new-lines. A sample prototype specification follows (line numbers have been added to aid in the explanation):

```
1.   /dev/rdsk/0s0
2.    4872 110
3.    d--777 3 1
4.    usr   d--777 3 1
5.          sh    ---755 3 1 /sbin/sh
6.          ken   d--755 6 1
7.                $
8.          b0    b--644 3 1 0 0
9.          c0    c--644 3 1 0 0
10.         slnk  l--777 2 2 /var/tmp
11.         $
12.   $
```

Line 1 in the example is the name of a file to be copied onto block zero as the bootstrap program.

Line 2 specifies the number of *physical* (512 byte) blocks the file system is to occupy and the number of i-nodes in the file system.

Lines 3-10 tell **mkfs** about files and directories to be included in this file system.

Line 3 specifies the root directory.

Lines 4-6 and 8-10 specify other directories and files.

Line 10 specifies the symbolic link **slnk** set up in **/usr** and containing **/var/tmp**.

The $ on line 7 tells **mkfs** to end the branch of the file system it is on, and continue from the next higher directory. The $ on lines 11 and 12 end the process, since no additional specifications follow.

File specifications give the mode, the user ID, the group ID, and the initial contents of the file. Valid syntax for the contents field depends on the first character of the mode.

The mode for a file is specified by a 6-character string. The first character specifies the type of the file. The character range is **-bcdl** to specify regular, block special, character special, directory, and symbolic link files respectively. The second character of the mode is either **u** or **-** to specify set-user-id mode or not. The third is **g** or **-** for the set-group-id mode. The rest of the mode is a 3 digit octal number giving the owner, group, and other read, write, execute permissions [see **chmod**(1)].

Two decimal number tokens come after the mode; they specify the user and group IDs of the owner of the file.

If the file is a regular file, the next token of the specification may be a path name whence the contents and size are copied. If the file is a block or character special file, two decimal numbers follow which give the major and minor device numbers. If the file is a directory, **mkfs** makes the entries **.** and **..** and then reads a list of names and (recursively) file specifications for the entries in the directory. As noted above, the scan is terminated with the token **$**.

The *gap blocks/cyl* argument in both forms of the command specifies the rotational gap and the number of blocks/cylinder. If the *gap* and *blocks/cyl* are not specified or are considered illegal values a default value of gap size 10 and 162 blocks/cyl is used.

NOTES

With a prototype file there is no way to specify hard links.

The maximum number of i-nodes configurable is 65500.

SEE ALSO

chmod(1), **dir**(4), **s5**-specific **fs**(4) generic **mkfs**(1M)

NAME

mkfs (sfs) – construct a **sfs** file system

SYNOPSIS

mkfs [-F sfs] [*generic_options*] [-o *specific_options*] *special* [*size*]

DESCRIPTION

generic_options are options supported by the generic **mkfs** command. *current_options* are options supported by the **s5**-specific module of the **mkfs** command.

mkfs constructs a file system by writing on the special file *special* unless the '**-o N**' flag has been specified. The numeric *size* specifies the number of sectors in the file system. **mkfs** builds a file system with a root directory and a **lost+found** directory [see **fsck**(1M)]. The number of inodes is calculated as a function of the file system size.

The options are:

-F sfs Specifies the **sfs**-FSType.

-o Specify the **sfs** specific options. The following options are available:

- **M** Specifies that the root of the file system is to be a multilevel directory.
- **N** Do not write the file system to the *special* file. This suboption gives all the information needed to create a file system but does not create it.
- **nsect=***n* *n* is the number of sectors per track on the disk. The default is **18**.
- **ntrack=***n* *n* is the number of tracks per cylinder on the disk. The default is **9**.
- **bsize=***n* The primary block size for files on the file system. *n* must be a power of two, currently selected from **2048** or **8192** (the default). The default block size will be the same as the machine page size, unless the page size is less than **2048**, in which case the default block size is **2048**.
- **fragsize=***n*

  The fragment size for files on the file system. *n* represents the smallest amount of disk space that will be allocated to a file. It must be a power of two currently selected from the range **512** to **8192**. The default fragment size will equal the block size if the block size is less than or equal to **2048**; otherwise, it is **1024**.
- **cgsize=***n* The number of disk cylinders per cylinder group. *n* must be in the range **1** to **32**. **cgsize** has different defaults, depending on the size of the cylinder group. If the cylinder group is less than 3/4 MB, **cgsize** defaults to **16**. If the cylinder group is between 3/4 and 1.5 MB,

cgsize defaults to 12. If the cylinder group is greater than 1.5 MB, cgsize defaults to 8.

free — The minimum percentage of free disk space allowed. Once the file system capacity reaches this threshold, only a privileged user is allowed to allocate disk blocks.

rps=*n* — *n* is the rotational speed of the disk, in revolutions per second. The default is 60.

nbpi=*n* — *n* is the number of bytes for which one inode block is allocated. This parameter is currently set at one inode block for every 1024 bytes.

opt=s|t — Space or time optimization preference; **s** specifies optimization for space, **t** specifies optimization for time. The default is **t**.

apc=*n* — *n* is the number of alternates per cylinder (SCSI devices only). The default is 0.

gap=*n* — *n* is the expected time (in milliseconds) to service a transfer completion interrupt and initiate a new transfer on the same disk. It is used to decide how much rotational spacing to place between successive blocks in a file. The default is 4.

C — Some applications that pre-date SVR4 do not work on file systems with more than 64K inodes. Therefore, when the number of inodes for the file system being built exceeds the 64K limit, **mkfs** prompts the user to confirm that he or she indeed wants the large number of inodes. The **-o C** option silences this **mkfs** prompt and limits the number of inodes to a maximum of 64K, ensuring perfect binary compatibility with the pre-Release 4 UNIX System.

L — When the number of inodes for the file system being built exceeds the 64K limit, **mkfs** prompts the user to confirm that he or she indeed wants the large number of inodes. The **-o L** option silences this prompt and allows the user to create a file system with more than 64K inodes.

NOTES

The number of inodes is calculated as a function of the file system size, but can be modified with the **nbpi** option. For those who want a file system suitable for lots of tiny files (smaller than one block), the **nbpi** parameter may be used to increase the number of inodes.

SEE ALSO

fsck(1M), generic **mkfs**(1M), **dirent**(4)

NAME

mkfs (ufs) – construct a **ufs** file system

SYNOPSIS

mkfs [**-F ufs**] [*generic_options*] *special*
mkfs [**-F ufs**] [*generic_options*] [**-o** *specific_options*] *special size*

DESCRIPTION

generic_options are options supported by the generic **mkfs** command.

mkfs constructs a file system by writing on the special file *special* unless the '**-o N**' flag has been specified. The numeric *size* specifies the number of sectors in the file system. **mkfs** builds a file system with a root directory and a **lost+found** directory [see **fsck**(1M)].

The options are:

-F ufs Specifies the **ufs**-FSType.

-o Specify **ufs** file system specific options. The following options are available:

- **N** Do not write the file system to the *special* file. This suboption gives all the information needed to create a file system but does not create it.
- **nsect=***n* The number of sectors per track on the disk. The default is **18**.
- **ntrack=***n* The number of tracks per cylinder on the disk. The default is **9**.
- **bsize=***n* The primary block size for files on the file system. It must be a power of two, currently selected from **4096** (the default) or **8192**.
- **fragsize=***n* The fragment size for files on the file system. The **fragsize** represents the smallest amount of disk space that will be allocated to a file. It must be a power of two currently selected from the range **512** to **8192**. The default is **1024**.
- **cgsize=***n* The number of disk cylinders per cylinder group. *n* must be in the range **1** to **32**. **cgsize** has different defaults, depending on the size of the cylinder group. If the cylinder group is less than 3/4 MB, **cgsize** defaults to **16**. If the cylinder group is between 3/4 and 1.5 MB, **cgsize** defaults to **12**. If the cylinder group is greater than 1.5 MB, **cgsize** defaults to **8**.
- **nbpi=***n* The number of bytes for which one inode block is allocated. The default currently set at one inode block for every 2048 bytes.
- **free=***n* The minimum percentage of free disk space allowed. Once the file system capacity reaches this threshold, only a privileged user is allowed to allocate disk blocks. The default value is **10%**. It is inadvisable to reduce the

allocation of free space below the default level because this may adversely affect performance.

rps=*n* The rotational speed of the disk, in revolutions per second. The default is 60.

opt=s|t Space or time optimization preference; **s** specifies optimization for space, **t** specifies optimization for time. The default is **t**.

apc=*n* The number of alternates per cylinder (SCSI devices only). The default is 0.

gap=*n* The expected time (in milliseconds) to service a transfer completion interrupt and initiate a new transfer on the same disk. It is used to decide how much rotational spacing to place between successive blocks in a file. The default is 4.

C Some applications that pre-date SVR4 do not work on file systems with more than 64K inodes. Therefore, when the number of inodes for the file system being built exceeds the 64K limit, **mkfs** prompts the user to confirm that he or she indeed wants the large number of inodes. The **-o C** option silences this **mkfs** prompt and limits the number of inodes to a maximum of 64K, ensuring perfect binary compatibility with the pre-Release 4 UNIX System.

L When the number of inodes for the file system being built exceeds the 64K limit, **mkfs** prompts the user to confirm that he or she indeed wants the large number of inodes. The **-o L** option silences this prompt and allows the user to create a file system with more than 64K inodes.

NOTES

The number of inodes is calculated as a function of the file system size, but can be modified with the **nbpi** option. For those who want a file system suitable for lots of tiny files (smaller than one block), the **nbpi** parameter may be used to increase the number of inodes.

SEE ALSO

dir(4), **fsck**(1M), generic **mkfs**(1M), **ufs**-specific **fs**(4)

NAME

mkfs (vxfs) – construct a **vxfs** file system

SYNOPSIS

mkfs [**-F vxfs**] [*generic_options*] [**-o** *specific_options*] *special size*

DESCRIPTION

generic_options are options supported by the generic **mkfs** command. *specific_options* are options supported by the **vxfs**-specific module of the **mkfs** command.

mkfs constructs a file system by writing on the special file *special* unless the **-o N** flag has been specified. The numeric *size* specifies the number of sectors in the file system. **mkfs** builds a file system with a root directory and a **lost+found** directory [see **fsck**(1M)]. The number of inodes is calculated as a function of the file system size. **mkfs** typically constructs file systems with any number of inodes, whether that number is the default (1/4 of the available blocks) or is specified by the *ninode=num* option. However, some applications that pre-date System V Release 4 do not work on file systems with more than 64K inodes. When the number of inodes for the file system to be built exceeds the 64K limit, **mkfs** prompts the user for confirmation that the file system should be built with the large number of inodes and offers the option of truncating the number to 64K. The **-o C** and **-o L** options suppress this prompting. No boot program is initialized by **mkfs**.

The options are:

-F vxfs Specify the **vxfs** FSType.

-o Specify the **vxfs** file system specific options in a comma-separated list. The following options are available:

- **C** Limit the number of inodes to no more than 65,536. Ensures compatibility with UNIX Systems prior to System V Release 4. diskadd calls mkfs with this option. Use of this option suppresses the confirmation prompting when the number of inodes exceeds 65,536. Note that the **C** and **L** options are mutually exclusive.
- **L** Do not limit the number of inodes to 65,536. Use of this option suppresses the confirmation prompting when the number of inodes exceeds 65,536. The **L** option forces the build of the file system with the given number of inodes, even if that number exceeds 65,536. Note that the **C** and **L** options are mutually exclusive.
- **N** Do not write the file system to the *special* file. This option gives all the information needed to create a file system but does not create it.
- **bsize=***bsize* *bsize* is the block size for files on the file system and represents the smallest amount of disk space that will be allocated to a file. *bsize* must be a power of 2 currently selected from the range **1024** to **8192**. The default is **1024**.

ninode=*n* *n* is the number of inodes on the file system, rounded down. The default is the total number of blocks in allocation units divided by **4**.

nau=*n* *n* is the number of allocation units on the file system. The number of allocation units should not exceed 10 because some structures and operations exist on a per-allocation basis. No more than 8 allocation units should be produced by default.

ausize=*n* *n* is the size, in blocks of size *bsize,* of an allocation unit. This is an alternate way of specifying the number of allocations units. This option may not be used in conjunction with the **nau** option. With this option, the last allocation unit on the file system may be shorter than the others. If the last allocation unit on the file system is not long enough to contain an entire allocation unit header, the resulting size of the file system will be to the end of the last complete allocation unit.

aufirst=*n* *n* is the starting block number, in blocks of size *bsize,* of the first allocation unit. This option allows the allocation units to be aligned to a particular boundary, such as a cylinder boundary.

aupad=*n* *n* is the size, in blocks of size *bsize,* to leave between the end of the inode list and the first data block in each allocation unit. This option allows the data blocks of an allocation unit to be aligned to a particular boundary, such as a cylinder boundary.

logsize=*n* *n* is the number of blocks to allocate for an activity logging area. *n* must be in the range **32** to **1024**. The default is **512** blocks. If the file system is less than 4 megabytes, **logsize** will be reduced to avoid wasting space. The log size is 64 blocks for file systems less than 4 megabytes and 32 blocks for those less than 2 megabytes.

SEE ALSO

dir(4), **vxfs**-specific **fs**(4), **fsck**(1M), generic **mkfs**(1M)

NAME

mkmsgs – create message files for use by **gettxt**

SYNOPSIS

mkmsgs [-o] [-i *locale*] *inputstrings msgfile*

DESCRIPTION

The **mkmsgs** utility is used to create a file of text strings that can be accessed using the text retrieval tools [see **gettxt**(1), **srchtxt**(1), **exstr**(1), and **gettxt**(3C)]. It will take as input a file of text strings for a particular geographic locale [see **setlocale**(3C)] and create a file of text strings in a format that can be retrieved by both **gettxt**(1) and **gettxt**(3C). By using the **-i** option, you can install the created file under the **/usr/lib/locale/***locale***/LC_MESSAGES** directory (*locale* corresponds to the language in which the text strings are written).

inputstrings the name of the file that contains the original text strings.

msgfile the name of the output file where **mkmsgs** writes the strings in a format that is readable by **gettxt**(1) and **gettxt**(3C). The name of *msgfile* can be up to 14 characters in length, but may not contain either \ **0** (null) or the ASCII code for **/** (slash) or **:** (colon).

-i *locale* install *msgfile* in the **/usr/lib/locale/***locale***/LC_MESSAGES** directory. Only a privileged user or a member of group **bin** can create or overwrite files in this directory. Directories under **/usr/lib/locale** will be created if they don't exist.

-o overwrite *msgfile*, if it exists.

The input file contains a set of text strings for the particular geographic locale. Text strings are separated by a newline character. Nongraphic characters must be represented as alphabetic escape sequences. Messages are transformed and copied sequentially from *inputstrings* to *msgfile*. To generate an empty message in *msgfile*, leave an empty line at the correct place in *inputstrings*.

Strings can be changed simply by editing the file *inputstrings*. New strings must be added only at the end of the file; then a new *msgfile* file must be created and installed in the correct place. If this procedure is not followed, the retrieval function will retrieve the wrong string and software compatibility will be broken.

EXAMPLES

The following example shows an input message source file **C.str**:

```
File %s:\t cannot be opened\n
%s: Bad directory\n
        .
        .
        .
write error\n
        .
        .
```

The following command uses the input strings from **C.str** to create text strings in the appropriate format in the file **UX** in the current directory:

```
mkmsgs C.str UX
```

The following command uses the input strings from **FR.str** to create text strings in the appropriate format in the file **UX** in the directory **/usr/lib/locale/french/LC_MESSAGES/UX**.

```
mkmsgs -i french FR.str UX
```

These text strings would be accessed if you had set the environment variable **LC_MESSAGES=french** and then invoked one of the text retrieval tools listed at the beginning of the DESCRIPTION section.

FILES

/usr/lib/locale/*locale***/LC_MESSAGES/*** message files created by **mkmsgs**

SEE ALSO

exstr(1), **gettxt**(1), **gettxt**(3C), **setlocale**(3C), **srchtxt**(1)

mknod (1M)

NAME

mknod – make a special file

SYNOPSIS

mknod *name* **b** | **c** *major minor*
mknod *name* **p**

DESCRIPTION

mknod makes a directory entry for a special file.

name is the special file to be created. The second argument is either **b**, to indicate a block-type special file, or **c**, to indicate a character-type. The last two arguments are numbers specifying the *major* and *minor* device numbers; these may be either decimal or octal. The assignment of major device numbers is specific to each system. You must be a privileged user to use this form of the command.

The second case is used to create a FIFO (named pipe).

NOTES

If **mknod** is used to create a device in a remote directory (Remote File Sharing), the major and minor device numbers are interpreted by the server.

SEE ALSO

mknod(2)

NAME

mknod – (XENIX) make a special file

SYNOPSIS

mknod *name* **b** | **c** *major minor*
mknod *name* **p**
mknod *name* **m**
mknod *name* **s**

DESCRIPTION

mknod makes a directory entry for a special file.

In the first case, *name* is the special file to be created. The second argument is either **b** to indicate a block-type special file or **c** to indicate a character-type. The last two arguments are numbers specifying the *major* and *minor* device numbers; these may be either decimal or octal [see **mknod(2)** for information on minor device number values]. The assignment of major device numbers is specific to each system. You must be the super-user to use this form of the command.

The second case, **p**, is used to create a FIFO (named pipe).

The third case, **m**, is used to create XENIX shared memory handles.

The fourth case, **s**, is used to create XENIX semaphore handles.

NOTES

If **mknod** is used to create a device in a remote directory (Remote File Sharing), the major and minor device numbers are interpreted by the server.

SEE ALSO

mknod(2)

NAME

mkpart – disk maintenance utility

SYNOPSIS

/etc/mkpart [**-f** *filename*] [**-p** *partition*] . . . [**-P** *partition*] . . . [**-b**]
[**-B** *filename*] [**-A** *sector*] ... [**-V**] [**-v**] [**-i**] [**-x** *file*]
[**-t** [**vpa**]] *device*

/etc/mkpart -F *interleave raw_device*

DESCRIPTION

mkpart will not be supported in a future release. See "NOTES" below.

This program allows the system administrator to display and modify the data structures that the disk driver uses to access disks. These structures describe the number, size, and type of the partitions, as well as the physical characteristics of the disk drive itself.

The user maintains a file of stanzas, each of which contains comments and parameters. The stanzas are of two varieties: those that describe disk partitions and disk devices. Stanzas may refer to other stanzas of the same type so that common device or partition types may be customized. By default, the stanza file is named **/etc/partitions**. The required parameter, *device,* specifies the device stanza for the disk to be used.

The following options may be used with **mkpart**:

-f *filename* specifies the partition and device specification stanza file. If not present, **/etc/partitions** is assumed.

-p *partition* removes a partition from the vtoc on the specified device. The *partition* is a stanza that indicates the partition to be removed by its partition number parameter; no comparisons are made by attribute. Note: Alternate partitions cannot be removed.

-P *partition* adds a partition to the vtoc on the specified device. *partition* is a stanza which contains and/or refers to other stanzas that contain all of the necessary parameters for a vtoc partition.

-b causes only the boot program to be updated, unless other options are specified.

-B *filename* specifies a different boot program than the one given by the device stanza.

-A *sector* marks the specified sector as bad and assigns it an alternate if possible. *sector* is a zero-based absolute sector number from the beginning of the drive. To compute a sector number given cylinder, head, and (0-based) sector in track, the formula is cylinder * (sectors-per-track * heads-per-cylinder) + head * (sectors-per-track) + sector.

-V causes a complete surface-analysis pass to be run. This first writes a data pattern (currently 0xe5 in every byte) to each sector of the disk, then reads each sector. Any errors are noted and the bad sectors found are added to the alternates table if possible.

-v causes a non-destructive surface-analysis pass to be run. This just reads every sector of the disk, noting bad sectors as above.

-i initializes the VTOC on the drive to default values, clearing any existing partition and bad-sector information which may have existed. This is the only way to remove an alternate partition and can be used to re-initialize a drive which may have obsolete or incorrect VTOC data on it.

-x *file* writes a complete *device* and partition stanza list for the specified *device* to file.
Note: The tags in the file are pseudo names used to identify the slice.

-t [*vpa*] creates a listing of the current vtoc. The sub-parameters specify pieces to be printed: a - alternate sectors, **p** - *partitions,* and **v** - *vtoc* and related structures.

The *partitions* file is composed of blank-line-separated stanzas. (Blank lines have only tabs and spaces between new-lines). Commentary consists of all text between a '#' and a *new-line.* Stanzas begin with an identifier followed by a ':', and are followed by a comma-separated list of parameters. Each parameter has a keyword followed by an '=' followed by a value. The value may be a number, another stanza's name, a double quoted string, or a parenthesis-surrounded, comma-separated list of numbers or ranges of numbers, as appropriate for the keyword. Numbers may be written as decimal, octal, or hexadecimal constants in the form familiar to C programmers.

Device specification stanzas may contain the following parameters:

usedevice = *name* causes the named stanza's parameters to be included in the device definition.

boot = *string* indicates that the string is the filename of a bootstrap program to install on the disk.

device = *string* gives the filename of the character special device for the disk.

heads = *number* specifies the number of tracks per cylinder on the device.

cyls = *number* is the number of cylinders on the disk.

sectors = *number* is the number of sectors per track.

bpsec = *number* is the number of bytes per sector.

dserial = *string* is an arbitrary string which is recorded in the volume label. (Multibus systems only)

vtocsec = *number* gives the sector number to use for the volume table of contents.
Note: for AT386 systems, this number must be 17.

altsec = *number* is the sector to use for the alternate block table.

badsec = *number-list* lists the known bad sectors. These are appended to any specified in the command line or found during surface analysis.

Partition stanzas may have the following parameters:

usepart = *name* refers to another partition stanza.

partition = *number* gives this partition's entry number in the vtoc.

tag = *tagname* A partition tag specifies the purpose of the partition. The *tagnames* are reserved words which are presently used for identification purposes only:

- **BACKUP** means the entire disk.
- **ROOT** is a root file system partition.
- **BOOT** is a bootstrap partition.
- **SWAP** is a partition that does not contain a file system.
- **USR** is a partition that does contain a file system.
- **ALTS** contains alternate sectors to which the driver remaps bad sectors. Currently a maximum of 62 alternate sectors is supported.
- **OTHER** is a partition that the UNIX system does not know how to handle, such as MS-DOS space.

perm = *permname* specifies a permission type for the partition. Permissions are not mutually exclusive.
RO indicates that the partition cannot be written upon. Normally, write access is granted (standard UNIX system file permissions notwithstanding).
NOMOUNT disallows the driver from mounting the file system that may be contained in the partition.
VALID indicates that the partition contains valid data. Any partition added with the **-A** flag will be marked VALID.

start = *number* is the starting sector number for the partition.
Note: For AT386 systems, the root file system should start at the *second* track of the cylinder which is the beginning of the active UNIX system '**fdisk**' partition. This allows space for the writing of the boot code.

size = *number* is the size, in sectors, of the partition.

When **mkpart** is run, it first attempts to read the volume label (for multibus systems) or the '**fdisk**' table (for AT386 systems), the VTOC block, and the alternate sector table. If any of the structures is invalid or cannot be read, or if the **-i** flag is specified, the internal tables are initialized to default values for the device specified (taken from the device stanza in the partition file). If the **-F** flag is specified, the device is formatted. If either the **-V** or **-v** flag is specified, the appropriate surface analysis is performed. After these steps, partitions are deleted or added as required. Next, any bad sectors specified in the partition file, found during surface analysis, or specified in the command line with **-A** flags are merged into the alternate sectors table. Note that an alternate partition must exist for any bad-sector marking to occur, as bad sectors are assigned good alternates at this point. Finally, the boot program is written to track 0 of cylinder 0 (Multibus systems) or the cylinder where the active UNIX system '**fdisk**' partition starts (AT386 systems). If **-b** was not the only parameter specified, the updated VTOC and alternates tables are written, and the disk driver is instructed to re-read the tables when the drive is opened the next time. When only **-t** is specified, only a listing is created and no updating occurs.

-F *interleave* causes the entire device to be hardware formatted. This process re-writes all the sector headers on each track of the disk, enabling subsequent access using normal reads and writes. *interleave* is the distance in physical sectors between each successive logical sector. Normal values are 1 for track-cache controllers, 3–4 for standard controllers. The device for this option must be a raw UNIX system device. The **-F** option precludes all other options, thus should be used alone.

Files

/etc/partitions /etc/boot /dev/rdsk/*s0

NOTES

The **mkpart** command will not be supported in a future release. Use **prtvtoc**(1M) and **edvtoc**(1M) instead.

Currently, very little consistency checking is done. No checks are made to ensure that the '**fdisk**' partition table is consistent with the UNIX system partitions placed in the VTOC. If a DOS '**fdisk**' partition is started at cylinder 0, DOS will happily overwrite the UNIX system VTOC.

REFERENCES

edvtoc(1M), **prtvtoc**(1M)

modadmin (1M)

NAME

modadmin – loadable kernel module administration

SYNOPSIS

modadmin -l *modname . . .* | *pathname . . .*

modadmin -u *modid . . .*

modadmin -U *modname . . .*

modadmin -q *modid . . .*

modadmin -Q *modname . . .*

modadmin -s | **S**

modadmin -d *dirname* | **D**

DESCRIPTION

modadmin is the administrative command for loadable kernel modules. It performs the following functions:

load a loadable module into a running system

unload a loadable module from a running system

display the status of a loadable module(s) that is currently loaded

modify the loadable modules search path

The loadable modules feature lets you add a module to a running system without rebooting the system or rebuilding the kernel. When the module is no longer needed, this feature also lets you dynamically remove the module, thereby freeing system resources for other use.

Types of modules that can be dynamically loaded include:

device drivers (block, character, STREAMS and pseudo)

Host Bus Adapter (HBA) drivers

Direct Coupled Device (DCD) controller drivers

STREAMS modules

file systems

miscellaneous modules, such as modules containing code for support routines shared among multiple loadable modules which are not needed in the statically configured kernel

Loadable modules are maintained in individual object files (**.o** files) in the same manner as statically configured modules. Unlike static modules, loadable modules:

are not linked to the kernel until they are needed

must be preconfigured into the system and registered with the running kernel using the **idbuild**(1M) command with the **-M** option before they can be loaded

must be preconfigured in loadable form (requires writing additional module initialization or "wrapper" code)

can be loaded and unloaded by the user, as required, using the **modadmin** command, or by **init**(1M), during every system reboot, using the **idmodload**(1M) command (called a demand load/unload) can be loaded and unloaded by the kernel itself (called an auto load/unload—see NOTES section)

The **modadmin** options have the following meanings:

-l *modname* Load the named module(s) *modname* using the current value of the loadable modules search path to locate the module's object file on disk.

This option searches for a matching file in all directories specified in the loadable modules search path. By default, the search pathname is **/etc/conf/mod.d**.

The load operation performs all tasks associated with link editing the module to the kernel and making the module accessible to the system. If the module depends on other loadable modules (as defined in **/etc/conf/mdevice.d**), and these modules are not currently loaded, **modadmin** will automatically load the dependent modules during the load operation.

When loading completes, an integer *modid* prints on the standard output to identify the module(s) that was loaded.

-l *pathname* Same as **-l** *modname*, except the absolute pathname *pathname* is used to locate the module's object file.

-u *modid* Unload the module(s) identified by the integer value *modid*.

If *modid* specifies **0** (zero), **modadmin** attempts to unload all loadable modules.

The unload operation performs all tasks associated with disconnecting the module from the kernel and releasing any memory acquired by the module. When unloading completes, an integer *modid* prints on the standard output to identify the module(s) that was unloaded.

If the module(s) to be unloaded are currently in-use, are dependents of a loadable module that is currently loaded, or are currently being loaded or unloaded, the unload request will fail.

-U *modname* Same as **-u** *modid*, except the module(s) to be unloaded is specified by name *modname*.

-q *modid* Print the status of the loaded module(s) identified by the integer value *modid*.

Information returned by this option includes:

module identifier (*modid*)
the module's pathname
the module's virtual load address
amount of memory the module occupies
the module's reference count

the module's dependent count

the module's unload delay value

the module's descriptive name

the type of module

depending on the type of module, either the module's character major number, block major number, file system switch number, or STREAMS switch number

-Q *modname* Same as **-q** *modid*, except the module(s) for which status information is to be reported is specified by name *modname*.

-s Print an abbreviated status for all modules currently loaded.

This option returns a listing of module names and module identifiers only.

-S Print the full status for all modules currently loaded.

This option returns status information of the form returned by the **-q** option.

-d *pathname* Prepend the pathname *pathname* to the current loadable modules search path, where *pathname* specifies directories that should be searched:

for all subsequent demand loads initiated by a **modadmin** command with the option **-l** and a named *modname*

for all subsequent loads performed by the kernel's auto-load mechanism (see NOTES section)

prior to searching any directories already prepended to the search path by a prior **modadmin** command with the option **-d**

prior to searching the default search path **/etc/conf/mod.d**, which is always searched, and is always searched last

pathname must specify an absolute pathname or a list of absolute pathnames delimited by colons. The directories identified by *pathname* do not have to exist on the system at the time the request to modify the search path using **modadmin** is made. If these directories do not exist at the time a load takes place, the load operation ignores them.

All modifications to the search path made using this option take effect immediately and affect all subsequent loads (demand and auto-load) and all users on the system.

-D Reset the loadable modules search path to its default value, **/etc/conf/mod.d**. The reset takes effect immediately and affects all subsequent loads (demand and auto-load) and all users on the system.

ERRORS

UX:modadmin: ERROR: Incorrect usage
Command line input contained one or more syntax errors. See the SYNOPSIS section for the correct usage.

UX:modadmin: ERROR: *modid*: **No such file or directory**
Unable to load the module *modid* because the module does not exist.

UX:modadmin: ERROR: Device busy
Unable to load a module because the module is currently in-use.

UX:modadmin: ERROR: Non-numeric ID string: *string*
Unable to unload or obtain status for a module because the module id *string* specified a non-numeric value.

UX:modadmin: ERROR: modstat: Invalid argument
Unable to unload or obtain status for module *modid* because the module does not exist.

UX:modadmin: ERROR: Module: *modid*, **not found**
Unable to obtain status for module *modid* because the module is currently unloaded.

FILES

/etc/conf/mod.d/*

NOTES

Auto Loading

Auto-load occurs when the kernel detects a particular loadable module is required to accomplish some task, but is not currently loaded. For example, if the task were a mount of a file system, and the loadable module that supports the file system was not loaded, the kernel would automatically load the file system module. Once the module was loaded, the mount would take place.

Auto-unload occurs when the kernel detects that the amount of available memory is low. At this time, the kernel begins unloading all modules that are not currently in-use—and that have not been used for some predetermined amount of time—to reclaim the memory allocated to these modules. Unloading continues until the amount of available memory reaches a predetermined high water mark, or the list of modules that are candidates for unloading is exhausted. The amount of time that must elapse before unused modules are considered candidates for unloading is controlled by the value of the global tunable parameter **DEF_UNLOAD_DELAY** in **/etc/conf/mtune.d**. Individual modules can override the value of the global auto-unload delay by specifying their own auto-unload delay value in their **Mtune** files.

Modules that are demand loaded using the **modadmin** command cannot be auto unloaded by the kernel. If a demand-loaded module is no longer needed in the system, it must be demand-unloaded. If a demand unload for a loaded module fails (because the module is in-use, for example) the unload mechanism will add the module to a list of modules that are candidates for the next auto-unload.

Loadable HBA Driver Considerations

Loadable HBA drivers:

must be demand loaded by the user via the **modadmin** command, or (during system reboot) demand loaded by **init** via the **idmodload** command

can not be auto loaded

can not be unloaded (demand or auto)

Loadable DCD Controller Driver Considerations

Loadable DCD controller drivers can not be demand loaded. They are auto loaded/unloaded by the kernel as required.

System Profiler

When the system profiler **prf** is turned on, loadable modules are locked into memory and cannot be unloaded. Modules can continue to be loaded with profiling enabled, but these modules will also become locked. When profiling is disabled, the locks for all loadable modules are removed.

SEE ALSO

idbuild(1M), **idmodload**(1M), **idmodreg**(1M), **idtune**(1M), **init**(1M), **modload**(2), **moduload**(2), **modpath**(2), **modstat**(2), **prf**(7)

NAME

montbl – create monetary database

SYNOPSIS

montbl [**-o** *outfile*] *infile*

DESCRIPTION

The **montbl** command takes as input a specification file, *infile*, that describes the formatting conventions for monetary quantities for a specific locale.

-o *outfile* Write the output on *outfile*; otherwise, write the output on a file named **LC_MONETARY**.

The output of **montbl** is suitable for use by the **localeconv** function [see **localeconv**(3C)]. Before *outfile* can be used by **localeconv**, it must be installed in the **/usr/lib/locale/***locale* directory with the name **LC_MONETARY** by a user with appropriate privilege or a member of group **bin**. *locale* is the locale whose monetary formatting conventions are described in *infile*. This file must be readable by user, group, and other; no other permissions should be set. To use formatting conventions for monetary quantities described in this file, use **setlocale**(3C) to change the locale for category **LC_MONETARY** to *locale* [see **setlocale**(3C)].

Once installed, this file will be used by the **localeconv** function to initialize the monetary specific fields of a structure of type **struct lconv**. For a description of each field in this structure, see **localeconv**(3C).

```
struct     lconv      {
      char *decimal_point;        /* "." */
      char *thousands_sep;        /* "" (zero length string) */
      char *grouping;             /* "" */
      char *int_curr_symbol;      /* "" */
      char *currency_symbol;      /* "" */
      char *mon_decimal_point;    /* "" */
      char *mon_thousands_sep;    /* "" */
      char *mon_grouping;         /* "" */
      char *positive_sign;        /* "" */
      char *negative_sign;        /* "" */
      char int_frac_digits;       /* CHAR_MAX */
      char frac_digits;           /* CHAR_MAX */
      char p_cs_precedes;         /* CHAR_MAX */
      char p_sep_by_space;        /* CHAR_MAX */
      char n_cs_precedes;         /* CHAR_MAX */
      char n_sep_by_space;        /* CHAR_MAX */
      char p_sign_posn;           /* CHAR_MAX */
      char n_sign_posn;           /* CHAR_MAX */
};
```

The specification file specifies the value of each **struct lconv** member, except for the first three members, *decimal_point*, *thousands_sep*, and *grouping*, which are set by the **LC_NUMERIC** category of **setlocale**(3C). Each member's value is given on a line with the following format:

keyword <white space> *value*

where *keyword* is identical to the **struct lconv** field name and *value* is a quoted string for those fields that are a **char** * and an integer for those fields that hold an integer value. For example,

```
int_curr_symbol       "ITL."
int_frac_digits       0
```

will set the international currency symbol and the number of fractional digits to be displayed in an internationally formatted monetary quantity to **ITL.** and **0**, respectively.

Blank lines and lines starting with a **#** are taken to be comments and are ignored. A character in a string may be in octal or hex representation. For example, **\141** or **\x61** could be used to represent the letter 'a'. If there is no specification line for a given structure member, then the default **"C"** locale value for that member is used (see the values in comments in the **struct lconv** definition above).

Given below is an example of what the specification file for Italy would look like:

```
# Italy

int_curr_symbol       "ITL."
currency_symbol       "L."
mon_decimal_point     ""
mon_thousands_sep     "."
mon_grouping          "\3"
positive_sign         ""
negative_sign         "-"
int_frac_digits       0
frac_digits           0
p_cs_precedes         1
p_sep_by_space        0
n_cs_precedes         1
n_sep_by_space        0
p_sign_posn           1
n_sign_posn           1
```

The first three elements of the **lconv** structure, **decimal_point, thousand_sep,** and **grouping** are set by the **LC_NUMERIC** category of **setlocale**(3C). The **chrtbl**(1M) utility can be used to generate the **LC_NUMERIC** data containing this information.

FILES

/usr/lib/locale/*locale***/LC_MONETARY**
  LC_MONETARY database for *locale*

/usr/lib/locale/C/montbl_C
  input file used to construct **LC_MONETARY** in the default locale

SEE ALSO

localeconv(3C), **setlocale**(3C)

NAME

more, **page** – browse or page through a text file

SYNOPSIS

more [**-cdflrsuw**] [-*lines*] [+*linenumber*] [**+/***pattern*] [*filename* . . .

page [**-cdflrsuw**] [-*lines*] [+*linenumber*] [**+/***pattern*] [*filename* . . .

DESCRIPTION

more is a filter that displays the contents of a text file on the terminal, one screenful at a time. It normally pauses after each screenful, and prints **--More--** at the bottom of the screen. **more** provides a two-line overlap between screens for continuity. If **more** is reading from a file rather than a pipe, the percentage of characters displayed so far is also shown.

more scrolls up to display one more line in response to a RETURN character; it displays another screenful in response to a SPACE character. Other commands are listed below.

page clears the screen before displaying the next screenful of text; it only provides a one-line overlap between screens.

more sets the terminal to *noecho* mode, so that the output can be continuous. Commands that you type do not normally show up on your terminal, except for the **/** and **!** commands.

If the standard output is not a terminal, **more** acts just like **cat**(1), except that a header is printed before each file in a series.

OPTIONS

The following options are available with **more**:

-c Clear before displaying. Redrawing the screen instead of scrolling for faster displays. This option is ignored if the terminal does not have the ability to clear to the end of a line.

-d Display error messages rather than ringing the terminal bell if an unrecognized command is used. This is helpful for inexperienced users.

-f Do not fold long lines. This is useful when lines contain nonprinting characters or escape sequences, such as those generated when **nroff**(1) output is piped through **ul**(1).

-l Do not treat FORMFEED characters (CTRL-d) as page breaks. If **-l** is not used, **more** pauses to accept commands after any line containing a **^L** character (CTRL-d). Also, if a file begins with a FORMFEED, the screen is cleared before the file is printed.

-r Normally, **more** ignores control characters that it does not interpret in some way. The **-r** option causes these to be displayed as ^C where C stands for any such control character.

-s Squeeze. Replace multiple blank lines with a single blank line. This is helpful when viewing **nroff**(1) output, on the screen.

-u	Suppress generation of underlining escape sequences. Normally, **more** handles underlining, such as that produced by **nroff**(1), in a manner appropriate to the terminal. If the terminal can perform underlining or has a stand-out mode, **more** supplies appropriate escape sequences as called for in the text file.
-w	Normally, **more** exits when it comes to the end of its input. With **-w**, however, **more** prompts and waits for any key to be struck before exiting.
-lines	Display the indicated number of *lines* in each screenful, rather than the default (the number of lines in the terminal screen less two).
+*linenumber*	Start up at *linenumber*.
+/*pattern*	Start up two lines above the line containing the regular expression *pattern*. Note: unlike editors, this construct should *not* end with a '**/**'. If it does, then the trailing slash is taken as a character in the search pattern.

USAGE

Environment

more uses the terminal's **/usr/share/lib/terminfo/?/*** for the terminal descriptions and looks in the environment variable for any preset options. For instance, to page through files using the **-c** mode by default, set the value of this variable to **-c**. (Normally, the command sequence to set up this environment variable is placed in the **.login** or **.profile** file).

Commands

The commands take effect immediately; it is not necessary to type a carriage return. Up to the time when the command character itself is given, the user may type the line kill character to cancel the numerical argument being formed. In addition, the user may type the erase character to redisplay the '**--More--(***xx***%)**' message.

In the following commands, *i* is a numerical argument (**1** by default).

*i*SPACE	Display another screenful, or *i* more lines if *i* is specified.
*i*RETURN	Display another line, or *i* more lines, if specified.
*i***^D**	(CTRL-d) Display (scroll down) 11 more lines. If *i* is given, the scroll size is set to *i* .
*i*d	Same as **^D**.
*i***z**	Same as SPACE, except that *i* , if present, becomes the new default number of lines per screenful.
*i***s**	Skip *i* lines and then print a screenful.
*i***f**	Skip *i* screenfuls and then print a screenful.
*i***^B**	(CTRL-b) Skip back *i* screenfuls and then print a screenful.
b	Same as **^B** (CTRL-d).

q
Q Exit from **more**.

= Display the current line number.

v Drop into the editor indicated by the **EDITOR** environment variable, at the current line of the current file. The default editor is **ed**(1).

h Help. Give a description of all the **more** commands.

i/*pattern* Search forward for the *i* th occurrence of the regular expression *pattern*. Display the screenful starting two lines before the line that contains the *i* th match for the regular expression *pattern*, or the end of a pipe, whichever comes first. If **more** is displaying a file and there is no such match, its position in the file remains unchanged. Regular expressions can be edited using erase and kill characters. Erasing back past the first column cancels the search command.

*i***n** Search for the *i* th occurrence of the last *pattern* entered.

' Single quote. Go to the point from which the last search started. If no search has been performed in the current file, go to the beginning of the file.

!*command* Invoke a shell to execute *command* . The characters **%** and **!**, when used within *command* are replaced with the current filename and the previous shell command, respectively. If there is no current filename, **%** is not expanded. Prepend a backslash to these characters to escape expansion.

*i***:n** Skip to the *i* th next filename given in the command line, or to the last filename in the list if *i* is out of range.

*i***:p** Skip to the *i* th previous filename given in the command line, or to the first filename if *i* is out of range. If given while **more** is positioned within a file, go to the beginning of the file. If **more** is reading from a pipe, **more** simply rings the terminal bell.

:f Display the current filename and line number.

:q
:Q Exit from **more** (same as **q** or **Q**).

. Dot. Repeat the previous command.

^ Halt a partial display of text. **more** stops sending output, and displays the usual **--More--** prompt. Unfortunately, some output is lost as a result.

FILES

/usr/share/lib/terminfo/?/* terminal data base
/usr/lib/more.help help file

SEE ALSO

cat(1), **csh**(1), **environ**(5), **man**(1), **script**(1), **sh**(1), **term**(4), **terminfo**(4)

NOTES

Skipping backwards is too slow on large files.

NAME

mount, **umount** (generic) – mount or unmount file systems and remote resources

SYNOPSIS

mount [**-v** | **-p**]
mount [**-F** *FSType*] [**-V**] [*current_options*] [**-o** *specific_options*] {*special* | *mount_point*}
mount [**-F** *FSType*] [**-V**] [*current_options*] [**-o** *specific_options*] *special mount_point*
umount [**-V**] [**-o** *specific_options*] {*special* | *mount_point*}

DESCRIPTION

File systems other than **root** (**/**) are considered removable in the sense that they can be either available to users or unavailable. **mount** notifies the system that *special*, a block special device or a remote resource, is available to users from the *mount_point* which must already exist; it becomes the name of the root of the newly mounted *special* or resource.

mount, when entered with arguments, validates all arguments except the device name and invokes an *FSType* specific **mount** module. If invoked with no arguments, **mount** lists all the mounted file systems from the mount table. If invoked with any of the following partial argument lists (for example, one of *special* or *mount_point* or when both arguments are specified but no *FSType* is specified), **mount** will search **/etc/vfstab** to fill in the missing arguments: *FSType*, *special*, *mount_point*, *specific_options*. It will then invoke the *FSType*-specific **mount** module.

Most *FSTypes* do not have a **umount** specific module. If one exists, it is executed; otherwise, the generic module unmounts the file system. If the **-o** option is specified, the **umount** specific module is always executed.

current_options are options supported by the **s5**-specific module of **mount** and **umount**. Other *FSTypes* do not necessarily support these options. *specific_options* indicate suboptions specified in a comma-separated list of suboptions and/or keyword-attribute pairs for interpretation by the *FSType*-specific module of the command.

The options are:

-v Print the output in a new style. The new output has the *FSType* and flags displayed in addition to the old output. The *mount_point* and *special* fields are reversed.

-p Print the list of mounted file systems in the **/etc/vfstab** format.

-F Specify the *FSType* on which to operate. The *FSType* must be specified or must be determinable from **/etc/vfstab** while mounting a file system.

-V Echo the complete command line, but do not execute the command. The command line is generated by using the options and arguments provided by the user and adding to them information derived from **/etc/vfstab**. This option should be used to verify and validate the command line.

-o Specify *FSType*-specific options.

Exit Codes

The following values are returned by the generic **mount** command:

0	Successful exit
1	Usage error
2	Invalid combinations of options
4	Invalid arguments for options
5	FSType exceeds MAX characters
6	More than one FSType specified
7	Cannot open **vfstab**
8	**getvfsany**() error
9	Cannot open **mnttab**
10	Cannot lock **mnttab**
11	**getmntent**() error
12	Cannot stat mount point
13	Mount point cannot be determined
14	Mount point is not an absolute pathname
15	Mount point does not exist
18	*special* device cannot be determined
19	Device not found in device database
21	Cannot access device database
27	**malloc**() error - unable to allocate memory
28	**wait**() error - unexpected problem with file system dependent mount
29	**fork**() error - Unable to create a process
30	**exec**() error - Invalid file system type
31	**exec**() error - Permission denied

The following values are returned by the generic **umount** command:

0	Success
1	Usage error
2	FSType name exceeds maximum characters
3	Cannot execute path
4	Cannot open **mnttab**
5	Cannot lock **mnttab**
6	Line in **mnttab** exceeds max chars

7	Line in mnttab has too few entries
8	Miscellaneous errors from getmntent()
9	Cannot open temp file
10	Cannot write to temp file
11	umount() - permission denied
12	umount() - no such device
13	umount() - no such directory
14	umount() - not mounted
15	umount() - mount pt busy
16	umount() - block device required
17	umount() - broken link detected
18	umount() - misc error

NOTES

mount does not prevent you from mounting a file system on a directory that is not empty.

The old output format will be phased out in a future release and all output will be in the new **-v** format. The most significant changes are the addition of two new fields to show the *FSType* and flags, and the reversal of the *mount_point* and *special* name.

mount adds an entry to the mount table **/etc/mnttab**; **umount** removes an entry from the table.

FILES

/etc/mnttab	mount table
/etc/vfstab	list of default parameters for each file system

SEE ALSO

fumount(1M), **bfs**-specific **mount**(1M), **cdfs**-specific **mount**(1M), **nfs**-specific **mount**(1M), **rfs**-specific **mount**(1M), **s5**-specific **mount**(1M), **sfs**-specific **mount**(1M), **ufs**-specific **mount**(1M), **vxfs**-specific **mount**(1M), **mnttab**(4), **rmount**(1M), **setmnt**(1M), **vfstab**(4)

NAME

mountall, umountall – mount, unmount multiple file systems

SYNOPSIS

/sbin/mountall [**-F** *FSType*] [**-l** | **-r**] [*file_system_table*]
/sbin/umountall [**-F** *FSType*] [**-k**] [**-l** | **-r**]

DESCRIPTION

These commands may be executed only by a privileged user.

mountall is used to mount file systems according to a *file_system_table*. (**/etc/vfstab** is the default file system table.) The special file name "–" reads from the standard input. If the dash is specified, then the standard input must be in the same format as **/etc/vfstab**. With no arguments **mountall** restricts the mount to all systems with **automnt** field set to **yes** in the *file_system_table*.

Before each file system is mounted, a sanity check is done using **fsck** [see **fsck(1M)**] to see if it appears mountable. If the file system does not appear mountable, it is fixed, using **fsck**, before the mount is attempted.

umountall causes all mounted file systems except **root**, **/proc**, **/stand**, and **/dev/fd** to be unmounted. If the *FSType* is specified **mountall** and **umountall** limit their actions to the *FSType* specified.

The options are:

- **-F** Specify the File System type to be mounted or unmounted. If *FSType* is specified the action is limited to file systems of this *FSType*.
- **-l** Limit the action to local file systems.
- **-r** Limit the action to remote file system types.
- **-k** Send a *SIGKILL* signal to processes that have files opened.

DIAGNOSTICS

No messages are printed if the file systems are mountable and clean.

Error and warning messages come from **fsck**(1M) and **mount**(1M).

SEE ALSO

fsck(1M), **fuser**(1M), **mnttab**(4), **mount**(1M), **signal**(2), **vfstab**(4)

mountd (1M)

NAME

mountd – NFS mount request server

SYNOPSIS

`/usr/lib/nfs/mountd [-n]`

DESCRIPTION

mountd is an RPC server that answers file system mount requests. It reads the file **/etc/dfs/sharetab**, described in **sharetab**(4), to determine which file systems are available for mounting by which machines. It also provides information as to what file systems are mounted by which clients. This information can be printed using the **dfmounts**(1M) command.

The **mountd** daemon is automatically invoked in run level 3.

With the **-n** option, **mountd** does not check that the clients are root users. Though this option makes things slightly less secure, it does allow older versions (pre-3.0) of client NFS to work.

Only a privileged user can execute this command.

FILES

/etc/dfs/sharetab

SEE ALSO

dfmounts(1M), **nfsping**(1M), **sharetab**(4)

NAME

mount (bfs) - mount **bfs** file systems

SYNOPSIS

mount [-F bfs] [*generic_options*] **[-r]** [**-o** *specific_options*] {*special* | *mount_point*}
mount [-F bfs] [*generic_options*] **[-r]** [**-o** *specific_options*] *special mount_point*

DESCRIPTION

generic_options are options supported by the generic **mount** command.

mount attaches a **bfs** file system, referenced by *special*, to the file system hierarchy at the pathname location *mount_point*, which must already exist. If *mount_point* has any contents prior to the **mount** operation, these are hidden until the file system is unmounted.

The options are:

-F bfs Specify the **bfs**-FSType

-r Mount the file system read-only

-o Specify the options specific to the **bfs** file system. Available options are:

  rw | ro Read/write or read-only. Default is read/write.

Only a privileged user can mount file systems.

FILES

/etc/mnttab mount table

SEE ALSO

generic **mount**(1M), **mount**(2), **mnttab**(4)

NAME

mount (cdfs) – mount cdfs file system

SYNOPSIS

mount [-F cdfs] [*generic_options*] -r [-o *cdfs_options*] [*special* | *mount_point*]
mount [-F cdfs] [*generic_options*] -r [-o *cdfs_options*] *special mount_point*

DESCRIPTION

The **mount** command attaches the **cdfs** file system to the file system hierarchy at the location specified by *mount_point*, which must already exist and must be a directory. If *mount_point* already has contents prior to the **mount** operation, the contents remain hidden until the **cdfs** file system is unmounted. The *generic_options* are the options supported by the generic **mount** command (see the generic **mount**(1M) command for information about these options.) The **cdfs**-specific options affect the mode of operation of the CD-ROM and are used to set default values.

The CD-ROM media may or may not have values set for items such as the User ID (UID), Group ID (GID), permissions, etc. If a value is not recorded on the CD-ROM, a default value is assigned by the software. The default value is either taken from the **/etc/conf/pack.d/cdfs/space.c** file, or from the value specified with the **-o** option of the **mount** command.

Once the media is mounted, a default value can only be changed by using the **cddevsuppl**(1M) or **cdmntsuppl**(1M) commands, or by unmounting/remounting the media and specifying the desired values using the **-o** option.

Options

The **cdfs**-specific options are:

-F cdfs Specifies the **cdfs** file system type. (Required)

-r Mounts the file system as read-only. This option or the **-o ro** option is required.

-o Specifies the **cdfs**-specific options in a comma-separated list of options from the list below. The default values that are set when the CD-ROM is mounted include **suid**, **susp**, and **rrip**, and the values defined in the **/etc/conf/pack.d/cdfs/space.c** file.

In the list below, replace the words shown in italics with the desired value:

ro Mounts the resource read-only. This option or the 1-**r** option are required.

suid|nosuid Allows or disallows execution of Setuid programs. The default is **suid**.

susp|nosusp Enables/disables the processing of all System Use Sharing Protocol (SUSP) compliant extensions to the ISO-9660/High-Sierra specification. The SUSP defines a mechanism for which the System Use Area of a Directory Record may be shared by multiple independent organizations, for example, Rock

Ridge Interchange Protocol (RRIP). The **nosusp** flag prevents the processing of all SUSP-compliant extensions, even if recorded on the media.

rrip|norrip Enables/disables the processing of all the Rock Ridge Interchange Protocol (RRIP) extensions to the ISO-9660/High-Sierra specification. The RRIP is a SUSP-compliant set of extensions that provide POSIX file semantics within the context of an ISO-9660/High-Sierra file-system. The **rrip** flag requires that the **susp** flag also be set. The **norrip** flag prevents the processing of all RRIP extensions even if recorded on the media.

noextend Disallows the processing of all extensions to the ISO-9660/High-Sierra specification (SUSP and non-SUSP alike), even if recorded on the media. Currently, **noextend** is equivalent to **nosusp,norrip**. However, **noextend** will apply to future ISO-9660/High-Sierra extensions.

sectsz=<*value*> Defines the logical sector size of the media, as defined by the ISO-9660 and/or the High Sierra specifications. If not specified, the system will automatically determine the logical sector size of the media. The user need not specify this option. However, if specified, the value must exactly match the media being mounted.

uid=*owner* Defines the default UID to be used for the files and/or directories that do not have a UID recorded on the CD-ROM. *owner* is a numeric UID value or a user name. See the **cdmntsuppl**(1M) command for more information.

gid=*group* Defines the default GID to be used for the files and/or directories that do not have a GID recorded on the CD-ROM. *group* is a numeric GID value or a group name. See the **cdmntsuppl**(1M) command in the X/Open *CD-ROM Support Component Preliminary Specification* for more information.

fperm=*mode* Defines the default file permissions to be used for the files that do not have permissions recorded on the CD-ROM. The value *mode* is an absolute value (a 4-digit octal), or symbolic value. See the **chmod**(1) and **cdmntsuppl**(1M) commands

dperm=*mode* Defines the default directory permissions to be used for the directories that do not have permissions recorded on the CD-ROM. The value *mode* is an absolute value (a 4-digit octal), or symbolic value. See the **chmod**(1) and **cdmntsuppl**(1M) commands.

uidmap=*filename* Sets User ID mappings. The UID and user names associated with a file or directory on the CD-ROM might not be valid on the host system. The **uidmap** function maps the CD-ROM UID's to valid host system UID's.

Entries in *filename* are specified as the value recorded on the CD-ROM, colon (:), followed by the UID or user name as found in the user database. Multiple entries are separated by new lines.

For example, *filename* may contain the entries:

```
1500:418
1006:stanley
```

The first entry maps the UID of 1500 (on the CD-ROM) to a UID of 418. The second entry maps the UID of 1006 (on the CD-ROM) to the user named **stanley**. See the **cdmntsuppl**(1M) command.

The maximum number of mappings allowed is defined in **sys/cdrom.h**.

gidmap=*filename* Sets Group ID mappings. The GID and group names associated with a file or directory on the CD-ROM might not be valid on the host system. The **gidmap** function maps the CD-ROM GID's to valid host system GID's.

Entries in *filename* are specified as the value recorded on CD-ROM, colon (:), followed by the GID or group name as found in the group database. Multiple entries are separated by new lines. See the **cdmntsuppl**(1M) command.

The maximum number of mappings allowed is defined in **sys/cdrom.h**.

nmconv=*a* Sets the file name conversion mode for the ISO-9660/High-Sierra file and directory names recorded on the CD-ROM. The **nmconv** option lets you specify how the file and directory names are seen by the user on the host system. Non-ISO-9660 and non-High-Sierra names are not converted.

a is some combination of the following:

- **c** Names are not converted; the names used are the ones recorded on the CD-ROM.
- **l** Converts upper case letters to lower case.

m Suppresses the version number and the separator (;). See the **cdmntsuppl**(1M) page for more information.

dsearch=*b* Defines how the directory's search permissions (the execute bit) are to be determined. *b* is one of the following:

x Search permission is granted only if the user has "execute" permissions (as recorded on the CD-ROM or using the **dperm** option above). See the **cdmntsuppl**(1M) command for more information.

s Search permission is granted only if the user has "read" or "execute" permissions (as recorded on the CD-ROM or using the **dperm** option above). See the **cdmntsuppl**(1M) command for more information.

devmap=*filename* Maps the CD-ROM major and minor numbers assigned to device nodes to valid host system major and minor numbers. The value for *filename* is a file that contains one entry for each device file in the form:

device_file_path new_major new_minor

Fields are separated by white space (tabs or spaces) and entries are separated by a new line. Anything beyond the third field in a line is treated as a comment. See the **cddevsuppl**(1M) command for more information.

Examples

For example, the command line:

```
mount -F cdfs -r -o nosuid,dperm=544,nmconv=l
```

mounts **cdfs** read-only (required), disallows setuid, sets the default directory permissions to 544 (read/execute for owner, read for group and others), and converts upper case filenames to lower case.

Exit Codes

The **mount** command exits with one of the following values:

0 Successful completion.

1 The mount point or device file specified does not exist.

1 Device does not contain a CD-ROM file system.

1 Access is denied.

2 Only a privileged user can change any settings.

3 Too many user, group, or file mappings. The **sys/cdrom.h** header file defines the maximum number of mappings allowed. (See the **devmap**, **gidmap**, and **uidmap** options.)

4 Parameter error.

4 Bad format in *filename* (used when setting/resetting the UID, GID and major/minor numbers).

5 The file name specified with the **devmap** option is not a device file.

NOTES

Only a privileged user can mount file systems.

REFERENCES

cddevsuppl(1M), **cd_idmap**(3X), **cdmntsuppl**(1M) **cd_nmconv**(3X) **cd_setdevmap**(3X), **chmod**(1), generic **mount**(1M)
The X/Open *CD-ROM Support Component Preliminary Specification*.

NAME

mount, **umount** – mount or unmount remote NFS resources

SYNOPSIS

mount [-F nfs] [-r] [-o *specific_options*] {*server*:*path* | *mountpoint*}
mount [-F nfs] [-r] [-o *specific_options*] *server*:*path mountpoint*
umount [-o *specific_options*] {*server*:*path* | *mountpoint*}

DESCRIPTION

The **mount** command attaches a named *path* residing on machine *server* to the file system hierarchy at the pathname location *mountpoint*, which must already exist. If *mountpoint* has any contents prior to the **mount** operation, the contents remain hidden until the *server*:*path* is once again unmounted.

If *server*:*path* is listed in the **vfstab** file, the command line can specify either *server*:*path* or *mountpoint*, and **mount** will consult **vfstab** for more information.

mount maintains a table of mounted file systems in **/etc/mnttab**, described in **mnttab**(4).

The NFS-specific **umount** command is located in **/usr/lib/fs/nfs/umount** and is called by the generic **umount** [see **mount**(1M)] command. **umount** unmounts a file system and removes the appropriate entry from **/etc/mnttab**.

If the directory on which a file system is to be mounted is a symbolic link, the file system is mounted on *the directory to which the symbolic link refers* , rather than being mounted on top of the symbolic link itself.

Only a privileged user can execute these commands.

Options

The following options are available to the **mount** command:

-F Specifies the File System Type (FSType). If the **-F** option is omitted, **mount** will take the file system type from **/etc/vfstab** if an entry exists in **/etc/vfstab** for the file system being mounted.

-r Mount the specified file system read-only.

-o Specify file system specific options in a comma-separated list of words from the list below.

rw | **ro**
server:*path* is mounted read-write or read-only. The default is **rw**.

suid | **nosuid**
Execution of setuid allowed or disallowed. The default is **suid**.

remount
If a file system is mounted read-only, remounts the file system read-write.

bg | **fg**
If the first attempt fails, retry as a background process, or, as a foreground process. The default is **fg**.

retry=*n*
The number of times to retry the mount operation. The default is 10000.

port=*n*
The server IP port number. The default is **NFS_PORT**.

grpid Create a file with its GID set to the effective GID of the calling process. This behavior may be overridden on a per-directory basis by setting the set-GID bit of the parent directory; in this case, the GID is set to the GID of the parent directory [see **open**(2) and **mkdir**(2)]. Files created on file systems that are *not* mounted with the **grpid** option will obey BSD semantics; that is, the GID is unconditionally inherited from that of the parent directory.

rsize=*n*
Set the read buffer size to *n* bytes.

wsize=*n*
Set the write buffer size to *n* bytes.

timeo=*n*
Set the NFS timeout to *n* tenths of a second.

retrans=*n*
Set the number of NFS retransmissions to *n*.

soft | **hard**
Return an error if the server does not respond, or continue the retry request until the server responds.

intr Allow keyboard interrupts to kill a process that is hung while waiting for a response on a hard-mounted file system.

secure
Use a more secure protocol for NFS transactions.

noac Suppress attribute caching.

acregmin=*n*
Hold cached attributes for at least *n* seconds after file modification.

acregmax=*n*
Hold cached attributes for no more than *n* seconds after file modification.

acdirmin=*n*
Hold cached attributes for at least *n* seconds after directory update.

acdirmax=*n*
Hold cached attributes for no more than *n* seconds after directory update.

actimeo=*n*
Set *min* and *max* times for regular files and directories to *n* seconds.

The following options are available to the NFS-specific **mount** and **umount** commands:

server:path
: Where *server* is the machine that has the remote resource and *path* is the pathname of the resource.

mountpoint
: The name of the local directory where the remote resource has been mounted.

Files

/etc/mnttab	table of mounted file systems
/etc/dfs/fstypes	default distributed file system type
/etc/vfstab	table of automatically mounted resources

Exit Codes

The following values are returned by the NFS-specific **mount** command:

0	Successful exit
47	Could not open mnttab
48	Could not lock mnttab
70	Retry **mount** operation
32	Usage error
72	Specify *host:path*
73	Invalid option
74	Server not responding
75	Could not get nfs service addr
76	Could not negotiate secure protocol
77	Access denied
71	Gave up retrying **mount** operation
78	No such directory

The following values are returned by the NFS-specific **umount** command:

0	Successful exit
33	Usage error
34	Permission denied
35	Directory/Resource not mounted
36	Mount point busy

USAGE

Background vs. Foreground

NFS File systems mounted with the **bg** option indicate that **mount** is to retry as a background process if the server's mount daemon [**mountd**(1M)] does not respond. **mount** retries the request up to the count specified in the **retry=***n* option. Once the file system is mounted, each NFS request made in the kernel waits **timeo=***n* tenths of a second for a response. If no response arrives, the time-out is multiplied by **2** and the request is retransmitted. When the number of retransmissions has reached the number specified in the **retrans=***n* option, a file system mounted with the **soft** option returns an error on the request; one mounted with the **hard** option prints a warning message and continues to retry the request.

Read-Write vs. Read-Only

NFS File systems that are mounted **rw** (read-write) should use the **hard** option. If the server goes down when a user is writing a file, the write will continue when the serve comes back up, and the data being written will not be lost.

Secure File Systems

The **secure** option must be given if the server requires secure mounting for the NFS file system.

File Attributes

The attribute cache retains file attributes on the client. Attributes for a file are assigned a time to be flushed (updated). If the file is modified before the flush time, then the flush time is extended by the time since the last modification (under the assumption that files that changed recently are likely to change soon). There is a minimum and maximum flush time extension for regular files and for directories. Setting **actimeo=***n* extends flush time by *n* seconds for both regular files and directories.

Examples

To mount a remote file system:

```
mount -F nfs serv:/usr/src /usr/src
```

To soft mount a remote file system:

```
mount -F nfs -o soft serv:/usr/src /usr/src
```

To hard mount a remote file system:

```
mount -F nfs -o hard serv:/usr/src /usr/src
```

To mount a file system with **rsize** set to 1024 bytes:

```
mount -F nfs -o rsize=1024 serv:/usr/src /usr/src
```

To mount a file system and allow the mount command to only be retried 3 times:

```
mount -F nfs -o retry=3 serv:/usr/src /usr/src
```

To unmount a remote file system with *server:path*

```
umount serv:/usr/src
```

where **serv** is the name of the *server* and **/usr/src** is the name of the *path*.

To unmount a remote file system with *mountpoint*

```
umount /usr/src
```

where **/usr/src** is the *mountpoint* of the mounted resource.

Notes

There is a potential RPC authentication error that can occur with NFS clients/servers that are running different releases of UNIX (pre-SVR4.0).

In pre-SVR4.0 systems, the number of groups that the "root" user could belong to was limited to eight. In UNIX SVR4.2, the "root" user belongs to more than eight groups.

The following is an example of an error than can occur:

> **nfs mount:** *server*:*path* **server not responding: RPC: Authentication error; why = Invalid client credential.**

If you need to use NFS with pre-SVR4.0 systems, you need to limit the "root" user to no more than eight groups. To modify the groups that a user belongs to, use **groupmod**. For information on **groupmod**, see **groupmod**(1M).

Choose the groups that you limit the "root" user to with caution. There is a possibility that you could impact system operations if the "root" user is limited to no more than eight groups.

If you are mounting resources from a fast server, it is advised that you use **rsize=1024,wsize=1024 mount** options. This should be used because fast servers cause data overruns on the ethernet driver on slow client machines. One symptom of this problem has the following message being written to the console of the client machines:

> **RPC: Timed out**

Another symptom of this problem may be that the client machine appears to be hung, with the following message being written to the console of the client machine:

> **NFS server** *hostname* **not responding, still trying**

REFERENCES

groupmod(1M), **mnttab**(4), **mount**(1M), **mount**(2), **mountall**(1M), **open**(2), **umount**(2)

NOTICES

When a single file is mounted over NFS, it cannot be opened with the **O_CREAT** flag. See **open**(2) for information on **O_CREAT**.

NAME

mount – mount remote resources

SYNOPSIS

mount [-F rfs] [-cr] [-o *specific_options*] *resource directory*
mount [-F rfs] [-cr] [-o *specific_options*] {*resource* | *directory*}

DESCRIPTION

This command is obsolete and will not be supported after this release. The **mount** command makes a remote *resource* available to users from the mount point *directory*. The command adds an entry to the table of mounted devices, **/etc/mnttab**.

If the resource is listed in the **vfstab** file, the command line can specify either *resource* or *directory*, and **mount** will consult **vfstab** for more information. If the **-F** option is omitted, **mount** will take the file system type from **vfstab**.

If multiple transport providers are installed and network administrators attempt to mount a resource over them, the transport providers should be specified as network IDs in the **/etc/netconfig** file. The NETPATH environment variable can be used to specify the sequence of transport providers **mount** will use to attempt a connection to a server machine (**NETPATH=***transport1***:***transport2*, where *transport#* is replaced by a valid transport provider (for example, **tcp**)). If only one transport provider is installed and **/etc/netconfig** has not been set up, all resources will be mounted over this transport provider by default.

The following options are available:

-F rfs Specifies **rfs** as the file system type.

-c Disable client caching. This is the same as **-o nocaching**.

-r *resource* is to be mounted read-only. If the *resource* is write-protected, this flag or the **-o ro** specific option must be used.

-o Specify the **rfs** file system specific options in a comma-separated list. The available options are:

nocaching Disable client caching.

rw|ro *resource* is to be mounted read/write or read-only. The default is read/write.

suid|nosuid Set-uid bits are to be obeyed or ignored, respectively, on execution. The default is **nosuid**.

Note that mounting a resource from an untrusted server introduces possible security risks. While the use of **nosuid** protects against some risks, it is not completely effective. The best defense against such security risks is to avoid such mounts.

Only a privileged user can execute this command.

FILES

```
/etc/mnttab        mount table
/etc/netconfig     network configuration database
/etc/vfstab        table of automatically mounted resources
```

SEE ALSO

dfmounts(1M), dfshares(1M), fuser(1M), mnttab(4), mount(1M), netconfig(4), share(1M), unshare(1M), vfstab(4)

NAME

mount (s5) – mount an **s5** file system

SYNOPSIS

mount [**-F s5**] [*generic_options*] [**-r**] [**-o** *specific_options*] {*special* | *mount_point*}
mount [**-F s5**] [*generic_options*] [**-r**] [**-o** *specific_options*] *special mount_point*

DESCRIPTION

generic_options are options supported by the generic **mount** command.

mount notifies the system that *special*, an **s5** block special device, is available to users from the *mount_point* which must exist before **mount** is called; it becomes the name of the root of the newly mounted *special*.

The options are:

-F s5 Specify an **s5** FSType.

-r Mount the file system read-only.

-o Specify the **s5** file-specific options in a comma-separated list. The available options are:

- **rw** | **ro** Read/write or read-only. Default is **rw**.
- **suid** | **nosuid**
  Setuid is honored or ignored on execution. Default is **suid**.

  Note that a **mount** of an unprotected medium (such as a floppy disk) introduces possible security risks. While the use of **nosuid** protects against some risks, it is not completely effective. The best defense against such security risks is to avoid mounting unprotected media.
- **remount** Used in conjunction with **rw**. A file system mounted read-only can be *remounted* read-write. Fails if the file system is not currently mounted or if the file system is mounted **rw**. Option is in force only when specified.

FILES

/etc/mnttab mount table

SEE ALSO

mnttab(4), generic **mount**(1M), **mount**(2), **setmnt**(1M), **setuid**(2)

NAME

mount (sfs) – mount **sfs** file systems

SYNOPSIS

mount [**-F sfs**] [*generic_options*] [**-r**] [**-o** *specific_options*] { *special* | *mount_point* }
mount [**-F sfs**] [*generic_options*] [**-r**] [**-o** *specific_options*] *special mount_point*

DESCRIPTION

mount attaches a **sfs** file system to the file system hierarchy at the pathname location *mount_point*, which must already exist. If *mount_point* has any contents prior to the **mount** operation, these remain hidden until the file system is once again unmounted.

The options are:

-F sfs Specifies the **sfs**-FSType.

-r Mount the file system read-only.

-o Specify **sfs** file system specific options. If invalid options are specified, a warning message is printed and the invalid options are ignored. The following options are available:

- **f** Fake an **/etc/mnttab** entry, but do not actually mount any file systems. Parameters are not verified.
- **n** Mount the file system without making an entry in **/etc/mnttab**.
- **rw** | **ro** Read/write or read-only. Default is **rw**.
- **nosuid** By default the file system is mounted with setuid execution allowed. Specifying **nosuid** overrides the default and causes the file system to be mounted with setuid execution disallowed.

  Note that mounting an unprotected medium (such as a floppy disk) introduces possible security risks. While the use of **nosuid** protects against some risks, it is not completely effective. The best defense against such security risks is to avoid mounting unprotected media.
- **remount** Used in conjunction with **rw**. A file system mounted read-only can be *remounted* read-write. Fails if the file system is not currently mounted or if the file system is mounted **rw**.

NOTES

If the directory on which a file system is to be mounted is a symbolic link, the file system is mounted on the directory to which the symbolic link refers, rather than on top of the symbolic link itself.

FILES

/etc/mnttab table of mounted file systems

SEE ALSO

mkdir(2), **mnttab**(4), generic **mount**(1M), **mount**(2), **umount**(2), **open**(2)

NAME

mount (ufs) – mount **ufs** file systems

SYNOPSIS

mount [**-F ufs**] [*generic_options*] [**-r**] [**-o** *specific_options*] { *special* | *mount_point* }
mount [**-F ufs**] [*generic_options*] [**-r**] [**-o** *specific_options*] *special mount_point*

DESCRIPTION

generic_options are options supported by the generic **mount** command. **mount** attaches a **ufs** file system, referenced by *special*, to the file system hierarchy at the pathname location *mount_point*, which must already exist. If *mount_point* has any contents prior to the **mount** operation, these remain hidden until the file system is once again unmounted.

The options are:

-F ufs Specifies the **ufs**-FSType.

-r Mount the file system read-only.

-o Specify the **ufs** file system specific options in a comma-separated list. If invalid options are specified, a warning message is printed and the invalid options are ignored. The following options are available:

- **f** Fake an **/etc/mnttab** entry, but do not actually mount any file systems. Parameters are not verified.
- **n** Mount the file system without making an entry in **/etc/mnttab**.
- **rw** | **ro** Read/write or read-only. Default is **rw**.
- **nosuid** By default the file system is mounted with setuid execution allowed. Specifying **nosuid** overrides the default and causes the file system to be mounted with setuid execution disallowed.
- **remount** Used in conjunction with **rw**. A file system mounted read-only can be *remounted* read-write. Fails if the file system is not currently mounted or if the file system is mounted **rw**.

NOTES

If the directory on which a file system is to be mounted is a symbolic link, the file system is mounted on the directory to which the symbolic link refers, rather than on top of the symbolic link itself.

FILES

/etc/mnttab mount table

SEE ALSO

mkdir(2), **mnttab**(4), generic **mount**(1M), **mount**(2), **open**(2), **umount**(2)

NAME

mount (vxfs) – mount a **vxfs** file system

SYNOPSIS

mount [**-F vxfs**] [*generic_options*] [**-r**] [**-o** *specific_options*] {*special* | *mount_point*}
mount [**-F vxfs**] [*generic_options*] [**-r**] [**-o** *specific_options*] *special mount_point*

DESCRIPTION

generic_options are options supported by the generic **mount** command.

mount notifies the system that *special*, a **vxfs** block special device, is available to users from *mount_point*, which must exist before **mount** is called. *mount_point* becomes the name of the root of the newly mounted *special*.

The options are:

-F vxfs Specify the **vxfs** FSType.

-r Mount the file system read-only.

-o Specify the **vxfs** file system specific options in a comma-separated list. The available options are:

rw | **ro** Read/write or read-only. The default is **rw**.

suid | **nosuid** Setuid is honored or ignored on execution. The default is **suid**.

log | **delaylog** | **tmplog** | **nolog**
Control intent logging. File system integrity across system failure requires that logging be enabled. The default is **log**. In **log** mode, file system structural changes are logged to disk before the system call returns to the application. If the system crashes, **vxfs** will complete the operations.

In **delaylog** mode, some system calls return before the intent log is written. This improves the performance of the system, but some changes are not guaranteed until a short time later when the intent log is written. This mode approximates traditional UNIX system guarantees for correctness in case of system failures.

In **tmplog** mode, the intent log is almost always delayed. This improves performance, but recent changes may disappear if the system crashes. This mode is only recommended for temporary file systems.

In **nolog** mode, the intent log is disabled. All I/O requests, including synchronous I/O, are performed asynchronously. The other three logging modes provide fast file system recovery; **nolog** does not provide fast file system recovery. With **nolog** mode, a full structural check must be performed after a crash; this may result in loss of substantial portions of the file system, depending upon activity at the time of the crash. Usually, a **nolog** file system should be rebuilt with **mkfs**(1M) after a crash. The **nolog** mode should only be used for memory resident or very temporary file systems.

NOTE: **nolog** is available with the VxFS Advanced package only.

`blkclear`
Ensure that all data extents are cleared before being allocated to a file (requires synchronous zeroing of certain newly allocated extents).

`remount`
Used in conjunction with **rw**. A file system mounted read-only can be *remounted* read-write. **remount** fails if the file system is not currently mounted or if the file system is mounted **rw**.

snapof=*snapof_special*
Mount the file system as a snapshot of *snapof_special*, where *snapof_special* is the block special file of a mounted **vxfs** file system.

NOTE: snapof=*snapof_special* is available with the VxFS Advanced package only.

snapsize=*size*
Used in conjunction with **snapof**. *size* is the size in sectors of the snapshot file system being mounted. This option is required only when the device driver is incapable of determining the size of *snapof_special*, and will default to the entire device if not specified.

NOTE: **snapsize**=*size* is available with the VxFS Advanced package only.

`mincache=direct`|**dsync**|**closesync**
This option is used to alter the caching behavior of the file system. The **direct** value will cause any writes without the **O_SYNC** flag and all reads to be handled as if the **VX_DIRECT** caching advisory had been set. The **dsync** value will cause any writes without either the **O_SYNC** flag or the **VX_DIRECT** caching advisory to be handled as if the **VX_DSYNC** caching advisory had been set. The **closesync**, **dsync** and **direct** values all cause the equivalent of an **fsync**(2) to be run when the file is closed. See **vxfsio**(7) for an explanation of **VX_DIRECT** and **VX_DSYNC**.

NOTE: **mincache=direct** and **mincache=dsync** are available with the VxFS Advanced package only.

`convosync=direct`|**dsync**|**closesync**
This option is used to alter the caching behavior of the file system for **O_SYNC** I/O operations. The **direct** value will cause any reads or writes with the **O_SYNC**

flag to be handled as if the **VX_DIRECT** caching advisory had been set instead. The **dsync** value will cause any writes with the **O_SYNC** flag to be handled as if the **VX_DSYNC** caching advisory had been set instead. The **closesync** value causes **O_SYNC** writes to be delayed rather than to take effect immediately. The **closesync**, **dsync** and **direct** values all cause the equivalent of an **fsync**(2) to be run when any file accessed with the **O_SYNC** flag is closed.

NOTE: **convosync=direct**, **convosync=dsync**, and **convosync=closesync** are available with the VxFS Advanced package only.

datainlog | **nodatainlog**

Normally, the **vxfs** file system will do **O_SYNC** writes by logging the data and the time change to the inode (**datainlog**). If the **nodatainlog** option is used, the logging of synchronous writes is disabled. Then, the **O_SYNC** writes will write the data into the file and update the inode synchronously before returning to the user.

NOTE: **datainlog** is available with the VxFS Advanced package only.

NOTES

Only a privileged user can mount file systems.

Unlike some file system commands, multiple **-o** options to mount is an error.

FILES

/etc/mnttab

SEE ALSO

vxfs-specific **fs**(4), **mnttab**(4), **mount**(2), generic **mount**(1M), **setmnt**(1M), **setuid**(2)

mouseadmin (1)

NAME

`mouseadmin` – mouse administration

SYNOPSIS

`mouseadmin -l`

`mouseadmin [ -nb ] [ -i` *interrupt* `] [ -a` *terminal* `]` *mouse*

`mouseadmin [ -nb ] [ -d` *terminal* `]`

`mouseadmin -t`

DESCRIPTION

`mouseadmin` allows any user with system administrator privileges to add or delete mouse devices. Users without appropriate privileges will only be allowed to list the current mouse and display assignments. The **`mouseadmin`** command issued without arguments will execute in menu mode, providing the user with a listing of current assignments and a selection menu of operations. After configuring the mouse, choose the `U` option to update the mouse configuration and then quit. Once the new mouse configuration has been updated, you can used the `-t` command line option or the `T` menu option to test the newly configured mouse.

OPTIONS

The command line arguments are defined as follows:

- `-a` assign mouse device (PS2, BUS, tty00, s0tty0, . . .) to terminal (console, s0vt00, . . .).
- `-b` do not validate for BUS mouse in system configuration. (This option should only be used within install scripts.)
- `-d` delete terminal assignment.
- `-i` specify an interrupt vector for a BUS mouse. When using the **`-i`** option *mouse* must be **`BUS`**.
- `-l` list mouse/display assignments.
- `-n` build mouse/display pair table without downloading to driver. (This option should only be used within install scripts.)
- `-t` test currently configured mouse. If the mouse is there and detected, the return will be `0`; otherwise, the return will be `1` or higher.

EXAMPLES

`mouseadmin -a console PS2`

mouseadmin -a console BUS
mouseadmin -a s0vt00 tty00
mouseadmin -a s0vt00 tty01

FILES

`/usr/bin/mouseadmin`
`/usr/lib/mousemgr`

SEE ALSO

`mouse`(7)

NAME

mv – move files

SYNOPSIS

mv [**-f**] [**-i**] [**-e** *extent_opt*] *file1* [*file2* . . .] *target*

DESCRIPTION

The **mv** command moves *filen* to *target*. *filen* and *target* may not have the same name. (Care must be taken when using **sh**(1) metacharacters). If *target* is not a directory, only one file may be specified before it; if it is a directory, more than one file may be specified. If *target* does not exist, **mv** creates a file named *target*. If *target* exists and is not a directory, its contents are overwritten. If *target* is a directory the file(s) are moved to that directory.

If **mv** determines that the mode of *target* forbids writing, it will print the mode [see **chmod**(2)], ask for a response, and read the standard input for one line. If the line begins with **y**, the **mv** occurs, if permissible; otherwise, the command exits. When the parent directory of *filen* is writable and has the sticky bit set, one or more of the following conditions must be true:

the user must own the file
the user must own the directory
the file must be writable by the user
the user must be a privileged user

The following options are recognized:

-i **mv** will prompt for confirmation whenever the move would overwrite an existing *target*. A **y** answer means that the move should proceed. Any other answer prevents **mv** from overwriting the *target*.

-f **mv** will move the file(s) without prompting even if it is writing over an existing *target*. This option overrides the **-i** option. Note that this is the default if the standard input is not a terminal.

-e *extent_opt*
Specify how to handle a **vxfs** file that has extent attribute information. Extent attributes include reserved space, a fixed extent size, and extent alignment. It may not be possible to preserve the information if the destination file system does not support extent attributes, has a different block size than the source file system, or lacks free extents appropriate to satisfy the extent attribute requirements. Valid values for *extent_opt* are:

warn Issue a warning message if extent attribute information cannot be kept (default).

force Fail the move if extent attribute information cannot be kept.

ignore Ignore extent attribute information entirely.

If *filen* is a directory, *target* must be a directory in the same physical file system. *target* and *filen* do not have to share the same parent directory.

If *filen* is a file and *target* is a link to another file with links, the other links remain and *target* becomes a new file.

FILES

/usr/lib/locale/*locale*/LC_MESSAGES/uxcore.abi
language-specific message file [See **LANG** on **environ** (5).]

SEE ALSO

chmod(1), **cp**(1), **cpio**(1), **ln**(1), **rm**(1)

NOTES

If *filen* and *target* are on different file systems, **mv** copies the file and deletes the original; any links to other files are lost.

A -- permits the user to mark explicitly the end of any command line options, allowing **mv** to recognize filename arguments that begin with a -. As an aid to BSD migration, **mv** will accept - as a synonym for --. This migration aid may disappear in a future release. If a -- and a - both appear on the same command line, the second will be interpreted as a filename.

NAME

mvdir – move a directory

SYNOPSIS

/usr/sbin/mvdir *dirname name*

DESCRIPTION

mvdir moves directories within a file system. *dirname* must be a directory. If *name* does not exist, it will be created as a directory. If *name* does exist, and is a directory, *dirname* will be created as *name/dirname. dirname* and *name* may not be on the same path; that is, one may not be subordinate to the other. For example:

```
mvdir x/y x/z
```

is legal, but

```
mvdir x/y x/y/z
```

is not.

SEE ALSO

mkdir(1), **mv**(1)

NOTES

Only the super-user can use **mvdir**.

NAME

named, **in.named** – Internet domain name server

SYNOPSIS

in.named [**-d** *level*] [**-p** *port*] [[**-b**] *bootfile*]

DESCRIPTION

named is the Internet domain name server. It is used by hosts on the Internet to provide access to the Internet distributed naming database. See RFC 1034 and RFC 1035 for more details. With no arguments **named** reads **/etc/named.boot** for any initial data, and listens for queries on a privileged port.

The following options are available:

-d *level* Print debugging information. *level* is a number indicating the level of messages printed. *level* is a number from 1 to 9. Higher numbers give more detailed debugging information.

-p *port* Use a different *port* number.

-b *bootfile* Use *bootfile* rather than **/etc/named.boot**.

EXAMPLE

Note that all domain names in the *bootfile* must not contain a trailing "." (dot).

```
;
;     boot file for name server
;
; type          domain            source file or host
;
domain          berkeley.edu
primary         berkeley.edu      named.db
secondary       cc.berkeley.edu 10.2.0.78 128.32.0.10
cache           .                 named.ca
```

The **domain** line specifies that **berkeley.edu** is the domain of the given server.

The **primary** line states that the file **named.db** contains authoritative data for **berkeley.edu**. The file **named.db** contains data in the master file format, described in RFC 1035, except that all domain names are relative to the origin; in this case, **berkeley.edu** (see below for a more detailed description).

The **secondary** line specifies that all authoritative data under **cc.berkeley.edu** is to be transferred from the name server at **10.2.0.78**. If the transfer fails it will try **128.32.0.10**, and continue for up to 10 tries at that address. The secondary copy is also authoritative for the domain.

The **cache** line specifies that data in **named.ca** is to be placed in the cache (typically such data as the locations of root domain servers). The file **named.ca** is in the same format as **named.db**.

The master file consists of entries of the form:

$INCLUDE < *filename* >
$ORIGIN < *domain* >
< *domain* > < *opt_ttl* > < *opt_class* > < *type* > < *resource_record_data* >

where *domain* is "**.**" for the root, "**@**" for the current origin, or a standard domain name. If *domain* is a standard domain name that does not end with "**.**", the current origin is appended to the domain. Domain names ending with "**.**" are unmodified. When you need to specify a fully qualified domain name (such as **somehost.berkeley.edu.**), be sure to include the trailing "." (dot).

The *opt_ttl* field is an optional integer number for the time-to-live field. It defaults to zero.

The *opt_class* field is currently one token, **IN** for the Internet.

The *type* field is one of the following tokens; the data expected in the *resource_record_data* field is in parentheses.

A	A host address (dotted quad).
NS	An authoritative name server (domain).
MX	A mail exchanger (domain).
CNAME	The canonical name for an alias (domain).
SOA	Marks the start of a zone of authority (5 numbers). See RFC 1035.
MB	A mailbox domain name (domain).
MG	A mail group member (domain).
MR	A mail rename domain name (domain).
NULL	A null resource record (no format or data).
WKS	A well know service description (not implemented yet).
PTR	A domain name pointer (domain).
HINFO	Host information (cpu_type OS_type).
MINFO	Mailbox or mail list information (request_domain error_domain).

FILES

/etc/named.boot	name server configuration boot file
/etc/named.pid	the process ID
/var/tmp/named.run	debug output
/var/tmp/named_dump.db	dump of the name servers database

SEE ALSO

kill(1), **resolv.conf**(4), **resolver**(3N), **signal**(3)

Mockapetris, Paul, *Domain Names - Concepts and Facilities*, RFC 1034, Network Information Center, SRI International, Menlo Park, Calif., November 1987

Mockapetris, Paul, *Domain Names - Implementation and Specification*, RFC 1035, Network Information Center, SRI International, Menlo Park, Calif., November 1987

Mockapetris, Paul, *Domain System Changes and Observations*, RFC 973, Network Information Center, SRI International, Menlo Park, Calif., January 1986

Partridge, Craig, *Mail Routing and the Domain System*, RFC 974, Network Information Center, SRI International, Menlo Park, Calif., January 1986

NOTES

The following signals have the specified effect when sent to the server process using the **kill**(1) command.

SIGHUP	Reads **/etc/named.boot** and reloads database.
SIGINT	Dumps the current database and cache to **/var/tmp/named_dump.db**.
SIGUSR1	Turns on debugging; each subsequent **SIGUSR1** increments debug level.
SIGUSR2	Turns off debugging completely.

NAME

nawk – pattern scanning and processing language

SYNOPSIS

nawk [-**f** *progfile* | *'prog'*] [-**F***fieldsep*] [-**v** *var=value*] [*file* . . .]

DESCRIPTION

nawk scans each input *file* for lines that match any of a set of patterns specified in *prog*. The *prog* string must be enclosed in single quotes (') to protect it from the shell. Patterns are arbitrary Boolean combinations of regular expressions and relational expressions. For each pattern in *prog* there may be an associated action performed when a line of a *file* matches the pattern. The set of pattern-action statements may appear literally as *prog* or in a file specified with the **-f** *progfile* option. Input files are read in order; if there are no files, the standard input is read. The file name - means the standard input.

nawk processes supplementary code set characters in pattern-action statements and comments, and recognizes supplementary code set characters as field separators (see below) according to the locale specified in the **LC_CTYPE** environment variable [see **LANG** on **environ**(5)]. In regular expressions, pattern searches are performed on characters, not bytes, as described on **ed**(1).

Each input line is matched against the pattern portion of every pattern-action statement; the associated action is performed for each matched pattern. Any *file* of the form **var**=*value* is treated as an assignment, not a filename, and is executed at the time it would have been opened if it were a filename, and is executed at the time it would have been opened if it were a filename. The option **-v** followed by **var**=*value* is an assignment to be done before *prog* is executed; any number of **-v** options may be present.

An input line is normally made up of fields separated by white space. (This default can be changed by using the **FS** built-in variable or the **-F***fieldsep* option.) The fields are denoted **$1**, **$2**, . . . ; **$0** refers to the entire line.

A pattern-action statement has the form:

pattern { *action* }

Either pattern or action may be omitted. If there is no action with a pattern, the matching line is printed. If there is no pattern with an action, the action is performed on every input line. Pattern-action statements are separated by newlines or semicolons.

As noted, patterns are arbitrary Boolean combinations (**!**, ||, **&&**, and parentheses) of relational expressions and regular expressions. A relational expression is one of the following:

expression relop expression
expression matchop regular_expression
expression **in** *array-name*
(*expression*,*expression*, ...) **in** *array-name*

where a *relop* is any of the six relational operators in C, and a *matchop* is either ~ (contains) or **!~** (does not contain). An *expression* is an arithmetic expression, a relational expression, the special expression

var **in** *array*

or a Boolean combination of these.

Regular expressions are as in **egrep**(1). In patterns they must be surrounded by slashes. Isolated regular expressions in a pattern apply to the entire line. Regular expressions may also occur in relational expressions. A pattern may consist of two patterns separated by a comma; in this case, the action is performed for all lines between an occurrence of the first pattern and the next occurrence of the second pattern.

The special patterns **BEGIN** and **END** may be used to capture control before the first input line has been read and after the last input line has been read respectively. These keywords do not combine with any other patterns.

A regular expression may be used to separate fields by using the **-F** *fieldsep* option or by assigning the expression to the built-in variable FS. The default is to ignore leading blanks and to separate fields by blanks and/or tab characters. However, if FS is assigned a value, leading blanks are no longer ignored.

Other built-in variables include:

ARGC	command line argument count
ARGV	command line argument array
ENVIRON	array of environment variables; subscripts are names
FILENAME	name of the current input file
FNR	ordinal number of the current record in the current file
FS	input field separator regular expression (default blank and tab)
NF	number of fields in the current record
NR	ordinal number of the current record
OFMT	output format for numbers (default **%.6g**)
OFS	output field separator (default blank)
ORS	output record separator (default new-line)
RS	input record separator (default new-line)
SUBSEP	separates multiple subscripts (default is 034)

The field separators specified with the **-F** option or with the variables **OFS**, **ORS**, and **FS** may be supplementary code set characters.

An action is a sequence of statements. A statement may be one of the following:

if (*expression*) *statement* [**else** *statement*]
while (*expression*) *statement*
do *statement* **while** (*expression*)
for (*expression* ; *expression* ; *expression*) *statement*

for (*var* **in** *array*) *statement*
delete *array*[*subscript*] #delete an array element
break
continue
{ [*statement*] ... }
expression # commonly variable = expression
print [*expression-list*] [>*expression*]
printf *format* [, *expression-list*] [>*expression*]
next # skip remaining patterns on this input line
exit [**expr**] # skip the rest of the input; exit status is expr
return [**expr**]

Statements are terminated by semicolons, new-lines, or right braces. An empty expression-list stands for the whole input line. Expressions take on string or numeric values as appropriate, and are built using the operators **+**, **-**, *****, **/**, **%**, **^** and concatenation (indicated by a blank). The operators **++ -- += -= *= /= %= ^= > >= < <= == != ?:** are also available in expressions. Variables may be scalars, array elements (denoted x[i]), or fields. Variables are initialized to the null string or zero. Array subscripts may be any string, not necessarily numeric; this allows for a form of associative memory. Multiple subscripts such as **[i,j,k]** are permitted; the constituents are concatenated, separated by the value of **SUBSEP**. String constants are quoted (**""**), with the usual C escapes recognized within.

The **print** statement prints its arguments on the standard output, or on a file if >*expression* is present, or on a pipe if | *cmd* is present. The arguments are separated by the current output field separator and terminated by the output record separator. The **printf** statement formats its expression list according to the format [see **printf**(3S)]. The built-in function **close**(*expr*) closes the file or pipe *expr*.

The mathematical functions: **atan2**, **cos**, **exp**, **log**, **sin**, **sqrt**, are built-in.

Other built-in functions include:

gsub(*for, repl, in*) behaves like **sub** (see below), except that it replaces successive occurrences of the regular expression (like the **ed** global substitute command).

index(*s, t*) returns the position in string *s* where string *t* first occurs, or 0 if it does not occur at all.

int truncates to an integer value.

length(*s*) returns the length in bytes of its argument taken as a string, or of the whole line if there is no argument.

match(*s, re*) returns the position in string *s* where the regular expression *re* occurs, or 0 if it does not occur at all. **RSTART** is set to the starting position (which is the same as the returned value), and **RLENGTH** is set to the length of the matched string.

rand random number on (0, 1).

split(*s, a, fs*) splits the string *s* into array elements *a*[*1*], *a*[*2*], *a*[*n*], and returns *n*. The separation is done with the regular expression *fs* or with the field separator **FS** if *fs* is not given.

srand sets the seed for **rand**

sprintf(*fmt*, *expr*, *expr*, ...)
formats the expressions according to the **printf**(3S) format given by *fmt* and returns the resulting string.

sub(*for*, *repl*, *in*) substitutes the string *repl* in place of the first instance of the regular expression *for* in string *in* and returns the number of substitutions. If *in* is omitted, **nawk** substitutes in the current record (**$0**).

substr(*s*, *m*, *n*) returns the *n*-byte substring of *s* that begins at position *m*.

The input/output built-in functions are:

close(*filename*) closes the file or pipe named *filename*.

cmd | **getline** pipes the output of *cmd* into **getline**; each successive call to *getline* returns the next line of output from *cmd*.

getline sets **$0** to the next input record from the current input file.

getline <*file* sets **$0** to the next record from *file*.

getline *x* sets variable *x* instead.

getline *x* <*file* sets *x* from the next record of *file*.

system(*cmd*) executes *cmd* and returns its exit status.

All forms of **getline** return 1 for successful input, 0 for end of file, and –1 for an error.

nawk also provides user-defined functions. Such functions may be defined (in the pattern position of a pattern-action statement) as

function *name*(*args*,...) { *stmts* }

or

func *name*(*args*,...) { *stmts* }

Function arguments are passed by value if scalar and by reference if array name. Argument names are local to the function; all other variable names are global. Function calls may be nested and functions may be recursive. The **return** statement may be used to return a value.

EXAMPLES

Print lines longer than 72 characters:

```
length > 72
```

Print first two fields in opposite order:

```
{ print $2, $1 }
```

Same, with input fields separated by comma and/or blanks and tabs:

```
BEGIN { FS = ",[ \t]*|[ \t]+" }
      { print $2, $1 }
```

Add up first column, print sum and average:

```
        { s += $1 }
END     { print "sum is", s, " average is", s/NR }
```

Print fields in reverse order:

```
{ for (i = NF; i > 0; --i) print $i }
```

Print all lines between start/stop pairs:

```
/start/, /stop/
```

Print all lines whose first field is different from previous one:

```
$1 != prev { print; prev = $1 }
```

Simulate **echo**(1):

```
BEGIN {
        for (i = 1; i < ARGC; i++)
                printf "%s", ARGV[i]
        printf "\n"
        exit
        }
```

Print a file, filling in page numbers starting at 5:

```
/Page/     { $2 = n++; }
           { print }
```

Assuming this program is in a file named **prog**, the following command line prints the file **input** numbering its pages starting at 5: **nawk -f prog n=5 input**.

FILES

/usr/lib/locale/*locale***/LC_MESSAGES/uxawk**
language-specific message file [See **LANG** on **environ**(5).]

SEE ALSO

egrep(1), **grep**(1), **lex**(1), **printf**(3S), **sed**(1)
A. V. Aho, B. W. Kernighan, P. J. Weinberger, *The awk Programming Language* Addison-Wesley, 1988

NOTES

nawk is a new version of **awk** that provides capabilities unavailable in previous versions. This version will become the default version of **awk** in the next major UNIX system release.

Input white space is not preserved on output if fields are involved.

There are no explicit conversions between numbers and strings. To force an expression to be treated as a number add 0 to it; to force it to be treated as a string concatenate the null string ("") to it.

ncheck (1M)

NAME

ncheck (generic) – generate a list of path names vs i-numbers

SYNOPSIS

/usr/sbin/ncheck [**-F** *FSType*] [**-V**] [*current_options*] [**-o** *specific_options*] [*special* . . .]

DESCRIPTION

ncheck with no options generates a path-name vs. i-number list of all files on *special*. If *special* is not specified on the command line the list is generated for all *specials* in **/etc/vfstab** for entries which have a numeric *fsckpass*. *special* is a character special device on which the file system exists.

current_options are options supported by the **s5**-specific module of **ncheck**. Other *FSTypes* do not necessarily support these options. *specific_options* indicate suboptions specified in a comma-separated list of suboptions and/or keyword-attribute pairs for interpretation by the *FSType*-specific module of the command.

The options are:

-F Specify the *FSType* on which to operate. The *FSType* should either be specified here or be determinable from **/etc/vfstab** by finding an entry in the table that has a numeric *fsckpass* field and a matching *special* if specified.

-V Echo the complete command line, but do not execute the command. The command line is generated by using the options and arguments provided by the user and adding to them information derived from **/etc/vfstab**. This option should be used to verify and validate the command line.

-o used to specify *FSType* specific options if any.

FILES

/etc/vfstab list of default parameters for each file system

SEE ALSO

s5-specific **ncheck**(1M), **sfs**-specific **ncheck**(1M), **ufs**-specific **ncheck**(1M), **vxfs**-specific **ncheck**(1M), **vfstab**(4)

NOTES

This command may not be supported for all *FSTypes*.

NAME

ncheck (s5) – generate path names versus i-numbers for **s5** file systems

SYNOPSIS

ncheck [**-F s5**] [*generic_options*] [**-i** *i-number* . . .] [**-a**] [**-s**] [*special* . . .]

DESCRIPTION

generic_options are options supported by the generic **ncheck** command.

ncheck generates a path-name vs. i-number list of all files on the specified *special* device(s). Names of directory files are followed by "**/.**" .

The options are:

-F s5 Specifies the **s5**-FSType.

-i *i-number*
: Limits the report to those files whose i-numbers follow. The *i-numbers* must be separated by commas without spaces.

-a Allows printing of the names "**.**" and "**..**", which are ordinarily suppressed.

-s Limits the report to special files and files with set-user-ID mode. This option may be used to detect violations of security policy.

DIAGNOSTICS

If the file system structure is not consistent, **??** denotes the parent of a parentless file and a path-name beginning with . . . denotes a loop.

SEE ALSO

generic **ncheck**(1M)

NAME

ncheck (sfs) – generate pathnames versus i-numbers for **sfs** file systems

SYNOPSIS

ncheck [**-F sfs**] [*generic_options*] [**-i** *i-list*] **[-a] [-s] [-o m]** [*special* . . .]

DESCRIPTION

generic_options are options supported by the generic **ncheck** command.

ncheck generates a pathname versus i-number list of files for the **sfs** file system. Names of directory files are followed by "**/.** ".

Note that in the **sfs**-FSType, only even i-numbers are valid.

The options are:

-F sfs
: Specifies the **sfs**-FSType.

-i *i-list*
: Limits the report to the files on the i-list that follows. The i-list must be separated by commas without spaces.

-a
: Allows printing of the names "." and "..", which are ordinarily suppressed.

-s
: Limits the report to special files and files with set-user-ID mode. This option may be used to detect violations of security policy.

-o
: Specify **sfs** file system specific options. The available option is:

  m Print mode information.

DIAGNOSTICS

When the file system structure is improper, '**??**' denotes the parent of a parentless file and a pathname beginning with '**. . .**' denotes a loop.

SEE ALSO

generic **ncheck**(1M)

NAME

ncheck (ufs) – generate pathnames versus i-numbers for **ufs** file systems

SYNOPSIS

ncheck [**-F ufs**] [*generic_options*] [**-i** *i-list*] **[-a] [-s] [-o m]** [*special* . . .]

DESCRIPTION

generic_options are options supported by the generic **ncheck** command.

ncheck generates a pathname versus i-number list of files for the **ufs** file system. Names of directory files are followed by "**/.** ".

The options are:

-F ufs Specifies the **ufs**-FSType.

-i *i-list* Limits the report to the files on the i-list that follows. The i-list must be separated by commas without spaces.

-a Allows printing of the names "." and "..", which are ordinarily suppressed.

-s Limits the report to special files and files with set-user-ID mode. This option may be used to detect violations of security policy.

-o Specify **ufs** file system specific options. The available option is:

m Print mode information.

DIAGNOSTICS

When the file system structure is improper, **??** denotes the parent of a parentless file and a pathname beginning with . . . denotes a loop.

SEE ALSO

generic **ncheck**(1M)

NAME

ncheck (vxfs) – generate pathnames from inumbers for **vxfs** file systems

SYNOPSIS

ncheck [**-F vxfs**] [*generic_options*] [**-i** *ilist*] [**-a**] [**-s**] [**-o m,b=***blk#*] *special* . . .

DESCRIPTION

generic_options are options supported by the generic **ncheck** command.

ncheck generates a pathname versus inumber list of files for the **vxfs** file system. Names of directory files are followed by "**/.** ".

The options are:

-F vxfs Specifies the **vxfs** FSType.

-i *ilist* Limits the report to the files on the ilist that follows. The ilist must be separated by commas without spaces.

-a Allows printing of the names "." and "..", which are ordinarily suppressed.

-s Limits the report to special files and files with set-user-ID mode. This option may be used to detect violations of security policy.

-o Specify **vxfs** file system specific options. The available options are:

- **m** Print mode information. (Used in conjunction with **-i** option.)
- **b=***blk#* Print pathname containing block number *blk#*.

DIAGNOSTICS

When the file system structure is improper, "**???**" denotes the parent of a parentless file and a pathname beginning with "**. . .**" denotes a loop. A pathname beginning with "*******" denotes a directory entry whose "**. .**" entry is not in accord with the directory in which it was found.

SEE ALSO

vxfs-specific **fs**(4), **fsck**(1M), generic **ncheck**(1M), **sort**(1)

NAME

netinfo – interface to add/list/remove entries in **/etc/confnet.d/netdrivers**

SYNOPSIS

/usr/sbin/netinfo [**-l dev**] [**-l proto**] [**-d** *device*] [**-p** *protocol*]
/usr/sbin/netinfo [**-u -l dev**] [**-u -l proto**]
/usr/sbin/netinfo [**-a -d** *device*] [**-a -d** *device* **-p** *protocol*]
/usr/sbin/netinfo [**-r -d** *device*] [**-r -p** *protocol*] [**-r -d** *device* **-p** *protocol*]

DESCRIPTION

The **netinfo** command provides the interface to the **netdrivers** file to allow packages and applications to update the file without being dependent on the format of the file. This command will only update the **netdrivers** file. It will not take any action to configure or unconfigure a device or protocol.

Options

The following options are available to **netinfo**:

-l dev
List all of the devices in **netdrivers**.

-l proto
List all of the protocols currently mapped to devices in **netdrivers**.

-u -l dev
List all of the devices that are not mapped to any protocol in **netdrivers**. If no information is returned, all the device(s) in the machine are mapped to an installed protocol.

-u -l proto
List all protocols that are not mapped to any device(s) in **netdrivers**. If no information is returned, all of the installed protocols are mapped to device(s) that are installed in the machine.

-d *device*
List the protocols currently configured for the specified *device*.

-p *protocol*
List the devices currently configured for the specified *protocol*.

-a -d *device*
Add an entry for *device* to the **netdrivers** file.

-a -d *device* **-p** *protocol*
add an entry in the **netdrivers** file indicating a mapping between *device* and *protocol*.

-r -d *device*
remove all entries for the specified *device* from the **netdrivers** file. This option would be used if you were removing the *device* from the machine.

-r -p *protocol*
remove all entries for the specified *protocol* from the **netdrivers** file.

-r -d *device* **-p** *protocol*
remove the entry mapping for the specified *device* to *protocol* from the **netdrivers** file.

Files

`/etc/confnet.d/netdrivers`

REFERENCES

generic **configure**(1M), INET-specific **configure**(1M), *protocol-specific* **configure**(1M), **netdrivers**(4)

NAME

netstat – show network status

SYNOPSIS

netstat [-Aainrs] [-f *address_family*] **[-I** *interface*] **[system] [core]**
netstat [-I *interface*] *interval* **[system] [core]**

DESCRIPTION

netstat displays the contents of various network-related data structures in various formats, depending on the options you select.

The first form of the command displays a list of active sockets for each protocol. The second form selects one from among various other network data structures. The third form displays running statistics of packet traffic on configured network interfaces; the *interval* argument indicates the number of seconds in which to gather statistics between displays.

The default value for the **system** argument is **/unix**; for *core*, the default is **/dev/kmem**.

The following options are available:

-a Show the state of all sockets; normally sockets used by server processes are not shown.

-A Show the address of any protocol control blocks associated with sockets; used for debugging.

-i Show the state of interfaces that have been auto-configured. Interfaces that are statically configured into a system, but not located at boot time, are not shown.

-n Show network addresses as numbers. **netstat** normally displays addresses as symbols. This option may be used with any of the display formats.

-r Show the routing tables. When used with the **-s** option, show routing statistics instead.

-s Show per-protocol statistics. When used with the **-r** option, show routing statistics.

-f *address_family*
Limit statistics or address control block reports to those of the specified *address_family*, which can be one of:

inet For the AF_INET address family, or
unix For the AF_UNIX family.

-I *interface*
Highlight information about the indicated *interface* in a separate column; the default (for the third form of the command) is the interface with the most traffic since the system was last rebooted. *interface* can be any valid interface listed in the system configuration file, such as **emd1** or **lo0**.

DISPLAYS

Active Sockets (First Form)

The display for each active socket shows the protocol, the receive and send queue size (in bytes), the local and foreigh address, and the internal state of the protocol.

The symbolic format normally used to display socket addresses is either:

hostname.*port*

when the name of the host is specified, or:

network.*port*

if a socket address specifies a network but no specific host. Each **hostname** and *network* is shown according to its entry in the **/etc/hosts** or the **/etc/networks** file, as appropriate.

If the network or hostname for an address is not known (or if the **-n** option is specified), the numerical network address is shown. Unspecified, or wildcard, addresses and ports appear as *. For more information regarding the Internet naming conventions, refer to **inet**(7).

TCP Sockets

The possible state values for TCP sockets are as follows:

CLOSED	Closed. The socket is not being used.
LISTEN	Listening for incoming connections.
SYN_SENT	Actively trying to establish connection.
SYN_RECEIVED	Initial synchronization of the connection under way.
ESTABLISHED	Connection has been established.
CLOSE_WAIT	Remote shut down; waiting for the socket to close.
FIN_WAIT_1	Socket closed; shutting down connection.
CLOSING	Closed, then remote shutdown; awaiting acknowledgement.
LAST_ACK	Remote shut down, then closed; awaiting acknowledgement.
FIN_WAIT_2	Socket closed; waiting for shutdown from remote.
TIME_WAIT	Wait after close for remote shutdown retransmission.

Network Data Structures (Second Form)

The form of the display depends upon which of the **-i** or **-r** options you select. If you specify more than one of these options, **netstat** selects one in the order listed here.

Routing Table Display

The routing table display lists the available routes and the status of each. Each route consists of a destination host or network, and a gateway to use in forwarding packets. The *flags* column shows the status of the route (**U** if up), whether the route is to a gateway (**G**), whether the route was created dynamically by a redirect (**D**), and whether an individual host address (**H**) is used, rather than a network address. For example, the loopback transport provider, **lo0**, has the **H** flag associated with it.

Direct routes are created for each interface attached to the local host; the gateway field for such entries shows the address of the outgoing interface.

The **refcnt** column gives the current number of active uses per route. Connection-oriented protocols normally hold on to a single route for the duration of a connection, whereas connectionless protocols obtain a route while sending to the same destination.

The **use** column displays the number of packets sent per route.

The *interface* entry indicates the network interface utilized for the route.

Cumulative Traffic Statistics (Third Form)

When the *interval* argument is given, **netstat** displays a table of cumulative statistics regarding packets transferred, errors and collisions. The first line of data displayed, and every 24th line thereafter, contains cumulative statistics from the time the system was last rebooted. Each subsequent line shows incremental statistics for the *interval* (specified on the command line) since the previous display.

SEE ALSO

hosts(4), **networks**(4), **protocols**(4), **services**(4), **trpt**(1M)

NOTES

The kernel's tables can change while **netstat** is examining them, creating incorrect or partial displays.

NAME

newaliases – (BSD) rebuild the data base for the mail aliases file

SYNOPSIS

/usr/ucb/newaliases

DESCRIPTION

newaliases rebuilds the random access data base for the mail aliases file **/usr/ucblib/aliases**. **newaliases** should be run whenever the **/usr/ucblib/aliases** file is updated.

FILES

/usr/ucblib/aliases
/usr/ucblib/aliases.dir
/usr/ucblib/aliases.pag

SEE ALSO

aliases(4), **sendmail**(1M)

NAME

newform – change the format of a text file

SYNOPSIS

newform [**-s**] [**-i***tabspec*] [**-o***tabspec*] [**-b***n*] [**-e***n*] [**-p***n*] [**-a***n*] [**-f**] [**-c***char*] [**-l***n*] [*files*]

DESCRIPTION

newform reads lines from the named *files*, or the standard input if no input file is named, and reproduces the lines on the standard output. Lines are reformatted in accordance with command line options in effect. **newform** processes supplementary code set characters according to the locale specified in the **LC_CTYPE** environment variable [see **LANG** on **environ**(5)], except as noted under the **-c** option below.

Except for **-s**, command line options may appear in any order, may be repeated, and may be intermingled with the optional *files*. Command line options are processed in the order specified. This means that option sequences like "**-e**15 **-l**60" will yield results different from "**-l**60 **-e**15". Options are applied to all *files* on the command line. References to "characters" below should be interpreted as "bytes" in multibyte character environments.

-s Shears off leading characters on each line up to the first tab and places up to 8 of the sheared characters at the end of the line. If more than 8 characters (not counting the first tab) are sheared, the eighth character is replaced by a * and any characters to the right of it are discarded. The first tab is always discarded.

An error message and program exit will occur if this option is used on a file without a tab on each line. The characters sheared off are saved internally until all other options specified are applied to that line. The characters are then added at the end of the processed line.

For example, to convert a file with leading digits, one or more tabs, and text on each line, to a file beginning with the text, all tabs after the first expanded to spaces, padded with spaces out to column 72 (or truncated to column 72), and the leading digits placed starting at column 73, the command would be:

newform -s -i -l -a -e *file-name*

-i*tabspec* Input tab specification: expands tabs to spaces, according to the tab specifications given. *tabspec* accepts four types of tab specifications: canned, repetitive, arbitrary and file. *–n* represents the repetitive tab specification. This format can be used to replace each tab in a file with *n* spaces. For example,

newform -i-4 *file-name*

replaces tabs with 4 spaces. For more information about the *tabspec* formats see **tabs**(1). In addition, *tabspec* may be **--**, in which **newform** assumes that the tab specification is to be found in the first line read from the standard input (see **fspec**(4)). If no *tabspec* is given, *tabspec* defaults to **-8**. A *tabspec* of **-0** expects no tabs; if any are found, they are treated as **-1**.

-o*tabspec* Output tab specification: replaces spaces by tabs, according to the tab specifications given. The tab specifications are the same as for **-i***tabspec*. If no *tabspec* is given, *tabspec* defaults to **-8**. A *tabspec* of **-0** means that no spaces will be converted to tabs on output.

-b*n* Truncate *n* characters from the beginning of the line when the line length is greater than the effective line length (see **-l***n*). Default is to truncate the number of characters necessary to obtain the effective line length. The default value is used when **-b** with no *n* is used. This option can be used to delete the sequence numbers from a COBOL program as follows:

newform -l1 -b7 *file-name*

-e*n* Same as **-b***n* except that characters are truncated from the end of the line.

-p*n* Prefix *n* characters (see **-c***k*) to the beginning of a line when the line length is less than the effective line length. Default is to prefix the number of characters necessary to obtain the effective line length.

-a*n* Same as **-p***n* except characters are appended to the end of a line.

-f Write the tab specification format line on the standard output before any other lines are output. The tab specification format line which is printed will correspond to the format specified in the *last* **-o** option. If no **-o** option is specified, the line which is printed will contain the default specification of **-8**.

-c*k* Change the prefix/append character to *k*. Default character for *k* is a space. *k* must be a single-byte character.

-l*n* Set the effective line length to *n* characters. If *n* is not entered, **-l** defaults to 72. The default line length without the **-l** option is 80 characters. Note that tabs and backspaces are considered to be one character (use **-i** to expand tabs to spaces).

The **-l1** must be used to set the effective line length shorter than any existing line in the file so that the **-b** option is activated.

SEE ALSO

csplit(1), **fspec**(4), **tabs**(1)

DIAGNOSTICS

All diagnostics are fatal.

UX:newform:ERROR:usage: . . .
newform was called with a bad option.

UX:newform:ERROR:not -s format
There was no tab on one line.

UX:newform:ERROR:can't open file
Self-explanatory.

UX:newform:ERROR:internal line too long
A line exceeds 512 characters after being expanded in the internal work buffer.

UX:newform:ERROR:tabspec in error
A tab specification is incorrectly formatted, or specified tab stops are not ascending.

UX:newform:ERROR:tabspec indirection illegal
A *tabspec* read from a file (or standard input) may not contain a *tabspec* referencing another file (or standard input).

0 – normal execution
1 – for any error

NOTES

newform normally only keeps track of physical characters; however, for the **-i** and **-o** options, **newform** will keep track of backspaces in order to line up tabs in the appropriate logical columns.

newform will not prompt the user if a *tabspec* is to be read from the standard input (by use of **-i--** or **-o--**).

If the **-f** option is used, and the last **-o** option specified was **-o--**, and was preceded by either a **-o--** or a **-i--**, the tab specification format line will be incorrect.

NAME

newgrp – log in to a new group

SYNOPSIS

newgrp [-] [group]

DESCRIPTION

newgrp changes a user's real and effective group ID. The user remains logged in and the current directory is unchanged. The user is given a new shell, replacing the current shell by **newgrp**, unless the current user ID or specified group ID is invalid, or the exec of the login shell fails.

Exported variables retain their values after invoking **newgrp**; however, all unexported variables are either reset to their default value or set to null. System variables (such as **PS1**, **PS2**, **PATH**, **MAIL**, and **HOME**), unless exported by the system or explicitly exported by the user, are reset to default values. For example, a user has a primary prompt string (**PS1**) other than **$** (default) and has not exported **PS1**. After an invocation of **newgrp**, successful or not, the user's **PS1** will now be set to the default prompt string **$**. Note that the shell command **export** [see the **sh**(1) manual page] is the method to export variables so that they retain their assigned value when invoking new shells.

With no arguments, **newgrp** changes the user's group IDs (real and effective) back to the group specified in the user's password file entry. This is a way to exit the effect of an earlier **newgrp** command.

If the first argument to **newgrp** is a **-**, the environment is changed to what would be expected if the user actually logged in again as a member of the new group.

A password is demanded if the group has a password and the user is not listed in **/etc/group** as being a member of that group.

FILES

/etc/group
system's group file

/etc/passwd
system's password file

/usr/lib/locale/*locale***/LC_MESSAGES/uxcore.abi**
language-specific message file [See **LANG** on **environ** (5).]

NOTES

The ability of the user to enter a password when using this command will be removed in a future release.

SEE ALSO

environ(5), **group**(4), **intro**(2), **login**(1), **passwd**(4), **sh**(1)

NAME

newkey – create a new key in the publickey database

SYNOPSIS

newkey -h *hostname*

newkey -u *username*

DESCRIPTION

The **newkey** command is normally run by the RPC administrator on the machine that contains the **publickey**(4) database, to establish public keys for users and privileged users on the network. These keys are needed when using secure RPC or secure NFS.

newkey will prompt for a password for the given *username* or *hostname* and then create a new public/secret key pair for the user or host in **/etc/publickey**, encrypted with the given password.

The following options are available:

-h *hostname* Create a new public/secret key pair for the privileged user at the given *hostname*. Prompts for a password for the given *hostname*.

-u *username* Create a new public/secret key pair for the given *username*. Prompts for a password for the given *username*.

SEE ALSO

chkey(1), **keylogin**(1), **keylogout**(1), **keyserv**(1M), **publickey**(4)

news(1)

NAME

news – print news items

SYNOPSIS

news [**-a**] [**-n**] [**-s**] [*items*]

DESCRIPTION

news is used to keep the user informed of current events. By convention, these events are described by files in the directory **/var/news**.

When invoked without arguments, **news** prints the contents of all current files in **/var/news**, most recent first, with each preceded by an appropriate header. **news** stores the "currency" time as the modification date of a file named **.news_time** in the user's home directory (the identity of this directory is determined by the environment variable **$HOME**); only files more recent than this currency time are considered "current."

-a option causes **news** to print all items, regardless of currency. In this case, the stored time is not changed.

-n option causes **news** to report the names of the current items without printing their contents, and without changing the stored time.

-s option causes **news** to report how many current items exist, without printing their names or contents, and without changing the stored time. It is useful to include such an invocation of **news** in one's **.profile** file, or in the system's **/etc/profile**.

All other arguments are assumed to be specific news items that are to be printed.

If a *delete* is typed during the printing of a news item, printing stops and the next item is started. Another *delete* within one second of the first causes the program to terminate.

FILES

/etc/profile
/var/news/*
$HOME/.news_time
/usr/lib/locale/*locale***/LC_MESSAGES/uxcore**
    language-specific message file [See **LANG** on **environ**(5).]

SEE ALSO

environ(5), **profile**(4)

NAME

newvt – opens virtual terminals.

SYNOPSIS

newvt [**-e** *prog*] [**-n** *vt_number*]

DESCRIPTION

Use the **newvt** command to open a new virtual terminal. The newly opened virtual terminal will inherit your environment.

-e Specifies a program (*prog*) to execute in the new virtual terminal. Without the **-e** option, the program pointed to by the **$SHELL** environment variable is started in the new virtual terminal. If **$SHELL** is NULL or points to a nonexecutable program, then **/bin/sh** is invoked. The new virtual terminal will exit on exiting the program.

-n Specifies a particular virtual terminal (*vt_number*) to open. If the **-n** option is not specified, then the next available virtual terminal is opened. Close virtual terminals by pressing CTRL-d (control d). Repeat CTRL-d until all open virtual terminals are closed.

DIAGNOSTICS

The **newvt** command will fail under the following conditions:

If an invalid option is specified.
If the device cannot be opened.
If **newvt** is invoked from a remote terminal.
If no virtual terminals are available (**-n** option not specified).
If the requested virtual terminal is not available (**-n** option specified).
If the requested virtual terminal cannot be opened.
If the specified command cannot be executed (**-e** option specified).
If the **$SHELL** program cannot be executed (**$SHELL** set and **-e** option not specified).
If **/dev/vtmon** cannot be opened.

SEE ALSO

vtgetty(1M), **vtlmgr**(1)

nfsd (1M)

NAME

nfsd – NFS daemon

SYNOPSIS

/usr/lib/nfs/nfsd [-a] [-p *protocol***] [-t** *transport***] [***nservers***]**

DESCRIPTION

nfsd starts the daemons that handle client file system requests.

The **nfsd** daemons are automatically invoked in run level 3.

Only a privileged user can execute this command.

Options

The following options are available to the **nfsd** command:

-a	Start **nfsd**'s over all available connectionless transports.
-p *protocol*	Start **nfsd**'s over the specified protocol.
-t *transport*	Start **nfsd**'s for the transport specified by *transport*.
nservers	The number of file system request daemons to start. *nservers* should be based on the load expected on this server. Four is the usual number of *nservers*.

Files

.nfs*XXX*	client machine pointer to an open-but-unlinked file (in the same directory as the original file)

REFERENCES

biod(1M), **mountd**(1M), **nfsping**(1M), **sharetab**(4)

NAME

`nfsping` – check status of the NFS daemons

SYNOPSIS

`/usr/sbin/nfsping [-a | -s | -c | -o` *name* `]`

DESCRIPTION

`nfsping` allows any user to check the status of the NFS daemons, and to see if they are running.

Options

The following options are available to the `nfsping` command:

`-a` Check that all NFS daemons (`nfsd`, `biod`, `rpcbind`, `mountd`, `lockd`, `statd`, `bootparamd`, and `pcnfsd`) are running.

`-s` Check that the `nfsd`, `rpcbind`, `mountd`, `lockd`, and `statd` NFS daemons are running.

`-c` Check that the `biod`, `rpcbind`, `lockd`, and `statd` NFS daemons are running.

`-o` *name*
Check that the NFS daemon specified by *name* is running.

Only one option may be used at a time. If no options are specified, a usage message is printed.

Exit Codes

The following values are returned by the `nfsping` command:

0 All NFS daemons are running

32 No NFS daemons are running

33 Only the rpcbind daemon is running

34 System is running in bootserver mode

35 System is running in pc server mode

36 System is only running in server mode

37 System is only running in client mode

38 System is running in bootserver and client mode

39 System is running in client and pc server mode

40 System is running in server and client mode

41 The rpcbind daemon is not running

42 Usage message printed

43 More than one option has been specified

50 Could not get network configuration for udp

51 The status daemon (`statd`) is not running

52 Invalid daemon name specified with `-o`

USAGE

Examples

The `nfsping -a` command reports the following:

```
nfsping: nfsd is running
nfsping: biod is running
nfsping: rpcbind is running
nfsping: mountd is running
nfsping: lockd is running
nfsping: statd is running
nfsping: bootparamd is running
nfsping: pcnfsd is running
```

The `nfsping -o statd` produces the following output:

```
nfsping: statd is running
```

REFERENCES

biod(1M), **bootparamd**(1M), **lockd**(1M), **mountd**(1M), **nfsd**(1M), **pcnfsd**(1M), **rpcbind**(1M), **statd**(1M)

NAME

nfsstat – Network File System statistics

SYNOPSIS

nfsstat [-csnrz] [*unix*] [*core*]

DESCRIPTION

nfsstat displays statistical information about the NFS (Network File System) and RPC (Remote Procedure Call), interfaces to the kernel. It can also be used to reinitialize this information. If no options are given the default is

```
nfsstat -csnr
```

That is, display everything, but reinitialize nothing.

Options

The options for **nfsstat** are as follows:

-c Display client information. Only the client side NFS and RPC information will be printed. Can be combined with the **-n** and **-r** options to print client NFS or client RPC information only.

-s Display server information.

-n Display NFS information. NFS information for both the client and server side will be printed. Can be combined with the **-c** and **-s** options to print client or server NFS information only.

-r Display RPC information.

-z Zero (reinitialize) statistics. This option is for use by a privileged user only, and can be combined with any of the above options to zero particular sets of statistics after printing them.

unix Specifiy an alternate location for the UNIX kernel. The default is **/stand/unix**.

core Specifiy an alternate location of the special file from where to read kernel memory. The default is **/dev/kmem**.

Displays

The server RPC display includes the fields:

calls total number of RPC calls received

badcalls total number of calls rejected

nullrecv number of times no RPC packet was available when trying to receive

badlen number of packets that were too short

xdrcall number of packets that had a malformed header

The server NFS display shows the number of NFS calls received (**calls**) and rejected (**badcalls**), and the counts and percentages for the various calls that were made.

The client RPC display includes the following fields:

`calls`	total number of RPC calls sent
`badcalls`	total of calls rejected by a server
`retrans`	number of times a call had to be retransmitted
`badxid`	number of times a reply did not match the call
`timeout`	number of times a call timed out
`wait`	number of times a call had to wait on a busy **`CLIENT`** handle
`newcred`	number of times authentication information had to be refreshed

The client NFS display shows the number of calls sent (**`calls`**) and rejected (**`badcalls`**), as well as the number of times a **`CLIENT`** handle was received (**`nclget`**), the number of times a call had to sleep while awaiting a handle (**`nclsleep`**), as well as a count of the various calls and their respective percentages.

FILES

`/stand/unix`	system namelist
`/dev/kmem`	kernel memory

NAME

nice – run a command at low priority

SYNOPSIS

nice [-*increment*] *command* [*arguments*]

DESCRIPTION

nice executes *command* with a lower CPU scheduling priority. The **priocntl** command is a more general interface to scheduler functions.

The invoking process (generally the user's shell) must be in the time-sharing scheduling class. The *command* is executed in the time-sharing class.

If the *increment* argument (in the range 1–19) is given, it is used; if not, an increment of 10 is assumed.

The super-user may run commands with priority higher than normal by using a negative increment, for example, **--10**.

SEE ALSO

nice(2), **nohup**(1), **priocntl**(1)

DIAGNOSTICS

nice returns the exit status of *command*.

NOTES

An *increment* larger than 19 is equivalent to 19.

nl(1)

NAME

nl – line numbering filter

SYNOPSIS

nl [**-b***type*] [**-f***type*] [**-h***type*] [**-v***start#*] [**-i***incr*] [**-p**] [**-l***num*] [**-s***sep*] [**-w***width*] [**-n***format*] [**-d***delim*] [*file*]

DESCRIPTION

nl reads lines from the named *file*, or the standard input if no *file* is named, and reproduces the lines on the standard output. Lines are numbered on the left in accordance with the command options in effect. **nl** processes supplementary code set characters according to the locale specified in the **LC_CTYPE** environment variable [see **LANG** on **environ**(5)], except as noted below. In regular expressions, pattern searches are performed on characters, not bytes, as described on **ed**(1).

nl views the text it reads in terms of logical pages. Line numbering is reset at the start of each logical page. A logical page consists of a header, a body, and a footer section. Empty sections are valid. Different line numbering options are independently available for header, body, and footer. For example, **-bt** (the default) numbers non-blank lines in the body section and does not number any lines in the header and footer sections.

The start of logical page sections are signaled by input lines containing nothing but the following delimiter character(s):

Line contents	*Start of*
\:\:\:	header
\:\:	body
\:	footer

Unless optioned otherwise, **nl** assumes the text being read is in a single logical page body.

Command options may appear in any order and may be intermingled with an optional file name. Only one file may be named. The options are:

-b*type* Specifies which logical page body lines are to be numbered. Recognized *type*s and their meanings are:

- **a** number all lines
- **t** number lines with printable text only
- **n** no line numbering
- **p***exp* number only lines that contain the regular expression specified in *exp* [see **ed**(1)]

Default *type* for logical page body is **t** (text lines numbered). All supplementary code set characters are considered printable.

-f*type* Same as **-b***type* except for footer. Default *type* for logical page footer is **n** (no lines numbered). All supplementary code set characters are considered printable.

-h*type* Same as **-b***type* except for header. Default *type* for logical page header is **n** (no lines numbered). All supplementary code set characters are considered printable.

-v*start#* *start#* is the initial value used to number logical page lines. Default *start#* is **1**.

-i*incr* *incr* is the increment value used to number logical page lines. Default *incr* is **1**.

-p Do not restart numbering at logical page delimiters.

-l*num* *num* is the number of blank lines to be considered as one. For example, **-l2** results in only the second adjacent blank being numbered (if the appropriate **-ha**, **-ba**, and/or **-fa** option is set). Default *num* is **1**.

-s*sep* *sep* is the character(s) used in separating the line number and the corresponding text line. Default *sep* is a tab. *sep* must be a single-byte character or characters.

-w*width* *width* is the number of characters to be used for the line number. Default *width* is **6**. The maximum for *width* is 100. If a number greater than the maximum is specified for *width*, the maximum is automatically used.

-n*format* *format* is the line numbering format. Recognized values are: **ln**, left justified, leading zeroes suppressed; **rn**, right justified, leading zeroes suppressed; **rz**, right justified, leading zeroes kept. Default *format* is **rn** (right justified).

-d*delim* The two delimiter characters specifying the start of a logical page section may be changed from the default characters (\:) to two user-specified characters. If only one character is entered, the second character remains the default character (:). No space should appear between the **-d** and the delimiter characters. To enter a backslash, use two backslashes. *delim* must be a single-byte character or characters.

EXAMPLE

The command:

```
nl -v10 -i10 -d!+ file1
```

will cause the first line of the page body to be numbered **10**, the second line of the page body to be numbered **20**, the third **30**, and so forth. The logical page delimiters are !+.

FILES

/usr/lib/locale/*locale***/LC_MESSAGES/uxdfm**
language-specific message file [See **LANG** on **environ**(5).]

SEE ALSO

ed(1), **pr**(1)

NAME

nlsadmin – network listener service administration

SYNOPSIS

/usr/sbin/nlsadmin -x
/usr/sbin/nlsadmin [*options*] *net_spec*
/usr/sbin/nlsadmin [*options*] **-N** *port_monitor_tag*
/usr/sbin/nlsadmin -V
/usr/sbin/nlsadmin -c *cmd* | **-o** *pipename* [**-p** *modules*] [**-A** *address* | **-D**] [**-R** *prognum***:***versnum*]

DESCRIPTION

nlsadmin is the administrative command for the network listener process(es) on a machine. Each network has at least one instance of the network listener process associated with it; each instance (and thus, each network) is configured separately. The listener process "listens" to the network for service requests, accepts requests when they arrive, and invokes servers in response to those service requests. The network listener process may be used with any network (more precisely, with any connection-oriented transport provider) that conforms to the transport provider specification.

nlsadmin can establish a listener process for a given network, configure the specific attributes of that listener, and start and kill the listener process for that network. **nlsadmin** can also report on the listener processes on a machine, either individually (per network) or collectively.

The list below shows how to use **nlsadmin**. In this list, *net_spec* represents a particular listener process. Specifically, *net_spec* is the relative path name of the entry under **/dev** for a given network (that is, a transport provider); *net_spec* must be specified in ASCII characters. *address* is a transport address on which to listen and is interpreted using a syntax that allows for a variety of address formats. By default, *address* is interpreted as the symbolic ASCII representation of the transport address. An *address* preceded by a **\x** will let you enter an address in hexadecimal notation. Note that *address* must appear as a single word to the shell and thus must be quoted if it contains any blanks.

nlsadmin processes supplementary code set characters in the *cmd* given to the **-c** option and the *comment* given to the **-y** option (see below) according to the locale specified in the **LC_CTYPE** environment variable [see **LANG** on **environ**(5)].

Changes to the list of services provided by the listener or the addresses of those services are put into effect immediately.

nlsadmin may be used with the following combinations of options and arguments:

nlsadmin gives a brief usage message.

nlsadmin -x reports the status of all of the listener processes installed on this machine.

nlsadmin *net_spec*
prints the status of the listener process for *net_spec*.

nlsadmin -q *net_spec*
queries the status of the listener process for the specified network, and reflects the result of that query in its exit code. If a listener process is active, **nlsadmin** will exit with a status of 0; if no process is active, the exit code will be 1; the exit code will be greater than 1 in case of error.

nlsadmin -v *net_spec*
prints a verbose report on the servers associated with *net_spec*, giving the service code, status, command, and comment for each. It also specifies the **uid** the server will run as, the authentication scheme, and the list of modules to be pushed, if any, before the server is started.

nlsadmin -z *service_code net_spec*
prints a report on the server associated with *net_spec* that has service code *service_code*, giving the same information as in the **-v** option.

nlsadmin -q -z *service_code net_spec*
queries the status of the service with service code *service_code* on network *net_spec*, and exits with a status of 0 if that service is enabled, 1 if that service is disabled, and greater than 1 in case of error.

nlsadmin -l *address net_spec*
changes or sets the transport address on which the listener listens (the general listener service). This address can be used by remote processes to access the servers available through this listener (see the **-a** option, below).

If *address* is just a dash ("-"), **nlsadmin** will report the address currently configured, instead of changing it.

A change of address takes effect immediately.

nlsadmin -t *address net_spec*
changes or sets the address on which the listener listens for requests for terminal service but is otherwise similar to the **-l** option above. A terminal service address should not be defined unless the appropriate remote login software is available. The terminal service must be configured as service code 1 (see the **-a** option, below).

nlsadmin -i *net_spec*
initializes an instance of the listener for the network specified by *net_spec*; that is, creates and initializes the files required by the listener as well as starting that instance of the listener. Note that a particular instance of the listener should be initialized only once. The listener must be initialized before assigning addresses or services.

nlsadmin -a *service_code* [**-p** *modules*] [**-w** *name*] **-c** *cmd* **-y** *comment net_spec*
adds a new service to the list of services available through the indicated listener. *service_code* is the code for the service, *cmd* is the command to be invoked in response to that service code, comprised of the full path name of the server and its arguments, and *comment* is a brief (free-form) description of the service for use in various reports.

Note that *cmd* must appear as a single word to the shell; if arguments are required, the *cmd* and its arguments must be enclosed in quotation marks. The *comment* must also appear as a single word to the shell. When a service is added, it is initially enabled (see the **-e** and **-d** options, below). *cmd* and *comment* may contain supplementary code set characters.

Service codes are alphanumeric strings. The numeric service codes 0 through 100 are reserved for internal use by the listener. Service code 0 is assigned to the nlps server, which is the service invoked on the general listening address. In particular, code 1 is assigned to the remote login service, which is the service automatically invoked for connections to the terminal login address.

If the **-p** option is specified, then *modules* will be interpreted as a list of STREAMS modules for the listener to push before starting the service being added. The modules are pushed in the order they are specified. *modules* should be a comma-separated list of modules, with no white space included. *modules* must be specified in ASCII characters.

If the **-w** option is specified, then *name* is interpreted as the user name from **/etc/passwd** that the listener should look up. From the user name, the listener obtains the user ID, the group ID(s), and the home directory for use by the server. If **-w** is not specified, the default is to use the user name **listen**.

A service must explicitly be added to the listener for each network on which that service is to be available. This operation will normally be performed only when the service is installed on a machine, or when populating the list of services for a new network.

nlsadmin -r *service_code net_spec*
: removes the entry for the *service_code* from that listener's list of services. This is normally done only in conjunction with the deinstallation of a service from a machine.

nlsadmin -e *service_code net_spec*
nlsadmin -d *service_code net_spec*
: enables or disables (respectively) the service indicated by *service_code* for the specified network. The service must previously have been added to the listener for that network (see the **-a** option, above). Disabling a service will cause subsequent service requests for that service to be denied, but the processes from any prior service requests that are still running will continue unaffected.

nlsadmin -s *net_spec*
nlsadmin -k *net_spec*
: starts and kills (respectively) the listener process for the indicated network. These operations will normally be performed as part of the system startup and shutdown procedures. Before a listener can be started for a particular network, it must first have been initialized (see the **-i** option, above). When a listener is killed, processes that

are still running as a result of prior service requests will continue unaffected.

Under the Service Access Facility, it is possible to have multiple instances of the listener on a single *net_spec*. In any of the above commands, the option **-N** *port_monitor_tag* may be used in place of the *net_spec* argument. This argument specifies the tag by which an instance of the listener is identified by the Service Access Facility. If the **-N** option is not specified (that is, the *net_spec* is specified in the invocation), then it will be assumed that the last component of the *net_spec* represents the tag of the listener for which the operation is destined. In other words, it is assumed that there is at least one listener on a designated *net_spec*, and that its tag is identical to the last component of the *net_spec*. This listener may be thought of as the primary, or default, listener for a particular *net_spec*.

nlsadmin is also used in conjunction with the Service Access Facility commands. In that capacity, the following combinations of options can be used:

nlsadmin -V writes the current version number of the listener's administrative file to the standard output. It is used as part of the **sacadm**(1M) command line when **sacadm** adds a listener to the system.

nlsadmin -c *cmd* | **-o** *pipename* [**-p** *modules*] [**-A** *address* | **-D**] [**-R** *prognum* **:** *versnum*]

formats the port monitor-specific information to be used as an argument to **pmadm**(1M).

The **-c** option specifies the full path name of the server and its arguments. *cmd* must appear as a single word to the shell; its arguments must be surrounded by quotes. *cmd* may contain supplementary code set characters.

The **-o** option specifies the full path name of a FIFO or named STREAM through which a standing server is actually receiving the connection.

If the **-p** option is specified, then *modules* will be interpreted as a list of STREAMS modules for the listener to push before starting the service being added. The modules are pushed in the order in which they are specified. *modules* must be a comma-separated list, with no white space included.

If the **-A** option is specified, then *address* will be interpreted as the server's private address. The listener will monitor this address on behalf of the service and will dispatch all calls arriving on this address directly to the designated service. This option may not be used in conjunction with the **-D** option.

If the **-D** option is specified, then the service is assigned a private address dynamically, that is, the listener will have the transport provider select the address each time the listener begins listening on behalf of this service. For RPC services, this option will be often be used in conjunction with the **-R** option to register the dynamically assigned address with the rpcbinder. This option may not be used in conjunction with the **-A** option.

When the `-R` option is specified, the service is an RPC service whose address, program number, and version number should be registered with the rpcbinder for this transport provider. This registration is performed each time the listener begins listening on behalf of the service. *prognum* and *versnum* are the program number and version number, respectively, of the RPC service.

`nlsadmin` may be invoked by any user to generate reports.

The options specific to the Service Access Facility may not be mixed with any other options.

SEE ALSO

`listen`(1M), `pmadm`(1M), `rpcbind`(1M), `sacadm`(1M)

NOTES

Dynamically assigned addresses are not displayed in reports as are statically assigned addresses.

NAME

nm – print name list of an object file

SYNOPSIS

nm [**-oxhvnefurplVT**] *files*

DESCRIPTION

The **nm** command displays the symbol table of each ELF or COFF object file, specified by *file(s)*. The file may be a relocatable or absolute ELF or COFF object file; or it may be an archive of relocatable or absolute ELF or COFF object files. For each symbol, the following information will be printed:

Index The index of the symbol. (The index appears in brackets.)

Value The value of the symbol is one of the following: a section offset for defined symbols in a relocatable file; alignment constraints for symbols whose section index is **SHN_COMMON**; a virtual address in executable and dynamic library files.

Size The size in bytes of the associated object.

Type A symbol is of one of the following types: **NOTYPE** (no type was specified), **OBJECT** (a data object such as an array or variable), **FUNC** (a function or other executable code), **SECTION** (a section symbol), or **FILE** (name of the source file).

Bind The symbol's binding attributes. **LOCAL** symbols have a scope limited to the object file containing their definition; **GLOBAL** symbols are visible to all object files being combined; and **WEAK** symbols are essentially global symbols with a lower precedence than **GLOBAL**.

Other A field reserved for future use, currently containing 0.

Shndx Except for three special values, this is the section header table index in relation to which the symbol is defined. The following special values exist: **ABS** indicates the symbol's value will not change through relocation; **COMMON** indicates an unallocated block and the value provides alignment constraints; and **UNDEF** indicates an undefined symbol.

Name The name of the symbol.

The output of **nm** may be controlled using the following options:

-o Print the value and size of a symbol in octal instead of decimal.

-x Print the value and size of a symbol in hexadecimal instead of decimal.

-h Do not display the output heading data.

-v Sort external symbols by value before they are printed.

-n Sort external symbols by name before they are printed.

-e See NOTES below.

-f See NOTES below.

-u Print undefined symbols only.

-r Prepend the name of the object file or archive to each output line.

-p [-l] Produce terse output that can be parsed easily. Each symbol name is preceded by its value (blanks if undefined) and one of the letters **U** (undefined), **N** (symbol has no type), **D** (data object symbol), **T** (text symbol), **S** (section symbol), or **F** (file symbol). If the symbol's binding attribute is **LOCAL**, the key letter is lower case; if the symbol's binding attribute is **WEAK**, the key letter is upper case (if the **-l** modifier is specified, the upper case key letter is followed by an *****); if the symbol's binding attribute is **GLOBAL**, the key letter is upper case.

-C Print C++ names decoded.

-V Print on the standard error output the version number of the **nm** command being executed.

-T See NOTES below.

Options may be used in any order, either singly or in combination, and may appear anywhere in the command line. When conflicting options are specified (such as **nm -v -n**) the first is taken and the second ignored with a warning message to the user.

SEE ALSO

a.out(4), ar(4), as(1), cc(1), dump(1), ld(1)

NOTES

The following options are obsolete because of changes to the object file format and will be deleted in a future release.

-e Print only external and static symbols. The symbol table now contains only static and external symbols. Automatic symbols no longer appear in the symbol table. They do appear in the debugging information produced by **cc -g**, which may be examined using **dump**(1).

-f Produce full output. Redundant symbols (such as .text, .data, and so on) which existed previously do not exist and producing full output will be identical to the default output.

-T By default, **nm** prints the entire name of the symbols listed. Since symbol names have been moved to the last column, the problem of overflow is removed and it is no longer necessary to truncate the symbol name.

NAME

nohup – run a command immune to hangups and quits

SYNOPSIS

nohup *command* [*arguments*]

DESCRIPTION

nohup executes *command* with hangups and quits ignored. If output is not redirected by the user, both standard output and standard error are sent to **nohup.out**. If **nohup.out** is not writable in the current directory, output is redirected to **$HOME/nohup.out**.

EXAMPLE

It is frequently desirable to apply **nohup** to pipelines or lists of commands. This can be done only by placing pipelines and command lists in a single file, called a shell procedure. One can then issue: **nohup sh** *file*

and the **nohup** applies to everything in *file*. If the shell procedure *file* is to be executed often, then the need to type **sh** can be eliminated by giving *file* execute permission. Add an ampersand and the contents of *file* are run in the background with interrupts also ignored [see **sh**(1)]:

nohup *file* **&**

An example of what the contents of *file* could be is: **sort ofile > nfile**

FILES

/usr/lib/locale/*locale***/LC_MESSAGES/uxue**
language-specific message file [See **LANG** on **environ**(5).]

SEE ALSO

chmod(1), **nice**(1), **sh**(1), **signal**(2)

NOTES

In the case of the following command

```
nohup command1; command2
```

nohup applies only to **command1**. The command

```
nohup (command1; command2)
```

is syntactically incorrect.

notify(1)

NAME

notify – notify user of the arrival of new mail

SYNOPSIS

notify -y
notify [**-n**]

DESCRIPTION

When a new mail message arrives, the **mail** command first checks the recipient's forwarding file, **/var/mail/:forward/***user*, to see if the message is to be forwarded elsewhere (to some other recipient or as the input to some command). **notify** is used to set up forwarding so that the new message is saved both into the mailbox and, if the user is currently logged in, he or she is notified immediately of the arrival of new mail.

Command-line options are:

-y	Install mail notification facility
-n	Remove mail notification facility

If invoked with no arguments, **notify** reports whether automatic mail notification is activated or not.

The notification is done by looking in **/var/adm/utmp** to determine if the recipient is currently logged in, and if so, on which terminal device. Then the terminal device is opened for writing and the user is notified about the new message. The notification will indicate who the message is from. If the message contains a **Subject:** header line it will be included.

For security, all unprintable characters within the header will be converted to an exclamation point. This prevents **notify** from writing an escape sequence to a "smart" terminal which could potentially cause the terminal to be programmed through a mail message.

If the user is logged in multiple times he or she will get multiple notifications, one per terminal. To disable notifications to a particular login session, the **mesg**(1) command can be used to disable writing to that terminal.

If there are multiple machines connected together via a distributed filesystem, **notify** will look up the **/var/adm/utmp** files on the other systems as well. To do this, the file **/etc/mail/notify.sys** will be consulted, which will contain two columns, the first being the name of a system and the second being a path to find the root filesystem for that machine.

If **notify** has troubles delivering the mail to the specified mailfile, **notify** will deliver the file to the user's regular mailfile.

FILES

/tmp/notif*	temporary file
/var/mail/*	users' standard mailboxes
/var/mail/:forward/*	users' forwarding information
/usr/lib/mail/notify2	program that performs the notification

`/etc/mail/notify.sys`
list of machines and paths to their root filesystems

`/var/adm/utmp` list of users who are logged in

SEE ALSO

mail(1), **mailcheck**(1), **mesg**(1)

NOTES

notify uses the "**Forward to** >|*command*" facility of **mail** to implement notifications.

NAME

nroff – (BSD) format documents for display or line-printer

SYNOPSIS

/usr/ucb/nroff [**-ehiqz**] [**-F***dir*] [**-m***name*] [**-n***N*] [**-o***list*] [**-r***aN*] [**-s***N*] [**-T***name*] [**-u***N*] [*file* . . .]

DESCRIPTION

nroff formats text in the named *file* for typewriter-like devices. [See also **troff**(1)].

If no *file* argument is present, **nroff** reads the standard input. An argument consisting of a '–' is taken to be a file name corresponding to the standard input.

The following options may appear in any order, but must appear before the files.

-e Produce equally-spaced words in adjusted lines, using full terminal resolution.

-h Use output TAB characters during horizontal spacing to speed output and reduce output character count. TAB settings are assumed to be every 8 nominal character widths.

-i Read the standard input after the input files are exhausted.

-q Invoke the simultaneous input-output mode of the **rd** request.

-F*dir* Search directory *dir* for font tables instead of the system-dependent default.

-m*name* Prepend the macro file **/usr/ucblib/doctools/tmac/***name* to the input files.

-n*N* Number first generated page *N* .

-o*list* Print only pages whose page numbers appear in the comma-separated *list* of numbers and ranges. A range *N–M* means pages *N* through *M*; an initial *–N* means from the beginning to page *N*; and a final *N–* means from *N* to the end.

-r*aN* Set register *a* (one-character) to *N*.

-s*N* Stop every *N* pages. **nroff** will halt prior to every *N* pages (default *N*=**1**) to allow paper loading or changing, and will resume upon receipt of a NEWLINE.

-T*name* Prepare output for a device of the specified *name*. Known *name*s are:

37	Teletype Corporation Model 37 terminal — this is the default.
lp | **tn300**	GE TermiNet 300, or any line printer or terminal without half-line capability.
300	DASI-300.
300-12	DASI-300 — 12-pitch.
300S | **300s**	DASI-300S.

300S-12 | **300s-12**
DASI-300S.

382 DASI-382 (fancy DTC 382).

450 DASI-450 (Diablo Hyterm).

450-12 DASI-450 (Diablo Hyterm) — 12-pitch.

832 AJ 832.

-u*N* Set emboldening factor for the font mounted on position 3 to **N**. Emboldening is accomplished by overstriking the specified number of times.

-z Suppress formatted output. The only output will consist of diagnostic messages from **nroff** and messages output with the **.tm** request.

EXAMPLE

The following command:

```
nroff -s4 -me users.guide
```

formats **users.guide** using the **-me** macro package, and stopping every 4 pages.

FILES

/var/tmp/tr*	temporary file
/usr/ucblib/doctools/tmac/*	standard macro files
/usr/ucblib/doctools/nterm/tab.*	terminal driving tables for **nroff**

SEE ALSO

checknr(1), **col**(1), **eqn**(1), **man**(5), **me**(5), **ms**(5), **tbl**(1), **term**(4), **troff**(1)

nslookup (1M)

NAME

nslookup – query name servers interactively

SYNOPSIS

nslookup
nslookup - *server*
nslookup *host*
nslookup *host server*

DESCRIPTION

nslookup is an interactive program to query ARPA Internet domain name servers. The user can contact servers to request information about a specific host or print a list of hosts in the domain.

OPTIONS

– *server*	runs **nslookup** in interactive mode using the specified *server*.
host	looks up the specified *host* using the default *server* and exits.
host server	looks up the specified *host* using the specified *server* and exits.

When **nslookup** is used with no options, it is run in interactive mode using the default *server*.

USAGE

Overview

The Internet domain name-space is tree-structured, with four top-level domains at present:

COM	commercial establishments
EDU	educational institutions
GOV	government agencies
MIL	MILNET hosts

If you are looking for a specific host, you need to know something about the host's organization in order to determine the top-level domain it belongs to. For instance, if you want to find the Internet address of a machine at UCLA , do the following:

Connect with the root server using the **root** command. The root server of the name space has knowledge of the top-level domains.

Since UCLA is a university, its domain name is **ucla.edu**. Connect with a server for the **ucla.edu** domain with the command **server ucla.edu**. The response will print the names of hosts that act as servers for that domain. Note: the root server does not have information about **ucla.edu**, but knows the names and addresses of hosts that do. Once located by the root server, all future queries will be sent to the UCLA name server.

To request information about a particular host in the domain (for instance, **locus**), just type the host name. To request a listing of hosts in the UCLA domain, use the **ls** command. The **ls** command requires a domain name (in this case, **ucla.edu**) as an argument.

If you are connected with a name server that handles more than one domain, all lookups for host names must be fully specified with its domain. For instance, the domain **harvard.edu** is served by **seismo.css.gov**, which also services the **css.gov** and **cornell.edu** domains. A lookup request for the host **aiken** in the **harvard.edu** domain must be specified as **aiken.harvard.edu**. However, the

set domain = *name*

and

set defname

commands can be used to automatically append a domain name to each request.

After a successful lookup of a host, use the **finger** command to see who is on the system, or to finger a specific person. To get other information about the host, use the

set querytype = *value*

command to change the type of information desired and request another lookup. (**finger** requires the type to be A.)

Commands

To exit, type Ctrl-D (EOF). The command line length must be less than 80 characters. An unrecognized command will be interpreted as a host name.

host [*server*]
: Look up information for *host* using the current default server or using *server* if it is specified.

server *domain*
lserver *domain*
: Change the default server to *domain*. **lserver** uses the initial server to look up information about *domain* while **server** uses the current default server. If an authoritative answer can't be found, the names of servers that might have the answer are returned.

root
: Changes the default server to the server for the root of the domain name space. Currently, the host **sri-nic.arpa** is used; this command is a synonym for **lserver sri-nic.arpa**.) The name of the root server can be changed with the **set root** command.

finger [*username*]
: Connect with the finger server on the current host, which is defined by a previous successful lookup for a host's address information (see the **set** *querytype* **=A** command). If *username* is provided, **finger** is run for that specific user. As with the shell, output can be redirected to a named file using > and >>.

ls [*domain***]**
: List the information available for *domain*. The default output contains host names and their Internet addresses. As with the shell, output can be redirected to a named file using > and >>. When output is directed to a file, hash marks are printed for every 50 records received from the server.

view *filename*
Sort and list the output of the **ls** command with **more**(1).

help

? Print a brief summary of commands.

set *keyword* [= *value*] This command is used to change state information that affects the lookups. Valid keywords are:

all Prints the current values of the various options to **set**. Information about the current default server and host is also printed.

[**no**] **deb**[**ug**]
Turn debugging mode on. A lot more information is printed about the packet sent to the server and the resulting answer. The default is **nodebug**.

[**no**] **def** [*name*]
Append the default domain name to every lookup. The default is **nodefname**.

do [**main**] = *filename*
Change the default domain name to *filename*. The default domain name is appended to all lookup requests if **defname** option has been set. The default is the value in **/etc/resolv.conf**.

q [**querytype**] = *value*
Change the type of information returned from a query to one of:

A	The host's Internet address (the default).
CNAME	The canonical name for an alias.
HINFO	The host CPU and operating system type.
MX	The mail exchanger.
MB	The mailbox domain name.
MG	The mail group member.
MINFO	The mailbox or mail list information.

(Other types specified in the RFC883 document are valid, but are not very useful.)

[**no**] **recurse**
Tell the name server to query other servers if it does not have the information. The default is **recurse**.

ret [**ry**] = *count*
Set the number of times to retry a request before giving up to *count*. When a reply to a request is not received within a certain amount of time (changed with **set timeout**), the request is resent. The default is *count* is **2**.

ro [**ot**] = *host*
Change the name of the root server to *host*. This affects the **root** command. The default root server is **sri-nic.arpa**.

`t [ timeout ] =` *interval*
: Change the time-out for a reply to *interval* seconds. The default *interval* is **10** seconds.

`[ no ] v[ c ]`
: Always use a virtual circuit when sending requests to the server. The default is **novc**.

FILES

`/etc/resolv.conf` initial domain name and name server addresses.

SEE ALSO

named(1M), **resolv.conf**(4), **resolver**(3N), RFC 882, RFC 883

DIAGNOSTICS

If the lookup request was not successful, an error message is printed. Possible errors are:

Time-out
: The server did not respond to a request after a certain amount of time (changed with **set timeout** = *value*) and a certain number of retries (changed with **set retry** = *value*).

No information
: Depending on the query type set with the **set querytype** command, no information about the host was available, though the host name is valid.

Non-existent domain
: The host or domain name does not exist.

Connection refused
Network is unreachable
: The connection to the name or finger server could not be made at the current time. This error commonly occurs with **finger** requests.

Server failure
: The name server found an internal inconsistency in its database and could not return a valid answer.

Refused
: The name server refused to service the request.

The following error should not occur and it indicates a bug in the program.

Format error
: The name server found that the request packet was not in the proper format.

NOTES

The *server* must be a valid Internet address in the standard "dot" notation.

NAME

nsquery – Remote File Sharing name server query

SYNOPSIS

nsquery [-h] [*name*]

DESCRIPTION

This command is obsolete and will not be supported after this release. **nsquery** provides information about resources available to the host from both the local domain and from other domains. All resources are reported, regardless of whether the host is authorized to access them. When used with no options, **nsquery** identifies all resources in the domain that have been advertised as sharable. A report on selected resources can be obtained by specifying *name*, where *name* is:

nodename The report will include only those resources available from *nodename*.

domain. The report will include only those resources available from *domain*.

domain.nodename The report will include only those resources available from *domain.nodename*.

When the name does not include the delimiter ".", it will be interpreted as a *nodename* within the local domain. If the name ends with a delimiter ".", it will be interpreted as a domain name.

The information contained in the report on each resource includes its advertised name (*domain.resource*), the read/write permissions, the server (*nodename.domain*) that advertised the resource, the transport provider used, and a brief textual description (if a description was specified when the resource was made available).

The output of **nsquery** consists of an optional header line (suppressed with the **-h** flag) followed by a list of lines containing whitespace-separated fields. For each line listed by the **nsquery** command, the fields are:

resource access server transport description

where

resource Specifies the resource name that must be given to the **mount**(1M) command.

access Specifies the access permissions granted to the client systems, either **ro** (for read-only) or **rw** (for read and write).

server Specifies the system that is making the resource available.

transport Specifies the transport provider over with the *resource* is shared.

description Describes the resource. This field may be null (blank).

A remote domain must be listed in your **rfmaster** file in order to query that domain.

If your host cannot contact the domain name server, an error message will be sent to standard error.

Output

If no entries are found when **nsquery** is executed, the report header is printed.

REFERENCES

rfmaster(4), **RFS**-specific **share**(1M), **RFS**-specific **unshare**(1M)

od(1)

NAME

od – octal dump

SYNOPSIS

od [**-bcDdFfOoSsvXx**] [*file*] [[+]*offset*] [**.** | **b** | **x**]

DESCRIPTION

od displays *file* in one or more formats, as selected by the first argument. If the first argument is missing, **-o** is default. If no *file* is specified, the standard input is used. For the purposes of this description, "word" refers to a 16-bit unit, independent of the word size of the machine; "long word" refers to a 32-bit unit, and "double long word" refers to a 64-bit unit. **od** processes supplementary code set characters according to the locale specified in the **LC_CTYPE** environment variable [see **LANG** on **environ**(5)]. The meanings of the format options are:

-b Interpret bytes in octal.

-c Interpret bytes as single-byte characters. Multibyte characters are treated as non-graphic characters. Certain non-graphic characters appear as C-language escapes: null=**\0**, backspace=**\b**, form-feed=**\f**, new-line=**\n**, return=**\r**, tab=**\t**; others appear as 3-digit octal numbers. For example:

```
echo "hello world" | od -c
0000000   h   e   l   l   o       w   o   r   l   d  \n
0000014
```

-D Interpret long words in unsigned decimal.

-d Interpret words in unsigned decimal.

-F Interpret double long words in extended precision.

-f Interpret long words in floating point.

-O Interpret long words in unsigned octal.

-o Interpret words in octal.

-S Interpret long words in signed decimal.

-s Interpret words in signed decimal.

-v Show all data (verbose).

-X Interpret long words in hex.

-x Interpret words in hex.

offset specifies an offset from the beginning of *file* where the display will begin. *offset* is normally interpreted as octal bytes. If **.** is appended, *offset* is interpreted in decimal. If **x** is appended, *offset* is interpreted in hexadecimal. If *offset* is omitted, the **.** and **x** can still be used to display decimal and hexadecimal addresses, respectively. If **b** is appended, *offset* is interpreted in blocks of 512 bytes. If *file* is omitted, *offset* must be preceded by **+**.

The display continues until an end-of-file is reached.

FILES

/usr/lib/locale/*locale***/LC_MESSAGES/uxdfm**
language-specific message file [See **LANG** on **environ**(5).]

NAME

.olsetup - execute **desktop** from a **.profile**

SYNOPSIS

$HOME/.olsetup

DESCRIPTION

The **.olsetup** command is a front end shell script that invokes **desktop** from a user's **$HOME/.profile**. It will check the value of the shell variable **DT**. If this variable is set to **yes**, it will start the UNIX Desktop. There is one copy of the script **$HOME/.olsetup** for each desktop user. **.olsetup** will also set the **XWINFONTPATH** variable to include the standard OPEN LOOK or MOTIF fonts.

If logging in remotely (not from the console), and **$REMOTE** is set and responds to a ping, **.olsetup** querys if the user is logging in from **$REMOTE**.

If logging in remotely, **.olsetup** querys if the desktop should be displayed, and, if yes, invokes **dtm** rather than **desktop**.

Environment

The **.olsetup** command uses or affects the following environment variables:

DESKTOPDIR	users desktop home directory
DISPLAY	display type
DT	begin desktop on login if yes
LD_LIBRARY_PATH	modified by **.olsetup**
PATH	modified by **.olsetup**
REMOTE	remote location user generally logs in from
XDM_LOGIN	use graphical login
XGUI	graphical user interface
XNETACCESS	allow remote machines to access the server
XWINHOME	default XWIN home, **/usr/X**
XWINFONTPATH	default font path

Files

$HOME/.profile

SEE ALSO

desktop(1), **dtm**(1), **dtadduser**(1M)

NAME

`olwm` - OPEN LOOK Window Manager

SYNOPSIS

`olwm` [`-motif`] [`-openlook`]

DESCRIPTION

`olwm` is the desktop window manager. It supports applications using the MOTIF, MoOLIT, or OPEN LOOK toolkits, and checks the **`$HOME/.Xdefaults`** file or the **`$XWINHOME/lib/app-defaults/`***app* directory for toolkit properties. It allows the user to create, move, resize, raise, lower, iconify, and delete windows.

RESOURCES

The following table lists the `olwm` resources:

`olwm` Resources				
Resource	Type	Class	Range of Values	Default Value
`XtNbackground`	`Pixel`	`XtCBackground`	color	`WHITE`
`XtNforeground`	`Pixel`	`XtCForeground`	color	`BLACK`
`XtNfont`	`String`	`XtCFont`	any legal font	MOTIF font
`XtNiconBackground`†	`Pixel`	`XtCBackground`	color	`WHITE`
`XtNiconBorder`	`Boolean`	`XtCIconBorder`	True, False	`TRUE`
`XtNiconForeground`†	`Pixel`	`XtCForeground`	color	`BLACK`
`XtNiconGravity`	`String`	`XtCIconGravity`	north, south, east, west	`SOUTH`
`XtNiconParentRelative`†	`Boolean`	`XtCIconParentRelative`	True,False	`FALSE`
`XtNinputWindowHeader`	`Pixel`	`XtCInputWindowHeader`	color	`White`
`XtNmoveOpaque`†	`Boolean`	`XtCmoveOpaque`	True, False	`FALSE`
`XtNpassKeys`	`Boolean`	`XtCpassKeys`	True, False	`FALSE`
`XtNpointerFocus`	`Boolean`	`XtCPointerFocus`	True, False	`FALSE`
`XtNscale`	`int`	`XtCScale`	10, 12, 14, 19 (points)	`12`
`XtNselectDoesPreview`	`Boolean`	`XtCSelectDoesPreview`	True, False	`TRUE`
`XtNwindowLayering`	`Boolean`	`XtCWindowLayering`	True, False	`TRUE`

† These resources can not be set from one of `dtm`'s property sheets, but all others can be.

Most `olwm` resources can be set through one of `dtm`'s property sheets or through an X resource file, such as **`.Xdefaults`**.

XtNbackground

The **`XtNbackground`** resource determines the color used with most decorations provided by `olwm`, including the window menu mark or pushpin and the decoration frame background.

XtNfont

The **`XtNfont`** resource determines the font of window titles. The default is the MOTIF or OPEN LOOK default font depending on which look and feel is selected.

XtNforeground

The **`XtNforeground`** resource determines the color of the applications title in the window header or icon.

XtNiconBorder

The **XtNiconBorder** resource determines if an icon border is used. If **TRUE**, a border is always drawn around icons. If the icon is selected, then the border is 3 points thick; otherwise, the border is 2 points thick. If **FALSE**, no border is drawn.

XtNiconParentRelative

The **XtNiconParentRelative** resource determines the icon display relative to its parent. If **TRUE**, the icon is displayed with the background pixmap of ParentRelative, and the icon background color is the background workspace. If **FALSE**, the icon background is, in order, **XtNiconBackground** or the **XtNiconParentRelative** class default.

XtNiconGravity

The **XtNiconGravity** resource controls the default placement of icons. Icon placement starts and continues at an area of the screen based on the value of this resource:

SOUTH Placement starts at the lower left hand corner of the screen and proceeds to the right. If the next positioned icon would overrun the right edge of the screen, icon placement resumes at the left and above the previous icon row.

WEST Placement starts at the upper left corner of the screen and proceeds downward. If the next positioned icon would overrun the bottom edge, icon placement resumes at the top and right of the previous icon column.

NORTH Placement starts at the upper left corner of the screen and proceeds to the right. If the next positioned icon would overrun the right edge, icon placement resumes at the left, just below the previous row.

EAST Placement starts at the upper right corner of the screen and proceeds downward. If the next positioned icon would overrun the bottom edge, it is placed at the top, left of the previous column.

XtNinputWindowHeader

The **XtNinputWindowHeader** resource provides the color that **olwm** uses in the header of windows that have input focus. In the OPEN LOOK look and feel only, if the **XtNpointerFocus** resource is **TRUE**, additional lines are drawn (one at the top and one at the bottom of the header) with **XtNinputWindowHeader** color, and the header background color remains the same.

XtNpassKeys

The **XtNpassKeys** resource controls whether window menu operations are passed on to the application. If **TRUE**, then window menu operations are passed to the application except

if the window menu is posted, accelerators are not passed

if the client is iconified, accelerators are consumed and window menu operations are handled by **olwm** independent of the state of the window menu

The following keys are never passed to the client:

`OL_WINDOWMENU`
post the window menu

`OL_NEXTAPP`
transfer focus to the next application

`OL_PREVAPP`
transfer focus to the previous application

`OL_NEXTWIN`
transfer focus to the next window

`OL_PREVWIN`
transfer focus to the next window

XtNpointerFocus

The **XtNpointerFocus** resource controls the method input focus is distributed. If **TRUE**, then "focus follows the mouse", that is, moving the pointer into a window will give it input focus (if it accepts it), and moving the pointer out of a window removes focus.

In the MOTIF look and feel, no special visual feedback is provided. In the OPEN LOOK look and feel, **olwm** provides a special visual feedback to denote input focus. A real-estate based focus mode is assumed (for example, the focus follows the mouse). When the pointer enters the border of a window capable of gaining input focus, two additional lines are drawn into the header with the **XtNinputWindow-Header** color, and the window is considered selected.

All mouseless operations are now directed to the selected window. Moving the pointer out of the window and onto the workspace will remove input focus (for example, the two lines in the header will disappear) but the window will remain selected until the pointer enters a different window.

If **FALSE**, then "click-to-type", that is, the user must click the mouse on the window header to give it focus, or traverse to it using keyboard commands.

XtNscale

The **XtNscale** resource scales the relative size of widgets and decorations used in the toolkit. The integer value supplied for this resource represents a point size that maps to a scale for the applications widgets. In the MOTIF look and feel, the available integer value is 12. In the OPEN LOOK look and feel, the following table describes the scales available:

OPEN LOOK scales	
Point Size	Scale
10	Small
12	Medium
14	large
19	X-large

olwm supports the use of all four scales; however, the OPEN LOOK toolkit currently provides widgets with the medium (12 point) scale only.

XtNselectDoesPreview

This resource has effect only in the OPEN LOOK look and feel. The **XtNselectDoesPreview** resource determines how **MenuButton** and **Abbreviated-MenuButton** react to the user clicking SELECT over them. Although this is a toolkit feature, it affects **olwm** in two areas: the window menu button in the header of base windows, and the Dismiss menu button on the limited (popup window) menu.

XtNwindowLayering

The **XtNwindowLayering** resource affects the **olwm** Window Move operation. The Move operation is initiated by pressing SELECT on the window header and dragging the window to a new location, or through either the window menu (the Move button) or the keyboard.

If a window is moved using **olwm**, then:

FALSE only the window the Move operation is initiated on will get moved

TRUE moving a window (for example, the target window) will also move any windows that has the **window_group** field in it's **WM_HINTS** property set to the target window. In effect, the target window becomes a leader, and any window with a **WM_HINTS.window_group** value equal to the target window becomes a follower. When **XtNwindowLayering** is **TRUE**, moving a leader always results in moving a follower relative to the position of the leader. However, moving a follower will never result in the leader moving. For example, moving the leader 25 pixels to the right and 20 pixels down will result in the follower moving 25 pixels to the right and 20 pixels down.

XtNiconBackground

The **XtNiconBackground** resource specifies the color of the icons' background

XtNiconForeground

The **XtNiconForeground** resource is useful with applications that supply an icon pixmap. The pixmap is really a bitmap, with **olwm** supplying a default foreground color. If a color is specified for this resource, it will be used with all application supplied icon bitmaps.

XtNmoveOpaque

The **XtNmoveOpaque** resource affects how the Window Move operation is done. Unless changed by the user, the resource default is **FALSE**, and the Move operation proceeds under the usual circumstances:

> For the duration of the Move operation, only an outline (for example, a floating border) of the window appears to move as directed by the users actions with the mouse or keyboard. When the operation completes, the window is moved to the outline.
>
> The move is immediate – there is no floating border, and the actual window moves in direct response to the users actions (with the keyboard or mouse).
>
> **olwm** must grab the server prior to drawing the floating border on the root window, and the server grab is maintained until the operation is completed or aborted. While the server is grabbed, other applications running on the workstation can not send or receive events, and in effect their event processing is frozen.

NOTES

Not all MOTIF properties are supported at this time.

SEE ALSO

x(1)

NAME

pack, **pcat**, **unpack** – compress and expand files

SYNOPSIS

pack [–] [**-f**] *name* . . .

pcat *name* . . .

unpack *name* . . . .

DESCRIPTION

pack attempts to store the specified files in a compressed form. Wherever possible (and useful), each input file *name* is replaced by a packed file *name*.**z** with the same access modes, access and modified dates, and owner as those of *name*. The **-f** option will force packing of *name*. This is useful for causing an entire directory to be packed even if some of the files will not benefit. If **pack** is successful, *name* will be removed. Packed files can be restored to their original form using **unpack** or **pcat**.

pack uses Huffman (minimum redundancy) codes on a byte-by-byte basis. If the – argument is used, an internal flag is set that causes the number of times each byte is used, its relative frequency, and the code for the byte to be printed on the standard output. Additional occurrences of – in place of *name* will cause the internal flag to be set and reset.

The amount of compression obtained depends on the size of the input file and the character frequency distribution. Because a decoding tree forms the first part of each **.z** file, it is usually not worthwhile to pack files smaller than three blocks, unless the character frequency distribution is very skewed, which may occur with printer plots or pictures.

Typically, text files are reduced to 60-75% of their original size. Load modules, which use a larger character set and have a more uniform distribution of characters, show little compression, the packed versions being about 90% of the original size.

pack returns a value that is the number of files that it failed to compress.

No packing will occur if:

the file appears to be already packed;
the file has links;
the file is a directory;
the file cannot be opened;
no disk storage blocks will be saved by packing;
a file called *name*.**z** already exists;
the **.z** file cannot be created;
an I/O error occurred during processing;
the file size is over 16 MB;
the file name has more than **NAME_MAX** minus two characters - **pack** uses two characters to append **.z** to the file name.

pcat does for packed files what **cat**(1) does for ordinary files, except that **pcat** cannot be used as a filter. The specified files are unpacked and written to the standard output. Thus to view a packed file named **name.z** use:

```
pcat name.z
```

or just:

```
pcat name
```

To make an unpacked copy, say **nnn**, of a packed file named **name.z** (without destroying **name.z**) use the command:

```
pcat name >nnn
```

pcat returns the number of files it was unable to unpack. Failure may occur if:

the file name (including the **.z**) has more than **NAME_MAX** characters;
the file cannot be opened;
the file does not appear to be the output of **pack**.

unpack expands files created by **pack**. For each file *name* specified in the command, a search is made for a file called *name*.**z** (or just *name*, if *name* ends in **.z**). If this file appears to be a packed file, it is replaced by its expanded version. The new file has the **.z** suffix stripped from its name, and has the same access modes, access and modification dates, and owner as those of the packed file.

unpack returns a value that is the number of files it was unable to unpack. Failure may occur for the same reasons that it may in **pcat**, as well as for the following:

a file with the "unpacked" name already exists;
if the unpacked file cannot be created.

FILES

/usr/lib/locale/*locale***/LC_MESSAGES/uxdfm**
language-specific message file [See **LANG** on **environ**(5).]

SEE ALSO

cat(1), **compress**(1)

NAME

`pagesize` – (BSD) display the size of a page of memory

SYNOPSIS

`/usr/ucb/pagesize`

DESCRIPTION

`pagesize` prints the size of a page of memory in bytes, as returned by `getpagesize`. This program is useful for constructing portable shell scripts.

REFERENCES

`getpagesize`(3)

partsize (1M)

NAME

partsize – returns the size of the active UNIX System partition

SYNOPSIS

partsize [**-ds**] *raw-device*

DESCRIPTION

The function of **partsize** is to print the size of the active UNIX System partition for the raw-device disk drive. The size value returned is in megabytes (MB = 2E20 bytes). This command is intended for use with the installation scripts, but is available for general use. If the system cannot retrieve a valid partition table, there will be a non-zero exit value. If a valid partition table is found, but no active UNIX system partition is found, it will display a value of zero.

raw-device the required raw-device argument is the character special device for the disk drive to be accessed. It should be the slice 0 device to represent the entire device (for example, **/dev/rdsk/0s0** or **/dev/rdsk/c0t0d0s0**).

Options

partsize takes the following options:

-d Displays the disk geometry and the configuration layout of the four optional disk partitions. Disk partitions are initialized using the **fdisk**(1M) command. Unused partition entries contain the value **100** in the OS field.

-s Displays the size of the entire disk in megabytes. The value can be greater than the size of the UNIX System partition if multiple partitions were allocated.

Files

/dev/rdsk/0s0
/dev/rdsk/1s0
/dev/rdsk/c?t?d?s0

REFERENCES

fdisk(1M)

NAME

passwd – change login password and password attributes

SYNOPSIS

passwd [*login_name*]

passwd [**-l** | **-d**] [**-f**] [**-x** *max*] [**-n** *min*] [**-w** *warn*] *login_name*

passwd -s [**-a**]

passwd -s [*login_name*]

DESCRIPTION

The **passwd** command lets any user change the password or get a list of the current password attributes for his or her *login_name*. Privileged users may run **passwd** to perform these functions for any user, and to set the password attributes for any user.

A password is usually assigned by an administrator while creating a user account for the owner of the login name *login_name*. Later the user can change the password either by running the **passwd** command without any options or by invoking the **-p** option to the login procedure.

To use the latter method, enter a **-p** immediately after the login prompt (before entering *login_name*):

login: -p *login_name*

The **login** scheme then calls the **passwd** command.

See **login**(1) for details.

Command Syntax

Any user may use the **-s** option:

-s Show password attributes for the user's own *login_name*.

Only a privileged user may use the following options:

-l Lock the password entry for *login_name*.

-d Delete the password for *login_name* so user *login_name* is not prompted for a password.

-f Force the user to change the password at the next login by expiring the password for *login_name*.

-x *max* Specify the number of days the password is valid for user *login_name*.

-n *min* Specify the minimum number of days between password changes for user *login_name*. Always use this option with the **-x** option unless *max* is set to –1 (aging turned off). In that case, *min* need not be set.

-w *warn* Specify the number of days (relative to *max*) on which user *login_name* will be warned before the password expires.

-s Show password attributes for *login_name*.

-s -a Show the password attributes for all users.

Password Construction

Passwords must be constructed to meet the following requirements:

Each password must have at least **PASSLENGTH** characters as defined in **/etc/default/passwd**. **PASSLENGTH** must be at least 3. Only the first eight characters are significant.

Each password must contain at least two alphabetic characters and at least one numeric or special character. (In this case, "alphabetic" includes all uppercase and lowercase letters.)

Each password must differ from the user's login *name* and any reverse or circular shift of that login *name*. (Corresponding uppercase and lowercase letters are considered equivalent.)

A new password must differ from the old one by at least three characters.

If a password generator program has been specified for a user through the **useradd** (or **usermod**) command, **passwd** calls the password generator program to generate possible passwords for the user to select; when a password generator is used, none of the normally required password construction rules are enforced.

Operation

When used to change a password, **passwd** prompts ordinary users for their old password, if any. If sufficient time has passed since the old password was set, **passwd** then prompts the user twice for the new password; otherwise it terminates. Next, **passwd** checks to make sure the new password meets construction requirements. When the new password is entered a second time, the two copies of the new password are compared. If the two copies are not identical, the cycle of prompting for the new password is repeated a maximum of twice.

Privileged users may change any password; the **passwd** command does not prompt a privileged user for an old password. Privileged users are not forced to comply with password aging and password construction requirements. Such users can create a null password by pressing RETURN in response to the prompt for a new password. (This differs from **passwd -d** because the **Password:** prompt will still be displayed.)

Password Aging

Passwords are valid for finite periods (defined by the system administrator), after which they must be changed. Therefore a record must be kept of each password and the period for which it's active. As the expiration date for a password approaches, its owner is warned to choose a new password before a specified number of days elapses. The process of monitoring password schedules and notifying users about their passwords, when necessary, is called password aging.

Information about the password for each user on the system is kept in a file called **/etc/shadow**, which is readable only by privileged users.

Each user's line in **/etc/shadow** has four parameters that affect password aging:

lastchanged: The date on which the password for the user was last changed. (Note that this date is determined using Greenwich Mean Time and, therefore, may differ by as much as a day in other time zones.)

minimum: The number of days that must elapse after the **lastchanged** date before the password for the user can be changed.

maximum: The number of days for which the password for the user will be valid after the **lastchanged** date (after which it will be necessary to change the password). This number does not include the day on which the password is set.

warn: The number of days the user will receive warnings about the impending expiration of his or her password. Thus, for example, if the value of *warn* is 7, the owner of *login_name* will start receiving warnings a week before the password expires.

The last three of these parameters may be set by the command line options **-n**, **-x**, and **-w**, respectively. In the absence of command options, their values are set from the **/etc/default/passwd** file. The "Defaults" section describes these parameters.

If *minimum* is greater than *maximum*, the user may not change the password. Aging for *login_name* is turned off immediately if *maximum* is set to -1. If *maximum* is set to 0, the user is forced to change the password at the next login session after the **lastchanged** date, and aging is turned off at that time.

Password aging is never turned off directly by the command line "**passwd -x** 0 *login_name*". Instead, this command sets the **maximum** field to 0. If the **lastchanged** field is not 0, the aging fields will be cleared the next time the **passwd** command is used to change the user's password. If, however, the **lastchanged** field is set to 0, the aging fields are not changed.

If you expect the aging fields to be cleared and they're not, the explanation could be that the **lastchanged** field has been set to 0 without your realizing it. There are two possible explanations.

You (the administrator) may have expired a user's password by running the command **passwd -f** *login_name*. In this case, the value of **lastchanged** would have been set to 0.

The **maximum** field may have been clear when you issued the command **passwd -x** 0 *login_name*. In this case, the **passwd** command itself would have set the value of **lastchanged** to 0.

Displaying Password Attributes

When the **passwd** command is used to show password attributes, the format of the display is:

login_name status lastchanged minimum maximum warn

or, if password aging information is not present,

login_name status

The fields are defined as follows:

login_name The login ID of the user.

status The password status of *login_name*: **PS** stands for "passworded," **LK** stands for locked, and **NP** stands for "no password."

The last four fields are as defined under "Password Aging".

Defaults

By assigning values to a set of parameters in the file **/etc/default/passwd**, an administrator can control the aging and length of passwords. The following four parameters are available.

MINWEEKS	Minimum number of weeks before a password can be changed. In a delivered system, the value is **0**.
MAXWEEKS	Maximum number of weeks a password can be unchanged. In a delivered system, the value is **24**.
WARNWEEKS	Number of weeks before a password expires that the user is to be warned. In a delivered system, the value is **1**.
PASSLENGTH	Minimum number of characters in a password. In a delivered system, the value is **6**.

Note that the **passwd** command option arguments *min*, *max*, and *warn* and the corresponding **/etc/shadow** fields **minimum**, **maximum**, and **warn** treat aging in terms of days; the corresponding **/etc/default/passwd** fields, **MINWEEKS**, **MAXWEEKS**, and **WARNWEEKS**, in terms of weeks.

When password aging is off for a user but default aging values exist in **/etc/default/passwd**, then password aging will be turned on when the user's password is changed.

DIAGNOSTICS

The **passwd** command exits with a return code of 0 upon successful completion. Following are reasons for failure:

permission denied

invalid combination of options

unexpected failure; password file unchanged

unexpected failure; password file(s) missing

password file(s) busy; try again later

invalid argument to option

unexpected failure

unknown ID

aging disabled

FILES

/etc/shadow
/etc/passwd
/etc/oshadow
/etc/opasswd
/etc/default/passwd
/usr/lib/locale/*locale***/LC_MESSAGES/uxcore.abi**

language-specific message file [See **LANG** on **environ**(5).]

/etc/security/ia/index	index into **/etc/security/ia/master**
/etc/security/ia/master	contains all I&A information about users

NOTES

If root runs the **passwd -d** command to delete a password for a user for whom password aging is in effect, that user will not be allowed to add a new password until the **NULL** password has been aged. This is true even if the **PASSREQ** flag in **/etc/default/login** is set to **YES**. This results in a user without a password. We recommend you use the **-f** option whenever you use **-d** to delete a password. By doing so, you'll ensure the user is forced to change his or her password when he or she next logs in.

SEE ALSO

crypt(3C), **id**(1M), **login**(1), **passwd**(4), **pwconv**(1M), **shadow**(4), **su**(1M), **useradd**(1M), **userdel**(1M), **usermod**(1M)

paste(1)

NAME

paste – merge same lines of several files or subsequent lines of one file

SYNOPSIS

paste – | *file1* – | *file2* . . .
paste -d*list* – | *file1* – | *file2* . . .
paste -s [-d*list*] – | *file1* . . .

DESCRIPTION

In the first two forms, **paste** concatenates corresponding lines of the given input files *file1*, *file2*, and so on. It treats each file as a column or columns of a table and pastes them together horizontally (parallel merging). If you will, it is the counterpart of **cat**(1) which concatenates vertically, that is, one file after the other. In the last form above, **paste** replaces the function of an older command with the same name by combining subsequent lines of the input file (serial merging). If more than one file is specified with the **-s** option, **paste**(1) concatenates the merged files one below the other. In all cases, lines are glued together with the *tab* character, or with characters from an optionally specified *list*. Output is to the standard output, so it can be used as the start of a pipe, or as a filter, if – is used in place of a file name. **paste** processes supplementary code set characters in *files*, and recognizes supplementary code set characters in the *list* given to the **-d** option (see below) according to the locale specified in the **LC_CTYPE** environment variable [see **LANG** on **environ**(5)].

The meanings of the options are:

-d Without this option, the new-line characters of each but the last file (or last line in case of the **-s** option) are replaced by a *tab* character. This option allows replacing the *tab* character by one or more alternate characters (see below).

list One or more characters immediately following **-d** replace the default *tab* as the line concatenation character. The list is used sequentially and circularly: first, the first element on the list is used to concatenate the lines, then the next, and so on; when all elements have been used, the list is reused starting from the first element. In parallel merging (that is, no **-s** option), the lines from the last file are always terminated with a new-line character, not from the *list*. The list may contain the special escape sequences: **\n** (new-line), **\t** (tab), **** (backslash), and **\0** (empty string, not a null character). Quoting may be necessary, if characters have special meaning to the shell (for example, to get one backslash, use *–d* \\\\""). *list* may contain supplementary code set characters.

-s Merge subsequent lines rather than one from each input file. Use *tab* for concatenation, unless a *list* is specified with **-d** option. Regardless of the *list*, the very last character of the file is forced to be a new-line.

– May be used in place of any file name, to read a line from the standard input. (There is no prompting.)

EXAMPLES

`ls	paste -d" " -`	Lists directory in one column
`ls	paste - - - -`	Lists directory in four columns
`paste -d"\t\n"` *file1 file2*	Lists *file1* in column 1 and *file2* in column 2. The columns are separated by a tab.
`paste -s -d"\t\n"` *file1 file2*	Merges pairs of subsequent lines first in *file1*, then in *file2*. Concatenates the merged *file2* below *file1*.

FILES

/usr/lib/locale/*locale***/LC_MESSAGES/uxdfm**
language-specific message file [See **LANG** on **environ**(5).]

SEE ALSO

cut(1), **grep**(1), **pr**(1)

DIAGNOSTICS

UX:paste:ERROR:line too long
Output lines are restricted to 511 bytes.

UX:paste:ERROR:too many files
Except for **-s** option, no more than 12 input files may be specified.

pathconv (1F)

NAME

pathconv – search FMLI criteria for filename

SYNOPSIS

pathconv [**-f**] [**-v** *alias*]
pathconv [**-t**] [**-l**] [**-n***num*] [**-v** *string*]

DESCRIPTION

The **pathconv** function converts an alias to its pathname. By default, it takes the alias as a string from *stdin*.

-f If **-f** is specified, the full path will be returned (this is the default).

-t If **-t** is specified, **pathconv** will truncate a pathname specified in *string* in a format suitable for display as a frame title. This format is a shortened version of the full pathname, created by deleting components of the path from the middle of the string until it is under **DISPLAYW - 6** characters in length, and then inserting ellipses (**. . .**) between the remaining pieces. Ellipses are also used to show truncation at the ends of the strings if necessary, unless the **-l** option is given.

- **-l** If **-l** is specified, **<** and **>** will be used instead of ellipses (**...**) to indicate truncation at the ends of the string generated by the **-t** option. Truncation in the middle of the string is still indicated with ellipses. Using **-l** allows display of the longest possible string while still notifying users it has been truncated.

- **-n***num* If **-n** is specified, *num* is the maximum length of the string (in characters) generated by the **-t** option. The argument *num* can be any integer from 1 to 255.

-v *arg* If the **-v** option is used, then *alias* or *string* can be specified when **pathconv** is called. The argument *alias* must be an alias defined in the *alias_file* named when **fmli** was invoked. The argument *string* can only be used with the **-t** option and must be a pathname.

EXAMPLES

Here is a menu descriptor that uses **pathconv** to construct the menu title. It searches for **MYPATH** in the *alias_file* named when **fmli** was invoked:

```
menu=`pathconv -v MYPATH/ls`
    .
    .
    .
```

where there is a line in *alias_file* that defines **MYPATH**. For example, **MYPATH=$HOME/bin:/usr/bin**.

Here is a menu descriptor that takes *alias* from *stdin*.

```
menu=`echo MYPATH/ls | pathconv`
    .
    .
    .
```

SEE ALSO

`fmli`(1)

pchown (1M)

NAME

`pchown` – change owner of mail files

SYNOPSIS

posixchown –m *username*

posixchown –m *:dirname*

posixchown –s *username*

posixchown –T

posixchown –S [*dirname*]

posixchown –a *alias.t*

DESCRIPTION

/usr/lib/mail/surrcmd/pchown changes the owner and group of files associated with the mail sytem. It is only used by the mail program on systems in which the **chown**(2) system call is restricted to privileged programs.

The –m option is used to either change the ownership and group of a user's file to the given user and group **mail**, or, if the name starts with a colon, the given directory name to user **root** and group **mail**.

The –s option is used to change the ownership and group of a user's temporary file under **/var/mail/:saved** to the given user and group **mail**.

The –T option changes the ownership and group of **/etc/mail/Tmailsurr** to user **bin** and group **mail**.

The –S option is used to change **/var/spool/smtpq** or **/var/spool/smtpq/***dirname* to user **smtp** and group **mail**.

The –a option is used to change **/etc/mail/***alias.t* to user **bin** and group **mail**.

This program is intended to be used from within the **mail** command.

SEE ALSO

mail(1), **chown**(2).

NAME

`pciconsvr.ip` – manages the connection between the personal computer and the host

SYNOPSIS

`/usr/pci/bin/pciconsvr` [`-DFILNnTx`]

DESCRIPTION

The **pciconsvr** daemon has two jobs: to broadcast the message "pciconsvr *hostname* here" every 30 seconds and to manage the connection between the personal computer and the host. The broadcast messages are used by the **pcimapsvr** daemon to keep the list of available hosts up to date.

The host connection process includes several subordinate tasks. The connection management process begins when the **pciconsvr** daemon receives a connection request. from LOGIN. It assigns a port number for use in subsequent communication with the personal computer and spawns a new process, **/usr/pci/bin/pcidossvr.ip**.

All of the options below can be set on the command line:

-D Specifies the debug level for the **pciconsvr.ip** daemon. 0 means no debugging and –Dffff means full debugging.

-F Specifies a feature file. This file contains the feature information used by the **pciconsvr**.

-I Is used to specify the interface list. The interface list consists of a local address, a broadcast address, and a subnet mask.

The syntax is:

```
local,broadcast,subnet;local,broadcast,subnet; ...
```

This is generated by **loadpci**. Each address is specified in the INTERNET standard format of A.B.C.D. All components are numeric. The exact format depends on the **inet_addr()** library function.

-L Specifies the debug level for **pcidossvr.ip**.

-N Specifies the network device name.

-n Specifies the network descriptor to use. This is an open file descriptor that is passed from **loadpci**.

-T Specifies the "pciconsvr here" retransmission time.

-x Tells **pciconsvr.ip** not to disconnect **pcidossvr.ip** when they time out.

pcidebug (1M)

NAME

pcidebug – controls log output of the executing DOS server

SYNOPSIS

/usr/pci/bin/pcidebug *pid* [[*op*] *channels*] [child] [on] [off] [close]

DESCRIPTION

The **pcidebug** command controls log output of the executing DOS server (**pcidossvr**) and monitors the bidirectional communication between the personal computer and the host components of PC-Interface. It is also a mechanism for tracing the operations of the host component in response to personal computer requests.

There are 32 debugging output channels that can be controlled independently from the command line when **pcidebug** is invoked. Each channel controls the output of specific information about the process being logged. If a channel is activated, **pcidebug** outputs the data associated with that channel. If a channel is not activated, **pcidebug** does not output the data associated with that channel.

pcidebug generates formatted debug output for all activated channels and sends it to the host log file **/usr/spool/pcilog/dossvr**.*pid*, where *pid* is the process number of the executing server. Output is generated only if at least one channel is enabled. The debug channels that monitor a running server can be changed while the server is running by invoking **pcidebug** with the desired set of channels activated.

The fields in the invocation are:

op One of the following four symbols indicating the operation to be done on the channels listed in the *channels* field:

- = Enable these channels.
- + Add these channels to the enabled set.
- – Remove these channels from the enabled set.
- ~ Toggle the state of these channels.

channels A comma-separated list of integers between 1 and 32 representing up to 32 channels. 1 refers to the least significant bit of the **dbgEnable** bit mask and 32 refers to the most significant bit.

The keyword arguments are:

CHILD Manipulate the channels for the child processes, that is, for **pcidossvrs** that are started from the **pciconsvr**.

ON Turn all channels on. If this argument is given, a list of *channels* is redundant.

OFF Turn all channels off. If this argument is given, a list of *channels* is redundant.

CLOSE Tell the server to close its log file. This argument allows space used by the log file to be freed without killing the server. CLOSE is typically invoked together with the OFF argument to turn off all channels and close the log file at the same time.

NAME

pcidossvr – maintains an exclusive dialog with the bridge driver (BRIDGE.DRV) on the personal computer

SYNOPSIS

`/usr/pci/bin/pcidossvr` [`-D`]

DESCRIPTION

The **pcidossvr** program (either **/usr/pci/bin/pcidossvr.ip** or **/usr/pci/pcidossvr.232**) maintains an exclusive dialog with BRIDGE.DRV on a personal computer.

pcidossvr on the remote host translates the user's standard DOS system calls into appropriate UNIX operating system calls, executes them on behalf of the user, translates the results back into standard DOS, and returns the results to the user via BRIDGE.DRV. The extension (**.ip** or **.232**) identifies whether the connection is over a LAN or RS-232.

The options can be entered from the command line. The **-D** option specifies the debug level of **pcidossvr.ip**. Other options may be generated by **pciconsvr.ip**.

pcimapsvr (1M)

NAME

pcimapsvr.ip – listens for broadcasts from the connection server daemons.

SYNOPSIS

/usr/pci/bin/pcimapsvr [**-DINnS**]

DESCRIPTION

The **pcimapsvr.ip** daemon listens for broadcast requests for site tables and for broadcasts from connection-server daemons (**pciconsvr.ip**) announcing their presence.

The following options can be entered at the command line:

-D Debug level of the **pcimapsvr.ip**.

-I Interface list, which consists of a local address, a broadcast address, and a subnet mask. The syntax is:

```
local,broadcast,subnet;local,broadcast,subnet; ...
```

This is generated by **loadpci**. Each address is specified in the Internet standard format of A.B.C.D. All components are numeric. The exact format depends on the **inet_addr()** library function.

-N Network device name.

-n Network descriptor. This is an open file descriptor that is passed from **loadpci**.

-S Use subnet masks when determining which servers to return to the personal computer.

NAME

`pciprint` – sample print program

SYNOPSIS

`/usr/pci/bin/pciprint`

DESCRIPTION

The **`pciprint`** shell script is used as the default print program for print jobs sent from the personal computer.

pcistart (1M)

NAME

pcistart – starts the PC-Interface daemons on the host.

SYNOPSIS

/usr/pci/bin/pcistart [debug]

DESCRIPTION

A **pcistart** script is run when the system begins multi-user mode. This sets environment parameters that affect all processes spawned by **pciconsvr**. Some of the items set are: UMASK, TIME ZONE, default UNIX printer program, and the maximum file size that can be translated between the host and personal computer.

The default print program is defined in **pcistart**. The default settings must be appropriate for your system. You may want to change the default system printer to suit the needs of your community.

Changing the default system printer involves editing the **pcistart** file and then stopping and restarting PC-Interface to make the change effective. Be sure to warn PC-Interface users before you run **pcistop** and **pcistart**. Editing **pcistart** is described in Chapter 4.

The script **/usr/pci/bin/pcistart** sets the **umask** when PC-Interface is initialized. This **umask** is inherited by the connection server (**/usr/pci/bin/pciconsvr.ip**) and applies to all PC-Interface LAN file service users. Refer to Chapter 4 for further information.

The option **debug** creates log files in **/usr/spool/pcilog**. The three files are **mapsvr_log**, **consvr_log**, and **loadpci_log**. These log files contain traces of bidirectional packet information from the personal computer and the server. The **debug** option should only be used with the assistance of your vendor's technical support personnel.

NAME

pcistop – terminates PC-Interface execution on the host.

SYNOPSIS

/usr/pci/bin/pcistop

DESCRIPTION

pcistop kills **pciconsvr.ip** and **pcimapsvr.ip** deamons and echoes that it has done so. It does not stop RS-232 processes.

All **pcidossvr.ip** processes are also killed.

NAME

pcnfsd – NFS daemon for PC–NFS user authentication and remote printing

SYNOPSIS

/usr/lib/nfs/pcnfsd

DESCRIPTION

pcnfsd starts the daemon that handles PC–NFS user authentication and remote printing from DOS client machines.

This command has no options.

The pcnfsd daemon is automatically invoked in run level 3.

Only a privileged user can execute this command.

REFERENCES

nfsping(1M)

See the documentation that comes with your PC–NFS software.

NAME

pdiadd – add new disk, tape, or SCSI devices to the UNIX System kernel

SYNOPSIS

/etc/scsi/pdiadd [**-d** *dma_channel*] [**-v** *vector*] [**-i** *i/o_address*] [**-m** *memory_address*] [**-R** *ROOT*] *device*

DESCRIPTION

This script, **pdiadd**, adds support for a new disk, tape, or SCSI device to the UNIX system kernel by modifying the current system configuration in **/etc/conf**. After you run this command, you need to reboot the machine. A kernel reconfiguration will take place during this reboot. Note that **pdiadd** does not use the shell variable **ROOT** from the user environment as its starting path. You may specify a value for **ROOT** by using the **-R** option. The **-R** option should not be used except for the special case of kernel development in a non-root source tree.

Please note that if all you are trying to do is add a new mass-storage device to an existing, working disk controller or SCSI host bus adapter already installed in your UNIX System, you do not need to use this command. Simply shutdown your system, power it off, install the new mass-storage device and turn your system back on. Any reconfiguration that must take place to support your device will be automatic.

If the device you are adding is a disk device, you also need to use the **diskadd**(1M) utility to setup your new disk device and create filesystems on it. Do not attempt to run **diskadd** until after you have shutdown and restarted your UNIX System.

If the device you are about to install is or requires a new controller, you must be able to determine some of the basic characteristics of your new controller. If you do not understand the terms DMA channel, interrupt vector, and memory address, please read the documentation that came with your new device carefully. This should provide you with enough data to successfully install your new device in the UNIX System.

Options

pdiadd takes the following options:

-d *dma_channel*
: Use this value instead of the default DMA channel specified in the **disk.cfg** file for the device you want to add. *dma_channel* should be an integer in the range 0 to 7 on ISA-bus machines. The value 0 here implies that the device does not use a DMA channel. This option is unnecessary on Micro-Channel Architecture® machines.

-v *vector*
: Use this value instead of the default interrupt vector specified in the **disk.cfg** file for the device you want to add. *vector* should be an integer in the range 0 to 15. The value 0 here implies that the device does not use an interrupt vector.

-i *i/o_address*
: Use this value instead of the default starting I/O address specified in the **disk.cfg** file for the device you want to add. *i/o_address* should be a 3-digit hexadecimal number on AT-bus machines, or a 3- or 4-digit hexadecimal number on Micro-Channel Architecture® machines.

-m *memory_address*
Use this value instead of the default starting memory address specified in the **disk.cfg** file for the device you want to add. *memory_address* should be a 5-digit hexadecimal number on ISA-bus machines and Micro-Channel Architecture® machines. The value **0** here implies that the device does not use a region of memory.

device This required argument specifies the new controller you want to add. For a list of the devices supported by your release of the UNIX System, simply execute **pdiadd** without any arguments and a list will be displayed.

Return Values

Because **pdiadd** calls other system commands to perform system reconfiguration, it reports all errors encountered by those commands, then cleans up intermediate files created in the process. In general, an exit value greater than **0** indicates an error was encountered by **pdiadd**. An exit value of **0** indicates success.

NOTES

pdiadd is an administrative command and must be run in single user mode. See **init**(1M) for information on switching the machine to single user mode.

Any configuration changes made with **pdiadd** will not be reflected in the output of **pdiconfig**(1M) until the current UNIX System kernel is rebuilt and the system is rebooted. The UNIX System kernel will be rebuilt automatically for you when you use the shutdown command to reboot your system.

Because **pdiadd** does not support the large I/O addresses required by EISA-bus controllers, you should install the controller manually. The manual installation procedure can be found in the UNIX System administration documentation.

REFERENCES

disk.cfg(4), **diskadd**(1M), **idbuild**(1M), **idcheck**(1M), **pdirm**(1M)

NAME

pdiconfig – determine which PDI disk, tape, and SCSI controllers are present

SYNOPSIS

/etc/scsi/pdiconfig [**-R** *ROOT*] [*filename*]

DESCRIPTION

pdiconfig queries the Portable Device Interface (PDI) subsystem to determine which disk, tape, and SCSI controllers are present. **pdiconfig** reads the Equipped Device Table (EDT) built by the PDI drivers to determine which disk, tape, and SCSI controllers are present. This information is output in a format suitable for piping directly to **diskcfg**.

Options

pdiconfig accepts the following options:

-R *ROOT*
: Uses this value instead of **/** for the root of a kernel source tree.

filename
: Directs output to *filename* instead of to standard output.

Output

The output includes all of the information needed by **diskcfg** to reconfigure the System files so that a kernel can be built containing only those drivers needed for devices actually present on the system.

The format of the output for **pdiconfig** is:

```
driver name
long driver name
driver type
configure flag
unit number
dma channel 1
dma channel 2
ipl level
interrupt vector
interrupt sharing flag
starting I/O address
ending I/O address
starting memory address
ending memory address
```

Each field has a value present and is tab separated. If an error occurs while trying to retrieve the EDT or configuration information, or if no devices are found in the EDT, **pdiconfig** will terminate with a non-zero return value.

Note that **pdiconfig** does not use the shell variable *ROOT* from the user's environment as its starting path. You can specify a value for *ROOT* by using the **-R** option. The **-R** option should not be used except for the special case of kernel development in a non-root source tree.

Return Values

pdiconfig exits with a return code of zero on success and non-zero on failure.

NOTES

pdiconfig is an administrative command and must be run in single user mode. See **init**(1M) for information on switching the machine to single user mode.

Any loadable target drivers, such as **st01**(7), **sc01**(7), or **sw01**(7), that deal with PDI devices, must be demand loaded before executing **pdiconfig**. See **modadmin**(1M) for information on loading loadable drivers.

REFERENCES

disk.cfg(4), **diskcfg**(1M), **init**(1M), **pdiadd**(1M), **pdirm**(1M)

NAME

pdimkdev – generate device nodes for the Portable Device Interface (PDI) subsystem

SYNOPSIS

/etc/scsi/pdimkdev [**-fis**] [**-d***filename*]

DESCRIPTION

pdimkdev reads the Equipped Device Table (EDT) built by the PDI drivers and makes any device nodes needed for access to the disk, tape, and SCSI controllers that are present on the system. Since the device nodes that are created for each device are unique to that device type, template files are used to specify the device naming conventions. The location of the template files is specified in a target controller index file, which may be supplied as a command line argument. By default, any time a new device is detected, a message is printed on standard output describing the device.

pdimkdev keeps a record of the EDT from invocation to invocation in **/etc/scsi/pdi_edt**. If the EDT obtained by **pdimkdev** during execution is identical to the one in **/etc/scsi/pdi_edt**, no action is taken and **pdimkdev** exits. If the EDT has changed since the last invocation, **pdimkdev** checks every node for every device in the EDT and creates any missing nodes.

Options

pdimkdev takes the following options:

-f Forces **pdimkdev** to run at a time other than from **init**(1M). **pdimkdev** is designed to be run from **init**; to force its execution at any other time, you must use the **-f** option.

-i Forces **pdimkdev** to ignore the existing record of this machine's configuration in **/etc/scsi/pdi_edt** and update all PDI device nodes, as if a new device had been added to the system.

-s Suppress the standard output message from **pdimkdev** indicating that new device nodes were just created for a device.

-d *filename*
Use *filename* instead of **/etc/scsi/tc.index** to determine which template file to use for each device.

Return Values

pdimkdev exits with a return code of zero when it detects new devices on the system. If there are no new devices since the last time **pdimkdev** was executed, it exits with a positive return code. If an error is detected, it exits with a negative return code.

Files

/etc/scsi/mkdev.d/*,
/etc/scsi/pdi_edt,
/etc/scsi/tc.index

NOTES

pdimkdev is an administrative command and must be run in single user mode. See **init**(1M) for information on switching the machine to single user mode.

Any loadable target drivers, such as **st01**(7), **sc01**(7), or **sw01**(7), that deal with PDI devices, must be demand loaded before executing **pdimkdev**. See **modadmin**(1M) for information on loading loadable drivers.

REFERENCES

init(1M) **modadmin**(1M) **pdimkdtab**(1M)

NAME

pdimkdtab – update the device table entries for the Portable Device Interface (PDI) subsystem

SYNOPSIS

/etc/scsi/pdimkdtab [**-fi**] [**-d** *filename*]

DESCRIPTION

pdimkdtab reads the Equipped Device Table (EDT) built by the PDI drivers and updates the device table entries in **/etc/device.tab** for any disk, tape, and SCSI controllers that are present on the system. Since the device table entries that are created for each device are unique to that device type, template files are used to specify the device table entries. The location of the template files is specified in a target controller index file, which may be supplied as a command line argument.

pdimkdtab keeps a record of the EDT from invocation to invocation in **/etc/scsi/pdi_edt**. If the EDT obtained by **pdimkdtab** during execution is identical to the one in **/etc/scsi/pdi_edt**, no action is taken and **pdimkdtab** exits. If the EDT has changed since the last invocation of either **pdimkdev** or **pdimkdtab**, **pdimkdtab** updates the device table entries for every device in the EDT.

Options

pdimkdtab takes the following options:

-i Forces **pdimkdtab to run at a time other than from init(1M). pdimkdtab is designed to be run from init; to force its execution at any other time, you must use the -f option.**

-i Forces **pdimkdtab** to ignore the existing record of this machine's configuration in **/etc/scsi/pdi_edt** and update **/etc/device.tab**, as if a new device had been added to the system.

-d *filename*
Use *filename* instead of **/etc/scsi/tc.index** to determine which template file to use for each device.

Return Values

pdimkdtab exits with a return code of zero when it detects new devices on the system. If there are no new devices since the last time either **pdimkdev** or **pdimkdtab** were executed, it exits with a positive return code. If an error is detected, it exits with a negative return code.

NOTICES

When **pdimkdtab** is run immediately after **pdimkdev**, it must be run with the **-i** option or no updates will take place, because the EDT in **/etc/scsi/pdi_edt** will be the one created by **pdimkdev** and will be up to date.

pdimkdtab is an administrative command and must be run in single user mode. See **init**(1M) for information on switching the machine to single user mode.

Any loadable target drivers, such as **st01**(7), **sc01**(7), or **sw01**(7), which deal with PDI devices, must be demand loaded before executing **pdimkdtab**. See **modadmin**(1M) for information on loading loadable drivers.

Files

/etc/device.tab
/etc/scsi/mkdev.d/*
/etc/scsi/pdi_edt
/etc/scsi/tc.index

REFERENCES

init(1M), modadmin(1M), pdimkdev(1M)

NAME

pdirm – remove existing disk, tape, or SCSI devices from the UNIX System kernel

SYNOPSIS

/etc/scsi/pdirm [**-d** *dma_channel*] [**-v** *vector*] [**-i** *i/o_address*] [**-m** *memory_address*] [**-R** *ROOT*] *device*

DESCRIPTION

This script, **pdirm**, removes support for a existing disk, tape, or SCSI device from the UNIX System kernel by modifying the current system configuration in **/etc/conf**. Once you run command, you need to reboot the machine. A kernel reconfiguration will take place during this reboot. Note that **pdirm** does not use the shell variable **ROOT** from the user environment as its starting path. You may specify a value for the **ROOT** variable using the **-R** option. The **-R** option should not be used except for the special case of kernel development in a non-root source tree.

Please note that if all you are trying to do is remove an existing mass-storage device from an existing, working disk controller or SCSI host bus adapter already installed in your UNIX System, you do not need to use this command. Simply shutdown your system, power it off, remove the mass-storage device and turn your system back on. Any reconfiguration that must take place to support your device will be automatic.

If the device you are removing is a disk device, make sure that none of the critical parts of the UNIX System reside on it. This will only be true if you specified that the device be used during the initial installation of the UNIX System on your machine.

If the device you are about to remove is not an existing mass-storage device on a disk controller or SCSI host bus adapter, you must be able to determine the name used by the UNIX System to represent your controller or storage device before you can remove it. For a list of the devices supported by your release of the UNIX System, simply execute **pdirm** without any arguments and a list will be displayed.

Options

pdirm takes the following options:

-d *dma_channel*
: Use this value instead of the default DMA channel specified in the **disk.cfg** file for the device you want to remove to uniquely identify the device. *dma_channel* should be an integer in the range `0` to `7` on AT-bus machines. The value `0` here implies that the device does not use a DMA channel. This option is unnecessary on Micro-Channel Architecture® machines.

-v *vector*
: Use this value instead of the default interrupt vector specified in the **disk.cfg** file for the device you want to remove to uniquely identify the device. *vector* should be an integer in the range `0` to `15`. The value `0` here implies that the device does not use an interrupt vector.

-i *i/o_address*
: Use this value instead of the default starting I/O address specified in the **disk.cfg** file for the device you want to remove to uniquely identify the device. *i/o_address* should be a 3-digit hexadecimal number on ISA-bus

machines, or a 3- or 4-digit hexadecimal number on Micro-Channel Architecture® machines.

-m *memory_address*
Use this value instead of the default starting memory address specified in the **disk.cfg** file for the device you want to remove to uniquely identify the device. *memory_address* should be a 5-digit hexadecimal number. number on ISA-bus machines and Micro-Channel Architecture® machines. The value **0** here implies that the device does not use a region of memory.

device This required argument specifies the new controller you want to add. For a list of the devices supported by your release of the UNIX System, simply execute **pdirm** without any arguments and a list will be displayed. If there is more than one instance of this device installed on your system, you may need to more explicitly identify the correct device using one or more of the command line options above. However, this should be unnecessary in most cases.

Return Values

Because **pdirm** calls other system commands to perform the system reconfiguration, it reports all errors encountered by those commands, then cleans up intermediate files created in the process. In general, an exit value greater than **0** indicates an error was encountered by **pdirm**. An exit value of **0** indicates success.

NOTES

pdirm is an administrative command and must be run in single user mode. See **init**(1M) for information on switching the machine to single user mode.

Any configuration changes made with **pdirm** will not be reflected in the output of **pdiconfig**(1M) until the current UNIX System kernel is rebuilt and the system is rebooted. The UNIX System kernel will be rebuilt automatically for you when you use the shutdown command to reboot your system.

REFERENCES

disk.cfg(4), **diskadd**(1M), **idbuild**(1M), **idcheck**(1M), **pdiadd**(1M)

NAME

pfb2pfa – convert PostScript Type 1 outline fonts from binary to ASCII

SYNOPSIS

pfb2pfa < *pfb-file* > *pfa-file*

DESCRIPTION

The **pfb2pfa** utility converts Type 1 outline fonts from their binary form to their ASCII form. The binary form is usually the form in which they appear on retail DOS diskettes; the ASCII form is the form in which they are stored on the system for use with XWIN and **lp**. Both forms are encrypted.

The utility takes no options and reads and writes only standard input and output.

USAGE

Examples

```
pfb2pfa  <  HOBO.PFB  > HOBO.PFA
```

Installing Type 1 Fonts Using the UNIX Desktop

The Font Setup application of the UNIX Desktop allows most Type 1 fonts packaged for the retail DOS Windows® market to be installed using a graphical user interface, via the Install selection of the Actions menu button. This installation mechanism works for Type 1 fonts:

- whose filenames have a suffix of **.PFB**, and
- whose files are in the topmost directory of the diskette or in a subdirectory named **PSFONTS**

If a font has an associated AFM (Adobe Font Metrics) file, the Font Setup installation process also copies it to the system (Type 1 fonts are installed in the directory **/usr/X/lib/fonts/type1** and AFM files are installed in the **afm** subdirectory there).

Installing Type 1 Fonts Using UNIX Utilities

If you have a Type 1 fonts diskette in DOS format that cannot be installed using the graphical interface (it would give you a message like "Diskette does not contain Type 1 fonts in a recognizable format"), the fonts can still be installed using a sequence of UNIX utilities. Use the following steps:

1. Open a terminal window ("xterm") from the Applications folder.
2. Ensure that the diskette can be read using the DOS diskette utilities. Use the **dosdir** command:
   ```
   dosdir a:  # use b: for second diskette drive
   ```
   If this displays a list of filenames in the format of a DOS **dir** command, then the diskette is a DOS diskette.
3. If any of the files shown in the output of the **dosdir** command are directories (marked **<DIR>** in the output), then you need to repeat the **dosdir** command with the directory name as part of the argument. For example:
   ```
   dosdir a:/FONTS
   ```

If at least one of the files shown from either of these **dosdir** commands has a file name suffix of **.PFB** or **.PFA**, then proceed; otherwise; the diskette has no usable Type 1 fonts.

4. **su - root**
5. **cd /usr/X/lib/fonts/type1**
6. For each **.PFB** file on the diskette, do the following sequence:
   doscp a:*filename***.PFB .** or **doscp a:/FONTS/***filename***.PFB**
   pfb2pfa < *filename***.PFB >** *filename***.pfa**
   rm *filename***.PFB**

   If there are **.PFA** files on the diskette, those can be copied as well; just skip the use of the **pfb2pfa** command to convert the file (it is already in ASCII form) and the **rm** command.
7. For each **.AFM** file on the diskette:
   doscp a:*filename***.AFM afm**

This puts the font metric files in the appropriate directory.

8. **LD_LIBRARY_PATH=/usr/X/lib mkfontscale && mkfontdir**
9. **xset fp rehash**
10. Use **exit** to return to your non-**root** login.

Steps 8 and 9, which update the list of fonts available to the X server, can also be accomplished using the Integrity Check selection on the Actions menu button of the Font Setup client; this method causes the **DERIVED_INSTANCE_PS** environment variable to be used for the **mkfontscale** utility (it is set from the value in the configuration file **/usr/X/defaults/Xwinfont**) [see **mkfontscale**(1)].

SEE ALSO

desktop(1), **download**(1), **mkfontdir**(1), **mkfontscale**(1)

NOTES

Portions of this page are derived from material which is copyright © 1987-1991 by Adobe Systems Incorporated.

NAME

pfmt – display error message in standard format

SYNOPSIS

pfmt [-l *label*] [-s *severity*] [-g *catalog*:*msgid*] *format* [*args*]

DESCRIPTION

pfmt uses *format* for **printf** style formatting of *args*. **pfmt** encapsulates the output in the standard error message format and displays it on **stderr**.

The following options are available.

-l *label* Specify the label string to be displayed with the message (for example, **"UX:cat"**). *label* is a character string no more than 25 characters in length; it will be automatically suffixed with a colon (**:**). When unspecified, no label is displayed as part of the message.

-s *severity* Specify the severity string to be displayed with the message. Acceptable strings include the standard severities in either their print string (that is, **HALT**, **ERROR**, **INFO**, **WARNING**, and **"TO FIX"**) or keyword (that is, **halt**, **error**, **info**, **warn**, and **action**) forms, or any other user-defined string. A user-defined string will be assigned the integer severity value of 5. The severity will be suffixed with a colon (**:**). The **ERROR** severity will be used if no severity is specified.

-g *catalog*:*msgid*

Specify that a localized version of *format* should be retrieved from a locale-specific message database. *catalog* indicates the message database that contains the localized version of the *format* string. *catalog* must be limited to 14 characters. These characters must be selected from a set of all characters values, excluding **\0** (**NULL**) or the characters **/** (slash) and **:** (colon).

msgid is a positive number that indicates the index of the string into the message database.

If *catalog* does not exist in the current locale (identified by the **LC_MESSAGES** or **LANG** environment variables), or if *msgid* is out of bounds, **pfmt** will attempt to retrieve the message from the C locale. If this second retrieval fails, **pfmt** uses the *format* string as passed on the command line.

pfmt will output **Message not found!!\n** as the *format* string if *msgid* is not a valid number.

Standard Error Message Format

pfmt displays error messages in the following format:

label: *severity*: *text*

If no *label* was defined using the **-l** *label* option, the message is displayed in the format:

severity: *text*

If **pfmt** is called twice to display an error message and a helpful *action* or recovery message, the output can look like the following:

> *label*: *severity*: *text*
> *label*: **TO FIX:** *text*

EXAMPLE

Example 1:

```
pfmt -l UX:test -s error "Syntax error\n"
```

displays the message:

```
UX:test: ERROR: Syntax error
```

SEE ALSO

gettxt(1), **printf**(1), **pfmt**(3C), **environ**(5)

DIAGNOSTICS

Upon success, **pfmt** exits with code 0.

Upon failure, **pfmt** exits with the following codes:

1 write error

3 syntax error

NAME

pg – file perusal filter for CRTs

SYNOPSIS

pg [*–number*] [**-p** *string*] [**-cefnrs**] [*+linenumber*] [**+/***pattern***/**] [*file* . . .]

DESCRIPTION

The **pg** command is a filter that allows the examination of *files* one screenful at a time on a CRT. (If no *file* is specified or if it encounters the file name **-**, **pg** reads from standard input.) Each screenful is followed by a prompt. If the user types a carriage return, another page is displayed; other possibilities are listed below. **pg** processes supplementary code set characters in *files*, and recognizes supplementary code set characters in the *string* given to the **-p** option (see below) according to the locale specified in the **LC_CTYPE** environment variable [see **LANG** on **environ**(5)]. In regular expressions, pattern searches are performed on characters, not bytes, as described on **ed**(1).

This command is different from previous paginators in that it allows you to back up and review something that has already passed. The method for doing this is explained below.

To determine terminal attributes, **pg** scans the **terminfo**(4) data base for the terminal type specified by the environment variable **TERM**. If **TERM** is not defined, the terminal type **dumb** is assumed.

The command line options are:

–number
: An integer specifying the size (in lines) of the window that **pg** is to use instead of the default. (On a terminal containing 24 lines, the default window size is 23).

-c
: Home the cursor and clear the screen before displaying each page. This option is ignored if **clear_screen** is not defined for this terminal type in the **terminfo**(4) data base.

-e
: Causes **pg** not to pause at the end of each file.

-f
: Normally, **pg** splits lines longer than the screen width at characters, but some sequences of characters in the text being displayed (for example, escape sequences for underlining) generate undesirable results. The **-f** option inhibits **pg** from splitting lines.

-n
: Normally, commands must be terminated by a *newline* character. This option causes an automatic end of command as soon as a command letter is entered.

-p *string*
: Causes **pg** to use *string* as the prompt. If the prompt string contains a **%d**, the first occurrence of **%d**' in the prompt will be replaced by the current page number when the prompt is issued. The default prompt string is "**:**". *string* may contain supplementary code set characters.

-r Restricted mode. The shell escape is disallowed. **pg** will print an error message but does not exit.

-s Causes **pg** to print all messages and prompts in standout mode (usually inverse video).

+*linenumber*
Start up at *linenumber*.

+/*pattern*/
Start up at the first line containing the regular expression pattern.

The responses that may be typed when **pg** pauses can be divided into three categories: those causing further perusal, those that search, and those that modify the perusal environment.

Commands that cause further perusal normally take a preceding *address*, an optionally signed number indicating the point from which further text should be displayed. This *address* is interpreted in either pages or lines depending on the command. A signed *address* specifies a point relative to the current page or line, and an unsigned *address* specifies an address relative to the beginning of the file. Each command has a default address that is used if none is provided.

The perusal commands and their defaults are as follows:

(+1)<*newline*> or <*blank*>
This causes one page to be displayed. The address is specified in pages.

(+1) **l** With a relative address this causes **pg** to simulate scrolling the screen, forward or backward, the number of lines specified. With an absolute address this command prints a screenful beginning at the specified line.

(+1) **d** or **^D**
Simulates scrolling half a screen forward or backward.

*i***f** Skip *i* screens of text.

*i***z** Same as *newline* except that *i*, if present, becomes the new default number of lines per screenful.

The following perusal commands take no *address*.

. or **^L**
Typing a single period causes the current page of text to be redisplayed.

$ Displays the last windowful in the file. Use with caution when the input is a pipe.

The following commands are available for searching for text patterns in the text. The regular expressions described in **ed**(1) are available. They must always be terminated by a *newline*, even if the *–n* option is specified.

i/*pattern*/
Search forward for the *i*th (default *i*=1) occurrence of *pattern*. Searching begins immediately after the current page and continues to the end of the current file, without wrap-around.

i^*pattern*^
i?*pattern*?

Search backwards for the *i*th (default *i*=1) occurrence of *pattern*. Searching begins immediately before the current page and continues to the beginning of the current file, without wrap-around. The ^ notation is useful for Adds 100 terminals which will not properly handle the ?.

After searching, **pg** will normally display the line found at the top of the screen. This can be modified by appending **m** or **b** to the search command to leave the line found in the middle or at the bottom of the window from now on. The suffix **t** can be used to restore the original situation.

The user of **pg** can modify the environment of perusal with the following commands:

*i***n** Begin perusing the *i*th next file in the command line. The *i* is an unsigned number, default value is 1.

*i***p** Begin perusing the *i*th previous file in the command line. *i* is an unsigned number, default is 1.

*i***w** Display another window of text. If *i* is present, set the window size to *i*.

s *filename*

Save the input in the named file. Only the current file being perused is saved. The white space between the **s** and *filename* is optional. This command must always be terminated by a *newline*, even if the *–n* option is specified.

h Help by displaying an abbreviated summary of available commands.

q or **Q** Quit **pg**.

!*command*

Command is passed to the shell, whose name is taken from the **SHELL** environment variable. If this is not available, the default shell is used. This command must always be terminated by a *newline*, even if the *–n* option is specified.

At any time when output is being sent to the terminal, the user can press the quit key (normally CTRL-\) or the interrupt (break) key. This causes **pg** to stop sending output, and display the prompt. The user may then enter one of the above commands in the normal manner. Unfortunately, some output is lost when this is done, because any characters waiting in the terminal's output queue are flushed when the quit signal occurs.

If the standard output is not a terminal, then **pg** acts just like **cat**(1), except that a header is printed before each file (if there is more than one).

EXAMPLE

The following command line uses **pg** to read the system news:

```
news | pg -p "(Page %d):"
```

FILES

/usr/share/lib/terminfo/?/*
terminal information database

/tmp/pg*
temporary file when input is from a pipe

/usr/lib/locale/*locale*/LC_MESSAGES/uxcore.abi
language-specific message file [See **LANG** on **environ** (5).]

SEE ALSO

ed(1), **grep**(1), **more**(1), **terminfo**(4)

NOTES

While waiting for terminal input, **pg** responds to BREAK, DEL, and CTRL-\ by terminating execution. Between prompts, however, these signals interrupt **pg**'s current task and place the user in prompt mode. These should be used with caution when input is being read from a pipe, since an interrupt is likely to terminate the other commands in the pipeline.

The terminal /, ^, or ? may be omitted from the searching commands.

If terminal tabs are not set every eight positions, undesirable results may occur.

When using **pg** as a filter with another command that changes the terminal I/O options, terminal settings may not be restored correctly.

NAME

ping – send ICMP **ECHO_REQUEST** packets to network hosts

SYNOPSIS

/usr/sbin/ping *host* [*timeout*]

/usr/sbin/ping -s [-drvRl] *host* [*data size*] [*npackets*]

DESCRIPTION

ping utilizes the ICMP protocol's **ECHO_REQUEST** datagram to elicit an ICMP **ECHO_RESPONSE** from the specified *host* or network gateway. If *host* responds, **ping** will print *host* **is alive** on the standard output and exit. Otherwise after *timeout* seconds, it will write **no answer from** *host*. The default value of *timeout* is 20 seconds.

When the **-s** flag is specified, **ping** sends one datagram per second, and prints one line of output for every **ECHO_RESPONSE** that it receives. No output is produced if there is no response. In this second form, **ping** computes round trip times and packet loss statistics; it displays a summary of this information upon termination or timeout. The default datagram packet size is 64 bytes, or you can specify a size with the *datasize* command-line argument. If an optional *npackets* is given, **ping** sends only that number of requests.

When using **ping** for fault isolation, first ping the local host to verify that the local network interface is running.

OPTIONS

-d Debug mode. Prints the *ping* statistics to "standard output" (**stdout**). The **-d** option can be used with *datasize* and/or *npackets*. If *npackets* is not specified, the command will execute indefinitely. Use the BREAK key to interrupt the continuous output.

-l Loose source route. Use this option in the IP header to send the packet to the given host and back again. Usually specified with the **-R** option. The **-l** option is only valid when the *host* is **localhost** or **`uname -n`**.

-r Bypass the normal routing tables and send directly to a host on an attached network. If the host is not on a directly-attached network, an error is returned. This option can be used to **ping** a local host through an interface that has been dropped by the router daemon [see **routed**(1M)].

-R Record route. Sets the IP record route option, which will store the route of the packet inside the IP header. The contents of the record route will only be printed if the **-v** option is given, and only be set on return packets if the target host preserves the record route option across echos, or the **-l** option is given.

-v Verbose output. List any ICMP packets, other than **ECHO_RESPONSE**, that are received.

SEE ALSO

icmp(7), **ifconfig**(1M), **netstat**(1M), **rpcinfo**(1M)

NAME

pkgadd – transfer software package or set to the system

SYNOPSIS

pkgadd [**-d** *device*] [**-r** *response*] [**-n**] [**-q**] [**-l**] [**-a** *admin*] [**-p**] [*pkginst1* [*pkginst2*[. . .]]]

pkgadd -s *spool* [**-d** *device*] [**-q**] [**-l**] [**-p**] [*pkginst1* [*pkginst2*[. . .]]]

DESCRIPTION

pkgadd transfers the contents of a software package or set from the distribution medium or directory to install it onto the system. A package is a collection of related files and executables that can be independently installed. A set is made up of a special-purpose package, referred to as a Set Installation Package (SIP), and a collection of one or more packages that are members of the set. The SIP controls the installation of the set.

Used without the **-d** option, **pkgadd** looks in the default spool directory for the package (**/var/spool/pkg**). Used with the **-s** option, it writes the package to a spool directory instead of installing it.

Error messages are always logged (see **-l**, below). In addition, when **pkgadd** terminates, it will send mail (by default, to **root**) with all the error messages and a summary of which packages installed completely, partially, or not at all.

-d *device* Installs or copies a package/set from *device*. *device* can be: (a) the full pathname to a directory, file, or named pipe (such as **/var/tmp**); (b) the device identifiers for tape or disk devices (such as **/dev/rmt/*** or **/dev/dsk/***) [see **intro**(7)]; or (c) a device alias (such as **diskette1**). The default device is the installation spool directory (**/var/spool/pkg**).

For device identifiers, the device specified (either by pathname or alias), must have an entry in the device table (**/etc/device.tab**). If no entry exists in the device table, **pkgadd** will abort.

A device alias is the unique name by which a device is known. (For example, the alias for a cartridge tape drive might be **ctape1**.) The name must be limited in length to 64 characters (**DDB_MAXALIAS**) and can contain only alphanumeric characters and/or any of the following special characters: underscore (_), dollar sign (**$**), hyphen (**-**), and period (**.**). No two devices in the database can share the same alias.

-r *response* Identifies a file or directory, *response*, which contains the answers to questions posed by a "request script" during a previous **pkgask** session conducted in interactive mode [see **pkgask**(1M)]. When *pkginst* is a package, *response* can be a full pathname or a directory; when *pkginst* is a SIP, *response* must be a directory. For a complete description of request scripts and response files, see your system administration or software packaging guides.

-n Installation occurs in non-interactive mode. The default mode is interactive.

-q Installation is performed in quiet mode. Only prompts requesting user input and error messages are displayed on the screen.

-l Error messages are not sent to the standard error output; they are only logged to **/var/sadm/install/logs/***pkginst***.log**.

-a *admin* Defines an installation administration file, *admin*, to be used in place of the default administration file to specify whether installation checks (such as the check on the amount of space, the system state, and so on) are done. [For a description of the format of an *admin* file, see **admin**(4).] The token **none** overrides the use of any *admin* file, and thus forces interaction with the user. Unless a full pathname is given, **pkgadd** looks in the **/var/sadm/install/admin** directory for the file. By default, the file **default** in that directory is used. **default** specifies that no checking will be done, except to see if there is enough room to install the package and if there are dependencies on other packages. The **-a** option cannot be used if *pkginst* is a SIP.

-p Do not give the initial prompt to the user to insert the distribution medium. All other prompts will continue normally.

pkginst A short string used to designate a package/set. It is composed of one or two parts: *pkg* (an abbreviation for the package/set name) or, if more than one instance of that package exists, *pkg* plus *inst* (an instance identifier). (The term "package instance" is used loosely: it refers to all instantiations of *pkginst*, even those that do not include instance identifiers.)

The package name abbreviation (*pkg*) is the mandatory part of *pkginst*. [See **pkginfo**(1), **pkginfo**(4).]

If *pkginst* is a SIP, the SIP controls installation of the set by using request scripts and preinstall scripts. The SIP request script, not the package installation tools, is responsible for prompting the user for responses and taking the appropriate actions. If the request script fails, only the SIP will be processed. For a complete description of request and preinstall scripts, see your system administration and/or software packaging guides.

The second part (*inst*), which is required only if you have more than one instance of the package in question, is a suffix that identifies the instance. This suffix is either a number (preceded by a period) or any short mnemonic string you choose. If you don't assign your own instance identifier when one is required, the system assigns a numeric one by default. For example, if you have three instances of the Advanced Commands package and you don't create your own mnemonic identifiers (such as **old** and **beta**), the system adds the suffixes **.2** and **.3** to the second and third packages, automatically.

To indicate all instances of a package, specify **'***pkginst***.*'**, enclosing the command line in single quotes, as shown, to prevent the shell from interpreting the * character. Use the token **all** to refer to all packages available on the source medium.

-s *spool* Reads the package into the directory *spool* instead of installing it.

NOTES

The **-r** option can be used to indicate a directory name as well as a filename. The directory can contain numerous *response* files, each sharing the name of the package with which it should be associated. This would be used, for example, when adding multiple interactive packages with one invocation of **pkgadd**. Each package that had a request script would need a *response* file. If you create response files with the same name as the package (for example, *package1* and *package2*) then, after the **-r** option, name the directory in which these files reside.

The **-n** option will cause the installation to halt if any interaction is needed to complete it.

When invoked with no *pkginst* specified on the command line, *pkgadd* only displays the names of sets if at least one SIP exists on the media. Because of this, you shouldn't include packages on the same media if some are members of sets and some are not. If you do, the packages which are not members of sets can be installed only if their *pkginst* names are provided on the command line.

The **pkgadd** command checks to see if any of the files in *pkginst* are already installed on the system and, if any are, saves this fact before continuing with installation. Later, **pkgadd** won't reinstall these files on the system. If one of the package's installation scripts removes such a file, the result will be that the file will no longer be on the system when package installation completes.

FILES

/etc/device.tab	device table
/var/sadm/install/admin/default	default package administration file
/var/sadm/install/logs/*pkginst***.log**	error message log
/var/spool/pkg	default spool directory

SEE ALSO

admin(4), **compver**(4), **copyright**(4), **depend**(4), **installf**(1M), **intro**(7), **pkgask**(1M), **pkgchk**(1M), **pkginfo**(1), **pkginfo**(4), **pkgmap**(4), **pkgparam**(1), **pkgrm**(1M), **putdev**(1M), **removef**(1M), **setinfo**(4), **space**(4)

NAME

pkgask – stores answers to a request script

SYNOPSIS

pkgask [**-d** *device*] **-r** *response* [*pkginst* [*pkginst* [. . .]]

DESCRIPTION

pkgask allows an administrator to store answers to an interactive package (one with a request script) or a set of packages. A set is made up of a special-purpose package, referred to as a Set Installation Package (SIP), and a collection of one or more packages that are members of the set. The SIP controls the installation of the set.

Invoking **pkgask** generates a *response* file that is then used as input at installation time. The use of this *response* file prevents any interaction from occurring during installation since the file already contains all of the information the package needs.

-d *device* Runs the request script for a package on *device*. *device* can be (a) the full pathname to a directory (such as **/var/tmp**), (b) the full pathname to a device (such as **/dev/rmt/*** or **/dev/dsk/***) [see **intro**(7)], or (c) a device alias. The default device is the installation spool directory (**/var/spool/pkg**).

An alias is the unique name by which a device is known. (For example, the alias for a cartridge tape drive might be **ctape1**.) The name must be limited in length to 64 characters (**DDB_MAXALIAS**) and may contain only alphanumeric characters and/or any of the following special characters: underscore (_), dollar sign (**$**), hyphen (-), and period (**.**). No two devices in the database may share the same alias.

-r *response* Identifies a file or directory, *response*, which should be created to contain the responses to interactions with the package's request script. The file, or directory of files, can later be used as input to the **pkgadd** command [see **pkgadd**(1M)]. When *pkginst* is a package, *response* can be a full pathname or a directory; when *pkginst* is a SIP, *response* must be a directory. For a complete description of request scripts and response files, see your system administration or software packaging guides.

pkginst A short string used to designate a package/set. It is composed of one or two parts: *pkg* (an abbreviation for the package/set name) or, if more than one instance of that package exists, *pkg* plus *inst* (an instance identifier). (The term "package instance" is used loosely: it refers to all instantiations of *pkginst*, even those that do not include instance identifiers.)

The package name abbreviation (*pkg*) is the mandatory part of *pkginst*. To create such an abbreviation, assign it with the **PKG** parameter. For example, to assign the abbreviation **cmds** to the Advanced Commands package, enter **PKG=cmds**.

If *pkginst* specifies a SIP, all request scripts for packages which are members of that set are run (if any) and the resulting response files are placed in the directory provided to the **-r** option.

The second part (*inst*), which is required only if you have more than one instance of the package in question, is a suffix that identifies the instance. This suffix is either a number (preceded by a period) or any short mnemonic string you choose. If you don't assign your own instance identifier when one is required, the system assigns a numeric one by default. For example, if you have three instances of the Advanced Commands package and you don't create your own mnemonic identifiers (such as **old** and **beta**), the system adds the suffixes **.2** and **.3** to the second and third packages, automatically.

To indicate all instances of a package, specify '*pkginst*.*', enclosing the command line in single quotes, as shown, to prevent the shell from interpreting the * character. Use the token **all** to refer to all packages available on the source medium.

NOTES

You can use the **-r** option to indicate a directory name as well as a filename. The directory name is used to create numerous *response* files, each sharing the name of the package with which it should be associated. This is useful, for example, when you add multiple interactive packages with one invocation of **pkgadd**. Each package needs a *response* file. To create multiple response files with the same name as the package instance, name the directory in which the files should be created and supply multiple instance names with the **pkgask** command. When installing the packages, you can identify this directory to the **pkgadd** command.

FILES

/var/spool/pkg	default spool directory

SEE ALSO

compver(4), **copyright**(4), **depend**(4), **installf**(1M), **intro**(7), **pkgadd**(1M), **pkgchk**(1M), **pkginfo**(1), **pkginfo**(4), **pkgmap**(4), **pkgmk**(1), **pkgparam**(1), **pkgproto**(1), **pkgtrans**(1), **pkgrm**(1M), **removef**(1M), **setinfo**(4), **space**(4)

NAME

pkgchk – check accuracy of installation

SYNOPSIS

pkgchk [**-l** | **-acfqv**] [**-nx**] [**-p** *path1*[**,** *path2* . . .] [**-i** *file*] [*pkginst* . . .]

pkgchk -d *device* [**-l** | **v**] [**-p** *path1*[**,** *path2* . . .] [**-i** *file*] [*pkginst* . . .]

pkgchk -m *pkgmap* [**-e** *envfile*] [**-l** | **-acfqv**] [**-nx**] [**-i** *file*] [**-p** *path1*[**,** *path2* . . .]]

DESCRIPTION

pkgchk checks the accuracy of installed files or, by use of the **-l** option, displays information about package files. The command checks the integrity of directory structures and the files. Discrepancies are reported on **stderr** along with a detailed explanation of the problem.

The first synopsis defined above is used to list or check the contents and/or attributes of objects that are currently installed on the system. Package names may be listed on the command line, or by default the entire contents of a machine will be checked.

The second synopsis is used to list or check the contents of a package which has been spooled on the specified device, but not installed. Note that attributes cannot be checked for spooled packages.

The third synopsis is used to list or check the contents and/or attributes of objects which are described in the indicated *pkgmap*.

The option definitions are:

-l Lists information on the selected files that make up a package. It is not compatible with the **a**, **c**, **f**, **g**, and **v** options.

-a Audits the file attributes only, does not check file contents. Default is to check both.

-c Audits the file contents only, does not check file attributes. Default is to check both.

-f Corrects file attributes if possible. If used with the **-x** option, it removes hidden files. When **pkgchk** is invoked with this option it creates directories, named pipes, links, and special devices if they do not already exist.

-q Quiet mode. Does not give messages about missing files.

-v Verbose mode. Files are listed as processed.

-n Does not check volatile files. This should be used for most post-installation checking.

-x Searches exclusive directories only, looking for files that exist that are not in the installation software database or the indicated *pkgmap* file. (An exclusive directory is a directory created by and for a package; it should contain only files delivered with a package. If any non-package files are found in an exclusive directory, **pkgchk** reports an error.) If **-x** is used with the **-f** option, hidden files are removed; no other checking is done.

-p Only checks the accuracy of the pathname or pathnames listed. *pathname* can be one or more pathnames separated by commas (or by white space, if the list is quoted).

-i Reads a list of pathnames from *file* and compares this list against the installation software database or the indicated *pkgmap* file. Pathnames that are not contained in *inputfile* are not checked.

-d Specifies the device on which a spooled package resides. *device* can be a directory pathname or the identifiers for a tape or other removable medium (for example, **/var/tmp** or **/dev/rmt/ctape1**).

-m Requests that the package be checked against the pkgmap file *pkgmap*.

-e Requests that the pkginfo file named as *envfile* be used to resolve parameters noted in the specified pkgmap file.

pkginst A short string used to designate a package. It is composed of one or two parts: *pkg* (an abbreviation for the package name) or, if more than one instance of that package exists, *pkg* plus *inst* (an instance identifier). (The term "package instance" is used loosely: it refers to all instantiations of *pkginst*, even those that do not include instance identifiers.)

The package name abbreviation (*pkg*) is the mandatory part of *pkginst*. [See **pkginfo**(1), **pkginfo**(4).]

The second part (*inst*), which is required only if you have more than one instance of the package in question, is a suffix that identifies the instance. This suffix is either a number (preceded by a period) or any short mnemonic string you choose. If you don't assign your own instance identifier when one is required, the system assigns a numeric one by default. For example, if you have three instances of the Advanced Commands package and you don't create your own mnemonic identifiers (such as **old** and **beta**), the system adds the suffixes **.2** and **.3** to the second and third packages, automatically.

To indicate all instances of a package, specify '*pkginst*.*', enclosing the command line in single quotes, as shown, to prevent the shell from interpreting the * character. Use the token **all** to refer to all packages available on the source medium.

NOTES

To remove hidden files only, use the **-f** and **-x** options together. To remove hidden files and check attributes and contents of files, use the **-f**, **-x**, **-c**, and **-a** options together.

SEE ALSO

compver(4), **copyright**(4), **depend**(4), **installf**(1M), **pkgadd**(1M), **pkgask**(1M), **pkginfo**(1), **pkginfo**(4), **pkgmap**(4), **pkgrm**(1M), **pkgtrans**(1), **space**(4)

NAME

pkginfo – display software package and/or set information

SYNOPSIS

pkginfo [**-q**] [**x** | **l**] [**-p** | **i**] [**-a** *arch*] [**-v** *version*]
[**-c** *category1*,[*category2*[, ...]]] [*pkginst*[,*pkginst*[, ...]]]

pkginfo [**-d** *device* [**-q**] [**x** | **l**] [**-a** *arch*] [**-v** *version*]
[**-c** *category1*,[*category2*[, ...]]] [*pkginst*[,*pkginst*[, ...]]]

DESCRIPTION

pkginfo displays information about software packages or sets that are installed on the system (as requested in the first synopsis) or that reside on a particular device or directory (as requested in the second synopsis). A package is a collection of related files and executables that can be independently installed. A set is made up of a special-purpose package, referred to as a Set Installation Package (SIP), and a collection of one or more packages that are members of the set. The SIP controls the installation of the set.

When run without options, **pkginfo** displays one line of information about every installed package (whether installed completely or partially) whose category is not the value "set." The information displayed includes the primary category, package instance, and name of the package. For UNIX software packages produced before UNIX System V Release 4, **pkginfo** displays only the package name and abbreviation. For XENIX software packages, **pkginfo** prints the heading "Custom Installed Packages," followed by a list of XENIX packages. The list identifies the package name and abbreviation, with the word **yes** in place of the package instance, to indicate that the package is installed.

The **-p** and **-i** options are meaningless if used in conjunction with the **-d** option. The **-p** and **-i** options are mutually exclusive. The **-x** and **-l** options are mutually exclusive.

The options for this command are:

-q Do not list any information. This option overrides the **-x, -l, -p, and -i options. (Can be invoked by a program to query whether or not a package has been installed.)**

-x Extract and display the following information about the specified package: abbreviation, name, and, if available, architecture and version.

-l Display a "long format" report (that is, one that includes all available information) about the specified package(s).

-p Display information only for partially installed packages.

-i Display information only for fully installed packages.

-a *arch* Specify the architecture of the package as *arch*.

-v *version* Specify the version of the package as *version*. All compatible versions can be requested by preceding the version name with a tilde (~). The list produced by **-v** will include pre-Release 4 and XENIX software packages (with which no version numbers are associated). Multiple white spaces are replaced with a single space during version comparison.

-c *category . . .*
Display information about packages that belong to category *category*. (Categories are defined in the category field of the **pkginfo** file; see **pkginfo**(4) for details.) More than one category may be specified (as long as they're separated by white space). A package is required to belong to only one category, even when multiple categories are specified. The package-to-category match is case-specific.

If the category specified is "set," **pkginfo** will display information about Set Installation Packages (SIPs).

pkginst A short string used to designate a package/set. It is composed of one or two parts: *pkg* (an abbreviation for the package/set name) or, if more than one instance of that package exists, *pkg* plus *inst* (an instance identifier). (The term "package instance" is used loosely: it refers to all instantiations of *pkginst*, even those that do not include instance identifiers.)

The package name abbreviation (*pkg*) is the mandatory part of *pkginst*. [See **pkginfo**(4).]

The second part (*inst*), which is required only if you have more than one instance of the package in question, is a suffix that identifies the instance. This suffix is either a number (preceded by a period) or any short mnemonic string you choose. If you don't assign your own instance identifier when one is required, the system assigns a numeric one by default. For example, if you have three instances of the Advanced Commands package and you don't create your own mnemonic identifiers (such as **old** and **beta**), the system adds the suffixes **.2** and **.3** to the second and third packages, automatically.

To indicate all instances of a package, specify **'***pkginst***.*'**, enclosing the command line in single quotes, as shown, to prevent the shell from interpreting the * character. Use the token **all** to refer to all packages available on the source medium.

If *pkginst* is a SIP, information about the packages with which the SIP is associated will be displayed.

-d *device* Display information from packages/sets that reside on *device*. *device* can be (a) the full pathname to a directory (such as **/var/tmp**), (b) the full pathname to a device (such as **/dev/rmt/*** or **/dev/dsk/***) [see **intro**(7)], or (c) a device alias. The default device is the installation spool directory (**/var/spool/pkg**).

An alias is the unique name by which a device is known. (For example, the alias for a cartridge tape drive might be **ctape1**.) The name must be limited in length to 64 characters (**DDB_MAXALIAS**) and may contain only alphanumeric characters and/or any of the following special characters: underscore (_), dollar sign (**$**), hyphen (-), and period (**.**). No two devices in the database may share the same alias.

NOTES

pkginfo cannot tell if a pre-UNIX System V Release 4 or XENIX software package is only partially installed. It is assumed that all pre-Release 4 and XENIX software packages are fully installed.

If **pkginfo** is invoked to obtain information on packages that are members of sets located on tape media, all options to **pkginfo** are allowed since the information on these packages is readily available on the tape. In the case of diskettes, if the SIP and each of its member packages are on separate disks, not all information on these packages is available. In this case, the **pkginfo** command will only display a short listing. For this reason, the **-a**, **-l** and **-v** options will not work for sets whose packages span over several diskettes.

FILES

/var/spool/pkg default spool directory

SEE ALSO

intro(7), **pkgadd**(1M), **pkgask**(1M), **pkgchk**(1M), **pkginfo**(4), **pkgrm**(1M), **pkgtrans**(1), **setinfo**(4)

pkgmk(1)

NAME

pkgmk – produce an installable package

SYNOPSIS

pkgmk [**-o**] [**-c**] [**-d** *device*] [**-r** *rootpath*] [**-b** *basedir*] [**-l** *limit*] [**-a** *arch*]
[**-v** *version*] [**-p** *pstamp*] [**-f** *prototype*] [*variable=value* . . .] [*pkginst*]

DESCRIPTION

pkgmk produces an installable package to be used as input to the **pkgadd** command. The package contents will be in directory structure format. A package is a collection of related files and executables that can be independently installed.

The command uses the package **prototype** file as input and creates a **pkgmap** file. The contents for each entry in the **prototype** file is copied to the appropriate output location. Information concerning the contents (checksum, file size, modification date) is computed and stored in the **pkgmap** file, along with attribute information specified in the **prototype** file.

-o Overwrites the same instance, package instance will be overwritten if it already exists.

-c Compresses non-information files.

-d *device* Creates the package on *device*. *device* can be a full pathname to a directory or the identifier for a removable block device (for example, **diskette1**). The default device is the installation spool directory.

-r *rootpath* Uses the indicated *rootpath* with the source pathname in the **prototype** file appended to locate objects on the source machine.

-b *basedir* Prepends the indicated *basedir* to locate relocatable objects on the source machine.

-l *limit* Specifies the maximum size in 512-byte blocks of the output device as *limit*. By default, if the output file is a directory or a mountable device, **pkgmk** will employ the **df** command to dynamically calculate the amount of available space on the output device. Useful in conjunction with **pkgtrans** to create package with datastream format.

-a *arch* Overrides the architecture information provided in the **pkginfo** file with *arch*.

-v *version* Overrides version information provided in the **pkginfo** file with *version*.

-p *pstamp* Overrides the production stamp definition in the **pkginfo** file with *pstamp*.

-f *prototype* Uses the file *prototype* as input to the command. The default name for this file is either **Prototype** or **prototype**.

variable=value Places the indicated variable in the packaging environment. [See **prototype**(4) for definitions of packaging variables.]

pkginst Specifies the package by its instance. **pkgmk** will automatically create a new instance if the version and/or architecture is different. A user should specify only a package abbreviation; a particular instance should not be specified unless the user is overwriting it.

NOTES

Entries in the **prototype** file that reference relative paths above the rootpath specification will not be compressed.

When the **-c** option is specified, any **!search** commands found in the **prototype**(4) file will not work. The **-c** option should not be used when the argument to the **-d** option is used to specify a removable block device.

SEE ALSO

pkginfo(4), **pkgparam**(1), **pkgproto**(1), **pkgtrans**(1), **setinfo**(4)

pkgparam(1)

NAME

pkgparam – displays package parameter values

SYNOPSIS

pkgparam [**-v**] [**-d** *device*] *pkginst* [*param*[. . .]]
pkgparam -d *device* [**-v**] [*param*[. . .]]
pkgparam -f *file* [**-v**] [*param*[. . .]]

DESCRIPTION

pkgparam displays the value associated with the parameter or parameters requested on the command line. The values are located in one of the following places: (a) in the **pkginfo** file for *pkginst*, (b) on the *device* named with the **-d** option, or (c) on the specific file named with the **-f** option. When a *device* is given, but a *pkginst* is not (as shown in the second synopsis), parameter information for all packages residing on *device* is shown.

One parameter value is shown per line. Only the value of a parameter is given unless the **-v** option is used. With this option, the output of the command is in this format:

parameter1='*value1*'
parameter2='*value2*'
parameter3='*value3*'

If no parameters are specified on the command line, values for all parameters associated with the package are shown.

Options and arguments for this command are:

-v Specifies verbose mode. Displays name of parameter and its value.

-d *device* Specifies the *device* on which a *pkginst* is stored. *device* can be (a) the full pathname to a directory (such as **/var/tmp**), (b) the full pathname to a device (such as **/dev/rmt/*** or **/dev/dsk/***) [see **intro**(7)], or (c) a device alias. The default device is the installation spool directory (**/var/spool/pkg**).

An alias is the unique name by which a device is known. (For example, the alias for a cartridge tape drive might be **ctape1**.) The name must be limited in length to 64 characters (**DDB_MAXALIAS**) and can contain only alphanumeric characters and/or any of the following special characters: underscore (_), dollar sign (**$**), hyphen (**-**), and period (**.**). No two devices in the database can share the same alias.

-f Requests that the command read *file* for parameter values.

pkginst Defines a specific package instance for which parameter values should be displayed. The format *pkginst*.* can be used to indicate all instances of a package. When using this format, enclose the command line in single quotes to prevent the shell from interpreting the * character.

param Defines a specific parameter whose value should be displayed.

EXIT CODES

If parameter information is not available for the indicated package, the command exits with a non-zero status.

NOTES

The `-f` synopsis allows you to specify the file from which parameter values should be extracted. This file should be in the same format as a **pkginfo** file. As an example, such a file might be created during package development and used while testing software during this stage.

FILES

/var/spool/pkg	default spool directory

SEE ALSO

intro(7), **pkginfo**(4), **pkgmk**(1), **pkgproto**(1), **pkgtrans**(1)

pkgproto (1)

NAME

pkgproto – generate a **prototype** file

SYNOPSIS

pkgproto [**-i**] [**-c** *class*] [*path1*[=*path2*] . . .]

DESCRIPTION

pkgproto scans the indicated paths and generates a **prototype** file that may be used as input to the **pkgmk** command.

- **-i** Ignores symbolic links and records the paths as **ftype=f** (a file) versus **ftype=s**(symbolic link)
- **-c** Maps the class of all paths to *class*.
- *path1* Path of directory where objects are located.
- *path2* Path that should be substituted on output for *path1*.

If no paths are specified on the command line, standard input is assumed to be a list of paths. If the path listed on the command line is a directory, the contents of the directory are searched. However, if input is read from **stdin**, a directory specified as a path will not be searched.

The **protoype** file attributes **mac**, **fixed**, and **inherited**, cannot be determined by **pkgproto**; to add these attributes to the **prototype** file, you must add them to the file manually. See **prototype**(4).

NOTES

By default, **pkgproto** creates symbolic link entries for any symbolic link encountered (**ftype=s**). When you use the **-i** option, **pkgproto** creates a file entry for symbolic links (**ftype=f**). The **prototype** file must be edited to assign file types such as **v** (volatile), **e** (editable), or **x** (exclusive directory). **pkgproto** detects linked files. If multiple files are linked together, the first path encountered is considered the source of the link.

EXAMPLE

The following two examples show uses of **pkgproto** and a partial listing of the output produced.

Example 1:

```
$ pkgproto /usr/bin=bin /usr/usr/bin=usrbin /etc=etc
f none bin/sed=/bin/sed 0775 bin bin
f none bin/sh=/bin/sh 0755 bin daemon
f none bin/sort=/bin/sort 0755 bin bin
f none usrbin/sdb=/usr/bin/sdb 0775 bin bin
f none usrbin/shl=/usr/bin/shl 4755 bin bin
d none etc/master.d 0755 root daemon
f none etc/master.d/kernel=/etc/master.d/kernel 0644 root daemon
f none etc/rc=/etc/rc 0744 root daemon
```

Example 2:

```
$ find / -type d -print | pkgproto
d none / 755 root root
d none /usr/bin 755 bin bin
d none /usr 755 root root
d none /usr/bin 775 bin bin
d none /etc 755 root root
d none /tmp 777 root root
```

SEE ALSO

pkginfo(4), pkgmk(1), pkgparam(1), pkgtrans(1)

NAME

pkgrm – removes a package or set from the system

SYNOPSIS

pkgrm [**-n**] [**-a** *admin*] [*pkginst1* [*pkginst2*[. . .]]]

pkgrm -s *spool* [*pkginst*]

DESCRIPTION

pkgrm will remove a previously installed or partially installed package/set from the system. A package is a collection of related files and executables that can be independently installed. A set is made up of a special-purpose package, referred to as a Set Installation Package (SIP), and a collection of one or more packages that are members of the set.

A check is made to determine if any other packages depend on the one being removed. The action taken if a dependency exists is defined in the *admin* file (see the **-a** option, below).

The default state for the command is interactive mode, meaning that prompt messages are given during processing to allow the administrator to confirm the actions being taken. Non-interactive mode can be requested with the **-n** option.

The **-s** option can be used to specify the directory from which spooled packages should be removed.

The options and arguments for this command are:

-n Non-interactive mode. If there is a need for interaction, the command will exit. Use of this option requires that at least one package instance be named upon invocation of the command.

-a *admin* Defines an installation administration file, *admin*, to be used in place of the default administration file. [For a description of the format of an *admin* file, see **admin**(4).] The token **none** overrides the use of any *admin* file, and thus forces interaction with the user. Unless a full pathname is given, **pkgrm** looks in the **/var/sadm/install/admin** directory for the file. By default, the file **default** in that directory is used.

-s *spool* Removes the specified package(s) from the directory *spool*.

pkginst A short string used to designate a package/set. It is composed of one or two parts: *pkg* (an abbreviation for the package/set name) or, if more than one instance of that package exists, *pkg* plus *inst* (an instance identifier). (The term "package instance" is used loosely: it refers to all instantiations of *pkginst*, even those that do not include instance identifiers.)

The package name abbreviation (*pkg*) is the mandatory part of *pkginst*. [See **pkginfo**(1), **pkginfo**(4).]

If *pkginst* specifies a SIP, all installed packages which are members of the set, and the SIP itself, are removed in reverse dependency order.

The second part (*inst*), which is required only if you have more than one instance of the package in question, is a suffix that identifies the instance. This suffix is either a number (preceded by a period) or any short mnemonic string you choose. If you don't assign your own instance identifier when one is required, the system assigns a numeric one by default. For example, if you have three instances of the Advanced Commands package and you don't create your own mnemonic identifiers (such as **old** and **beta**), the system adds the suffixes **.2** and **.3** to the second and third packages, automatically.

To indicate all instances of a package, specify **'***pkginst***.*'**, enclosing the command line in single quotes, as shown, to prevent the shell from interpreting the * character. Use the token **all** to refer to all packages available on the source medium.

SEE ALSO

admin(4), **compver**(4), **copyright**(4), **depend**(4), **installf**(1M), **pkgadd**(1M), **pkgask**(1M), **pkgchk**(1M), **pkginfo**(1), **pkginfo**(4), **pkgmap**(4), **pkgmk**(1), **pkgparam**(1), **pkgproto**(1), **pkgtrans**(1), **removef**(1M), **setinfo**(4), **space**(4)

NAME

pkgtrans – translate package format

SYNOPSIS

pkgtrans [**-ions**] [-z blocksize] *device1 device2* [*pkginst1* [*pkginst2* [. . .]]]

DESCRIPTION

pkgtrans translates an installable package from one format to another. It translates:

a file system format to a datastream

a datastream to a file system format

a file system format to another file system format

For removable filesystem media, **pkgtrans** will optionally allow the user to format and place a filesystem on the media, and write a label on the media before transferring the package to the media.

The options and arguments for this command are:

-i	Copies the **pkginfo** and **pkgmap** files. If the package's category is defined as **set**, for Set Installation Packages (SIPs) [see **setinfo**(4)], then that package's **setinfo** file is also copied.
-o	Overwrites the same instance on the destination device, package instance will be overwritten if it already exists.
-n	Creates a new instance if any instance of this package already exists.
-s	Indicates that the package should be written to *device2* as a datastream rather than as a file system. The default behavior is to write to *device2* in the file system format.
-z blocksize	Indicates the blocksize to be used when transferring to cartridge tape. Packages that have been written to tape using the **-z** option and a value not equal to 512 are always read using a blocksize of 32768. Thus, the **-z** option is not applicable when reading from cartridge tape.
device1	Indicates the source device. The package or packages on this device will be translated and placed on *device2*.
device2	Indicates the destination device. Translated packages will be placed on this device.
pkginst	Specifies which package instance or instances on *device1* should be translated. The token **all** may be used to indicate all packages. *pkginst*.* can be used to indicate all instances of a package. If no packages are defined, a prompt shows all packages on the device and asks which to translate. If a set is being transferred to datastream format, the *pkginst* arguments should begin with the SIP and be followed by the packages listed in the SIP's **setinfo** file, in the order in which they appear in that file.

NOTES

Device specifications can be either the special node name (**/dev/diskette**) or the device alias (**diskette1**). The device **spool** indicates the default spool directory. Source and destination devices may not be the same.

By default, **pkgtrans** will not transfer any instance of a package if any instance of that package already exists on the destination device. Use of the **-n** option will create a new instance if an instance of this package already exists. Use of the **-o** option will overwrite the same instance if it already exists. Neither of these options are useful if the destination device is a datastream, since the entire datastream is overwritten anyway.

pkgtrans will optionally create packages on either **ufs** or **s5** file systems, with **ufs** being the default.

pkgtrans depends on the integrity of the **/etc/device.tab** file to determine whether a device can support a datastream and/or file system formats. Problems in transferring a device in a particular format could mean corruption of **/etc/device.tab**.

EXAMPLE

The following example translates all packages located on the floppy drive **/dev/diskette** and places the translations on **/tmp**.

```
pkgtrans /diskette1 /tmp all
```

The next example translates packages **pkg1** and **pkg2** located on **/tmp** and places their translations (that is, a datastream) on the **9track1** output device.

```
pkgtrans /tmp 9track1 pkg1 pkg2
```

The next example translates **pkg1** and **pkg2** on **tmp** and places them on the diskette in a datastream format.

```
pkgtrans -s /tmp /diskette1 pkg1 pkg2
```

FILES

/etc/device.tab

SEE ALSO

installf(1M), **pkgadd**(1M), **pkgask**(1M), **pkginfo**(1), **pkginfo**(4), **pkgmk**(1), **pkgparam**(1), **pkgproto**(1), **pkgrm**(1M), **removef**(1M)

NAME

plot, **aedplot**, **atoplot**, **bgplot**, **crtplot**, **dumbplot**, **gigiplot**, **hpplot**, **implot**, **plottoa**, **t300**, **t300s**, **t4013**, **t450**, **tek** – (BSD) graphics filters for various plotters

SYNOPSIS

/usr/ucb/plot [**-T***terminal*]

DESCRIPTION

plot reads plotting instructions [see **plot**(1)] from the standard input and produces plotting instructions suitable for a particular *terminal* on the standard output.

If no *terminal* is specified, the environment variable **TERM** is used. The default *terminal* is **tek**.

ENVIRONMENT

Except for **ver**, the following terminal-types can be used with **lpr -g** (see **lpr**) to produce plotted output:

2648 | **2648a** | **h8** | **hp2648** | **hp2648a**
: Hewlett Packard® 2648 graphics terminal.

300
: DASI 300 or GSI terminal (Diablo® mechanism).

300s | **300S**
: DASI 300s terminal (Diablo mechanism).

450
: DASI Hyterm 450 terminal (Diablo mechanism).

4013
: Tektronix® 4013 storage scope.

4014 | **tek**
: Tektronix 4014 and 4015 storage scope with Enhanced Graphics Module. (Use 4013 for Tektronix 4014 or 4015 without the Enhanced Graphics Module).

aed
: AED 512 color graphics terminal.

bgplot | **bitgraph**
: BBN bitgraph graphics terminal.

crt
: Any crt terminal capable of running **vi**(1).

dumb | **un** | **unknown**
: Dumb terminals without cursor addressing or line printers.

gigi | **vt125**
: DEC® vt125 terminal.

h7 | **hp7** | **hp7221**
: Hewlett Packard 7221 graphics terminal.

implot
: Imagen plotter.

var
: Benson Varian printer-plotter

ver
: Versatec® D1200A printer-plotter. The output is scan-converted and suitable input to **lpr -v**.

FILES

/usr/ucb/aedplot
/usr/ucb/atoplot
/usr/ucb/bgplot
/usr/ucb/crtplot
/usr/ucb/dumbplot
/usr/ucb/gigiplot
/usr/ucb/hpplot
/usr/ucb/implot
/usr/ucb/plot
/usr/ucb/plottoa
/usr/ucb/t300
/usr/ucb/t300s
/usr/ucb/t4013
/usr/ucb/t450
/usr/ucb/tek
/usr/ucb/vplot
/var/ucb/vplot*nnnnnn*

SEE ALSO

lpr(1), vi(1)

pmadm (1M)

NAME

pmadm – port monitor administration

SYNOPSIS

pmadm -a [-p *pmtag* | -t *type*] -s *svctag* [-i id] -m "*pmspecific*" -v *version* [-f xu] [-S "*scheme*"] [-y "*comment*"] [-z *script*]

pmadm -r -p *pmtag* -s *svctag*

pmadm -e -p *pmtag* -s *svctag*

pmadm -d -p *pmtag* -s *svctag*

pmadm -l [-p *pmtag* | -t *type*] [-s *svctag*]

pmadm -L [-p *pmtag* | -t *type*] [-s *svctag*]

pmadm -g -p *pmtag* -s *svctag* [-z *script*]

pmadm -g -s *svctag* -t *type* -z *script*

pmadm -c -S "*scheme*" [-i *id*] -p *pmtag* -s *svctag*

pmadm -c -i *id* [-S "*scheme*"] -p *pmtag* -s *svctag*

DESCRIPTION

pmadm is the administrative command for the lower level of the Service Access Facility hierarchy, that is, for service administration. A port may have only one service associated with it although the same service may be available through more than one port. In order to uniquely identify an instance of a service the **pmadm** command must identify both the port monitor or port monitors through which the service is available (-p or -t) and the service (-s). See the option descriptions below.

pmadm performs the following functions:

- add or remove a service
- enable or disable a service
- add or delete authentication scheme and user ID information
- install or replace a per-service configuration script
- print requested service information

Any user on the system may invoke **pmadm** to request service status (-l or -L) or to print per-service configuration scripts (-g without the -z option).

The options have the following meanings:

-a Add a service. **pmadm** adds an entry for the new service to the port monitor's administrative file. Because of the complexity of the options and arguments that follow the -a option, it may be convenient to use a command script or the menu system to add services. If you use the menu system, enter **sysadm ports**, then choose the **port_services** option.

-c Used with -i or -S to change the authentication scheme or user ID associated with the named service. To identify the service, both -p and -s options are required. -c may be used with either -i or -S separately or it may be used with both options. See -i and -S.

-d Disable a service. Add **x** to the flag field in the entry for service *svctag* in the port monitor's administrative file. See the **-f** option, below, for a description of the flags available.

-e Enable a service. Remove **x** from the flag field in the entry for service *svctag* in the port monitor administrative file. See the **-f** option, below, for a description of the flags available.

-f xu Used with the **-a** option. The **-f** option specifies one or both of the two flags listed below. The flags are then included in the flag field of the port monitor administrative file entry for the new service. If the **-f** option is not included, no flags are set and the default conditions prevail. By default, a new service is enabled and no **utmp** entry is created for it. A **-f** option without a following argument is illegal.

- **x** Disable the service *svctag* available through port monitor *pmtag*. When **x** is present in the flag field, the service is no started until explicitly enabled.
- **u** Create a **utmp** entry for service *svctag* available through port monitor *pmtag*.

-g Used with the options described below, the **-g** option prints, installs, or replaces a per-service configuration script.

-g -p *pmtag* **-s** *svctag*
Prints the per-service configuration script for service *svctag* available through port monitor *pmtag*.

-g -p pmtag **-s** *svctag* **-z** *script*
Installs the per-service configuration script contained in the file *script* as the per-service configuration script for service *svctag* available through port monitor *pmtag*.

-g -s *svctag* **-t** *type* **-z** *script*
Installs the file *script* as the per-service configuration script for service *svctag* available through any port monitor of type *type*.

Other combinations of options with **-g** are invalid.

-i *id* Used with **-a** or **-c**. *id* is the identity that is to be assigned to service *svctag* when it is started. *id* must be an entry in **/etc/passwd**.

The **-i** argument is optional when a service is being added (that is, with the **-a** option). If the **-i** option is omitted, the port monitor determines the user ID from information supplied by the authentication scheme. If the **-i** option is omitted and no authentication scheme is specified, an error is returned when the service is executed. When the user ID is specified using **-i** and an authentication scheme is also specified, the port monitor performs the authentication using the scheme-supplied identity. The identity specified by the **-i** option takes precedence when the service is invoked.

Used with the **-c** option, the argument to **-i** replaces the user ID in the port monitor-generic field of the port monitor administrative file entry for the named service. If *id* is not the **NULL** string, **pmadm** ensures that it is a valid user ID on the machine. Changing a user ID to the **NULL** string (**" "**) removes the ID from the port monitor administrative file entry for the service.

`-l` The `-l` option requests service information. Used by itself and with the options described below it provides a filter for extracting information in several different groupings.

`-l` By itself, the `-l` option lists all services on the system.

`-l -p` *pmtag* Lists all services available through port monitor *pmtag*.

`-l -s` *svctag* Lists all services with tag *svctag*.

`-l -p` *pmtag* `-s` *svctag*
Lists service *svctag* available through the port monitor *pmtab*.

`-l -t` *type* Lists all services available through port monitors of type *type*.

`-l -t` *type* `-s` *svctag*
Lists all services with tag *svctag* available through a port monitor of type *type*.

Other combinations of options with `-l` are invalid.

`-L` The `-L` option is identical to the `-l` option except that output is printed in a condensed format and without column headers.

`-m` "*pmspecific*"
pmspecific is a port monitor-specific command. Every port monitor running under the Service Access Facility must have such a command to supply information for the port monitor-specific field of the port monitor administrative file entry for the service. The command and its options are enclosed in back quotes (`). See **ttyadm**(1M), the port monitor-specific command for **ttymon**, and **nlsadmin**(1M), the port monitor-specific command for **listen**.

`-p` *pmtag*
Specifies the tag associated with the port monitor through which a service (specified as `-s` *svctag*) is available.

`-r` Remove a service. When **pmadm** removes a service, the entry for the service is removed from the port monitor's administrative file.

`-s` *svctag*
Specifies the service tag associated with a given service. The service tag is assigned by the system administrator and is part of the entry for the service in the port monitor's administrative file.

`-S` "*scheme*"
Used with `-a` or `-c`. The `-S` option specifies the authentication scheme to be associated with *svctag*. *scheme* may be a simple authentication scheme name or the full pathname of the authentication scheme and can have arguments associated with it.

Used with **-c**, **-S** replaces the authentication scheme name and arguments in the *scheme* field of the port monitor's administrative file with the new scheme name (and arguments, if any).

Changing an authentication scheme name to the **NULL** string removes the scheme from the port monitor administrative file entry for the service.

-t *type* Used with the **-a**, or **-l**, or **-g** option. **-t** specifies the port monitor type.

-v *version*

Specifies the version number of the port monitor administrative file. The version number may be given as

```
-v `pmspec -V`
```

where *pmspec* is the administrative command for port monitor *pmtag*. This command is **ttyadm** for **ttymon** and **nlsadmin** for **listen**. The version stamp of the port monitor is known by the command and is returned when *pmspec* is invoked with a **-V** option.

-y "*comment*"

Associate *comment* with the service entry in the port monitor administrative file.

-z *script*

Used with the **-g** option to specify the name of the file that contains the per-service configuration script. The **-z** option overwrites the existing script. It is suggested that you do the following three steps when you modify/replace a configuration script. First a copy of the existing script should be made (**-g** alone). Then the copy should be edited. Finally, the copy is put in place over the existing script (**-g** with **-z**).

OUTPUT

If successful, **pmadm** will exit with a status of **0**. If it fails for any reason, it will exit with a nonzero status.

Options that request information write the requested information to the standard output. A request for information using the **-l** option prints column headers and aligns the information under the appropriate headings. In this format, a missing field is indicated by a hyphen. A request for information in the condensed format using the **-L** option prints the information in colon-separated fields; missing fields are indicated by two successive colons. **#** is the comment character.

If the *id* argument is specified and the user ID given is not the **NULL** string and is not a valid user ID on the machine, **pmadm** will fail and will print the following error message:

```
invalid user identity
```

EXAMPLES

Add a service to a port monitor with tag **pmtag**. Give the service the tag **svctag**. Port monitor-specific information is generated by **specpm**. The service defined by **svctag** will be invoked with identity **root**.

```
pmadm -a -p pmtag -s svctag -i root -m `specpm -a arg1 -b arg2` \
   -v `specpm -V`
```

Add the same service to the same port monitor, but instead of specifying the user ID **root**, specify an authentication scheme (**-S scheme**), which will determine the user ID.

```
pmadm -a -p pmtag -s svctag -S scheme -m `specpm -a arg1 \
      -b arg2` -v `specpm -V`
```

Add a service with service tag **svctag**, identity **guest**, and port monitor-specific information generated by **specpm** to all port monitors of type **type**:

```
pmadm -a -s svctag -t type -i guest -m `specpm -a arg1 -b arg2` \
      -v `specpm -V`
```

Remove the service **svctag** from port monitor **pmtag**:

```
pmadm -r -p pmtag -s svctag
```

Enable the service **svctag** available through port monitor **pmtag**:

```
pmadm -e -p pmtag -s svctag
```

Disable the service **svctag** available through port monitor **pmtag**:

```
pmadm -d -p pmtag -s svctag
```

List status information for all services:

```
pmadm -l
```

List status information for all services available through the port monitor with tag **ports**:

```
pmadm -l -p ports
```

List the same information in condensed format:

```
pmadm -L -p ports
```

List status information for all services available through port monitors of type **listen**:

```
pmadm -l -t listen
```

Print the per-service configuration script associated with the service **svctag** available through port monitor **pmtag**:

```
pmadm -g -p pmtag -s svctag
```

Associate authentication scheme **scheme** with the service **svctag** on port monitor **pmtag**. The service runs with user ID **id**:

```
pmadm -c -S "scheme" -i id -p pmtag -s svctag
```

Remove the authentication scheme from the **svctag** service on port monitor **pmtag**:

```
pmadm -c -S "" -p pmtag -s svctag
```

A network service tag is unique for a given port monitor. If the administrator of a server machine wants to offer a network service with more than one authentication scheme, a unique service tag is required for each service/authentication scheme combination. Similarly, if the administrator wants to change the authentication scheme for a service, allowing a period of time when both old and new authentication schemes are available, then two unique service tags are required.

FILES

/etc/saf/*pmtag***/_config**
/etc/saf/*pmtag***/***svctag*
/var/saf/*pmtag***/***

SEE ALSO

doconfig(3N), **sac**(1M), **sacadm**(1M)

postdaisy (1)

NAME

postdaisy – PostScript translator for Diablo 630 files

SYNOPSIS

/usr/lib/lp/postscript/postdaisy [*options*] [*files*]

DESCRIPTION

The **postdaisy** filter translates Diablo 630 daisy-wheel *files* into PostScript and writes the results on the standard output. If no *files* are specified, or if – is one of the input *files*, the standard input is read. The following *options* are understood:

-c *num* Print *num* copies of each page. By default only one copy is printed.

-f *name* Print *files* using font *name*. Any PostScript font can be used, although the best results will be obtained only with constant-width fonts. The default font is Courier.

-h *num* Set the initial horizontal motion index to *num*. Determines the character advance and the default point size, unless the **-s** option is used. The default is 12.

-m *num* Magnify each logical page by the factor *num*. Pages are scaled uniformly about the origin, which is located near the upper left corner of each page. The default magnification is 1.0.

-n *num* Print *num* logical pages on each piece of paper, where *num* can be any positive integer. By default, *num* is set to 1.

-o *list* Print pages whose numbers are given in the comma-separated *list*. The list contains single numbers *N* and ranges *N1* – *N2*. A missing *N1* means the lowest numbered page, a missing *N2* means the highest.

-p *mode* Print *files* in either portrait or landscape *mode*. Only the first character of *mode* is significant. The default *mode* is portrait.

-r *num* Selects carriage return and line feed behavior. If *num* is 1, a line feed generates a carriage return. If *num* is 2, a carriage return generates a line feed. Setting *num* to 3 enables both modes.

-s *num* Use point size *num* instead of the default value set by the initial horizontal motion index.

-v *num* Set the initial vertical motion index to *num*. The default is 8.

-x *num* Translate the origin *num* inches along the positive x axis. The default coordinate system has the origin fixed near the upper left corner of the page, with positive x to the right and positive y down the page. Positive *num* moves everything right. The default offset is 0.25 inches.

-y *num* Translate the origin *num* inches along the positive y axis. Positive *num* moves text up the page. The default offset is –0.25 inches.

DIAGNOSTICS

An exit status of 0 is returned if *files* were successfully processed.

FILES

`/usr/lib/lp/postscript/postdaisy.ps`
`/usr/lib/lp/postscript/forms.ps`
`/usr/lib/lp/postscript/ps.requests`

SEE ALSO

`download`(1), `dpost`(1), `postdmd`(1), `postio`(1), `postmd`(1), `postprint`(1), `postreverse`(1), `posttek`(1)

postdmd (1)

NAME

postdmd – PostScript translator for DMD bitmap files

SYNOPSIS

/usr/lib/lp/postscript/postdmd [*options*] [*files*]

DESCRIPTION

postdmd translates DMD bitmap *files*, as produced by *dmdps*, or *files* written in the Ninth Edition **bitfile** format into PostScript and writes the results on the standard output. If no *files* are specified, or if – is one of the input *files*, the standard input is read. The following *options* are understood:

-b *num* Pack the bitmap in the output file using *num* byte patterns. A value of 0 turns off all packing of the output file. By default, *num* is 6.

-c *num* Print *num* copies of each page. By default only one copy is printed.

-f Flip the sense of the bits in *files* before printing the bitmaps.

-m *num* Magnify each logical page by the factor *num*. Pages are scaled uniformly about the origin, which by default is located at the center of each page. The default magnification is 1.0.

-n *num* Print *num* logical pages on each piece of paper, where *num* can be any positive integer. By default *num* is set to 1.

-o *list* Print pages whose numbers are given in the comma-separated *list*. The list contains single numbers *N* and ranges *N1* – *N2*. A missing *N1* means the lowest numbered page, a missing *N2* means the highest.

-p *mode* Print *files* in either portrait or landscape *mode*. Only the first character of *mode* is significant. The default *mode* is portrait.

-x *num* Translate the origin *num* inches along the positive x axis. The default coordinate system has the origin fixed at the center of the page, with positive x to the right and positive y up the page. Positive *num* moves everything right. The default offset is 0 inches.

-y *num* Translate the origin *num* inches along the positive y axis. Positive *num* moves everything up the page. The default offset is 0.

Only one bitmap is printed on each logical page, and each of the input *files* must contain complete descriptions of at least one bitmap. Decreasing the pattern size using the **-b** option may help throughput on printers with fast processors (such as PS-810s), while increasing the pattern size will often be the right move on older models (such as PS-800s).

DIAGNOSTICS

An exit status of 0 is returned if *files* were successfully processed.

FILES

/usr/lib/lp/postscript/postdmd.ps
/usr/lib/lp/postscript/forms.ps
/usr/lib/lp/postscript/ps.requests

SEE ALSO

download(1), **dpost**(1), **postdaisy**(1), **postio**(1), **postmd**(1), **postprint**(1), **postreverse**(1), **posttek**(1)

postio(1)

NAME

postio – serial interface for PostScript printers

SYNOPSIS

postio -l *line* [*options*] [*files*]

DESCRIPTION

postio sends *files* to the PostScript printer attached to *line*. If no *files* are specified the standard input is sent. The first group of *options* should be sufficient for most applications:

-b *speed* — Transmit data over *line* at baud rate *speed*. Recognized baud rates are 1200, 2400, 4800, 9600, and 19200. The default *speed* is 9600 baud.

-l *line* — Connect to the printer attached to *line*. In most cases there is no default and **postio** must be able to read and write *line*. If the *line* doesn't begin with a / it may be treated as a Datakit destination.

-q — Prevents status queries while *files* are being sent to the printer. When status queries are disabled a dummy message is appended to the log file before each block is transmitted.

-B *num* — Set the internal buffer size for reading and writing *files* to *num* bytes. By default *num* is 2048 bytes.

-D — Enable debug mode. Guarantees that everything read on *line* will be added to the log file (standard error by default).

-L *file* — Data received on *line* gets put in *file*. The default log *file* is standard error. Printer or status messages that don't show a change in state are not normally written to *file* but can be forced out using the **-D** option.

-P *string* — Send *string* to the printer before any of the input files. The default *string* is simple PostScript code that disables timeouts.

-R *num* — Run *postio* as a single process if *num* is 1 or as separate read and write processes if *num* is 2. By default **postio** runs as a single process.

The next two *options* are provided for users who expect to run **postio** on their own. Neither is suitable for use in spooler interface programs:

-i — Run the program in interactive mode. Any *files* are sent first and followed by the standard input. Forces separate read and write processes and overrides many other options. To exit interactive mode use your interrupt or quit character. To get a friendly interactive connection with the printer type **executive** on a line by itself.

-t — Data received on *line* and not recognized as printer or status information is written to the standard output. Forces separate read and write processes. Convenient if you have a PostScript program that will be returning useful data to the host.

The last option is not generally recommended and should only be used if all else fails to provide a reliable connection:

-S Slow the transmission of data to the printer. Severely limits throughput, runs as a single process, disables the **-q** option, limits the internal buffer size to 1024 bytes, can use an excessive amount of CPU time, and does nothing in interactive mode.

The best performance will usually be obtained by using a large internal buffer (the **-B** option) and by running the program as separate read and write processes (the **-R 2** option). Inability to fork the additional process causes **postio** to continue as a single read/write process. When one process is used, only data sent to the printer is flow controlled.

The *options* are not all mutually exclusive. The **-i** option always wins, selecting its own settings for whatever is needed to run interactive mode, independent of anything else found on the command line. Interactive mode runs as separate read and write processes and few of the other *options* accomplish anything in the presence of the **-i** option. The **-t** option needs a reliable two way connection to the printer and therefore tries to force separate read and write processes. The **-S** option relies on the status query mechanism, so **-q** is disabled and the program runs as a single process.

In most cases **postio** starts by making a connection to *line* and then attempts to force the printer into the IDLE state by sending an appropriate sequence of **^T** (status query), **^C** (interrupt), and **^D** (end of job) characters. When the printer goes IDLE, *files* are transmitted along with an occasional **^T** (unless the **-q** option was used). After all the *files* are sent the program waits until it's reasonably sure the job is complete. Printer generated error messages received at any time except while establishing the initial connection (or when running interactive mode) cause **postio** to exit with a non-zero status. In addition to being added to the log file, printer error messages are also echoed to standard error.

EXAMPLES

Run as a single process at 9600 baud and send *file1* and *file2* to the printer attached to **/dev/tty01**:

postio -l /dev/tty01 *file1 file2*

Same as above except two processes are used, the internal buffer is set to 4096 bytes, and data returned by the printer gets put in file *log*:

postio -R2 -B4096 -l/dev/tty01 -L*log file1 file2*

Establish an interactive connection with the printer at Datakit destination *my/printer*:

postio -i -l *my/printer*

Send file program to the printer connected to **/dev/tty22**, recover any data in file results, and put log messages in file *log*:

postio -t -l /dev/tty22 -L *log program* >*results*

NOTES

The input *files* are handled as a single PostScript job. Sending several different jobs, each with their own internal end of job mark (`^D`) is not guaranteed to work properly. **postio** may quit before all the jobs have completed and could be restarted before the last one finishes.

All the capabilities described above may not be available on every machine or even across the different versions of the UNIX system that are currently supported by the program. For example, the code needed to connect to a Datakit destination may work only on System V and may require that the DKHOST software package be available at compile time.

There may be no default *line*, so using the **-l** option is strongly recommended. If omitted, **postio** may attempt to connect to the printer using the standard output. If Datakit is involved, the **-b** option may be ineffective and attempts by **postio** to impose flow control over data in both directions may not work. The **-q** option can help if the printer is connected to RADIAN. The **-S** option is not generally recommended and should be used only if all other attempts to establish a reliable connection fail.

DIAGNOSTICS

An exit status of 0 is returned if the files ran successfully. System errors (such as an inability to open the line) set the low order bit in the exit status, while PostScript errors set bit 1. An exit status of 2 usually means the printer detected a PostScript error in the input *files*.

SEE ALSO

download(1), **dpost**(1), **postdaisy**(1), **postdmd**(1), **postmd**(1), **postprint**(1), **postreverse**(1), **posttek**(1)

NAME

postmd – matrix display program for PostScript printers

SYNOPSIS

/usr/lib/lp/postscript/postmd [*options*] [*files*]

DESCRIPTION

The **postmd** filter reads a series of floating point numbers from *files*, translates them into a PostScript gray scale image, and writes the results on the standard output. In a typical application the numbers might be the elements of a large matrix, written in row major order, while the printed image could help locate patterns in the matrix. If no *files* are specified, or if – is one of the input *files*, the standard input is read. The following *options* are understood:

-b *num* Pack the bitmap in the output file using *num* byte patterns. A value of 0 turns off all packing of the output file. By default, *num* is 6.

-c *num* Print *num* copies of each page. By default, only one copy is printed.

-d *dimen* Sets the default matrix dimensions for all input *files* to *dimen*. The *dimen* string can be given as rows or rows**x**columns. If *columns* is omitted it will be set to rows. By default, **postmd** assumes each matrix is square and sets the number of rows and columns to the square root of the number of elements in each input file.

-g *list* *List* is a comma or space separated string of integers, each lying between 0 and 255 inclusive, that assigns PostScript gray scales to the regions of the real line selected by the **-i** option. 255 corresponds to white, and 0, to black. The **postmd** filter assigns a default gray scale that omits white (that is, 255) and gets darker as the regions move from left to right along the real line.

-i *list* *List* is a comma, space or slash(/) separated string of *N* floating point numbers that partition the real line into 2*N*+1 regions. The *list* must be given in increasing numerical order. The partitions are used to map floating point numbers read from the input *files* into gray scale integers that are either assigned automatically by **postmd** or arbitrarily selected using the **-g** option. The default interval *list* is **-1,0,1**, which partions the real line into seven regions.

-m *num* Magnify each logical page by the factor *num*. Pages are scaled uniformly about the origin which, by default, is located at the center of each page. The default magnification is 1.0.

-n *num* Print *num* logical pages on each piece of paper, where *num* can be any positive integer. By default, *num* is set to 1.

-o *list* Print pages whose numbers are given in the comma separated *list*. The list contains single numbers *N* and ranges *N1* – *N2*. A missing *N1* means the lowest numbered page, a missing *N2* means the highest.

-p *mode* Print *files* in either portrait or landscape *mode*. Only the first character of *mode* is significant. The default *mode* is portrait.

-w *window* *Window* is a comma or space separated list of four positive integers that select the upper left and lower right corners of a submatrix from each of the input *files*. Row and column indices start at 1 in the upper left corner and the numbers in the input *files* are assumed to be written in row major order. By default, the entire matrix is displayed.

-x *num* Translate the origin *num* inches along the positive x axis. The default coordinate system has the origin fixed at the center of the page, with positive x to the right and positive y up the page. Positive *num* moves everything right. The default offset is 0 inches.

-y *num* Translate the origin *num* inches along the positive y axis. Positive *num* moves everything up the page. The default offset is 0.

Only one matrix is displayed on each logical page, and each of the input *files* must contain complete descriptions of exactly one matrix. Matrix elements are floating point numbers arranged in row major order in each input file. White space, including newlines, is not used to determine matrix dimensions. By default, **postmd** assumes each matrix is square and sets the number of rows and columns to the square root of the number of elements in the input file. Supplying default dimensions on the command line with the **-d** option overrides this default behavior, and in that case the dimensions apply to all input *files*.

An optional header can be supplied with each input file and is used to set the matrix dimensions, the partition of the real line, the gray scale map, and a window into the matrix. The header consists of keyword/value pairs, each on a separate line. It begins on the first line of each input file and ends with the first unrecognized string, which should be the first matrix element. Values set in the header take precedence, but apply only to the current input file. Recognized header keywords are **dimension**, **interval**, **grayscale**, and **window**. The syntax of the value string that follows each keyword parallels what's accepted by the **-d**, **-i**, **-g**, and **-w** options.

EXAMPLES

For example, suppose file initially contains the 1000 numbers in a 20x50 matrix. Then you can produce exactly the same output by completing three steps. First, issue the following command line:

```
postmd -d20x50 -i"-100 100" -g0,128,254,128,0 file
```

Second, prepend the following header to *file*:

```
dimension 20x50
interval  -100.0 .100e+3
grayscale 0 128 254 128 0
```

Third, issue the following command line:

```
postmd file
```

The interval list partitions the real line into five regions and the gray scale list maps numbers less than –100 or greater than 100 into 0 (that is, black), numbers equal to –100 or 100 into 128 (that is, 50 percent black), and numbers between –100 and 100 into 254 (that is, almost white).

NOTES

The largest matrix that can be adequately displayed is a function of the interval and gray scale lists, the printer resolution, and the paper size. A 600x600 matrix is an optimistic upper bound for a two element interval list (that is, five regions) using 8.5x11 inch paper on a 300 dpi printer.

Using white (that is, 255) in a gray scale list is not recommended and won't show up in the legend and bar graph that **postmd** displays below each image.

DIAGNOSTICS

An exit status of 0 is returned if *files* were successfully processed.

FILES

`/usr/lib/lp/postscript/postmd.ps`
`/usr/lib/lp/postscript/forms.ps`
`/usr/lib/lp/postscript/ps.requests`

SEE ALSO

dpost(1), **postdaisy**(1), **postdmd**(1), **postio**(1), **postprint**(1), **postreverse**(1), **posttek**(1)

postplot(1)

NAME

postplot – PostScript translator for **plot** graphics files

SYNOPSIS

/usr/lib/lp/postscript/postplot [*options*] [*files*]

DESCRIPTION

The **postplot** filter translates **plot**(1) graphics *files* into PostScript and writes the results on the standard output. If no *files* are specified, or if – is one of the input *files*, the standard input is read. The following *options* are understood:

-c *num* — Print *num* copies of each page. By default, only one copy is printed.

-f *name* — Print text using font *name*. Any PostScript font can be used, although the best results will be obtained only with constant width fonts. The default font is Courier.

-m *num* — Magnify each logical page by the factor *num*. Pages are scaled uniformly about the origin which, by default, is located at the center of each page. The default magnification is 1.0.

-n *num* — Print *num* logical pages on each piece of paper, where *num* can be any positive integer. By default, *num* is set to 1.

-o *list* — Print pages whose numbers are given in the comma-separated *list*. The list contains single numbers *N* and ranges *N1* – *N2*. A missing *N1* means the lowest numbered page, a missing *N2* means the highest.

-p *mode* — Print *files* in either portrait or landscape *mode*. Only the first character of *mode* is significant. The default *mode* is landscape.

-w *num* — Set the line width used for graphics to *num* points, where a point is approximately 1/72 of an inch. By default, *num* is set to 0 points, which forces lines to be one pixel wide.

-x *num* — Translate the origin *num* inches along the positive x axis. The default coordinate system has the origin fixed at the center of the page, with positive x to the right and positive y up the page. Positive *num* moves everything right. The default offset is 0.0 inches.

-y *num* — Translate the origin *num* inches along the positive y axis. Positive *num* moves everything up the page. The default offset is 0.0.

DIAGNOSTICS

An exit status of 0 is returned if *files* were successfully processed.

NOTES

The default line width is too small for write-white print engines, such as the one used by the PS-2400.

FILES

/usr/lib/lp/postscript/postplot.ps
/usr/lib/lp/postscript/forms.ps
/usr/lib/lp/postscript/ps.requests

SEE ALSO

download(1), **dpost**(1), **postdaisy**(1), **postdmd**(1), **postio**(1), **postmd**(1), **postprint**(1), **postreverse**(1), **plot**(1)

postprint(1)

NAME

`postprint` – PostScript translator for text files

SYNOPSIS

`/usr/lib/lp/postscript/postprint` [*options*] [*files*]

DESCRIPTION

The `postprint` filter translates text *files* into PostScript and writes the results on the standard output. If no *files* are specified, or if – is one of the input *files*, the standard input is read. The following *options* are understood:

`-c` *num* — Print *num* copies of each page. By default, only one copy is printed.

`-f` *name* — Print *files* using font *name*. Any PostScript font can be used, although the best results will be obtained only with constant width fonts. The default font is Courier.

`-l` *num* — Set the length of a page to *num* lines. By default, *num* is 66. Setting *num* to 0 is allowed, and will cause *postprint* to guess a value, based on the point size that's being used.

`-m` *num* — Magnify each logical page by the factor *num*. Pages are scaled uniformly about the origin, which is located near the upper left corner of each page. The default magnification is 1.0.

`-n` *num* — Print *num* logical pages on each piece of paper, where *num* can be any positive integer. By default, *num* is set to 1.

`-o` *list* — Print pages whose numbers are given in the comma-separated *list*. The *list* contains single numbers *N* and ranges *N1* – *N2*. A missing *N1* means the lowest numbered page, a missing *N2* means the highest.

`-p` *mode* — Print *files* in either portrait or landscape *mode*. Only the first character of *mode* is significant. The default *mode* is portrait.

`-r` *num* — Selects carriage return behavior. Carriage returns are ignored if *num* is 0, cause a return to column 1 if *num* is 1, and generate a newline if *num* is 2. The default *num* is 0.

`-s` *num* — Print *files* using point size *num*. When printing in landscape mode *num* is scaled by a factor that depends on the imaging area of the device. The default size for portrait mode is 10.

`-t` *num* — Assume tabs are set every *num* columns, starting with the first column. By default, tabs are set every 8 columns.

`-x` *num* — Translate the origin *num* inches along the positive x axis. The default coordinate system has the origin fixed near the upper left corner of the page, with positive x to the right and positive y down the page. Positive *num* moves everything right. The default offset is 0.25 inches.

`-y` *num* — Translate the origin *num* inches along the positive y axis. Positive *num* moves text up the page. The default offset is –0.25 inches.

A new logical page is started after 66 lines have been printed on the current page, or whenever an ASCII form feed character is read. The number of lines per page can be changed using the `-l` option. Unprintable ASCII characters are ignored, and lines that are too long are silently truncated by the printer.

EXAMPLES

To print *file1* and *file2* in landscape mode, issue the following command:

postprint -pland *file1 file2*

To print three logical pages on each physical page in portrait mode:

postprint -n3 *file*

DIAGNOSTICS

An exit status of 0 is returned if *files* were successfully processed.

FILES

/usr/lib/lp/postscript/postprint.ps
/usr/lib/lp/postscript/forms.ps
/usr/lib/lp/postscript/ps.requests

SEE ALSO

download(1), **dpost**(1), **postdaisy**(1), **postdmd**(1), **postio**(1), **postmd**(1), **postreverse**(1), **posttek**(1)

postreverse (1)

NAME

postreverse – reverse the page order in a PostScript file

SYNOPSIS

/usr/lib/lp/postscript/postreverse [*options*] [*file*]

DESCRIPTION

The **postreverse** filter reverses the page order in files that conform to Adobe's Version 1.0 or Version 2.0 file structuring conventions, and writes the results on the standard output. Only one input *file* is allowed and if no *file* is specified, the standard input is read. The following *options* are understood:

-o *list* Select pages whose numbers are given in the comma-separated *list*. The *list* contains single numbers *N* and ranges *N1* – *N2*. A missing *N1* means the lowest numbered page, a missing *N2* means the highest.

-r Don't reverse the pages in *file*.

The **postreverse** filter can handle a limited class of files that violate page independence, provided all global definitions are bracketed by **%%BeginGlobal** and **%%EndGlobal** comments. In addition, files that mark the end of each page with **%%EndPage: label ordinal** comments will also reverse properly, provided the prologue and trailer sections can be located. If **postreverse** fails to find an **%%EndProlog** or **%%EndSetup** comment, the entire *file* is copied, unmodified, to the standard output.

Because global definitions are extracted from individual pages and put in the prologue, the output file can be minimally conforming, even if the input *file* wasn't.

EXAMPLES

To select pages 1 to 100 from *file* and reverse the pages:

postreverse -o1-100 *file*

To print four logical pages on each physical page and reverse all the pages:

postprint -n4 *file* **| postreverse**

To produce a minimally conforming file from output generated by **dpost** without reversing the pages:

dpost *file* **| postreverse -r**

DIAGNOSTICS

An exit status of 0 is returned if *file* was successfully processed.

NOTES

No attempt has been made to deal with redefinitions of global variables or procedures. If standard input is used, the input *file* will be read three times before being reversed.

SEE ALSO

download(1), **dpost**(1), **postdaisy**(1), **postdmd**(1), **postio**(1), **postmd**(1), **postprint**(1), **posttek**(1)

NAME

posttek – PostScript translator for tektronix 4014 files

SYNOPSIS

/usr/lib/lp/postscript/posttek [*options*] [*files*]

DESCRIPTION

The **posttek** filter translates tektronix 4014 graphics *files* into PostScript and writes the results on the standard output. If no *files* are specified, or if – is one of the input *files*, the standard input is read. The following *options* are understood:

-c *num* Print *num* copies of each page. By default, only one copy is printed.

-f *name* Print text using font *name*. Any PostScript font can be used, although the best results will be obtained only with constant width fonts. The default font is Courier.

-m *num* Magnify each logical page by the factor *num*. Pages are scaled uniformly about the origin which, by default, is located at the center of each page. The default magnification is 1.0.

-n *num* Print *num* logical pages on each piece of paper, where *num* can be any positive integer. By default, *num* is set to 1.

-o *list* Print pages whose numbers are given in the comma-separated *list*. The *list* contains single numbers *N* and ranges *N1* – *N2*. A missing *N1* means the lowest numbered page, a missing *N2* means the highest.

-p *mode* Print *files* in either portrait or landscape *mode*. Only the first character of *mode* is significant. The default *mode* is landscape.

-w *num* Set the line width used for graphics to *num* points, where a point is approximately 1/72 of an inch. By default, *num* is set to 0 points, which forces lines to be one pixel wide.

-x *num* Translate the origin *num* inches along the positive x axis. The default coordinate system has the origin fixed at the center of the page, with positive x to the right and positive y up the page. Positive *num* moves everything right. The default offset is 0.0 inches.

-y *num* Translate the origin *num* inches along the positive y axis. Positive *num* moves everything up the page. The default offset is 0.0.

DIAGNOSTICS

An exit status of 0 is returned if *files* were successfully processed.

NOTES

The default line width is too small for write-white print engines, such as the one used by the PS-2400.

FILES

/usr/lib/lp/postscript/posttek.ps
/usr/lib/lp/postscript/forms.ps
/usr/lib/lp/postscript/ps.requests

SEE ALSO

download(1), **dpost**(1), **postdaisy**(1), **postdmd**(1), **postio**(1), **postmd**(1), **postprint**(1), **postreverse**(1)

NAME

pr – print files

SYNOPSIS

pr [-*columns* [-**w***width*] [-**a**]] [-**e***ck*] [-**i***ck*] [-**drtfp**] [+*page*] [-**n***ck*] [-**o***offset*] [-**l***length*] [-**s***separator*] [-**h** *header*] [-**F**] [*file* . . .]

pr [-**m** [-**w***width*]] [-**e***ck*] [-**i***ck*] [-**drtfp**] [+*page*] [-**n***ck*] [-**o***offset*] [-**l***length*] [-**s***separator*] [-**h** *header*] [-**F**] [*file1 file2* . . .]

DESCRIPTION

The **pr** command formats and prints the contents of a file. If *file* is **-**, or if no files are specified, **pr** assumes standard input. The named files are printed on standard output. **pr** processes supplementary code set characters in *files*, and recognizes supplementary code set characters in the *header* given to the **-h** option (see below) according to the locale specified in the **LC_CTYPE** environment variable [see **LANG** on **environ**(5)], except as noted below. References to "character positions" below assume single-byte characters.

By default, the listing is separated into pages, each headed by the page number, the date and time that the file was last modified, and the name of the file. Page length is 66 lines which includes 10 lines of header and trailer output. The header is composed of 2 blank lines, 1 line of text (can be altered with **-h**), and 2 blank lines; the trailer is 5 blank lines. For single column output, line width may not be set and is unlimited. For multicolumn output, line width may be set and the default is 72 columns. Diagnostic reports (failed options) are reported at the end of standard output associated with a terminal, rather than interspersed in the output. Pages are separated by series of line feeds rather than form feed characters.

By default, columns are of equal width, separated by at least one space; lines which do not fit are truncated. If the **-s** option is used, lines are not truncated and columns are separated by the *separator* character.

Either *–columns* or **-m** should be used to produce multi-column output. **-a** should only be used with *–columns* and not **-m**.

Command line options are

+*page*	Begin printing with page numbered *page* (default is 1).
-*columns*	Print *columns* columns of output (default is 1). Output appears as if **-e** and **-i** are on for multi-column output. May not use with **-m**.
-a	Print multi-column output across the page one line per column. *columns* must be greater than one. If a line is too long to fit in a column, it is truncated.
-m	Merge and print all files simultaneously, one per column. The maximum number of files that may be specified is eight. If a line is too long to fit in a column, it is truncated. May not use with *–column*.
-d	Double-space the output. Blank lines that result from double-spacing are dropped when they occur at the top of a page.

-e*ck* Expand input tabs to character positions k+1, 2∗k+1, 3∗k+1, and so on. If k is 0 or is omitted, default tab settings at every eighth position are assumed. Tab characters in the input are expanded into the appropriate number of spaces. If *c* is given, it is treated as the input tab character (default for *c* is the tab character). *c* must be a non-digit single-byte character.

-i*ck* In output, replace white space wherever possible by inserting tabs to character positions k+1, 2∗k+1, 3∗k+1, and so on. If k is 0 or is omitted, default tab settings at every eighth position are assumed. If *c* is given, it is treated as the output tab character (default for *c* is the tab character). *c* must be a non-digit single-byte character.

-n*ck* Provide k-digit line numbering (default for k is 5). The number occupies the first k+1 character positions of each column of single column output or each line of **-m** output. If *c* is given, it is appended to the line number to separate it from whatever follows (default for *c* is a tab). *c* must be a non-digit single-byte character.

-w*width* Set the width of a line to *width* character positions (default is 72). This is effective only for multi-column output (-*columns* and **-m**). There is no line limit for single column output.

-o*offset* Offset each line by *offset* character positions (default is 0). The number of character positions per line is the sum of the width and offset.

-l*length* Set the length of a page to *length* lines (default is 66). A *length* of 0 specifies the default length. By default, output contains 5 lines of header and 5 lines of trailer leaving 56 lines for user-supplied text. When **-l***length* is used and *length* exceeds 10, then *length*–10 lines are left per page for user supplied text. When *length* is 10 or less, header and trailer output is omitted to make room for user supplied text; see the **-t** option.

-h *header* Use *header* as the text line of the header to be printed instead of the file name. **-h** is ignored when **-t** is specified or **-l***length* is specified and the value of *length* is 10 or less. (**-h** is the only **pr** option requiring space between the option and argument.)

-p Pause before beginning each page if the output device is a terminal. **pr** rings the terminal bell and waits for a carriage return.

-f Use a single form-feed character for new pages (default is to use a sequence of line feeds). Pause before beginning the first page if the standard output is associated with a terminal.

-r Print no diagnostic reports on files that cannot be opened.

-t Print neither the five-line identifying header nor the five-line trailer normally supplied for each page. Quit printing after the last line of each file without spacing to the end of the page. Use of **-t** overrides the **-h** option.

-s*separator* Separate columns by the single character *separator* instead of by the appropriate number of spaces (default for *separator* is a tab). Prevents truncation of lines on multicolumn output unless **-w** is specified. *separator* must be a single-byte character.

-F Fold the lines of the input file. When used in multi-column mode (with the **-a** or **-m** options) lines will be folded to fit the current column's width, otherwise they will be folded to fit the current line width (80 columns).

EXAMPLES

Print **file1** and **file2** as a double-spaced, three-column listing headed by "**file list**":

```
pr -3dh "file list" file1 file2
```

Copy **file1** to **file2**, expanding tabs to columns 10, 19, 28, 37, . . . :

```
pr -e9 -t < file1 > file2
```

Print **file1** and **file2** simultaneously in a two-column listing with no header or trailer where both columns have line numbers:

```
pr -t -n file1 | pr -t -m -n file2 -
```

FILES

/dev/tty*
: If standard output is directed to one of the special files **/dev/tty***, then other output directed to this terminal is delayed until standard output is completed. This prevents error messages from being interspersed throughout the output.

/usr/lib/locale/*locale***/LC_MESSAGES/uxcore**
: language-specific message file [See **LANG** on **environ**(5).]

NOTE

The **pr** command automatically converts ^Ls (form feeds) into multiple newlines. It also will interpret control characters that **printf**(3S) interprets.

SEE ALSO

cat(1), **fold**(1), **more**(1), **pg**(1) **printf**(3S)

printf(1)

NAME

printf – print formatted output

SYNOPSIS

printf *format* [*arg* . . .]

DESCRIPTION

The **printf** command converts, formats, and prints its *arg*s under control of the *format*. It fully supports conversion specifications for strings (**%s** descriptor); however, the results are undefined for the other conversion specifications supported by **printf**(3S).

format a character string that contains three types of objects: 1) plain characters, which are simply copied to the output stream; 2) conversion specifications, each of which results in fetching zero or more *arg*s; and 3) C-language escape sequences, which are translated into the corresponding characters.

arg string(s) to be printed under the control of *format*. The results are undefined if there are insufficient *arg*s for the format. If the format is exhausted while *arg*s remain, the excess *arg*s are simply ignored.

Each conversion specification is introduced by the character %. After the %, the following appear in sequence:

An optional field, consisting of a decimal digit string followed by a **$**, specifying the next *arg* to be converted. If this field is not provided, the *arg* following the last *arg* converted is used.

An optional decimal digit string specifying a minimum *field width*. If the converted value has fewer characters than the field width, it is padded on the left (or right, if the left-adjustment flag '-' has been given) to the field width. The padding is with blanks unless the field width digit string starts with a zero, in which case the padding is with zeros.

An optional *precision* that gives the maximum number of characters to be printed from a string in **%s** conversion. The precision takes the form of a period (**.**) followed by a decimal digit string; a null digit string is treated as zero (nothing is printed). Padding specified by the precision overrides the padding specified by the field width. That is, if *precision* is specified, its value controls the number of characters printed.

A field width or precision or both may be indicated by an asterisk (*) instead of a digit string. In this case, an integer *arg* supplies the field width or precision. The *arg* that is actually converted is not fetched until the conversion letter is seen, so the *arg*s specifying field width or precision must appear *before* the *arg* (if any) to be converted. A negative field width argument is taken as a **'-'** (left-adjustment) flag followed by a positive field width. If the precision argument is negative, it is changed to zero (nothing is printed). A non-existent or small field width does not cause truncation of a field; if the result of a conversion is wider than the field width, the field is simply expanded to contain the conversion result.

The conversion characters and their meanings are:

`%s` The *arg* is taken to be a string and characters from the string are printed until a null character (`\0`) is encountered or the number of characters shown by the precision specification is reached. If the precision is missing, it is taken to be infinite, so all characters up to the first null character are printed. A null value for *arg* yields undefined results.

`%%` Print a `%`; no argument is converted.

EXAMPLES

The command

```
printf '%s %s %s\n' Good Morning World
```

results in the output:

```
Good Morning World
```

The following command produces the same output.

```
printf '%2$s %s %1$s\n' World Good Morning
```

Here is an example that prints the first 6 characters of **$PATH** left-adjusted in a 10-character field:

```
printf 'First 6 chars of %s are %-10.6s.\n' $PATH $PATH
```

If **$PATH** has the value **/usr/bin:/usr/local/bin**, then the above command would print the following output:

```
First 6 chars of /usr/bin:/usr/local/bin are /usr/b    .
```

REFERENCES

`printf`(3S)

prof(1)

NAME

`prof` – display profile data

SYNOPSIS

`prof` [`-t` | `c` | `a` | `n`] [`-o` | `x`] [`-g` | `l`] [`-z`] [`-h`] [`-s`] [`-m` *mdata*] `-V` [*prog*]

DESCRIPTION

The **`prof`** command interprets a profile file produced by the **`monitor`** function. The symbol table in the object file *prog* (**`a.out`** by default) is read and correlated with a profile file (**`mon.out`** by default). For each external text symbol the percentage of time spent executing between the address of that symbol and the address of the next is printed, together with the number of times that function was called and the average number of milliseconds per call.

The mutually exclusive options **`-t`**, **`-c`**, **`-a`**, and **`-n`** determine the type of sorting of the output lines:

`-t` Sort by decreasing percentage of total time (default).

`-c` Sort by decreasing number of calls.

`-a` Sort by increasing symbol address.

`-n` Sort lexically by symbol name.

The mutually exclusive options **`-o`** and **`-x`** specify the printing of the address of each symbol monitored:

`-o` Print each symbol address (in octal) along with the symbol name.

`-x` Print each symbol address (in hexadecimal) along with the symbol name.

The mutually exclusive options **`-g`** and **`-l`** control the type of symbols to be reported. The **`-l`** option must be used with care; it applies the time spent in a static function to the preceding (in memory) global function, instead of giving the static function a separate entry in the report. If all static functions are properly located (see example below), this feature can be very useful. If not, the resulting report may be misleading.

Assume that **`A`** and **`B`** are global functions and only **`A`** calls static function **`S`**. If **`S`** is located immediately after **`A`** in the source code (that is, if **`S`** is properly located), then, with the **`-l`** option, the amount of time spent in **`A`** can easily be determined, including the time spent in **`S`**. If, however, both **`A`** and **`B`** call **`S`**, then, if the **`-l`** option is used, the report will be misleading; the time spent during **`B`**'s call to **`S`** will be attributed to **`A`**, making it appear as if more time had been spent in **`A`** than really had. In this case, function **`S`** cannot be properly located.

`-g` Include static (non-global) functions.

`-l` Do not include static (non-global) functions (default).

The following options may be used in any combination:

`-z` Include all symbols in the profile range, even if associated with zero number of calls and zero time.

-h Suppress the heading normally printed on the report. (This is useful if the report is to be processed further.)

-s Print a summary of several of the monitoring parameters and statistics on the standard error output.

-m *mdata*
Use file *mdata* instead of **mon.out** as the input profile file.

-V Print **prof** version information on the standard error output.

A program creates a profile file if it has been link edited with the **-p** option of **cc**. This option to the **cc** command arranges for calls to **monitor** at the beginning and end of execution. It is the call to **monitor** at the end of execution that causes the system to write a profile file. The number of calls to a function is tallied if the **-p** option was used when the file containing the function was compiled.

The name of the file created by a profiled program is controlled by the environmental variable **PROFDIR**. If **PROFDIR** is not set, **mon.out** is produced in the directory current when the program terminates. If **PROFDIR=***string*, *string***/***pid***.***progname* is produced, where *progname* consists of **argv[0]** with any path prefix removed, and *pid* is the process ID of the program. If **PROFDIR** is set, but null, no profiling output are produced.

A single function may be split into subfunctions for profiling by means of the **MARK** macro [see **prof**(5)].

FILES

mon.out	default profile file
a.out	default namelist (object) file

SEE ALSO

cc(1), **exit**(2), **lprof**(1), **monitor**(3C), **prof**(5) **profil**(2),

NOTES

The times reported in successive identical runs may show variances because of varying cache-hit ratios that result from sharing the cache with other processes. Even if a program seems to be the only one using the machine, hidden background or asynchronous processes may blur the data. In rare cases, the clock ticks initiating recording of the program counter may "beat" with loops in a program, grossly distorting measurements. Call counts are always recorded precisely, however.

Only programs that call **exit** or return from **main** are guaranteed to produce a profile file, unless a final call to **monitor** is explicitly coded.

The times for static functions are attributed to the preceding external text symbol if the **-g** option is not used. However, the call counts for the preceding function are still correct; that is, the static function call counts are not added to the call counts of the external function.

If more than one of the options **-t**, **-c**, **-a**, and **-n** is specified, the last option specified is used and the user is warned.

Profiling may be used with dynamically linked executables, but care must be applied. Currently, shared objects cannot be profiled with **prof**. Thus, when a profiled, dynamically linked program is executed, only the "main" portion of the image is sampled. This means that all time spent outside of the "main" object, that is, time spent in a shared object, will not be included in the profile summary; the total time reported for the program may be less than the total time used by the program.

Because the time spent in a shared object cannot be accounted for, the use of shared objects should be minimized whenever a program is profiled with **prof**. If possible, the program should be linked statically before being profiled.

Consider an extreme case. A profiled program dynamically linked with the shared C library spends 100 units of time in some **libc** routine, say, **malloc**. Suppose **malloc** is called only from routine **B** and **B** consumes only 1 unit of time. Suppose further that routine **A** consumes 10 units of time, more than any other routine in the "main" (profiled) portion of the image. In this case, **prof** will conclude that most of the time is being spent in **A** and almost no time is being spent in **B**. From this it will be almost impossible to tell that the greatest improvement can be made by looking at routine **B** and not routine **A**. The value of the profiler in this case is severely degraded; the solution is to use archives as much as possible for profiling.

NAME

profiler: **prfld**, **prfstat**, **prfdc**, **prfsnap**, **prfpr** – UNIX system profiler

SYNOPSIS

/usr/sbin/prfld
/usr/sbin/prfstat on
/usr/sbin/prfstat off
/usr/sbin/prfdc *file* [*period* [*off_hour*]]
/usr/sbin/prfsnap *file*
/usr/sbin/prfpr [**-t**] *file* [*cutoff*]

DESCRIPTION

prfld, **prfstat**, **prfdc**, **prfsnap**, and **prfpr** form a system of programs to facilitate an activity study of the UNIX operating system.

prfld is used to initialize the recording mechanism in the system. It generates a table containing the starting address of each system subroutine as extracted from **/stand/unix** and the modules in **/etc/conf/mod.d**. It locks all currently loaded modules into memory. It is no longer necessary to use **prfld**, as this is done automatically by **prfstart on**, **prfsnap**, and **prfdc**. To unlock modules after profiling activities are complete, be sure to run **prfstat off**.

prfstat is used to enable or disable the sampling mechanism. Profiler overhead is less than 4% as calculated for 3000 text addresses. **prfstat** will also reveal the number of text addresses being measured.

prfdc and **prfsnap** perform the data collection function of the profiler by copying the current value of all the text address counters to a file where the data can be analyzed. **prfdc** will store the counters into *file* every *period* minutes and will turn off at *off_hour* (valid values for *off_hour* are **0–24**). **prfsnap** collects data at the time of invocation only, appending the counter values to *file*.

prfpr formats the data collected by **prfdc** or **prfsnap**. Each text address is converted to the nearest text symbol and is printed if the percent activity for that range is greater than *cutoff*. *cutoff* can be any decimal value greater than or equal to zero. The **-t** option reports time in clock ticks instead of in percentages.

FILES

/dev/prf interface to profile data and text addresses

/stand/unix system namelist file for non-loadable modules.

/etc/conf/mod.d/*
system namelists for loadable modules.

NAME

prs – print an SCCS file

SYNOPSIS

prs [**-d**[*dataspec*]] [**-r**[*SID*]] [**-e**] [**-l**] [**-c**[*date–time*]] [**-a**] *file* . . .

DESCRIPTION

prs prints, on the standard output, parts or all of an SCCS file [see **sccsfile**(4)] in a user-supplied format. If a directory is named, **prs** prints the files in that directory, except the non-SCCS files (last component of the path name does not begin with **s.**) and unreadable files. If a name of – is given, the standard input is read; each line of the standard input is taken to be the name of an SCCS file or directory to be processed. **prs** silently ignores non-SCCS files and unreadable files.

Arguments to **prs**, which may appear in any order, consist of keyletter arguments and file names.

The keyletter arguments apply independently to each named file:

-d[*dataspec*] Specifies the output data specification. The *dataspec* is a string consisting of SCCS file data keywords (see the "Data Keywords" section) interspersed with optional user-supplied text.

-r[*SID*] Specifies the SCCS identification (SID) string of a delta for which information is desired. The default is the top delta.

-e Requests information for all deltas created earlier than and including the delta designated via the **-r** keyletter or the date given by the **-c** option.

-l Requests information for all deltas created later than and including the delta designated via the **-r** keyletter or the date given by the **-c** option.

-c[*date–time*] The cutoff date–time in the form:

YY[*MM*[*DD*[*HH*[*MM*[*SS*]]]]]

Units omitted from the date–time default to their maximum possible values; for example, **-c7502** is equivalent to **-c750228235959**. Any number of non-numeric characters may separate the fields of the cutoff date; for example, **"-c77/2/2 9:22:25"**.

-a Requests printing of information for both removed, that is, delta type = R, [see **rmdel**(1)] and existing, that is, delta type = D, deltas. If the **-a** keyletter is not specified, information for existing deltas only is provided.

Data Keywords

Data keywords specify those parts of an SCCS file that are to be retrieved and output. All parts of an SCCS file [see **sccsfile**(4)] have an associated data keyword. There is no limit on the number of times a data keyword may appear in a *dataspec*.

The information printed by **prs** consists of: (1) the user-supplied text; and (2) appropriate values (extracted from the SCCS file) substituted for the recognized data keywords in the order of appearance in the *dataspec*. The format of a data keyword value is either "Simple" (S), in which keyword substitution is direct, or "Multi-line" (M), in which keyword substitution is followed by pressing RETURN.

User-supplied text is any text other than recognized data keywords. A tab is specified by `\t` and RETURN/new-line is specified by `\n`. The default data keywords are:

`":Dt:\t:DL:\nMRs:\n:MR:COMMENTS:\n:C:"`

Keyword	Data Item	File Section	Value	Format
`:Dt:`	Delta information	Delta Table	See below*	S
`:DL:`	Delta line statistics	"	`:Li:/:Ld:/:Lu:`	S
`:Li:`	Lines inserted by Delta	"	*nnnnn*	S
`:Ld:`	Lines deleted by Delta	"	*nnnnn*	S
`:Lu:`	Lines unchanged by Delta	"	*nnnnn*	S
`:DT:`	Delta type	"	`D` *or* `R`	S
`:I:`	SCCS ID string (SID)	"	`:R:.:L:.:B:.:S:`	S
`:R:`	Release number	"	*nnnn*	S
`:L:`	Level number	"	*nnnn*	S
`:B:`	Branch number	"	*nnnn*	S
`:S:`	Sequence number	"	*nnnn*	S
`:D:`	Date Delta created	"	`:Dy:/:Dm:/:Dd:`	S
`:Dy:`	Year Delta created	"	*nn*	S
`:Dm:`	Month Delta created	"	*nn*	S
`:Dd:`	Day Delta created	"	*nn*	S
`:T:`	Time Delta created	"	`:Th:::Tm:::Ts:`	S
`:Th:`	Hour Delta created	"	*nn*	S
`:Tm:`	Minutes Delta created	"	*nn*	S
`:Ts:`	Seconds Delta created	"	*nn*	S
`:P:`	Programmer who created Delta	"	*logname*	S
`:DS:`	Delta sequence number	"	*nnnn*	S
`:DP:`	Predecessor Delta seq-no.	"	*nnnn*	S
`:DI:`	Seq-no. of deltas incl., excl., ignored	"	`:Dn:/:Dx:/:Dg:`	S
`:Dn:`	Deltas included (seq #)	"	`:DS: :DS:`...	S
`:Dx:`	Deltas excluded (seq #)	"	`:DS: :DS:`...	S
`:Dg:`	Deltas ignored (seq #)	"	`:DS: :DS:`...	S
`:MR:`	MR numbers for delta	"	*text*	M
`:C:`	Comments for delta	"	*text*	M
`:UN:`	User names	User Names	*text*	M
`:FL:`	Flag list	Flags	*text*	M

Keyword	Data Item	File Section	Value	Format
`:Y:`	Module type flag	"	*text*	S
`:MF:`	MR validation flag	"	`yes` or `no`	S
`:MP:`	MR validation pgm name	"	*text*	S
`:KF:`	Keyword error/warning flag	"	`yes` or `no`	S
`:KV:`	Keyword validation string	"	*text*	S
`:BF:`	Branch flag	"	`yes` or `no`	S
`:J:`	Joint edit flag	"	`yes` or `no`	S
`:LK:`	Locked releases	"	`:R:` ...	S
`:Q:`	User-defined keyword	"	*text*	S
`:M:`	Module name	"	*text*	S
`:FB:`	Floor boundary	"	`:R:`	S
`:CB:`	Ceiling boundary	"	`:R:`	S
`:Ds:`	Default SID	"	`:I:`	S
`:ND:`	Null delta flag	"	`yes` or `no`	S
`:FD:`	File descriptive text	Comments	*text*	M
`:BD:`	Body	Body	*text*	M
`:GB:`	Gotten body	"	*text*	M
`:W:`	A form of what(1) string	N/A	`:Z::M:\t:I:`	S
`:A:`	A form of what(1) string	N/A	`:Z::Y: :M: :I::Z:`	S
`:Z:`	what(1) string delimiter	N/A	`@(#)`	S
`:F:`	SCCS file name	N/A	*text*	S
`:PN:`	SCCS file path name	N/A	*text*	S

* `:Dt: = :DT: :I: :D: :T: :P: :DS: :DP:`

EXAMPLES

The command

```
prs -d"Users and/or user IDs for :F: are:\n:UN:" s.file
```

may produce on the standard output:

```
Users and/or user IDs for s.file are:
xyz
131
abc
```

The command

```
prs -d"Newest delta for pgm :M:: :I: Created :D: By :P:" -r
s.file
```

may produce on the standard output:

```
Newest delta for pgm main.c: 3.7 Created 77/12/1 By cas
```

The default case:

```
prs s.file
```

produces on the standard output:

```
D 1.1 77/12/1 00:00:00 cas 1 000000/00000/00000
MRs:
bl78-12345
bl79-54321
COMMENTS:
this is the comment line for s.file initial delta
```

for each delta table entry of the "D" type. The only keyletter argument allowed to be used with the "special case" is the **-a** keyletter.

FILES

`/var/tmp/pr?????`

SEE ALSO

admin(1), **delta**(1), **get**(1), **help**(1), **sccsfile**(4)

DIAGNOSTICS

Use **help**(1) for explanations.

NAME

prt – (BSD) display the delta and commentary history of an SCCS file

SYNOPSIS

/usr/ucb/prt [**-abdefistu**] [**-y**[*SID*]] [**-c**[*cutoff*] [**-r**[*rev-cutoff*]] *file* . . .

DESCRIPTION

Note: the **prt** command is an older version of **prs**(1) that in most circumstances is more convenient to use, but is less flexible than **prs**.

prt prints part or all of an SCCS file in a useful format. If a directory is named, **prt** behaves as though each file in the directory were specified as a named file, except that non-SCCS files (last component of the pathname does not begin with **s.**) and unreadable files are silently ignored. If a name of '–' is given, the standard input is read; each line of the standard input is taken to be the name of an SCCS file to be processed. Again, non-SCCS files and unreadable files are silently ignored.

The following options are available with **prt :**

-a Print those types of deltas normally not printed by the **d** keyletter. These are types **R** (removed). This keyletter is effective only if the **d** keyletter is also specified (or assumed).

-b Print the body of the SCCS file.

-d This keyletter normally prints delta table entries of the **D** type.

-e This keyletter implies the **d**, **i**, **u**, **f**, and **t** keyletters and is provided for convenience.

-f Print the flags of the named file.

-i Print the serial numbers of those deltas included, excluded, and ignored. This keyletter is effective only if the **d** keyletter is also specified (or assumed).

The following format is used to print those portions of the SCCS file as specified by the above keyletters. The printing of each delta table entry is preceded by a NEWLINE.

- Type of delta (**D** or **R**).
- SPACE.
- SCCS identification string (SID).
- TAB.
- Date and time of creation (in the form YY/MM/DD HH:MM:SS).
- SPACE.
- Creator.
- TAB.
- Serial number.
- SPACE.
- Predecessor delta's serial number.
- TAB.
- Statistics (in the form inserted/deleted/unchanged).

- NEWLINE.
- "Included:TAB", followed by SID's of deltas included, followed by NEWLINE (only if there were any such deltas and if **i** keyletter was supplied).
- "Excluded:TAB", followed by SID's of deltas excluded, followed by NEWLINE (see note above).
- "Ignored:TAB", followed by SID's of deltas ignored, followed by NEWLINE (see note above).
- "MRs:TAB", followed by MR numbers related to the delta, followed by NEWLINE (only if any MR numbers were supplied).
- Lines of comments (delta commentary), followed by newline (if any were supplied).

-s Print only the first line of the delta table entries; that is, only up to the statistics. This keyletter is effective only if the **d** keyletter is also specified (or assumed).

-t Print the descriptive text contained in the file.

-u Print the login-names and/or numerical group IDs of those users allowed to make deltas.

-y[*SID*]
Print the delta table entries to stop when the delta just printed has the specified SID. If no delta in the table has the specified SID, the entire table is printed. If no SID is specified, the first delta in the delta table is printed. This keyletter will print the entire delta table entry for each delta as a single line (the NEWLINE in the normal multi-line format of the **d** keyletter are replaced by SPACE characters) preceded by the name of the SCCS file being processed, followed by a **:**, followed by a TAB. This keyletter is effective only if the **d** keyletter is also specified (or assumed).

-c[*cutoff*]
Stop printing the delta table entries if the delta about to be printed is older than the specified cutoff date-time (see **get**(1) for the format of date-time). If no date-time is supplied, the epoch 0000 GMT Jan. 1, 1970 is used. As with the **y** keyletter, this keyletter will cause the entire delta table entry to be printed as a single line and to be preceded by the name of the SCCS file being processed, followed by a **:**, followed by a tab. This keyletter is effective only if the **d** keyletter is also specified (or assumed).

-r[*rev-cutoff*]
Begin printing the delta table entries when the delta about to be printed is older than or equal to the specified cutoff date-time (see **get**(1) for the format of date-time). If no date-time is supplied, the epoch 0000 GMT Jan. 1, 1970 is used. (In this case, nothing will be printed). As with the **y** keyletter, this keyletter will cause the entire delta table entry to be printed as a single line and to be preceded by the name of the SCCS file being processed, followed by a **:**, followed by a tab. This keyletter is effective only if the **d** keyletter is also specified (or assumed).

If any keyletter but **y**, **c**, or **r** is supplied, the name of the file being processed (preceded by one NEWLINE and followed by two NEWLINE characters) is printed before its contents.

If none of the **u**, **f**, **t**, or **b** keyletters is supplied, the **d** keyletter is assumed.

Note: the **s** and **i** keyletters, and the **c** and **r** keyletters are mutually exclusive; therefore, they may not be specified together on the same **prt** command.

The form of the delta table as produced by the **y**, **c**, and **r** keyletters makes it easy to sort multiple delta tables in chronological order.

When both the **y** and **c** or the **y** and **r** keyletters are supplied, **prt** will stop printing when the first of the two conditions is met.

SEE ALSO

admin(1), **delta**(1), **get**(1), **prs**(1), **sccs**(1), **sccsfile**(4), **what**(1)

NAME

prtvtoc – disk information display utility

SYNOPSIS

prtvtoc [**-aep**] [**-f** *vtoc-file*] *raw-device*

DESCRIPTION

The default and primary function of **prtvtoc** is to display the contents of the VTOC (Volume Table Of Contents). The information displayed for each valid slice includes slice number, slice tag, slice flag/permissions, slice start sector, slice size (in sectors).

Options

-a Print the alternates tables (bad tracks and bad sectors).

-e Creates or add information to the **/etc/partitions** file. This option is provided to allow support for **mkpart**(1M). Dependence on this feature is not suggested since it will not be supported in a future release.

-p Print the information contained in the **pdinfo** structure.

-f *vtoc-file*
Write the current contents of the VTOC into the *vtoc-file* in a condensed format. The format of the file is slice number, slice tag value, slice flag value, slice start sector, slice size (in sectors). The purpose of this file is to be input for the **edvtoc** command.

raw-device
The character special device for the disk drive to be accessed. It must be the slice 0 device to represent the entire device (for example, **/dev/rdsk/0s0** or **/dev/rdsk/c0t0d0s0**).

Files

/dev/rdsk/c?t?d?s0

USAGE

When editing the VTOC, the following entries are the valid slice tags and slice permission flags.

Slice Tags

```
#define V_BOOT     0x01   /* Boot slice */
#define V_ROOT     0x02   /* Root filesystem */
#define V_SWAP     0x03   /* Swap filesystem */
#define V_USR      0x04   /* Usr filesystem */
#define V_BACKUP   0x05   /* full disk */
#define V_ALTS     0x06   /* alternate sector space */
#define V_OTHER    0x07   /* non-unix space */
#define V_ALTTRK   0x08   /* alternate track space */
#define V_STAND    0x09   /* Stand slice */
#define V_VAR      0x0a   /* Var slice */
#define V_HOME     0x0b   /* Home slice */
#define V_DUMP     0x0c   /* dump slice */
```

Slice Permission Flags		
`#define V_UNMNT`	`0x01`	/* Unmountable partition */
`#define V_RONLY`	`0x10`	/* Read only */
`#define V_VALID`	`0x200`	/* Partition is valid to use */

The start and size value are in absolute sector numbers where the first sector on the drive is 0 (which is reserved for the partition table). Slices should start and end on a cylinder boundary if possible. The head, cylinder and sectors/track information provided by **prtvtoc -p** will assist in the calculations. Slices should not overlap (slice 0 is the exception, it describes the entire UNIX partition).

REFERENCE

edvtoc(1M), **sd01**(7)

NAME

ps – report process status

SYNOPSIS

ps [*options*]

DESCRIPTION

ps prints information about active processes. Without *options*, **ps** prints information about processes associated with the controlling terminal. The output contains only the process ID, terminal identifier, cumulative execution time, and the command name. Otherwise, the information that is displayed is controlled by the *options*.

Some options accept lists as arguments. Items in a list can be either separated by commas or else enclosed in double quotes and separated by commas or spaces. Values for *proclist* and *grplist* must be numeric.

The *options* are:

-e Print information about **e**very process now running.

-d Print information about all processes except session leaders.

-a Print information about **a**ll processes most frequently requested: all those except session leaders and processes not associated with a terminal.

-j Print session ID and process group ID.

-f Generate a **f**ull listing. (See below for significance of columns in a full listing.)

-l Generate a **l**ong listing. (See below.)

-c Print information in a format that reflects scheduler properties as described in **priocntl**(1). The **-c** option affects the output of the **-f** and **-l** options, as described below.

-t *termlist* List only process data associated with the terminal given in *termlist*. Terminal identifiers may be specified in one of two forms: the device's file name (for example, **term/04**) or, if the device's file name starts with **term**, just the digit identifier (for example, **04**).

-p *proclist* List only process data whose process ID numbers are given in *proclist*.

-u *uidlist* List only process data whose user ID number or login name is given in *uidlist*. In the listing, the numerical user ID will be printed unless you give the **-f** option, which prints the login name.

-g *grplist* List only process data whose group leader's ID number(s) appears in *grplist*. (A group leader is a process whose process ID number is identical to its process group ID number.

-s *sesslist* List information on all session leaders whose IDs appear in *sesslist*.

Under the **-f** option, **ps** tries to determine the command name and arguments given when the process was created by examining the user block. Failing this, the command name is printed, as it would have appeared without the **-f** option, in square brackets.

The column headings and the meaning of the columns in a **ps** listing are given below; the letters **f** and **l** indicate the option (**f**ull or **l**ong, respectively) that causes the corresponding heading to appear; **all** means that the heading always appears.

Note that these two options determine only what information is provided for a process; they do not determine which processes will be listed.

`F`	(l)	Flags (hexadecimal and additive) associated with the process 00 Process has terminated: process table entry now available. 01 A system process: always in primary memory. 02 Parent is tracing process. 04 Tracing parent's signal has stopped process: parent is waiting [**ptrace**(2)]. 08 Process is currently in primary memory. 10 Process currently in primary memory: locked until an event completes. 20 Process cannot be swapped.
`S`	(l)	The state of the process: O Process is running on a processor. S Sleeping: process is waiting for an event to complete. R Runnable: process is on run queue. I Idle: process is being created. Z Zombie state: process terminated and parent not waiting. T Traced: process stopped by a signal because parent is tracing it. X SXBRK state: process is waiting for more primary memory.
`UID`	(f,l)	The user ID number of the process owner (the login name is printed under the `-f` option).
`PID`	(all)	The process ID of the process (this datum is necessary in order to kill a process).
`PPID`	(f,l)	The process ID of the parent process.
`C`	(f,l)	Processor utilization for scheduling. Not printed when the `-c` option is used.
`CLS`	(f,l)	Scheduling class. Printed only when the `-c` option is used.
`PRI`	(l)	The priority of the process. Without the `-c` option, higher numbers mean lower priority. With the `-c` option, higher numbers mean higher priority.
`NI`	(l)	Nice value, used in priority computation. Not printed when the `-c` option is used. Only processes in the time-sharing class have a nice value.
`ADDR`	(l)	The memory address of the process.
`SZ`	(l)	The size (in pages or clicks) of the virtual address space of the process.

WCHAN	(l)	The address of an event for which the process is sleeping, or in SXBRK state, (if blank, the process is running).
STIME	(f)	The starting time of the process, given in hours, minutes, and seconds. (A process begun more than twenty-four hours before the **ps** inquiry is executed is given in months and days.)
TTY	(all)	The controlling terminal for the process (the message, **?**, is printed when there is no controlling terminal).
TIME	(all)	The cumulative execution time for the process.
COMMAND	(all)	The command name (the full command name and its arguments are printed under the **-f** option).

A process that has exited and has a parent, but has not yet been waited for by the parent, is marked **<defunct>**.

FILES

/dev
/dev/sxt/*
/dev/term/*
/dev/xt/* terminal ("tty") names searcher files
/dev/kmem kernel virtual memory
/dev/swap the default swap device
/dev/mem memory
/etc/passwd UID information supplier
/etc/ps_data internal data structure
/usr/lib/locale/*locale***/LC_MESSAGES/uxcore**
language-specific message file [See **LANG** on **environ**(5).]

SEE ALSO

getty(1M), **kill**(1), **nice**(1), **priocntl**(1)

NOTES

Things can change while **ps** is running; the snap-shot it gives is true only for a split-second, and it may not be accurate by the time you see it. Some data printed for defunct processes is irrelevant.

If no *termlist*, *proclist*, *uidlist*, or *grplist* is specified, **ps** checks **stdin**, **stdout**, and **stderr** in that order, looking for the controlling terminal and will attempt to report on processes associated with the controlling terminal. In this situation, if **stdin**, **stdout**, and **stderr** are all redirected, **ps** will not find a controlling terminal, so there will be no report.

On a heavily loaded system, **ps** may report an **lseek** error and exit. **ps** may seek to an invalid user area address: having obtained the address of a process' user area, **ps** may not be able to seek to that address before the process exits and the address becomes invalid.

ps -ef may not report the actual start of a tty login session, but rather an earlier time, when a getty was last respawned on the tty line.

NAME

ps – (BSD) display the status of current processes

SYNOPSIS

/usr/ucb/ps [**-acglnrSuUvwx**] [**-t***term*] [*num*]

DESCRIPTION

The **ps** command displays information about processes. Normally, only those processes that are running with your effective user ID and are attached to a controlling terminal (see **termio**(7)) are shown. Additional categories of processes can be added to the display using various options. In particular, the **-a** option allows you to include processes that are not owned by you (that do not have your user ID), and the **-x** option allows you to include processes without control terminals. When you specify both **-a** and **-x**, you get processes owned by anyone, with or without a control terminal. The **-r** option restricts the list of processes printed to running and runnable processes.

ps displays the process ID, under PID; the control terminal (if any), under TT; the cpu time used by the process so far, including both user and system time, under TIME; the state of the process, under S; and finally, an indication of the COMMAND that is running.

The state is given by a single letter from the following:

O	Process is running on a processor.
S	Sleeping. Process is waiting for an event to complete.
R	Runnable. Process is on run queue.
I	Idle. Process is being created.
Z	Zombie state. Process terminated and parent not waiting.
T	Traced. Process stopped by a signal because parent is tracing it.
X	**SXBRK** state. Process is waiting for more primary memory.

The following options must all be combined to form the first argument:

-a Include information about processes owned by others.

-c Display the command name, as stored internally in the system for purposes of accounting, rather than the command arguments, which are kept in the process' address space. This is more reliable, if less informative, since the process is free to destroy the latter information.

-g Display all processes. Without this option, **ps** only prints interesting processes. Processes are deemed to be uninteresting if they are process group leaders. This normally eliminates top-level command interpreters and processes waiting for users to login on free terminals.

-l Display a long listing, with fields **F**, **PPID**, **CP**, **PRI**, **NI**, **SZ**, **RSS** and **WCHAN** as described below.

-n Produce numerical output for some fields. In a user listing, the **USER** field is replaced by a **UID** field.

-r Restrict output to running and runnable processes.

-S Display accumulated CPU time used by this process and all of its reaped children.

-u Display user-oriented output. This includes fields **USER**, **SZ**, **RSS** and **START** as described below.

-U Update the private database (**/etc/ps_data**) where **ps** keeps system information. This option may be used solely by privileged users.

-v Display a version of the output containing virtual memory. This includes fields **SIZE** and **RSS**, described below.

-w Use a wide output format (132 columns rather than 80); if repeated, that is, **-ww**, use arbitrarily wide output. This information is used to decide how much of long commands to print.

-x Include processes with no controlling terminal.

-t*term* List only process data associated with the terminal, *term*. Terminal identifiers may be specified in one of two forms: the device's file name (for example, **tty04** or **term/14**) or, if the device's file name starts with **tty**, just the digit identifier (for example, **04**).

num A process number may be given, in which case the output is restricted to that process. This option must be supplied last.

DISPLAY FORMATS

Fields that are not common to all output formats:

USER Name of the owner of the process.

NI Process scheduling increment [see **getpriority**(3) and **nice**(3C)].

SIZE
SZ The combined size of the data and stack segments (in kilobyte units)

RSS Real memory (resident set) size of the process (in kilobyte units).

UID Numerical user-ID of process owner.

PPID Numerical ID of parent of process.

CP Short-term CPU utilization factor (used in scheduling).

PRI The priority of the process (higher numbers mean lower priority).

START The starting time of the process, given in hours, minutes, and seconds. A process begun more than 24 hours before the **ps** inquiry is executed is given in months and days.

WCHAN The address of an event for which the process is sleeping, or in **SXBRK** state (if blank, the process is running).

F Flags (hexadecimal and additive) associated with the process:

- **00** Process has terminated. Process table now available.
- **01** A system process, always in primary memory.
- **02** Parent is tracing process.
- **04** Tracing parent's signal has stopped process. Parent is waiting, see **ptrace**(2).

08	Process is currently in primary memory.
10	Process currently in primary memory, locked until an event is completed.

A process that has exited and has a parent, but has not yet been waited for by the parent is marked <**defunct**>; otherwise, **ps** tries to determine the command name and arguments given when the process was created by examining the user block.

FILES

/dev	
/dev/sxt/*	
/dev/tty*	
/dev/xt/*	terminal (**tty**) names searcher files
/dev/kmem	kernel virtual memory
/dev/swap	default swap device
/dev/mem	memory
/etc/passwd	UID information supplier
/etc/ps_data	internal data structure

SEE ALSO

getpriority(3), **kill**(1), **lseek**(2), **nice**(3C), **whodo**(1M)

NOTES

Things can change while **ps** is running; the picture it gives is only a close approximation to the current state. Some data printed for defunct processes is irrelevant.

If no *term* or *num* is specified, **ps** checks the standard input, the standard output, and the standard error in that order, looking for the controlling terminal and will attempt to report on processes associated with the controlling terminal. In this situation, if the standard input, the standard output, and the standard error are all redirected, **ps** will not find a controlling terminal, so there will be no report.

On a heavily loaded system, **ps** may report an **lseek**(2) error and exit. **ps** may seek to an invalid user area address, having obtained the address of process' user area, **ps** may not be able to seek to that address before the process exits and the address becomes invalid.

NAME

pseudo – STREAMS interface for non-STREAMS devices

SYNOPSIS

pseudo [-l] [-m *line***]**

DESCRIPTION

The **pseudo** command provides a STREAMS interface on non-STREAMS tty devices. It opens a master pseudo-tty device (**/dev/ptmx**) and a slave pseudo-tty device (**/dev/pts/???**). It pushes the pseudo-terminal emulation module **ptem**(7), then a line discipline module, **ldterm**(7) by default, onto the slave to connect the master and the slave. (The stream may be subsequently manipulated with other commands to provide the desired configuration.) **pseudo** then forks to become two processes. One reads from the user's tty line and writes to the pseudo-tty; the other reads from the pseudo-tty and writes to the user's tty. On the pseudo-tty side, a shell is executed.

pseudo accepts the following options:

-l Execute a "login shell" (executed as **-sh**). By default, **pseudo** executes a simple interactive shell (**sh -i**).

-m *line* Push line discipline module *line* instead of the default **ldterm** module. At most one line discipline is pushed.

The effect of running **pseudo** is that the user obtains an interactive shell with the standard I/O files connected to a STREAMS device that behaves as a real tty. This is useful in situations where a STREAMS device is desired but a non-STREAMS device driver is being used.

When the executed shell exits, **pseudo** exits and control returns to the original tty with the original **termio**(7) parameters.

FILES

/dev/ptmx	pseudo-terminal master device
/dev/pts/*	pseudo-terminal slave devices

SEE ALSO

ldterm(7), **ptem**(7), **pty**(7)

putdev (1M)

NAME

putdev – creates and updates the device database

SYNOPSIS

putdev -a *alias* [*secdev=value*] [*attribute=value* [. . .]]

putdev -m *device attribute=value* [*attribute=value* [. . .]]

putdev -d *device* [*attribute* [. . .]]

putdev -p *device attribute=value*[**,** *value* . . .]

putdev -r *device attribute=value*[**,** *value* . . .]

DESCRIPTION

The **putdev** command is used to add a new device to the Device Database (DDB), modify an existing device's attributes, or remove a device entry from the DDB. It also allows appending new values to attributes that take value-lists (separated by commas), and removal of specific values from value-lists.

Options

putdev takes the following options:

-a *alias*
: Add a *device* to the DDB using the specified *attributes.* The *device* must be referenced by its *alias.*

-m *device*
: Modify a *device* entry in the DDB, using the specified attribute values. If a specified attribute does not exist in the device entry, **putdev** adds the specified *attribute* to the entry. It also modifies *attributes* that already have a value with the *value* specified.

-d *device*
: Remove a *device* entry from the DDB, when executed without the *attributes* argument. If the *attribute* argument is specified, the *attribute* and its value are deleted from the device entry.

-p *device*
: Append the list of values to the *attribute* value-list of the *device.* If the *value* item is multiply defined in the input value-list or already defined in the DDB, **putdev** fails and prints an error message.

-r *device*
: Remove the list of values from the *attribute* value-list, of the *device.* The command succeeds, even if the *value* has been removed or is not defined for the *attribute* in the DDB.

Arguments

alias must be unique throughout the DDB. *alias* is limited to 64 characters (**DDB_MAXALIAS**) and should contain only alphanumeric characters and any of the following special characters: **.** (period), _ (underscore), **$** (dollar sign), and - (hyphen).

device designates the absolute pathname or alias name of the device whose attribute is to be added, modified, or removed. If *device* is a pathname, then the attributes of the alias to which it maps are updated.

attribute designates a device attribute to be added, modified, or deleted. This prevents an accidental modification or deletion of a device's alias from the DDB.

value designates the value to be assigned to a device's attribute. If any of the values are invalid, then **putdev** fails and prints an error message.

Whenever the attributes in a Device Database file are updated, the old version of the of the file is saved to a file with the capital letter "O" prefixed to the file name. If there are errors in the modification of device attributes, you can recover the old versions of the Device Database files.

Attributes

Following are all of the attributes which can be defined for a device:

alias The unique name by which a device is known. No two devices in the database may share the same alias name. The name is limited in length to 64 characters (**DDB_MAXALIAS**) and should contain only alphanumeric characters and any of the special characters: underscore (_), dollar sign (**$**), hyphen (-), and period (**.**).

bdevice
: The absolute pathname to the block special device node associated with the device, if any, with maximum length of **PATH_MAX**. This attribute is optional.

bdevlist
: A list of additional pathnames of block device special files which map to the same logical or secure device. Each item in the list is separated by a comma, and each must be an absolute pathname of the device special file, with a maximum length of **PATH_MAX**. Since, this attribute takes a list of values, **putdev -p|-r** can be used for this attribute. This attribute is optional.

capacity
: The capacity of the device or of the typical volume, if removable.

cdevice
: The absolute pathname to the character special device node associated with the device, if any, with maximum length of **PATH_MAX**. This attribute is optional.

cdevlist
: It contains a list of additional pathnames of character device special files mapping to the same logical or secure device. Each item in the list is separated by a comma, and each must be an absolute pathname of the device special file, with a maximum length of **PATH_MAX**. Since, this attribute takes a list of values, **putdev -p|-r** can be used for this attribute. This attribute is optional.

cyl Used by the command specified in the **mkfscmd** attribute.

desc A description of any instance of a volume associated with this device (such as floppy diskette).

dpartlist
The list of disk partitions associated with this device. Used only if **type=disk**. The list should contain device aliases, each of which must have **type=dpart**.

dparttype
The type of disk partition represented by this device. Used only if **type=dpart**. It should be either **fs** (for filesystem) or **dp** (for data partition).

erasecmd
The command string that, when executed, erases the device.

fmtcmd
The command string that, when executed, formats the device.

fsname
The filesystem name on the file system administered on this partition, as supplied to the **/usr/sbin/labelit** command. This attribute is specified only if **type=dpart** and **dparttype=fs**.

gap Used by the command specified in the **mkfscmd** attribute.

mkfscmd
The command string that, when executed, places a file system on a previously formatted device.

mountpt
The default mount point to use for the device. Used only if the device is mountable. For disk partitions where **type=dpart** and **dparttype=fs**, this attribute should specify the location where the partition is normally mounted.

nblocks
The number of blocks in the filesystem administered on this partition. Used only if **type=dpart** and **dparttype=fs**.

ninodes
The number of inodes in the filesystem administered on this partition. Used only if **type=dpart** and **dparttype=fs**.

norewind
The name of the character special device node that allows access to the serial device without rewinding when the device is closed.

pathname
Defines the pathname to an i-node describing the device (used for non-block or character device pathnames, such as directories).

type A token that represents inherent qualities of the device. Standard types include: 9-track, ctape, disk, directory, diskette, dpart, and qtape.

`volname`

The volume name on the filesystem administered on this partition, as supplied to the **/usr/sbin/labelit** command. Used only if **type=dpart** and **dparttype=fs**.

`volume`

A text string used to describe any instance of a volume associated with this device. This attribute should not be defined for devices which are not removable.

Return Values

If the command is successful, it returns an exit code of zero (0). Otherwise, it returns one of the following exit codes and prints the corresponding error message:

n `incorrect usage`

```
USAGE: putdev -a alias [attribute=value] ...
    putdev -m device attribute=value [attribute=value [...]]
    putdev -d device [attribute[ . . . ]]
    putdev -p device attribute=value[,value . . . ]
    putdev -r device attribute=value[,value. . . ]
```

2 `Device Database in inconsistent state - notify administrator`

2 `Device Database could not be accessed or created`

3 *alias* `already exists in Device Database`

3 *device* `does not exist in Device Database`

? "*dsf*" `already exists in Device Database`

6 `invalid alias or invalid pathname` "*device*"

4 `hilevel does not dominate lolevel in attribute range`

4 `invalid value for attribute` "*attr*"
    `level=` "*level*" `not defined in LTDB`

6 `invalid value for attribute` "*attr*"
    `user/uid=` "*uid*" `not defined in system`

6 `invalid value for attribute` "*attr*"
    `group/gid=` "*group*" `not defined in system`

6 `invalid value for attribute` "*attr*"
    `invalid permissions specified` "*perm*"

6 `invalid value for attribute` "*attr*"
    `invalid delimiter specified in` "*value*"

6 "*value*" `multiply defined for attribute` "*attr*"

6 `Device Database in use.  Try again later.`

3 "*alias*" `not defined in Device Database`

5 `system service not installed`

Files

/etc/device.tab

REFERENCES

devattr(1M), getdev(1M)

NAME

putdgrp – edits device group table

SYNOPSIS

putdgrp [**-d**] *dgroup* [*device* [. . .]]

DESCRIPTION

putdgrp modifies the device group table. It can modify the table by creating a new device group or by removing a device group. It can also change group definitions by adding or removing a device from the group definition.

When **putdgrp** is executed with only a *dgroup* specification, the command adds the specified group name to the device group table if it does not already exist. If the **-d** option is also used with only the *dgroup* specification, the command deletes the group from the table.

When **putdgrp** is executed with both a *dgroup* and a *device* specification, it adds the given device name (or names) to the group definition. When invoked with both arguments and the **-d** option, the command deletes the device name (or names) from the group definition.

When **putdgrp** is executed with both a *dgroup* and a *device* specification and the device group does not exist, it creates the group and adds the specified devices to that new group.

Options

The options and arguments for this command are:

-d Delete the group or, if used with *device*, the device from a group definition.

dgroup
Specify a device group name.

device Specify the pathname or alias of the device that is to added to or deleted from the device group.

Return Values

The command will exit with one of the following values:

0 Successful completion of the task

1 Command syntax incorrect, invalid option used, or internal error occurred.

2 Device group table could not be opened for reading or a new device group table could not be created.

3 If executed with the **-d** option, indicates that an entry in the device group table for the device group *dgroup* does not exist and so cannot be deleted. Otherwise, indicates that the device group *dgroup* already exists and cannot be added.

4 If executed with the **-d** option, indicates that the device group *dgroup* does not have as members one or more of the specified devices. Otherwise, indicates that the device group *dgroup* already has one or more of the specified devices as members.

Files

/etc/dgroup.tab

USAGE

Examples

To add a new device group: **putdgrp floppies** To add a device to a device group:

```
putdgrp floppies diskette2
```

To delete a device group:

```
putdgrp -d floppies
```

To delete a device from a device group:

```
putdgrp -d floppies diskette2
```

REFERENCES

listdgrp(1M), **putdev**(1M)

NAME

pwck, **grpck** – password/group file checkers

SYNOPSIS

/usr/sbin/pwck [*file*]
/usr/sbin/grpck [*file*]

DESCRIPTION

pwck scans the password file and notes any inconsistencies. The checks include validation of the number of fields, login name, user ID, group ID, and whether the login directory and the program-to-use-as-shell exist. The default password file is **/etc/passwd**.

grpck verifies all entries in the group file. This verification includes a check of the number of fields, group name, group ID, whether any login names belong to more than **NGROUPS_MAX** groups and that all login names appear in the password file. The default group file is **/etc/group**.

FILES

/etc/group
/etc/passwd

SEE ALSO

group(4), **passwd**(4)

DIAGNOSTICS

Group entries in **/etc/group** with no login names are flagged.

NAME

pwck – (BSD) check password database entries

SYNOPSIS

/usr/ucb/pwck [*file*]

DESCRIPTION

pwck checks a password file for errors. If specified, *file* is checked, otherwise **/etc/passwd** is checked.

This command differs from **/usr/sbin/pwck** in its ability to correctly parse YP entries in **/etc/passwd**.

DIAGNOSTICS

Too many/few fields
An entry in the password file does not have the proper number of fields.

No login name
The login name field of an entry is empty.

Bad character(s) in login name
The login name in an entry contains characters other than lowercase letters and digits.

First char in login name not lower case alpha
The login name in an entry does not begin with a lowercase letter.

Login name too long
The login name in an entry has more than 8 characters.

Invalid UID
The user ID field in an entry is not numeric or is greater than 65535.

Invalid GID
The group ID field in an entry is not numeric or is greater than 65535.

No login directory
The login directory field in an entry is empty.

Login directory not found
The login directory field in an entry refers to a directory that does not exist.

Optional shell file not found.
The login shell field in an entry refers to a program or shell script that does not exist.

No netgroup name
The entry is a Yellow Pages entry referring to a netgroup, but no netgroup is present.

Bad character(s) in netgroup name
The netgroup name in a Yellow Pages entry contains characters other than lowercase letters and digits.

First char in netgroup name not lower case alpha
The netgroup name in a Yellow pages entry does not begin with a lowercase letter.

FILES

/etc/passwd

SEE ALSO

group(4), passwd(4)

pwconv(1M)

NAME

pwconv – install and update /etc/shadow with information from /etc/passwd

SYNOPSIS

pwconv

DESCRIPTION

The pwconv command creates and updates /etc/shadow with information from /etc/passwd.

If the /etc/shadow file does not exist, pwconv creates /etc/shadow with information from /etc/passwd. The command populates /etc/shadow with the user's login name, password, and password aging information. If password aging information does not exist in /etc/passwd for a given user, none is added to /etc/shadow. However, the last changed information is always updated.

If the /etc/shadow file does exist, the following tasks are performed:

> Entries that are in the /etc/passwd file and not in the /etc/shadow file are added to the /etc/shadow file.
>
> Entries that are in the /etc/shadow file and not in the /etc/passwd file are removed from /etc/shadow.
>
> Password attributes (for example, password and aging information) in an /etc/passwd entry are moved to the corresponding entry in /etc/shadow.

The pwconv program is a privileged system command that cannot be executed by ordinary users.

FILES

/etc/passwd, /etc/shadow, /etc/opasswd, /etc/oshadow

SEE ALSO

passwd(1)

DIAGNOSTICS

The pwconv command exits with 0 on success, or non-zero on one of the following error conditions:

```
Permission denied.
Invalid command syntax.
Unexpected failure.  Conversion not done.
Unexpected failure.  Password file(s) missing.
Password file(s) busy.  Try again later.
```

NAME

pwd – working directory name

SYNOPSIS

pwd

DESCRIPTION

pwd prints the path name of the working (current) directory.

FILES

/usr/lib/locale/*locale***/LC_MESSAGES/uxcore.abi**
language-specific message file [See **LANG** on **environ**(5).]

SEE ALSO

cd(1)

DIAGNOSTICS

```
UX:pwd:ERROR: cannot open ...
UX:pwd:ERROR: read error in ...
```

indicate possible file system trouble and should be referred to a UNIX system administrator.

NOTES

If you move the current directory or one above it, **pwd** may not give the correct response. Use the **cd**(1) command with a full path name to correct this situation.

quot (1M)

NAME

`quot` – summarize `ufs` file system ownership

SYNOPSIS

`/usr/sbin/quot` [`-acfhnv`] [*filesystem* . . .]

DESCRIPTION

`quot` displays the number of blocks (1024 bytes) in the named *filesystem* currently owned by each user. There is a limit of 2048 blocks. Files larger than this will be counted as a 2048 block file, but the total blocks count will be correct.

The options are:

`-a` Generate a report for all mounted file systems.

`-c` Display three columns giving a file size in blocks, the number of files of that size, and a cumulative total of blocks containing files of that size or a smaller size. Files exceeding 499 blocks are listed as 499 blocks. The last line always lists 499 blocks, even if there are no files of that size.

`-f` Display count of number of files as well as space owned by each user. This option is incompatible with the `-c` and `-v` options.

`-h` Estimate the number of blocks in the file — this does not account for files with holes in them.

`-n` Attach names to the list of files read from standard input. `quot -n` cannot be used alone, because it expects data from standard input. For example, the pipeline

```
ncheck filesystem | sort +0n | quot -n filesystem
```

will produce a list of all files and their owners. This option is incompatible with all other options.

`-v` In addition to the default output, display three columns containing the number of blocks not accessed in the last 30, 60, and 90 days.

FILES

`/etc/mnttab` mounted file systems
`/etc/passwd` to get user names

SEE ALSO

`du`(1M)

NAME

quota – display a user's disk quota and usage on **ufs** file system

SYNOPSIS

/usr/sbin/quota [**-v**] [*username*]

DESCRIPTION

quota displays users' disk usage and limits. Only a privileged user may use the optional *username* argument to view the limits of other users.

quota without options displays only warnings about mounted file systems where quotas are turned on and usage is over quota. Remotely mounted file systems which do not have quotas turned on are ignored.

username can be numeric, corresponding to the uid of a user.

The **-v** option displays user's quotas on all mounted file systems where quotas are turned on.

FILES

/etc/mnttab list of currently mounted filesystems

SEE ALSO

edquota(1M), **quotaon**(1M)

quotacheck (1M)

NAME

quotacheck – **ufs** file system quota consistency checker

SYNOPSIS

/usr/sbin/quotacheck [**-v**] [**-p**] *filesystem* . . .
/usr/sbin/quotacheck -a [**-p**] [**-v**]

DESCRIPTION

quotacheck examines each file system, builds a table of current disk usage, and compares this table against that stored in the disk quota file for the file system. If any inconsistencies are detected, both the quota file and the current system copy of the incorrect quotas are updated (the latter only occurs if an active file system is checked).

quotacheck expects each file system to be checked to have a quota file named **quotas** in the root directory. If none is present, **quotacheck** will ignore the file system.

quotacheck accesses the character special device in calculating the actual disk usage for each user. Thus, the file systems checked should be quiescent while **quotacheck** is running.

The options are:

-v Indicate the calculated disk quotas for each user on a particular file system. **quotacheck** normally reports only those quotas modified.

-a Check the file systems indicated in **/etc/mnttab** to be read-write. Only those file systems that have "rq" in the **mntopts** field of the **/etc/vfstab** file are checked.

-p Run parallel passes on the required file systems.

FILES

/etc/mnttab	mounted file systems
/etc/vfstab	list of default parameters for each file system

SEE ALSO

quotaon(1M)

NAME

quotaon, **quotaoff** – turn **ufs** file system quotas on and off

SYNOPSIS

/usr/sbin/quotaon [**-v**] *filesystem* . . .

/usr/sbin/quotaon -a [**-v**] *filesystem* . . .

/usr/sbin/quotaoff [**-v**] *filesystem* . . .

/usr/sbin/quotaoff -a [**-v**] *filesystem* . . .

DESCRIPTION

quotaon announces to the system that disk quotas should be enabled on one or more file systems. The file systems specified must be mounted at the time. The file system quota files must be present in the root directory of the specified file system and be named **quotas**.

quotaoff announces to the system that file systems specified should have any disk quotas turned off.

The option for **quotaon**:

-v Displays a message for each file system where quotas are turned on.

The option for **quotaoff**:

-v Displays a message for each file system affected.

For both **quotaon** and **quoatoff**, the option:

-a Reports on all mounted file systems that have **rq** in the **mntopts** field of the **/etc/vfstab** file.

These commands update the status field of devices located in **/etc/mnttab** to indicate when quotas are on or off for each file system.

FILES

/etc/mnttab	mounted file systems
/etc/vfstab	list of default parameters for each file system

SEE ALSO

mnttab(4), **vfstab**(4)

NAME

random – (XENIX) generate a random number

SYNOPSIS

random [**-s**] [*scale*]

DESCRIPTION

random generates a random number on the standard output, and returns the number as its exit value. By default, this number is either 0 or 1. If *scale* is given a value between 1 and 255, then the range of the random value is from 0 to *scale*. If *scale* is greater than 255, an error message is printed.

When the **-s** (silent) option is given, then the random number is returned as an exit value, but is not printed on the standard output. If an error occurs, **random** returns an exit value of zero.

SEE ALSO

rand(3C)

NOTES

This command does not perform any floating point computations. **random** uses the time of day as a seed.

NAME

rarpd – DARPA Reverse Address Resolution Protocol server

SYNOPSIS

/usr/sbin/in.rarpd [-d] *device* [*hostname*]

/usr/sbin/in.rarpd -a [-d]

DESCRIPTION

rarpd starts a daemon that responds to Reverse Address Resolution Protocol (RARP) requests. The daemon forks a copy of itself that runs in background. It must be run as root.

RARP is used by machines at boot time to discover their Internet Protocol (IP) address. The booting machine provides its Ethernet Address in a RARP request message. Using the **ethers** and **hosts** databases, **rarpd** maps this Ethernet Address into the corresponding IP address which it returns to the booting machine in an RARP reply message. The booting machine must be listed in both databases for **rarpd** to locate its IP address. **rarpd** issues no reply when it fails to locate an IP address.

In the first synopsis, the *device* parameter names the network interface upon which **rarpd** is to listen for requests. The *device* parameter takes the "name unit" form used by **ifconfig**(1M). The second argument, *hostname*, is used to obtain the IP address of that interface. An IP address in "decimal dot" notation may be used for *hostname*. If *hostname* is omitted, the address of the interface will be obtained from the kernel. When the first form of the command is used, **rarpd** must be run separately for each interface on which RARP service is to be supported. A machine that is a router may invoke **rarpd** multiple times, for example:

```
/usr/sbin/in.rarpd wd0 host
/usr/sbin/in.rarpd wd1 host-backbone
```

In the second synopsis, the **-a** option of **rarpd** locates all of the network interfaces present on the system and starts a daemon process for each one that supports RARP.

The **-d** option (valid for both synopsis entries) turns on debugging, and debugging information is printed to "standard error" (**stderr**).

FILES

/etc/ethers
/etc/hosts

SEE ALSO

boot(1M), **ethers**(4), **hosts**(4), **ifconfig**(1M), **netconfig**(4)

Finlayson, Ross, Timothy Mann, Jeffrey Mogul, and Marvin Theimer, *A Reverse Address Resolution Protocol*, RFC 903, Network Information Center, SRI International, Menlo Park, Calif., June 1984

rc0 (1M)

NAME

`rc0`, `rc6` – run commands performed to stop the operating system

SYNOPSIS

`/sbin/rc0` [`firmware` | `off` | `reboot`]
`/sbin/rc6` [`firmware` | `off` | `reboot`]

DESCRIPTION

`rc0` is executed at each system state change that needs to have the system in an inactive state. It is responsible for those actions that bring the system to a quiescent state, traditionally called "shutdown". (For backwards compatibility, **`/sbin/rc0`** is linked to **`/sbin/rc6`**.)

Three system states require this procedure: state `0`, state `5`, and state `6`. Whenever a change to one of these states occurs, the `rc0` procedure is run. The options are used as follows:

`firmware`	Go to init state 5 (the firmware state)
`off`	Go to init state 0 (the system halt state)
`reboot`	Go to init state 6 (the reboot state)

The entries in **`/etc/inittab`**, which may vary slightly on different machine types, might read something like this:

```
r0:0:wait:/sbin/rc0 off 1>/dev/sysmsg 2>&1 </dev/console
r5:5:wait:/sbin/rc0 firm 1>/dev/sysmsg 2>&1 </dev/console
r6:6:wait:/sbin/rc0 reboot 1>/dev/sysmsg 2>&1 </dev/console
```

See `init`(1M) for complete details on init states.

Some of the actions performed by `rc0` are carried out by files beginning with `K` in `/etc/rc0.d`. These files are executed in ASCII order (see FILES below for more information), terminating some system service. The combination of commands in `rc0` and files in `/etc/rc0.d` determines how the system is shut down.

The recommended sequence for `rc0` is:

Stop System Services and Daemons.

Various system services (such as a Local Area Network or LP Spooler) are gracefully terminated.

New services are sometimes added that should be terminated when the system is shut down or that need to do cleanup before being terminated by a `SIGTERM` signal. For such services the appropriate files are installed in `/etc/rc0.d`.

Terminate Processes

`SIGTERM` signals are sent to all running processes by **`killall`**(1M). Most processes stop themselves cleanly if sent **`SIGTERM`**.

Kill Processes

`SIGKILL` signals are sent to all remaining processes; no process can resist `SIGKILL`.

At this point the only processes left are those associated with **rc0** and processes 0 and 1, which are special to the operating system.

Unmount All File Systems

Only the root file system (/) remains mounted.

Depending on which system state the systems end up in (0, 5, or 6), **rc0** determines what happens next: for system state 0, **uadmin 2 0** is run; for system state 5, **uadmin 2 2** is run; for system state 6, **uadmin 2 1** is run. If the **/etc/inittab** has not defined any other actions to be performed as in the case of system state 0, then the operating system will have nothing to do. It should not be possible to get the system's attention. The only thing that can be done is to turn off the power or possibly get the attention of a firmware monitor. The command can be used only by a privileged user.

FILES

The execution by **/usr/bin/sh** of any files in **/etc/rc0.d** occurs in ASCII sort-sequence order. See **rc2**(1M) for more information.

SEE ALSO

init(1M), **killall**(1M), **rc2**(1M), **shutdown**(1M), **uadmin**(1M), **uadmin**(2)

rc1 (1M)

NAME

rc1 – run commands to bring system to administrative state

SYNOPSIS

/sbin/rc1

DESCRIPTION

The shell script **rc1** is run whenever a transition to run state 1 is requested either through **init 1** or **shutdown -i 1**.

File systems required for multi-user operations will be mounted at the end of **rc1**.

When the system comes up from firmware mode into state 1, only the console is active; multi-user (state 2) services are unavailable. When the system is going from state 2 to state 1, some services are stopped and some processes are killed; otherwise, the system continues operating as it did in state 2.

Note that in this state, logins requiring access to multi-user file systems can be used, but other multi-user services are unavailable.

SEE ALSO

init(1M), **inittab**(4), **rc0**(1M), **rc2**(1M), **shutdown**(1M)

NAME

`rc2` – run commands performed for multi-user environment

SYNOPSIS

`/sbin/rc2`

DESCRIPTION

This file is executed via an entry in **/etc/inittab** and is responsible for those initializations that bring the system to a ready-to-use state, traditionally state **2**, called the "multi-user" state.

The actions performed by **rc2** are found in files in the directory **/etc/rc.d** and files beginning with **S** in **/etc/rc2.d**. These files are executed by **/usr/bin/sh** in ASCII sort–sequence order (see FILES for more information). When functions are added that need to be initialized when the system goes multi-user, an appropriate file should be added in **/etc/rc2.d**.

The functions done by the **rc2** command and associated **/etc/rc2.d** files include:

Setting and exporting the **TIMEZONE** variable.

Setting-up and mounting the user (**/usr**) file system.

Cleaning up (remaking) the **/tmp** and **/var/tmp** directories.

Loading the network interface and ports cards with program data and starting the associated processes.

Starting the **cron** daemon by executing **/usr/sbin/cron**.

Cleaning up (deleting) uucp locks status, and temporary files in the **/var/spool/uucp** directory.

Other functions can be added, as required, to support the addition of hardware and software features.

EXAMPLES

The following are prototypical files found in **/etc/rc2.d**. These files are prefixed by an **S** and a number indicating the execution order of the files.

MOUNTFILESYS

```
#    Set up and mount file systems
cd /
/sbin/mountall /etc/fstab
```

RMTMPFILES

```
# clean up /tmp
rm -rf /tmp
mkdir -m /tmp
chmod 1777 /tmp
chgrp bin /tmp
chown bin /tmp
```

uucp

```
#    clean-up uucp locks, status, and temporary files
rm -rf /usr/spool/locks/*
```

The file /etc/TIMEZONE is included early in rc2, thus establishing the default time zone for all commands that follow.

FILES

Here are some hints about files in /etc/rc.d:

The order in which files are executed is important. Since they are executed in ASCII sort–sequence order, using the first character of the file name as a sequence indicator will help keep the proper order. Thus, files starting with the following characters would be:

[0-9].	very early
[A-Z].	early
[a-n].	later
[o-z].	last

Files in /etc/rc.d that begin with a dot (.) will not be executed. This feature can be used to hide files that are not to be executed for the time being without removing them. The command can be used only by a privileged user.

Files in /etc/rc2.d must begin with an S or a K followed by a number and the rest of the file name. Upon entering run level 2, files beginning with S are executed with the start option; files beginning with K, are executed with the stop option. Files beginning with other characters are ignored.

SEE ALSO

inittab(4), shutdown(1M)

NAME

`rc3` – run commands to start distributed file sharing

SYNOPSIS

`/sbin/rc3`

DESCRIPTION

The shell script `rc3` is run whenever a transition to run state 3 is requested either through `init 3` or `shutdown -i 3`.

This state initializes networking and distributed file sharing operations.

SEE ALSO

`init`(1M), `inittab`(4), `rc0`(1M), `rc2`(1M), `shutdown`(1M)

NAME

rcp – remote file copy

SYNOPSIS

rcp [**-p**] *filename1 filename2*
rcp [**-pr**] *filename... directory*

DESCRIPTION

The **rcp** command copies files between machines. Each *filename* or *directory* argument is either a remote file name of the form:

hostname:*path*

or a local file name (containing no : characters, or a / before any : characters).

If a *filename* is not a full path name, it is interpreted relative to your home directory on *hostname*. A *path* on a remote host may be quoted (using \, ", or ') so that the metacharacters are interpreted remotely.

rcp does not prompt for passwords; your current local user name must exist on *hostname* and allow remote command execution by **rsh**(1).

rcp handles third party copies, where neither source nor target files are on the current machine. Hostnames may also take the form

username@*hostname*:*filename*

to use *username* rather than your current local user name as the user name on the remote host. **rcp** also supports Internet domain addressing of the remote host, so that:

username@*host*.*domain*:*filename*

specifies the username to be used, the hostname, and the domain in which that host resides. Filenames that are not full path names will be interpreted relative to the home directory of the user named *username*, on the remote host.

The destination hostname may also take the form *hostname*.*username*:*filename* to support destination machines that are running older versions of **rcp**.

The following options are available:

-p Attempt to give each copy the same modification times, access times, and modes as the original file.

-r Copy each subtree rooted at *filename*; in this case the destination must be a directory.

SEE ALSO

ftp(1), **rlogin**(1), **rsh**(1), **hosts.equiv**(4)

NOTES

rcp is meant to copy between different hosts; attempting to **rcp** a file onto itself, as with:

```
rcp tmp/file myhost:/tmp/file
```

results in a severely corrupted file.

rcp does not detect all cases where the target of a copy might be a file in cases where only a directory should be legal.

rcp requires that the source host have permission to execute commands on the remote host when doing third-party copies.

If you forget to quote metacharacters intended for the remote host you get an incomprehensible error message.

rdate(1M)

NAME

`rdate` – set system date from a remote host

SYNOPSIS

`rdate` *hostname*

DESCRIPTION

`rdate` sets the local date and time from the *hostname* given as an argument. You must be a privileged user on the local system. Typically **`rdate`** can be inserted as part of a startup script.

NAME

`readfile`, `longline` – reads file, gets longest line

SYNOPSIS

`readfile` *file*

`longline` [*file*]

DESCRIPTION

The `readfile` function reads *file* and copies it to *stdout*. No translation of NEWLINE is done. It keeps track of the longest line it reads and if there is a subsequent call to `longline`, the length of that line, including the NEWLINE character, is returned.

The `readfile` function primarily checks the system's locale. If it is not set to `C` (default), it tries to read file from *dirname*`/$LANG`. If no file can be found under *dirname*`/$LANG`, file will be read from *dirname*.

The `longline` function returns the length, including the NEWLINE character, of the longest line in *file*. If *file* is not specified, it uses the file named in the last call to `readfile`.

EXAMPLES

Here is a typical use of `readfile` and `longline` in a text frame definition file:

```
.
.
.
text="`readfile myfile`"
columns=`longline`
.
.
.
```

DIAGNOSTICS

If *file* does not exist, `readfile` will return `FALSE` (that is, the expression will have an error return).

`longline` returns 0 if a `readfile` has not previously been issued.

NOTES

More than one descriptor can call `readfile` in the same frame definition file. In text frames, if one of those calls is made from the `text` descriptor, then a subsequent use of `longline` will always get the longest line of the file read by the `readfile` associated with the `text` descriptor, even if it was not the most recent use of `readfile`.

SEE ALSO

`cat`(1)

NAME

reboot – (BSD) restart the operating system

SYNOPSIS

/usr/ucb/reboot [**-dlnq**] [*boot arguments*]

DESCRIPTION

reboot restarts the kernel. The kernel is loaded into memory by the PROM monitor, which transfers control to it.

Although **reboot** can be run by the privileged user at any time, **shutdown**(1M) is normally used first to warn all users logged in of the impending loss of service. See **shutdown**(1M) for details.

reboot performs a **sync**(1M) operation on the disks, and then a multiuser reboot is initiated. See **init**(1M) for details.

Executing **reboot -l** logs the reboot to the system log daemon, **syslogd**(1M), and places a shutdown record in the login accounting file **/var/adm/wtmp**. These actions are inhibited if the **-n** or **-q** options are present.

The following options are available:

-d Dump system core before rebooting. This option is provided for compatibility, but is not supported by the underlying **reboot**(3) call.

-l Logs a message to the system log indicating who rebooted the system.

-n Avoid the **sync**(1M). It can be used if a disk or the processor is on fire.

-q Quick. Reboots quickly and ungracefully, without first shutting down running processes.

boot arguments
These arguments are accepted for compatibility, but are ignored by **reboot**. See **boot**(1M) for details.

Power Fail and Crash Recovery

Normally, the system will reboot itself at power-up or after crashes.

FILES

/var/adm/wtmp login accounting file

SEE ALSO

boot(1M), **crash**(1M), **fsck**(1M), **halt**(1M), **init**(1M), **reboot**(3) **shutdown**(1M), **sync**(1M), **syslogd**(1M)

NAME

refer – (BSD) expand and insert references from a bibliographic database

SYNOPSIS

/usr/ucb/refer [**-b**] [**-e**] [**-n**] [**-a***r*] [**-c***string*] [**-k***x*] [**-l***m,n*]
[**-p** *filename*] [**-s***keys*] *filename* . . .

DESCRIPTION

refer is a preprocessor for **nroff**(1), or **troff**(1), that finds and formats references. The input files (standard input by default) are copied to the standard output, except for lines between '**.[**' and '**.]**' command lines. Such lines are assumed to contain keywords as for **lookbib**(1), and are replaced by information from a bibliographic data base. The user can avoid the search, override fields from it, or add new fields. The reference data, from whatever source, is assigned to a set of **troff** strings. Macro packages such as **ms**(5) print the finished reference text from these strings. A flag is placed in the text at the point of reference. By default, the references are indicated by numbers.

When **refer** is used with **eqn**(1), **neqn**, or **tbl**(1), **refer** should be used first in the sequence, to minimize the volume of data passed through pipes.

The following options are available:

-b Bare mode — do not put any flags in text (neither numbers or labels).

-e Accumulate references instead of leaving the references where encountered, until a sequence of the form:

```
.[
$LIST$
.]
```

is encountered, and then write out all references collected so far. Collapse references to the same source.

-n Do not search the default file.

-a*r* Reverse the first *r* author names (Jones, J. A. instead of J. A. Jones). If *r* is omitted, all author names are reversed.

-c*string*
Capitalize (with SMALL CAPS) the fields whose key-letters are in *string*.

-k*x* Instead of numbering references, use key labels as specified in a reference data line beginning with the characters %*x*; By default, **%***x* is **%L**.

-l*m,n* Instead of numbering references, use labels from the senior author's last name and the year of publication. Only the first *m* letters of the last name and the last *n* digits of the date are used. If either of *m* or *n* is omitted, the entire name or date, respectively, is used.

-p *filename*
Take the next argument as a file of references to be searched. The default file is searched last.

-s*keys* Sort references by fields whose key-letters are in the *keys* string, and permute reference numbers in the text accordingly. Using this option implies the **-e** option. The key-letters in *keys* may be followed by a number indicating how many such fields are used, with a **+** sign taken as a very large number. The default is **AD**, which sorts on the senior author and date. To sort on all authors and then the title, for instance, use the options '**-sA+T**'.

FILES

/usr/ucblib/reftools/papers	default publication lists and indexes
/usr/ucblib/reftools	programs

SEE ALSO

addbib(1), **eqn**(1), **indxbib**(1), **lookbib**(1), **nroff**(1), **roffbib**(1), **sortbib**(1), **tbl**(1), **troff**(1)

NAME

regcmp – regular expression compile

SYNOPSIS

regcmp [-] *file* . . .

DESCRIPTION

The **regcmp** command performs a function similar to **regcmp** and, in most cases, precludes the need for calling **regcmp** from C programs. Bypassing **regcmp** saves on both execution time and program size. The command **regcmp** compiles the regular expressions in *file* and places the output in *file*.**i**. If the **-** option is used, the output is placed in *file*.**c**. The format of entries in *file* is a name (C variable) followed by one or more blanks followed by one or more regular expressions enclosed in double quotes. The output of **regcmp** is C source code. Compiled regular expressions are represented as **extern char** vectors. *file*.**i** files may thus be **#include**d in C programs, or *file*.**c** files may be compiled and later loaded. In the C program that uses the **regcmp** output, **regex(abc,line)** applies the regular expression named **abc** to **line**. Diagnostics are self-explanatory. **regcmp** processes supplementary code set characters in *files* according to the locale specified in the **LC_CTYPE** environment variable [see **LANG** on **environ**(5)]. Pattern searches are performed on characters, not bytes, as described on **ed**(1).

EXAMPLES

```
name     "([A-Za-z][A-Za-z0-9_]*)$0"

telno    "\({0,1}([2-9][01][1-9])$0\){0,1} *"
         "([2-9][0-9]{2})$1[ -]{0,1}"
         "([0-9]{4})$2"
```

The three arguments to **telno** shown above must all be entered on one line.

In the C program that uses the **regcmp** output,

```
regex(telno, line, area, exch, rest)
```

applies the regular expression named **telno** to **line**.

SEE ALSO

ed(1), **regcmp**(3G)

regex(1F)

NAME

regex – match patterns against a string

SYNOPSIS

regex [-e] [-v "*string*"] [*pattern template*] . . . *pattern* [*template*]

DESCRIPTION

The **regex** command takes a string from *standard input*, and a list of *pattern / template* pairs, and runs the **regex** function defined in **regcmp**(3G) to compare the string against each *pattern* until there is a match. When a match occurs, **regex** writes the corresponding *template* to *stdout*. The last (or only) *pattern* does not need a template.

-e means **regex** will evaluate the corresponding template and write the result to *stdout*.

-v "*string*" If **-v** is specified, *string* will be used instead of *stdin* to match against patterns.

The argument *pattern* is a regular expression of the form described in **regcmp**(3G). In most cases *pattern* should be enclosed in single quotes to turn off special meanings of characters. Note that only the final *pattern* in the list may lack a *template*.

The argument *template* may contain the strings **$m0** through **$m9**, which will be expanded to the part of *pattern* enclosed in `( ... )$0` through `( ... )$9` constructs (see examples below). Note that if you use this feature, you must be sure to enclose *template* in single quotes so that FMLI doesn't expand **$m0** through **$m9** at parse time. This feature gives **regex** much of the power of **cut**(1), **paste**(1), and **grep**(1), and some of the capabilities of **sed**(1). If there is no *template*, the default is "**$m0$m1$m2$m3$m4$m5$m6$m7$m8$m9**".

EXAMPLES

To cut the 4th through 8th letters out of a string (this example will output **string**).

```
`regex -v "my string is nice" '^.{3}(.{5})$0' '$m0'`
```

In a form, to validate input to field 5 as an integer:

```
valid=`regex -v "$F5" '^[0-9]+$'`
```

In a form, to translate an environment variable which contains one of the numbers **1**, **2**, **3**, **4**, **5** to the letters **a**, **b**, **c**, **d**, **e**:

```
value=`regex -v "$VAR1" 1 a 2 b 3 c 4 d 5 e '.*' 'Error'`
```

Note the use of the pattern **'.*'** to mean "anything else."

In the example below, all three lines constitute a single backquoted expression. This expression, by itself, could be put in a menu definition file. Since backquoted expressions are expanded as they are parsed, and output from a backquoted expression (the **cat** command, in this example) becomes part of the definition file being parsed, this expression would read **/etc/passwd** and make a dynamic menu of all the login ids on the system.

```
`cat /etc/passwd | regex '^([^:]*)$0.*$' '
name=$m0
action=`message "$m0 is a user"`'`
```

NOTES

Patterns and templates must often be enclosed in single quotes to turn off the special meanings of characters. Especially if you use the **$m0** through **$m9** variables in the template, since FMLI will expand the variables (usually to "") before **regex** even sees them.

Single characters in character classes (inside **[ ]**) must be listed before character ranges, otherwise they will not be recognized. For example, **[a-zA-Z_/]** will not find underscores (_) or slashes (/), but **[_/a-zA-Z]** will.

The regular expressions accepted by **regcmp** differ slightly from other utilities (that is, **sed**, **grep**, **awk**, **ed**, and so on).

regex with the **-e** option forces subsequent commands to be ignored. In other words if a backquoted statement appears as follows:

```
`regex -e ...; command1; command2`
```

command1 and *command2* would never be executed. However, dividing the expression into two:

```
`regex -e ...``command1; command2`
```

would yield the desired result.

SEE ALSO

awk(1), **cut**(1), **grep**(1), **paste**(1), **sed**(1)

regcmp(3G)

reinit (1F)

NAME

reinit – runs an initialization file

SYNOPSIS

reinit *file*

DESCRIPTION

The **reinit** command is used to change the values of descriptors defined in the initialization file that was named when **fmli** was invoked and/or define additional descriptors. FMLI will parse and evaluate the descriptors in *file*, and then continue running the current application. The argument *file* must be the name of a valid FMLI initialization file.

The **reinit** command does not re-display the introductory frame or change the layout of screen labels for function keys.

NAME

removef – remove a file from software database

SYNOPSIS

removef *pkginst path1* [*path2* . . .]

removef *pkginst* -

removef -f *pkginst*

DESCRIPTION

removef informs the system that the user, or software, intends to remove a pathname. Output from **removef** is the list of input pathnames that may be safely removed (no other packages have a dependency on them).

When the second synopsis is used, the pathname descriptions will be read from standard input. These descriptions are the same as would be given in the first synopsis, but the information is given in the form of a list.

After all files have been processed, **removef** should be invoked with the **-f** option to indicate the removal phase is complete.

pkginst Name of package instance with which the pathname should be associated.

-f Indicates the removal phase is complete. This option is used with **removef** when all files have been processed.

EXAMPLE

The following shows the use of **removef** in an optional post-install script:

```
echo "The following files are no longer part of this package \
      and are being removed."
removef $PKGINST /dev/xt[0-9][0-9][0-9] |
while read pathname
do
      echo "$pathname"
      rm -f $pathname
done
removef -f $PKGINST || exit 2
```

NOTES

Using multiple invocations is discouraged if standard input style invocations can be used with a list of files. This will be much faster because the **contents** file must be searched for each entry.

SEE ALSO

compver(4), **copyright**(4), **depend**(4), **installf**(1M), **pkgadd**(1M), **pkgask**(1M), **pkgchk**(1M), **pkginfo**(1), **pkginfo**(4), **pkgmap**(4), **pkgmk**(1), **pkgproto**(1), **pkgtrans**(1), **space**(4)

rename (1)

NAME

rename – change the name of a file

SYNOPSIS

rename *old new*

DESCRIPTION

rename renames a file. *old* is the pathname of the file or directory to be renamed. *new* is the new pathname of the file or directory. Both *old* and *new* must be of the same type (either both files, or both directories) and must reside on the same file system.

If *new* already exists, it is removed. Thus, if *new* names an existing directory, the directory must not have any entries other than, possibly, "**.**" and "**..**". When renaming directories, the *new* pathname must not name a descendant of *old*. The implementation of **rename** ensures that upon successful completion a link named *new* will always exist.

If the final component of *old* is a symbolic link, the symbolic link is renamed, not the file or directory to which it points.

Write permission is required for both the directory containing *old* and the directory containing *new*.

NOTES

The system can deadlock if there is a loop in the file system graph. Such a loop takes the form of an entry in directory *a*, say *a/foo*, being a hard link to directory *b*, and an entry in directory *b*, say *b/bar*, being a hard link to directory *a*. When such a loop exists and two separate processes attempt to perform **rename** *a/foo b/bar* and **rename** *b/bar a/foo*, respectively, the system may deadlock attempting to lock both directories for modification. The system administrator should replace hard links to directories by symbolic links.

SEE ALSO

link(2), **rename**(2), **unlink**(2)

NAME

renice – (BSD) alter priority of running processes

SYNOPSIS

/usr/ucb/renice *priority pid* ...

/usr/ucb/renice *priority* [**-p** *pid* ...] [**-g** *pgrp* ...] [**-u** *username* ...]

DESCRIPTION

The **renice** command alters the scheduling priority of one or more running processes. By default, the processes to be affected are specified by their process IDs. *priority* is the new priority value.

The following options are available:

-p *pid* ... Specify a list of process IDs.

-g *pgrp* ... Specify a list of process group IDs. The processes in the specified process groups have their scheduling priority altered.

-u *user* ... Specify a list of user IDs or usernames. All processes owned by each *user* have their scheduling altered.

Users other than the privileged user may only alter the priority of processes they own, and can only monotonically increase their nice value within the range 0 to 20. This prevents overriding administrative fiats. The privileged user may alter the priority of any process and set the priority to any value in the range –20 to 20. Useful priorities are: 19 (the affected processes will run only when nothing else in the system wants to), 0 (the base scheduling priority) and any negative value (to make things go very fast).

If only the priority is specified, the current process (alternatively, process group or user) is used.

FILES

/etc/passwd map user names to user ID's

SEE ALSO

priocntl(1)

NOTES

If you make the priority very negative, then the process cannot be interrupted.

To regain control you must make the priority greater than zero.

Users other than the privileged user cannot increase scheduling priorities of their own processes, even if they were the ones that decreased the priorities in the first place.

The **priocntl** command subsumes the function of **renice**.

reportscheme (1M)

NAME

reportscheme – give authentication scheme information to client applications

SYNOPSIS

`reportscheme [-d]`

DESCRIPTION

/usr/sbin/reportscheme is a non-standing network service that tells client machine applications what authentication scheme to use for a specified network service. The **reportscheme** service must exist on each port monitor that offers network services if the server wishes to enforce authentication scheme invocation.

The Connection Server invokes the **reportscheme** service on the server machine on behalf of client applications and sends the name of the requested network service to be executed. On the server side, **reportscheme** receives the name of the network service, searches the current transport's **_pmtab** database and finds the first entry for the specified network service. If the service is not listed in the **_pmtab** file, **reportscheme** returns an error. The Connection Server will then fail the connection request for the network service over the current transport. If the service is found in the **_pmtab** file but no authentication information is listed a NULL authentication scheme is assumed.

reportscheme returns the following information:

- the name of the authentication scheme for the requested network service on the current port monitor
- an indication of whether the network service will invoke the authentication scheme as the imposer or the responder

Since **reportscheme** is used to report authentication schemes, there can be no authentication scheme associated with **reportscheme** itself. If there were, client machines would not be able to invoke the **reportscheme** service.

OPTIONS

-d is a debugging option. All debugging information is written to **/var/adm/log/cs.debug**. The debugging information related to **reportscheme** begins with an **rs:** tag.

EXAMPLES

The following is a **reportscheme** entry from a sample **_pmtab** file. **reportscheme** itself may not have an authentication scheme name in the *scheme* field of the **_pmtab** file, that is, it is always executed with a NULL authentication scheme. A line similar to this must appear in the **_pmtab** file of every port monitor that the Connection Server expects to connect to. If the **reportscheme** service is not entered in a port monitor's **_pmtab** file, a NULL authentication scheme is assumed for all services under that port monitor. The following represents a single, one-line entry in the **_pmtab** file; it is broken here so that it can be printed on the page.

```
reportscheme::root:reserved:reserved::\x00020b02c00b6c180000000000000000
   /usr/sbin/reportscheme#
```

FILES

/usr/sbin/reportscheme
/etc/saf/*pmtag***/_pmtab**

SEE ALSO

`cs_connect`(3N), `dial`(3N)

repquota (1M)

NAME

repquota – summarize quotas for a **ufs** file system

SYNOPSIS

repquota [**-v**] *filesystem* . . .
repquota -a [**-v**]

DESCRIPTION

repquota prints a summary of the disk usage and quotas for the specified file systems. For each user the current number of files and amount of space (in kilobytes) is printed, along with any quotas created with **edquota**.

An error message is returned if you run **repquota** on a filesystem that does not have a **quotas** file in the root directory.

The options are:

-a Report on all file systems that have "rq" in the **mntopts** field of the **/etc/vfstab** file.

-v Report all quotas, even if there is no usage.

Only privileged users may view quotas which are not their own.

SEE ALSO

edquota(1M), **quota**(1M), **quotacheck**(1M), **quotaon**(1M)

NAME

`reset` – reset the current form field to its default values

SYNOPSIS

`reset`

DESCRIPTION

The **`reset`** function causes the **`value`** descriptor of the current field to be re-evaluated, restoring the default value of the field if the current value is different. The descriptor is re-evaluated even if it has been modified by **`const`**.

resize (1)

NAME

`resize` - utility to set terminal settings to current window size

SYNOPSIS

`resize` [-uc] [-s [*row col*]]

DESCRIPTION

The **resize** command prints a shell command for setting the **TERM** and **TERMCAP** environment variables to indicate the current size of **xterm** window from which the command is run. For this output to take effect, **resize** must either be evaluated as part of the command line (usually done with a shell alias or function) or else redirected to a file which can then be read in. From the C shell (usually known as **/bin/csh**), the following alias could be defined in the user's **.cshrc**:

```
% alias rs 'set noglob; 'eval resize''
```

After resizing the window, the user would type:

```
% rs
```

Users of versions of the Bourne shell (usually known as **/bin/sh**) that don't have command functions will need to send the output to a temporary file and the read it back in with the "**.**" command:

```
$ resize >/tmp/out $  . /tmp/out
```

OptionS

The following options may be used with **resize**:

- `-u` generate Bourne shell commands even if the user's current shell isn't **/bin/sh**
- `-c` generate C shell commands even if the user's current shell isn't **/bin/csh**

Files

`/etc/termcap`	for the base termcap entry to modify
`/.cshrc`	user's alias for the command

SEE ALSO

csh(1), **tset**(1), **xterm**(1)

NOTES

Portions of the page are derived from material which is copyright Massachusetts Institute of Technology.

NAME

restore – initiate restores of file systems, data partitions, or disks

SYNOPSIS

restore -P [**-mn**] [**-s**|**v**] [**-o** *target*] [**-d** *date*] *partdev* . . .

restore -A [**-mn**] [**-s**|**v**] [**-o** *target*] [**-d** *date*] *diskdev* . . .

restore -S [**-mn**] [**-s**|**v**] [**-o** *target*] [**-d** *date*] *fsdev* . . .

restore [**-w**] [**-i**] [**-O**] [**-T**] [**-W** *device* | [*pattern*[*pattern*] . . .]

DESCRIPTION

Two restore facilities are delivered with UNIX System V Release 4.2: the basic version and the extended version. A basic **restore** command (providing five options) is delivered in the Foundation Set. It provides a facility that is adequate for most small machines and machines with a minimal amount of software installed. If you install the Extended Backup and Restore Package, however, you'll have access to the extended **restore** command. This section describes the options available with both facilities.

Although many options cannot be run unless a user has privileges to do so, some options to the basic **restore** command can be executed by any user without special privileges.

The Extended Restore Facility

restore posts requests for the restore of a data partition, a file system partition, or a disk from most system-maintained archives. (The exception is any archive created by specifying **-m ffile** or **-m incfile** on the **backup** command line. To restore an archive created in this way, run the **urestore** command.) If the appropriate archive containing the required partition is online, the partition is restored immediately. If not, a request to restore the specified archive of the partition is posted to a restore status table. The restore status table is **/etc/bkup/rsstatus.tab**. The restore request is assigned a **restore** jobid that can be used to monitor the progress of the restore or to cancel it. A restore request that has been posted must later be resolved by an operator [see **rsoper**(1M)].

If **restore -A** *partdev* is issued, the **fdisk**(1M) (full disk recovery) method is used to repartition and repopulate disk *partdev*. *partdev* is the name of the device that refers to the entire disk. For example, the name might be **/dev/rdsk/***, where the value of * is machine specific.

Options Available with the Foundation Set

-w A complete restore. All files on the tape are restored.

-T Indicates that the tape device is to be used. Must be used with the **-d** option when restoring from tape.

-W *device* *device* is the device special pathname to be used. It defaults to **/dev/rdsk/f0**. A raw device must be used to do multi-volume restore operations.

-i Retrieve the index file.

-o Overwrite the existing file.

Options Available with Extended Backup/Restore

-d *date* Restores the partition as of *date*. This may or may not be the latest archive. See **getdate**(3C) for valid date formats.

-i Gets the index file off of the medium. This works only when the archive was created using **backup**. The output is a list of all the files on the medium. No files are actually restored.

-m If the restore cannot be carried out immediately, this option notifies the invoking user [via **mail**(1)] when the request has been completed.

-n Displays a list of all archived versions of the object contained in the backup history log, but does not attempt to restore the object.

-o *target* Instead of restoring directly to the specified object (*partdev* or *fsdev*), this option restores the archive to *target*. *target* is of the form:

[*oname*][**:***odev*]

where *oname* is the name of the file system to be restored to (for **-S** archives) and *odev* is the name of the partition to be restored to (for **-P** and **-A** archives). This option allows you to overwrite files. If the file being restored already exists, it will not be restored unless this option is specified.

-s While a restore operation is occurring, displays a "." for each 100 (512-byte) blocks transferred from the destination device.

-v Displays the name of each object as it is restored. Only those archiving methods that restore named directories and files (**incfile, ffile**) support this option.

-A Initiates restore of the entire disk.

-O Overwrite existing files. If the file being restored already exists it will not be restored unless this option is specified.

-P Initiates restore of the data partition.

-S Initiates restore of the file system partition.

DIAGNOSTICS

The exit codes for the extended **restore** command are as follows:

0 = the task completed successfully
1 = one or more parameters to **restore** are invalid
2 = an error has occurred, causing **restore** to fail to complete *all* portions of its task

EXAMPLES

The following examples show several uses of the extended **restore** command.

Example 1:

```
restore -S -m /usr
```

posts a request to restore the most current archived version of **/usr**. If the restore cannot be carried out immediately, notify the invoking user when the request has been completed.

Example 2:

```
restore -P -o /dev/rdsk/* /dev/rdsk/y
```

posts a request that the archived data partition **/dev/rdsk/***y* be restored to the target device partition **/dev/rdsk/***, where the value of * and *y* are machine specific.

Example 3:

```
restore -A -d "december 1, 1987" /dev/rdsk/*
```

posts a request for the restore of the entire disk **/dev/rdsk/***, where the value of * is machine specific. The restore should be made as of December 1, 1987.

Example 4:

```
restore -P -n /dev/rdsk/*
```

requests the system to display the backup date and an **ls -l** listing from the backup history log of all archived versions of the data partition **/dev/rdsk/***, where the value of * is machine specific. The data partition is not restored.

FILES

The following files are used by the extended **restore** command.

/etc/bkup/bkhist.tab	lists the labels of all volumes that have been used for backup operations
/etc/bkup/rsstatus.tab	lists the status of all restore requests from users
/etc/bkup/rsnotify.tab	lists the email address of the operator to be notified whenever restore requests require operator intervention

SEE ALSO

fdisk(1M), **getdate**(3C), **mail**(1), **rsoper**(1M), **urestore**(1M)

NAME

restore – (XENIX) restore file to original directory

SYNOPSIS

restore [-c] [-i] [-o] [-t] [-d *device*] | [*pattern* [*pattern*]. . .]

DESCRIPTION

- **-c** complete restore. All files on the tape are restored.
- **-i** gets the index file off of the medium. This only works when the archive was created using **backup**. The output is a list of all the files on the medium. No files are actually restored.
- **-o** overwrite existing files. If the file being restored already exists it will not be restored unless this option is specified.
- **-t** indicates that the tape device is to be used. Must be used with the **-d** option when restoring from tape.
- **-d** *device* is the raw device to be used. It defaults to **dev/SA/diskette**

When doing a restore, one or more patterns can be specified. These patterns are matched against the files on the tape. When a match is found, the file is restored. Since backups are done using full pathnames, the file is restored to its original directory. Metacharacters can be used to match multiple files. The patterns should be in quotes to prevent the characters from being expanded before they are passed to the command. If no patterns are specified, it defaults to restoring all files. If a pattern does not match any file on the tape, a message is printed.

When end of medium is reached, the user is prompted for the next media. The user can exit at this point by typing **q**. (This may cause files to be corrupted if a file happens to span a medium.) In general, quitting in the middle is not a good idea.

If the file already exists and an attempt is made to restore it without the **-o** option, the file name will be printed on the screen followed by a question mark. This file will not be retored.

In order for multi-volume restores to work correctly, the raw device must be used.

SEE ALSO

sh(1)

NAME

rexec – execute a service remotely through REXEC

SYNOPSIS

rexec *host service* [*parameters*]
rx *host command*
rl *host*
rquery *host*
service host [*parameters*]

DESCRIPTION

rexec is the REXEC command that allows the user on a client machine to execute a service on a remote host. A user on a client machine can utilize any service on the host, provided the user is authorized to access the service. Although any service can be installed, REXEC generally provides the following standard services:

rx A remote command execution service, which allows the user to execute any command (provided the user has appropriate permissions) on the remote host. Any arguments required by the remote command need to be specified on the **rx** command line.

rl A remote login service, which effectively logs the user into the remote host, bypassing the login/password sequence.

rquery A service that lets the user query a remote host for a list of services the user is allowed to execute.

The arguments to the REXEC commands have the following meanings:

host The name of the remote host on which the service is defined.

service The name of the service to be executed on the remote host.

parameters Service arguments (i.e., options or option operands).

command The command to be executed remotely, including applicable arguments.

When the REXEC software is installed on the client machine, the standard services are linked to the **rexec** command. Once linked, the user can execute a service by specifying the service name, followed by the host name and the parameters to the service.

The user on the client machine can pass environment variables to a service by setting the **RXPORT** variable. The **RXPORT** variable contains a comma-separated list of exported variables. Only exported variables from the user's environment can be passed to the specified service. If the **RXPORT** variable consists only of the special character *, then all exported variables on the local system are passed to the remote service. By default, the remote service environment includes the variables PATH and HOME.

EXAMPLES

If a user wants to see who is logged into the remote host **strider**, the following command can be used:

```
$ rexec strider rx who
```

If **rexec** is linked to **rx**, the user can execute the following:

```
$ rx strider who
```

If a user wants to execute the **vi**(1) command on the remote host **aslan**, passing the environment variables **TERM** and **EXINIT** to the server, the user can execute the following:

```
$ RXPORT=TERM,EXINIT rx aslan vi main.c
```

SEE ALSO

rxlist(1M), **rxservice**(1M), **rexecve**(3N)

NOTES

rexec requires that **tirdwr** has been pushed onto the stream. If it hasn't been, **rexec** will exit and log a message in **/usr/adm/log/rexec.log**. If **tirdwr** is already pushed on the stream, execution will continue.

NAME

rexecd – remote execution server

SYNOPSIS

in.rexecd *host.port*

DESCRIPTION

rexecd is the server for the **rexec**(3N) routine. The server provides remote execution facilities with authentication based on user names and encrypted passwords. It is invoked automatically as needed by **inetd**(1M), and then executes the following protocol:

1) The server reads characters from the socket up to a null (`\0`) byte. The resultant string is interpreted as an ASCII number, base 10.

2) If the number received in step 1 is non-zero, it is interpreted as the port number of a secondary stream to be used for the **stderr**. A second connection is then created to the specified port on the client's machine.

3) A null terminated user name of at most 16 characters is retrieved on the initial socket.

4) A null terminated, encrypted, password of at most 16 characters is retrieved on the initial socket.

5) A null terminated command to be passed to a shell is retrieved on the initial socket. The length of the command is limited by the upper bound on the size of the system's argument list.

6) **rexecd** then validates the user as is done at login time and, if the authentication was successful, changes to the user's home directory, and establishes the user and group protections of the user. If any of these steps fail the connection is aborted with a diagnostic message returned.

7) A null byte is returned on the connection associated with the **stderr** and the command line is passed to the normal login shell of the user. The shell inherits the network connections established by **rexecd**.

SEE ALSO

inetd(1M)

DIAGNOSTICS

All diagnostic messages are returned on the connection associated with the **stderr**, after which any network connections are closed. An error is indicated by a leading byte with a value of 1 (0 is returned in step 7 above upon successful completion of all the steps prior to the command execution).

username too long
The name is longer than 16 characters.

password too long
The password is longer than 16 characters.

command too long
The command line passed exceeds the size of the argument list (as configured into the system).

`Login incorrect.`
No password file entry for the user name existed.

`Password incorrect.`
The wrong password was supplied.

`No remote directory.`
The **`chdir`** command to the home directory failed.

`Try again.`
A **`fork`** by the server failed.

`/usr/bin/sh: ...`
The user's login shell could not be started.

NOTES

Indicating **`Login incorrect`** as opposed to **`Password incorrect`** is a security breach which allows people to probe a system for users with null passwords.

A facility to allow all data exchanges to be encrypted should be present.

NAME

rfadmin – Remote File Sharing domain administration

SYNOPSIS

rfadmin

rfadmin -a *hostname*

rfadmin -r *hostname*

rfadmin -p [–t *transport1,transport2,. . .*]

rfadmin -q

rfadmin -o *option*

DESCRIPTION

This command is obsolete and will not be supported after this release. **rfadmin** is used to add and remove hosts, and their associated authentication information, from a *domain*/**passwd** file on a Remote File Sharing primary domain name server. It is also used to transfer domain name server responsibilities from one machine to another. Used with no options, **rfadmin** returns the *hostname* of the current domain name server for the local domain on each of the transport providers that span the domain.

rfadmin can only be used to modify domain files on the primary domain name server (**-a** and **-r** options). If domain name server responsibilities are temporarily passed to a secondary domain name server, that computer can use the **-p** option to pass domain name server responsibility back to the primary. The command can be directed to a specific set of transport providers by using the **-t** option with a comma-separated list of transport providers. Any host can use **rfadmin** with no options to print information about the domain. Only a privileged user can use this command, except in the case when the **-q** option is used.

-a *hostname* Add a host to a domain that is served by this domain name server. *hostname* must be of the form *domain.nodename*. It creates an entry for *hostname* in the *domain*/**passwd** file and prompts for an initial authentication password; the password prompting process conforms with that of **passwd**(1).

-r *hostname* Remove a host, *hostname*, from its domain by removing it from the *domain*/**passwd file.**

-p Used to pass the domain name server responsibilities back to a primary or to a secondary name server.

-t *transport1, transport2. . .*
Select transport provider(s). The **-t** option is used only with the **-p** option.

-q Tells if RFS is running.

-o *option* Sets RFS system option. *option* is one of the following:

loopback Enable loop back facility. This allows a resource advertised by a computer to be mounted by the same computer. **loopback** is off by default.

noloopback	Turn off the loop back facility. **noloopback** is the default.
loopmode	Check if the loop back facility is on or off.

ERRORS

When used with the **-a** option, if *hostname* is not unique in the domain, an error message will be sent to standard error.

When used with the **-r** option, if (1) *hostname* does not exist in the domain, (2) *hostname* is defined as a domain name server, or (3) there are resources advertised by *hostname,* a warning message will be sent to standard error.

When used with the **-p** option to change the domain name server, if there are no backup name servers defined for *domain,* an error message will be sent to standard error.

FILES

/etc/rfs/auth.info/*domain***/passwd**
For each *domain*, this file is created on the primary, copied to all secondaries, and copied to all hosts that want to do password verification of hosts in the *domain*.

SEE ALSO

dname(1M), **mount**(1M), **passwd**(1), **rfstart**(1M), **rfstop**(1M)

NAME

rfpasswd – change Remote File Sharing host password

SYNOPSIS

rfpasswd

DESCRIPTION

This command is obsolete and will not be supported after this release. **rfpasswd** updates the Remote File Sharing authentication password for a host; processing of the new password follows the same criteria as **passwd**(1). The updated password is registered at the domain name server (**/etc/rfs/auth.info/***domain***/passwd**) and replaces the password stored at the local host (**/etc/rfs/**<*transport*>**/loc.passwd** file).

Only a privileged user can execute this command.

NOTE: If you change your host password, make sure that hosts that validate your password are notified of this change. To receive the new password, hosts must obtain a copy of the *domain*/**passwd** file from the domain's primary name server. If this is not done, attempts to mount remote resources may fail!

ERRORS

If

1. the old password entered from this command does not match the existing password for this machine,
2. the two new passwords entered from this command do not match,
3. the new password does not satisfy the security criteria in **passwd**(1),
4. the domain name server does not know about this machine, or
5. the command is not run by a privileged user,

an error message will be sent to standard error. Also, Remote File Sharing must be running on your host and your domain's primary name server. A new password cannot be logged if a secondary is acting as the domain name server.

FILES

/etc/rfs/auth.info/*domain***/passwd**
/etc/rfs/<*transport*>**/loc.passwd**

SEE ALSO

passwd(1), **rfadmin**(1M), **rfstart**(1M)

NAME

rfstart – start Remote File Sharing

SYNOPSIS

rfstart [-v] [-p *primary_addr*]

DESCRIPTION

This command is obsolete and will not be supported after this release. **rfstart** starts Remote File Sharing and defines an authentication level for incoming requests. [This command can only be used after the domain name server is set up and your computer's domain name and network specification have been defined using **dname**(1M).]

-v Specifies that verification of all clients is required in response to initial incoming mount requests; any host not in the file **/etc/rfs/auth.info/***domain*/passwd for the **domain** they belong to, will not be allowed to mount resources from your host. If **-v** is not specified, hosts named in *domain*/passwd will be verified. Other hosts will be allowed to connect without verification.

-p *primary_addr*
Indicates the primary domain name server for your domain. *primary_addr* can specify any of the following: the network address of the primary name server for a domain (*addr*); a list of address tuples when RFS is used over multiple transport providers (*transport1:addr1,transport2:addr2, . . .*). An example of each type of specification follows:

-p *addr*
-p *transport1:addr1,transport2:addr2, . . .*

If the **-p** option is not specified, the address of the domain name server is taken from the associated **rfmaster** files. The **-p** *addr* specification is valid only when one transport provider is being used. See the **rfmaster**(4) manual page for a description of the valid address syntax.

If the host password has not been set, **rfstart** will prompt for a password. The password prompting process must match the password entered for your machine at the primary domain name server (see **rfadmin**(1M)). If you remove the **loc.passwd** file or change domains, you will also have to reenter the password.

Also, when **rfstart** is run on a domain name server, entries in the **rfmaster**(4) file are syntactically validated.

Only a privileged user can execute this command.

ERRORS

If syntax errors are found when validating an **rfmaster**(4) file, a warning describing each error will be sent to standard error.

An error message will be sent to standard error if any of the following conditions are true:

1. remote file sharing is already running
2. there is no communications network
3. a domain name server cannot be found
4. a domain name server does not recognize the machine
5. the command is run by an unprivileged user

Remote file sharing will not start if a host password in **/etc/rfs/**<*transport*>**/loc.passwd** is corrupted. If you suspect this has happened, remove the file and run **rfstart** again to reenter your password.

NOTE: **rfstart** will not fail if your host password does not match the password on the domain name server. You will simply receive a warning message. However, if you try to mount a resource from the primary, or any other host that validates your password, the mount will fail if your password does not match the one that the host has listed for your machine.

FILES

/etc/rfs/<*transport*>**/rfmaster**
/etc/rfs/<*transport*>**/loc.passwd**

SEE ALSO

dname(1M), **idload**(1M), **mount**(1M), **rfadmin**(1M), **rfmaster**(4) **rfstop**(1M), **share**(1M), **uname**(1), **unshare**(1M)

NOTES

You must run **idload**(1M) to put any non-default user and group mappings into place.

For RFS to work properly, the nodename of a system can be no longer than 8 characters and each nodename in a domain must be different. Valid characters consist of upper and lower case letters, digits, hyphens (–), and underscores (_). To set the nodename of your system, see **uname**(1).

rfstop (1M)

NAME

rfstop – stop the Remote File Sharing environment

SYNOPSIS

rfstop

DESCRIPTION

This command is obsolete and will not be supported after this release. **rfstop** disconnects a host from the Remote File Sharing environment until another **rfstart**(1M) is executed.

When executed on the domain name server, the domain name server responsibility is moved to a secondary name server as designated in the **rfmaster**(4) file. If there is no designated secondary name server **rfstop** will issue a warning message, Remote File Sharing will be stopped, and name service will no longer be available to the domain.

Only a privileged user can execute this command.

ERRORS

If

1. there are resources currently advertised by this host,
2. resources from this machine are still remotely mounted by other hosts,
3. there are still remotely mounted resources in the local file system tree,
4. **rfstart**(1M) had not previously been executed, or
5. the command is run by an unprivileged user,

an error message will be sent to standard error and Remote File Sharing will not be stopped.

SEE ALSO

mount(1M), **rfadmin**(1M), **rfstart**(1M), **rfmaster**(4), **RFS**-specific **share**(1M), **RFS**-specific **unshare**(1M)

NAME

rfuadmin – Remote File Sharing notification shell script

SYNOPSIS

/etc/rfs/rfuadmin *message remote_resource* [*seconds*]

DESCRIPTION

This command is obsolete and will not be supported after this release. The **rfuadmin** administrative shell script responds to unexpected Remote File Sharing events, such as broken network connections and forced unmounts, picked up by the **rfudaemon** process. This command is not intended to be run directly from the shell.

The response to messages received by **rfudaemon** can be tailored to suit the particular system by editing the **rfuadmin** script. The following paragraphs describe the arguments passed to **rfuadmin** and the responses. **rfuadmin** processes supplementary code set characters in *message* according to the locale specified in the **LC_CTYPE** environment variable [see **LANG** on **environ**(5)].

disconnect *remote_resource*

A link to a remote resource has been cut. **rfudaemon** executes **rfuadmin**, passing it the message **disconnect** and the name of the disconnected resource. **rfuadmin** sends this message to all terminals using **wall**(1M):

Remote_resource **has been disconnected from the system.**

Then it executes **fuser**(1M) to kill all processes using the resource, unmounts the resource [for **umount**, see **mount**(1M)] to clean up the kernel, and starts **rmount** to try to remount the resource.

fumount *remote_resource*

A remote server machine has forced an unmount of a resource a local machine has mounted. The processing is similar to processing for a disconnect.

fuwarn *remote_resource seconds*

This message notifies **rfuadmin** that a resource is about to be unmounted. **rfudaemon** sends this script the **fuwarn** message, the resource name, and the number of seconds in which the forced unmount will occur. **rfuadmin** sends this message to all terminals:

Remote_resource **is being removed from the system in** # **seconds.**

SEE ALSO

fumount(1M), **rfstart**(1M), **rfudaemon**(1M), **rmount**(1M), **wall**(1M)

NOTES

The console must be on when Remote File Sharing is running. If it's not, **rfuadmin** will hang when it tries to write to the console (**wall**) and recovery from disconnected resources will not complete.

NAME

rfudaemon – Remote File Sharing daemon process

SYNOPSIS

/etc/rfs/rfudaemon

DESCRIPTION

This command is obsolete and will not be supported after this release. The **rfudaemon** command is started automatically by **rfstart**(1M) and runs as a daemon process as long as Remote File Sharing is active. Its function is to listen for unexpected events, such as broken network connections and forced unmounts, and execute appropriate administrative procedures.

When such an event occurs, **rfudaemon** executes the administrative shell script **rfuadmin**, with arguments that identify the event. This command is not intended to be run from the shell. Here are the events:

RFUD_DISCONNECT
: A link to a remote resource has been cut. **rfudaemon** executes **rfuadmin**, with two arguments: **disconnect** and the name of the disconnected resource.

RFUD_FUMOUNT
: A remote server machine has forced an unmount of a resource a local machine has mounted. **rfudaemon** executes **rfuadmin**, with two arguments: **fumount** and the name of the disconnected resource.

RFUD_GETUMSG
: A remote user-level program has sent a message to the local **rfudaemon**. Currently the only message sent is *fuwarn*, which notifies **rfuadmin** that a resource is about to be unmounted. It sends **rfuadmin** the *fuwarn*, the resource name, and the number of seconds in which the forced unmount will occur.

RFUD_LASTUMSG
: The local machine wants to stop the **rfudaemon** [**rfstop**(1M)]. This causes **rfudaemon** to exit.

SEE ALSO

rfstart(1M), **rfuadmin**(1M)

NAME

rlogin – remote login

SYNOPSIS

rlogin [**-L**] [**-8**] [**-e***x*] [**-l** *username*] *hostname*

DESCRIPTION

rlogin establishes a remote login session from your terminal to the remote machine named *hostname*.

Hostnames are listed in the *hosts* database, which may be contained in the **/etc/hosts** file, the Internet domain name server, or in both. Each host has one official name (the first name in the database entry), and optionally one or more nicknames. Either official hostnames or nicknames may be specified in *hostname.*

Each remote machine may have a file named **/etc/hosts.equiv** containing a list of trusted hostnames with which it shares usernames. Users with the same username on both the local and remote machine may **rlogin** from the machines listed in the remote machine's **/etc/hosts.equiv** file without supplying a password. Individual users may set up a similar private equivalence list with the file **.rhosts** in their home directories. Each line in this file contains two names: a *hostname* and a *username* separated by a space. An entry in a remote user's **.rhosts** file permits the user named *username* who is logged into *hostname* to log in to the remote machine as the remote user without supplying a password. If the name of the local host is not found in the **/etc/hosts.equiv** file on the remote machine, and the local username and hostname are not found in the remote user's **.rhosts** file, then the remote machine will prompt for a password. Hostnames listed in **/etc/hosts.equiv** and **.rhosts** files must be the official hostnames listed in the hosts database; nicknames may not be used in either of these files.

To counter security problems, the **.rhosts** file must be owned by either the remote user or by root.

The remote terminal type is the same as your local terminal type (as given in your environment **TERM** variable). The terminal or window size is also copied to the remote system if the server supports the option, and changes in size are reflected as well. All echoing takes place at the remote site, so that (except for delays) the remote login is transparent. Flow control using **CTRL-S** and **CTRL-Q** and flushing of input and output on interrupts are handled properly.

The following options are available:

-L Allow the **rlogin** session to be run in litout mode.

-8 Pass eight-bit data across the net instead of seven-bit data.

-e*x* Specify a different escape character, *c*, for the line used to disconnect from the remote host.

-l *username*
Specify a different *username* for the remote login. If you do not use this option, the remote username used is the same as your local username.

Escape Sequences

Lines that you type which start with the tilde character are escape sequences (the escape character can be changed using the **-e** options):

~. Disconnect from the remote host — this is not the same as a logout, because the local host breaks the connection with no warning to the remote end.

susp Suspend the login session (only if you are using a shell with Job Control). **susp** is your suspend character, usually see **tty**(1).

FILES

/etc/passwd	
/usr/hosts/*	for *hostname* version of the command
/etc/hosts.equiv	list of trusted hostnames with shared usernames
$HOME/.rhosts	private list of trusted hostname/username combinations

SEE ALSO

rsh(1), **stty**(1), **tty**(1), **named**(1M), **hosts**(4), **hosts.equiv**(4)

NOTES

When a system is listed in **hosts.equiv**, its security must be as good as local security. One insecure system listed in **hosts.equiv** can compromise the security of the entire system.

When a line of the form *hostname username* appears in **hosts.equiv**, the user named may log in as anyone in the local password file by using the command

rlogin -l *username hostname*

where *username* is any valid username in the **passwd** file.

This implementation can only use the TCP network service.

NAME

rlogind – remote login server

SYNOPSIS

in.rlogind

DESCRIPTION

rlogind is the server for the **rlogin**(1) program. The server provides a remote login facility with authentication based on privileged port numbers.

rlogind is invoked by **inetd**(1M) when a remote login connection is established, and executes the following protocol:

1. The server checks the remote client's source port. If the port is not in the range 0-1023, the server aborts the connection.
2. The server checks the remote client's source address. If an entry for the client exists in both **/etc/hosts** and **/etc/hosts.equiv**, a user logging in from the client is not prompted for a password. If the address is associated with a host for which no corresponding entry exists in **/etc/hosts**, the user is prompted for a password, regardless of whether or not an entry for the remote client is present in **/etc/hosts.equiv** [see **hosts**(4) and **hosts.equiv**(4)].

Once the source port and address have been checked, **rlogind** allocates a pseudo-terminal and manipulates file descriptors so that the slave half of the pseudo-terminal becomes the **stdin**, **stdout**, and **stderr** for a login process.

The login process is an instance of the **in.login** program, which is based on **login**(1). The login process is invoked with the **-R** option to indicate that it is originated by **rlogind**. The login process proceeds with the authentication process as described in **rshd**(1M), but if automatic authentication fails, it reprompts the user to login as one finds on a standard terminal line.

rlogind manipulates the master side of the pseudo-terminal, operating as an intermediary between the login process and the remote client's **rlogin** program. In normal operation, a packet protocol is invoked to provide **Ctrl-S** / **Ctrl-Q** type facilities and propagate interrupt signals to the remote programs. The login process propagates the client terminal's baud rate and terminal type, as found in the environment variable, **TERM**; see **environ**(4).

SEE ALSO

inetd(1M), **hosts**(4), **hosts.equiv**(4)

DIAGNOSTICS

All diagnostic messages are returned on the connection associated with the **stderr**, after which any network connections are closed. An error is indicated by a leading byte with a value of 1.

Hostname for your address unknown.

No entry in the host name database existed for the client's machine.

Try again.

A *fork* by the server failed.

/usr/bin/sh: ...
The user's login shell could not be started.

NOTES

The authentication procedure used here assumes the integrity of each client machine and the connecting medium. This is insecure, but is useful in an "open" environment.

A facility to allow all data exchanges to be encrypted should be present.

NAME

rm, **rmdir** – remove files or directories

SYNOPSIS

rm [**-f**] [**-i**] *file* ...

rm -r [**-f**] [**-i**] **dirname** . . . [*file* . . .]

rmdir [**-p**] [**-s**] **dirname** . . .

DESCRIPTION

rm removes the entries for one or more files from a directory. If a file has no write permission and the standard input is a terminal, the full set of permissions (in octal) for the file are printed followed by a question mark. This is a prompt for confirmation. If the answer begins with **y** (for yes), the file is deleted, otherwise the file remains.

If *file* is a symbolic link, the link will be removed, but the file or directory to which it refers will not be deleted. A user does not need write permission on a symbolic link to remove it, provided they have write permissions in the directory.

Note that if the standard input is not a terminal, the command will operate as if the **-f** option is in effect.

Three options apply to **rm**:

-f This option causes the removal of all files (whether write-protected or not) in a directory without prompting the user. In a write-protected directory, however, files are never removed (whatever their permissions are), but no messages are displayed. If the removal of a write-protected directory is attempted, this option will not suppress an error message.

-r This option causes the recursive removal of any directories and subdirectories in the argument list. The directory will be emptied of files and removed. Note that the user is normally prompted for removal of any write-protected files which the directory contains. The write-protected files are removed without prompting, however, if the **-f** option is used, or if the standard input is not a terminal and the **-i** option is not used.

Symbolic links that are encountered with this option will not be traversed.

If the removal of a non-empty, write-protected directory is attempted, the command will always fail (even if the **-f** option is used), resulting in an error message.

-i With this option, confirmation of removal of any file occurs interactively, regardless of whether the file is write-protected. It overrides the **-f** option and remains in effect even if the standard input is not a terminal.

Two options apply to **rmdir**:

-p This option allows users to remove the directory *dirname* and its parent directories which become empty. A message is printed on standard output about whether the whole path is removed or part of the path remains for some reason.

-s This option is used to suppress the message printed on standard error when **-p** is in effect.

FILES

/usr/lib/locale/*locale***/LC_MESSAGES/uxcore.abi**
language-specific message file [See **LANG** on **environ** (5).]

SEE ALSO

rmdir(2), **unlink**(2)

DIAGNOSTICS

All messages are generally self-explanatory.

It is forbidden to remove the files "**.**" and "**..**" in order to avoid the consequences of inadvertently doing something like the following:

```
rm -r .*
```

Both **rm** and **rmdir** return exit codes of 0 if all the specified directories are removed successfully. Otherwise, they return a non-zero exit code.

NOTES

A **--** permits the user to mark explicitly the end of any command line options, allowing **rm** to recognize filename arguments that begin with a **-**. As an aid to BSD migration, **rm** will accept **-** as a synonym for **--**. This migration aid may disappear in a future release. If a **--** and a **-** both appear on the same command line, the second will be interpreted as a filename.

NAME

rmdel – remove a delta from an SCCS file

SYNOPSIS

rmdel -r*SID file* . . .

DESCRIPTION

rmdel removes the delta specified by the *SID* (SCCS identification string) from each named SCCS *file*. The delta to be removed must be the newest (most recent) delta in its branch in the delta chain of each named SCCS *file*. In addition, the delta specified must not be that of a version being edited for the purpose of making a delta; that is, if a **p.***file* exists for the named SCCS file [see **get**(1)], the delta specified must not appear in any entry of the **p.***file*.

The **-r** option specifies the *SID* level of the delta to be removed.

If a directory is named, **rmdel** behaves as though each file in the directory were specified as a named file, except that non-SCCS files (last component of the path name does not begin with **s.**) and unreadable files are silently ignored. If a name of **-** is given, the standard input is read; each line of the standard input is taken to be the name of an SCCS file to be processed; non-SCCS files and unreadable files are silently ignored.

The rules governing the removal of a delta are as follows: if you make a delta and have appropriate file permissions, you can remove it; if you own the file and directory in which a new delta file resides, you can remove the delta.

FILES

x.*file* [See **delta**(1)]
z.*file* [See **delta**(1)]

SEE ALSO

delta(1), **get**(1), **help**(1), **prs**(1), **sccsfile**(4)

DIAGNOSTICS

Use **help**(1) for explanations.

rmntstat (1M)

NAME

rmntstat – display mounted resource information

SYNOPSIS

rmntstat [**-h**] [*resource*]

DESCRIPTION

This command is obsolete and will not be supported after this release. When used with no options, **rmntstat** displays a list of all local Remote File Sharing resources that are remotely mounted, the local path name, and the corresponding clients. **rmntstat** returns the remote mount data regardless of whether a resource is currently advertised; this ensures that resources that have been unadvertised but are still remotely mounted are included in the report. When a *resource* is specified, **rmntstat** displays the remote mount information only for that resource. The **-h** option causes header information to be omitted from the display.

Only a privileged user can execute this command.

EXIT STATUS

If no local resources are remotely mounted, **rmntstat** will return a successful exit status.

ERRORS

If *resource*

1. does not physically reside on the local machine or
2. is an invalid resource name,

an error message will be sent to standard error.

SEE ALSO

mount(1M), **fumount**(1M), **RFS**-specific **unshare**(1M)

NAME

rmnttry – attempt to mount queued remote resources

SYNOPSIS

/etc/rfs/rmnttry [*resource* . . .]

DESCRIPTION

This command is obsolete and will not be supported after this release. **rmnttry** sequences through the pending mount requests stored in **/etc/rfs/rmnttab**, trying to mount each resource. If a mount succeeds, the resource entry is removed from the **/etc/rfs/rmnttab** file.

If one or more resource names are supplied, mounts are attempted only for those resources, rather than for all pending mounts. Mounts are not attempted for resources not present in the **/etc/rfs/rmnttab** file (see **rmount**(1M)). If a mount invoked from **rmnttry** takes over 3 minutes to complete, **rmnttry** aborts the mount and issues a warning message.

rmnttry is typically invoked from a cron entry in **/var/spool/cron/crontabs/root** to attempt mounting queued resources at periodic intervals. The default strategy is to attempt mounts at 15 minute intervals. The cron entry for this is:

```
10,25,40,55 * * * * $TFADMIN /etc/rfs/rmnttry >/dev/null
```

Only a privileged user can execute this command.

FILES

/etc/rfs/rmnttab pending mount requests

SEE ALSO

crontab(1), **mnttab**(4), **mount**(1M), **rmount**(1M), **rumount**(1M)

DIAGNOSTICS

An exit code of 0 is returned if all requested mounts succeeded, 1 is returned if one or more mounts failed, and 2 is returned for bad usage.

NAME

rmount – queue remote resource mounts

SYNOPSIS

/usr/sbin/rmount [-F rfs] [-dcr] [-o *specific_options*]
resource directory

DESCRIPTION

This command is obsolete and will not be supported after this release. **rmount** queues a remote resource for mounting. The command enters the resource request into the **/etc/rfs/rmnttab** file. The file's format is identical to **mnttab**(4). **rmnttry**(1M) is used to poll entries in this file.

Any user can execute **rmount** without arguments; **rmount** prints a list of resources with pending mounts along with their destined directories, modes, and date of request. The resources are listed chronologically, with the oldest resource request appearing first.

Only a privileged user can execute **rmount** with the following options:

-F rfs Specifies **rfs** as the file system type.

-d Indicates that the resource is a remote resource to be mounted on directory.

-c Disable client caching. This is the same as **-o nocaching**.

-r *resource* is to be mounted read-only. If the *resource* is write-protected, this flag or the **-o ro** specific option must be used.

-o Specify the **rfs** file system specific options in a comma-separated list. The available options are:

- **nocaching** Disable client caching.
- **rw|ro** *resource* is to be mounted read/write or read-only. The default is read/write.
- **suid|nosuid** Set-uid bits are to be obeyed or ignored, respectively, on execution. The default is **nosuid**.

  Note that mounting a resource from an untrusted server introduces possible security risks. While the use of **nosuid** protects against some risks, it is not completely effective. The best defense against such security risks is to avoid such mounts.

FILES

/etc/rfs/rmnttab pending mount requests

SEE ALSO

mount(1M), **rmnttry**(1M), **rumount**(1M), **rmountall**(1M), **mnttab**(4)

DIAGNOSTICS

An exit code of 0 is returned upon successful completion of **rmount**. Otherwise, a non-zero value is returned.

NAME

rmountall, **rumountall** – mount, unmount Remote File Sharing resources

SYNOPSIS

/usr/sbin/rmountall [–] "*file-system-table*" [. . .]
/usr/sbin/rumountall [-k]

DESCRIPTION

This command is obsolete and will not be supported after this release. **rmountall** is a Remote File Sharing command used to mount remote resources according to a *file-system-table*. (**/etc/vfstab** is the recommended *file-system-table*.) **rmountall** also invokes the **rmnttry** command, which attempts to mount queued resources. The special file name "**-**" reads from the standard input.

rumountall causes all mounted remote resources to be unmounted and deletes all resources that were queued from **rmount**. The **-k** option sends a **SIGKILL** signal, via **fuser**, to processes that have files open.

Only a privileged user can execute these commands.

The format of the *file-system-table* is as follows:

column 1	block special file name of file system
column 2	file system name for **fsck** (ignored)
column 3	mount-point directory
column 4	file system type (must be **rfs**)
column 5	file system check option (ignored)
column 6	automount option (must be **yes**)
column 7	mount flags (**ro** for read-only, **rw** for read-write, – for read-write)

Columns are separated by white space. Lines beginning with a pound sign (**#**) are comments. Empty lines are ignored.

SEE ALSO

fuser(1M), **mount**(1M), **rfstart**(1M), **rmnttry**(1M), **rmount**(1M), **signal**(2), **sysadm**(1M)

DIAGNOSTICS

No messages are printed if the remote resources are mounted successfully.

Error and warning messages come from **mount**(1M).

NAME

roffbib – (BSD) format and print a bibliographic database

SYNOPSIS

/usr/ucb/roffbib [**-e**] [**-h**] [**-Q**] [**-x**] [**-m** *name*] [**-n***p*] [**-o***list*] [**-r***aN*] [**-s***N*] [**-T***term*] [*file*] . . .

DESCRIPTION

The **roffbib** command prints out all records in a bibliographic database, in bibliography format rather than as footnotes or endnotes. Generally it is used in conjunction with **sortbib**(1):

```
example% sortbib  database | roffbib
```

If abstracts or comments are entered following the **%X** field key, **roffbib** will format them into paragraphs for an annotated bibliography. Several **%X** fields may be given if several annotation paragraphs are desired.

roffbib accepts most options understood by **nroff**(1), as well as others defined below:

-e Produce equally-spaced words in adjusted lines using full terminal resolution.

-h Use output tabs during horizontal spacing to speed output and reduce output character count. TAB settings are assumed to be every 8 nominal character widths.

-Q Queue output for the phototypesetter. Page offset is set to 1 inch.

-x Suppress printing of abstracts.

-m *name* Prepend the macro file **/usr/ucblib/doctools/tmac/***name* to the input files. There should be a space between the **-m** and the macro filename. This set of macros will replace the ones defined in **/usr/ucblib/doctools/tmac/bib**.

-n*p* Number first generated page *p*.

-o*list* Print only page numbers that appear in the comma-separated *list* of numbers and ranges. A range *N*–*M* means pages *N* through *M*; an initial -*N* means from the beginning to page *N*; a final *N*– means from page *N* to end.

-r*aN* Set register *a* (one-character) to *N*. The command-line argument **-rN1** will number the references starting at 1.

Four command-line registers control formatting style of the bibliography, much like the number registers of **ms**(5). The flag **-rV2** will double space the bibliography, while **-rV1** will double space references but single space annotation paragraphs. The line length can be changed from the default 6.5 inches to 6 inches with the **-rL6i** argument, and the page offset can be set from the default of 0 to one inch by specifying **-rO1i** (capital O, not zero).

-s*N* Halt prior to every *N* pages for paper loading or changing (default *N* =1). To resume, enter NEWLINE or RETURN.

-T*term* Specify *term* as the terminal type.

FILES

/usr/ucblib/doctools/tmac/bib file of macros used by **nroff/troff**

SEE ALSO

addbib(1), **indxbib**(1), **lookbib**(1), **nroff**(1) **refer**(1), **sortbib**(1), **troff**(1)

NOTES

Users have to rewrite macros to create customized formats.

route(1M)

NAME

route – manually manipulate the routing tables

SYNOPSIS

route [**-fn**] { **add** | **delete** } { *destination* | **default** } [**host** | **net**] [*gateway* [*metric*]]

DESCRIPTION

route manually manipulates the network routing tables normally maintained by the system routing daemon, **routed**(1M), or through default routes and redirect messages from routers. **route** allows a privileged user to operate directly on the routing table for the specific host or network indicated by *destination*. **default** is available for gateways to use after all other routes have been attempted. The *gateway* argument, if present, indicates the network gateway to which packets should be addressed. The *metric* argument indicates the number of hops to the *destination*. The *metric* is required for *add* commands; it must be zero if the destination is on a directly-attached network, and nonzero if the route utilizes one or more gateways.

The **add** command instructs **route** to add a route to *destination*. **delete** deletes a route.

Routes to a particular host must be distinguished from those to a network. The optional keywords **net** and **host** force the destination to be interpreted as a network or a host, respectively. Otherwise, if the destination has a local address part of **INADDR_ANY**, then the route is assumed to be to a network; otherwise, it is presumed to be a route to a host. If the route is to a destination connected by a gateway, the *metric* parameter should be greater than 0. If adding a route with metric 0, the gateway given is the address of this host on the common network, indicating the interface to be used directly for transmission. All symbolic names specified for a *destination* (except **default**) or *gateway* are looked up in the hosts database using **gethostbyname**() [see **gethostent**(3N)]. If this lookup fails, then the name is looked up in the networks database using **getnetbyname**() [see **getnetent**(3N)].

netstat(1M) can be used to display available routes and the status each route in the routing table.

OPTIONS

-f Flush the routing tables of all gateway entries. If this is used in conjunction with one of the commands described above, **route** flushes the gateways before performing the command.

-n Prevents attempts to print host and network names symbolically when reporting actions. This is useful, for example, when all name servers are down on your local net, so you need a route before you can contact the name server.

FILES

/etc/hosts
/etc/networks

SEE ALSO

ioctl(2), **gethostent**(3N), **getnetent**(3N), **netstat**(1M), **routed**(1M), **routing**(4)

DIAGNOSTICS

add [**host** | **net**] *destination*:*gateway*

The specified route is being added to the tables. The values printed are from the routing table entry supplied in the `ioctl`(2) call.

delete [**host** | **net**] *destination*:*gateway*

The specified route is being deleted.

destination **done**

When the **-f** flag is specified, each routing table entry deleted is indicated with a message of this form.

Network is unreachable

An attempt to add a route failed because the gateway listed was not on a directly-connected network. Give the next-hop gateway instead.

not in table

A delete operation was attempted for an entry that is not in the table.

routing table overflow

An add operation was attempted, but the system was unable to allocate memory to create the new entry.

routed (1M)

NAME

routed – network routing daemon

SYNOPSIS

in.routed [**-qstv**] [*logfile*]

DESCRIPTION

routed is invoked at boot time to manage the network routing tables. The routing daemon uses a variant of the Xerox NS Routing Information Protocol in maintaining up to date kernel routing table entries.

In normal operation **routed** listens on **udp**(7) socket 520 (decimal) for routing information packets. If the host is an internetwork router, it periodically supplies copies of its routing tables to any directly connected hosts and networks.

When **routed** is started, it uses the **SIOCGIFCONF** **ioctl**(2) to find those directly connected interfaces configured into the system and marked up (the software loopback interface is ignored). If multiple interfaces are present, it is assumed the host will forward packets between networks. **routed** then transmits a *request* packet on each interface (using a broadcast packet if the interface supports it) and enters a loop, listening for *request* and *response* packets from other hosts.

When a *request* packet is received, **routed** formulates a reply based on the information maintained in its internal tables. The *response* packet generated contains a list of known routes, each marked with a hop count metric (a count of 16, or greater, is considered infinite). The metric associated with each route returned provides a metric relative to the sender.

request packets received by **routed** are used to update the routing tables if one of the following conditions is satisfied:

(1) No routing table entry exists for the destination network or host, and the metric indicates the destination is reachable (that is, the hop count is not infinite).

(2) The source host of the packet is the same as the router in the existing routing table entry. That is, updated information is being received from the very internetwork router through which packets for the destination are being routed.

(3) The existing entry in the routing table has not been updated for some time (defined to be 90 seconds) and the route is at least as cost effective as the current route.

(4) The new route describes a shorter route to the destination than the one currently stored in the routing tables; the metric of the new route is compared against the one stored in the table to decide this.

When an update is applied, **routed** records the change in its internal tables and generates a *response* packet to all directly connected hosts and networks. **routed** waits a short period of time (no more than 30 seconds) before modifying the kernel's routing tables to allow possible unstable situations to settle.

In addition to processing incoming packets, **routed** also periodically checks the routing table entries. If an entry has not been updated for 3 minutes, the entry's metric is set to infinity and marked for deletion. Deletions are delayed an additional 60 seconds to insure the invalidation is propagated throughout the internet.

Hosts acting as internetwork routers gratuitously supply their routing tables every 30 seconds to all directly connected hosts and networks.

Supplying the **-s** option forces **routed** to supply routing information whether it is acting as an internetwork router or not. The **-q** option is the opposite of the **-s** option. If the **-t** option is specified, all packets sent or received are printed on the standard output. In addition, **routed** will not divorce itself from the controlling terminal so that interrupts from the keyboard will kill the process. Any other argument supplied is interpreted as the name of file in which **routed**'s actions should be logged. This log contains information about any changes to the routing tables and a history of recent messages sent and received which are related to the changed route. The **-v** option allows a logfile to be created showing the changes made to the routing tables with a timestamp.

In addition to the facilities described above, **routed** supports the notion of distant *passive* and *active* gateways. When **routed** is started up, it reads the file **gateways** to find gateways which may not be identified using the **SIOGIFCONF ioctl**. Gateways specified in this manner should be marked passive if they are not expected to exchange routing information, while gateways marked active should be willing to exchange routing information (that is, they should have a **routed** process running on the machine). Passive gateways are maintained in the routing tables forever and information regarding their existence is included in any routing information transmitted. Active gateways are treated equally to network interfaces. Routing information is distributed to the gateway and if no routing information is received for a period of the time, the associated route is deleted.

The **gateways** is comprised of a series of lines, each in the following format:

< **net** | **host** > *filename1* **gateway** *filename2* **metric** *value* < **passive** | **active** >

The **net** or **host** keyword indicates if the route is to a network or specific host.

filename1 is the name of the destination network or host. This may be a symbolic name located in **networks** or **hosts**, or an Internet address specified in dot notation; see **inet**(3N).

filename2 is the name or address of the gateway to which messages should be forwarded.

value is a metric indicating the hop count to the destination host or network.

The keyword **passive** or **active** indicates if the gateway should be treated as passive or active (as described above).

FILES

`/etc/gateways`	for distant gateways
`/etc/networks`	
`/etc/hosts`	

SEE ALSO

ioctl(2), **inet**(7), **udp**(7)

NOTES

The kernel's routing tables may not correspond to those of **routed** for short periods of time while processes utilizing existing routes exit; the only remedy for this is to place the routing process in the kernel.

routed should listen to intelligent interfaces, such as an IMP, and to error protocols, such as ICMP, to gather more information.

NAME

rpcbind – universal addresses to RPC program number mapper

SYNOPSIS

rpcbind

DESCRIPTION

rpcbind is a server that converts RPC program numbers into universal addresses. It must be running to make RPC calls.

When an RPC service is started, it will tell **rpcbind** at what address it is listening, and what RPC program numbers it is prepared to serve. When a client wishes to make an RPC call to a given program number, it will first contact **rpcbind** on the server machine to determine the address where RPC packets should be sent.

Normally, standard RPC servers are started by port monitors, so **rpcbind** must be started before port monitors are invoked.

rpcbind is restricted to users with the **root** user ID.

NOTES

If **rpcbind** crashes, all RPC servers must be restarted.

WARNINGS

If the **rpcbind** daemon fails to start, the name of the machine may be different from that in the **/etc/net/*/hosts** files. This can occur if the machine name is changed with the **uname**(1) command.

To see if **rpcbind** is running, enter

nfsping -o rpcbind

If a message is displayed that states **rpcbind** is not running, check the name of the system (**uname -n**) with the entries in the **/etc/net/*/hosts** files, and see if they match.

If they do not match, your machine has had its name changed with the **uname** command, and the hostname entries in the **/etc/net/*/hosts** files must be manually updated.

For example, if the machine's hostname was **hulk** (use **uname -n**), the first entry in each of the **/etc/net/*/hosts** files should look like:

hulk hulk

If the first entry in each of the **/etc/net/*/hosts** files do not match the machine's hostname, you must update the first entry in the **/etc/net/*/hosts** files, and restart the **rpcbind** daemon. To restart **rpcbind**, enter:

/usr/sbin/rpcbind

SEE ALSO

nfsping(1M), **rpcinfo**(1M), **uname**(1)

rpcgen (1)

NAME

rpcgen – an RPC protocol compiler

SYNOPSIS

rpcgen *infile*
rpcgen [-D*name*[=*value*]] [-T] [-K *secs*] *infile*
rpcgen -c|-h|-l|-m|-t [-o *outfile*] *infile*
rpcgen -s *nettype* [-o *outfile*] *infile*
rpcgen -n *netid* [-o *outfile*] *infile*

DESCRIPTION

rpcgen is a tool that generates C code to implement an RPC protocol. The input to **rpcgen** is a language similar to C known as RPC Language (Remote Procedure Call Language).

rpcgen is normally used as in the first synopsis where it takes an input file and generates up to four output files. If the *infile* is named **proto.x**, then **rpcgen** will generate a header file in **proto.h**, XDR routines in **proto_xdr.c**, server-side stubs in **proto_svc.c**, and client-side stubs in **proto_clnt.c**. With the **-T** option, it will also generate the RPC dispatch table in **proto_tbl.i**.

The server created can be started both by the port monitors (for example, **inetd** or **listen**) or by itself. When it is started by a port monitor, it creates servers only for the transport for which the file descriptor **0** was passed. The name of the transport must be specified by setting up the environment variable **PM_TRANSPORT**. When the server generated by **rpcgen** is executed, it creates server handles for all the transports specified in **NETPATH** environment variable, or if it is not set, it creates server handles for all the visible transports from **/etc/netconfig** file. Note: the transports are chosen at run time and not at compile time. When the server is self-started, it backgrounds itself by default. A special symbol, **RPC_SVC_FG**, can be defined at compilation time to make the server process run in foreground.

The second synopsis provides special features which allow for the creation of more sophisticated RPC servers. These features include support for user provided **#defines** and RPC dispatch tables. The entries in the RPC dispatch table contain:

- pointers to the service routine corresponding to that procedure,
- a pointer to the input and output arguments
- the size of these routines

A server can use the dispatch table to check authorization and then to execute the service routine; a client library may use it to deal with the details of storage management and XDR data conversion.

The other three synopses shown above are used when one does not want to generate all the output files, but only a particular one. Some examples of their usage is described in the EXAMPLE section below. When **rpcgen** is executed with the **-s** option, it creates servers for that particular class of transports. When executed with the **-n** option, it creates a server for the transport specified by *netid*. If *infile* is not specified, **rpcgen** accepts the standard input.

The C preprocessor, **cc -E** [see cc(1)], is run on the input file before it is actually interpreted by **rpcgen**. For each type of output file, **rpcgen** defines a special preprocessor symbol for use by the **rpcgen** programmer:

RPC_HDR	defined when compiling into header files
RPC_XDR	defined when compiling into XDR routines
RPC_SVC	defined when compiling into server-side stubs
RPC_CLNT	defined when compiling into client-side stubs
RPC_TBL	defined when compiling into RPC dispatch tables

Any line beginning with '%' is passed directly into the output file, uninterpreted by **rpcgen**.

For every data type referred to in *infile*, **rpcgen** assumes that there exists a routine with the string **xdr_** prepended to the name of the data type. If this routine does not exist in the RPC/XDR library, it must be provided. Providing an undefined data type allows customization of XDR routines.

The following options are available:

-c Compile into XDR routines.

-D*name* [=*value*]
Define a symbol *name*. Equivalent to the **#define** directive in the source. If no *value* is given, *value* is defined as 1. This option may be specified more than once.

-h Compile into C data-definitions (a header file). **-T** option can be used in conjunction to produce a header file which supports RPC dispatch tables.

-K *secs*
By default, services created using **rpcgen** wait 120 seconds after servicing a request before exiting. That interval can be changed using the **-K** flag. To create a server that exits immediately upon servicing a request, **-K 0** can be used. To create a server that never exits, the appropriate argument is **-K -1**.

When monitoring for a server, some portmonitors, like **listen**(1M), *always* spawn a new process in response to a service request. If it is known that a server will be used with such a monitor, the server should exit immediately on completion. For such servers, **rpcgen** should be used with **-K -1**.

-l Compile into client-side stubs.

-m Compile into server-side stubs, but do not generate a main routine. This option is useful for doing callback-routines and for users who need to write their own main routine to do initialization.

-n *netid*
Compile into server-side stubs for the transport specified by *netid*. There should be an entry for *netid* in the netconfig database. This option may be specified more than once, so as to compile a server that serves multiple transports.

-o *outfile*
Specify the name of the output file. If none is specified, standard output is used (**-c**, **-h**, **-l**, **-m**, **-n**, **-s** and **-t** modes only).

-s *nettype*
Compile into server-side stubs for all the transports belonging to the class *nettype*. The supported classes are **netpath**, **visible**, **circuit_n**, **circuit_v**, **datagram_n**, **datagram_v**, **tcp**, and **udp** [see **rpc**(3N) for the

meanings associated with these classes]. This option may be specified more than once. Note: the transports are chosen at run time and not at compile time.

- `-t` Compile into RPC dispatch table.
- `-T` Generate the code to support RPC dispatch tables.

The options **-c**, **-h**, **-l**, **-m**, **-s** and **-t** are used exclusively to generate a particular type of file, while the options **-D** and **-T** are global and can be used with the other options.

NOTES

The RPC Language does not support nesting of structures. As a work-around, structures can be declared at the top-level, and their name used inside other structures in order to achieve the same effect.

Name clashes can occur when using program definitions, since the apparent scoping does not really apply. Most of these can be avoided by giving unique names for programs, versions, procedures and types.

The server code generated with **-n** option refers to the transport indicated by *netid* and hence is very site specific.

EXAMPLE

The following example:

```
$ rpcgen -T prot.x
```

generates all the five files: **prot.h**, **prot_clnt.c**, **prot_svc.c**, **prot_xdr.c** and **prot_tbl.i**.

The following example sends the C data-definitions (header file) to the standard output.

```
$ rpcgen -h prot.x
```

To send the test version of the **-DTEST**, server side stubs for all the transport belonging to the class **datagram_n** to standard output, use:

```
$ rpcgen -s datagram_n -DTEST prot.x
```

To create the server side stubs for the transport indicated by *netid* **tcp**, use:

```
$ rpcgen -n tcp -o prot_svc.c prot.x
```

SEE ALSO

cc(1)

NAME

rpcinfo – report RPC information

SYNOPSIS

rpcinfo [*host*]
rpcinfo -p [*host*]
rpcinfo -T *transport host program version*
rpcinfo [**-n** *portnum*] **-u** *host program version*
rpcinfo [**-n** *portnum*] **-t** *host program version*
rpcinfo -a *serv_address* **-T** *transport program* [*version*]
rpcinfo -b [**-T** *transport*] *program version*
rpcinfo -d [**-T** *transport*] *program version*

DESCRIPTION

rpcinfo makes an RPC call to an RPC server and reports what it finds.

In the first synopsis, **rpcinfo** lists all RPC services registered with **rpcbind** on *host*. If *host* is not specified, **rpcinfo** defaults to the local host. In the second synopsis, or if **rpcinfo** cannot contact **rpcbind**, **rpcinfo** lists all RPC services registered with portmapper. The format in which the information is printed is different for the first and second synopses since the first gets its information from **rpcbind** (version 3) and the second from **portmap** (version 2).

The third synopsis makes an RPC call to procedure **0** of *program* with version number *version* on *host* and reports whether a response was received. *transport* is the transport which is to be used for contacting the service. The remote address of the service is obtained by making a call to remote **rpcbind**.

See the EXAMPLES section for other ways of using **rpcinfo**.

The following options are available:

-T *transport* Specifies the transport on which the service is required. If this option is not specified, **rpcinfo** uses the transport specified in the **NETPATH** environment variable, or if that is unset or null, in the **netconfig** database. This is a generic option and can be used in conjunction with any other option. If it is used with the **-b** option, however, it will succeed only with a transport that supports broadcasting.

-a *serv_address* Use *serv_address* as the (universal) address for the service on *transport*, **ping**(1M) procedure **0** of the specified *program*, and report whether a response was received. The use of the **-T** option is required with the **-a** option.

If *version* is not specified, **rpcinfo** tries to **ping** all the available version numbers for that program number. This option avoids calls to remote **rpcbind** to find the address of the service. *serv_address* is specified in the universal address format of the given transport.

-b Make an RPC broadcast to procedure **0** of *program* with version number *version* and report all hosts that respond. If *transport* is specified, **rpcinfo** broadcasts its request only on that transport. If broadcasting is not supported by *transport*, an error message is printed. Only UDP transports support broadcasting.

-d Delete registration for the RPC service of the specified *program* and *version*. If *transport* is specified, unregister the service on only that transport, otherwise unregister the service on all the transports on which it was registered. This option can be exercised only by a privileged user.

-n *portnum* Use *portnum* as the port number for the **-t** and **-u** options instead of the port number given by the portmapper. Use of this option avoids a call to the remote portmapper to find out the address of the service.

-p Probe the portmapper on *host*, and print a list of all registered RPC programs. If *host* is not specified, **rpcinfo** defaults to the local host.

-t Make an RPC call to procedure 0 of *program* on the specified *host*, using TCP; report whether a response was received.

-u Make an RPC call to procedure 0 of *program* on the specified *host*, using UDP; report whether a response was received.

The *program* argument is a number.

The version number is required for **-T**, **-u**, **-t**, **-b**, and **-d** options. When a *version* is specified, **rpcinfo** attempts to call that version of *program*. If *version* is not specified, **rpcinfo** attempts to find all the registered version numbers for the specified *program* by calling version 0, which is presumed not to exist. If version 0 exists, **rpcinfo** attempts to find all *program*'s registered version numbers by calling an extremely high version number instead, and then attempts to call each registered version.

EXAMPLES

Print all RPC services registered on the local machine:

rpcinfo

Print all RPC services registered with **rpcbind** on the machine named **klaxon**:

rpcinfo klaxon

To find out if the RPC service with program number *prog_no* and version *vers* is registered on machine **klaxon** for the transport **tcp**:

rpcinfo -T tcp klaxon *prog_no vers*

Print all RPC services registered with the portmapper on the local machine:

rpcinfo -p

ping version 2 of **rpcbind** (program number **100000**) on host **sparky**:

rpcinfo -t sparky 100000 2

Delete the registration for version `1` of the **`walld`** service (program number `100008`) for all transports (this option requires privileged access):

```
rpcinfo -d 100008 1
```

SEE ALSO

`rpcbind`(1M), **`rpc`**(4)

NAME

rsh – remote shell

SYNOPSIS

rsh [**-n**] [**-l** *username*] *hostname command*

rsh *hostname* [**-n**] [**-l** *username*] *command*

hostname [**-n**] [**-l** *username*] *command*

DESCRIPTION

rsh connects to the specified *hostname* and executes the specified *command*. **rsh** copies its standard input to the remote command, the standard output of the remote command to its standard output, and the standard error of the remote command to its standard error. Interrupt, quit and terminate signals are propagated to the remote command; **rsh** normally terminates when the remote command does.

If you omit *command*, instead of executing a single command, **rsh** logs you in on the remote host using **rlogin**(1). Shell metacharacters which are not quoted are interpreted on the local machine, while quoted metacharacters are interpreted on the remote machine. See EXAMPLES.

Hostnames are given in the *hosts* database, which may be contained in the **/etc/hosts** file, the Internet domain name database, or both. Each host has one official name (the first name in the database entry) and optionally one or more nicknames. Official hostnames or nicknames may be given as *hostname*.

If the name of the file from which **rsh** is executed is anything other than **rsh**, **rsh** takes this name as its *hostname* argument. This allows you to create a symbolic link to **rsh** in the name of a host which, when executed, will invoke a remote shell on that host. By creating a directory and populating it with symbolic links in the names of commonly used hosts, then including the directory in your shell's search path, you can run **rsh** by typing *hostname* to your shell.

Each remote machine may have a file named **/etc/hosts.equiv** containing a list of trusted hostnames with which it shares usernames. Users with the same username on both the local and remote machine may **rsh** from the machines listed in the remote machine's **/etc/hosts** file. Individual users may set up a similar private equivalence list with the file **.rhosts** in their home directories. Each line in this file contains two names: a *hostname* and a *username* separated by a space. The entry permits the user named *username* who is logged into *hostname* to use **rsh** to access the remote machine as the remote user. If the name of the local host is not found in the **/etc/hosts.equiv** file on the remote machine, and the local username and hostname are not found in the remote user's **.rhosts** file, then the access is denied. The hostnames listed in the **/etc/hosts.equiv** and **.rhosts** files must be the official hostnames listed in the **hosts** database; nicknames may not be used in either of these files.

rsh will not prompt for a password if access is denied on the remote machine unless the *command* argument is omitted.

OPTIONS

-l *username*

Use *username* as the remote username instead of your local username. In the absence of this option, the remote username is the same as your local username.

-n Redirect the input of **rsh** to **/dev/null**. You sometimes need this option to avoid unfortunate interactions between **rsh** and the shell which invokes it. For example, if you are running **rsh** and invoke a **rsh** in the background without redirecting its input away from the terminal, it will block even if no reads are posted by the remote command. The **-n** option will prevent this.

The type of remote shell (**sh**, the restricted shell—**/usr/lib/rsh**, or other) is determined by the user's entry in the file **/etc/passwd** on the remote system.

EXAMPLES

The command:

```
rsh lizard cat lizard.file >> example.file
```

appends the remote file **lizard.file** from the machine called "lizard" to the file called **example.file** on the local machine, while the command:

```
rsh lizard cat lizard.file ">>" lizard.file2
```

appends the file **lizard.file** on the machine called "lizard" to the file **lizard.file2** which also resides on the machine called "lizard."

FILES

/etc/hosts
/etc/passwd

SEE ALSO

rlogin(1), **vi**(1), **named**(1M), **hosts**(4), **hosts.equiv**(4)

NOTES

When a system is listed in **hosts.equiv**, its security must be as good as local security. One insecure system listed in **hosts.equiv** can compromise the security of the entire system.

You cannot run an interactive command [such as **vi**(1)]; use **rlogin** if you want to do so.

Stop signals stop the local **rsh** process only; this is arguably wrong, but currently hard to fix for reasons too complicated to explain here.

The current local environment is not passed to the remote shell.

Sometimes the **-n** option is needed for reasons that are less than obvious. For example, the command:

```
rsh somehost dd if=/dev/nrmt0 bs=20b | tar xvpBf -
```

will put your shell into a strange state. Evidently, what happens is that the **tar** terminates before the **rsh**. The **rsh** then tries to write into the "broken pipe" and, instead of terminating neatly, proceeds to compete with your shell for its standard input. Invoking **rsh** with the **-n** option avoids such incidents.

This bug occurs only when **rsh** is at the beginning of a pipeline and is not reading standard input. Do not use the **-n** if **rsh** actually needs to read standard input. For example,

```
tar cf - . | rsh sundial dd of=/dev/rmt0 obs=20b
```

does not produce the bug. If you were to use the **-n** in a case like this, **rsh** would incorrectly read from **/dev/null** instead of from the pipe.

Prior to Release 4, the **rsh** command invoked the restricted shell. This restricted shell command is **/usr/lib/rsh** and can be executed by using the full pathname.

NAME

rshd – remote shell server

SYNOPSIS

in.rshd *host.port*

DESCRIPTION

rshd is the server for the **rsh**(1) program. The server provides remote execution facilities with authentication based on privileged port numbers.

rshd is invoked by **inetd**(1M) each time a shell service is requested, and executes the following protocol:

1) The server checks the client's source port. If the port is not in the range 0-1023, the server aborts the connection. The clients host address (in hex) and port number (in decimal) are the argument passed to **rshd.**

2) The server reads characters from the socket up to a null (**\0**) byte. The resultant string is interpreted as an ASCII number, base 10.

3) If the number received in step 1 is non-zero, it is interpreted as the port number of a secondary stream to be used for the **stderr**. A second connection is then created to the specified port on the client's machine. The source port of this second connection is also in the range 0-1023.

4) The server checks the client's source address. If the address is associated with a host for which no corresponding entry exists in the host name data base [see **hosts**(4)], the server aborts the connection.

5) A null terminated user name of at most 16 characters is retrieved on the initial socket. This user name is interpreted as a user identity to use on the **server**'s machine.

6) A null terminated user name of at most 16 characters is retrieved on the initial socket. This user name is interpreted as the user identity on the **client**'s machine.

7) A null terminated command to be passed to a shell is retrieved on the initial socket. The length of the command is limited by the upper bound on the size of the system's argument list.

8) **rshd** then validates the user according to the following steps. The remote user name is looked up in the password file and a **chdir** is performed to the user's home directory. If the lookup or fails, the connection is terminated. If the **chdir** fails, it does a **chdir** to **/** (root). If the user is not **root** (UID is 0), the file **/etc/hosts.equiv** is consulted for a list of hosts considered equivalent. If the client's host name is present in this file, the authentication is considered successful. If the lookup fails, or the user is a privileged user, then the file **.rhosts** in the home directory of the remote user is checked for the machine name and identity of the user on the client's machine. If this lookup fails, the connection is terminated.

9) A null byte is returned on the connection associated with the **stderr** and the command line is passed to the normal login shell of the user. The shell inherits the network connections established by **rshd**.

FILES

/etc/hosts.equiv

SEE ALSO

rsh(1)

DIAGNOSTICS

The following diagnostic messages are returned on the connection associated with the **stderr**, after which any network connections are closed. An error is indicated by a leading byte with a value of 1 (0 is returned in step 9 above upon successful completion of all the steps prior to the command execution).

`locuser too long`
: The name of the user on the client's machine is longer than 16 characters.

`remuser too long`
: The name of the user on the remote machine is longer than 16 characters.

`command too long`
: The command line passed exceeds the size of the argument list (as configured into the system).

`Hostname for your address unknown.`
: No entry in the host name database existed for the client's machine.

`Login incorrect.`
: No password file entry for the user name existed.

`Permission denied.`
: The authentication procedure described above failed.

`Can't make pipe.`
: The pipe needed for the **stderr** was not created.

`Try again.`
: A *fork* by the server failed.

NOTES

The authentication procedure used here assumes the integrity of each client machine and the connecting medium. This is insecure, but is useful in an open environment.

If a remote user does not have a home directory, the root directory (/) becomes the user's home directory.

A facility to allow all data exchanges to be encrypted should be present.

NAME

rsnotify – display or modify the information identifying the individual in charge of restore requests

SYNOPSIS

rsnotify [**-u** *user*]

DESCRIPTION

rsnotify without options displays the name of the person who is to receive **mail**(1) notifications whenever restore requests require operator intervention. The display includes the date the individual was assigned.

rsnotify may be executed only by a privileged user.

Options

-u *user* Assign *user* to be the one to receive restore notifications. *user* is the user's login ID. If *user* is null, **rsnotify** mails the notices to root. *user* must be in the **passwd** file.

DIAGNOSTICS

The exit codes for **rsnotify** are the following:

0 The task completed successfully.
1 One or more parameters to **rsnotify** are invalid.
2 An error has occurred, causing **rsnotify** to fail to complete all portions of its task

EXAMPLES

Assign the individual with login ID **oper3** as the one to be notified when a restore request needing operator intervention is initiated:

```
rsnotify -u oper3
```

FILES

/etc/bkup/rsnotify.tab electronic mail address of the operator to be notified whenever restore requests require operator intervention

/etc/bkup/rsstatus.tab status of all restore requests from users

SEE ALSO

getvol(1M), **restore**(1M), **rsstatus**(1M), **urestore**(1M)

rsstatus (1M)

NAME

rsstatus – report the status of posted restore requests

SYNOPSIS

rsstatus [**-h**] [**-d** *ddev*] [**-f** *field_separator*] [**-j** *jobids*] [**-u** *users*]

DESCRIPTION

With no options, **rsstatus** reports the status of all pending restore requests that are posted in the restore status table.

rsstatus may be executed only by a privileged user.

Volume labels marked with an asterisk in the output of this command are table of contents volumes.

Options

-d *ddev* Restricts the report to pending restore jobs that could be satisfied by the specified device type or volumes. *ddev* describes the device or volumes used to select requests to be restored. *ddev* is of the form:

[*dtype*][**:***dlabels*]

dtype is a device type (such as diskette, cartridge tape, or 9-track tape). If specified, restrict the report to posted requests that could be satisfied by volumes of the type specified.

dlabels is a list of volume names corresponding to the *volumename* displayed by the **labelit** command. *dlabels* may be either comma-separated or blank-separated and surrounded by quotes. If specified, restrict the report to posted requests that could be satisfied by an archive residing on the specified volumes.

-f *field_separator*

Suppresses field wrap and specifies an output field separator to be used. *field_separator* is the character that will appear as the field separator in the output displayed. To make sure the output is clear, avoid using a character (for a separator) that is likely to appear in a field. For example, do not use a colon as a field separator if the display will contain dates in which a colon is used to separate hours from minutes.

-h Suppresses the header for the report.

-j *jobids* Restricts the report to the jobs specified. *jobids* is a list of restore job IDs (either comma-separated or blank-separated and surrounded by quotes).

-u *users* Restricts the report to requests submitted by the specified *users* (either comma-separated or blank-separated and surrounded by quotes). *users* must be listed in the **passwd** file.

DIAGNOSTICS

The exit codes for **rsstatus** are the following:

0 = successful completion of the task
1 = one or more parameters to **rsstatus** are invalid.
2 = an error has occurred which caused **rsstatus** to fail to complete all portions of its task.

EXAMPLES

Example 1:

```
rsstatus -d diskette
```

reports the status of those posted restore requests that can be satisfied by inserting diskettes into a diskette drive.

Example 2:

```
rsstatus -j rest-354a,rest-429b
```

reports the status of only the two posted restore requests for which job IDs are specified.

FILES

/etc/bkup/rsstatus.tab — tracks the status of all restore requests from users

SEE ALSO

restore(1M), **urestore**(1M), **ursstatus**(1M), **volcopy**(1M)

rsoper (1M)

NAME

rsoper – service pending restore requests and service media insertion prompts

SYNOPSIS

rsoper -d *ddev* [**-j** *jobids*] [**-u** *user*] [**-m** *method*] [**-n**] [**-s** | **v**] [**-t**]
[**-o** *oname*[:*odevice*]]

rsoper -r *jobid*

rsoper -c *jobid*

DESCRIPTION

rsoper -d identifies media containing backup archives of file systems and data partitions, and allows an operator to complete pending **restore**(1M) and **urestore**(1M) requests. **rsoper** takes information about the archive entered on the command line and matches it against pending **restore** or **urestore** requests in the restore status table. **rsoper** then invokes the proper archiving method to read the archive and extract requested files, directories, and data partitions. As subsequent archive volumes are needed, the operator is requested to insert or mount the appropriate archive volumes. See **getvol**(1M).

Depending on the information available in **bkhist.tab** and the volume labeling technique (internal or external), all options and arguments listed below may not be required. If required fields are omitted, **rsoper** issues an error message indicating the information that is needed. The command can then be reissued with the appropriate fields specified.

rsoper may be executed only by a privileged user.

rsoper -r removes a pending restore job from the restore status table and notifies the requesting user that the job has been marked complete.

rsoper -c removes a pending restore job from the restore status table and notifies the requesting user that the job has been canceled.

Options

-c *jobid* Cancels a pending restore request and notifies the originating user that the request has been canceled.

-d *ddev* Describes the device that will be used to read the archive containing the required file system or data partition. *ddev* is of the form:

ddevice[**:**[*dchar*][**:**[*dmnames*]]]

ddevice is the device name for the device. *dchar* describes characteristics associated with the device. *dchar* is of the form:

[**density=***density*] [**blk_fac=***blockingfactor*] [**mntpt=***dir*]

If **mntpt=***dir* is specified, *ddevice* is assumed to be a file system partition and *dir* is the place in the UNIX directory structure where *ddevice* will be mounted. This is valid only for **fimage** archives. *dmnames* is a list of volume labels, separated by either commas or blanks. If the list is blank separated, the entire *ddev* argument must be surrounded by quotes.

-j *jobids* Limits the scope of the request to the jobs specified. *jobids* is a list of restore job IDs (either comma separated or blank separated and surrounded by quotes).

-m *method* Assumes the archive on the first volume in the destination device was created by the *method* archiving operation. Valid *methods* are: **incfile**, **ffile**, **fimage**, **fdp**, **fdisk**, and any customized methods in the **/etc/bkup/method** directory. This option is required if the backup history log is not available, if the log does not include information about the specified archive or if **rsoper** cannot determine the format of the archive.

-n Displays attributes of the specified destination device but does not attempt to service pending restore requests.

-o *oname*[**:***odevice*] [**,***oname*[**:***odevice*]]
Specifies the multiple file system partitions or data partitions to be restored. *oname* is the name of the the originating file system. It may be null. *odevice* is the device name of the originating file system or data partition. This option is required if the backup history log is not available or does not include information about the specified archive.

-r *jobid* Removes the restore request for the specified job.

-s While a restore operation is occurring, this option displays a period (**.**) for each 100 (512-byte) blocks transferred from the destination device.

-t Assumes that the volume inserted in the destination device contains a table of contents for an archive. This option is required if the backup history log is not available, if the log does not include information about the specified archive, or if **rsoper** cannot determine the format of the volume.

-u *user* Restricts restores to those requested by the user specified.

-v Displays the name of each object as it is restored. Only those archiving methods that restore named directories and files (**incfile** and **ffile**) support this option.

DIAGNOSTICS

The exit codes for **rsoper** are the following:

0 = the task completed successfully
1 = one or more parameters to **rsoper** are invalid
2 = an error has occurred, causing **rsoper** to fail to complete all portions of its task

If a method reports that no part of a restore request was completed, **rsoper** reports this fact to the user.

EXAMPLES

Example 1:

```
rsoper -d /dev/tape/c4d0s2
```

asks the restore service to read the archive volume that has been inserted into the device **/dev/tape/c4d0s2**. The service will attempt to resolve any restore requests that can be satisfied by the archive volume.

Example 2:

The following example assumes that the backup history table contains a record of backups performed and that the restore status table contains a record of the restore requests. The command line

```
rsoper -d /dev/ctape:density=1600:USRLBL1 -v -u clerk1
```

instructs the restore service to perform only pending restore requests from the **rsstatus.tab** table issued by **clerk1**. The restore procedures are to be done from the cartridge tape labeled USRLBL1, with a density of 1600 bps. The restore service will display on the operator terminal the names of the files and directories as they are successfully restored.

Example 3:

The following example assumes that the backup history table no longer contains a log of the requested backup operations. With that assumption:

```
rsoper -d /dev/diskette2:blk_fac=2400:arc.dec79 -m incfile -o /usr2
```

instructs the restore service to perform a restore of the **/usr2** file system using the incremental restore method. The **/usr2** file system is to be restored from archived diskettes with a blocking factor of 2400. The diskettes containing the archive are labeled "arc.dec79.a," "arc.dec79.b," and "arc.dec79.c."

Example 4:

```
rsoper -c rest-737b
```

cancels the restore request with the job ID **rest-737b**.

FILES

/etc/bkup/bkhist.tab	–	lists the labels of all volumes that have been used for backup operations
/etc/bkup/rsstatus.tab	–	lists the status of all restore requests from users
/etc/bkup/rsnotify.tab	–	lists the electronic mail address of the operator to be notified whenever restore requests require operator intervention
/etc/bkup/method	–	a directory that contains the programs used for various backup methods

SEE ALSO

getdate(3C), **getvol**(1M), **mail**(1), **restore**(1M), **urestore**(1M)

NAME

rumount – cancel queued remote resource request

SYNOPSIS

/etc/rfs/rumount *resource* . . .

DESCRIPTION

rumount cancels a request for one or more resources that are queued for mount. The entries for the resources are deleted from **/etc/rfs/rmnttab**.

Only a privileged user can execute this command.

FILES

/etc/rfs/rmnttab — pending mount requests

SEE ALSO

mnttab(4), **mount**(1M), **rmnttry**(1M), **rmount**(1M), **rmountall**(1M)

DIAGNOSTICS

An exit code of **0** is returned if **rumount** completes successfully. A **1** is returned if the resource requested for dequeuing is not in **/etc/rfs/rmnttab**. A **2** is returned for bad usage or an error in reading or writing **/etc/rfs/rmnttab**.

run (1F)

NAME

run – run an executable

SYNOPSIS

run [-**s**] [-**e**] [-**n**] [-**t** *string*] *program*

DESCRIPTION

The **run** function runs *program*, using the PATH variable to find it. By default, when *program* has completed, the user is prompted (**Press ENTER to continue:**), before being returned to FMLI. The argument *program* is a UNIX system executable followed by its options (if any).

-**e** If -**e** is specified the user will be prompted before returning to FMLI only if there is an error condition

-**n** If -**n** is specified the user will never be prompted before returning to FMLI (useful for programs like **vi**, in which the user must do some specific action to exit in the first place).

-**s** The -**s** option means "silent," implying that the screen will not have to be repainted when *program* has completed. NOTE: The -**s** option should only be used when *program* does not write to the terminal. In addition, when -**s** is used, *program* cannot be interrupted, even if it recognizes interrupts.

-**t** *string* If -**t** is specified, *string* is the name this process will have in the pop-up menu generated by the **frm-list** command. This feature requires the executable **facesuspend**, (currently only available with the FACE product), to suspend the UNIX system process and return to the FMLI application.

EXAMPLE

Here is a menu that uses **run**:

```
menu="Edit special System files"

name="Password file"
action=`run -e vi /etc/passwd`

name="Group file"
action=`run -e vi /etc/group`

name="My .profile"
action=`run -n vi $HOME/.profile`
```

NAME

runacct – run daily accounting

SYNOPSIS

/usr/lib/acct/runacct [*mmdd* [*state*]]

DESCRIPTION

runacct is the main daily accounting shell procedure. It is normally initiated via **cron**. **runacct** processes connect, fee, disk, and process accounting files. It also prepares summary files for **prdaily** or billing purposes. **runacct** is distributed only to source code licensees.

runacct takes care not to damage active accounting files or summary files in the event of errors. It records its progress by writing descriptive diagnostic messages into *active*. When an error is detected, a message is written to **/dev/console**, mail [see **mail**(1)] is sent to **root** and **adm**, and **runacct** terminates. **runacct** uses a series of lock files to protect against re-invocation. The files **lock** and **lock1** are used to prevent simultaneous invocation, and **lastdate** is used to prevent more than one invocation per day.

runacct breaks its processing into separate, restartable *states* using *statefile* to remember the last *state* completed. It accomplishes this by writing the *state* name into *statefile*. **runacct** then looks in *statefile* to see what it has done and to determine what to process next. *states* are executed in the following order:

SETUP	Move active accounting files into working files.
WTMPFIX	Verify integrity of **wtmp** file, correcting date changes if necessary.
CONNECT	Produce connect session records in **tacct.h** format.
PROCESS	Convert process accounting records into **tacct.h** format.
MERGE	Merge the connect and process accounting records.
FEES	Convert output of **chargefee** into **tacct.h** format and merge with connect and process accounting records.
DISK	Merge disk accounting records with connect, process, and fee accounting records.
MERGETACCT	Merge the daily total accounting records in **daytacct** with the summary total accounting records in **/var/adm/acct/sum/tacct**.
CMS	Produce command summaries.
USEREXIT	Any installation dependent accounting programs can be included here.
CLEANUP	Clean up temporary files and exit.

To restart **runacct** after a failure, first check the *active* file for diagnostics, then fix any corrupted data files, such as **pacct** or **wtmp**. The **lock**, **lock1**, and **lastdate** files must be removed before **runacct** can be restarted. The argument *mmdd* is necessary if **runacct** is being restarted, and specifies the month and day for which **runacct** will rerun the accounting. The entry point for processing is based on the contents of *statefile*; to override this, include the desired *state* on the command line to designate where processing should begin.

EXAMPLES

To start **runacct**:

```
nohup runacct 2> /var/adm/acct/nite/fd2log &
```

To restart **runacct**:

```
nohup runacct 0601 2>> /var/adm/acct/nite/fd2log &
```

To restart **runacct** at a specific *state*:

```
nohup runacct 0601 MERGE 2>> /var/adm/acct/nite/fd2log &
```

FILES

/var/adm/wtmp
/var/adm/pacct*incr*
/usr/src/cmd/acct/tacct.h
/usr/src/cmd/acct/ctmp.h
/var/adm/acct/nite/active
/var/adm/acct/nite/daytacct
/var/adm/acct/nite/lock
/var/adm/acct/nite/lock1
/var/adm/acct/nite/lastdate
/var/adm/acct/nite/statefile

SEE ALSO

acct(1M), **acct**(2), **acct**(4), **acctcms**(1M), **acctcom**(1), **acctcon**(1M), **acctmerg**(1M), **acctprc**(1M), **acctsh**(1M), **cron**(1M), **fwtmp**(1M), **mail**(1), **utmp**(4)

NOTES

Normally it is not a good idea to restart **runacct** in the **SETUP** *state*. Run **SETUP** manually and restart via:

runacct *mmdd* **WTMPFIX**

If **runacct** failed in the **PROCESS** *state*, remove the last **ptacct** file because it will not be complete.

NAME

ruptime – show host status of local machines

SYNOPSIS

ruptime [**-alrtu**]

DESCRIPTION

ruptime gives a status line like **uptime** for each machine on the local network; these are formed from packets broadcast by each host on the network once a minute.

Machines for which no status report has been received for 5 minutes are shown as being down.

Normally, the listing is sorted by host name, but this order can be changed by specifying one of the options listed below.

The following options are available:

-a Count even those users who have been idle for an hour or more.

-l Sort the display by load average.

-r Reverse the sorting order.

-t Sort the display by up time.

-u Sort the display by number of users.

FILES

/var/spool/rwho/whod.* data files

SEE ALSO

rwho(1), **rwhod**(1M)

NOTES

For **rwho** to work properly, the directory **/var/spool/rwho** must exist on the system.

rusers (1)

NAME

rusers – who's logged in on local machines

SYNOPSIS

rusers [**-ahilu**] *host . . .*

DESCRIPTION

The **rusers** command produces output similar to **who**(1), but for remote machines. The listing is in the order that responses are received, but this order can be changed by specifying one of the options listed below.

The default is to print out the names of the users logged in. When the **-l** flag is given, additional information is printed for each user, including idle time, when user logged in, and tty.

A remote host will only respond if it is running the **rusersd**(1M) daemon, which may be started up from **inetd**(1M) or **listen**(1M).

The following options are available:

-a Give a report for a machine even if no users are logged on.

-h Sort alphabetically by host name.

-i Sort by idle time.

-l Give a longer listing in the style of **who**(1).

-u Sort by number of users.

SEE ALSO

inetd(1M), **listen**(1M), **pmadm**(1M), **rusersd**(1M), **sacadm**(1M), **who**(1)

NAME

rpc.rusersd – network username server

SYNOPSIS

/usr/lib/netsvc/rusers/rpc.rusersd

DESCRIPTION

rusersd is a server that returns a list of users on the host. The **rusersd** daemon may be started by **inetd**(1M) or **listen**(1M).

SEE ALSO

inetd(1M), **listen**(1M), **pmadm**(1M), **sacadm**(1M)

rwall (1M)

NAME

rwall – write to all users over a network

SYNOPSIS

/usr/sbin/rwall *hostname* . . .

DESCRIPTION

rwall reads a message from standard input until EOF. It then sends this message, preceded by the line:

```
Broadcast Message ...
```

to all users logged in on the specified host machines.

A machine can only receive such a message if it is running **rwalld**(1M), which may be started by **inetd**(1M) or **listen**(1M).

NOTES

The timeout is fairly short to allow transmission to a large group of machines (some of which may be down) in a reasonable amount of time. Thus the message may not get through to a heavily loaded machine.

SEE ALSO

inetd(1M), **listen**(1M), **pmadm**(1M), **rwalld**(1M), **sacadm**(1M), **wall**(1M)

NAME

rpc.rwalld – network rwall server

SYNOPSIS

/usr/lib/netsvc/rwall/rpc.rwalld

DESCRIPTION

rwalld is a server that handles **rwall**(1M) requests. It is implemented by calling **wall**(1M) on all the appropriate network machines. The **rwalld** daemon may be started by **inetd**(1M) or **listen**(1M).

SEE ALSO

inetd(1M), **listen**(1M), **rwall**(1M), **wall**(1M)

NAME

rwho – who's logged in on local machines

SYNOPSIS

rwho [**-a**]

DESCRIPTION

The **rwho** command produces output similar to **who**(1), but for all machines on your network. If no report has been received from a machine for 5 minutes, **rwho** assumes the machine is down, and does not report users last known to be logged into that machine.

If a user has not typed to the system for a minute or more, **rwho** reports this idle time. If a user has not typed to the system for an hour or more, the user is omitted from the output of **rwho** unless the **-a** flag is given.

The **-a** option reports all users whether or not they have typed to the system in the past hour.

FILES

/var/spool/rwho/whod.*	information about other machines

SEE ALSO

finger(1), **ruptime**(1), **who**(1), **rwhod**(1M)

NOTES

Does not work through gateways.

This is unwieldy when the number of machines on the local net is large.

The **rwho** service daemon, **rwhod**(1M), must be enabled for this command to return useful results.

For **rwho** to work properly, the directory **/var/spool/rwho** must exist on the system.

NAME

rwhod, **in.rwhod** – system status server

SYNOPSIS

in.rwhod

DESCRIPTION

rwhod is the server which maintains the database used by the **rwho**(1) and **ruptime**(1) programs. Its operation is predicated on the ability to broadcast messages on a network.

rwhod operates as both a producer and consumer of status information. As a producer of information it periodically queries the state of the system and constructs status messages which are broadcast on a network. As a consumer of information, it listens for other **rwhod** servers' status messages, validating them, then recording them in a collection of files located in the directory **/var/spool/rwho**.

The **rwho** server transmits and receives messages at the port indicated in the **rwho** service specification, see **services**(4). The messages sent and received, are of the form:

```
struct      outmp {
        char out_line[8];     /* tty name */
        char out_name[8];     /* user id */
        long out_time;  /* time on */
};

struct      whod {
        char wd_vers;
        char wd_type;
        char wd_fill[2];
        int  wd_sendtime;
        int  wd_recvtime;
        char wd_hostname[32];
        int  wd_loadav[3];
        int  wd_boottime;
             struct     whoent {
             struct     outmp we_utmp;
             int   we_idle;
        } wd_we[1024 / sizeof (struct whoent)];
};
```

All fields are converted to network byte order prior to transmission. The load averages are as calculated by the w(1) program, and represent load averages over the 5, 10, and 15 minute intervals prior to a server's transmission. The host name included is that returned by the **gethostname**(3) system call. The array at the end of the message contains information about the users logged in to the sending machine. This information includes the contents of the **utmp**(4) entry for each non-idle terminal line and a value indicating the time since a character was last received on the terminal line.

Messages received by the **rwho** server are discarded unless they originated at a **rwho** server's port. In addition, if the host's name, as specified in the message, contains any unprintable ASCII characters, the message is discarded. Valid messages received by **rwhod** are placed in files named **whod.***hostname* in the directory **/var/spool/rwho**. These files contain only the most recent message, in the format described above.

Status messages are generated approximately once every 60 seconds. **rwhod** performs an **nlist**(3E) on **/stand/unix** every 10 minutes to guard against the possibility that this file is not the system image currently operating.

FILES

/var/spool/rwho

SEE ALSO

gethostname(3), **nlist**(3E), **ruptime**(1), **rwho**(1), **utmp**(4), **w**(1)

NOTES

This service takes up progressively more network bandwidth as the number of hosts on the local net increases. For large networks, the cost becomes prohibitive.

rwhod should relay status information between networks. People often interpret the server dying as a machine going down.

For **rwho** to work properly, the directory **/var/spool/rwho** must exist on the system.

NAME

rxlist – list available REXEC services

SYNOPSIS

/usr/lib/rexec/rxlist [**-l**] [**-h**]

DESCRIPTION

rxlist is a command that lists REXEC services currently defined on the system. A remote user invokes the command indirectly through the **rquery** service. When a user invokes **rxlist** through **rquery**, **rxlist** reports only the services currently available to the invoking user [see **rexec**(1)].

The options to **rxlist** have the following meanings:

-l Indicates that a long listing should be generated.

-h Indicates that a listing should be generated with headings. The headings, in order of appearance, are: SERVICE, DESCRIPTION, UTMP, and DEFINITION.

If no options are given, a two-column table of defined services is printed, where the first column contains the service name and the second column contains a text description of the service.

A long listing consists of a four-column table, where the columns contain the following:

Column 1: The service name.

Column 2: A text description of the service.

Column 3: A **u** if the **-u** option was specified with the **rxservice** command when the service was defined, or a hyphen if it was not.

Column 4: The service definition.

FILES

/etc/rexec/services REXEC services database

SEE ALSO

rexec(1), **rexecve**(3N), **rxservice**(1M)

NAME

rxservice – add or remove an REXEC service

SYNOPSIS

rxservice –a *servicename* [–d *description*] [–u] *servicedef*
rxservice –r *servicename...*
rxservice –l

DESCRIPTION

The **rxservice** command provides an administrator with a way of adding and removing REXEC services.

Options

The following options are available to the **rxservice** command:

-a *servicename*
Add an REXEC service. *servicename* is the name of the REXEC service being defined. Users on a client machine invoke the service via the service name. The service name is restricted to 14 characters and must be alphanumeric.

-d *description*
A text description (up to 256 characters in length) that describes the service.

-u Specifies that a **utmp** entry is to be made on the remote host containing the mapped user's login name.

servicedef
A service definition, consisting of a character string composed of the command (with parameters) that is executed when the service is invoked. The command must be a full path name. The parameters are parsed as tokens separated by white space, tokens enclosed in double quote (") characters, or tokens enclosed in single quote (') characters. If the double quote or single quote character is to be interpreted literally, it must be preceded by a backslash (\) character. If a token is enclosed in single quote characters, then every character of that token is interpreted literally. If you need to use a quote in the service definition, use a different one than is used in the service argument. For example, if you use double quotes in the service argument, use single quotes in the service definition. The character string is limited to 256 characters. The command line is interpreted first by the shell, then by **rxservice**, and then by the remote shell.

-r *servicename*
Remove one or more REXEC services. *servicename* is the name of the service or services to be deleted.

-l Displays the contents of the services file.

Files

/etc/rexec/services REXEC services database

USAGE

The following rules apply when creating a service definition:

The service definition can take parameters from the client machine; these parameters are referenced in the service definition via the macros **%0** for the service name, **%1** for the first parameter, **%2** for the second, and so on, up to **%9** for the ninth parameter.

The parameter macros are parsed as tokens consisting of the **%** character, followed immediately by a single-digit integer representing the position of the parameter.

The special macro **%*** is used to reference all parameters (except **%0**).

If the **%** character is to be interpreted literally, it must be preceded by a backslash (\) character, be contained in a token enclosed within single-quote characters, or be contained in an undefined macro name.

If a service definition must reference more than nine parameters, the **%*** macro can be used to pass all the parameters to a shell script.

The REXEC facility defines the following macros, which can be used by any service:

%m The address of the client machine.

%t The name of the transport provider used to connect to the remote host.

%s The shell for the mapped user, obtained from the **/etc/passwd** file.

Service definitions are required to begin with a slash (**/**) or a percent (**%**) character.

Examples

The following defines a service called **rlookup**, which accesses a local database via a command called **dblook**:

```
rxservice -a rlookup -d 'Remote database lookup' \
        '/usr/bin/dblook %*'
```

The following defines a service called **rsetup**, which modifies database tables via a local command called **setdb**. The **setdb** command takes the address of the client machine as a parameter.

```
rxservice -a rsetdb -d 'remote setup service' \
        '/usr/bin/setdb %m'
```

REFERENCES

rexec(1), **rexecve**(3N), **rxlist**(1M)

NAME

sac – service access controller

SYNOPSIS

/usr/lib/saf/sac -t *sanity_interval*

DESCRIPTION

The Service Access Controller (SAC) is the overseer of the server machine. **sac** is started with a *sanity_interval* of 300 seconds from **/etc/inittab** when the server machine enters multiuser mode. The SAC performs several important functions as explained below.

Customizing the SAC environment

When **sac** is invoked, it first looks for the per-system configuration script **/etc/saf/_sysconfig**. **sac** interprets **_sysconfig** to customize its own environment. The modifications made to the SAC environment by **_sysconfig** are inherited by all the children of the SAC. This inherited environment may be modified by the children.

Starting port monitors

After it has interpreted the **_sysconfig** file, the **sac** reads its administrative file **/etc/saf/_sactab**. **_sactab** specifies which port monitors are to be started. For each port monitor to be started, **sac** forks a child [fork(2)] and creates a **utmp** entry with the *type* field set to **LOGIN_PROCESS**. Each child then interprets its per-port monitor configuration script **/etc/saf/***pmtag***/_config**, if the file exists. These modifications to the environment affect the port monitor and will be inherited by all its children. Finally, the child process **exec**s the port monitor, using the command found in the **_sactab** entry. (See **sacadm**; this is the command given with the **-c** option when the port monitor is added to the system.)

Polling port monitors to detect failure

The **-t** option sets the frequency (in seconds) with which **sac** polls the port monitors on the system. This time may also be thought of as half of the maximum latency required to detect that a port monitor has failed and that recovery action is necessary.

Administrative functions

The Service Access Controller represents the administrative point of control for port monitors. Its administrative tasks are explained below.

When queried (**sacadm** with either **-l** or **-L**), the Service Access Controller returns the status of the port monitors specified, which **sacadm** prints on the standard output. A port monitor may be in one of six states:

ENABLED The port monitor is currently running and is accepting connections. See **sacadm**(1M) with the **-e** option.

DISABLED The port monitor is currently running and is not accepting connections. See **sacadm** with the **-d** option, and see **NOTRUNNING**, below.

STARTING The port monitor is in the process of starting up. **STARTING** is an intermediate state on the way to **ENABLED** or **DISABLED**.

FAILED The port monitor was unable to start and remain running.

STOPPING The port monitor has been manually terminated but has not completed its shutdown procedure. **STOPPING** is an intermediate state on the way to **NOTRUNNING**.

NOTRUNNING The port monitor is not currently running. (See **sacadm** with **-k**.) This is the normal "not running" state. When a port monitor is killed, all ports it was monitoring are inaccessible. It is not possible for an external user to tell whether a port is not being monitored or the system is down. If the port monitor is not killed but is in the **DISABLED** state, it may be possible (depending on the port monitor being used) to write a message on the inaccessible port telling the user who is trying to access the port that it is disabled. This is the advantage of having a **DISABLED** state as well as the **NOTRUNNING** state.

When a port monitor terminates, the SAC frees the **utmp** entry for that port monitor.

The SAC receives all requests to enable, disable, start, or stop port monitors and takes the appropriate action.

The SAC is responsible for restarting port monitors that terminate. Whether or not the SAC will restart a given port monitor depends on two things:

- the restart count specified for the port monitor when the port monitor was added. See **sacadm**(1M).
- the number of times the port monitor has already been restarted

FILES

/etc/saf/_sactab
/etc/saf/_sysconfig
/etc/inittab
/var/adm/utmp
/var/saf/_log

SEE ALSO

inittab(4), **pmadm**(1M), **sacadm**(1M)

sacadm (1M)

NAME

sacadm – service access controller administration

SYNOPSIS

sacadm -a -p *pmtag* **-t** *type* **-c** *cmd* **-v** *ver* **[-f dx] [-n** *count***] **
[-y "*comment***"] [-z** *script***]**

sacadm -r -p *pmtag*

sacadm -s -p *pmtag*

sacadm -k -p *pmtag*

sacadm -e -p *pmtag*

sacadm -d -p *pmtag*

sacadm -l [-p *pmtag* **| -t** *type***]**

sacadm -L [-p *pmtag* **| -t** *type***]**

sacadm -g -p *pmtag* **[-z** *script***]**

sacadm -G [-z *script***]**

sacadm -x [-p *pmtag***]**

DESCRIPTION

sacadm is the administrative command for the upper level of the Service Access Facility hierarchy, that is, for port monitor administration. **sacadm** performs the following functions:

- adds or removes a port monitor
- starts or stops a port monitor
- enables or disables a port monitor
- installs or replaces a per-system configuration script
- installs or replaces a per-port monitor configuration script
- prints requested port monitor information

Any user on the system may invoke **sacadm** to request port monitor status (**-l** and **-L**) and to print per-port monitor and per-system configuration scripts (**-g** and **-G** without the **-z** option).

The options have the following meanings:

-a Add a port monitor. When adding a port monitor, **sacadm** creates the supporting directory structure in **/etc/saf** and **/var/saf** and adds an entry for the new port monitor to **/etc/saf/_sactab**. The file **_sactab** already exists on the delivered system. Initially, it is empty except for a single line, which contains the version number of the Service Access Controller.

Unless the command line that adds the new port monitor includes a **-f** option with the argument **x**, the new port monitor will be started. Because of the complexity of the options and arguments that follow the **-a** option, it may be convenient to use a command script or the menu system to add port monitors. If you use the menu system, enter **sysadm ports** and then choose the **port_monitors** option.

-c *cmd* The command (*cmd*) to execute when the port monitor is started. If the command includes arguments, the string must be enclosed with double quote characters.

-d Disable the port monitor *pmtag*.

-e Enable the port monitor *pmtag*.

-f dx The **-f** option specifies one or both of the following two flags which are then included in the flags field of the **_sactab** entry for the new port monitor. If the **-f** option is not included on the command line, no flags are set and the default conditions prevail. By default, a port monitor is started and enabled. A **-f** option with no following argument is illegal.

- **d** Do not enable the new port monitor.
- **x** Do not start the new port monitor.

-g The **-g** option is used to request output or to install or replace the per-port monitor configuration script **/etc/saf/***pmtag***/_config**. **-g** requires a **-p** option. The **-g** option with only a **-p** option prints the per-port monitor configuration script for port monitor *pmtag*. The **-g** option with a **-p** option and a **-z** option installs the file **script** as the per-port monitor configuration script for port monitor *pmtag*. Other combinations of options with **-g** are invalid.

-G The **-G** option is used to request output or to install or replace the per-system configuration script **/etc/saf/_sysconfig**. The **-G** option by itself prints the per-system configuration script. The **-G** option in combination with a **-z** option installs the file **script** as the per-system configuration script. Other combinations of options with a **-G** option are invalid.

-k Stop port monitor *pmtag*.

-l The **-l** option is used to request port monitor information. The **-l** by itself lists all port monitors on the system. The **-l** option in combination with the **-p** option lists only the port monitor specified by *pmtag*. A **-l** in combination with the **-t** option lists all port monitors of type *type*. Any other combination of options with the **-l** option is invalid.

-L The **-L** option is identical to the **-l** option except that the output appears in a condensed format.

-n *count*

Set the restart count to *count*. If a restart count is not specified, count is set to **0**. A count of **0** indicates that the port monitor is not to be restarted if it fails.

-p *pmtag*

Specifies the tag associated with a port monitor.

-r Remove port monitor *pmtag*. **sacadm** removes the port monitor entry from **/etc/saf/_sactab**. If the removed port monitor is not running, then no further action is taken. If the removed port monitor is running, the Service Access Controller (SAC) sends it **SIGTERM** to indicate that it should shut down. Note that the port monitor's directory structure remains intact.

-s Start a port monitor. The SAC starts the port monitor *pmtag*.

-t *type* Specifies the port monitor type.

-v *ver* Specifies the version number of the port monitor. This version number may be given as

-v `*pmspec* **-V**`

where *pmspec* is the special administrative command for port monitor *pmtag*. This special command is **ttyadm** for **ttymon** and **nlsadmin** for **listen**. The version stamp of the port monitor is known by the command and is returned when *pmspec* is invoked with a **-V** option.

-x The **-x** option by itself tells the SAC to read its database file (**_sactab**). The **-x** option with the **-p** option tells port monitor *pmtag* to read its administrative file.

-y "*comment*"
Include *comment* in the **_sactab** entry for port monitor *pmtag*.

-z *script*
Used with the **-g** and **-G** options to specify the name of a file that contains a configuration script. With the **-g** option, **script** is a per-port monitor configuration script; with **-G** it is a per-system configuration script. The **-z** option overwrites the existing script. It is suggested that you do the following three steps when you modify/replace a configuration script. First a copy of the existing script should be made (**-g** or **-G**). Then the copy should be edited. Finally, the copy is put in place over the existing script (**-g** or **-G** with **-z**).

OUTPUT

If successful, **sacadm** will exit with a status of 0. If **sacadm** fails for any reason, it will exit with a nonzero status. Options that request information will write the information on the standard output. In the condensed format (**-L**), port monitor information is printed as a sequence of colon-separated fields; empty fields are indicated by two successive colons. The standard format (**-l**) prints a header identifying the columns, and port monitor information is aligned under the appropriate headings. In this format, an empty field is indicated by a hyphen. The comment character is **#**.

EXAMPLES

The following command line adds a port monitor. The port monitor tag is **tcp**; its type is **listen**; if necessary, it will restart three times before failing; its administrative command is **nlsadmin**; and the configuration script to be read is in the file **script**:

```
sacadm -a -p tcp -t listen -c "/usr/lib/saf/listen -m inet/tcp tcp"
   -v `nlsadmin -V` -n 3 -z script
```

Remove a port monitor whose tag is **pmtag**:

```
sacadm -r -p pmtag
```

Start the port monitor whose tag is **pmtag**:

```
sacadm -s -p pmtag
```

Stop the port monitor whose tag is **pmtag**:

```
sacadm -k -p pmtag
```

Enable the port monitor whose tag is **pmtag**:

```
sacadm -e -p pmtag
```

Disable the port monitor whose tag is **pmtag**:

```
sacadm -d -p pmtag
```

List status information for all port monitors:

```
sacadm -l
```

List status information for the port monitor whose tag is **pmtag**:

```
sacadm -l -p pmtag
```

List the same information in condensed format:

```
sacadm -L -p pmtag
```

List status information for all port monitors whose type is **listen**:

```
sacadm -l -t listen
```

Replace the per-port monitor configuration script associated with the port monitor whose tag is **pmtag** with the contents of the file **file.config**:

```
sacadm -g -p pmtag -z file.config
```

FILES

/etc/saf/_sactab
/etc/saf/_sysconfig
/etc/saf/*pmtag***/_config**

SEE ALSO

doconfig(3N), **pmadm**(1M), **sac**(1M)

sact(1)

NAME

sact – print current SCCS file editing activity

SYNOPSIS

sact *file* . . .

DESCRIPTION

sact informs the user of any impending deltas to a named SCCS file. This situation occurs when **get** with the **-e** option has been previously executed without a subsequent execution of **delta**. If a directory is named on the command line, **sact** behaves as though each file in the directory were specified as a named file, except that non-SCCS files and unreadable files are silently ignored. If a name of – is given, the standard input is read with each line being taken as the name of an SCCS file to be processed.

The output for each named file consists of five fields separated by spaces.

Field 1 specifies the SID of a delta that currently exists in the SCCS file to which changes will be made to make the new delta.

Field 2 specifies the SID for the new delta to be created.

Field 3 contains the logname of the user who will make the delta (that is, executed a **get** for editing).

Field 4 contains the date that **get -e** was executed.

Field 5 contains the time that **get -e** was executed.

SEE ALSO

delta(1), **diff**(1), **get**(1), **help**(1), **unget**(1)

DIAGNOSTICS

Use **help**(1) for explanations.

NAME

sadc, **sa1**, **sa2** – system activity report package

SYNOPSIS

/usr/lib/sa/sadc [*t n*] [*ofile*]

/usr/lib/sa/sa1 [*t n*]

/usr/lib/sa/sa2 [**-ubdycwaqvmpgrkxDSAC**] [**-s** *time*] [**-e** *time*] [**-i** *sec*]

DESCRIPTION

System activity data can be accessed at the special request of a user [see **sar**(1M)] and automatically, on a routine basis, as described here. The operating system contains several counters that are incremented as various system actions occur. These include counters for CPU utilization, buffer usage, disk and tape I/O activity, TTY device activity, switching and system-call activity, file-access, queue activity, inter-process communications, paging, and Remote File Sharing.

sadc and two shell procedures, **sa1** and **sa2**, are used to sample, save, and process this data.

sadc, the data collector, samples system data *n* times, with an interval of *t* seconds between samples, and writes in binary format to *ofile* or to standard output. The sampling interval *t* should be greater than 5 seconds; otherwise, the activity of **sadc** itself may affect the sample. If *t* and *n* are omitted, a special record is written. This facility is used at system boot time, when booting to a multiuser state, to mark the time at which the counters restart from zero. For example, the **/etc/init.d/perf** file writes the restart mark to the daily data by the command entry:

```
su sys -c "$TFADMIN /usr/lib/sa/sadc /var/adm/sa/sadate +%d"
```

The shell script **sa1**, a variant of **sadc**, is used to collect and store data in the binary file **/var/adm/sa/sa***dd*, where *dd* is the current day. The arguments *t* and *n* cause records to be written *n* times at an interval of *t* seconds, or once if omitted. The following entries in **/var/spool/cron/crontabs/sys** produce records every 20 minutes during working hours and hourly otherwise:

```
0 * * * 0-6 $TFADMIN /usr/lib/sa/sa1
20,40 8-17 * * 1-5 $TFADMIN /usr/lib/sa/sa1
```

See **crontab**(1) for details.

The shell script **sa2**, a variant of **sar**, writes a daily report in the file **/var/adm/sa/sar***dd*. The options are explained in **sar**(1M). The following entry in **/var/spool/cron/crontabs/sys** reports important activities hourly during the working day:

```
5 18 * * 1-5 $TFADMIN /usr/lib/sa/sa2 -s 8:00 -e 18:01 -i 1200 -A
```

FILES

/var/adm/sa/sa*dd*	daily data file
/var/adm/sa/sar*dd*	daily report file

SEE ALSO

crontab(1), **sar**(1M), **timex**(1)

NAME

sadp – disk access profiler

SYNOPSIS

sadp [**-th**] [**-d** *device*[–*drive*]] *s* [*n*]

DESCRIPTION

sadp reports disk access location and seek distance, in tabular or histogram form. It samples disk activity once every second during an interval of *s* seconds. This is done *n* times if *n* is specified. Cylinder usage and disk distance are recorded in units of 8 cylinders.

The only valid name for *device* is **sd01**, which is for Small Computer Systems Interface (SCSI) disks.

drive specifies the disk drives and it may be:

> a drive number in the range supported by **device**,
> two numbers separated by a minus (indicating an inclusive range),

or

> a list of drive numbers separated by commas.

Up to 56 disk drives may be reported for device type **sd01**. If *drive* is not specified, **sadp** profiles all the disk drives specifed by *device*, up to the maximum of 56 for **sd01**.

The **-t** flag causes the data to be reported in tabular form. The **-h** flag produces a histogram of the data. The default is **-t**.

EXAMPLE

The command:

```
sadp -d sd01-0 900 4
```

will generate four tabular reports, each describing cylinder usage and seek distance of **sd01** disk drive 0 during a 15-minute interval.

FILES

/dev/kmem

SEE ALSO

mem(7)

NAME

sar – system activity reporter

SYNOPSIS

sar [**-ubdycwaqvtmpgrkxDSAC**] [**-o** *file*] *t* [*n*]

sar [**-ubdycwaqvtmpgrkxDSAC**] [**-s** *time*] [**-e** *time*] [**-i** *sec*] [**-f** *file*]

DESCRIPTION

In the first synopsis line, **sar** samples cumulative activity counters in the operating system at *n* intervals of *t* seconds, where *t* should be 5 or greater and the default value of *n* is 1. (Note that if the sampling interval is less than 5, the activity of **sar** itself may affect the sample.) If the **-o** option is specified, **sar** saves the samples in *file* in binary format. The type of command shown in the first synopsis line immediately sends the output for every option specified to standard output, without organizing it into a rational format; data for different options appears in an undifferentiated jumble and is difficult to read. Therefore, when running **sar** in the format of the first synopsis line, we recommend (a) specifying only one option, and (b) avoiding the **-A** option (which is equivalent to specifying all options).

In the second synopsis line, with no sampling interval specified, **sar** extracts data from a previously recorded *file*, either the one specified by the **-f** option or, by default, the standard system activity daily data file **/var/adm/sa/sa***dd* for the current day *dd*. The starting and ending times of the report can be bounded using the **-s** and **-e** *time* arguments of the form *hh*[:*mm*[:*ss*]]. The **-i** option selects records at *sec* second intervals. Otherwise, all intervals found in the data file are reported.

In either case, subsets of data to be printed are specified by option:

-u Report processor utilization (the default):

- **%usr** portion of time running in user mode
- **%sys** portion of time running in system mode
- **%wio** portion of time idle with some process waiting for block I/O
- **%idle** portion of time otherwise idle

When used with **-D**, **%sys** is split into percentage of time servicing requests from remote machines via RFS (**%sys remote**) and all other system time (**%sys local**).

-b Report buffer activity:

- **bread/s, bwrit/s** transfers per second of data between system buffers and disk or other block devices
- **lread/s, lwrit/s** accesses per second of system buffers
- **%rcache, %wcache** cache hit ratios, such as (**1-bread/lread**) as a percentage
- **pread/s, pwrit/s** transfers per second by means of raw (physical) device mechanism

When used with **-D**, buffer caching is reported for locally-mounted RFS remote resources.

-d Report activity for hard disks. When data is displayed, the device specification *dsk-* is generally used to represent a disk drive. The data reported is:

%busy percentage of time disk was busy servicing a transfer request

avque The average number of requests outstanding during the monitored period (the number of requests being serviced). This number is the ratio of total time for all requests to complete to total time disk was busy servicing the requests minus 1.

r+w/s number of data transfers to or from disk per second

blks/s number of 512-byte blocks transferred to or from the disk per second

avwait average time in milliseconds that transfer requests wait idly on queue

avserv average time in milliseconds for a transfer request to be completed by the disk (including seek, rotational latency, and data transfer times)

-y Report TTY device activity (per second):

rawch/s input characters

canch/s input characters processed by canon

outch/s output characters

rcvin/s receiver hardware interrupts

xmtin/s transmitter hardware interrupts

mdmin/s modem interrupts

-c Report system calls (per second):

scall/s system calls of all types

sread/s, **swrit/s**, **fork/s**, **exec/s**
specific system calls (**read**, **write**, **fork**, and **exec**)

rchar/s characters (bytes) transferred by **read** system calls

wchar/s characters (bytes) transferred by **write** system calls

When used with **-D**, the system calls are split into RFS incoming, RFS outgoing, and local calls. No RFS incoming or outgoing **fork** and **exec** calls are reported.

-w Report system swapping and switching activity (per second):

swpin/s, **swpot/s**
number of transfers to and from memory

pswin/s, pswot/s
number of 512-byte blocks transferred for swapins and swapouts

pswch/s process switches

-a Report use of file access system routines (per second):

iget/s number of S5, SFS, and UFS files located by inode entry

namei/s number of file system path searches

dirblk/s number of S5 directory block reads issued

-q Report average queue length while occupied, and percentage of time occupied:

runq-sz run queue of processes in memory and runnable

%runocc percentage of time run queue is occupied

swpq-sz the average number of processes in the swap queue when there were processes in the queue If there were no processes in the swap queue, this field is blank.

%swpocc the percent of time during the sample that there were processes in the swap queue. If there were no processes in the swap queue, this field is blank.

-v Report status of process, i-node, file, and file and record locking tables for each file system:

proc-sz, inod-sz, file-sz, lock-sz
entries/size for each table, evaluated once at sampling point.

ov overflows that occur between sampling points for each table.

-t Report usage by file system type:

fstype file system type (either **s5**, **vxfs**, or combined **ufs** and **sfs**)

inodes

inuse current number of inode table entries being used by processes.

alloc current number of inode table entries existing (both in use and free).

limit maximum limit of inodes that can be allocated. (This is a soft upper limit, so **alloc** may exceed **limit**.)

fail number of inode allocation failures that occur between sampling points. (This can occur when the limit is exceeded or when memory for inodes is unavailable.)

ipf the percentage of inodes taken off the freelist by **iget** that had reusable pages associated with them. These pages are flushed and cannot be reclaimed by processes. Thus, this is the percentage of **iget**s that cause page flushes.

-m Report message and semaphore activities:

msg/s, sema/s
: primitives per second

-p Report paging activities:

atch/s page faults per second that are satisfied by reclaiming a page currently in memory (attaches per second)

pgin/s page-in requests per second

ppgin/s pages paged-in per second

pflt/s page faults from protection errors per second (invalid access to page or "copy-on-writes")

vflt/s address translation page faults per second (valid page not in memory)

slock/s faults per second caused by software lock requests requiring physical I/O

-g Report paging activities:

pgout/s page-out requests per second

ppgout/s pages paged-out per second

pgfree/s pages per second placed on the freelist by the page stealing daemon

pgscan/s pages per second scanned by the page stealing daemon

-r Report unused memory pages and disk blocks:

freemem average pages available to user processes

freeswap disk blocks available for page swapping

-k Report kernel memory allocation (KMA) activities:

Information about the memory pool reserving and allocating space for small requests (less than 256 bytes):

sml_mem the amount of memory in bytes KMA has for the small pool

alloc the number of bytes allocated to satisfy requests for small amounts of memory

fail the number of requests for small amounts of memory that were not satisfied (failed)

Information for the large memory pool:

lg_mem, alloc, fail
: (analogous to the information for the small memory pool)

Information for oversized requests (because oversized memory is allocated dynamically, there is not a pool):

`ovsz_alloc` the amount of memory allocated for oversize requests

`fail` the number of oversize requests that could not be satisfied

-x Report remote file sharing (RFS) operations:

`open/s` the number of open operations made per second by clients (incoming) and by the server (outgoing)

`create/s` the number of create operations made per second by clients (incoming) and by the server (outgoing)

`lookup/s` the number of lookup operations made per second by clients (incoming) and by the server (outgoing)

`readdir/s` the number of readdir operations made per second by clients (incoming) and by the server (outgoing)

`getpage/s` the number of getpage operations made per second by clients (incoming) and by the server (outgoing)

`putpage/s` the number of putpage operations made per second by clients (incoming) and by the server (outgoing)

`other/s` the number of other operations made per second by clients (incoming) and the server (outgoing)

-D Report Remote File Sharing activity:

When used in combination with **-u**, **-b**, or **-c**, it causes **sar** to produce the remote file sharing version of the corresponding report. **-Du** is assumed when only **-D** is specified.

-S Report server and request queue status:

`serv/`*lo-hi* average number of Remote File Sharing servers on the system (*lo* and *hi* are the minimum and maximum number of servers respectively)

`request %busy`
percentage of time receive descriptors are on the request queue

`request avg lgth`
average number of receive descriptors waiting for service when queue is occupied

`server %avail`
percentage of time there are idle servers

`server avg avail`
average number of idle servers when idle ones exist

-A Report all data (equivalent to **-udqbwcayvtmpgrkxCSD**).

-C Report Remote File Sharing data caching overhead:

`snd-inv/s` number of invalidation messages per second sent by your machine as a server

snd-msg/s	total outgoing RFS messages sent per second
rcv-inv/s	number of invalidation messages received from the remote server
rcv-msg/s	total number of incoming RFS messages received per second
dis-bread/s	number of read messages that would be eligible for caching if caching had not been turned off because of an invalidation message. (Indicates the penalty incurred because of the invalidation message).
blk-inv/s	number of pages removed from the client cache in response to cache invalidation messages

EXAMPLES

To see today's processor activity so far:

```
sar
```

To watch processor activity evolve for ten minutes and save data:

```
sar -o temp 60 10
```

To later review disk activity from that period:

```
sar -d -f temp
```

FILES

/var/adm/sa/sa*dd* daily data file, where *dd* are digits representing the day of the month

SEE ALSO

sadc(1M)

NOTES

The start (**-s**) and end (**-e**) times cannot overlap at midnight.

NAME

sccs – (BSD) front end for the Source Code Control System (SCCS)

SYNOPSIS

/usr/ucb/sccs [**-r**] [**-d***prefixpath*] [**-p***finalpath*] *command* [*SCCS-flags* . . .]
[*file* . . .]

DESCRIPTION

The **sccs** command is a front end to the utility programs of the Source Code Control System (SCCS).

sccs normally prefixes each *file*, or the last component of each *file*, with the string '**SCCS/s.**', because you normally keep your SCCS database files in a directory called **SCCS**, and each database file starts with an '**s.**' prefix. If the environment variable PROJECTDIR is set, and is an absolute pathname (that is, begins with a slash) **sccs** will search for SCCS files in the directory given by that variable. If it is a relative pathname (that is, does not begin with a slash), it is treated as the name of a user, and **sccs** will search in that user's home directory for a directory named **src** or **source**. If that directory is found, **sccs** will search for SCCS files in the directory given by that variable.

sccs program options must appear before the *command* argument. Flags to be passed to the actual SCCS command (utility program) must appear after the *command* argument. These flags are specific to the *command* being used.

sccs also includes the capability to run "set user ID" to another user to provide additional protection. Certain commands (such as **admin**(1)) cannot be run "set user ID" by all users, since this would allow anyone to change the authorizations. Such commands are always run as the real user.

OPTIONS

-r Run **sccs** as the real user rather than as whatever effective user **sccs** is "set user ID" to.

-d*prefixpath*
Define the prefix portion of the pathname for the SCCS database files. The default prefix portion of the pathname is the current directory. *prefixpath* is prefixed to the entire pathname. See EXAMPLE.

This flag overrides any directory specified by the **PROJECTDIR** environment variable.

-p*finalpath*
Define the name of a lower directory in which the SCCS files will be found; SCCS is the default. *finalpath* is appended before the final component of the pathname. See EXAMPLES.

USAGE

Additional sccs Commands

Several "pseudo-commands" are available in addition to the usual SCCS commands. These are:

create **create** is used when creating new **s.** files. For example, given a C source language file called '**obscure.c**', **create** would perform the following actions: (1) create the '**s.**' file called '**s.obscure.c**' in the SCCS directory; (2) rename the original source file to '**,obscure.c**'; (3)

do an '**sccs get**' on '**obscure.c**'. Compared to the SCCS **admin** command, **create** does more of the startup work for you and should be used in preference to **admin**.

enter — **enter** is just like **create**, except that it does not do the final '**sccs get**'. It is usually used if an '**sccs edit**' is to be performed immediately after the **enter**.

edit — Get a file for editing.

delget — Perform a **delta** on the named files and then **get** new versions. The new versions have ID keywords expanded, and so cannot be edited.

deledit — Same as **delget**, but produces new versions suitable for editing. **deledit** is useful for making a "checkpoint" of your current editing phase.

fix — Remove the named delta, but leaves you with a copy of the delta with the changes that were in it. **fix** must be followed by a **-r** flag. **fix** is useful for fixing small compiler bugs, and so on. Since **fix** does not leave audit trails, use it carefully.

clean — Remove everything from the current directory that can be recreated from SCCS files. **clean** checks for and does not remove any files being edited. If '**clean -b**' is used, branches are **not** checked to see if they are currently being edited. Note: **-b** is dangerous if you are keeping the branches in the same directory.

unedit — "Undo" the last **edit** or '**get -e**' and return a file to its previous condition. If you **unedit** a file being edited, all changes made since the beginning of the editing session are lost.

info — Display a list of all files being edited. If the **-b** flag is given, branches (that is, SID's with two or fewer components) are ignored. If the **-u** flag is given (with an optional argument), only files being edited by you (or the named user) are listed.

check — Check for files currently being edited, like **info**, but returns an exit code rather than a listing: nothing is printed if nothing is being edited, and a non-zero exit status is returned if anything is being edited. **check** may thus be included in an "install" entry in a makefile, to ensure that everything is included in an SCCS file before a version is installed.

tell — Display a list of files being edited on the standard output. Filenames are separated by NEWLINE characters. Take the **-b** and **-u** flags like **info** and **check**.

diffs — Compare (in **diff**-like format) the current version of the program you have out for editing and the versions in SCCS format. **diffs** accepts the same arguments as **diff**, except that the **-c** flag must be specified as **-C** instead, because the **-c** flag is taken as a flag to **get** indicating which version is to be compared with the current version.

print Print verbose information about the named files. **print** does an '**sccs prs -e**' followed by an '**sccs get -p -m**' on each file.

EXAMPLES

The command:

```
sccs  -d/usr/include  get sys/inode.h
```

converts to:

```
get  /usr/include/sys/SCCS/s.inode.h
```

The intent here is to create aliases such as:

```
alias  syssccs  sccs  -d/usr/src
```

which will be used as:

```
syssccs  get  cmd/who.c
```

The command:

```
sccs  -pprivate  get  usr/include/stdio.h
```

converts to:

```
get  usr/include/private/s.stdio.h
```

To put a file called **myprogram.c** into SCCS format for the first time, assuming also that there is no SCCS directory already existing:

```
$ mkdir SCCS
$ sccs create myprogram.c
$ myprogram.c:
1.1
14 lines
$
```

To get a copy of **myprogram.c** for editing, edit that file, then place it back in the SCCS database:

```
$ sccs edit myprogram.c
1.1
new delta 1.2
14 lines
$ vi myprogram.c
your editing session
$ sccs delget myprogram.c
comments? Added responses for compatibility
1.2
7 inserted
7 deleted
7 unchanged
1.2
14 lines
$
```

To get a file from another directory:

```
sccs -p/usr/src/sccs/  get cc.c
```

or:

```
sccs get /usr/src/sccs/cc.c
```

To make a delta of a large number of files in the current directory:

```
sccs delta *.c
```

To get a list of files being edited that are not on branches:

```
sccs info -b
```

To delta everything that you are editing:

```
$ sccs delta `sccs tell -u`
```

In a makefile, to get source files from an SCCS file if it does not already exist:

```
SRCS = <list of source files>
$(SRCS):
        sccs get $(REL) $@
```

Regular sccs Commands

The "regular" SCCS commands are described very briefly below. It is unlikely that you ever need to use these commands because the user interface is so complicated, and the **sccs** front end command does 99.9% of the interesting tasks for you.

admin Create new SCCS files and changes parameters of existing SCCS files. You can use '**sccs create**' to create new SCCS files, or use '**sccs admin**' to do other things.

cdc Change the commentary material in an SCCS delta.

comb Combine SCCS deltas and reconstructs the SCCS files.

delta Permanently introduces changes that were made to a file previously retrieved using '**sccs get**'. You can use '**sccs delget**' as the more useful version of this command since '**sccs delget**' does all of the useful work and more.

get Extract a file from the SCCS database, either for compilation, or for editing when the **-e** option is used. Use '**sccs get**' if you really need it, but '**sccs delget**' will normally have done this job for you. Use **sccs edit** instead of **get** with the **-e** option.

help Supposed to help you interpret SCCS error messages.

prs Display information about what is happening in an SCCS file.

rmdel Remove a delta from an SCCS file.

sccsdiff Compare two versions of an SCCS file and generates the differences between the two versions.

val Determine if a given SCCS file meets specified criteria. If you use the **sccs** command, you should not need to use **val**, because its user interface is unbelievable.

what	Display SCCS identification information.

FILES

/usr/sccs/*

SEE ALSO

admin(1), **cdc**(1), **comb**(1), **delta**(1), **get**(1), **help**(1), **prs**(1), **rmdel**(1), **sact**(1), **sccsdiff**(1), **sccsfile**(4), **unget**(1), **val**(1), **what**(1)

NOTES

The **help** command usually just parrots SCCS error messages and is generally not considered very helpful.

sccsdiff (1)

NAME

sccsdiff – compare two versions of an SCCS file

SYNOPSIS

sccsdiff -r*SID1* **-r***SID2* [**-p**] [**-s***n*] *file . . .*

DESCRIPTION

sccsdiff compares two versions of an SCCS file and generates the differences between the two versions. Any number of SCCS files may be specified, but arguments apply to all files.

-r*SID1* -r*SID2*
: *SID1* and *SID2* specify the deltas of an SCCS file that are to be compared. Versions are passed to **bdiff** in the order given.

-p
: pipe output for each file through **pr**.

-s*n*
: *n* is the file segment size that **bdiff** will pass to **diff**. This option is useful when **diff** fails due to a high system load.

FILES

/var/tmp/get????? temporary files

SEE ALSO

bdiff(1), **diff**(1), **get**(1), **help**(1), **pr**(1)

NAME

scompat – (XENIX) set up XENIX system compatibility environment for console applications

SYNOPSIS

scompat [-r *interpretnumber*] [*command_line*]

DESCRIPTION

COFF- or ELF-based applications developed for SCO UNIX System V/386 3.2 (or later releases) that use graphics may not work correctly on the system VGA/EGA/CGA console or Fiber Optic Workstations, which are STREAMS-based beginning with UNIX System V/386 Release 4.

The **scompat** command sets up the workstation environment so that these applications may function correctly. While the environment is in effect, access to the workstation as a STREAMS device will not work correctly unless the **-r** option is used with the argument **4** (see below).

For COFF or ELF executables, **scompat** may be invoked with no arguments to give you XENIX™ system **ioctl** interpretation [see **ioctl**(2)]. In this case, a sub-shell is created. For the lifetime of the shell, the compatibility environment is in effect on the workstation.

The options and arguments for this command are:

-r *interpretnumber*, where *interpretnumber* is:

- 3 UNIX System V/386 Release 3.2 **ioctl** interpretation for XENIX system applications
- 4 STREAMS **ioctl** interpretation for COFF executables or XENIX system applications

command_line a shell command line (for example,, **scompat ls -l**). The command line will be executed with the compatibility environment in effect. When the command completes execution, the compatibility environment is restored to its previous state.

SEE ALSO

ioctl(2), **sh**(1), **uname**(1)

NOTES

For computers based on Intel™ microprocessors, if the shell environment variable **SCOMPAT** is set to **3.2**, **uname -a** gives a value of **3.2** for *release* and a value of **2** for *version*.

To set **SCOMPAT** to any other version, use the syntax

SCOMPAT=*release***:***version*

To return to the beginning state, unset **SCOMPAT**.

In all cases, when **SCOMPAT** is set, it must be exported [see **sh**(1)].

script(1)

NAME

script – make typescript of a terminal session

SYNOPSIS

script [**-a**] [*file*]

DESCRIPTION

script makes a typescript of everything printed on your terminal, including prompts. The typescript is written to *file*, or appended to *file* if the **-a** option is given. If no file name is given, the typescript is saved in the file **typescript**.

The script ends when the forked shell exits or when CTRL-**d** is typed.

NAME

sdb – symbolic debugger

SYNOPSIS

sdb [-e] [-s *signo*] [-V] [-W] [-w] [*objfile* [*corfile [directory-list*]]]

DESCRIPTION

sdb is obsolete and will no longer be available after this release. Use **debug**(1) instead. **sdb** is a symbolic debugger for C and assembly programs. **sdb** may be used to examine executable program files and core files. It may also be used to examine live processes in a controlled execution environment.

The *objfile* argument is the name of an executable program file. To take full advantage of the symbolic capabilities of **sdb**, this file should be compiled with the **-g** (debug) option. If it has not been compiled with the **-g** option, the symbolic capabilities of **sdb** will be limited, but the file can still be examined and the program debugged. *objfile* may also be a path name in the **/proc** directory, in which case the currently executing process denoted by that path name is controlled by **sdb**.

The *corfile* argument is the name of a core image file. A core image file is produced by the abnormal termination of *objfile* or by the use of **gcore**. A core image file contains a copy of the segments of a program. The default for *corfile* is **core**. A core image file need not be present to use **sdb**. Using a hyphen (–) instead of *corfile* forces **sdb** to ignore an existing core image file.

The *directory-list* argument is a colon-separated list of directories that is used by **sdb** to locate source files used to build *objfile*. If no directory list is specified, **sdb** will look in the current directory.

sdb processes supplementary code set characters according to the locale specified in the **LC_CTYPE** environment variable [see **LANG** on **environ**(5)]. In regular expressions, pattern searches are performed on characters, not bytes, as described on **ed**(1). Variables of type **wchar_t** can be specified; process codes can be displayed as characters, or characters can be entered by process code representation.

The following options are recognized by **sdb**:

-e Ignore symbolic information and treat nonsymbolic addresses as file offsets.

-s *signo* Where *signo* is a decimal number that corresponds to a signal number [see **signal**(2)], do not stop live processes under control of **sdb** that receive the signal. This option may be used more than once on the **sdb** command line.

-V Print version information. If no *objfile* argument is specified on the command line, **sdb** will exit after printing the version information.

-W Suppress warnings about *corfile* being older than *objfile* or about source files that are older than *objfile*.

-w Allow user to write to *objfile* or *corfile*.

sdb recognizes a current line and a current file. When **sdb** is examining an executable program file without a core file, the current line and current file are initially set to the line and file containing the first line of **main**. If *corfile* exists, then current line and current file are initially set to the line and file containing the source statement where the process terminated. The current line and current file change automatically as a live process executes. They may also be changed with the source file examination commands.

Names of variables are written as in C. Variables local to a procedure may be accessed using the form *procedure*`:`*variable*. If no procedure name is given, the procedure containing the current line is used by default.

Structure members may be referred to as *variable*`.`*member*, pointers to structure members as *variable*`->`*member*, and array elements as *variable*`[`*number*`]`. Pointers may also be dereferenced by using the form *pointer*`[`*number*`]`. Combinations of these forms may also be used. The form *number*`->`*member* may be used where *number* is the address of a pointer, and *number*`.`*member* where *number* is interpreted as the address of a structure instance. The template of the structure type used in this case will be the last structure type referenced. When **sdb** displays the value of a structure, it does so by displaying the value of all elements of the structure. The address of a structure is displayed by displaying the address of the structure instance rather than the addresses of individual elements.

Elements of a multidimensional array may be referred to as *variable* `[`*number*`]` `[`*number*`]`. . ., or as *variable* `[`*number*`,`*number*`,`. . .`]`. In place of *number*, the form *number*`;`*number* may be used to indicate a range of values, * may be used to indicate all legitimate values for that subscript, or subscripts may be omitted entirely if they are the last subscripts and the full range of values is desired. If no subscripts are specified, **sdb** will display the value of all elements of the array.

A particular instance of a variable on the stack is referred to as *procedure*`:`*variable*`,`*number*. The *number* is the occurrence of the specified procedure on the stack, with the topmost occurrence being 1. The default procedure is the one containing the current line.

Addresses may be used in **sdb** commands as well. Addresses are specified by decimal, octal, or hexadecimal numbers.

Line numbers in the source program are specified by the form *filename*`:`*number* or *procedure*`:`*number*. In either case, the *number* is relative to the beginning of the file and corresponds to the line number used by text editors or the output of **pr**. A number used by itself implies a line in the current file.

While a live process is running under **sdb**, all addresses and identifiers refer to the live process. When **sdb** is not examining a live process, the addresses and identifiers refer to *objfile* or *corfile*.

Commands

The commands for examining data in the program are:

`t` Prints a stack trace of the terminated or halted program. The function invoked most recently is at the top of the stack. For C programs, the stack ends with **_start**, which is the startup routine that invokes **main**.

`T` Prints the top line of the stack trace.

variable/clm

Print the value of *variable* according to length *l* and format *m*. The numeric count *c* indicates that a region of memory, beginning at the address implied by *variable*, is to be displayed. The length specifiers are:

b one byte

h two bytes (half word)

l four bytes (long word)

Legal values for *m* are:

c character

d signed decimal

u unsigned decimal

o octal

x hexadecimal

f 32-bit single precision floating point

g 64-bit double precision floating point

s Assumes that *variable* is a string pointer and prints characters starting at the address pointed to by the variable.

a Prints characters starting at the variable's address. Do not use this with register variables.

p pointer to procedure

i Disassembles machine-language instruction with addresses printed numerically and symbolically.

I Disassembles machine-language instruction with addresses printed numerically only.

Length specifiers are effective with formats **c**, **d**, **u**, **o**, **x**. The length specifier determines the output length of the value to be displayed. This value may be truncated. The count specifier *c* displays that many units of memory, starting at the address of the *variable*. The number of bytes in the unit of memory is determined by *l* or by the size associated with the variable. If the specifiers *c*, *l*, and *m* are omitted, **sdb** uses defaults. If a count specifier is used with the **s** or **a** command, then that many characters are printed. Otherwise, successive characters are printed until either a null byte is reached or 128 characters are printed. The last variable may be redisplayed with the **./** command.

For a limited form of pattern matching, use the **sh** metacharacters * and **?** within procedure and variable names. (**sdb** does not accept these metacharacters in file names, as the function name in a line number when setting a breakpoint, in the function call command, or as the argument to the **e** command.) If no procedure name is supplied, **sdb** matches both local and global variables. If the procedure name is specified, then **sdb** matches only local variables. To match global variables only, use **:***pattern*. To print all variables, use ***:***.

*linenumber***?***lm*
*variable***:?***lm*

Prints the value at the address from the executable or text space given by *linenumber* or *variable* (procedure name), according to the format *lm*. The default format is **i**.

variable=*lm*
linenumber=*lm*
number=*lm*

Prints the address of *variable* or *linenumber*, or the value of *number*. *l* specifies length and *m* specifies the format. If no format is specified, then **sdb** uses **lx** (four-byte hex). *m* allows you to convert between decimal, octal, and hexadecimal.

variable!*value*

Sets *variable* to the given *value*. The value may be a number, a character constant, or a variable. The value must be well-defined; structures are allowed only if assigning to another structure variable of the same type. Character constants are denoted ´*character*. Numbers are viewed as integers unless a decimal point or exponent is used. In this case, they are treated as having the type **double**. Registers, except the floating point registers, are viewed as integers. Register names are identical to those used by the assembler (for example, %*regname* where *regname* is the name of a register). If the address of a variable is given, it is regarded as the address of a variable of type **int**. C conventions are used in any type conversions necessary to perform the indicated assignment.

x Prints the machine registers and the current machine-language instruction.

X Prints the current machine-language instruction.

The commands for examining source files are:

e
e *procedure*
e *filename*
e *directory*/

e, without arguments, prints the name of the current file. The second form sets the current file to the file containing the procedure. The third form sets the current file to *filename*. The current line is set to the first line in the named procedure or file. Source files are assumed to be in the directories in the directory list. The fourth form adds *directory* to the end of the directory list.

/*regular expression*/

Searches forward from the current line for a line containing a string matching *regular expression*, as in **ed**. The trailing / may be omitted, except when associated with a breakpoint.

?*regular expression*?

Searches backward from the current line for a line containing a string matching *regular expression*, as in **ed**. The trailing ? may be omitted, except when associated with a breakpoint.

p Prints the current line.

z Prints the current line and the following nine lines. Sets the current line to the last line printed.

w Prints the 10 lines (the window) around the current line.

number
Specifies the current line. Prints the new current line.

count+
Advances the current line by *count* lines. Prints the new current line.

count–
Resets the current line by *count* lines back. Prints the new current line.

The commands for controlling the execution of the source program are:

count **r** *args*
count **R**
Runs the program with the given arguments. The **r** command with no arguments reuses the previous arguments to the program. The **R** command runs the program with no arguments. An argument beginning with < or > redirects the standard input or output, respectively. Full **sh** syntax is accepted. If *count* is given, it specifies the number of breakpoints to be ignored. If *count* is 1, the program stops at the next breakpoint.

linenumber **c** *count*
linenumber **C** *count*
Continues execution. **sdb** stops when it encounters *count* breakpoints. If *count* is 1, the program stops at the next breakpoint. The signal that stopped the program is reactivated with the **C** command and ignored with the **c** command. If a line number is specified, then a temporary breakpoint is placed at the line and execution continues. The breakpoint is deleted when the command finishes.

linenumber **g** *count*
Continues with execution resumed at the given line. If *count* is given, it specifies the number of breakpoints to be ignored. If *count* is 1, the program stops at the next breakpoint.

s *count*
S *count*
s single steps the program through *count* lines or if no *count* is given, then the program runs for one line. **s** will step from one function into a called function. **S** also steps a program, but it will not step into a called function. It steps over the function called.

i *count*
I *count*
Single steps by *count* machine-language instructions. The signal that caused the program to stop is reactivated with the **I** command and ignored with the **i** command.

*variable***$m** *count*
*address***:m** *count*
Single steps (as with **s**) until the specified location is modified with a new value. If *count* is omitted, it is, in effect, infinity. *Variable* must be accessible from the current procedure. This command can be very slow.

level **v**

Toggles verbose mode. This is for use when single stepping with **S**, **s**, or **m**. If *level* is omitted, then just the current source file and/or function name is printed when either changes. If *level* is 1 or greater, each C source line is printed before it executes. If *level* is 2 or greater, each assembler statement is also printed. A **v** turns verbose mode off.

k Kills the program being debugged.

procedure(*arg1*,*arg2*,. . .)
procedure(*arg1*,*arg2*,. . .)/*m*

Executes the named procedure with the given arguments. Arguments can be register names, integer, character, or string constants, or names of variables accessible from the current procedure. The second form causes the value returned by the procedure to be printed according to format *m*. If no format is given, it defaults to **d**.

linenumber **b** *commands*

Sets a breakpoint at the given line. If a procedure name without a line number is given (for example, *proc*:), a breakpoint is placed at the first line in the procedure even if it was not compiled with the **-g** option. If no *linenumber* is given, a breakpoint is placed at the current line. If no *commands* are given, execution stops at the breakpoint and control is returned to **sdb**. Otherwise the *commands* are executed when the breakpoint is encountered. Multiple commands are specified by separating them with semicolons. Nested associated commands are not permitted; setting breakpoints within the associated environments is permitted.

B Prints a list of the currently active breakpoints.

linenumber **d**

Deletes a breakpoint at the given line. If no *linenumber* is given, then the breakpoints are deleted interactively. Each breakpoint location is printed and a line is read from the standard input. If the line begins with a **y** or **d**, then the breakpoint is deleted.

D Deletes all breakpoints.

l Prints the last executed line.

linenumber **a**

Announces a line number. If *linenumber* is of the form *proc*:*number*, the command effectively does a *linenumber*:**b l;c**. If *linenumber* is of the form *proc*:, the command effectively does a *proc*:**b T;c**.

Miscellaneous commands:

#*rest-of-line*

The *rest-of-line* represents comments that are ignored by **sdb**.

!*command*

The *command* is interpreted by **sh**.

new-line
If the previous command printed a source line, then advance the current line by one line and print the new current line. If the previous command displayed a memory location, then display the next memory location. If the previous command disassembled an instruction, then disassemble the next instruction.

end-of-file character
Scrolls the next 10 lines of instructions, source, or data depending on which was printed last. The end-of-file character is usually CTRL-d.

< *filename*
Read commands from *filename* until the end of file is reached, and then continue to accept commands from standard input. Commands are echoed, preceded by two asterisks, just before being executed. This command may not be nested; < may not appear as a command in a file.

M Prints the address maps.

" *string* "
Prints the given string. The C escape sequences of the form *character*, *octal-digits*, or **\x***hexdigits* are recognized, where *character* is a nonnumeric character. The trailing quote may be omitted.

q Exits the debugger.

v Prints version stamping information.

SEE ALSO

a.out(4), **cc**(1), **core**(4), **debug**(1), **ed**(1), **gcore**(1), **sh**(1), **signal**(2)

NOTES

If *objfile* is a dynamically linked executable, variables, function names, and so on that are defined in shared objects may not be referenced until the shared object in which the variable, etc., is defined is attached to the process. For shared objects attached at startup (for example, **libc.so.1**, the default C library), this implies that such variables may not be accessed until **main** is called.

The *objfile* argument is accessed directly for debugging information while the process is created via the **PATH** variable.

sdiff (1)

NAME

sdiff – print file differences side-by-side

SYNOPSIS

sdiff [*options*] *file1 file2*

DESCRIPTION

sdiff uses the output of the **diff** command to produce a side-by-side listing of two files indicating lines that are different. Lines of the two files are printed with a blank gutter between them if the lines are identical, a **<** in the gutter if the line appears only in *file1*, a **>** in the gutter if the line appears only in *file2*, and a **|** for lines that are different. For example:

```
x     |     y
a           a
b     <
c     <
d           d
      >     c
```

sdiff processes supplementary code set characters in *files* according to the locale specified in the **LC_CTYPE** environment variable [see **LANG** on **environ**(5)].

Valid options are:

-w *n* — Use the argument *n* as the width of the output line. The default line length is 130 columns.

-l — Print only the left side of any lines that are identical.

-s — Do not print identical lines.

-o *output* — Use the argument *output* as the name of a third file that is created as a user-controlled merge of *file1* and *file2*. Identical lines of *file1* and *file2* are copied to *output*. Sets of differences, as produced by **diff**, are printed; where a set of differences share a common gutter character. After printing each set of differences, **sdiff** prompts the user with a **%** and waits for one of the following user-typed commands:

l	Append the left column to the output file.
r	Append the right column to the output file.
s	Turn on silent mode; do not print identical lines.
v	Turn off silent mode.
e l	Call the editor with the left column.
e r	Call the editor with the right column.
e b	Call the editor with the concatenation of left and right.
e	Call the editor with a zero length file.
q	Exit from the program.

On exit from the editor, the resulting file is concatenated to the end of the *output* file.

SEE ALSO

diff(1), **ed**(1)

NAME

sed – stream editor

SYNOPSIS

sed [**-n**] [**-e** *script*] [**-f** *sfile*] [*file* . . .]

DESCRIPTION

sed copies the named *file* (standard input default) to the standard output, edited according to a script of commands. The **-f** option causes the script to be taken from file *sfile;* these options accumulate. If there is just one **-e** option and no **-f** options, the flag **-e** may be omitted. The **-n** option suppresses the default output.

sed processes supplementary code set characters, and recognizes supplementary code set characters in *script* file comments (see below) according to the locale specified in the **LC_CTYPE** environment variable [see **LANG** on **environ**(5)], except as noted under the **y** command below. In regular expressions, pattern searches are performed on characters, not bytes, as described on **ed**(1).

A script consists of editing commands, one per line, of the following form:

[*address* [, *address*]] *function* [*arguments*]

In normal operation, **sed** cyclically copies a line of input into a *pattern space* (unless there is something left after a **D** command), applies in sequence all commands whose *addresses* select that pattern space, and at the end of the script copies the pattern space to the standard output (except under **-n**) and deletes the pattern space.

Some of the commands use a *hold space* to save all or part of the *pattern space* for subsequent retrieval.

An *address* is either a decimal number that counts input lines cumulatively across files, a **$** that addresses the last line of input, or a context address, that is, a /*regular expression*/ in the style of **ed**(1) modified thus:

> In a context address, the construction \?*regular expression?*, where *?* is any character, is identical to /*regular expression*/. Note that in the context address **\xabc\xdefx**, the second **x** stands for itself, so that the regular expression is **abcxdef**.
>
> The escape sequence **\n** matches a new-line *embedded* in the pattern space.
>
> A period (.) matches any character except the *terminal* new-line of the pattern space.
>
> A command line with no addresses selects every pattern space.
>
> A command line with one address selects each pattern space that matches the address.
>
> A command line with two addresses selects the inclusive range from the first pattern space that matches the first address through the next pattern space that matches the second address. (If the second address is a number less than or equal to the line number selected by the first address, only the line corresponding to the first address is selected.) Thereafter the process is repeated, looking again for the first address.

Editing commands can be applied only to non-selected pattern spaces by use of the negation function **!** (below).

In the following list of functions the maximum number of permissible addresses for each function is indicated in parentheses.

The *text* argument consists of one or more lines, all but the last of which end with \ to hide the new-line. Backslashes in text are treated like backslashes in the replacement string of an **s** command. The *rfile* or *wfile* argument must terminate the command line and must be preceded by exactly one blank. Each *wfile* is created before processing begins. There can be at most 10 distinct *wfile* arguments.

(1) **a**
text Append. Place *text* on the output before reading the next input line.

(2) **b** *label* Branch to the **:** command bearing the *label*. If *label* is empty, branch to the end of the script.

(2) **c**
text Change. Delete the pattern space. Place *text* on the output. Start the next cycle.

(2) **d** Delete the pattern space. Start the next cycle.

(2) **D** Delete the initial segment of the pattern space through the first new-line. Start the next cycle.

(2) **g** Replace the contents of the pattern space by the contents of the hold space.

(2) **G** Append the contents of the hold space to the pattern space.

(2) **h** Replace the contents of the hold space by the contents of the pattern space.

(2) **H** Append the contents of the pattern space to the hold space.

(1) **i**
text Insert. Place *text* on the standard output.

(2) **l** List the pattern space on the standard output in an unambiguous form. Non-printable characters are displayed in octal notation and long lines are folded.

(2) **n** Copy the pattern space to the standard output. Replace the pattern space with the next line of input.

(2) **N** Append the next line of input to the pattern space with an embedded new-line. (The current line number changes.)

(2) **p** Print. Copy the pattern space to the standard output.

(2) **P** Copy the initial segment of the pattern space through the first new-line to the standard output.

(1) **q** Quit. Branch to the end of the script. Do not start a new cycle.

(2) **r** *rfile* Read the contents of *rfile*. Place them on the output before reading the next input line.

(2) **s** / *regular expression* / *replacement* / *flags*
Substitute the *replacement* string for instances of the *regular expression* in the pattern space. Any character may be used instead of **/**. For a fuller description see **ed**(1). *flags* is zero or more of:

n	*n*= 1 - 512. Substitute for just the *n*th occurrence of the *regular expression*.
g	Global. Substitute for all nonoverlapping instances of the *regular expression* rather than just the first one.
p	Print the pattern space if a replacement was made.
w *wfile*	Write. Append the pattern space to *wfile* if a replacement was made.

(2) **t** *label* Test. Branch to the **:** command bearing the *label* if any substitutions have been made since the most recent reading of an input line or execution of a **t**. If *label* is empty, branch to the end of the script.

(2) **w** *wfile* Write. Append the pattern space to *wfile*. The first occurrence of **w** will cause *wfile* to be cleared. Subsequent invocations of **w** will append. Each time the **sed** command is used, *wfile* is overwritten.

(2) **x** Exchange the contents of the pattern and hold spaces.

(2) **y/** *string1* **/** *string2* **/**

Transform. Replace all occurrences of characters in *string1* with the corresponding characters in *string2*. *string1* and *string2* must have the same number of characters. The result is not guaranteed when supplementary code set characters are specified in the strings.

(2) **!** *function*

Don't. Apply the *function* (or group, if *function* is **{**) only to lines *not* selected by the address(es).

(0) **:** *label* This command does nothing; it bears a *label* for **b** and **t** commands to branch to.

(1) **=** Place the current line number on the standard output as a line.

(2) **{** Execute the following commands through a matching **}** only when the pattern space is selected.

(0) An empty command is ignored.

(0) **#** If a **#** appears as the first character on a line of a script file, then that entire line is treated as a comment, with one exception: if a **#** appears on the first line and the character after the **#** is an **n**, then the default output will be suppressed. The rest of the line after **#n** is also ignored. A script file must contain at least one non-comment line. Comments may contain supplementary code set characters.

FILES

/usr/lib/locale/*locale***/LC_MESSAGES/uxcore.abi**
language-specific message file [See **LANG** on **environ** (5).]

SEE ALSO

awk(1), **ed**(1), **grep**(1)

NAME

sendmail – (BSD) send mail over the internet

SYNOPSIS

/usr/ucblib/sendmail [**-ba**] [**-bd**] [**-bi**] [**-bm**] [**-bp**] [**-bs**] [**-bt**] [**-bv**] [**-bz**] [**-C***file*] [**-d***X*] [**-F***fullname*] [**-f***name*] [**-h***N*] [**-n**] [**-o x***value*] [**-q** [*time*]] [**-r***name*] [**-t**] [**-v**] [*address* . . .]

DESCRIPTION

sendmail sends a message to one or more people, routing the message over whatever networks are necessary. **sendmail** does internetwork forwarding as necessary to deliver the message to the correct place.

sendmail is not intended as a user interface routine; other programs provide user-friendly front ends; **sendmail** is used only to deliver pre-formatted messages.

With no flags, **sendmail** reads its standard input up to an EOF, or a line with a single dot and sends a copy of the letter found there to all of the addresses listed. It determines the network to use based on the syntax and contents of the addresses.

Local addresses are looked up in the local **aliases**(4) file, or by using the YP name service, and aliased appropriately. In addition, if there is a **.forward** file in a recipient's home directory, **sendmail** forwards a copy of each message to the list of recipients that file contains. Aliasing can be prevented by preceding the address with a backslash. Normally the sender is not included in alias expansions, for example, if 'john' sends to 'group', and 'group' includes 'john' in the expansion, then the letter will not be delivered to 'john'.

sendmail will also route mail directly to other known hosts in a local network. The list of hosts to which mail is directly sent is maintained in the file **/usr/lib/mailhosts**.

The following options are available:

-ba Go into ARPANET mode. All input lines must end with a CR-LF, and all messages will be generated with a CR-LF at the end. Also, the "From:" and "Sender:" fields are examined for the name of the sender.

-bd Run as a daemon, waiting for incoming SMTP connections.

-bi Initialize the alias database.

-bm Deliver mail in the usual way (default).

-bp Print a summary of the mail queue.

-bs Use the SMTP protocol as described in RFC 821. This flag implies all the operations of the **-ba** flag that are compatible with SMTP.

-bt Run in address test mode. This mode reads addresses and shows the steps in parsing; it is used for debugging configuration tables.

-bv Verify names only — do not try to collect or deliver a message. Verify mode is normally used for validating users or mailing lists.

-bz Create the configuration freeze file.

-C*file* Use alternate configuration file.

-d*X* Set debugging value to *X*.

-F*fullname* Set the full name of the sender.

-f*name* Sets the name of the "from" person (that is, the sender of the mail). **-f** can only be used by "trusted" users (who are listed in the config file).

-h*N* Set the hop count to *N*. The hop count is incremented every time the mail is processed. When it reaches a limit, the mail is returned with an error message, the victim of an aliasing loop.

-M*id* Attempt to deliver the queued message with message-id **id**.

-n Do not do aliasing.

-o*x value* Set option *x* to the specified *value*. Options are described below.

-q[*time*] Processed saved messages in the queue at given intervals. If *time* is omitted, process the queue once. *Time* is given as a tagged number, with **s** being seconds, **m** being minutes, **h** being hours, **d** being days, and **w** being weeks. For example, **-q1h30m** or **-q90m** would both set the timeout to one hour thirty minutes.

-r*name* An alternate and obsolete form of the **-f** flag.

-R*string* Go through the queue of pending mail and attempt to deliver any message with a recipient containing the specified string. This is useful for clearing out mail directed to a machine which has been down for awhile.

-t Read message for recipients. "To:", "Cc:", and "Bcc:" lines will be scanned for people to send to. The "Bcc:" line will be deleted before transmission. Any addresses in the argument list will be suppressed.

-v Go into verbose mode. Alias expansions will be announced, and so on.

PROCESSING OPTIONS

There are also a number of processing options that may be set. Normally these will only be used by a system administrator. Options may be set either on the command line using the **-o** flag or in the configuration file. The options are:

A*file* Use alternate alias file.

c On mailers that are considered "expensive" to connect to, do not initiate immediate connection. This requires queuing.

d*x* Set the delivery mode to *x*. Delivery modes are **i** for interactive (synchronous) delivery, **b** for background (asynchronous) delivery, and **q** for queue only — that is, actual delivery is done the next time the queue is run.

D	Run **newaliases**(1M) to automatically rebuild the alias database, if necessary.
e*x*	Set error processing to mode *x*. Valid modes are **m** to mail back the error message, **w** to "write" back the error message (or mail it back if the sender is not logged in), **p** to print the errors on the terminal (default), 'q' to throw away error messages (only exit status is returned), and 'e' to do special processing for the BerkNet. If the text of the message is not mailed back by modes **m** or **w** and if the sender is local to this machine, a copy of the message is appended to the file **dead.letter** in the sender's home directory.
F*mode*	The mode to use when creating temporary files.
f	Save UNIX-system-style "From" lines at the front of messages.
g*N*	The default group ID to use when calling mailers.
H*file*	The **SMTP** help file.
i	Do not take dots on a line by themselves as a message terminator.
L*n*	The log level.
m	Send to "me" (the sender) also if I am in an alias expansion.
o	If set, this message may have old style headers. If not set, this message is guaranteed to have new style headers (that is, commas instead of spaces between addresses). If set, an adaptive algorithm is used that will correctly determine the header format in most cases.
Q*queuedir*	Select the directory in which to queue messages.
r*timeout*	The timeout on reads; if none is set, **sendmail** will wait forever for a mailer.
S*file*	Save statistics in the named file.
s	Always instantiate the queue file, even under circumstances where it is not strictly necessary.
T*time*	Set the timeout on messages in the queue to the specified time. After sitting in the queue for this amount of time, they will be returned to the sender. The default is three days.
t*stz,dtz*	Set the name of the time zone.
u*N*	Set the default user id for mailers.

If the first character of the user name is a vertical bar, the rest of the user name is used as the name of a program to pipe the mail to. It may be necessary to quote the name of the user to keep **sendmail** from suppressing the blanks from between arguments.

sendmail returns an exit status describing what it did. The codes are defined in **sysexits.h**.

EX_OK	Successful completion on all addresses.
EX_NOUSER	User name not recognized.
EX_UNAVAILABLE	Catchall meaning necessary resources were not available.
EX_SYNTAX	Syntax error in address.
EX_SOFTWARE	Internal software error, including bad arguments.
EX_OSERR	Temporary operating system error, such as cannot fork.
EX_NOHOST	Host name not recognized.
EX_TEMPFAIL	Message could not be sent immediately, but was queued.

If invoked as **newaliases**, **sendmail** rebuilds the alias database. If invoked as *mailq*, **sendmail** prints the contents of the mail queue.

FILES

Except for **/usr/ucblib/sendmail.cf**, these pathnames are all specified in **/usr/ucblib/sendmail.cf**. Thus, these values are only approximations.

/usr/bin/uux	to deliver uucp mail
/usr/ucblib/binmail	to deliver local mail
/var/spool/mqueue/*	temp files and queued mail
~/.forward	list of recipients for forwarding messages

SEE ALSO

aliases(4), **biff**(1), **mail**(1), **mailstats**(1M), **mconnect**(1M), **newaliases**(1M)

Su, Zaw-Sing, and Jon Postel, *The Domain Naming Convention for Internet User Applications*, RFC 819, Network Information Center, SRI International, Menlo Park, Calif., August 1982
Postel, Jon, *Simple Mail Transfer Protocol*, RFC 821, Network Information Center, SRI International, Menlo Park, Calif., August 1982
Crocker, Dave, *Standard for the Format of ARPA-Internet Text Messages*, RFC 822, Network Information Center, SRI International, Menlo Park, Calif., August 1982

NOTES

Do not use the **-bz** option if you plan to run **sendmail** as a daemon, that is, with the **-bd** option.

If the frozen configuration file, **/usr/ucblib/sendmail.fc**, was created with the **-bz** option, running **sendmail** as a daemon (with the **-bd** option) fails with a core dump.

set (1F)

NAME

set, **unset** – set and unset local or global environment variables

SYNOPSIS

set [**-l** *variable*[=*value*]] . . .
set [**-e** *variable*[=*value*]] . . .
set [**-f***file variable*[=*value*]] . . .

unset -l *variable* . . .
unset -f*file variable* . . .

DESCRIPTION

The **set** command sets *variable* in the environment, or adds *variable=value* to *file*. If *variable* is not equated it to a value, **set** expects the value to be on standard input. The **unset** command removes *variable*. Note that the FMLI predefined, read-only variables (such as **ARG1**), may not be set or unset.

FMLI inherits the UNIX environment when invoked:

-l sets or unsets the specified variable in the local environment. Variables set with **-l** will not be inherited by processes invoked from FMLI.

-e sets the specified variable in the UNIX environment. Variables set with **-e** will be inherited by any processes started from FMLI. Note that these variables cannot be **unset**.

-f*file*
sets or unsets the specified variable in the global environment. The argument *file* is the name, or pathname, of a file containing lines of the form *variable=value*. *file* will be created if it does not already exist. Note that no space intervenes between **-f** and *file*.

Note that at least one of the above options must be used for each variable being set or unset. If you set a variable with the **-f***filename* option, you must thereafter include *filename* in references to that variable. For example, **${(***file***)***VARIABLE***}**.

EXAMPLE

Storing a selection made in a menu:

```
name=Selection 2
action=`set -l SELECTION=2`close
```

NOTES

Variables set to be available to the UNIX environment (those set using the **-e** option) can only be set for the current **fmli** process and the processes it calls.

When using the **-f** option, unless *file* is unique to the process, other users of FMLI on the same machine will be able to expand these variables, depending on the read/write permissions on *file*.

A variable set in one frame may be referenced or unset in any other frame. This includes local variables.

When a variable is evaluated that does not specifically reference a file, the local environment and UNIX system environment are searched in that order. (When a **set -l** and a **set -e** is done for the same variable, the variable evaluates to the value used in the **set -l** command.)

SEE ALSO

env(1), **sh**(1)

setclk (1M)

NAME

setclk – set system time from hardware clock

SYNOPSIS

`/sbin/setclk`

DESCRIPTION

setclk is used to set the internal system time from the hardware time-of-day clock. The command can be used only by a privileged user. It is normally executed by an entry in the **/etc/inittab** file when the system is initialized at boot time. Note that **setclk** checks the Nonvolatile Random Access Memory (NVRAM) only for the date. If the date is set, **setclk** runs silently. If the date is not set, **setclk** prompts the user to use **sysadm datetime** [see **sysadm**(1M)] for the proper setting of the hardware clock].

SEE ALSO

sysadm(1M)

NAME

setcolor – redefine or create a color

SYNOPSIS

setcolor *color red_level green_level blue_level*

DESCRIPTION

The **setcolor** command takes four arguments: *color*, which must be a string naming the color; and the arguments *red_level*, *green_level*, and *blue_level*, which must be integer values defining, respectively, the intensity of the red, green, and blue components of *color*. Intensities must be in the range of 0 to 1000. If you are redefining an existing color, you must use its current name (default color names are: **black**, **blue**, **green**, **cyan**, **red**, **magenta**, **yellow**, and **white**). **setcolor** returns the color's name string.

EXAMPLE

```
`setcolor blue 100 24 300`
```

setcolor (1)

NAME

`setcolor`, `setcolour` – set screen color

SYNOPSIS

setcolor [-**nbrgopc**] *argument* [*argument*]
setcolour [-**nbrgopc**] *argument* [*argument*]

DESCRIPTION

setcolor and **setcolour** allow the user to set the screen to a specific color. Both foreground and background colors can be set independently in a range of 16 colors. **setcolor** can also set the reverse video and graphics character colors. **setcolor** with no arguments produces a usage message that displays all available colors, then resets the screen to its previous state.

For example, the following strings are possible colors:

blue	magenta	brown	black
lt_blue	lt_magenta	yellow	gray
cyan	white	green	red
lt_cyan	hi_white	lt_green	lt_red

Options

The following options are available for **setcolor** and **setcolour**. In the arguments below, *color* is taken from the above list.

-n	Sets the screen to normal white characters on black background.
color [*color*]	Sets the foreground to the first color. Sets background to second color if a second color choice is specified.
-b *color*	Sets the background to the specified color.
-r *color color*	Set the foreground reverse video characters to the first color. Set reverse video characters' background to second color.
-g *color color*	Set the foreground graphics characters to the first color. Set graphics characters' background to second color.
-o *color*	Sets the color of the screen border (over scan region). To reset border color, use **-o black**.
-p *pitch duration*	Set the pitch and duration of the bell. Pitch is the period in microseconds, and duration is measured in fifths of a second. When using this option, a control-G (bell) must be echoed to the screen for the command to work. For example:

```
setcolor -p 2500 2
echo ^G
```

-c*first last*	Set the first and last scan lines of the cursor.

NOTES

The ability of **setcolor** to set any of these described functions is ultimately dependent on the ability of devices to support them. For example, the **-o** option does not work on the Color Graphics Adapter (CGA).

`setcolor` emits an escape sequence that may or may not have an effect on monochrome devices.

Occasionally changing the screen color can help prolong the life of your monitor.

NAME

setext (vxfs) – set extent attributes

SYNOPSIS

setext [**-e** *extent_size*] [**-r** *reservation*] [**-f** *flags*] *file*

DESCRIPTION

setext allows space to be reserved to a file, and a fixed extent size to be specified for a file. The file must already exist.

The options are:

-e *extent_size*
: Specify a fixed extent size. The extent size is specified in file system blocks.

-r *reservation*
: Preallocate space for a file. The reservation is specified in file system blocks.

-f *flags*
: The available flags are:

-f align	Specify that all extents must be aligned on *extent_size* boundaries relative to the start of allocation units.
-f chgsize	Specify that the reservation is to be immediately incorporated into the file. The file's on-disk inode is updated with size and block count information that is increased to include the reserved space.
-f contig	Specify that the reservation must be allocated contiguously.
-f noextend	Specify that the file may not be extended once the preallocated space has been used.
-f noreserve	Specify that the reservation is to be made as a non-persistent allocation to the file. The on-disk inode is not updated with the reservation information. The reservation is associated with the file until the last close of the file, when it is trimmed to the current file size.
-f trim	Specify that the reservation is trimmed to the current file size upon last close by all processes that have the file open.

NOTES

setext is available with the VxFS Advanced package only.

Multiple flags may be specified by specifying multiple instances of **-f** on a command line.

SEE ALSO

getext(1), **vxfsio**(7)

NAME

setkey – assigns the function keys

SYNOPSIS

setkey *keynum string*

DESCRIPTION

The **setkey** command assigns the given ANSI *string* to be the output of the computer function key given by *keynum*. For example, the command:

```
setkey 1 date
```

assigns the string **date** as the output of function key 1. The *string* can contain control characters, such as a newline character, and should be quoted to protect it from processing by the shell. For example, the command:

```
setkey 2 "pwd; lc\n"
```

assigns the command sequence **pwd; lc** to function key 2. The newline character is embedded in the quoted string, so that the commands are executed when you press function key 2. If the newline character is not included in the quoted string, you must press the Enter key after pressing the function key.

setkey translates ^ into ^^, which, when passed to the screen driver, is interpreted as a right angle bracket (>), or greater than key.

NOTES

setkey applies to the console keyboard only.

Function keys are defined in the string mapping table. This table is an array of 512 bytes (**typedef strmap_t**) where null terminated strings redefine function keys. The first null terminated string is assigned to the first string key, the second to the second string key, and so on. There is one string mapping table per multiscreen.

Although the size of the **setkey** string mapping table is 512 bytes, 30 characters is the maximum size for any individual function key assignment.

Assigning more than 512 characters to the string mapping table causes the function key buffer to overflow. When this happens, the sequences sent by the arrow keys are overwritten, effectively disabling them. Once the function key buffer overflows, the only way to enable the arrow keys is to reboot the system.

The table below lists the *keynum* values for the function keys:

Function key	*keynum*	Function key	*keynum*
F1	1	Ctrl-F10	34
F2	2	Ctrl-F11	35
F3	3	Ctrl-F12	36
F4	4	Ctrl-Shift-F1	37
F5	5	Ctrl-Shift-F2	38
F6	6	Ctrl-Shift-F3	39
F7	7	Ctrl-Shift-F4	40
F8	8	Ctrl-Shift-F5	41
F9	9	Ctrl-Shift-F6	42
F10	10	Ctrl-Shift-F7	43
F11	11	Ctrl-Shift-F8	44
F12	12	Ctrl-Shift-F9	45
Shift-F1	13	Ctrl-Shift-F10	46
Shift-F2	14	Ctrl-Shift-F11	47
Shift-F3	15	Ctrl-Shift-F12	48
Shift-F4	16		
Shift-F5	17	Numeric Key-Pad	*keynum*
Shift-F6	18		
Shift-F7	19	7	49
Shift-F8	20	8	50
Shift-F9	21	9	51
Shift-F10	22	-	52
Shift-F11	23	4	53
Shift-F12	24	5	54
Ctrl-F1	25	6	55
Ctrl-F2	26	+	56
Ctrl-F3	27	1	57
Ctrl-F4	28	2	58
Ctrl-F5	29	3	59
Ctrl-F6	30	0	60
Ctrl-F7	31		
Ctrl-F8	32		
Ctrl-F9	33		

For a table of the escape sequences, see **keyboard**(7).

FILES

/usr/bin/setkey

SEE ALSO

keyboard(7)

NAME

`setmnt` – establish mount table

SYNOPSIS

`/sbin/setmnt`

DESCRIPTION

`setmnt` creates the `/etc/mnttab` table which is needed for both the `mount` and `umount` commands. `setmnt` reads standard input and creates a `mnttab` entry for each line. Input lines have the format:

filesys node

where *filesys* is the name of the file system's "special file" (such as `/dev/dsk/c?t?d?s?`) and *node* is the root name of that file system. Thus *filesys* and *node* become the first two strings in the mount table entry.

FILES

`/etc/mnttab`

SEE ALSO

`mount`(1M)

NOTES

Problems may occur if *filesys* or *node* are longer than 32 characters.
`setmnt` silently enforces an upper limit on the maximum number of `mnttab` entries.

setsizecvt(1)

NAME

setsizecvt – generates files in the **space** format for sets

SYNOPSIS

setsizecvt

DESCRIPTION

The **setsizecvt** command generates files in the **space** format for sets. Before sets were included as packaging objects, the installation tools used **space** files to specify any additional space the packages required, in addition to that listed in the entries in that package's **pkgmap** file.

The **setsizecvt** command was designed to be as simple as possible; the packaging tools process the sets in much the same way they process packages.

Executing in a set's installation directory, **setsizecvt** collects the **space** file (if it exists) and the **setsize** file from each of the packages included in that set. The **setsize** file is a file whose entries are formatted as follows:

pkg:/path/name *#blks* *#inodes*

where *pkg* is the short form of the package name, and the rest is the directory and number of blocks and inodes used in that directory. This **setsize** file is created when the sets are created. Typically, the **setsize** file for a given set would be created from the **pkgmap** files for all of the packages in that set.

setsizecvt selects those entries in the **setsize** file for packages (in the current set) that the user wants to install. Those entries are then collected in a new file called **space**.

pkgadd uses the **space** file to see if there is enough space on the disk to install the set. The **space** file for a set is treated the same way as it is in a package.

SEE ALSO

space(4)

NAME

settime – (XENIX) change the access and modification dates of files

SYNOPSIS

settime *mmddhhmm*[*yy*] [**-f** *fname*] *name*. . .

DESCRIPTION

settime sets the access and modification dates for one or more files. The dates are set to the specified date, or to the access and modification dates of the file specified via **-f**. Exactly one of these methods must be used to specify the new date(s). The first *mm* is the month number; *dd* is the day number in the month; *hh* is the hour number (24 hour system); the second *mm* is the minute number; *yy* is the last two digits of the year and is optional. For example:

```
settime 1008004592 ralph pete
```

sets the access and modification dates of files **ralph** and **pete** to Oct. 8, 12:45 AM, 1992. Another example:

```
settime -f ralph john
```

This sets the access and modification dates of the file **john** to those of the file **ralph**.

NOTES

Use of **touch** in place of **settime** is encouraged.

NAME

setuname – changes machine information

SYNOPSIS

setuname [**-s** *name*] [**-n** *node*] [**-t**]

DESCRIPTION

setuname changes the parameter value for the system name and the network node name. One or both of the **-s** and **-n** options must be given.

The options and arguments for this command are:

-s Changes the system name. *name* specifies the new system name and can consist of alphanumeric characters and the special characters dash, underbar, and dollar sign.

-n Changes the node name. *node* specifies the new network node name and can consist of alphanumeric characters and the special characters dash, underbar, and dollar sign. The node name is the name by which this system is known to other computers in a networked environment.

Be aware that if you change the network node name, other software may break unexpectedly, so it is good practice not to change a node name once it is set. For example, networking software and application packages may save the node name of your system at the time the package is installed. Therefore, each time you change the node name, you will need to locate all the files where it has been saved and change its value. See your system administration guide for further advice.

-t Temporary change. No attempt will be made to create a permanent change.

The system architecture may place requirements on the size of the system name and network node name. The command will issue a fatal warning message and an error message if the name entered is incompatible with the system requirements.

FILES

/etc/rc2.d/S18setuname script that sets system and node names when the system is booted

etc/nodename file containing the network node name

SEE ALSO

sysinfo(2), **uname**(1), **uname**(2)

NOTES

setuname attempts to change the parameter values in the running kernel and in files used during a system reboot. A temporary change changes only the running kernel.

NAME

sh, **jsh**, **rsh** – shell, the standard, job control, and restricted command interpreter

SYNOPSIS

sh [**-acefhiknprstuvx**] [*args*]
jsh [**-acefhiknprstuvx**] [*args*]
/usr/lib/rsh [**-acefhiknprstuvx**] [*args*]

DESCRIPTION

sh is a command programming language that executes commands read from a terminal or a file. The shell **/sbin/sh** is the only shell that is trusted for administrative use when the Enhanced Security Utilities are installed and running on your system.

The command **jsh** is an interface to the shell which provides all of the functionality of **sh** and enables Job Control (see "Job Control," below). **/usr/lib/rsh** is a restricted version of the standard command interpreter **sh**; it is used to restrict logins to execution environments whose capabilities are more controlled than those of the standard shell. See "Invocation", below for the meaning of arguments to the shell.

sh, **jsh**, and **rsh** process supplementary code set characters in command arguments, as values of variables and field separators, in prompt strings, comments, and pipes, and in scripts according to the locale specified in the **LC_CTYPE** environment variable [see **LANG** on **environ**(5)]. Pattern searches are performed on characters, not bytes, as described in "File Name Generation" below.

Definitions

A *blank* is a tab or a space. A *name* is a sequence of letters, digits, or underscores, beginning with a letter or an underscore. A *parameter* is a name, a digit, or any of the characters *, **@**, **#**, **?**, **–**, **$**, and **!**.

Commands

A *simple-command* is a sequence of non-blank *words* separated by *blanks*. The first *word* specifies the name of the command to be executed. Except as specified below, the remaining *words* are passed as arguments to the invoked command. The command name is passed as argument 0 [see **exec**(2)]. The *value* of a *simple-command* is its exit status if it terminates normally, or (octal) **200**+*status* if it terminates abnormally; see **signal**(5) for a list of status values.

A *pipeline* is a sequence of one or more *commands* separated by **|**. The standard output of each *command* but the last is connected by a **pipe**(2) to the standard input of the next *command*. Each *command* is run as a separate process; the shell waits for the last *command* to terminate. The exit status of a *pipeline* is the exit status of the last command in the *pipeline*.

A *list* is a sequence of one or more *pipelines* separated by **;**, **&**, **&&**, or **||**, and optionally terminated by **;** or **&**. Of these four symbols, **;** and **&** have equal precedence, which is lower than that of **&&** and **||**. The symbols **&&** and **||** also have equal precedence. A semicolon (**;**) causes sequential execution of the preceding *pipeline* (i.e., the shell waits for the *pipeline* to finish before executing any commands following the semicolon); an ampersand (**&**) causes asynchronous execution of the preceding pipeline (i.e., the shell does *not* wait for that pipeline to finish). The symbol **&&** (**||**) causes the *list* following it to be executed only if the preceding pipeline returns a zero (non-zero) exit status. An arbitrary number of new-lines may appear in a *list*, instead of semicolons, to delimit commands.

A *command* is either a *simple-command* or one of the following. Unless otherwise stated, the value returned by a command is that of the last *simple-command* executed in the command.

for *name* [**in** *word* ...] **do** *list* **done**
: Each time a **for** command is executed, *name* is set to the next *word* taken from the **in** *word* list. If **in** *word* ... is omitted, then the **for** command executes the **do** *list* once for each positional parameter that is set (see "Parameter Substitution," below). Execution ends when there are no more words in the list.

case *word* **in** [*pattern* [| *pattern*] ... **)** *list* **;;**] ... **esac**
: A **case** command executes the *list* associated with the first *pattern* that matches *word*. The form of the patterns is the same as that used for file-name generation (see "File Name Generation") except that a slash, a leading dot, or a dot immediately following a slash need not be matched explicitly.

if *list* **then** *list* [**elif** *list* **then** *list*] ... [**else** *list*] **fi**
: The *list* following **if** is executed and, if it returns a zero exit status, the *list* following the first **then** is executed. Otherwise, the *list* following **elif** is executed and, if its value is zero, the *list* following the next **then** is executed. Failing that, the **else** *list* is executed. If no **else** *list* or **then** *list* is executed, then the **if** command returns a zero exit status.

while *list* **do** *list* **done**
: A **while** command repeatedly executes the **while** *list* and, if the exit status of the last command in the list is zero, executes the **do** *list*; otherwise the loop terminates. If no commands in the **do** *list* are executed, then the **while** command returns a zero exit status; **until** may be used in place of **while** to negate the loop termination test.

(*list***)**
: Execute *list* in a sub-shell.

{ *list***;}**
: *list* is executed in the current (that is, parent) shell. The **{** must be followed by a space.

name **()** **{** *list***;}**
: Define a function which is referenced by *name*. The body of the function is the *list* of commands between **{** and **}**. The *list* may appear on the same line as the **{**. If it does, the **{** and *list* must be separated by a space. The **}** may not be on the same line as *list*; it must be on a newline. Execution of functions is described below (see "Execution"). The **{** and **}** are unnecessary if the body of the function is a simple *command* as defined above, under "Commands."

The following words are only recognized as the first word of a command and when not quoted:

if then else elif fi case esac for while until do done { }

Comments

A word beginning with **#** causes that word and all the following characters up to a new-line to be ignored.

Command Substitution

The shell interprets commands from the string between two grave accents (**` `**) and the standard output from these commands may be used as all or part of a word. Trailing new-lines from the standard output are removed.

No interpretation is done on the string before the string is read, except to remove backslashes (\) used to escape other characters. Backslashes may be used to escape a grave accent (**`**) or another backslash (\) and are removed before the command string is read. Escaping grave accents allows nested command substitution. If the command substitution lies within a pair of double quotes (**" . . .` . . .` . . . "**), a backslash used to escape a double quote (**\"**) will be removed; otherwise, it will be left intact.

If a backslash is used to escape a new-line character (**\new-line**), both the backslash and the new-line are removed (see the later section on "Quoting"). In addition, backslashes used to escape dollar signs (**\$**) are removed. Since no parameter substitution is done on the command string before it is read, inserting a backslash to escape a dollar sign has no effect. Backslashes that precede characters other than \, **`**, **"**, **new-line**, and **$** are left intact when the command string is read.

Parameter Substitution

The character **$** is used to introduce substitutable *parameters*. There are two types of parameters, positional and keyword. If *parameter* is a digit, it is a positional parameter. Positional parameters may be assigned values by **set**. Keyword parameters (also known as variables) may be assigned values by writing:

name=*value* [*name*=*value*] . . .

Pattern-matching is not performed on *value*. There cannot be a function and a variable with the same *name*.

${*parameter***}**
: The value, if any, of the parameter is substituted. The braces are required only when *parameter* is followed by a letter, digit, or underscore that is not to be interpreted as part of its name. If *parameter* is * or **@**, all the positional parameters, starting with **$1**, are substituted (separated by spaces). Parameter **$0** is set from argument zero when the shell is invoked.

${*parameter***:-***word***}**
: If *parameter* is set and is non-null, substitute its value; otherwise substitute *word*.

${*parameter***:=***word***}**
: If *parameter* is not set or is null set it to *word*; the value of the parameter is substituted. Positional parameters may not be assigned in this way.

${_parameter_**:?**_word_**}**
If _parameter_ is set and is non-null, substitute its value; otherwise, print _parameter: word_ and exit from the shell. If _word_ is omitted, the message "parameter null or not set" is printed.

${_parameter_**:+**_word_**}**
If _parameter_ is set and is non-null, substitute _word_; otherwise substitute nothing.

In the above, _word_ is not evaluated unless it is to be used as the substituted string, so that, in the following example, **pwd** is executed only if **d** is not set or is null:

```
echo ${d:-`pwd`}
```

If the colon (**:**) is omitted from the above expressions, the shell only checks whether _parameter_ is set or not.

The following parameters are automatically set by the shell.

- * Expands to the positional parameters, beginning with 1.
- **@** Expands to the positional parameters, beginning with 1, except when expanded within double quotes, in which case each positional parameter expands as a separate field.
- **#** The number of positional parameters in decimal.
- **-** Flags supplied to the shell on invocation or by the **set** command.
- **?** The decimal value returned by the last synchronously executed command.
- **$** The process number of this shell. **$** reports the process ID of the parent shell in all shell constructs, including pipelines, and in parenthesized sub-shells.
- **!** The process number of the last background command invoked.

The following parameters are used by the shell. The parameters in this section are also referred to as environment variables.

HOME
The default argument (home directory) for the **cd** command, set to the user's login directory by **login**(1) from the password file [see **passwd**(4)].

PATH The search path for commands (see "Execution," below). The user may not change _PATH_ if executing under **/usr/lib/rsh**.

CDPATH
The search path for the **cd** command.

MAIL If this parameter is set to the name of a mail file _and_ the _MAILPATH_ parameter is not set, the shell informs the user of the arrival of mail in the specified file.

MAILCHECK
This parameter specifies how often (in seconds) the shell will check for the arrival of mail in the files specified by the _MAILPATH_ or _MAIL_ parameters. The default value is **600** seconds (10 minutes). If set to **0**, the shell will check before each prompt.

MAILPATH
: A colon (**:**) separated list of file names. If this parameter is set, the shell informs the user of the arrival of mail in any of the specified files. Each file name can be followed by **%** and a message that will be printed when the modification time changes. The default message is **you have mail**.

PS1 Primary prompt string, by default "**$** ".

PS2 Secondary prompt string, by default "**>** ".

IFS Internal field separators, normally **space**, **tab**, and **new-line** (see "Blank Interpretation"). The user can modify **IFS** to allow additional field separators, but space, tab and new-line are always included in the list of field separators.

LANG If this parameter is set, the shell will use it to determine the current locale; see **environ**(5), **setlocale**(3C).

SHACCT
: If this parameter is set to the name of a file writable by the user, the shell will write an accounting record in the file for each shell procedure executed.

SHELL
: When the shell is invoked, it scans the environment (see "Environment," below) for this name. If it is found and **rsh** is the file name part of its value, the shell becomes a restricted shell.

TIMEOUT
: A non-zero value for **TIMEOUT** causes the shell to exit after **$TIMEOUT** seconds of inactivity. The default value is site dependent.

The shell gives default values to *PATH, PS1, PS2, MAILCHECK,* and *IFS*. *HOME* and *MAIL* are set by **login**(1).

Blank Interpretation

After parameter and command substitution, the results of substitution are scanned for internal field separator characters (those found in *IFS*) and split into distinct arguments where such characters are found. Explicit null arguments (**""** or **' '**) are retained. Implicit null arguments (those resulting from *parameters* that have no values) are removed.

TIMEOUT
: A non-zero value for **TIMEOUT** causes the shell to exit after **$TIMEOUT** seconds of inactivity. The default value is site dependent. The original whitespace characters (space, tab, and newline) are always considered internal field separators.

Input/Output

A command's input and output may be redirected using a special notation interpreted by the shell. The following may appear anywhere in a *simple-command* or may precede or follow a *command* and are *not* passed on as arguments to the invoked command. Note that parameter and command substitution occurs before *word* or *digit* is used.

<*word* — Use file *word* as standard input (file descriptor 0).

>*word* — Use file *word* as standard output (file descriptor 1). If the file does not exist, it is created; otherwise, it is truncated to zero length.

>>*word* — Use file *word* as standard output. If the file exists, output is appended to it (by first seeking to the end-of-file); otherwise, the file is created.

<<[-]*word* — After parameter and command substitution is done on *word*, the shell input is read up to the first line that literally matches the resulting *word*, or to an end-of-file. If, however, - is appended to <<:

1) leading tabs are stripped from *word* before the shell input is read (but after parameter and command substitution is done on *word*),
2) leading tabs are stripped from the shell input as it is read and before each line is compared with *word*, and
3) shell input is read up to the first line that literally matches the resulting *word*, or to an end-of-file.

If any character of *word* is quoted (see "Quoting," below), no additional processing is done to the shell input. If no characters of *word* are quoted:

1) parameter and command substitution occurs,
2) (escaped) **\new-line**s are removed, and
3) \ must be used to quote the characters \, $, and `.

The resulting document becomes the standard input.

<&*digit* — Use the file associated with file descriptor *digit* as standard input. Similarly for the standard output using >&*digit*.

<&- — The standard input is closed. Similarly for the standard output using >&-.

If any of the above is preceded by a digit, the file descriptor which will be associated with the file is that specified by the digit (instead of the default 0 or 1). For example:

```
... 2>&1
```

associates file descriptor 2 with the file currently associated with file descriptor 1.

The order in which redirections are specified is significant. The shell evaluates redirections left-to-right. For example:

```
... 1>xxx 2>&1
```

first associates file descriptor 1 with file *xxx*. It associates file descriptor 2 with the file associated with file descriptor 1 (i.e., *xxx*). If the order of redirections were reversed, file descriptor 2 would be associated with the terminal (assuming file descriptor 1 had been) and file descriptor 1 would be associated with file *xxx*.

Using the terminology introduced on the first page, under "Commands," if a *command* is composed of several *simple commands*, redirection will be evaluated for the entire *command* before it is evaluated for each *simple command*. That is, the shell evaluates redirection for the entire *list*, then each *pipeline* within the *list*, then each *command* within each *pipeline*, then each *list* within each *command*.

If a command is followed by **&** the default standard input for the command is the empty file **/dev/null**. Otherwise, the environment for the execution of a command contains the file descriptors of the invoking shell as modified by input/output specifications.

Redirection of output is not allowed in the restricted shell.

File Name Generation

Before a command is executed, each command *word* is scanned for the characters *, ?, and [. If one of these characters appears the word is regarded as a *pattern*. The word is replaced with alphabetically sorted file names that match the pattern. If no file name is found that matches the pattern, the word is left unchanged. The character . at the start of a file name or immediately following a /, as well as the character / itself, must be matched explicitly.

- `*` Matches any string, including supplementary code set characters and the null string.
- `?` Matches any single character, including supplementary code set characters.
- `[...]` Matches any one character in the string enclosed by square brackets, or any one character with a code value within the range designated using a minus (–) sign, including supplementary code set characters. When the characters in the range are from different code sets, one of the characters specifying the range is matched. If the first character following the opening [is a !, any character not enclosed is matched, including supplementary code set characters.

Note that all quoted characters (see below) must be matched explicitly in a filename.

Quoting

The following characters have a special meaning to the shell and cause termination of a word unless quoted:

; & ( ) | ^ < > new-line space tab

A character may be *quoted* (i.e., made to stand for itself) by preceding it with a backslash (\) or inserting it between a pair of quote marks (' ' or ""). During processing, the shell may quote certain characters to prevent them from taking on a special meaning. Backslashes used to quote a single character are removed from the word before the command is executed. The pair **\new-line** is removed from a word before command and parameter substitution.

All characters enclosed between a pair of single quote marks (' '), except a single quote, are quoted by the shell. Backslash has no special meaning inside a pair of single quotes. A single quote may be quoted inside a pair of double quote marks (for example, "'"), but a single quote can not be quoted inside a pair of single quotes.

Inside a pair of double quote marks (`""`), parameter and command substitution occurs and the shell quotes the results to avoid blank interpretation and file name generation. If **$*** is within a pair of double quotes, the positional parameters are substituted and quoted, separated by quoted spaces (`"$1 $2 ..."`); however, if **$@** is within a pair of double quotes, the positional parameters are substituted and quoted, separated by unquoted spaces (`"$1" "$2" ... )`. `\` quotes the characters `\`, `` ` ``, `"`, and `$`. The pair **\new-line** is removed before parameter and command substitution. If a backslash precedes characters other than `\`, `` ` ``, `"`, `$`, and new-line, then the backslash itself is quoted by the shell.

Prompting

When used interactively, the shell prompts with the value of **PS1** before reading a command. If at any time a new-line is typed and further input is needed to complete a command, the secondary prompt (i.e., the value of **PS2**) is issued.

Defaults

The file **/etc/default/sh** (which does not exist by default) can contain a value for the parameter **TIMEOUT**; this integer value specifies the number of seconds that can elapse without user activity before a shell will exit. If this value is `0`, undefined, or the file **/etc/default/sh** does not exist (the default), the shell will wait for user input until explicitly terminated.

Environment

The *environment* [see **environ**(5)] is a list of name-value pairs that is passed to an executed program in the same way as a normal argument list. The shell interacts with the environment in several ways. On invocation, the shell scans the environment and creates a parameter for each name found, giving it the corresponding value. If the user modifies the value of any of these parameters or creates new parameters, none of these affects the environment unless the **export** command is used to bind the shell's parameter to the environment (see also **set -a**). A parameter may be removed from the environment with the **unset** command. The environment seen by any executed command is thus composed of any unmodified name-value pairs originally inherited by the shell, minus any pairs removed by **unset**, plus any modifications or additions, all of which must be noted in **export** commands.

The environment for any *simple-command* may be augmented by prefixing it with one or more assignments to parameters. Thus:

> **TERM=450** *cmd* and
> **(export TERM; TERM=450;** *cmd*)

are equivalent as far as the execution of *cmd* is concerned if *cmd* is not a Special Command. If *cmd* is a Special Command, then

> **TERM=450** *cmd*

will modify the **TERM** variable in the current shell.

If the **-k** flag is set, *all* keyword arguments are placed in the environment, even if they occur after the command name. The following first prints **a=b c** and **c**:

```
echo a=b c
set -k
echo a=b c
```

Signals

When a command is run in the background (*cmd &*) under **sh**, it can receive **INTERRUPT** and **QUIT** signals but ignores them by default. [A background process can override this default behavior via trap or signal. For details, see the description of **trap**, below, or **signal**(2).] When a command is run in the background under **jsh**, however, it does not receive **INTERRUPT** or **QUIT** signals. Otherwise signals have the values inherited by the shell from its parent, with the exception of three signals: **11** (**SIGSEV**), **14** (**SIGALARM**), and **18** (**SIGCHILD**).

Execution

Each time a command is executed, the command substitution, parameter substitution, blank interpretation, input/output redirection, and filename generation listed above are carried out. If the command name matches the name of a defined function, the function is executed in the shell process (note how this differs from the execution of shell procedures). If the command name does not match the name of a defined function, but matches one of the *Special Commands* listed below, it is executed in the shell process. The positional parameters **$1**, **$2**, ... are set to the arguments of the function. If the command name matches neither a *Special Command* nor the name of a defined function, a new process is created and an attempt is made to execute the command via **exec**(2).

The shell parameter *PATH* defines the search path for the directory containing the command. Alternative directory names are separated by a colon (**:**). The default path is **/usr/bin**. The current directory is specified by a null path name, which can appear immediately after the equal sign, between two colon delimiters anywhere in the path list, or at the end of the path list. If the command name contains a **/** the search path is not used; such commands will not be executed by the restricted shell. Otherwise, each directory in the path is searched for an executable file. If the file has execute permission but is not an **a.out** file, it is assumed to be a file containing shell commands. A sub-shell is spawned to read it. A parenthesized command is also executed in a sub-shell.

For shell script files, in order for the "set user ID on execution" and/or the "set group ID on execution" mode to be effective, the first line of the file must be

```
#! /sbin/sh
```

The location in the search path where a command was found is remembered by the shell (to help avoid unnecessary *execs* later). If the command was found in a relative directory, its location must be re-determined whenever the current directory changes. The shell forgets all remembered locations whenever the *PATH* variable is changed or the **hash -r** command is executed (see below).

Special Commands

Input/output redirection is now permitted for these commands. File descriptor 1 is the default output location. When Job Control is enabled, additional *Special Commands* are added to the shell's environment (see "Job Control").

: No effect; the command does nothing. A zero exit code is returned.

. *file* Read and execute commands from *file* and return. The search path specified by *PATH* is used to find the directory containing *file*.

break [*n*]
Exit from the enclosing **for** or **while** loop, if any. If *n* is specified, break *n* levels.

continue [*n*]
Resume the next iteration of the enclosing **for** or **while** loop. If *n* is specified, resume at the *n*-th enclosing loop.

cd [*arg*]
Change the current directory to *arg*. The shell parameter *HOME* is the default *arg*. The shell parameter *CDPATH* defines the search path for the directory containing *arg*. Alternative directory names are separated by a colon (**:**). The default path is **<null>** (specifying the current directory). Note that the current directory is specified by a null path name, which can appear immediately after the equal sign or between the colon delimiters anywhere else in the path list. If *arg* begins with a **/** the search path is not used. Otherwise, each directory in the path is searched for *arg*. The **cd** command may not be executed by **/usr/lib/rsh**.

echo [*arg* ...]
Echo arguments. See **echo**(1) for usage and description.

eval [*arg* ...]
The arguments are read as input to the shell and the resulting command(s) executed.

exec [*arg* ...]
The command specified by the arguments is executed in place of this shell without creating a new process. Input/output arguments may appear and, if no other arguments are given, cause the shell input/output to be modified.

exit [*n*]
Causes a shell to exit with the exit status specified by *n*. If *n* is omitted the exit status is that of the last command executed (an end-of-file will also cause the shell to exit.)

export [*name* ...]
The given *name*s are marked for automatic export to the *environment* of subsequently executed commands. If no arguments are given, variable names that have been marked for export during the current shell's execution are listed. (Variable names exported from a parent shell are listed only if they have been exported again during the current shell's execution.) Function names are *not* exported.

getopts
Use in shell scripts to support command syntax standards [see **intro**(1)]; it parses positional parameters and checks for legal options. See **getopts**(1) for usage and description.

hash [**-r**] [*name* ...]
For each *name*, the location in the search path of the command specified by *name* is determined and remembered by the shell. The **-r** option causes the shell to forget all remembered locations. If no arguments are given, information about remembered commands is presented. *Hits* is the number of times a command has been invoked by the shell process. *Cost* is a measure

of the work required to locate a command in the search path. If a command is found in a "relative" directory in the search path, after changing to that directory, the stored location of that command is recalculated. Commands for which this will be done are indicated by an asterisk (*) adjacent to the *hits* information. *Cost* will be incremented when the recalculation is done.

mldmode

mldmode -r [*string*]

mldmode -v [*string*]

This command is available only if the Enhanced Security Utilities are installed. With no arguments, the current multilevel directory (MLD) mode is reported. If **-r** alone is specified, the MLD mode of the interactive shell is changed to *real* mode. If **-v** alone is specified, the MLD mode of the interactive shell is changed to *virtual* mode. If the **-r** or **-v** option is followed by a *string* specifying a command, that command alone is executed in the specified MLD mode. The default mode upon login is *virtual* mode.

newgrp [*arg*]

Equivalent to **exec newgrp** *arg*. See **newgrp**(1M) for usage and description.

priv [+|-*priv_name* . . .] *set_name* [. . .]

For each *set_name*, **priv** sets or displays the privileges contained in that privilege set. *set_name* may be either **max** for the maximum privilege set or **work** for the working set. *priv_name* is the name of a privilege [see **intro**(2)]. If *priv_names* are supplied, **priv** scans the list and turns off thoses privileges that are preceded by a minus sign and turns on those that are preceded by a plus sign in each of the sets listed. If no *priv_names* are supplied, the **priv** command prints the current list of privileges for each of the requested sets.

pwd Print the current working directory. See **pwd**(1) for usage and description.

read *name* . . .

One line is read from the standard input and, using the internal field separator, **IFS** (normally space or tab), to delimit word boundaries, the first word is assigned to the first *name*, the second word to the second *name*, etc., with leftover words assigned to the last *name*. Lines can be continued using **\new-line**. Characters other than **new-line** can be quoted by preceding them with a backslash. These backslashes are removed before words are assigned to *names*, and no interpretation is done on the character that follows the backslash. The return code is **0**, unless an end-of-file is encountered.

readonly [*name* . . .]

The given *names* are marked *readonly* and the values of the these *names* may not be changed by subsequent assignment. If no arguments are given, a list of all *readonly* names is printed.

return [*n*]

Causes a function to exit with the return value specified by *n*. If *n* is omitted, the return status is that of the last command executed.

set [**--aefhkntuvx** [*arg* ...]]

- **-a** Mark variables which are modified or created for export.
- **-e** Exit immediately if a command exits with a non-zero exit status.
- **-f** Disable file name generation
- **-h** Locate and remember function commands as functions are defined (function commands are normally located when the function is executed).
- **-k** All keyword arguments are placed in the environment for a command, not just those that precede the command name.
- **-n** Read commands but do not execute them.
- **-t** Exit after reading and executing one command.
- **-u** Treat unset variables as an error when substituting.
- **-v** Print shell input lines as they are read.
- **-x** Print commands and their arguments as they are executed.
- **--** Do not change any of the flags; useful in setting **$1** to **-**.

Using **+** rather than **-** causes these flags to be turned off. These flags can also be used upon invocation of the shell. The current set of flags may be found in **$-**. The remaining arguments are positional parameters and are assigned, in order, to **$1**, **$2**, ... If no arguments are given the values of all names are printed.

shift [*n*]

The positional parameters from **$***n***+1** ... are renamed **$1** .... If *n* is not given, it is assumed to be 1.

test

Evaluate conditional expressions. See **test**(1) for usage and description.

times

Print the accumulated user and system times for processes run from the shell.

trap [*arg*] [*n*] ...

The command *arg* is to be read and executed when the shell receives numeric or symbolic signal(s) (*n*). (Note that *arg* is scanned once when the trap is set and once when the trap is taken.) Trap commands are executed in order of signal number or corresponding symbolic names. Any attempt to set a trap on a signal that was ignored on entry to the current shell is ineffective. An error results when an attempt is made to trap on any of the following three signals: (1) signal **11** (**SIGSEV**—segmentation fault); (2) signal **14** (**SIGALRM**—alarm clock); and (3) signal **18** (**SIGCHILD**—child status changed). If *arg* is absent all trap(s) *n* are reset to their original values. If *arg* is the null string this signal is ignored by the shell and by the commands it invokes. If *n* is 0 the command *arg* is executed on exit from the shell. The **trap** command with no arguments prints a list of commands associated with each signal number.

type [*name* ...]
For each *name*, indicate how it would be interpreted if used as a command name.

ulimit [–[**HS**][**a** | **cdfnstv**]]

ulimit [–[**HS**][**c** | **d** | **f** | **n** | **s** | **t** | **v**]] *limit* **ulimit** prints or sets hard or soft resource limits. These limits are described in **getrlimit**(2).

If *limit* is not present, **ulimit** prints the specified limits. Any number of limits may be printed at one time. The **-a** option prints all limits.

If *limit* is present, **ulimit** sets the specified limit to *limit*. The string **unlimited** requests the largest valid limit. Limits may be set for only one resource at a time. Any user may set a soft limit to any value below the hard limit. Any user may lower a hard limit. Only a privileged user may raise a hard limit.

The **-H** option specifies a hard limit. The **-S** option specifies a soft limit. If neither option is specified, **ulimit** will set both limits and print the soft limit.

The following options specify the resource whose limits are to be printed or set. If no option is specified, the file size limit is printed or set.

-c	maximum core file size (in 512-byte blocks)
-d	maximum size of data segment or heap (in kbytes)
-f	maximum file size (in 512-byte blocks)
-n	maximum file descriptor plus 1
-s	maximum size of stack segment (in kbytes)
-t	maximum CPU time (in seconds)
-v	maximum size of virtual memory (in kbytes)

umask [*nnn*]
The user file-creation mask is set to *nnn* [see **umask**(1)]. If *nnn* is omitted, the current value of the mask is printed.

unset [*name* ...]
For each *name*, remove the corresponding variable or function value. The variables *PATH, PS1, PS2, MAILCHECK,* and *IFS* cannot be unset.

wait [*n*]
Wait for your background process whose process id is *n* and report its termination status. If *n* is omitted, all your shell's currently active background processes are waited for and the return code will be zero.

Invocation

If the shell is invoked through **exec**(2) and the first character of argument zero is **-**, commands are initially read from **/etc/profile** and from **$HOME/.profile**, if such files exist. Thereafter, commands are read as described below, which is also the case when the shell is invoked as **/usr/bin/sh**. The flags below are interpreted by the shell on invocation only. Note that unless the **-c** or **-s** flag is specified, the first argument is assumed to be the name of a file containing commands, and the remaining arguments are passed as positional parameters to that command file:

-c *string* If the **-c** flag is present commands are read from *string*.

-i If the **-i** flag is present or if the shell input and output are attached to a terminal, this shell is *interactive*. In this case TERMINATE is ignored (so that **kill 0** does not kill an interactive shell) and INTERRUPT is caught and ignored (so that **wait** is interruptible). In all cases, QUIT is ignored by the shell.

-p If the **-p** flag is present, the shell will not set the effective user and group *IDs* to the real user and group *IDs*.

-r If the **-r** flag is present the shell is a restricted shell.

-s If the **-s** flag is present or if no arguments remain, commands are read from the standard input. Any remaining arguments specify the positional parameters. Shell output (except for *Special Commands*) is written to file descriptor 2.

The remaining flags and arguments are described under the **set** command above.

Job Control (jsh)

When the shell is invoked as **jsh**, Job Control is enabled in addition to all of the functionality described previously for **sh**. Typically Job Control is enabled for the interactive shell only. Non-interactive shells typically do not benefit from the added functionality of Job Control.

With Job Control enabled every command or pipeline the user enters at the terminal is called a *job*. All jobs exist in one of the following states: foreground, background or stopped. These terms are defined as follows: 1) a job in the foreground has read and write access to the controlling terminal; 2) a job in the background is denied read access and has conditional write access to the controlling terminal [see **stty**(1)]; 3) a stopped job is a job that has been placed in a suspended state, usually as a result of a **SIGTSTP** signal [see **signal**(5)]. Jobs in the foreground can be stopped by **INTERRUPT** or **QUIT** signals from the keyboard; background jobs cannot be stopped by these signals.

Every job that the shell starts is assigned a positive integer, called a *job number* which is tracked by the shell and will be used as an identifier to indicate a specific job. Additionally the shell keeps track of the *current* and *previous* jobs. The *current job* is the most recent job to be started or restarted. The *previous job* is the first non-current job.

The acceptable syntax for a Job Identifier is of the form:

%*jobid*

where, *jobid* may be specified in any of the following formats:

% or + for the current job

– for the previous job

?<*string*> specify the job for which the command line uniquely contains *string*.

n for job number *n*, where *n* is a job number

pref where *pref* is a unique prefix of the command name (for example, if the command **ls -l foo** were running in the background, it could be referred to as **%ls**); *pref* cannot contain blanks unless it is quoted.

When Job Control is enabled, the following commands are added to the user's environment to manipulate jobs:

bg [%*jobid* ...]
: Resumes the execution of a stopped job in the background. If %*jobid* is omitted the current job is assumed.

fg [%*jobid* ...]
: Resumes the execution of a stopped job in the foreground, also moves an executing background job into the foreground. If %*jobid* is omitted the current job is assumed.

jobs [**-p**|**-l**] [%*jobid* . . .]

jobs -x *command* [*arguments*]
: Reports all jobs that are stopped or executing in the background. If %*jobid* is omitted, all jobs that are stopped or running in the background will be reported. The following options will modify/enhance the output of **jobs**:

- **-l** Report the process group *ID* and working directory of the jobs.
- **-p** Report only the process group *ID* of the jobs.
- **-x** Replace any *jobid* found in *command* or *arguments* with the corresponding process group *ID*, and then execute *command* passing it *arguments*.

kill [**-signal**] %*jobid*
: Builtin version of **kill** to provide the functionality of the **kill** command for processes identified with a *jobid*.

stop %*jobid* ...
: Stops the execution of a background job(s).

suspend
: Stops the execution of the current shell (but not if it is the login shell).

wait [%*jobid* ...]
: **wait** builtin accepts a job identifier. If %*jobid* is omitted **wait** behaves as described above under **Special Commands**.

Restricted Shell (/usr/lib/rsh) Only

/usr/lib/rsh is used to set up login names and execution environments whose capabilities are more controlled than those of the standard shell. The actions of **/usr/lib/rsh** are identical to those of **sh**, except that the following are disallowed:

changing directory [see **cd**(1)],
setting the value of *$PATH,*
specifying path or command names containing **/**,
redirecting output (**>** and **>>**).

The restrictions above are enforced after **.profile** is interpreted.

A restricted shell can be invoked in one of the following ways: (1) **rsh** is the filename part of the last entry in the **/etc/passwd** file [see **passwd**(4)]; (2) the environment variable **SHELL** exists and **rsh** is the filename part of its value; (3) the shell is invoked and **rsh** is the filename part of argument 0; (4) the shell is invoked with the **-r** option.

When a command to be executed is found to be a shell procedure, **/usr/lib/rsh** invokes **sh** to execute it. Thus, it is possible to provide to the end-user shell procedures that have access to the full power of the standard shell, while imposing a limited menu of commands; this scheme assumes that the end-user does not have write and execute permissions in the same directory.

The net effect of these rules is that the writer of the **.profile** [see **profile**(4)] has complete control over user actions by performing guaranteed setup actions and leaving the user in an appropriate directory (probably *not* the login directory).

The system administrator often sets up a directory of commands (i.e., **/usr/rbin**) that can be safely invoked by a restricted shell. Some systems also provide a restricted editor, **red**.

EXIT STATUS

Errors detected by the shell, such as syntax errors, cause the shell to return a non-zero exit status. If the shell is being used non-interactively execution of the shell file is abandoned. Otherwise, the shell returns the exit status of the last command executed (see also the **exit** command above).

jsh Only

If the shell is invoked as **jsh** and an attempt is made to exit the shell while there are stopped jobs, the shell issues one warning:

```
there are stopped jobs
```

This is the only message. If another exit attempt is made, and there are still stopped jobs they will be sent a **SIGHUP** signal from the kernel and the shell is exited.

FILES

/etc/profile
$HOME/.profile
/tmp/sh*
/dev/null
/usr/lib/locale/*locale***/LC_MESSAGES/uxcore.abi**
language-specific message file [See **LANG** on **environ**(5).]

SEE ALSO

cd(1), **dup**(2), **echo**(1), **environ**(5), **exec**(2), **fork**(2), **getopts**(1), **getrlimit**(2), **intro**(1), **intro**(2), **login**(1), **newgrp**(1M), **pipe**(2), **profile**(4), **pwd**(1), **setlocale**(3C), **signal**(5), **stty**(1), **test**(1), **ulimit**(2), **umask**(1), **wait**(1)

NOTES

Words used for filenames in input/output redirection are not interpreted for filename generation (see "File Name Generation," above). For example,

```
cat file1 >a*
```

will create a file named **a***.

Because commands in pipelines are run as separate processes, variables set in a pipeline have no effect on the parent shell.

If you get the error message

    cannot fork, too many processes,

try using the **wait**(1) command to clean up your background processes. If this doesn't help, the system process table is probably full or you have too many active foreground processes. (There is a limit to the number of process ids associated with your login, and to the number the system can keep track of.)

Only the last process in a pipeline can be waited for.

If a command is executed, and a command with the same name is installed in a directory in the search path before the directory where the original command was found, the shell will continue to **exec** the original command. Use the **hash** command to correct this situation. Prior to Release 4, the **rsh** command invoked the restricted shell. This restricted shell command is **/usr/lib/rsh** and it can be executed by using the full pathname. Beginning with Release 4, the **rsh** command is the remote shell [See **rsh**(1)].

share (1M)

NAME

share – make local resource available for mounting by remote systems

SYNOPSIS

share [**-F** *fstype*] [**-o** *specific_options*] [**-d** *description*] [*pathname* [*resourcename*]]

DESCRIPTION

The **share** command makes a resource available for mounting through a remote file system of type *fstype*. If the option **-F** *fstype* is omitted, the first file system type listed in file **/etc/dfs/fstypes** will be used as the default. *specific_options* as well as the semantics of *resourcename* are specific to the particular distributed file system associated with the specified file system type. When invoked with only a file system type, **share** displays all resources shared by the given file system to the local system. When invoked with no arguments, **share** displays all resources shared by the local system.

When sharing a resource, the **-d** flag may be used to provide a description of the resource being shared.

Only a privileged user can execute this command.

FILES

/etc/dfs/dfstab
/etc/dfs/sharetab
/etc/dfs/fstypes

SEE ALSO

nfs-specific **share**(1M), **rfs**-specific f4share(1M), **unshare**(1M)

NOTES

If you enter the **-d** option when you share an NFS resource, the description is stored in your **sharetab** file. However, clients will not see the description displayed when they use the **dfshares** command to list the resources shared on your system.

NAME

shareall, **unshareall** – share, unshare multiple resources

SYNOPSIS

shareall [**-F** *fstype*[,*fstype* . . .]] [**-** | *file*]
unshareall [**-F** *fstype*[,*fstype* . . .]]

DESCRIPTION

When used with no arguments, **shareall** shares all resources from *file*, which contains a list of **share** command lines. If the operand is a hyphen (–), then the **share** command lines are obtained from the standard input. Otherwise, if neither a *file* nor a hyphen is specified, then the file **/etc/dfs/dfstab** is used as the default.

Resources may be shared to specific file systems by specifying the file systems in a comma-separated list as an argument to **-F**.

unshareall unshares all currently shared resources. Without a **-F** flag, it unshares resources for all distributed file system types.

Only a privileged user can execute this command.

FILES

/etc/dfs/dfstab

SEE ALSO

share(1M), **unshare**(1M)

sharectl (1M)

NAME

sharectl – initializes, removes, and prints shared-memory information.

SYNOPSIS

/usr/pci/bin/sharectl [**-cdmor**] [*name=value*]. . .

DESCRIPTION

The **sharectl** command initializes, removes, or prints shared-memory information, depending on the options used. The following options can be entered from the command line:

-c Creates the shared memory segment.

-d Shows the default configuration (only).

-m Displays miscellaneous existing segment information.

-o Handles the old style (multisegment) shared memory.

-r Removes the shared memory segment.

Normal operation is to attach to the shared memory and not to display anything. This creates the default segment if it doesn't exist and verifies the ability to attach to it.

The **-d** option shows the default configuration and immediately exits.

Modifications to the default configuration parameters can be made by adding one or more "name=value" strings after the option. Note that this is only available for the new style shared memory.

NAME

share – make local NFS resource available for mounting by remote systems

SYNOPSIS

share -F nfs [**-o** *specific_options*] [**-d** *description*] *pathname [resource]*

DESCRIPTION

The **share** command makes local resources available for mounting by remote systems.

If no argument is specified, then **share** displays all of the NFS resources currently shared.

Options

The following options are available to the **share** command:

-F Specifies the File System Type (FSType). This option may be omitted if NFS is the first file system type listed in the **/etc/dfs/fstypes** file.

-o *specific_options*
: Specify options in a comma-separated list of keywords and attribute-value-assertions for interpretation by the file-system-type-specific command.

specific_options can be any combination of the following:

rw Sharing will be read-write to all clients.

rw=*client*[**:***client*]. . .
: Sharing will be read-write to the listed clients; overrides the **ro** suboption for the clients specified.

ro Sharing will be read-only to all clients.

ro=*client*[**:***client*]. . .
: Sharing will be read-only to the listed clients; overrides the **rw** suboption for the clients specified.

anon=*uid*
: Set *uid* to be the effective user ID of unauthenticated users if AUTH_DES authentication is used, or to be root if AUTH_UNIX authentication is used. By default, unknown users are given the effective user ID **UID_NOBODY**. If *uid* is set to **-1**, access is denied.

root=*host*[**:***host*] ...
: Only root users from the specified hosts will have root access. By default, no host has root access.

secure
: Clients must use the AUTH_DES authentication of RPC. AUTH_UNIX authentication is the default.

If *specific_options* is not specified, then by default sharing will be read-write to all clients.

-d *description*
: Provide a comment that describes the resource to be shared.

pathname

Specify the pathname of the resource to be shared.

resource

Specify the name of the *resource* to be shared.

The *specific_options* **ro=**, **rw=**, and **root=** are guaranteed to work over UDP but may not work over other transport providers.

Files

/etc/dfs/fstypes

/etc/dfs/sharetab

Exit Codes

0 Successful exit

33 Usage error

34 Could not add to sharetab

35 Could not delete from sharetab

36 Could not share

37 Error in options parsing

USAGE

If a resource is shared with a **ro=** list and a **root=** list, any host that is on the **root=** list will be given read-only access, regardless of whether that host is specified in the **ro=** list, unless **rw** is declared as the default, or the host is mentioned in a **rw=** list. The same is true if the resource is shared with **ro** as the default.

Examples

The following **share** commands will give read-only permissions to **hostb**:

```
share -F nfs -oro=hosta,root=hostb /var
share -F nfs -oro,root=hostb /var
```

While the following will give read/write permissions to hostb:

```
share -F nfs -oro=hosta,rw=hostb,root=hostb /var
share -F nfs -oroot=hostb /var
```

Notes

The **share** command will fail if both **ro** and **rw** (with no qualifiers) are specified. If the same client name exists in both the **ro=** and **rw=** lists, the **rw** will override the **ro**, giving read/write access to the client specified.

Granting root access to other hosts has far reaching security implications; use the **root=** option with extreme caution.

REFERENCES

unshare(1M)

NAME

share – make local RFS resource available for mounting by remote systems

SYNOPSIS

share [**-F** rfs] [**-o** *access_spec*] [**-d** *description*] [*pathname resourcename*]

DESCRIPTION

This command is obsolete and will not be supported after this release. The **share** command makes a resource available for mounting through Remote File Sharing. The **-F** flag may be omitted if rfs is the first file system type listed in the file **/etc/dfs/fstypes**. When invoked with only a file system type (or no arguments), **share** displays all local resources shared through Remote File Sharing.

The *access_spec* is used to control client access of the shared resource. Clients may be specified in any of the following forms:

domain.
domain.system
system

The *access_spec* can be one of the following:

rw
: *resourcename* is shared read/write to all clients. This is also the default behavior.

rw=*client*[*:client*]...
: *resourcename* is shared read/write only to the listed clients. No other systems can access *resourcename*.

ro
: *resourcename* is shared read-only to all clients.

ro=*client*[*:client*]...
: *resourcename* is shared read-only only to the listed clients. No other systems can access *resourcename*.

The **-d** flag may be used to provide a description of the resource being shared.

Only a privileged user can execute this command.

ERRORS

If the network is not up and running or *pathname* is not a full path, an error message will be sent to standard error. If *pathname* isn't on a file system mounted locally or the *client* is specified but syntactically incorrect, an error message will be sent to standard error. If the same *resource* name in the network over the same transport provider is to be shared more than once, an error message will be sent to standard error.

FILES

/etc/dfs/dfstab
/etc/dfs/sharetab
/etc/dfs/fstypes

SEE ALSO

unshare(1M)

NOTES

If the access privilege of the resource to be shared is being set, only one of the suboptions `rw`, `ro`, `rw=`, and `ro=` can be specified.

NAME

shell – run a command using shell

SYNOPSIS

shell *command* [*command*] . . .

DESCRIPTION

The **shell** function concatenates its arguments, separating each by a space, and passes this string to the UNIX system shell (**$SHELL** if set, otherwise **/usr/bin/sh**).

EXAMPLES

Since the Form and Menu Language does not directly support background processing, the **shell** function can be used instead.

```
'shell "build prog > /dev/null &"'
```

If you want the user to continue to be able to interact with the application while the background job is running, the output of an executable run by **shell** in the background must be redirected: to a file if you want to save the output, or to **/dev/null** if you don't want to save it (or if there is no output), otherwise your application may appear to be hung until the background job finishes processing.

shell can also be used to execute a command that has the same name as an FMLI built-in function.

NOTES

The arguments to **shell** will be concatenated using spaces, which may or may not do what is expected. The variables set in local environments will not be expanded by the shell because "local" means "local to the current process."

SEE ALSO

sh(1)

NAME

shl – shell layer manager

SYNOPSIS

shl

DESCRIPTION

shl allows a user to interact with more than one shell from a single terminal. The user controls these shells, known as **layers**, using the commands described below.

The current layer is the layer which can receive input from the keyboard. Other layers attempting to read from the keyboard are blocked. Output from multiple layers is multiplexed onto the terminal. To have the output of a layer blocked when it is not current, the **stty** option **loblk** may be set within the layer.

The **stty** character **swtch** (set to ^Z if NUL) is used to switch control to **shl** from a layer. **shl** has its own prompt, >>>, to help distinguish it from a layer.

A *layer* is a shell which has been bound to a virtual tty device (**/dev/sxt???**). The virtual device can be manipulated like a real tty device using **stty**(1) and **ioctl**(2). Each layer has its own process group id.

A layer processes supplementary code set characters as does the shell used in it [see **sh**(1), for example] according to the locale specified in the **LC_CTYPE** environment variable [see **LANG** on **environ**(5)]. Layer names given to **shl** commands (see below) must be specified with ASCII characters.

Definitions

A *name* is a sequence of characters delimited by a blank, tab or new-line. Only the first eight characters are significant. The *names* **(1)** through **(7)** cannot be used when creating a layer. They are used by **shl** when no name is supplied. They may be abbreviated to just the digit.

Commands

The following commands may be issued from the **shl** prompt level. Any unique prefix is accepted.

create [*name*]
: Create a layer called *name* and make it the current layer. If no argument is given, a layer will be created with a name of the form *(#)* where # is the last digit of the virtual device bound to the layer. The shell prompt variable **PS1** is set to the name of the layer followed by a space. A maximum of seven layers can be created.

block *name* [*name* ...]
: For each *name*, block the output of the corresponding layer when it is not the current layer. This is equivalent to setting the **stty** option **-loblk** within the layer.

delete *name* [*name* ...]
: For each *name*, delete the corresponding layer. All processes in the process group of the layer are sent the **SIGHUP** signal [see **signal**(2)].

help (or **?**)
: Print the syntax of the **shl** commands.

layers [**-l**] [*name* ...]
For each *name*, list the layer name and its process group. The **-l** option produces a **ps**(1)-like listing. If no arguments are given, information is presented for all existing layers.

resume [*name*]
Make the layer referenced by *name* the current layer. If no argument is given, the last existing current layer will be resumed.

toggle
Resume the layer that was current before the last current layer.

unblock *name* [*name* ...]
For each *name*, do not block the output of the corresponding layer when it is not the current layer. This is equivalent to setting the **stty** option **-loblk** within the layer.

quit Exit **shl**. All layers are sent the **SIGHUP** signal.

name Make the layer referenced by *name* the current layer.

FILES

/dev/sxt???
virtual tty devices

$SHELL
variable containing path name of the shell to use (default is **/bin/sh**)

/usr/lib/locale/*locale***/LC_MESSAGES/uxue**
language-specific message file [See **LANG** on **environ**(5).]

SEE ALSO

ioctl(2), **sh**(1), **signal**(2), **stty**(1), **sxt**(7)

NOTES

To avoid disabling the suspend character when in the job control environment, the **swtch** character must be redefined.

NAME

showmount – show all remote mounts

SYNOPSIS

/usr/sbin/showmount [**-ade**] [*hostname*]

DESCRIPTION

showmount lists all the clients that have remotely mounted a filesystem from *host*. This information is maintained by the **mountd**(1M) server on *host*, and is saved across crashes in the file **/etc/rmtab**. The default value for *host* is the value returned by **hostname**(1).

OPTIONS

-a Print all remote mounts in the format:

hostname : directory

where *hostname* is the name of the client, and *directory* is the root of the file system that has been mounted.

-d List directories that have been remotely mounted by clients.

-e Print the list of exported file systems.

FILES

/etc/rmtab

SEE ALSO

hostname(1), **exportfs**(1M), **mountd**(1M)

NOTES

If a client crashes, its entry will not be removed from the list until it reboots and executes **umount -a.**

NAME

showsnf - print contents of an SNF file

SYNOPSIS

showsnf [**-s**] [**-v**] [**-g**] [**-m**] [**-M**] [**-l**] [**-L**] [**-p***num*] [**-u***num*]

DESCRIPTION

The **showsnf** command displays the contents of font files in the Server Natural Format (SNF) produced by **bsdtosnf**. It is usually only to verify that a font file hasn't been corrupted or to convert the individual glyphs into arrays of characters for proofreading or for conversion to some other format.

Options

-s byte swap. This is needed for 6386 XWIN format, which is also used by the 730X.

-v print character bearings and sizes

-g print character glyph bitmaps

-m bit order of the font is MSBFirst (most significant bit first)

-l bit order of the font is LSBFirst (least significant bit first)

-M byte order of the font is MSBFirst (most significant byte first)

-L byte order of the font is LSBFirst (least significant byte first)

-p*num* glyph padding of the font (*num* is a number)

-u*num* scanline unit of the font

SEE ALSO

bdftosnf(1), **X**(1)

NOTES

There is no way to just print out a single glyph.

Portions of the page are derived from material which is copyright Massachusetts Institute of Technology.

shserv (1M)

NAME

shserv – provide the shell service as part of the login process

SYNOPSIS

shserv

DESCRIPTION

The **shserv** command sets up the basic environment, changes directories to the user's home directory, and executes the user's shell. **shserv** is invoked by the port monitor (**ttymon**) through an entry in the **_pmtab** file; see **ttymon**(1M) and **pmadm**(1M). The home directory, shell, and environment variables are provided to the command by the port monitor via a Stream module.

FILES

`/etc/security/ia/master`
`/etc/saf/ttymon[1-9]/_pmtab`

SEE ALSO

`login`(1), **pmadm**(1M), `ttymon`(1M)

DIAGNOSTICS

shserv provides the user's shell on success. On failure **shserv** exits with the value of 1 and one of the following messages:

```
failed retava in shserv
failed getava of SHELL
failed getava of HOMEDIR
unable to change directory to user's home directory
```

NOTES

This command cannot be run from the command line.

NAME

shutdown – shut down system, change system state

SYNOPSIS

shutdown [**-y**] [**-g***grace_period [* **-i***init_state*]

DESCRIPTION

This command is executed by a privileged user to change the state of the machine. In most cases, it is used to change from the multi-user state (state 2) to another state (see below).

By default, it brings the system to state **0**: the state in which it is safe to remove the power. This state is called the shutdown state.

The command sends a warning message and a final message before it starts actual shutdown activities. **shutdown** gets the default value for a *grace_period* following each of these messages from **/etc/default/shutdown**, if that file exists. The value of *grace_period* is implementation dependent. If **shutdown** cannot find the file or cannot read the value, it displays a warning and sets the grace period to 60 seconds. By default, the command asks for confirmation before it starts shutting down daemons and killing processes. The options are used as follows:

-y pre-answers the confirmation question so the command can be run without user intervention. A default *grace_period* is allowed between the warning message and the final message. Another *grace_period* is allowed between the final message and the confirmation.

-g*grace_period*
allows a privileged user to change the *grace_period* from the default.

-i*init_state*
specifies the state that **init** is to be put in following the warnings, if any. By default, system state **0** is used.

Other recommended system state definitions are:

state 0: Shut the machine down so it is safe to remove the power. If possible, have the machine remove the power. (The **rc0** procedure is invoked for this.)

state 1: State 1 is referred to as the administrative state. File systems required for multi-user operations are mounted and logins requiring access to multi-user file systems can be used. When the system comes up from firmware mode into state 1, only the console is active; multi-user (state 2) services are unavailable. When the system is going from state 2 to state 1, some services are stopped and some processes are killed; otherwise, the system continues operating as it did in state 2. (The **rc1** procedure is invoked for this.)

state s, S:
State s (or S) is referred to as the single-user state. All user processes are stopped and file systems required for multi-user logins are unmounted on transitions to this state. Thereafter, the system can be accessed only through the console; logins requiring access to multi-user file systems cannot be used. Run your system in this state to install or remove software utilities, or to back up, restore, or check a file system. The system enters state **s** automatically when the **/usr** file system is corrupted and cannot be

recovered. The set of file systems mounted while a system is in state **s** is not always the same; which file systems are mounted depends on the method by which the system entered state **s** and local computer site rules.

state 5: Stop the operating system and go to firmware mode if the processor (system) supports it. If firmware mode is supported: (a) run special firmware commands and programs that reside in NVRAM—such as making a floppy key, and (b) run programs that reside in the **/stand** file system under the control of the NVRAM—such as running **/stand/unix** to reboot the system.

If there is no firmware mode, shut the system down so it is safe to remove power. If possible, have the machine remove the power. (The **rc0** procedure is invoked for this.) See "state 0."

state 6: Stop and reboot the operating system to the state defined by the **initdefault** entry in **/etc/inittab**. If necessary, configure a new bootable operating system before the reboot. (Because **rc6** is linked to **rc0** for backward compatibility, the **rc0** procedure is invoked for this.)

FILES

/etc/default/shutdown

NOTES

shutdown(1M) behaves differently depending on the number of users logged in. If several users are logged in, three messages are displayed, warning, final, and confirmation, with *grace_period* between each message. If only the user issuing **shutdown** is logged in, or if **grace_period** is **0**, then no messages will be issued.

SEE ALSO

init(1M), **inittab**(4), **rc0**(1M), **rc2**(1M)

NAME

shutdown – (BSD) close down the system at a given time

SYNOPSIS

/usr/ucb/shutdown [**-fhknr**] *time* [*warning-message* ...]

DESCRIPTION

shutdown provides an automated procedure to notify users when the system is to be shut down. *time* specifies when **shutdown** will bring the system down; it may be the word **now** (indicating an immediate shutdown), or it may specify a future time in one of two formats: **+***number* and *hour***:***min.* The first form brings the system down in *number* minutes, and the second brings the system down at the time of day indicated in 24-hour notation.

At intervals that get closer as the apocalypse approaches, warning messages are displayed at terminals of all logged-in users, and of users who have remote mounts on that machine.

At shutdown time a message is written to the system log daemon, **syslogd**(1M), containing the time of shutdown, the instigator of the shutdown, and the reason. Then a terminate signal is sent to **init**, which brings the system down to init state **1**.

OPTIONS

As an alternative to the above procedure, these options can be specified:

-f Arrange, in the manner of **fastboot**(1M), that when the system is rebooted, the file systems will not be checked.

-h Execute **halt**(1M).

-k Simulate shutdown of the system. Do not actually shut down the system.

-n Prevent the normal **sync**(2) before stopping.

-r Execute **reboot**(1M).

FILES

/etc/xtab list of remote hosts that have mounted this host

SEE ALSO

fastboot(1M), **halt**(1M), **reboot**(1M), **syslogd**(1M), **sync**(2).

NOTES

Only allows you to bring the system down between **now** and 23:59 if you use the absolute time for shutdown.

NAME

size – print section sizes in bytes of object files

SYNOPSIS

size [**-F -f -n -o -V -x**] *files*

DESCRIPTION

The **size** command produces segment or section size information in bytes for each loaded section in ELF or COFF object files. **size** prints out the size of the text, data, and bss (uninitialized data) segments (or sections) and their total.

size processes ELF and COFF object files entered on the command line. If an archive file is input to the **size** command, the information for each object file in the archive is displayed.

When calculating segment information, the **size** command prints out the total file size of the non-writable segments, the total file size of the writable segments, and the total memory size of the writable segments minus the total file size of the writable segments.

If it cannot calculate segment information, **size** calculates section information. When calculating section information, it prints out the total size of sections that are allocatable, non-writable, and not NOBITS, the total size of the sections that are allocatable, writable, and not NOBITS, and the total size of the writable sections of type NOBITS. (NOBITS sections do not actually take up space in the *file*.)

If **size** cannot calculate either segment or section information, it prints an error message and stops processing the file.

-F Prints out the size of each loadable segment, the permission flags of the segment, then the total of the loadable segment sizes. If there is no segment data, **size** prints an error message and stops processing the file.

-f Prints out the size of each allocatable section, the name of the section, and the total of the section sizes. If there is no section data, **size** prints out an error message and stops processing the file.

-n Prints out non-loadable segment or non-allocatable section sizes. If segment data exists, **size** prints out the memory size of each loadable segment or file size of each non-loadable segment, the permission flags, and the total size of the segments. If there is no segment data, **size** prints out, for each allocatable and non-allocatable section, the memory size, the section name, and the total size of the sections. If there is no segment or section data, **size** prints an error message and stops processing.

-o Prints numbers in octal, not decimal.

-V Prints the version information for the **size** command on the standard error output.

-x Prints numbers in hexadecimal; not decimal.

EXAMPLES

The examples below are typical **size** output.

size *file*	`2724 + 88 + 0 =  2812`
size -f *file*	`26(.text) + 5(.init) + 5(.fini)  = 36`
size -F *file*	`2724(r-x) + 88(rwx) + 0(rwx) = 2812`

SEE ALSO

a.out(4), **ar**(4), **as**(1), **cc**(1), **ld**(1)

NOTES

Since the size of bss sections is not known until link-edit time, the **size** command does not give the true total size of pre-linked objects.

sleep (1)

NAME

sleep – suspend execution for an interval

SYNOPSIS

sleep *time*

DESCRIPTION

sleep suspends execution for *time* seconds. It is used to execute a command after a certain amount of time, as in:

```
(sleep 105; command)&
```

or to execute a command every so often, as in:

```
while true
do
        command
        sleep 37
done
```

FILES

/usr/lib/locale/*locale***/LC_MESSAGES/uxcore.abi**
language-specific message file [See **LANG** on **environ** (5).]

SEE ALSO

alarm(2), **sleep**(3C)

NAME

slink – streams linker

SYNOPSIS

slink [-v] [-f] [-p] [-u] [-c *file***] [func [***arg1 arg2* **. . .]]**

DESCRIPTION

slink is a STREAMS configuration utility which is used to link together the various STREAMS modules and drivers required for STREAMS TCP/IP. Input to **slink** is in the form of a script specifying the STREAMS operations to be performed. Input is normally taken from the file **/etc/strcf**.

The following options may be specified on the **slink** command line:

-c *file* Use *file* instead of **/etc/strcf**.

-v Verbose mode (each operation is logged to **stderr**).

-p Don't use persistent links (i.e., slink will remain in the background).

-f Don't use persistent links and don't fork (i.e., slink will remain in foreground).

-u Unlink persistent links (i.e., shut down network).

The configuration file contains a list of *functions*, each of which is composed of a list of *commands*. Each command is a call to one of the functions defined in the configuration file or to one of a set of built-in functions. Among the built-in functions are the basic STREAMS operations **open**, **link**, and **push**, along with several TCP/IP-specific functions.

slink processing consists of parsing the input file, then calling the user-defined function **boot**, which is normally used to set up the standard configuration at boot time. If a function is specified on the **slink** command line, that function will be called instead of **boot**.

By default, **slink** establishes streams with persistent links (**I_PLINK**) and exits following the execution of the specified function. If the **-p** flag is specified, **slink** establishes streams with regular links (**I_LINK**) and remains idle in the background, holding open whatever file descriptors have been opened by the configuration commands. If the **-f** flag is specified, **slink** establishes streams with regular links (**I_LINK**) and remains in the foreground, holding open whatever file descriptors have been opened by the configuration commands.

A function definition has the following form:

```
function-name {
      command1
      command2
      ...
}
```

The syntax for commands is:

function arg1 arg2 arg3 . . .

or

var = *function arg1 arg2 arg3 . . .*

The placement of newlines is important: a newline must follow the left and right braces and every command. Extra newlines are allowed, i.e. where one newline is required, more than one may be used. A backslash (\) followed immediately by a newline is considered equivalent to a space, i.e. may be used to continue a command on a new line. The use of other white space characters (spaces and tabs) is at the discretion of the user, except that there must be white space separating the function name and the arguments of a command.

Comments are delimited by **#** and newline, and are considered equivalent to a newline.

Function and variable names may be any string of characters taken from A-Z, a-z, 0-9, and _, except that the first character cannot be a digit. Function names and variable names occupy separate name spaces. All functions are global and may be forward referenced. All variables are local to the functions in which they occur.

Variables are defined when they appear to the left of an equals (=) on a command line; for example,

```
tcp = open /dev/tcp
```

The variable acquires the value returned by the command. In the above example, the value of the variable **tcp** will be the file descriptor returned by the **open** call.

Arguments to a command may be either variables, parameters, or strings.

A variable that appears as an argument must have been assigned a value on a previous command line in that function.

Parameters take the form of a dollar sign (**$**) followed by one or two decimal digits, and are replaced with the corresponding argument from the function call. If a given parameter was not specified in the function call, an error results (e.g. if a command references $3 and only two arguments were passed to the function, an execution error will occur).

Strings are sequences of characters optionally enclosed in double quotes (**"**). Quotes may be used to prevent a string from being interpreted as a variable name or a parameter, and to allow the inclusion of spaces, tabs, and the special characters **{**, **}**, **=**, and **#**. The backslash (\) may also be used to quote the characters **{**, **}**, **=**, **#**, **"**, and \ individually.

The following built-in functions are provided by **slink**:

open *path* — Open the device specified by pathname *path*. Returns a file descriptor referencing the open stream.

link *fd1 fd2* — Link the stream referenced by *fd2* beneath the stream referenced by *fd1*. Returns the link identifier associated with the link. Unless the **-f** or **-p** flag is specified on the command line, the streams will be linked with persistent links. Note: *fd2* cannot be used after this operation.

push *fd module* — Push the module *module* onto the stream referenced by *fd*.

sifname *fd link name* — Send a **SIOCSIFNAME** (set interface name) ioctl down the stream referenced by *fd* for the link associated with link identifier *link* specifying the name *name*.

unitsel *fd unit* — Send a **IF_UNITSEL** (unit select) ioctl down the stream referenced by *fd* specifying unit *unit*.

dlattach *fd unit* — Send a **DL_ATTACH_REQ** message down the stream referenced by *fd* specifying unit *unit*.

initqp *path qname lowat hiwat ...*

Send an **INITQPARMS** (initialize queue parameters) ioctl to the driver corresponding to pathname *path*. *qname* specifies the queue for which the low and high water marks will be set, and must be one of:

hd	stream head
rq	read queue
wq	write queue
muxrq	multiplexor read queue
muxwq	multiplexor write queue

lowat and *hiwat* specify the new low and high water marks for the queue. Both *lowat* and *hiwat* must be present. To change only one of these parameters, the other may be replaced with a dash (-). Up to five *qname lowat hiwat* triplets may be present.

strcat *str1 str2* — Concatenate strings *str1* and *str2* and return the resulting string.

return *val* — Set the return value for the current function to *val*.
Note: executing a **return** command does not terminate execution of the current function.

FILES

`/etc/strcf`

SEE ALSO

strcf(4)

NAME

smtp – send mail to a remote host using Simple Mail Transfer Protocol

SYNOPSIS

/usr/lib/mail/surrcmd/smtp [-D] [-N] [-u] [-d *domain***] [-H** *helohost***]** *sender targethost recip* **...**

/usr/lib/mail/surrcmd/smtpbatch [-D] [-N] *ctlfiles* **...**

DESCRIPTION

smtp sends a message to a remote host *targethost* using the Simple Mail Transfer Protocol (SMTP). The message is read from standard input. *sender* is used to identify the sender of the message, and the *recip*s are used as the recipients.

When establishing a connection, **smtp** first generates a list of "message exchangers" with which the mail may be forwarded. This list is generated by querying the nameserver for all MX records for the host *targethost* (as specified in RFC974). **smtp** then tries to connect to each host in preference order, until one accepts the call. The message is then delivered. The TCP port that is connected to is determined by using **getservbyname()** to lookup service "smtp" using protocol "tcp".

The options to *smtp* and their meanings are as follows:

-D This option turns on debugging. Debugging information is printed on standard error.

-N This option turns off the nameserver MX record lookup that normally occurs, and prevents *smtp* from using a nameserver for name to address mappings. This option will speed up processing if your host is not configured to use a nameserver (either local or remote).

-H *helohost* This option can be used to set the hostname used in the SMTP HELO message. If not specified, the hostname defaults to the system's name.

-d *domain* This option can be used to set the domain name to be used for this host.

-u If this option is specified, the message is not converted to RFC822 format as it is passed to the remote system (the message is transmitted in so-called "UNIX system mail" format).

smtp is normally run by the *smtpsched* process in order to deliver mail queued in **/var/spool/smtpq**.

smtpbatch is an alternate form of the **smtp** command. It is used if there are multiple mail messages which should be "batched" and sent over one TCP connection. The *ctlfiles* arguments are the names of the control files which **smtpqer** normally creates when queueing a message. **smtpbatch** will attempt to open a connection to the machine specified by the first control file, and will then send all messages to the remote machine over this one connection.

FILES

/etc/inet/services	list of TCP/UDP services
/var/spool/smtpq	where messages are queued
/var/spool/smtpq/*targethost***/C.***	control files for *targethost*

EXIT CODES

The following error codes may be returned from **smtp** or **smtpbatch**. They are normally logged in the SMTP logfile as "**smtpsched fail n**", where *n* is the error code.

0 Successful exit
1 Timer expired, or corrupt data file
64 Command line usage incorrect
65 Message format error
67 Addressee unknown, or error in address
68 Unknown host
69 Could not make a connection to the remote host
70 Miscellaneous error
72 "smtp" not defined in /etc/inet/services
74 Error in transport layer input/output
75 Temporary failure in TLI (may be out of resources)

SEE ALSO

cs(1M), **getservent**(3N), **smtpqer**(1M), **smtpsched**(1M)

RFC821 - Simple Mail Transfer Protocol

RFC974 - Mail Routing and the Domain System

smtpd (1M)

NAME

smtpd – receive incoming mail using Simple Mail Transfer Protocol

SYNOPSIS

smtpd [**-n**] [**-H** *helohost*] [**-h** *thishost*] [**-L** *loadlim*] [**-l** *maxprocs*] [**-r**]

in.smtpd [**-n**] [**-H** *helohost*] [**-h** *thishost*] [**-L** *loadlim*] [**-l** *maxprocs*] [**-r**]

DESCRIPTION

smtpd is a daemon that normally runs while in multi-user mode, waiting for requests from remote hosts to send mail. **smtpd** listens for these requests on the TCP port specified in */etc/inet/services* for the "smtp" service. As requests are received, **smtpd** will fork off child **smtpd** processes to handle each individual SMTP transaction.

The options to **smtpd** and their meanings are as follows:

-n Do not create **smtpsched** processes to process the incoming mail. Rely on the hourly **cron**(1M) invocation of **smtpsched** instead. This is useful if your installation receives heavy amounts of incoming SMTP mail, and you want to limit the number of **smtpsched**s which run simultaneously. **cron**(1M) can be adjusted to run **smtpsched** more frequently than once an hour, if necessary.

-H *helohost* This option can be used to specify the name to be used for the host in the initial SMTP "220" message which the daemon sends to the remote host. If it is not specified, the name used in the 220 message defaults to the system node name.

-h *thishost* Specify the network name to be prepended onto the sender path in the **From** line of the message. This feature is normally not used, but may be useful if you wish to configure mail to make routing decisions based upon the transport that mail arrived on.

-L *loadlim* This option is used to specify the maximum load at which **smtpd** will create children. If this option is not specified, there is no limit to the load at which children may run. The load is determined by reading the kernel variable *avenrun*. It can be determined independently by using the command *uptime*.

-l *maxprocs* This option is used to specify the maximum number of children of **smtpd** that can be running at once. Each child handles one SMTP conversation. If this option is not specified, there is no limit to the number of children that may run.

-r This option causes **smtpd** to not rewrite the addresses in **From:**, **To:**, **Cc:**, and **Bcc:** lines into **host!user** style. Normally, these addresses are rewritten in order to accommodate other mail software which cannot handle addresses of the form **user@domain**.

Mail which is successfully received is queued under the SMTP spool directory, **/var/spool/smtpq**. If the Enhanced Security Utilities are installed, **/var/spool/smtpq** is a multi-level directory, and mail is queued at the security level that **in.smtpd** was started at. An **smtpsched** process is then started to deliver the mail by invoking **rmail** on each incoming message. A log of all **smtpd**'s activities is kept in the file **/var/spool/smtpq/LOG**; if the Enhanced Security Utilities are installed, one log file is kept for each level at which **in.smtpd** was started. (Filenames for these log files are of the form **/var/spool/smtpq/***level***/LOG**, where *level* is the level of **in.smtpd**. The separate levels are only seen when in *real mode*.)

in.smtpd is an alternate version of this command which can be started by the *inetd* TCP/IP port monitor. It takes the same arguments as **smtpd**, but only runs as a result of an incoming connection request to *inetd* on the SMTP port. If the Enhanced Security Utilities are installed, *inetd* handles user authentication before starting the *in.smtpd* process.

After it handles the SMTP conversation, it exits. It is installed by placing the following line in *inetd*s configuration file (**/etc/inet/inetd.conf**):

```
smtp stream tcp nowait smtp /usr/lib/mail/surrcmd/in.smtpd
in.smtpd
```

Other options to *in.smtpd* (for example, the hostname option -H) may be appended to the above line.

FILES

/dev/kmem	to get the current machine load (avenrun)
/etc/inet/inetd.conf	*inetd* port monitor configuration
/etc/inet/services	list of TCP/UDP services (SMTP should be 25/tcp)
/var/spool/smtpq/LOG	log of smtpd transactions
/var/spool/smtpq/*host*	queue directory for remote host
/var/spool/smtpq/*host***/D.***	incoming mail messages
/var/spool/smtpq/*host***/X.***	control files for incoming mail messages

EXIT CODES

0 Successful exit
1 Memory error, or TLI error
2 Usage error

SEE ALSO

cron(1M), **inetd**(1M), **smtp**(1M), **smtpsched**(1M), **uptime**(1)

smtpqer (1M)

NAME

smtpqer – queue mail for delivery by SMTP

SYNOPSIS

smtpqer [**-B**] [**-D**] [**-N**] [**-n**] [**-u**] [**-a** *toaddr*] [**-d** domain]
[**-H** *helohost*] *sender host recip . . .*

DESCRIPTION

smtpqer queues the mail message it reads from standard input for eventual delivery by **smtp**. The message is queued for delivery to the host specified by *host*.

smtpqer should normally be invoked by the **mail** command by placing the following line in **/etc/mail/mailsurr**:

```
´.+´ ´([^!@]+)!(.+)´ ´< /usr/lib/mail/surrcmd/smtpqer %R \\1´ ´\\2´
```

smtpqer will check the host name *host*. If it is one which can be reached, the message will be queued, and **smtpqer** will exit with a return code of 0 (which means the mail was successfully queued). Otherwise, it will return with an exit code of 1, and the message will not be queued. Normally, **mail** will then try to deliver by using other mail surrogates in the **/etc/mail/mailsurr** file. **smtpqer** determines if the host can be reached by checking whether the host name can be looked up directly via **gethostbyname**() [see **gethostent**(3N)], or by seeing if there is at least one "message exchanger" for this host which can be reached.

Messages which are queued are stored as two files under the SMTP queue directory (**/var/spool/smtpq**). As such, messages are queued under the security level at which **smtpqer** is run. This, in turn, is determined by the invoking **mail** command.

A "C.*" file contains control information for the **smtp** command, and a 'D.*" file contains the actual mail message. Finally, **smtpqer** invokes the **smtpsched** program to deliver the mail.

The options to **smtpqer** and their meanings are as follows:

-u This option tells the SMTP subsystem not to convert the message to RFC822 format.

-H *helohost* The **-H** option is used to specify the host name that should be used in the SMTP HELO message. If no **-H** option is given, the full domain name of the local machine is used.

-N The **-N** option turns off the nameserver MX record lookup that normally occurs, and prevents **smtpqer** from using a nameserver for name to address mappings. This option will speed up processing if your host is not configured to use a nameserver (either local or remote). This option is passed through to the **smtp** process that delivers the mail.

-d *domain* This option is used to specify the domain name that should be used for your host. If this option is not used, and a domain has been specified in the mail configuration file **/etc/mail/mailcnfg**, that domain will be used instead.

-a *toaddr* The **-a** option is used to specify the "to address" that is passed to the **smtp** program.

-B This option is passed to the **smtpsched** which is invoked. This causes **smtpsched** to invoke **smtpbatch** rather then **smtp** to deliver mail.

-D This option turns on debugging output in the surrogate (which may be useful to see why a surrogate is rejecting your mail).

-n This option is used to prevent **smtpqer** from starting an **smtpsched** process to deliver the mail. This is useful if your installation sends large amounts of SMTP mail, and you want to limit the number of **smtpsched**s which run simultaneously. **cron**(1M) can be adjusted to run **smtpsched** more frequently than once an hour, if necessary.

FILES

/etc/inet/hosts	database of remote hosts
/etc/mail/mailcnfg	mail configuration file
/etc/mail/mailsurr	control file containing rule to invoke **smtpqer**
/usr/bin/rmail	where mail originates from [see **mail**(1)]
/usr/lib/mail/surrcmd/smtpsched	program to process message queues
/usr/lib/mail/surrcmd/smtp	program which passes message to remote host
/var/spool/smtpq	where messages are queued
/var/spool/smtpq/*host***/C.***	control files for *host*
/var/spool/smtpq/*host***/D.***	message files for *host*

EXIT CODES

0 Mail has been queued for delivery
1 Mail is not for SMTP

SEE ALSO

cron(1M), **gethostent**(3N), **mail**(1), **smtp**(1M), **smtpsched**(1M)
RFC822 - Standard for the Format of ARPA Internet Text Messages

smtpsched (1M)

NAME

smtpsched, **smtploop** – process messages queued in the SMTP mail queue

SYNOPSIS

smtpsched [**-B**] [**-c**] [**-v**] [**-t**] [**-s** *scheds*] [**-r** *days*] [**-w** *days*] [*queuename* . . .]

smtploop [**smtpsched** *options*]

DESCRIPTION

smtpsched is used to process the messages queued up in the mail queue **/var/spool/smtpq**. It is invoked automatically by the SMTP mail surrogate **smtpqer**, whenever mail is queued for SMTP delivery to a remote host, and by **smtpd** whenever incoming mail arrives. It should also be run once per hour (from **cron**(1M)) in order to attempt delivery of any mail which cannot be delivered immediately.

smtpsched will normally attempt to send all messages queued under all subdirectories of **/var/spool/smtpq**. However, if *queuenames* are specified, only those listed subdirectories of **/var/spool/smtpq** will be searched for messages to deliver. The subdirectories each refer to a different remote host.

The options to **smtpsched** are as follows:

-B Invoke **smtpbatch** rather than **smtp** to deliver mail to a remote host. If there are several messages queued for delivery, this option will cause the mail to be delivered more quickly.

-c Causes empty queue directories to be removed. This will also cause the logfile to be renamed LOG.*n*, where *n* is the day of the week (from 0 for Sunday to 6 for Saturday). Only the "**smtp**" user is allowed to use this option.

-v Causes verbose logging to occur.

-t Test mode. The actions **smtpsched** would take are logged but not performed.

-s *scheds* Specifies the maximum number of concurrent **smtpscheds** that may be running at once. If more than this number is running, **smtpsched** will exit. If this option is not specified, **smtpsched** will always run.

-r *days* Causes mail older than *days* days to be returned. Only the "smtp" user is allowed to use this option.

-w *days* Any mail older than *days* days will trigger a warning message, which is sent to the originator. Only the "smtp" user is allowed to use this option.

FILES

/usr/lib/mail/surrcmd/smtp	delivers the mail
/usr/lib/mail/surrcmd/smtpbatch	delivers the mail in batch mode
/usr/lib/mail/surrcmd/smtpqer	queues the mail
/var/spool/smtpq	queued mail messages
/var/spool/smtpq/*host*	mail messages queued for *host*
/var/spool/smtpq/LOG	the current SMTP log file
/var/spool/smtpq/LOG.*n*	older SMTP log files

EXIT CODES

0 Successful exit

1 Some error occurred

SEE ALSO

cron(1M), **smtp**(1M), **smtpqer**(1M)

NAME

soelim – (BSD) resolve and eliminate .so requests from nroff or troff input

SYNOPSIS

/usr/ucb/soelim [*filename* . . .]

DESCRIPTION

The **soelim** command reads the specified files or the standard input and performs the textual inclusion implied by the **nroff**(1) directives of the form

.so *somefile*

when they appear at the beginning of input lines. This is useful since programs such as **tbl**(1) do not normally do this; it allows the placement of individual tables in separate files to be run as a part of a large document.

An argument consisting of "–" is taken to be a file name corresponding to the standard input.

Note: inclusion can be suppressed by using " ´ " instead of " **.** ", that is,

```
´so /usr/ucblib/doctools/tmac/s
```

EXAMPLE

A sample usage of **soelim** would be

```
soelim exum?.n | tbl | nroff -ms | col | lpr
```

SEE ALSO

more(1), **nroff**(1), **tbl**(1)

NAME

sort – sort and/or merge files

SYNOPSIS

sort [**-cmu**] [**-o***output*] [**-y***kmem*] [**-z***recsz*] [**-dfiMnr**] [**-btx**] [**+***pos1* [**-***pos2*]] [*files*]

DESCRIPTION

The **sort** command sorts lines of all the named files together and writes the result on the standard output. The standard input is read if – is used as a filename or no input files are named.

Comparisons are based on one or more sort keys extracted from each line of input. By default, there is one sort key, the entire input line, and ordering is lexicographic by bytes in machine collating sequence.

sort processes supplementary code set characters according to the locale specified in the **LC_CTYPE** and **LC_COLLATE** environment variables [see **LANG** on **environ**(5)], except as noted below. Supplementary code set characters are collated in code order.

The following options alter the default behavior:

-c Check that the input file is sorted according to the ordering rules; give no output unless the file is out of sort.

-m Merge only, the input files are already sorted.

-u Unique: suppress all but one in each set of lines having equal keys.

-o*output*
The argument given is the name of an output file to use instead of the standard output. This file may be the same as one of the inputs. A blank may be left between **-o** and *output*.

-y*kmem*
The amount of main memory used by **sort** has a large impact on its performance. Sorting a small file in a large amount of memory is a waste. If this option is omitted, **sort** begins using a system default memory size, and continues to use more space as needed. If this option is presented with a value (*kmem*), **sort** will start using that number of kilobytes of memory, unless the administrative minimum or maximum is violated, in which case the corresponding extremum will be used. Thus, **-y**0 is guaranteed to start with minimum memory. By convention, **-y** (with no argument) starts with maximum memory.

-z*recsz*
The size of the longest line read is recorded in the sort phase so buffers can be allocated during the merge phase. If the sort phase is omitted via the **-c** or **-m** options, a popular system default size will be used. Lines longer than the buffer size will cause **sort** to terminate abnormally. Supplying the actual number of bytes in the longest line to be merged (or some larger value) will prevent abnormal termination.

If the sort phase is not omitted, then the maximum line size is calculated and used as the *recsz*, overriding the value of **-z**. Thus, the **-z** option is significant only when used with **-c** or **-m**.

The following options override the default ordering rules.

-d "Dictionary" order: only letters, digits, and blanks (spaces and tabs) are significant in comparisons. No comparison is performed for multibyte characters.

-f Fold lowercase letters into uppercase. Does not apply to multibyte characters.

-i Ignore non-printable characters. Multibyte characters are also ignored.

-M Compare as months. The first three non-blank characters of the field are folded to uppercase and compared. Month names are processed according to the locale specified in the **LC_TIME** environment variable [see **LANG** on **environ**(5)]. For example, in an English locale the sorting order would be "JAN" < "FEB" < . . . < "DEC." Invalid fields compare low to "JAN." The **-M** option implies the **-b** option (see below).

-n An initial numeric string, consisting of optional blanks, an optional minus sign, and zero or more digits with an optional decimal point, is sorted by arithmetic value. The **-n** option implies the **-b** option (see below). Note that the **-b** option is only effective when restricted sort key specifications are in effect.

-r Reverse the sense of comparisons.

When ordering options appear before restricted sort key specifications, the requested ordering rules are applied globally to all sort keys. When attached to a specific sort key (described below), the specified ordering options override all global ordering options for that key.

The notation **+***pos1* **-***pos2* restricts a sort key to one beginning at *pos1* and ending just before *pos2*. The characters at position *pos1* and just before *pos2* are included in the sort key (provided that *pos2* does not precede *pos1*). A missing **-***pos2* means the end of the line.

Specifying *pos1* and *pos2* involves the notion of a field, a minimal sequence of characters followed by a field separator or a newline. By default, the first blank (space or tab) of a sequence of blanks acts as the field separator. All blanks in a sequence of blanks are considered to be part of the next field; for example, all blanks at the beginning of a line are considered to be part of the first field. The treatment of field separators can be altered using the options:

-b Ignore leading blanks when determining the starting and ending positions of a restricted sort key. If the **-b** option is specified before the first **+***pos1* argument, it will be applied to all **+***pos1* arguments. Otherwise, the **b** flag may be attached independently to each **+***pos1* or **-***pos2* argument (see below).

-t*x* Use *x* as the field separator character; *x* is not considered to be part of a field (although it may be included in a sort key). Each occurrence of *x* is significant (for example, *xx* delimits an empty field). *x* may be a supplementary code set character.

pos1 and *pos2* each have the form **m.n** optionally followed by one or more of the flags **bdfinr**. A starting position specified by **+m.n** is interpreted to mean the *n*+1st character (column, in multibyte environments) in the *m*+1st field. A missing **.n** means **.0**, indicating the first character of the *m*+1st field. If the **b** flag is in effect *n* is counted from the first non-blank in the *m*+1st field; **+m.0b** refers to the first non-blank character in the *m*+1st field.

A last position specified by **-m.n** is interpreted to mean the *n*th character (including separators) after the last character of the *m*th field. A missing **.n** means **.0**, indicating the last character of the *m*th field. If the **b** flag is in effect *n* is counted from the last leading blank in the *m*+1st field; **-m.1b** refers to the first non-blank in the *m*+1st field.

When there are multiple sort keys, later keys are compared only after all earlier keys compare equal. Lines that otherwise compare equal are ordered with all bytes significant.

EXAMPLES

Sort the contents of *infile* with the second field as the sort key:

sort +1 -2 *infile*

Sort, in reverse order, the contents of *infile1* and *infile2*, placing the output in *outfile* and using the first character of the second field as the sort key:

sort -r -o *outfile* **+1.0 -1.2** *infile1 infile2*

Sort, in reverse order, the contents of *infile1* and *infile2* using the first non-blank character of the second field as the sort key:

sort -r +1.0b -1.1b *infile1 infile2*

Print the password file [**passwd**(4)] sorted by the numeric user ID (the third colon-separated field):

sort -t: +2n -3 /etc/passwd

Sort the contents of the password file using the group ID (third field) as the primary sort key and the user ID (second field) as the secondary sort key:

sort -t: +3 -4 +2 -3 /etc/passwd

Sort the contents of the password file using the group ID (third field) as the primary sort key and the user ID (second field) as the secondary sort key:

sort -t: +3 -4 +2 -3 /etc/passwd

Print the lines of the already sorted file *infile*, suppressing all but the first occurrence of lines having the same third field (the options **-um** with just one input file make the choice of a unique representative from a set of equal lines predictable):

sort -um +2 -3 *infile*

FILES

/var/tmp/stm???

/usr/lib/locale/*locale***/LC_MESSAGES/uxcore.abi**

language-specific message file [See **LANG** on **environ** (5).]

SEE ALSO

comm(1), join(1), uniq(1)

NOTES

sort prints diagnostics and exits with non-zero status for various trouble conditions (for example, when input lines are too long), and for disorder discovered under the -c option.

When the last line of an input file is missing a newline character, sort appends one, prints a warning message, and continues. sort does not guarantee preservation of relative line ordering on equal keys.

NAME

sortbib – (BSD) sort a bibliographic database

SYNOPSIS

/usr/ucb/sortbib [**-s***key-letters*] *database* . . .

DESCRIPTION

The **sortbib** command sorts files of records containing **refer** key-letters by user-specified keys. Records may be separated by blank lines, or by "**.[**" and "**.]**" delimiters, but the two styles may not be mixed together. This program reads through each *database* and pulls out key fields, which are sorted separately. The sorted key fields contain the file pointer, byte offset, and length of corresponding records. These records are delivered using disk seeks and reads, so **sortbib** may not be used in a pipeline to read standard input.

By default, **sortbib** alphabetizes by the first **%A** and the **%D** fields, which contain the senior author and date. The **-s** option is used to specify new *key-letters*. See **addbib** for a list of the most common key letters. For instance, **-sATD** will sort by author, title, and date, while **-sA+D** will sort by all authors, and date. Sort keys past the fourth are not meaningful. No more than 16 databases may be sorted together at one time. Records longer than 4096 characters will be truncated.

sortbib sorts on the last word on the **%A** line, which is assumed to be the author's last name. A word in the final position, such as "**jr.**" or "**ed.**", will be ignored if the name beforehand ends with a comma. Authors with two-word last names or unusual constructions can be sorted correctly by using the **nroff** convention "**\0**" in place of a blank. A **%Q** field is considered to be the same as **%A**, except sorting begins with the first, not the last, word. **sortbib** sorts on the last word of the **%D** line, usually the year. It also ignores leading articles (like "**A**" or "**The**") when sorting by titles in the **%T** or **%J** fields; it will ignore articles of any modern European language. If a sort-significant field is absent from a record, **sortbib** places that record before other records containing that field.

SEE ALSO

addbib(1), **indxbib**(1), **lookbib**(1), **refer**(1), **roffbib**(1)

NOTES

Records with missing author fields should probably be sorted by title.

spell (1)

NAME

spell, **hashmake**, **spellin**, **hashcheck**, **compress** – find spelling errors

SYNOPSIS

spell [**-v**] [**-b**] [**-x**] [**-l**] [+*local_file*] [*files*]

/usr/lib/spell/hashmake

/usr/lib/spell/spellin *n*

/usr/lib/spell/hashcheck

/usr/share/lib/spell/compress

DESCRIPTION

spell collects words from the named *files* and looks them up in a spelling list. Words that neither occur among nor are derivable (by applying certain inflections, prefixes, and/or suffixes) from words in the spelling list are printed on the standard output. If no *files* are named, words are collected from the standard input.

spell ignores most **troff**(1), **tbl**(1), and **eqn**(1) constructions. It also ignores punctuation marks and special characters (for example, _ and =).

-v All words not literally in the spelling list are printed, and plausible derivations from the words in the spelling list are indicated.

-b British spelling is checked. Besides preferring **centre**, **colour**, **programme**, **speciality**, **travelled**, and so on, this option insists upon *-ise* in words like **standardise**, Fowler and the OED (Oxford English Dictionary) to the contrary notwithstanding.

-x Every plausible stem is displayed, one per line, with = preceding each word.

-l Follow the chains of all included files. By default, **spell** (like **deroff**(1)) follows chains of included files (**.so** and **.nx** **troff**(1) requests), unless the names of such included files begin with **/usr/lib**.

+*local_file* Words found in *local_file* are removed from **spell**'s output. *local_file* is the name of a user-provided file that contains a sorted list of words, one per line. The list must be sorted with the ordering used by **sort**(1) (for example, upper case preceding lower case). If this ordering is not followed, some entries in *local_file* may be ignored. With this option, the user can specify a set of words that are correct spellings (in addition to **spell**'s own spelling list) for each job.

The spelling list is based on many sources, and while more haphazard than an ordinary dictionary, is also more effective with respect to proper names and popular technical words. Coverage of the specialized vocabularies of biology, medicine, and chemistry is light.

Alternate auxiliary files (spelling lists, stop list, history file) may be specified on the command line by using environment variables. These variables and their default settings are shown in the FILES section. Copies of all misspellings and entries that specify the login, tty, and time of each invocation of spell are accumulated in the *history* file. The *stop list* filters out misspellings (for example, **thier=thy-y+ier**) that would otherwise pass.

The following routines help maintain and check the hash lists used by **spell**:

hashmake Reads a list of words from the standard input and writes the corresponding nine-digit hash code on the standard output. This is the first step in creating a new spelling list or adding words to an existing list; it must be used prior to using **spellin**.

spellin Reads *n* hash codes (created by **hashmake**) from the standard input and writes a compressed spelling list on the standard output. The hash codes must be sorted before input to **spellin**. Use **spellin** to add words to an existing spelling list or create a new spelling list.

hashcheck Reads a compressed spelling_list and recreates the nine-digit hash codes for all the words in it; it writes these codes on the standard output. It takes as input an existing spelling list (**hlista** or **hlistb**) or a list created or modified by **spellin**. By using **hashcheck** on an existing compressed *spelling_list* and **hashmake** on a file of selected words, you can compare the two output files to determine if the selected words are present in the existing *spelling_list*.

compress When **spell** is executed, the misspelled words are added to a file called **spellhist**. This file may contain identical entries since the same word may be misspelled during different executions of **spell**. The **compress** program deletes redundant misspelled words in the **spellhist** file, thereby reducing the size of the file, making it easier to analyze.

FILES

D_SPELL=/usr/share/lib/spell/hlist[ab]
hashed spelling lists, American & British

S_SPELL=/usr/share/lib/spell/hstop
hashed stop list

H_SPELL=/var/adm/spellhist
history file

/usr/lib/spell/spellprog
program

NOTES

The spelling list's coverage is uneven; new installations will probably wish to monitor the output for several months to gather local additions. Typically, these are kept in a separate local file that is added to the hashed *spelling_list* via **spellin**.

SEE ALSO

deroff(1), **eqn**(1), **sed**(1), **sort**(1), **tbl**(1), **tee**(1), **troff**(1)

split (1)

NAME

split – split a file into pieces

SYNOPSIS

split [-*n*] [*file* [*name*]]

DESCRIPTION

split reads *file* and writes it in *n*-line pieces (default 1000 lines) onto a set of output files. The name of the first output file is *name* with **aa** appended, and so on lexicographically, up to **zz** (a maximum of 676 files). The maximum length of *name* is 2 characters less than the maximum filename length allowed by the file system. See **statvfs**(2). If no output name is given, **x** is default.

If no input file is given, or if – is given in its stead, then the standard input file is used.

FILES

/usr/lib/locale/*locale***/LC_MESSAGES/uxdfm**
language-specific message file [See **LANG** on **environ**(5).]

SEE ALSO

bfs(1), **csplit**(1), **statvfs**(2)

NAME

spray – spray packets

SYNOPSIS

/usr/sbin/spray [**-c** *count*] [**-d** *delay*] [**-l** *length*] [**-t** *nettype host*]

DESCRIPTION

spray sends a one-way stream of packets to *host* using RPC, and reports how many were received, as well as the the transfer rate. The *host* argument can be either a name or an Internet address.

The following options are available:

-c *count* — Specify how many packets to send. The default value of *count* is the number of packets required to make the total stream size 100000 bytes.

-d *delay* — Specify how many microseconds to pause between sending each packet. The default is 0.

-l *length* — The *length* parameter is the numbers of bytes in the Ethernet packet that holds the RPC call message. Since the data is encoded using XDR, and XDR only deals with 32 bit quantities, not all values of *length* are possible, and **spray** rounds up to the nearest possible value. When *length* is greater than 1514, then the RPC call can no longer be encapsulated in one Ethernet packet, so the *length* field no longer has a simple correspondence to Ethernet packet size. The default value of *length* is 86 bytes (the size of the RPC and UDP headers).

-t *nettype* — Specify class of transports. Defaults to **netpath**. See **rpc**(3N) for a description of supported classes.

SEE ALSO

sprayd(1M), **rpc**(3N)

sprayd (1M)

NAME

rpc.sprayd – spray server

SYNOPSIS

/usr/lib/netsvc/spray/rpc.sprayd

DESCRIPTION

rpc.sprayd is a server which records the packets sent by **spray**(1M). The **rpc.sprayd** daemon may be started by **inetd**(1M) or **listen**(1M).

SEE ALSO

inetd(1M) **listen**(1M), **pmadm**(1M), **sacadm**(1M), **spray**(1M)

NAME

srchtxt – display contents of, or search for a text string in, message data bases

SYNOPSIS

srchtxt [**-s**] [**-l** *locale*] [**-m** *msgfile*, ...] [*text*]

DESCRIPTION

The **srchtxt** utility is used to display all the text strings in message data bases, or to search for a text string in message data bases (see **mkmsgs**(1)). These data bases are files in the directory **/usr/lib/locale/***locale***/LC_MESSAGES** (see **setlocale**(3C)), unless a file name given with the **-m** option contains a **/**. The directory *locale* can be viewed as the name of the language in which the text strings are written. If the **-l** option is not specified, the files accessed will be determined by the value of the environment variable **LC_MESSAGES**. If **LC_MESSAGES** is not set, the files accessed will be determined by the value of the environment variable **LANG**. If **LANG** is not set, the files accessed will be in the directory **/usr/lib/locale/C/LC_MESSAGES**, which contains default strings.

If no *text* argument is present, then all the text strings in the files accessed will be displayed.

The meanings of the options are as follows:

-s suppress printing of the message sequence numbers of the messages being displayed

-l *locale* access files in the directory **/usr/lib/locale/***locale***/LC_MESSAGES**. If **-m** *msgfile* is also supplied, *locale* is ignored for *msgfile*s containing a **/**.

-m *msgfile* access file(s) specified by one or more *msgfile*s. If *msgfile* contains a **/** character, then *msgfile is* interpreted as a pathname; otherwise, it will be assumed to be in the directory determined as described above. To specify more than one *msgfile*, separate the file names using commas.

text search for the text string specified by *text* and display each one that matches. *text* can take the form of a regular expression (see **ed**(1)).

If the **-s** option is not specified, the displayed text is prefixed by message sequence numbers. The message sequence numbers are enclosed in angle brackets: **<***msgfile***:***msgnum***>.**

msgfile name of the file where the displayed text occurred

msgnum sequence number in *msgfile* where the displayed text occurred

This display is in the format used by **gettxt**(1) and **gettxt**(3C).

ERRORS

The error messages produced by **srchtxt** are intended to be self-explanatory. They indicate an error in the command line or errors encountered while searching for a particular locale and/or message file.

FILES

`/usr/lib/locale/C/LC_MESSAGES/*`	default files created by **mkmsgs**(1)
`/usr/lib/locale/`*locale*`/LC_MESSAGES/*`	message files created by **mkmsgs**(1)

EXAMPLES

The following examples show uses of **srchtxt**.

Example 1:

If message files have been installed in a locale named **french** by using **mkmsgs**(1), then you could display the entire set of text strings in the **french** locale (**/usr/lib/locale/french/LC_MESSAGES/***) by typing:

```
srchtxt -l french
```

Example 2:

If a set of error messages associated with the UNIX operating system have been installed in the file **UX** in the **french** locale (**/usr/lib/locale/french/LC_MESSAGES/UX**), then, using the value of the **LANG** environment variable to determine the locale to be searched, you could search that file in that locale for all error messages dealing with files by typing:

```
LANG=french; export LANG
srchtxt -m UX "[Ff]ichier"
```

If **/usr/lib/locale/french/LC_MESSAGES/UX** contained the following strings:

```
Erreur E/S\n
Liste d'arguments trop longue\n
Fichier inexistant\n
Argument invalide\n
Trop de fichiers ouverts\n
Fichier trop long\n
Trop de liens\n
Argument hors du domaine\n
Identificateur supprim\n
Etreinte fatale\n
  .
  .
  .
```

then the following strings would be displayed:

```
<UX:3>Fichier inexistant\n
<UX:5>Trop de fichiers ouverts\n
<UX:6>Fichier trop long\n
```

Example 3:

If a set of error messages associated with the UNIX operating system have been installed in the file **UX** and a set of error messages associated with the INGRESS data base product have been installed in the file **ingress**, both in the **german** locale, then you could search for the pattern **[Dd]atei** in both the files **UX** and **ingress** in the **german** locale by typing:

```
srchtxt -l german -m UX,ingress "[Dd]atei"
```

SEE ALSO

ed(1), **exstr**(1), **gettxt**(1), **gettxt**(3C), **mkmsgs**(1), **setlocale**(3C)

statd (1M)

NAME

`statd` – network status monitor

SYNOPSIS

`/usr/lib/nfs/statd`

DESCRIPTION

`statd` is a status monitor. It interacts with `lockd`(1M) to provide the crash and recovery functions for the locking services on NFS.

The `statd` daemon is automatically invoked in run level 3.

Only a privileged user can execute this command.

FILES

`/etc/sm`
`/etc/sm.bak`
`/etc/state`

SEE ALSO

`lockd`(1M), `nfsping`(1M)

NOTES

The crash of a site is only detected upon its recovery.

When NFS is restarted, `statd` will display notices on the system console if any machine which was involved in NFS file and record locking before the restart, is currently down. These messages can be avoided by removing all files from `/etc/sm` and `/etc/sm.bak` directories before restarting NFS.

NAME

strace – print STREAMS trace messages

SYNOPSIS

strace [*mid sid level*] . . .

DESCRIPTION

strace without arguments writes all STREAMS event trace messages from all drivers and modules to its standard output. These messages are obtained from the STREAMS log driver [**log**(7)]. If arguments are provided they must be in triplets of the form *mid, sid, level,* where *mid* is a STREAMS module ID number, *sid* is a sub-ID number, and *level* is a tracing priority level. Each triplet indicates that tracing messages are to be received from the given module/driver, sub-ID (usually indicating minor device), and priority level equal to or less than the given level. The token **all** may be used for any member to indicate no restriction for that attribute.

The format of each trace message output is:

<seq> <time> <ticks> <level> <flags> <mid> <sid> <text>

<seq>	trace sequence number
<time>	time of message in *hh:mm:ss*
<ticks>	time of message in machine ticks since boot
<level>	tracing priority level
<flags>	**E** : message is also in the error log **F** : indicates a fatal error **N** : mail was sent to the system administrator
<mid>	module ID number of source
<sid>	sub-ID number of source
<text>	formatted text of the trace message

Once initiated, **strace** will continue to execute until terminated by the user.

EXAMPLES

Output all trace messages from the module or driver whose module ID is 41:

```
strace  41 all all
```

Output those trace messages from driver/module ID 41 with sub-IDs 0, 1, or 2:

```
strace  41 0 1  41 1 1  41 2 0
```

Messages from sub-IDs 0 and 1 must have a tracing level less than or equal to 1. Those from sub-ID 2 must have a tracing level of 0.

SEE ALSO

log(7)

NOTES

Due to performance considerations, only one **strace** process is permitted to open the STREAMS log driver at a time. The log driver has a list of the triplets specified in the command invocation, and compares each potential trace message against this list to decide if it should be formatted and sent up to the **strace** process. Hence, long lists of triplets will have a greater impact on overall STREAMS performance.

Running **strace** will have the most impact on the timing of the modules and drivers generating the trace messages that are sent to the **strace** process. If trace messages are generated faster than the **strace** process can handle them, then some of the messages will be lost. This last case can be determined by examining the sequence numbers on the trace messages output.

NAME

strchg, **strconf** – change or query stream configuration

SYNOPSIS

strchg -h *module1*[,*module2* . . .]
strchg -p [**-a** | **-u** *module*]
strchg -f *file*
strconf [**-t** | **-m** *module*]

DESCRIPTION

These commands are used to alter or query the configuration of the stream associated with the user's standard input. The **strchg** command pushes modules on and/or pops modules off the stream. The **strconf** command queries the configuration of the stream. Only a privileged user or owner of a STREAMS device may alter the configuration of that stream.

With the **-h** option, **strchg** pushes modules onto a stream; it takes as arguments the names of one or more pushable streams modules. These modules are pushed in order; that is, *module1* is pushed first, *module2* is pushed second, and so on.

The **-p** option pops modules off the stream. With the **-p** option alone, **strchg** pops the topmost module from the stream. With the **-p** and **-a** options, all the modules above the topmost driver are popped. When the **-p** option is followed by **-u** *module*, then all modules above but not including *module* are popped off the stream. The **-a** and **-u** options are mutually exclusive.

With the **-f** option, the user can specify a *file* that contains a list of modules representing the desired configuration of the stream. Each module name must appear on a separate line where the first name represents the topmost module and the last name represents the module that should be closest to the driver. The **strchg** command will determine the current configuration of the stream and pop and push the necessary modules in order to end up with the desired configuration.

The **-h**, **-f** and **-p** options are mutually exclusive.

Invoked without any arguments, **strconf** prints a list of all the modules in the stream as well as the topmost driver. The list is printed with one name per line where the first name printed is the topmost module on the stream (if one exists) and the last item printed is the name of the driver. With the **-t** option, only the topmost module (if one exists) is printed. The **-m** option determines if the named *module* is present on a stream. If it is, **strconf** prints the message **yes** and returns zero. If not, **strconf** prints the message **no** and returns a non-zero value. The **-t** and **-m** options are mutually exclusive.

EXAMPLES

The following command pushes the module **ldterm** on the stream associated with the user's standard input:

```
strchg -h ldterm
```

The following command pops the topmost module from the stream associated with **/dev/term/24**. The user must be the owner of this device or a privileged user.

```
strchg -p < /dev/term/24
```

If the file **fileconf** contains the following:

```
compat
ldterm
ptem
```

then the command

```
strchg -f fileconf
```

will configure the user's standard input stream so that the module **ptem** is pushed over the driver, followed by **ldterm** and **compat** closest to the stream head.

The **strconf** command with no arguments lists the modules and topmost driver on the stream; for a stream that has only the module **ldterm** pushed above the **ports** driver, it would produce the following output:

```
ldterm
ports
```

The following command asks if **ldterm** is on the stream

```
strconf -m ldterm
```

and produces the following output while returning an exit status of 0:

```
yes
```

SEE ALSO

streamio(7)

DIAGNOSTICS

strchg returns zero on success. It prints an error message and returns non-zero status for various error conditions, including usage error, bad module name, too many modules to push, failure of an **ioctl** on the stream, or failure to open *file* from the **-f** option.

strconf returns zero on success (for the **-m** or **-t** option, "success" means the named or topmost module is present). It returns a non-zero status if invoked with the **-m** or **-t** option and the module is not present. It prints an error message and returns non-zero status for various error conditions, including usage error or failure of an **ioctl** on the stream.

NOTES

If the user is neither the owner of the stream nor a privileged user, the **strchg** command will fail. If the user does not have read permissions on the stream and is not a privileged user, the **strconf** command will fail.

If modules are pushed in the wrong order, one could end up with a stream that does not function as expected. For terminals, if the line discipline module is not pushed in the correct place, one could have a terminal that does not respond to any commands.

NAME

strclean – STREAMS error logger cleanup program

SYNOPSIS

strclean [**-d** *logdir*] [**-a** *age*]

DESCRIPTION

strclean is used to clean up the STREAMS error logger directory on a regular basis (for example, by using **cron**). By default, all files with names matching **error.*** in **/var/adm/streams** that have not been modified in the last three days are removed. A directory other than **/var/adm/streams** can be specified using the **-d** option. The maximum age in days for a log file can be changed using the **-a** option.

EXAMPLE

```
strclean -d /var/adm/streams -a 3
```

has the same result as running strclean with no arguments.

FILES

/var/adm/streams/error.*

SEE ALSO

cron(1M), **strerr**(1M)

NOTES

strclean is typically run from **cron** on a daily or weekly basis.

NAME

strerr – STREAMS error logger daemon

SYNOPSIS

strerr

DESCRIPTION

strerr receives error log messages from the STREAMS log driver [**log**(7)] and appends them to a log file. The error log files produced reside in the directory **/var/adm/streams**, and are named **error.***mm-dd*, where *mm* is the month and *dd* is the day of the messages contained in each log file.

The format of an error log message is:

<seq> <time> <ticks> <flags> <mid> <sid> <text>

<seq>	error sequence number
<time>	time of message in hh:mm:ss
<ticks>	time of message in machine ticks since boot priority level
<flags>	**T** : the message was also sent to a tracing process **F** : indicates a fatal error **N** : send mail to the system administrator
<mid>	module ID number of source
<sid>	sub-ID number of source
<text>	formatted text of the error message

Messages that appear in the error log are intended to report exceptional conditions that require the attention of the system administrator. Those messages which indicate the total failure of a STREAMS driver or module should have the **F** flag set. Those messages requiring the immediate attention of the administrator will have the **N** flag set, which causes the error logger to send the message to the system administrator via **mail**. The priority level usually has no meaning in the error log but will have meaning if the message is also sent to a tracer process.

Once initiated, **strerr** continues to execute until terminated by the user. It is commonly executed asynchronously.

FILES

/var/adm/streams/error.*mm-dd*

SEE ALSO

log(7)

NOTES

Only one **strerr** process at a time is permitted to open the STREAMS log driver.

If a module or driver is generating a large number of error messages, running the error logger will cause a degradation in STREAMS performance. If a large burst of messages are generated in a short time, the log driver may not be able to deliver some of the messages. This situation is indicated by gaps in the sequence numbering of the messages in the log files.

NAME

strings – find printable strings in an object file or binary

SYNOPSIS

strings [**-a**] [**-o**] [**-n** *number* | *-number*] *filename* . . .

DESCRIPTION

The **strings** command looks for ASCII strings in a binary file. A string is any sequence of 4 or more printing characters ending with a newline or a null character.

strings is useful for identifying random object files and many other things.

The following options are available:

-a	Look everywhere in the file for strings. If this flag is omitted, **strings** only looks in the initialized data space of object files.
-o	Precede each string by its offset in the file.
-n *number*	Use *number* as the minimum string length rather than 4.

SEE ALSO

od(1)

NOTES

The algorithm for identifying strings is extremely primitive.

For backwards compatibility, *-number* can be used in place of **-n** *number*. Similarly, the **-a** and a - option are interchangeable. The - and the *-number* variations are obsolescent.

NAME

strip – strip symbol table, debugging and line number information from an object file.

SYNOPSIS

strip [**-blrVx**] *file* . . .

DESCRIPTION

The **strip** command strips the symbol table, debugging information, and line number information from ELF object files; COFF object files can no longer be stripped. Once this stripping process has been done, no symbolic debugging access will be available for that file; therefore, this command is normally run only on production modules that have been debugged and tested.

If **strip** is executed on a common archive file [see **ar**(4)] in addition to processing the members, **strip** will remove the archive symbol table. The archive symbol table must be restored by executing the **ar**(1) command with the **-s** option before the archive can be linked by the **ld**(1) command. **strip** will produce appropriate warning messages when this situation arises.

The amount of information stripped from the ELF object file can be controlled by using any of the following options:

-b Same effect as the default behavior. This option is obsolete and will be removed in the next release.

-l Strip line number information only; do not strip the symbol table or debugging information.

-r Same effect as the default behavior. This option is obsolete and will be removed in the next release.

-V Print, on standard error, the version number of **strip**.

-x Do not strip the symbol table; debugging and line number information may be stripped.

strip is used to reduce the file storage overhead taken by the object file.

FILES

TMPDIR/strp*	temporary files
TMPDIR	usually **/var/tmp** but can be redefined by setting the environment variable **TMPDIR** [see **tempnam** in **tmpnam**(3S)].

SEE ALSO

a.out(4), **ar**(1), **ar**(4), **as**(1), **cc**(1), **ld**(1), **tmpnam**(3S)

NOTES

The symbol table section will not be removed if it is contained within a segment, or the file is either a relocatable or dynamic shared object.

The line number and debugging sections will not be removed if they are contained within a segment, or their associated relocation section is contained within a segment.

NAME

stty – set the options for a terminal

SYNOPSIS

stty [-a] [-g] [*options*]

DESCRIPTION

stty sets certain terminal I/O options for the device that is the current standard input; without arguments, it reports the settings of certain options.

In the input and output of **stty**, if a character is preceded by a caret (^), then the value of that option is the corresponding control character (for example, "**^h**" is CTRL-**h**; in this case, recall that CTRL-**h** is the same as the "backspace" key.) The sequence "^`" means that an option has a null value.

-a Report all option settings.

-g Report current settings in a form that can be used as an argument to another **stty** command.

For detailed information about the modes listed in sections "Control Modes" through "Local Modes" below, see **termio**(7). For detailed information about the modes listed in sections "Hardware Flow Control Modes" and "Clock Modes" below, see **termiox**(7). Options described in the "Combination Modes" section are implemented using options in the earlier sections. Note that many combinations of options make no sense, but no sanity checking is performed. Hardware flow control and clock modes options may not be supported by all hardware interfaces. The options are selected from the following:

Control Modes

parenb (**-parenb**) Enable (disable) parity generation and detection.

parext (**-parext**) Enable (disable) extended parity generation and detection for mark and space parity.

parodd (**-parodd**) Select odd (even) parity, or mark (space) parity if **parext** is enabled.

cs5 cs6 cs7 cs8 Select character size [see **termio**(7)].

0 Hang up line immediately.

110 300 600 1200 1800 2400 4800 9600 19200 38400
Set terminal baud rate to the number given, if possible. (All speeds are not supported by all hardware interfaces.)

ispeed 0 110 300 600 1200 1800 2400 4800 9600 19200 38400
Set terminal input baud rate to the number given, if possible. (Not all hardware supports split baud rates.) If the input baud rate is set to zero, the input baud rate will be specified by the value of the output baud rate.

ospeed 0 110 300 600 1200 1800 2400 4800 9600 19200 38400
Set terminal output baud rate to the number given, if possible. (Not all hardware supports split baud rates.) If the output baud rate is set to zero, the line will be hung up immediately.

hupcl (**-hupcl**) Hang up (do not hang up) connection on last close.

hup (**-hup**) Same as **hupcl** (**-hupcl**).

cstopb (**-cstopb**) Use two (one) stop bits per character.

cread (**-cread**) Enable (disable) the receiver.

clocal (**-clocal**) Assume a line without (with) modem control.

loblk (**-loblk**) Block (do not block) output from a non-current layer.

Input Modes

ignbrk (**-ignbrk**) Ignore (do not ignore) break on input.

brkint (**-brkint**) Signal (do not signal) INTR on break.

ignpar (**-ignpar**) Ignore (do not ignore) parity errors.

parmrk (**-parmrk**) Mark (do not mark) parity errors [see **termio**(7)].

inpck (**-inpck**) Enable (disable) input parity checking.

istrip (**-istrip**) Strip (do not strip) input characters to seven bits.

inlcr (**-inlcr**) Map (do not map) NL to CR on input.

igncr (**-igncr**) Ignore (do not ignore) CR on input.

icrnl (**-icrnl**) Map (do not map) CR to NL on input.

iuclc (**-iuclc**) Map (do not map) upper-case alphabetics to lower case on input.

ixon (**-ixon**) Enable (disable) START/STOP output control. Output is stopped by sending STOP control character and started by sending the START control character.

ixany (**-ixany**) Allow any character (only DC1) to restart output.

ixoff (**-ixoff**) Request that the system send (not send) START/STOP characters when the input queue is nearly empty/full.

imaxbel (**-imaxbel**) Echo (do not echo) BEL when the input line is too long.

KB_ENABLE Perform a **TIOCKBON**, which allows extended characters to be transmitted to the user's program. Extended characters are transmitted as a null byte followed by a second byte containing the character's extended code. [See **keyboard**(7).]

KB_DISABLE Perform a **TIOCKBOF**, which disables the transmission of extended characters. This is the default. [See **keyboard**(7).]

Output Modes

opost (**-opost**) Post-process output (do not post-process output; ignore all other output modes).

olcuc (**-olcuc**) Map (do not map) lower-case alphabetics to upper case on output.

onlcr (**-onlcr**) Map (do not map) NL to CR-NL on output.

ocrnl (**-ocrnl**) Map (do not map) CR to NL on output.

onocr (**-onocr**) Do not (do) output CRs at column zero.

onlret (**-onlret**) On the terminal NL performs (does not perform) the CR function.

ofill (**-ofill**) Use fill characters (use timing) for delays.

ofdel (**-ofdel**) Fill characters are DELs (NULs).

The following options set the delays for the output control characters. Selecting the 0 type option, such as **cr0**, causes no delay. **stty -a** does not report the 0 type options. For more information, see **termio**(7).

cr0 cr1 cr2 cr3 Select style of delay for carriage returns.

nl0 nl1 Select style of delay for line-feeds.

tab0 tab1 tab2 tab3 Select style of delay for horizontal tabs.

bs0 bs1 Select style of delay for backspaces.

ff0 ff1 Select style of delay for form-feeds.

vt0 vt1 Select style of delay for vertical tabs [see **termio**(7)].

Local Modes

isig (**-isig**) Enable (disable) the checking of characters against the special control characters INTR, QUIT, and SWTCH.

icanon (**-icanon**) Enable (disable) canonical input (ERASE and KILL processing).

xcase (**-xcase**) Canonical (unprocessed) upper/lower-case presentation.

echo (**-echo**) Echo back (do not echo back) every character typed.

echoe (**-echoe**) Echo (do not echo) ERASE character as a backspace-space-backspace string. This mode erases the ERASEed character on many terminals; however, it does not keep track of column position and, as a result, may be confusing on escaped characters, tabs, and backspaces.

echok (**-echok**) Echo (do not echo) NL after KILL character.

lfkc (**-lfkc**) The same as **echok** (**-echok**); obsolete.

echonl (**-echonl**) Echo (do not echo) NL.

noflsh (**-noflsh**) Disable (enable) flush after INTR, QUIT, or SWTCH.

stwrap (**-stwrap**) Disable (enable) truncation of lines longer than 79 characters on a synchronous line.

tostop (**-tostop**) Send (do not send) **SIGTTOU** when background processes write to the terminal.

echoctl (**-echoctl**) Echo (do not echo) control characters as ^*char*, delete as ^**?**

`echoprt` (`-echoprt`)	Echo (do not echo) erase character as character is "erased".
`echoke` (`-echoke`)	BS-SP-BS erase (do not BS-SP-BS erase) entire line on line kill.
`flusho` (`-flusho`)	Output is (is not) being flushed.
`pendin` (`-pendin`)	Retype (do not retype) pending input at next read or input character.
`iexten` (`-iexten`)	Enable (disable) extended (implementation-defined) functions for input data.
`stflush` (`-stflush`)	Enable (disable) flush on a synchronous line after every `write`(2).
`stappl` (`-stappl`)	Use application mode (use line mode) on a synchronous line.

Hardware Flow Control Modes

`rtsxoff` (`-rtsxoff`)	Enable (disable) RTS hardware flow control on input.
`ctsxon` (`-ctsxon`)	Enable (disable) CTS hardware flow control on output.
`dtrxoff` (`-dtrxoff`)	Enable (disable) DTR hardware flow control on input.
`cdxon` (`-cdxon`)	Enable (disable) CD hardware flow control on output.
`isxoff` (`-isxoff`)	Enable (disable) isochronous hardware flow control on input.

Clock Modes

`xcibrg`	Get transmit clock from internal baud rate generator.
`xctset`	Get transmit clock from transmitter signal element timing (DCE source) lead, CCITT V.24 circuit 114, EIA-232-D pin 15.
`xcrset`	Get transmit clock from receiver signal element timing (DCE source) lead, CCITT V.24 circuit 115, EIA-232-D pin 17.
`rcibrg`	Get receive clock from internal baud rate generator.
`rctset`	Get receive clock from transmitter signal element timing (DCE source) lead, CCITT V.24 circuit 114, EIA-232-D pin 15.
`rcrset`	Get receive clock from receiver signal element timing (DCE source) lead, CCITT V.24 circuit 115, EIA-232-D pin 17.
`tsetcoff`	Transmitter signal element timing clock is not provided.
`tsetcrbrg`	Output receive baud rate generator on transmitter signal element timing (DTE source) lead, CCITT V.24 circuit 113, EIA-232-D pin 24.
`tsetctbrg`	Output transmit baud rate generator on transmitter signal element timing (DTE source) lead, CCITT V.24 circuit 113, EIA-232-D pin 24.
`tsetctset`	Output transmitter signal element timing (DCE source) on transmitter signal element timing (DTE source) lead, CCITT V.24 circuit 113, EIA-232-D pin 24.

tsetcrset Output receiver signal element timing (DCE source) on transmitter signal element timing (DTE source) lead, CCITT V.24 circuit 113, EIA-232-D pin 24.

rsetcoff Receiver signal element timing clock is not provided.

rsetcrbrg Output receive baud rate generator on receiver signal element timing (DTE source) lead, CCITT V.24 circuit 128, no EIA-232-D pin.

rsetctbrg Output transmit baud rate generator on receiver signal element timing (DTE source) lead, CCITT V.24 circuit 128, no EIA-232-D pin.

rsetctset Output transmitter signal element timing (DCE source) on receiver signal element timing (DTE source) lead, CCITT V.24 circuit 128, no EIA-232-D pin.

rsetcrset Output receiver signal element timing (DCE source) on receiver signal element timing (DTE source) lead, CCITT V.24 circuit 128, no EIA-232-D pin.

Control Assignments

In the following assignments, if *c* is preceded by a caret (^) indicating an escape from the shell, then the value used is the corresponding control character (for example, "**^d**" is a CTRL-**d**). "**^?**" is interpreted as DEL and "**^-**" is interpreted as undefined. For more information on these special characters, see **termio**(7).

ctab *c* Set synchronous terminal tab character to *c*. Use with **-stappl**.

discard *c* Set discard character to *c*.

dsusp *c* Set to *c* character that suspends foreground process when process attempts to read *c*.

eof *c* Set end-of-file character to *c*.

eol *c* Set end-of-line character to *c*.

eol2 *c* Set secondary end-of-line character to *c*.

erase *c* Set erase character to *c*.

intr *c* Set interrupt character to *c*.

kill *c* Set kill character to *c*.

lnext *c* Set to *c* character that causes the special meaning of next character to be ignored.

quit *c* Set quit character to *c*.

reprint *c* Set reprint character to *c*.

start *c* Set start character to *c*.

stop *c* Set stop character to *c*.

susp *c* — Set suspend character to *c*.

swtch *c* — Set switch character to *c*.

werase *c* — Set word-erase character to *c*.

min *n* — Set the minimum number of characters that satisfy a read in non-canonical mode input processing (**-icanon**) to *n*.

time *n* — Set the intercharacter timer in non-canonical mode input processing (**-icanon**) to *n* ticks.

Combination Modes

evenp or **parity** — Enable **parenb** and **cs7**.

oddp — Enable **parenb**, **cs7**, and **parodd**.

spacep — Enable **parenb**, **cs7**, and **parext**.

markp — Enable **parenb**, **cs7**, **parodd**, and **parext**.

-parity, or **-evenp** — Disable **parenb**, and set **cs8**.

-oddp — Disable **parenb** and **parodd**, and set **cs8**.

-spacep — Disable **parenb** and **parext**, and set **cs8**.

-markp — Disable **parenb**, **parodd**, and **parext**, and set **cs8**.

raw (**-raw** or **cooked**)
Enable (disable) raw input and output (no ERASE, KILL, INTR, QUIT, SWTCH, EOT, or output post processing).

nl (**-nl**) — Unset (set) **icrnl**, **onlcr**. In addition **-nl** unset **inlcr**, **igncr**, **ocrnl**, and **onlret**.

lcase (**-lcase**) — Set (unset) **xcase**, **iuclc**, and **olcuc**.

LCASE (**-LCASE**) — Same as **lcase** (**-lcase**).

tabs (**-tabs** or **tab3**)
Preserve (expand to spaces) tabs when printing.

ek — Reset ERASE and KILL characters back to normal **#** and **@**.

sane — Reset all modes to some reasonable values.

term — Set all modes suitable for the terminal type *term*, where *term* is one of **tty33**, **tty37**, **vt05**, **tn300**, **ti700**, or **tek**.

async — Set normal asynchronous communications where clock settings are **xcibrg**, **rcibrg**, **tsetcoff** and **rsetcoff**.

Window Size

rows *n* — Set window size to *n* rows.

columns *n* — Set window size to *n* columns.

ypixels *n* — Set vertical window size to *n* pixels.

xpixels *n* — Set horizontal window size to *n* pixels.

Control Modes for the Video Monitor

`mono` Select the monochrome display as the output device for the console screen. This mode is valid if a standard monochrome adapter is present or if a standard enhanced graphics adapter (EGA) is present and the EGA is currently in one of the monochrome display modes.

`color` Select a standard regular color display as the output device for the console screen. This mode is valid if a color graphics adapter is present or if a standard EGA is present and is currently in one of the color graphics compatibility modes.

`enhanced` Select the enhanced color display as the output device for the console screen. This mode is valid if an EGA is present and is currently in a non-monochrome display mode.

`pro` Select the professional graphics adapter as the output device for the system console. This mode is valid if a VGA is present.

Control Modes for the Attached Display Devices

The **stty** command supports mode changes for the monochrome display adapter (MDA), color graphics adapter (CGA), enhanced graphics adapter (EGA), and video graphics array (VGA).

`MCAMODE` Reinitialize the monochrome graphics adapter.

`ENH_CGA` Select CGA hardware emulation, when an AT&T Super-Vu video controller is attached.

The following keyboard and display control modes are valid for the following configurations: standard color graphics adapter (CGA) attached to a standard regular color display; standard enhanced graphics adapter (EGA) (modes 0–6) attached to a standard regular color display or standard enhanced color display.

`B40x25` Select 40x25 (40 columns x 25 rows) black and white text display mode.

`C40x25` Select 40x25 color text display mode.

`B80x25` Select 80x25 black and white text display mode.

`C80x25` Select 80x25 color display text mode.

`BG320` Select 320x200 black and white graphics display mode.

`CG320` Select 320x200 color graphics display mode.

`BG640` Select 640x200 black and white graphics display mode.

The following options are valid only when an EGA is attached to a standard regular color display or an enhanced color display.

`CG320_D` Select EGA support for 320x200 graphics display mode (EGA mode D).

CG640_E	Select EGA support for 640x200 graphics display mode (EGA mode E).

The following options are valid only when a standard EGA is attached to an IBM monochrome display.

EGAMONO80x25	Select EGA Mode 7 as the display mode. Emulates the support provided by the standard monochrome display adapter.
EGAMONOAPA	Select EGA support for 640x350 graphics display mode (EGA mode F).
ENHMONOAPA2	Select EGA mode F*.

The following options are valid only when a standard EGA is attached to a standard enhanced color display.

ENH_B40x25	Select enhanced EGA support for 40x25 black and white text display mode (EGA mode 0*).
ENH_C40x25	Select enhanced EGA support for 40x25 color text display mode (EGA mode 1*).
ENH_B80x25	Select enhanced EGA support for 80x25 black and white text display mode (EGA mode 2*).
ENH_C80x25	Select enhanced EGA support for 80x25 color text display mode (EGA mode 3*).
ENH_B80x43	Select enhanced EGA support for 80x43 black and white text display mode.
ENH_C80x43	Select enhanced EGA support for 80x43 color text display mode.
CG640x350	Select EGA support for 640x350 graphics display mode (EGA mode 10).
ENH_CG640	Select EGA mode 10*.

The following options are valid only when a standard VGA is attached to a color display.

VGAMONO80x25	Select VGA Mode 7 as the display mode. Emulates the support provided by the standard monochrome display adapter.
VGA_C40x25	Select VGA 40x25 color text display mode.
VGA_C80x25	Select VGA 80x25 color text display mode.

FILES

/usr/lib/locale/*locale***/LC_MESSAGES/uxcore.abi**
language-specific message file [See **LANG** on **environ**(5).]

SEE ALSO

ioctl(2), **tabs**(1), **termio**(7), **termiox**(7)

NAME

stty – (BSD) set the options for a terminal

SYNOPSIS

/usr/ucb/stty [**-a**] [**-g**] [**-h**] [*options*]

DESCRIPTION

stty sets certain terminal I/O options for the device that is the current standard input; without arguments, it reports the settings of certain options.

In the input and output of **stty**, if a character is preceded by a caret (^), then the value of that option is the corresponding CTRL character (for example, "**^h**" is CTRL–**h**; in this case, recall that CTRL–**h** is the same as the "back-space" key.) The sequence "^'" means that an option has a null value.

-a reports all of the option settings;

-g reports current settings in a form that can be used as an argument to another **stty** command.

-h reports all the option settings with the control characters in an easy to read column format.

Options in the last group are implemented using options in the previous groups. Note that many combinations of options make no sense, but no sanity checking is performed. Hardware flow control and clock modes options may not be supported by all hardware interfaces. The options are selected from the following:

Special Requests

all Reports the same option settings as **stty** without arguments, but with the control characters in column format.

everything Everything **stty** knows about is printed. Same as **-h** option.

speed The terminal speed alone is reported on the standard output.

size The terminal (window) sizes are printed on the standard output, first rows and then columns. This option is only appropriate if currently running a window system.

size and **speed** always report on the settings of **/dev/tty**, and always report the settings to the standard output.

Control Modes

parenb (**-parenb**) enable (disable) parity generation and detection.

parext (**-parext**) enable (disable) extended parity generation and detection for mark and space parity.

parodd (**-parodd**) select odd (even) parity, or mark (space) parity if **parext** is enabled.

cs5 cs6 cs7 cs8 select character size [see **termio**(7)].

0 hang up line immediately.

110 300 600 1200 1800 2400 4800 9600 19200 exta 38400 extb
Set terminal baud rate to the number given, if possible. (All speeds are not supported by all hardware interfaces.)

ispeed 0 110 300 600 1200 1800 2400 4800 9600 19200 exta 38400 extb
Set terminal input baud rate to the number given, if possible. (Not all hardware supports split baud rates.) If the input baud rate is set to zero, the input baud rate will be specified by the value of the output baud rate.

ospeed 0 110 300 600 1200 1800 2400 4800 9600 19200 exta 38400 extb
Set terminal output baud rate to the number given, if possible. (Not all hardware supports split baud rates.) If the baud rate is set to zero, the line will be hung up immediately.

hupcl (**-hupcl**) hang up (do not hang up) connection on last close.

hup (**-hup**) same as **hupcl** (**-hupcl**).

cstopb (**-cstopb**) use two (one) stop bits per character.

cread (**-cread**) enable (disable) the receiver.

clocal (**-clocal**) assume a line without (with) modem control.

loblk (**-loblk**) block (do not block) output from a non-current layer.

Input Modes

ignbrk (**-ignbrk**) ignore (do not ignore) break on input.

brkint (**-brkint**) signal (do not signal) INTR on break.

ignpar (**-ignpar**) ignore (do not ignore) parity errors.

parmrk (**-parmrk**) mark (do not mark) parity errors [see **termio**(7)].

inpck (**-inpck**) enable (disable) input parity checking.

istrip (**-istrip**) strip (do not strip) input characters to seven bits.

inlcr (**-inlcr**) map (do not map) NL to CR on input.

igncr (**-igncr**) ignore (do not ignore) CR on input.

icrnl (**-icrnl**) map (do not map) CR to NL on input.

iuclc (**-iuclc**) map (do not map) upper-case alphabetics to lower case on input.

ixon (**-ixon**) enable (disable) START/STOP output control. Output is stopped by sending an STOP and started by sending an START.

ixany (**-ixany**) allow any character (only START) to restart output.

decctlq (**-decctlq**) Same as **-ixany**.

ixoff (**-ixoff**) request that the system send (not send) START/STOP characters when the input queue is nearly empty/full.

tandem (**-tandem**) Same as **ixoff**.

imaxbel (**-imaxbel**) echo (do not echo) BEL when the input line is too long.

iexten (**-iexten**) enable (disable) extended (implementation-defined) functions for input data.

Output Modes

opost (**-opost**) post-process output (do not post-process output; ignore all other output modes).

olcuc (**-olcuc**) map (do not map) lower-case alphabetics to upper case on output.

onlcr (**-onlcr**) map (do not map) NL to CR-NL on output.

ocrnl (**-ocrnl**) map (do not map) CR to NL on output.

onocr (**-onocr**) do not (do) output CRs at column zero.

onlret (**-onlret**) on the terminal NL performs (does not perform) the CR function.

ofill (**-ofill**) use fill characters (use timing) for delays.

ofdel (**-ofdel**) fill characters are DELs (NULs).

cr0 cr1 cr2 cr3 select style of delay for carriage returns [see **termio**(7)].

nl0 nl1 select style of delay for line-feeds [see **termio**(7)].

tab0 tab1 tab2 tab3
select style of delay for horizontal tabs [see **termio**(7)].

bs0 bs1 select style of delay for backspaces [see **termio**(7)].

ff0 ff1 select style of delay for form-feeds [see **termio**(7)].

vt0 vt1 select style of delay for vertical tabs [see **termio**(7)].

Local Modes

isig (**-isig**) enable (disable) the checking of characters against the special control characters INTR, QUIT, and SWTCH.

icanon (**-icanon**) enable (disable) canonical input (ERASE and KILL processing).

cbreak (**-cbreak**) Same as **-icanon**.

xcase (**-xcase**) canonical (unprocessed) upper/lower-case presentation.

echo (**-echo**) echo back (do not echo back) every character typed.

echoe (**-echoe**) echo (do not echo) ERASE character as a backspace-space-backspace string. Note: this mode will erase the ERASEed character on many CRT terminals; however, it does *not* keep track of column position and, as a result, may be confusing on escaped characters, tabs, and backspaces.

crterase (**-crterase**)
Same as **echoe**.

echok (**-echok**) echo (do not echo) NL after KILL character.

lfkc (**-lfkc**) the same as **echok** (**-echok**); obsolete.

echonl (**-echonl**) echo (do not echo) NL.

noflsh (**-noflsh**) disable (enable) flush after INTR, QUIT, or SWTCH.

stwrap (**-stwrap**) disable (enable) truncation of lines longer than 79 characters on a synchronous line.

tostop (**-tostop**) send (do not send) SIGTTOU for background processes.

echoctl (**-echoctl**) echo (do not echo) control characters as ^*char*, delete as ^?

ctlecho (**-ctlecho**) Same as **echoctl**.

echoprt (**-echoprt**) echo (do not echo) erase character as character is "erased".

prterase (**-prterase**)
Same as **echoprt**.

echoke (**-echoke**) BS-SP-BS erase (do not BS-SP-BS erase) entire line on line kill.

crtkill (**-crtkill**) Same as **echoke**.

flusho (**-flusho**) output is (is not) being flushed.

pendin (**-pendin**) retype (do not retype) pending input at next read or input character.

stflush (**-stflush**) enable (disable) flush on a synchronous line after every *write*(2).

stappl (**-stappl**) use application mode (use line mode) on a synchronous line.

Hardware Flow Control Modes

rtsxoff (**-rtsxoff**) enable (disable) RTS hardware flow control on input.

ctsxon (**-ctsxon**) enable (disable) CTS hardware flow control on output.

dterxoff (**-dterxoff**)
enable (disable) DTER hardware flow control on input.

rlsdxon (**-rlsdxon**) enable (disable) RLSD hardware flow control on output.

isxoff (**-isxoff**) enable (disable) isochronous hardware flow control on input.

Clock Modes

xcibrg get transmit clock from internal baud rate generator.

xctset get the transmit clock from transmitter signal element timing (DCE source) lead, CCITT V.24 circuit 114, EIA-232-D pin 15.

xcrset get transmit clock from receiver signal element timing (DCE source) lead, CCITT V.24 circuit 115, EIA-232-D pin 17.

rcibrg get receive clock from internal baud rate generator.

rctset get receive clock from transmitter signal element timing (DCE source) lead, CCITT V.24 circuit 114, EIA-232-D pin 15.

rcrset get receive clock from receiver signal element timing (DCE source) lead, CCITT V.24 circuit 115, EIA-232-D pin 17.

tsetcoff transmitter signal element timing clock not provided.

tsetcrc output receive clock on transmitter signal element timing (DTE source) lead, CCITT V.24 circuit 113, EIA-232-D pin 24, clock source.

tsetcxc output transmit clock on transmitter signal element timing (DTE source) lead, CCITT V.24 circuit 113, EIA-232-D pin 24, clock source.

rsetcoff receiver signal element timing clock not provided.

rsetcrc output receive clock on receiver signal element timing (DTE source) lead, CCITT V.24 circuit 128, no EIA-232-D pin, clock source.

rsetcxc output transmit clock on receiver signal element timing (DTE source) lead, CCITT V.24 circuit 128, no EIA-232-D pin, clock source.

Control Assignments

control-character c set *control-character* to *c*, where *control-character* is **intr**, **quit**, **erase**, **kill**, **eof**, **eol**, **eol2**, **swtch**, **start**, **stop**, **susp**, **dsusp**, **rprnt**, **flush**, **werase**, **lnext** **min**, **ctab**, **time**, or **brk**) [**ctab** is used with **-stappl**; **min** and **time** are used with **-icanon**; see **termio**(7)]. If *c* is preceded by an (escaped from the shell) caret (^), then the value used is the corresponding CTRL character (for example, "**^d**" is a **CTRL-d**); "**^?**" is interpreted as DEL and "**^-**" is interpreted as undefined.

line *i* set line discipline to *i* ($0 < i < 127$).

Combination Modes

evenp or **parity** enable **parenb** and **cs7**.

-evenp, or **-parity** disable **parenb**, and set **cs8**.

even (**-even**) Same as **evenp** (**-evenp**).

oddp enable **parenb**, **cs7**, and **parodd**.

-oddp disable **parenb** and **parodd**, and set **cs8**.

odd (**-odd**) Same as **oddp** (**-oddp**).

spacep enable **parenb**, **cs7**, and **parext**.

-spacep disable **parenb** and **parext**, and set **cs8**.

markp enable **parenb**, **cs7**, **parodd**, and **parext**.

-markp disable **parenb**, **parodd**, and **parext**, and set **cs8**.

raw (**-raw** or **cooked**)
enable (disable) raw input and output (no ERASE, KILL, INTR, QUIT, SWTCH, EOT, or output post processing).

nl (**-nl**) unset (set) **icrnl**, **onlcr**. In addition **-nl** unsets **inlcr**, **igncr**, **ocrnl**, and **onlret**.

lcase (**-lcase**) set (unset) **xcase**, **iuclc**, and **olcuc**.

LCASE (**-LCASE**) same as **lcase** (**-lcase**).

tabs (**-tabs** or **tab3**)
preserve (expand to spaces) tabs when printing.

ek — reset ERASE and KILL characters back to normal **#** and **@**.

sane — resets all modes to some reasonable values.

term — set all modes suitable for the terminal type *term*, where *term* is one of **tty33**, **tty37**, **vt05**, **tn300**, **ti700**, or **tek**.

async — set normal asynchronous communications where clock settings are **xcibrg**, **rcibrg**, **tsetcoff** and **rsetcoff**.

litout (-litout) — Disable (enable) **parenb**, **istrip**, and **opost**, and set **cs8** (**cs7**).

pass8 (-pass8) — Disable (enable) **parenb** and **istrip**, and set **cs8** (**cs7**).

crt — Set options for a CRT (**echoe**, **echoctl**, and, if >= 1200 baud, **echoke**.)

dec — Set all modes suitable for Digital Equipment Corp. operating systems users (**ERASE**, **KILL**, and **INTR** characters to **^?**, **^U**, and **^C**, **decctlq**, and **crt**.)

Window Size

rows *n* — set window size to *n* rows.

columns *n* — set window size to *n* columns.

cols *n* — An alias for **columns** *n*.

ypixels *n* — set vertical window size to *n* pixels.

xpixels *n* — set horizontal window size to *n* pixels.

SEE ALSO

ioctl(2), **tabs**(1), **termio**(7), **termiox**(7)

NAME

sttydefs – maintain line settings and hunt sequences for TTY ports

SYNOPSIS

/usr/sbin/sttydefs -a *ttylabel* [**-b**] [**-n** *nextlabel*] [**-i** *initial-flags*] [**-f** *final-flags*]

/usr/sbin/sttydefs -l [*ttylabel*]

/usr/sbin/sttydefs -r *ttylabel*

DESCRIPTION

sttydefs is an administrative command that maintains the line settings and hunt sequences for the system's TTY ports by making entries in and deleting entries from the **/etc/ttydefs** file.

sttydefs with a **-a** or **-r** option may be invoked only by a privileged user. **sttydefs** with **-l** may be invoked by any user on the system.

The options have the following meanings:

-l If a *ttylabel* is specified, **sttydefs** will display the record from **/etc/ttydefs** whose TTY label matches the specified *ttylabel*. If no *ttylabel* is specified, **sttydefs** will display the entire contents of **/etc/ttydefs**. **sttydefs** will verify that each entry it displays is correct and that the entry's *nextlabel* field references an existing *ttylabel*.

-a *ttylabel* Adds a record to the **ttydefs** file, using *ttylabel* as its label. The following describes the effect of the **-b**, **-n**, **-i**, or **-f** options when used in conjunction with the **-a** option:

-b Specifies that autobaud should be enabled. Autobaud allows the system to set the line speed of a given TTY port to the line speed of the device connected to the port without the user's intervention.

-n *nextlabel* Specifies the value to be used in the *nextlabel* field in **/etc/ttydefs**. If this option is not specified, **sttydefs** will set *nextlabel* equal to *ttylabel*.

-i *initial-flags* Specifies the value to be used in the *initial-flags* field in **/etc/ttydefs**. *initial-flags* must be in a format recognized by the **stty** command. These flags are used by **ttymon** when searching for the correct baud rate. They are set prior to writing the prompt.

If this option is not specified, **sttydefs** will set *initial-flags* equal to the **termio**(7) flag **9600**.

-f *final-flags* Specifies the value to be used in the *final-flags* field in **/etc/ttydefs**. *final-flags* must be in a format recognized by the **stty** command. *final-flags* are the **termio**(7) settings used by **ttymon** after receiving a successful connection request and immediately before invoking the service on the port. If this option is not specified, **sttydefs** will set *final-flags* equal to the **termio**(7) flags **9600** and **sane**.

-r *ttylabel* Removes any record in the **ttydefs** file that has *ttylabel* as its label.

EXAMPLES

The following command will list all the entries in the **ttydefs** file and print an error message for each invalid entry that is detected.

```
sttydefs -l
```

The following shows a command that requests information for a single label and its output:

```
# sttydefs -l 9600
-------------------------------------------------------------------
9600:9600 hupcl erase ^h:9600 sane ixany tab3 hupcl erase ^h::4800
-------------------------------------------------------------------

ttylabel:        9600
initial flags:   9600 hupcl erase ^h
final flags:     9600 sane ixany tab3 hupcl erase ^h
autobaud:        no
nextlabel:       4800
```

The following sequence of commands will add the labels **1200**, **2400**, **4800**, and **9600** and put them in a circular list:

```
sttydefs -a 1200 -n 2400 -i 1200 -f "1200 sane"
sttydefs -a 2400 -n 4800 -i 2400 -f "2400 sane"
sttydefs -a 4800 -n 9600 -i 4800 -f "4800 sane"
sttydefs -a 9600 -n 1200 -i 9600 -f "9600 sane"
```

FILES

/etc/ttydefs

/usr/lib/locale/*locale***/LC_MESSAGES/uxcore.abi**
language-specific message file [See **LANG** on **environ** (5).]

SEE ALSO

termio(7), **ttydefs**(4)

DIAGNOSTICS

If successful, **sttydefs** will exit with a status of **0**. **sttydefs -l** will generate the requested information and send it to the standard output.

NAME

su – become another user

SYNOPSIS

su [–] [*name* [*arg* . . .]

DESCRIPTION

su allows one to become another user without logging off. The default user *name* is **root**.

To use **su**, the appropriate password for the login *name* specified must be supplied (unless one is already **root**). The default password validation behavior can be altered via the **PROMPT** default parameter found in **/etc/default/su** (see FILES).

Upon successful execution, **su** will execute a new shell with the real and effective user and group IDs and supplementary group list set to that of the specified user. The new shell will be the optional program named in the shell field of the specified user's password file entry [see **passwd**(4)] or **/usr/bin/sh** if none is specified [see **sh**(1)].

To restore the normal user ID environment, type an EOF character (CTRL-d) to the new shell.

Any additional arguments given on the command line are passed to the program invoked as the shell. When using programs such as **sh**, an *arg* of the form **-c** *string* executes *string* via the shell and an arg of **-r** gives the user a restricted shell.

The following statements are true only if the optional program named in the shell field of the specified user's password file entry is like **sh**. If the first argument to **su** is a **-**, the environment will be changed to what would be expected if the user actually logged in as the specified user. This is done by invoking the program used as the shell with an *arg0* value whose first character is **-**, thus causing first the system's profile (**/etc/profile** for **sh** or**ksh**, or **/etc/.login** for **csh**) and then the specified user's profile (**.profile** in the new **HOME** directory) to be executed. Otherwise, the environment is passed along with the possible exception of **$PATH**, which is set to **/sbin:/usr/sbin:/usr/bin:/etc** for **root**. Note that if the optional program used as the shell is **/usr/bin/sh**, the user's **.profile** can check *arg0* for **-sh** or **-su** to determine if it was invoked by **login** or **su**, respectively. If the user's program is other than **/usr/bin/sh**, then **.profile** is invoked with an *arg0* of *–program* by both **login** and **su**.

Note that if you are using **csh**, **/etc/profile** is replaced by **/etc/.login** and **$HOME/.profile** is replaced by **$HOME/.login**.

All attempts to become another user using **su** are logged in the **log** file **/var/adm/sulog**.

EXAMPLES

To become user **bin** while retaining your previously exported environment, execute:

```
su bin
```

To become user **bin** but change the environment to what would be expected if **bin** had originally logged in, execute:

```
su - bin
```

To execute *command* with the temporary environment and permissions of user **bin**, type:

su - bin -c "*command args*"

FILES

/etc/passwd system's password file

/etc/security/ia/master
system's I&A data file

/etc/profile system's profile

/etc/.login system's profile

$HOME/.profile user's profile

$HOME/.login user's profile

/var/adm/sulog log file

/usr/lib/locale/*locale***/LC_MESSAGES/uxcore.abi**
language-specific message file [See **LANG** on **environ** (5).]

/etc/default/su default parameters in this file are:

SULOG: If defined, all attempts to **su** to another user are logged in the indicated file.

CONSOLE: If defined, all attempts to **su root** are logged on the console.

PATH: Default path.

SUPATH: Default path for a user invoking **su root**.

PROMPT: If this parameter exists and is set to **No**, the **su** command will not prompt for a password (even if one is defined for the login *name*); however, the invoking user must still have appropriate privilege to use **su** successfully. If this parameter does not exist, or is set to anything other than **No** (including **NULL**), **su** will prompt for a password when invoked and validate the password (if one is defined for the login *name*).

SEE ALSO

defadm(1M), **env**(1), **login**(1), **passwd**(4), **profile**(4), **sh**(1)

NAME

sulogin – access single-user mode

SYNOPSIS

sulogin

DESCRIPTION

sulogin is automatically invoked by **init** when the system is first started. It prompts the user to type the root password to enter system maintenance mode (single-user mode) or to type EOF (typically CTRL-d) for normal startup (multi-user mode). **sulogin** should never be invoked directly by the user.

FILES

/sbin/sulogin

SEE ALSO

init(1M)

sum(1)

NAME

sum – print checksum and block count of a file

SYNOPSIS

sum [**-r**] *file*

DESCRIPTION

sum calculates and prints a 16-bit checksum for the named file, and also prints the number of 512 byte blocks in the file. It is typically used to look for bad spots, or to validate a file communicated over some transmission line. The option **-r** causes an alternate algorithm to be used in computing the checksum.

FILES

/usr/lib/locale/*locale***/LC_MESSAGES/uxdfm**

language-specific message file [See **LANG** on **environ**(5).]

SEE ALSO

wc(1)

DIAGNOSTICS

"Read error" is indistinguishable from end of file on most devices; check the block count.

NAME

`sum` – (BSD) calculate a checksum for a file

SYNOPSIS

`/usr/ucb/sum` *filename*

DESCRIPTION

`sum` calculates and displays a 16-bit checksum for the named file, and also displays the size of the file in kilobytes. It is typically used to look for bad spots, or to validate a file communicated over some transmission line. The checksum is calculated by an algorithm which may yield different results on machines with 16-bit `int`s and machines with 32-bit `int`s, so it cannot always be used to validate that a file has been transferred between machines with different-sized `int`s.

SEE ALSO

`sum`(1), `wc`(1)

DIAGNOSTICS

`Read error` is indistinguishable from EOF on most devices; check the block count.

NOTES

Obsolescent.

NAME

swap – swap administrative interface

SYNOPSIS

/usr/sbin/swap -a *swapname swaplow swaplen*
/usr/sbin/swap -d *swapname swaplow*
/usr/sbin/swap -l [**-s**]
/usr/sbin/swap -s

DESCRIPTION

swap provides a method of adding, deleting, and monitoring the system swap areas used by the memory manager.

Options

swap takes following options:

-a Add the specified swap area. *swapname* is the name of the block special partition, for example, **/dev/dsk/***, where the value of * is machine dependent, or a regular file. *swaplow* is the offset in 512-byte blocks into the partition where the swap area should begin. If the offset value is omitted, an offset of zero is used. *swaplen* is the length of the swap area in 512-byte blocks. This option can only be used by a privileged user. If the size of the swap area is omitted, the size of the device is used, if available; if not available, the command will fail, reporting that an explicit size must be supplied for this device.

Swap areas are normally added by modifying the **/sbin/rc***n* file to include the **swap** command that is executed when the system is entering run level *n*. Generally, this occurrs during system start-up.

-d Delete the specified swap area. *swapname* is the name of block special partition, for example, **/dev/dsk/***, where the value of * is machine dependent, or a regular file. *swaplow* is the offset in 512-byte blocks into the partition specifying the beginning of the swap area to be deleted. Using this option marks the swap area as "INDEL" (in the process of being deleted). The system will not allocate any new blocks from the area, and will try to free swap blocks from it. The area will remain in use until all blocks from it are freed. This option can be used only by a privileged user.

-l List the status of all the swap areas. The output has five columns:

path The path name for the swap area.

dev The major/minor device number in decimal if it is a block special device; zeros otherwise.

swaplo The *swaplow* value for the area in 512-byte blocks.

blocks The *swaplen* value for the area in 512-byte blocks.

free The number of free 512-byte blocks in the area. If the swap area is being deleted, the word INDEL will be printed to the right of this number.

-s Print the following information about total swap space usage:

allocated The amount of swap space (in 512-byte blocks) allocated to private pages.

reserved The number of swap space (in 512-bytes blocks) not currently allocated, but claimed by memory mappings that have not yet created private pages.

used The total amount of swap space, in 512-byte blocks, that is either allocated or reserved.

available The total swap space, in 512-byte blocks, that is currently available for future reservation and allocation.

Example

The following **swap** example requests 10K of swap area (twenty 512-byte blocks) on the device **/dev/dsk/***, where the value of * is machine dependent.

```
/usr/sbin/swap -a /dev/dsk/* 0 20
```

NOTES

Privileged use of this command is restricted to maintenance mode. See the system administration documentation for a description of maintenance mode.

No check is done to see if a swap area being added overlaps with an existing file system.

sync(1M)

NAME

sync – update the super block

SYNOPSIS

sync

DESCRIPTION

sync executes the **sync** system primitive. If the system is to be stopped, **sync** must be called to insure file system integrity. It will flush all previously unwritten system buffers out to disk, thus assuring that all file modifications up to that point will be saved. See **sync**(2) for details.

NOTE

If you have done a write to a file on a remote machine in a Remote File Sharing environment, you cannot use **sync** to force buffers to be written out to disk on the remote machine. **sync** will only write local buffers to local disks.

REFERENCES

sync(2)

NAME

sysdef – output system definition

SYNOPSIS

/usr/sbin/sysdef [**-n** *namelist*]

/usr/sbin/sysdef -i

DESCRIPTION

sysdef outputs the current system definition in tabular form. It lists all hardware devices, their local bus addresses, and unit count, as well as pseudo devices, system devices, loadable modules, and the values of selected kernel tunable parameters.

It generates the output by analyzing the named bootable operating system file (*namelist*) and extracting the configuration information from it and files in the **master** directory. This directory contains the system configuration files used to build *namelist*.

The default system *namelist* is **/stand/unix**.

Valid options and parameters are:

-n *namelist* Specifies a *namelist* other than the default (**/stand/unix**). The *namelist* specified must be a valid bootable operating system

-i Allows you read the configuration information from the kernel that is currently in memory (that is, from **/dev/kmem**) rather than from a file.

DIAGNOSTICS

internal name list overflow
If the master table contains more than an internally specified number of entries for use by **nlist**(3C).

FILES

/stand/unix default operating system file (file that contains the system namelist)

SEE ALSO

master(4), **nlist**(3E)

sysadm (1M)

NAME

sysadm – visual interface for system administration

SYNOPSIS

sysadm [*menu name* | *task name*]

DESCRIPTION

This command, when invoked without an argument, presents a set of menus that help you do administrative work. If you specify a menu or task on the command line, one of two things happens: if the requested menu or task is unique, it is immediately displayed; if the menu or task is not unique, a menu of choices is displayed.

The **sysadm** command may be given a password. To assign a password, use the **password** task under the **system_setup** menu. To change a password after it is assigned, use the **passwd** command.

When you invoke **sysadm** on a computer running UNIX SVR4.2 the main menu appears as follows:

```
                         UNIX System V Administration

backup_service   - Backup Scheduling, Setup, and Control
file_systems     - File System Creation, Checking and Mounting
machine          - Machine Configuration, Display and Shutdown
network_services - Network Services Administration
ports            - Port Access Services and Monitors
preSVR4          - Peripherals Setup
printers         - Printer Configuration and Services
restore_service  - Restore From Backup Data
schedule_task    - Schedule Automatic Task
software         - Software Installation and Removal
storage_devices  - Storage Device Operations and Definitions
system_setup     - System Name, Date/Time and Initial Password Setup
users            - User Login and Group Administration
```

If, when you type **sysadm**, the main menu does not appear or if you cannot access a particular task, one or more of the **Menu.**∗ forms may have been corrupted, removed (accidentally), or not installed properly. If this happens, you can rebuild all the **Menu.**∗ forms that make up the administration menus by entering the following command:

```
/usr/sadm/install/bin/ie_build
```

The rest of this section describes each menu listed on the main menu.

`Backup Service Management`

This menu lists the available levels of administrative support for backup services.

`basic` (`Basic Backup Service`)
This menu provides functions for backup to removable media. Specifically, it allows you to view backup history, or to make a floppy disk or cartridge tape copy of the files you have on your computer's hard disk.

`extended` (`Extended Backup Service Management`)
This menu lists areas of administrative support for the backup services.

`backup` (`Start Backup Jobs`)
This task starts the backup scheduled for the current day based on the default backup control table or the specified backup control table.

`history` (`Backup History Management`)
This task lets you display reports of backup operations that have completed successfully.

`reminder` (`Schedule Backup Reminder`)
This menu lets you schedule messages that will be sent to you to remind you to do backups.

`respond` (`Respond to Backup Job Prompts`)
This task lets you reply to operator prompts from backup jobs.

`schedule` (`Schedule Automatic Backups`)
This menu lets you schedule backups so that they will run automatically. Because the backups are scheduled to run automatically and are not associated with a terminal, you must choose to run them in either automatic or background mode.

`setup` (`Backup Control Table Management`)
This menu lets you change or display backup registers.

`status` (`Backup Status Management`)
This menu lets you manage backup requests that are in progress.

`Manage File Systems`

This menu provides eleven tasks that are part of file system management. These tasks include checking for and repairing errors on a specific file system, monitoring disk usage for all file systems, tracking files based on age or size, listing all file systems currently mounted on your system, creating a new file system, and mounting and unmounting file systems.

`check` (`Check a File System`)
This task lets you check a file system for errors and fix them, either interactively or automatically.

`defaults` (`Manage Defaults`)
This task identifies the percentage of hard disks currently occupied by files.

diskuse (**Display Disk Usage**)
This task identifies the percentage of hard disks currently occupied by files. The information is presented as a list, organized by file system name.

display (**Display Installed Types**)
This task displays a list of the file system types installed on your system.

fileage (**List Files by Age**)
This task lets you print the names of old files in the directory you specify. If you do not specify an age, files older than 90 days are listed.

filesize (**List Files by Size**)
This task lets you print the names of the largest files in a specific directory. If you do not request a particular number of files, the ten largest files are listed.

identify (**Identify File System Type**)
This task tries to determine the type of any unmounted file system without damaging the data or the medium of the file system.

list (**List Mounted File Systems**)
This task lets you list all file systems mounted on your computer.

make (**Create a File System**)
This task lets you create a new file system on a removable medium where you can then store data you do not want to keep on hard disk. When mounted, the file system has all the properties of a file kept on hard disk.

mount (**Mount a File System**)
This task lets you mount a file system located on a removable medium and make it available to users on your system. The file system may be unmounted using the **unmount** task.

CAUTION: **(1) mount does not prevent you from mounting a file system on a directory that's not empty. (2) Do not remove the medium while the file system is still mounted.**

unmount (**Unmount a File System**)
This task lets you unmount a file system and thus lets you remove the medium on which it resides. Both **/** and **/usr** are excluded because unmounting these file systems would cause a system crash. Once a file system has been unmounted, you may remove the medium on which it resided.

Machine Configuration Display and Shutdown

This menu provides four tasks for functions such as turning off the computer, rebooting it, and changing to firmware mode.

configuration (**System Configuration Display**)
This task allows you to check the current configuration of the system.

shutdown (**Stops All Running Programs and Halts Machine**)
This task lets you stop all running programs, close any open files, write out information (such as directory information) to disk, and then bring the system down.

reboot (**Stops All Running Programs and Reboots Machine**)
This task lets you reboot the computer after all running programs have been stopped, any open files have been closed, and any necessary information (such as directory information) has been written out to disk, This procedure can be used to resolve some types of system trouble, such as a process that cannot be killed.

whos on (**Displays List of Users Logged onto Machine**)
This task prints the login ID, terminal device number, and sign-on time of all users who are currently using the computer.

Network Services Management

This menu provides functions for managing networks.

attr_map (**Attribute Mapping Administration**)
This menu allows you to set up and administer attribute mapping files.

basic_networking (**Basic Networking Utilities Management**)
This menu allows you to set up administrative files for UUCP utilities.

cr1 (**IAF Scheme cr1 Key Management**)
This menu allows you to set up and administer key files and start or stop the keymaster daemon.

name_map (**Name Mapping Administration**)
This menu allows you to set up and administer name mapping files.

remote_files (**Distributed File System Management**)
This menu allows you to set up administrative files for the Remote File Sharing (RFS) Utilities or the Network File Sharing (NFS) Utilities.

selection (**Network Selection Management**)
This menu allows you to set up administrative files for Network Selection; that is, for dynamically selecting a transport protocol.

name_to_address (**Machine and Service Address Management**)
This menu allows you to define machine addresses and service port information for the protocols that exist on the machine.

Service Access Management

This menu provides functions for managing service access to the system.

port_monitors (**Port Monitor Management**)
This menu provides functions for managing port monitors under the Service Access Facility. Specifically, it allows you to add, disable, enable, list, change, remove, start, and stop port monitors.

`port_services` (`Port Service Management`)
This menu provides functions for managing port services provides by port monitors. Specifically, it allows you to add, disable, enable, list, change, and remove port services.

`quick_terminal`(Quick Terminal Setup)
This menu provides functions for adding and removing a terminal to and from a port.

`tty_settings` (`Terminal Line Setting Management`)
This menu provides functions for managing tty line settings. Specifically, it allows you to create new tty settings and hunt sequences, and to display (on your screen) and remove those settings. To change an existing tty line setting, remove the entry and then recreate it, including the changes.

`Peripherals Setup`

This menu provides backwards compatibility for pre-SVR4 add-ons that install user interface forms and menus.

`Line Printer Services Configuration and Operation`

This menu lists

`classes` (`Manage Classes of Related Printers`)
This menu allows you to add a new class, list printers in classes, modify the membership of a class, or remove classes.

`filters` (`Manage Filters for Special Processing`)
This menu allows you to add new filters, list filter information, modify a filter, remove filters, or restore filters to factory settings.

`forms` (`Manage Pre-Printed Forms`)
This menu allows you to add a new form, list form attributes, modify a form, or remove forms.

`operations` (`Perform Daily Printer Service Operations`)
This menu allows you to accept print requests for classes or printers, control (stop) the printer service, disable a printer, enable a printer, set LP to always copy print request files, mount a form or font, reject print requests, set a default print destination, or unmount a form or printwheel.

`printers` (`Configure printers for the Printer Service`)
This menu allows you to add a new printer, list printer configurations, modify a printer configuration, or remove printers.

`priorities` (`Assign Print Queue Priorities to Users`)
This menu allows you to set a system default priority, list priority limits for users, remove priority limit from user(s), set a system priority limit, or set user(s) priority limit.

requests (**Manage Active Print Requests**)
This menu allows you to cancel, hold, move or release active print requests.

status (**Display Status of Printer Service**)
This menu allows you to display status of forms, printers, print requests, printwheels and character sets.

Restore Service Management

This menu lists the available levels of administrative support for restore services.

Basic (**Basic Restore Service**)
This menu enables you to restore files to your hard disk that were backed up to removable media. Specifically, it allows you to restore files that were backed up from your **HOME** directory or system files.

Extended Restore Service Management
This menu provides tasks for restoring directories, files, file systems, and data partitions from archive volumes.

operator (**Set/Display the Restore Operator**)
This task lets you set up and display the restore operator.

respond (**Respond to Restore Job Prompts**)
This task lets you respond to restore job prompts.

restore (**Restore from Backup Archives**)
This task lets you request the restoration of files, directories, file systems, and data partitions from an archived version.

status (**Modify/Report Pending Restore Request Status**)
This menu lets you display and change the status of pending restore requests.

Schedule Automatic Task

This menu provides functions for you to add, change, delete or display **cron** entries.

Software Installation and Information Management

The tasks in this menu provide functions for software package installation, removal, and management of information about software packages. They include the ability to install and remove packages, and to check the accuracy of package installation. In addition, they include the ability to set installation defaults, store interactions with a particular package, store a package without actually installing it, and to list all installed packages.

check (**Checks Accuracy of Installation**)
This task lets you check installed software packages for consistency, correct for inconsistencies, check for hidden files, and check the contents of files that are likely to have changed.

defaults (**Sets Installation Defaults**)
This task allows you to decide, ahead of time, the way that the system should respond to an installation problem.

install (**Installs Software Packages**)
This task lets you install software packages onto a spool, a hard disk, or a floppy diskette, and select the method that the system will use to respond to installation problems.

interact (**Stores Interactions with Package**)
This task allows you to interact with the software installation process.

list (**Displays Information about Packages**)
This task shows you the software packages that are installed on your system and tells you the name, location, and category of each.

read_in (**Stores Packages Without Installing**)
This task lets you read in software packages without installing them.

remove (**Removes Packages**)
This task lets you remove installed software packages.

Storage Device Operations and Definitions

This menu contains tasks for getting descriptions of device aliases and attributes and for assigning device groups.

add (**Add Storage Device**)
This task allows you to add a storage device.

copy (**Makes Duplicate Copies of Storage Volumes**)
This task allows you to copy a storage volume.

devices (**Device Alias and Attribute Management**)
This menu contains tasks for adding, listing, and removing device descriptions. This menu also provides access to device attribute management and device reservation services.

display (**Displays Information About Storage Devices**)
This task displays information about storage devices.

erase (**Erases the Contents of Storage Volumes**)
This task can be used to erase the contents of a storage volume.

format (**Formats Removable Volumes**)
This task can be used to format a storage volume.

groups (**Device Group Administration**)
This menu allows you to add a device group, list device groups, remove a device group; or add, list or remove members from a device group.

preSVR4 (**Disk Operations**)
This task allows you to perform pre-SVR4.2 disk operations.

remove (**Remove Storage Device**)
This task allows you to remove a storage device.

System Name, Date Time and Initial Password Setup

This menu lets you set up your machine. The tasks in this menu include setting the system date and time, setting the node name of your system, doing initial system setup, and assigning passwords to administrative logins on the system.

datetime (**System Date and Time Information**)
This task lets you tell the computer the date, time, time zone, and whether you observe Daylight Savings Time (DST). It is normally run once when the machine is first set up. If you observe DST, the computer automatically starts to observe it in the spring and returns to standard time in the fall. The machine must be turned off and turned back on again to guarantee that ALL times are reported correctly. Most times are correct the next time a user logs in. Date and time are processed according to the locale specified in the **LC_TIME** environment variable [see **LANG** on **environ**(5)].

file_maintenance (**Maintain Files in /etc/default**)
This task allows you to add, remove or change files in **/etc/default**.

nodename (**System Name and Network Node Name of the Machine**)
This task lets you change the node name and system name of this machine. These names are used by various communications networks to identify this machine.

password (**Assigns Administrative Login Passwords**)
This task lets you assign passwords to administrative logins.

setup (**Sets up System Information for First Time**)
This task lets you define the first login, set the initial passwords on administration logins, and set the time zone for your location.

User Login and Group Administration

This menu lets you manage the user IDs and groups on your machine. Tasks include the ability to add, change, and delete users or groups defined on your machine. You can place users in groups so that they can share access to files belonging to members of the group but protect these files from access by members of other groups. In addition, you can set defaults that are used for subsequent user definitions on your machine, and you can define or redefine user password information.

add (**Add Users or Groups**)
This task lets you define either a new user or a new group on your system.

defaults (**Define Defaults for Adding Users**)
This task lets you change some of the default values used when the **add user** task creates a new login. Changing the default values does not affect any existing logins; it affects only those added later.

list (**List Users or Groups**)
This task lets you examine the attributes of the users and groups on your system.

modify (**Modify Attributes of Users or Groups**)
This task lets you modify either a user definition or a group definition on your system.

password (**(Re-)define User Password Information**)
This task lets you define or change a user's password.

remove (**Remove Users or Groups**)
This task lets you remove a user from your system.

RETURN VALUES

The **sysadm** command exits with one of the following values:

- **0** Normal exit.
- **2** Invalid command syntax. Usage message of the **sysadm** command is displayed.
- **4** The menu or task name given as an argument does not exist.
- **5** The menu name given as an argument is an empty placeholder menu, and therefore not available for use.
- **7** The **sysadm** command is not available because it cannot invoke **fmli**. (FMLI may not have been installed.)

SEE ALSO

delsysadm(1M), **edsysadm**(1M), **shutdown**(1M),

Advanced Administration

NAME

syslogd – log system messages

SYNOPSIS

/usr/sbin/syslogd [**-d**] [**-f***configfile*] [**-m** *interval*] [**-p** *path*]

DESCRIPTION

syslogd reads and forwards system messages to the appropriate log files and/or users, depending upon the priority of a message and the system facility from which it originates. The configuration file **/etc/syslog.conf** [see **syslog.conf**(4)] controls where messages are forwarded. **syslogd** logs a mark (timestamp) message every *interval* minutes (default 20) at priority **LOG_INFO** to the facility whose name is given as **mark** in the **syslog.conf** file.

A system message consists of a single line of text, which may be prefixed with a priority code number enclosed in angle-brackets (**< >**); priorities are defined in **sys/syslog.h**.

syslogd reads from the STREAMS log driver, **/dev/log**, from any transport provider specified in **/etc/netconfig**, **/etc/net/***transport***/hosts**, and **/etc/net/***transport***/services**.

syslogd reads the configuration file when it starts up, and again whenever it receives a HUP signal, at which time it also closes all files it has open, re-reads its configuration file, and then opens only the log files that are listed in that file. **syslogd** exits when it receives a **TERM** signal.

As it starts up, **syslogd** creates the file **/etc/syslog.pid**, if possible, containing its process ID (PID).

The following options are available:

-d	Turn on debugging.
-f*configfile*	Specify an alternate configuration file.
-m *interval*	Specify an interval, in minutes, between mark messages.
-p *path*	Specify an alternate log (one other than **/dev/log**).

FILES

/etc/syslog.conf	configuration file
/etc/syslog.pid	process ID
/dev/log	STREAMS log driver
/etc/netconfig	specifies the transport providers available on the system
/etc/net/*transport***/hosts**	network hosts for each transport
/etc/net/*transport***/services**	network services for each transport

SEE ALSO

log(7), **logger**(1), **syslog**(3), **syslog.conf**(4)

NAME

tabs – set tabs on a terminal

SYNOPSIS

tabs [*tabspec*] [**-T***type*] [**+m***n*]

DESCRIPTION

tabs sets the tab stops on the user's terminal according to the tab specification *tabspec*, after clearing any previous settings. The user's terminal must have remotely settable hardware tabs.

tabspec Four types of tab specification are accepted for *tabspec*. They are described below: canned (-*code*), repetitive (-*n*), arbitrary (*n1, n2, . . .*), and file (--*file*). If no *tabspec* is given, the default value is **-8**, that is, UNIX system "standard" tabs. The lowest column number is 1. Note that for **tabs**, column 1 always refers to the left-most column on a terminal, even one whose column markers begin at 0, for example, the DASI 300, DASI 300s, and DASI 450.

–*code* Use one of the codes listed below to select a *canned* set of tabs. The valid codes and their meanings are as follows:

-a 1,10,16,36,72
Assembler, IBM S/370, first format

-a2 1,10,16,40,72
Assembler, IBM S/370, second format

-c 1,8,12,16,20,55
COBOL, normal format

-c2 1,6,10,14,49
COBOL compact format (columns 1-6 omitted). Using this code, the first typed character corresponds to card column 7, one space gets you to column 8, and a tab reaches column 12. Files using this tab setup should include a format specification as follows (see **fspec**(4)):

```
<:t-c2 m6 s66 d:>
```

-c3 1,6,10,14,18,22,26,30,34,38,42,46,50,54,58,62,67
COBOL compact format (columns 1-6 omitted), with more tabs than **-c2.** This is the recommended format for COBOL. The appropriate format specification is [see **fspec**(4)]:

```
<:t-c3 m6 s66 d:>
```

-f 1,7,11,15,19,23
FORTRAN

-p 1,5,9,13,17,21,25,29,33,37,41,45,49,53,57,61
PL/I

-s 1,10,55
SNOBOL

-u 1,12,20,44
UNIVAC 1100 Assembler

-n A *repetitive* specification requests tabs at columns 1+*n*, 1+2**n*, etc. Of particular importance is the value **8**: this represents the UNIX system "standard" tab setting, and is the most likely tab setting to be found at a terminal. Another special case is the value **0**, implying no tabs at all.

n1,n2,.. The *arbitrary* format permits the user to type any chosen set of numbers, separated by commas, in ascending order. Up to 40 numbers are allowed. If any number (except the first one) is preceded by a plus sign, it is taken as an increment to be added to the previous value. Thus, the formats **1,10,20,30**, and **1,10,+10,+10** are considered identical.

--file If the name of a *file* is given, **tabs** reads the first line of the file, searching for a format specification [see **fspec**(4)]. If it finds one there, it sets the tab stops according to it, otherwise it sets them as **-8**. This type of specification may be used to make sure that a tabbed file is printed with correct tab settings, and would be used with the **pr** command:

tabs **--***file*; **pr** *file*

Any of the following also may be used; if a given flag occurs more than once, the last value given takes effect:

-T*type* **tabs** usually needs to know the type of terminal in order to set tabs and always needs to know the type to set margins. *type* is a name listed in **term**(5). If no **-T** flag is supplied, **tabs** uses the value of the environment variable **TERM**. If **TERM** is not defined in the *environment* [see **environ**(5)], **tabs** tries a sequence that will work for many terminals.

+m*n* The margin argument may be used for some terminals. It causes all tabs to be moved over *n* columns by making column *n+1* the left margin. If **+m** is given without a value of *n*, the value assumed is **10**. For a TermiNet, the first value in the tab list should be **1**, or the margin will move even further to the right. The normal (leftmost) margin on most terminals is obtained by **+m0**. The margin for most terminals is reset only when the **+m** flag is given explicitly.

Tab and margin setting is performed via the standard output.

EXAMPLES

tabs -a example using *–code* (*canned* specification) to set tabs to the settings required by the IBM assembler: columns 1, 10, 16, 36, 72.

tabs -8 example of using *–n* (*repetitive* specification), where *n* is **8**, causes tabs to be set every eighth position:
1+(1*8), 1+(2*8), . . . which evaluate to columns 9, 17, . . .

tabs 1,8,36 example of using *n1,n2,..* (*arbitrary* specification) to set tabs at columns 1, 8, and 36.

tabs --$HOME/fspec.list/att4425
example of using *—file* (*file* specification) to indicate that tabs should be set according to the first line of **$HOME/fspec.list/att4425** [see **fspec**(4)].

FILES

/usr/lib/locale/*locale***/LC_MESSAGES/uxue**
language-specific message file [See **LANG** on **environ**(5).]

SEE ALSO

environ(5), **fspec**(4), **newform**(1), **pr**(1), **term**(5), **terminfo**(4), **tput**(1)

DIAGNOSTICS

UX:tabs:ERROR:illegal tabs	when arbitrary tabs are ordered incorrectly
UX:tabs:ERROR:illegal increment	when a zero or missing increment is found in an arbitrary specification
UX:tabs:ERROR:unknown tab code	when a *canned* code cannot be found
UX:tabs:ERROR:can't open	if *--file* option used, and file can't be opened
UX:tabs:ERROR:file indirection	if *--file* option used and the specification in that file points to yet another file. Indirection of this form is not permitted

NOTES

There is no consistency among different terminals regarding ways of clearing tabs and setting the left margin.

tabs clears only 20 tabs (on terminals requiring a long sequence), but is willing to set 64.

The *tabspec* used with the **tabs** command is different from the one used with the **newform** command. For example, **tabs -8** sets every eighth position; whereas **newform -i-8** indicates that tabs are set every eighth position.

NAME

tail – deliver the last part of a file

SYNOPSIS

tail [± *number* **lbcr**] [*file*]
tail [**-lbcr**] [*file*]
tail [± *number* **lbcf**] [*file*]
tail [**-lbcf**] [*file*]

DESCRIPTION

tail copies the named file to the standard output beginning at a designated place. If no file is named, the standard input is used.

Copying begins at distance **+***number* from the beginning, or **-***number* from the end of the input (if *number* is null, the value 10 is assumed). *Number* is counted in units of lines, blocks, or characters, according to the appended option **l**, **b**, or **c**. When no units are specified, counting is by lines. **tail** processes supplementary code set characters according to the locale specified in the **LC_CTYPE** environment variable [see **LANG** on **environ**(5)], except that multibyte characters may not be displayed correctly when the **-b** and **-c** options are specified.

With the **-f** (follow) option, if the input file is not a pipe, the program will not terminate after the line of the input file has been copied, but will enter an endless loop, wherein it sleeps for a second and then attempts to read and copy further records from the input file. Thus it may be used to monitor the growth of a file that is being written by some other process. For example, the command:

```
tail -f fred
```

will print the last ten lines of the file **fred**, followed by any lines that are appended to **fred** between the time **tail** is initiated and killed. As another example, the command:

```
tail -15cf fred
```

will print the last 15 characters of the file **fred**, followed by any lines that are appended to **fred** between the time **tail** is initiated and killed.

The **r** option copies lines from the end of the file in reverse order. *number* is the count of lines from the end of the file, regardless of the sign. The default for **r** is to print the entire file in reverse order.

The **r** option may not be used with **b**, **c** or **f**.

FILES

/usr/lib/locale/*locale***/LC_MESSAGES/uxcore.abi**
language-specific message file [See **LANG** on **environ** (5).]

SEE ALSO

cat(1), **dd**(1M), **head**(1), **more**(1), **pg**(1), **tail**(1)

NOTES

Tails relative to the end of the file are stored in a buffer, and thus are limited in length. Various kinds of anomalous behavior may happen with character special files.

talk(1)

NAME

talk – talk to another user

SYNOPSIS

talk *username* [*ttyname*]

DESCRIPTION

talk is a visual communication program that copies lines from your terminal to that of a user on the same or on another host. *username* is that user's login name.

The program is architecture dependent; it works only between machines of the same architecture.

If you want to talk to a user who is logged in more than once, the *ttyname* argument may be used to indicate the appropriate terminal name.

When first called, **talk** sends the message:

> **Message from TalkDaemon@** *her_machine* **at** *time* ...
> **talk: connection requested by** *your_name@your_machine*
> **talk: respond with: talk** *your_name@your_machine*

to the user you want to talk to. At this point, the recipient of the message should reply by typing:

> **talk** *your_name@your_machine*

It does not matter from which machine the recipient replies, as long as the login name is the same. Once communication is established, the two parties may type simultaneously, with their output appearing in separate windows. Typing CTRL-l redraws the screen, while your erase, kill, and word kill characters will work in **talk** as normal. To exit, just type your interrupt character; **talk** then moves the cursor to the bottom of the screen and restores the terminal.

Permission to talk may be denied or granted by use of the **mesg**(1) command. At the outset talking is allowed. Certain commands, such as **pr**(1), disallow messages in order to prevent messy output.

FILES

/etc/hosts	to find the recipient's machine
/var/adm/utmp	to find the recipient's tty

SEE ALSO

mail(1), **mesg**(1), **pr**(1), **who**(1), **write**(1), **talkd**(1M)

NAME

talkd, **in.talkd** – server for talk program

SYNOPSIS

in.talkd

DESCRIPTION

talkd is a server used by the **talk**(1) program. It listens at the UDP port indicated in the "talk" service description; see **services**(4). The actual conversation takes place on a TCP connection that is established by negotiation between the two machines involved.

SEE ALSO

talk(1), **inetd**(1M), **services**(4)

NOTES

The protocol is architecture dependent.

tape(1)

NAME

tape – magnetic tape maintenance

SYNOPSIS

tape *command* [*device*]

DESCRIPTION

tape sends commands to and receives status from the tape subsystem. **tape** can communicate with QIC-24/QIC-02 cartridge tape drives and SCSI tape drives.

tape reads **/etc/default/tape** to find the default device name for sending commands and receiving status. For example, the following line in **/etc/default/tape** will cause **tape** to communicate with the QIC-24/QIC-02 cartridge tape device:

```
device = /dev/rmt/c0s0
```

If a device name is specified on the command line, it overrides the default device.

COMMANDS

The following commands can be used with the various tape drivers supported under UNIX System V.

erase	Erase and retension the tape cartridge.
reset	Reset tape controller and tape drive. Clears error conditions and returns tape subsystem to power-up state.
reten	Retension tape cartridge. Should be used periodically to remedy slack tape problems. Tape slack can cause an unusually large number of tape errors.
rewind	Rewind to beginning of tape.
rfm	Wind tape forward to the next file mark.

FILES

Devices:

```
/dev/rmt/c0s0
/dev/rmt/c0s0n
/dev/rmt/c0s0r
/dev/rmt/c0s0nr
/dev/rmt/c0t3d0s0

/etc/default/tape
```

Include files:

```
/usr/include/sys/tape.h
```

NOTES

The **reset** command can be used while the tape is busy with other operations. All other commands wait until the currently executing command has been completed before proceeding.

When you are using the non-rewinding tape device or the **tape** command **rfm**, the tape drive light remains on after the command has been completed, indicating that more operations may be performed on the tape. The **tape rewind** command may be used to clear this condition.

REFERENCES

backup(1M), **cpio**(1), **dd**(1M), **restore**(1M), **tar**(1), **xrestore**(1M)

NAME

tapecntl – tape control for tape device

SYNOPSIS

tapecntl [**-abelrtuvw**] [**-d** *arg*] [**-f** *arg*] [**-p** *arg*] [**special**]

DESCRIPTION

tapecntl sends the optional commands to the tape device driver sub-device **/dev/rmt/ntape***. The sub-device **/dev/rmt/ctape*** provides a rewind on close capability, while **/dev/rmt/ntape*** allows for closing of the device without rewind. Error messages are written to standard error. **special** is the tape device, and defaults to **/dev/rmt/ntape1** if not specified.

Not all options are supported by all tape devices or all tape device drivers.

Options

tapecntl takes the following options:

-a Position the tape to the end of data (EOD) mark. This option is valid only for SCSI tape devices.

-b Read block length limits from the tape device and display them.

-e Erase the tape. The erase bar is activated while moving the tape from beginning to end, erasing all data tracks in a single pass over the tape.

-l Load the tape media and position the tape at the beginning of tape (BOT) mark.

-r Reset the tape device, initializing the tape controller registers and positioning the tape at the beginning of tape (BOT) mark. Note that if you use the **-r** option with DPT SCSI host bus adapters, the entire bus will be reset, not just the target tape driver; this limitation is specific to DPT SCSI adapters.

-t Retension the tape, moving the tape from beginning to end and back, thereby repacking the tape with the proper tension across its length.

-u Unload the tape media from the tape device. Depending on the device, unloading may include ejecting the cartridge.

-v Set the tape device to read and write variable length blocks. This option works only on devices that support variable length blocks.

-w Rewind the tape, moving the tape to the BOT mark.

-d[*n*] Set the tape density with argument *n*, where *n* is the numeric density code as defined in the SCSI-2 specification. This option works only with SCSI drives. The number specified must be in decimal. Common density codes include: 0 = the default value for the device, meaning autodetect; 4 = QIC-11; 5 = QIC-24; 15 = QIC-120; 16 = QIC-150. Zero is the recommended value. For DAT devices, 0 and 13 both denote the DDS format and are the only valid density codes.

-f[*n*] Set the tape device to read and write in fixed length blocks of *n* bytes, where *n* is some positive, non-zero integer. Individual devices have specific limitations and you should set this parameter only to a value supported by the device. This value should be set to 512 for cartridge tape devices. DAT devices, 8mm tape devices, and 9-track tape devices support other block sizes.

`-p`[*n*] Position tape past the end of file (EOF) mark *n*, where *n* is an integer, positive or negative, representing the number of EOF marks to move forward or backward. A positive integer moves the tape forward relative to its current position, to a point just after the specified EOF mark. A negative integer moves the tape backward in the same manner, to a point on the tape just before the specified EOF mark. So, for example, using `-p 2` will move the tape to the beginning of the third record; using `-p -1` will move the tape back past the previous file mark, putting the tape at the end of the record. For this reason, backward positioning cannot move to the beginning of a record, and because backward positioning is slow, rewinding and moving forward to the needed record is the recommended approach. Note, however, that backward positioning is not available on all devices. A positioning value of zero is ignored. Illegal or out-of-range values will leave the tape positioned at the last valid EOF mark.

Options can be used individually or strung together, with selected options executed sequentially from left to right in the command line.

Exit Codes

Exit codes and their meanings are as follows:

exit (1)
Device function could not initiate properly due to misconnected cables or poorly inserted tape cartridge.

exit (2)
Device function failed to complete properly due to unrecoverable error condition, either in the command setup or due to mechanical failure.

exit (3)
Device function failed due to the cartridge being write protected or to the lack of written data on the tape.

exit (4)
Device **/dev/rmt/ntape*** or **/dev/rmt/ctape*** failed to open properly due to already being opened or claimed by another process.

Files

/usr/bin/tapecntl
/dev/rmt/ntape*
/dev/rmt/ctape*

NAME

tar – file archiver

SYNOPSIS

/usr/sbin/tar -c[**vwfbLkFhienA**[*num*]] *device block volsize incfile files . . .*
/usr/sbin/tar -c[**vwfbLkXhienA**[*num*]] *device block volsize excfile files . . .*
/usr/sbin/tar -r[**vwfbLkFhienA**[*num*]] *device block volsize incfile files . . .*
/usr/sbin/tar -r[**vwfbLkXhienA**[*num*]] *device block volsize excfile files . . .*
/usr/sbin/tar -t[**vfLXien**[*num*] *device excfile* [*files . . .*]
/usr/sbin/tar -u[**vwfbLkXhienA**[*num*]] *device block volsize excfile files . . .*
/usr/sbin/tar -u[**vwfbLkFhienA**[*num*]] *device block volsize incfile files . . .*
/usr/sbin/tar -x[**lmovwfLXpienA**[*num*]] *device excfile* [*files . . .*]

DESCRIPTION

tar saves files on an archive medium (such as a floppy diskette or a tape) and restores them from that medium. Its actions are controlled by a string of characters containing one option (**c**, **r**, **t**, **u**, or **x**), and possibly followed by one or more modifiers (**v**, **w**, **f**, **b**, **L**, **k**, **F**, **X**, **h**, **i**, **e**, **n**, **A**, **l**, **m**, **o**, **p**, and *num*). Other arguments to the command are *files* (or directory names) specifying which files are to be dumped or restored. In all cases, appearance of a directory name refers to the files and (recursively) subdirectories of that directory.

tar uses the following criteria, listed in descending order of precedence, to determine which device to use:

> Is **-f** *device* specified on the command line?
>
> Is the **TAPE** environment variable set?
>
> Is the *num* modifier used on the command line? (**tar** looks up the specified device in **/etc/default/tar**.)
>
> If none of the above are true, **tar** uses the default device specified by the entry **''archive=''** in **/etc/default/tar**.

The options are as follows:

-c Create a new archive; writing begins at the beginning of the archive, instead of after the last file.

-r The named *files* are written on the end of an existing archive.

-t The names and other information for the specified files are listed each time they occur on the archive. The listing is similar to the format produced by the **ls -l** command. [See **ls**(1).] If no *files* argument is given, all the names in the archive are listed.

-u The named *files* are added to the archive if they are not already there, or have been modified since last written on that archive.

-x The named *files* are extracted from the archive. If a named file matches a directory whose contents have been written onto the archive, this directory is (recursively) extracted. Use the file or directory's relative path when appropriate, or **tar** will not find a match. The owner, modification time, and mode are restored (if possible). If no *files* argument is given, the entire contents of the archive are extracted.

The modifiers below may be used in the order shown in the synopsis.

num This modifier allows you to specify, via the file **/etc/default/tar**, the device to be used for creating or extracting an archive. Specify a number 0 through 9 as the value of *num*. **tar** looks for the **''archive***num*=**''** entry in **/etc/default/tar** and uses the device name specified there. By default (that is, if you specify neither **-f** nor *num* on the command line), **tar** looks for the **''archive=''** entry.

In addition to the device name, an entry in **/etc/default/tar** specifies the blocking factor and the volume size to be used for that device. For example, the default device entry in **/etc/default/tar** might look like:

```
archive=/dev/rdsk/f05ht 15 1200
```

where **15** is the blocking factor and **1200** is the volume size (in kilobytes).

v Normally, **tar** does its work silently. The **v** (verbose) modifier causes it to print the name of each file it treats, preceded by the option. With the **-t** option, **v** gives more information about the archive entries than just the name.

w This modifier causes **tar** to print the action to be taken, followed by the name of the file, and then wait for your confirmation. If a word beginning with **y** is given, the action is performed. Any other input means no. This is not valid with the **-t** option.

f This causes **tar** to use the *device* argument as the name of the archive instead of the default. If the name of the file is **-**, **tar** writes to the standard output or reads from the standard input, whichever is appropriate. Thus, **tar** can be used as the head or tail of a pipeline. **tar** can also be used to move hierarchies with the command:

cd *fromdir*; **tar cf - . | (cd** *todir*; **tar xf -)**

b This modifier causes **tar** to use the *block* argument as the blocking factor for archive records. The default is 20. This modifier should not be supplied when operating on regular archives or block special devices. It is mandatory however, when reading archives on raw magnetic tape archives (see **f** above). The blocking factor is determined automatically when reading tapes created on block special devices (options **x** and **t**).

l This modifier causes **tar** to complain if it cannot resolve all of the links to the files being dumped. If the **l** modifier is not specified, no error messages are printed.

m This modifier causes **tar** to not restore the modification times. The modification time of the file will be the time of extraction.

o This modifier causes extracted files to take on the user and group identifier of the user running the program, rather than those on tape. This is valid only with the **-x** option.

L Follow symbolic links. This modifier causes symbolic links to be followed. By default, symbolic links are not followed.

k This modifier, which must be used with multi-volume archives, uses the *volsize* argument as the size, in kilobytes per volume, for non-tape devices (such as floppy drives). The argument to **-k** should be a multiple of the blocking factor; if it isn't, **tar** will round it down to the nearest such multiple. A value of **0** for *volsize* causes multi-volume mode to be disabled (interpreted as an infinite volume size). This modifier may be used with the **-c**, **-r**, and **-u** options.

When restoring from a multi-volume archive, **tar** prompts for a new volume only if a split file has been partially restored. Otherwise **tar** exits at the end of the volume. If this happens, run the **tar** command again for the next volume.

F This modifier uses the *incfile* argument as a file containing a list of named files (or directories) to be included in the archive. This modifier may only be used with the **-c**, **-r**, and **-u** options. This modifier may not be used with the **X** modifier.

X This modifier uses the *excfile* argument as a file containing a list of named files (or directories) to be excluded. This modifier may not be used with the **F** modifier.

h This modifier causes **tar** to follow symbolic links as if they were normal files or directories. Normally **tar** does not follow symbolic links. The **h** modifier may be used with the **-c**, **-r**, and **-u** options.

p This modifier restores the named *file* arguments to their original modes, ignoring the present value returned by **umask**. [See **umask**(2).] **setuid** and sticky bit information are also restored if the effective user ID is root. This modifier may only be used with the **-x** option.

i This modifier causes **tar** to ignore directory checksum errors.

e This modifier causes **tar** to quit when certain minor errors are encountered. Otherwise **tar** will continue when minor errors are encountered.

n This modifier must be used when *device* is not a tape device.

A This modifier causes absolute pathnames for files to be suppressed, and may be used with the **-r**, **-c**, **-u**, and **-x** options. This causes all pathnames to be interpreted as relative to the current working directory.

EXAMPLES

If you set the **TAPE** environment variable to **/dev/rmt/ctape1n** and run the command **tar -cf /dev/rmt/ctape1**, the default device used will be **/dev/rmt/ctape1**.

If you set the **TAPE** environment variable to **/dev/rmt/ctape1n** and run the command **tar -c0h**, the device used will be **/dev/rmt/ctape1n** rather than the **0** entry of **/etc/default/tar**.

FILES

`/etc/default/tar`

`/tmp/tar*`

`/usr/lib/locale/`*locale***`/LC_MESSAGES/uxcore`** language-specific message file [See **LANG** on **environ**(5).]

SEE ALSO

ar(1), **cpio**(1), **ls**(1), **umask**(2)

DIAGNOSTICS

Complains about tape read/write errors.
Complains if insufficient memory is available to hold the link tables.

NOTES

There is no way to ask for the *n*-th occurrence of a file.

The **-b** modifier should not be used with archives that are going to be updated. The current magnetic tape driver cannot backspace raw magnetic tape. If the archive is on a disk file, the **-b** modifier should not be used at all, because updating an archive stored on disk can destroy it.

The current limit on file name length is 100 characters.

Because **cpio** can recognize archives that have been formatted with **tar**, it can be used as an alternative command for reading **tar** archives.

On a pre-Release 4 system, you cannot restore archives of directories, subdirectories, or files within directories that have been created with UNIX System V Release 4 **tar**. (That is, only files at the level of the current directory can be restored.) If you try to do so, you will get error messages saying files cannot be created.

NAME

tbl – (BSD) format tables for **nroff** or **troff**

SYNOPSIS

/usr/ucb/tbl [**-me**] [**-ms**] [**-TX**] [*file*] . . .

DESCRIPTION

The **tbl** command is a preprocessor for formatting tables for **nroff** or **troff**. The input *files* are copied to the standard output, except that lines between **.TS** and **.TE** command lines are assumed to describe tables and are reformatted.

If no arguments are given, **tbl** reads the standard input, so **tbl** may be used as a filter. When **tbl** is used with **eqn** or **neqn** the **tbl** command should be first, to minimize the volume of data passed through pipes.

-me This option copies the **-me** macro package to the front of the output file.

-ms This option copies the **-ms** macro package to the front of the output file.

-TX This option produces output that does not have fractional line motions in it.

Options

The following options must be placed immediately after the .TS line. Each option must be separated by a space, tab or comma and must end with a semicolon.

center centers the table (default is left-justified)

expand makes the table as wide as current line length

box encloses the table in a box

allbox encloses each data entry of the table in a box

tab(*x*) separates data entries by using *x* instead of tab

Format

The format section of the table specifies the layout of the columns. Each line in the format section corresponds to one line of table data except the last line, which corresponds to all succeeding data lines. Each line contains a key-letter for each column of the table. A dot (**.**) indicates the end of key letters.

l specifies a left-justified column entry

r specifies a right-justified column entry

c specifies a centered column entry

n specifies a numerical column entry

s specifies a spanned heading

w(*n*) **w** following a key-letter specifies a column width

EXAMPLE

Data entries are usually separated by pressing the TAB key, but in the following examples, a colon (**:**) is used as the tab character.

Input

```
.TS
center tab(:);
c s s
c c s
c c c
l n n.
Household Population
Town:Households
:Number:Size
Bedminster:789:3.26
Bernards Twp.:3087:3.74
Bernardsville:2018:3.30
.TE
```

Output

Household Population		
Town	Households	
	Number	Size
Bedminster	789	3.26
Bernards Twp.	3087	3.74
Bernardsville	2018	3.30

To include a block of text as a data entry, precede it by **T{** and follow it by **T}** as in the following example:

Input

```
.TS
center allbox tab(:);
c s s
c c c
l lw(1.5i) lw(1.5i).
New York Area Rocks
Era:Formation:Age (years)
Mesozoic:T{
Newark Basin, including
Stockton, Lockatong, and
Brunswick formations; also
Watchungs and Palisades.
T}:200 million
Cenozoic:Coastal Plain:T{
On Long Island 30,000 years;
Cretaceous sediments redeposited
by recent glaciation.
T}
.TE
```

Output

New York Area Rocks		
Era	Formation	Age (years)
Mesozoic	Newark Basin, including Stockton, Lockatong, and Brunswick formations; also Watchungs and Palisades.	200 million
Cenozoic	Coastal Plain	On Long Island 30,000 years; Cretaceous sediments redeposited by recent glaciation.

SEE ALSO

eqn(1), **nroff**(1), **troff**(1)

NAME

tee – pipe fitting

SYNOPSIS

tee [**-i**] [**-a**] [*file*] . . .

DESCRIPTION

tee transcribes the standard input to the standard output and makes copies in the *files*. The sole purpose of **tee** is to serve, as its name implies, as a ''T'' in a pipe. For example, the command

grep *pattern file1* **|** **tee** *file2* **|** **wc -l**

catches the output of **grep** in *file2* without having to reexecute the command.

The available options are:

-i ignore interrupts;

-a causes the output to be appended to the *files* rather than overwriting them.

FILES

/usr/lib/locale/*locale***/LC_MESSAGES/uxcore.abi**
language-specific message file [See **LANG** on **environ** (5).]

telnet(1)

NAME

telnet – user interface to a remote system using the TELNET protocol

SYNOPSIS

telnet [*host* [*port*]]

DESCRIPTION

telnet communicates with another host using the TELNET protocol. If **telnet** is invoked without arguments, it enters command mode, indicated by its prompt **telnet>**. In this mode, it accepts and executes the commands listed below. If it is invoked with arguments, it performs an **open** command (see "Telnet Commands" below) with those arguments.

Once a connection has been opened, **telnet** enters input mode. In this mode, text typed is sent to the remote host. The input mode entered will be either character at a time or line by line depending on what the remote system supports.

In character at a time mode, most text typed is immediately sent to the remote host for processing.

In line by line mode, all text is echoed locally, and (normally) only completed lines are sent to the remote host. The local echo character (initially **^E**) may be used to turn off and on the local echo (this would mostly be used to enter passwords without the password being echoed).

In either mode, if the *localchars* toggle is TRUE (the default in line mode; see below), the user's **quit**, **intr**, and **flush** characters are trapped locally, and sent as TELNET protocol sequences to the remote side. There are options (see **toggle**, **autoflush**, and **toggle**, **autosynch**) which cause this action to flush subsequent output to the terminal (until the remote host acknowledges the TELNET sequence) and flush previous terminal input (in the case of **quit** and **intr**).

While connected to a remote host, **telnet** command mode may be entered by typing the **telnet** escape character (initially **^]**). When in command mode, the normal terminal editing conventions are available.

USAGE

Telnet Commands

The following commands are available. Only enough of each command to uniquely identify it need be typed (this is also true for arguments to the **mode**, **set**, **toggle**, and **display** commands).

open *host* [*port*]
: Open a connection to the named host. If no port number is specified, **telnet** will attempt to contact a TELNET server at the default port. The host specification may be either a host name [see **hosts**(4)] or an Internet address specified in the dot notation [see **inet**(7)].

close
: Close any open TELNET session and exit **telnet**. An EOF (in command mode) will also close a session and exit.

quit
: Same as **close**, above.

z Suspend **telnet**. This command only works when the user is using a shell that supports job control, such as **sh**(1).

mode *type* *type* is either **line** (for line by line mode) or *character* (for character at a time mode). The remote host is asked for permission to go into the requested mode. If the remote host is capable of entering that mode, the requested mode will be entered.

status Show the current status of **telnet**. This includes the peer one is connected to, as well as the current mode.

display [*argument*. . .]
Display all, or some, of the **set** and **toggle** values (see **toggle**, *arguments*).

? [*command*]
Get help. With no arguments, **telnet** print a help summary. If a command is specified, **telnet** will print the help information for just that command.

send *arguments*
Send one or more special character sequences to the remote host. The following are the arguments which may be specified (more than one argument may be specified at a time):

escape Send the current **telnet** escape character (initially **^]**).

synch Send the TELNET **SYNCH** sequence. This sequence discards all previously typed (but not yet read) input on the remote system. This sequence is sent as TCP urgent data (and may not work if the remote system is a 4.2 BSD system — if it does not work, a lower case r may be echoed on the terminal).

brk Send the TELNET **BRK** (Break) sequence, which may have significance to the remote system.

ip Send the TELNET **IP** (Interrupt Process) sequence, which aborts the currently running process on the remote system.

ao Sends the TELNET **AO** (Abort Output) sequence, which flushes all output **from** the remote system **to** the user's terminal.

ayt Sends the TELNET **AYT** (Are You There) sequence, to which the remote system may or may not choose to respond.

ec Sends the TELNET **EC** (Erase Character) sequence, which erases the last character entered.

el Sends the TELNET **EL** (Erase Line) sequence, which should cause the remote system to erase the line currently being entered.

ga Sends the TELNET **GA** (Go Ahead) sequence, which likely has no significance to the remote system.

nop Sends the TELNET **NOP** (No Operation) sequence.

? Prints out help information for the **send** command.

set *argument value*

Set any one of a number of **telnet** variables to a specific value. The special value off turns off the function associated with the variable. The values of variables may be interrogated with the **display** command. The variables which may be specified are:

echo This is the value (initially **^E**) which, when in line by line mode, toggles between doing local echoing of entered characters (for normal processing), and suppressing echoing of entered characters (for example, entering a password).

escape This is the **telnet** escape character (initially **^]**) which enters **telnet** command mode (when connected to a remote system).

interrupt

If **telnet** is in **localchars** mode (see **toggle localchars**) and the **interrupt** character is typed, a TELNET **IP** sequence (see **send** and **ip**) is sent to the remote host. The initial value for the interrupt character is taken to be the terminal's **intr** character.

quit If **telnet** is in **localchars** mode (see **toggle localchars**) and the **quit** character is typed, a TELNET **BRK** sequence (see **send**, **brk**) is sent to the remote host. The initial value for the quit character is taken to be the terminal's **quit** character.

flushoutput

If **telnet** is in **localchars** mode (see **toggle localchars**) and the **flushoutput** character is typed, a TELNET **AO** sequence (see **send**, **ao**) is sent to the remote host. The initial value for the flush character is taken to be the terminal's **flush** character.

erase If **telnet** is in **localchars** mode (see **toggle localchars**), **and** if **telnet** is operating in character at a time mode, then when this character is typed, a TELNET **EC** sequence (see **send**, **ec**) is sent to the remote system. The initial value for the erase character is taken to be the terminal's **erase** character.

kill If **telnet** is in **localchars** mode (see **toggle localchars**), **and** if **telnet** is operating in character at a time mode, then when this character is typed, a TELNET **EL** sequence (see **send**, **el**) is sent to the remote system. The initial value for the kill character is taken to be the terminal's **kill** character.

eof If **telnet** is operating in line by line mode, entering this character as the first character on a line sends this character to the remote system. The initial value of the eof character is taken to be the terminal's **eof** character.

toggle *arguments...*

Toggle (between TRUE and FALSE) various flags that control how **telnet** responds to events. More than one argument may be specified. The state of these flags may be interrogated with the **display** command. Valid arguments are:

autoflush

If **autoflush** and **localchars** are both TRUE, then when the **ao**, **intr**, or **quit** characters are recognized (and transformed into

TELNET sequences; see **set** for details), **telnet** refuses to display any data on the user's terminal until the remote system acknowledges (using a TELNET **Timing Mark** option) that it has processed those TELNET sequences. The initial value for this toggle is TRUE if the terminal user had not done an stty noflsh, otherwise FALSE [see **stty**(1)].

autosynch

If **autosynch** and **localchars** are both TRUE, then when either the **intr** or *quit* characters are typed (see **set** for descriptions of the **intr** and **quit** characters), the resulting TELNET sequence sent is followed by the TELNET **SYNCH** sequence. This procedure **should** cause the remote system to begin throwing away all previously typed input until both of the TELNET sequences have been read and acted upon. The initial value of this toggle is FALSE.

crmod Toggle RETURN mode. When this mode is enabled, most RETURN characters received from the remote host will be mapped into a RETURN followed by a line feed. This mode does not affect those characters typed by the user, only those received from the remote host. This mode is not very useful unless the remote host only sends RETURN, but never LINEFEED. The initial value for this toggle is FALSE.

debug Toggle socket level debugging (useful only to the super-user). The initial value for this toggle is FALSE .

localchars

If this is TRUE , then the **flush**, **interrupt**, **quit**, **erase**, and **kill** characters (see **set**) are recognized locally, and transformed into appropriate TELNET control sequences (respectively **ao**, **ip**, **brk**, **ec**, and **el**; see **send**). The initial value for this toggle is TRUE in line by line mode, and FALSE in character at a time mode.

netdata Toggle the display of all network data (in hexadecimal format). The initial value for this toggle is FALSE.

`options`	Toggle the display of some internal **telnet** protocol processing (having to do with TELNET options). The initial value for this toggle is FALSE.
`?`	Display the legal **toggle** commands.

SEE ALSO

rlogin(1), **sh**(1), **stty**(1), **hosts**(4), **inet**(7)

NOTES

There is no adequate way for dealing with flow control.

On some remote systems, echo has to be turned off manually when in line by line mode.

There is enough settable state to justify a **.telnetrc** file.

In line by line mode, the terminal's EOF character is only recognized (and sent to the remote system) when it is the first character on a line.

NAME

`telnetd` – DARPA TELNET protocol server

SYNOPSIS

in.telnetd

DESCRIPTION

telnetd is a server which supports the DARPA standard TELNET virtual terminal protocol. **telnetd** is invoked by the internet server [see **inetd**(1M)], normally for requests to connect to the TELNET port as indicated by the **/etc/services** file [see **services**(4)].

telnetd operates by allocating a pseudo-terminal device for a client, then creating a login process which has the slave side of the pseudo-terminal as its standard input, output, and error. The login process is an instance of the **in.login** program, which is based on **login**(1). It is invoked with the **-H** option to indicate that it is originated by **telnetd**. **telnetd** manipulates the master side of the pseudo-terminal, implementing the TELNET protocol and passing characters between the remote client and the login process.

When a **TELNET** session is started up, **telnetd** sends TELNET options to the client side indicating a willingness to do *remote echo* of characters, to *suppress go ahead*, and to receive *terminal type information* from the remote client. If the remote client is willing, the remote terminal type is propagated in the environment of the created login process. The pseudo-terminal allocated to the client is configured to operate in cooked mode, and with **XTABS**, **ICRNL**, and **ONLCR** enabled [see **termio**(7)].

telnetd is willing to do: *echo*, *binary*, *suppress go ahead*, and *timing mark*.
telnetd is willing to have the remote client do: *binary*, *terminal type*, and *suppress go ahead*.

SEE ALSO

telnet(1)

Postel, Jon, and Joyce Reynolds, "Telnet Protocol Specification," RFC 854, Network Information Center, SRI International, Menlo Park, Calif., May 1983.

NOTES

Some TELNET commands are only partially implemented.

The TELNET protocol allows for the exchange of the number of lines and columns on the user's terminal, but **telnetd** doesn't make use of them.

Binary mode has no common interpretation except between similar operating systems

The terminal type name received from the remote client is converted to lower case.

The *packet* interface to the pseudo-terminal should be used for more intelligent flushing of input and output queues.

telnetd never sends TELNET *go ahead* commands. **telnetd** can only support 64 pseudo-terminals.

test (1F)

NAME

`test` – condition evaluation command

SYNOPSIS

`test` *expr*
`[`*expr*`]`

DESCRIPTION

`test` evaluates the expression *expr* and if its value is true, sets a zero (**`TRUE`**) exit status; otherwise, a non-zero (**`FALSE`**) exit status is set; `test` also sets a non-zero exit status if there are no arguments. When permissions are tested, the effective user ID of the process is used.

All operators, flags, and brackets (brackets used as shown in the second SYNOPSIS line) must be separate arguments to `test`. Normally these items are separated by spaces.

The following primitives are used to construct *expr*:

`-r` *file*	true if *file* exists and is readable.
`-w` *file*	true if *file* exists and is writable.
`-x` *file*	true if *file* exists and is executable.
`-f` *file*	true if *file* exists and is a regular file.
`-d` *file*	true if *file* exists and is a directory.
`-c` *file*	true if *file* exists and is a character special file.
`-b` *file*	true if *file* exists and is a block special file.
`-p` *file*	true if *file* exists and is a named pipe (fifo).
`-u` *file*	true if *file* exists and its set-user-ID bit is set.
`-g` *file*	true if *file* exists and its set-group-ID bit is set.
`-k` *file*	true if *file* exists and its sticky bit is set.
`-s` *file*	true if *file* exists and has a size greater than zero.
`-t` [*fildes*]	true if the open file whose file descriptor number is *fildes* (1 by default) is associated with a terminal device.
`-z` *s1*	true if the length of string *s1* is zero.
`-n` *s1*	true if the length of the string *s1* is non-zero.
s1 = *s2*	true if strings *s1* and *s2* are identical.
s1 `!=` *s2*	true if strings *s1* and *s2* are *not* identical.
s1	true if *s1* is *not* the null string.
n1 `-eq` *n2*	true if the integers *n1* and *n2* are algebraically equal. Any of the comparisons `-ne`, `-gt`, `-ge`, `-lt`, and `-le` may be used in place of `-eq`.

These primaries may be combined with the following operators:

!	unary negation operator.
-a	binary **and** operator.
-o	binary **or** operator (**-a** has higher precedence than **-o**).
\`( *expr* )\`	parentheses for grouping. Notice also that parentheses are meaningful to the shell and, therefore, must be quoted.

NOTES

If you test a file you own (the **-r**, **-w** , or **-x** tests), but the permission tested does not have the *owner* bit set, a non-zero (false) exit status will be returned even though the file may have the *group* or *other* bit set for that permission. The correct exit status will be set if you are super-user.

The = and **!=** operators have a higher precedence than the **-r** through **-n** operators, and = and **!=** always expect arguments; therefore, = and **!=** cannot be used with the **-r** through **-n** operators.

If more than one argument follows the **-r** through **-n** operators, only the first argument is examined; the others are ignored, unless a **-a** or a **-o** is the second argument.

SEE ALSO

find(1), **sh**(1)

NAME

test – condition evaluation command

SYNOPSIS

test *expr*
[*expr* **]**

DESCRIPTION

test evaluates the expression *expr* and, if its value is true, sets a zero (true) exit status; otherwise, a non-zero (false) exit status is set; **test** also sets a non-zero exit status if there are no arguments. When permissions are tested, the effective user ID of the process is used. **test** processes supplementary code set characters in *expr* according to the locale specified in the **LC_CTYPE** environment variable [see **LANG** on **environ**(5)].

All operators, flags, and brackets (brackets used as shown in the second SYNOPSIS line) must be separate arguments to the **test** command; normally these items are separated by spaces.

The following primitives are used to construct *expr*:

-r *file*	true if *file* exists and is readable.
-w *file*	true if *file* exists and is writable.
-x *file*	true if *file* exists and is executable.
-f *file*	true if *file* exists and is a regular file. Alternatively, if **/usr/bin/sh** users specify **/usr/ucb** before **/usr/bin** in their **PATH** environment variable, then **test** will return true if *file* exists and is not a directory. This is also the default for **/usr/bin/csh** users.
-d *file*	true if *file* exists and is a directory.
-h *file*	true if *file* exists and is a symbolic link. With all other primitives (except **-L** *file*), the symbolic links are followed by default.
-c *file*	true if *file* exists and is a character special file.
-b *file*	true if *file* exists and is a block special file.
-p *file*	true if *file* exists and is a named pipe (fifo).
-u *file*	true if *file* exists and its set-user-ID bit is set.
-g *file*	true if *file* exists and its set-group-ID bit is set.
-k *file*	true if *file* exists and its sticky bit is set.
-s *file*	true if *file* exists and has a size greater than zero.
-t [*fildes*]	true if the open file whose file descriptor number is *fildes* (1 by default) is associated with a terminal device.
-z *s1*	true if the length of string *s1* is zero.
-n *s1*	true if the length of the string *s1* is non-zero.
s1 **=** *s2*	true if strings *s1* and *s2* are identical.

s1 **!=** *s2*	true if strings *s1* and *s2* are *not* identical.
s1	true if *s1* is *not* the null string.
n1 **-eq** *n2*	true if the integers *n1* and *n2* are algebraically equal. Any of the comparisons **-ne**, **-gt**, **-ge**, **-lt**, and **-le** may be used in place of **-eq**.
-L *file*	true if *file* exists and is a symbolic link. With all other primitives (except **-h** *file*), the symbolic links are followed by default.

These primaries may be combined with the following operators:

!	unary negation operator.
-a	binary *and* operator.
-o	binary *or* operator (**-a** has higher precedence than **-o**).
(*expr*)	parentheses for grouping. Notice also that parentheses are meaningful to the shell and, therefore, must be quoted.

FILES

/usr/lib/locale/*locale***/LC_MESSAGES/uxcore.abi**
language-specific message file [See **LANG** on **environ** (5).]

SEE ALSO

find(1), **sh**(1)

NOTES

The not-a-directory alternative to the **-f** option is a transition aid for applications and may not be supported in future releases.

The **-L** option is a migration aid for users of other shells which have similar options and may not be supported in future releases.

If you test a file you own (the **-r**, **-w**, or **-x** tests), but the permission tested does not have the *owner* bit set, a non-zero (false) exit status will be returned even though the file may have the **group** or *other* bit set for that permission. The correct exit status will be set if you are a privileged user.

The = and **!=** operators have a higher precedence than the **-r** through **-n** operators, and = and **!=** always expect arguments; therefore, = and **!=** cannot be used with the **-r** through **-n** operators.

If more than one argument follows the **-r** through **-n** operators, only the first argument is examined; the others are ignored, unless a **-a** or a **-o** is the second argument.

NAME

test – (BSD) condition evaluation command

SYNOPSIS

/usr/ucb/test *expr*
[*expr* **]**

DESCRIPTION

test evaluates the expression *expr* and, if its value is true, sets a zero (true) exit status; otherwise, a non-zero (false) exit status is set; *test* also sets a non-zero exit status if there are no arguments. When permissions are tested, the effective user ID of the process is used.

All operators, flags, and brackets (brackets used as shown in the second SYNOPSIS line) must be separate arguments to the *test* command; normally these items are separated by spaces.

The following primitives are used to construct *expr*:

-r *file*	true if *file* exists and is readable.
-w *file*	true if *file* exists and is writable.
-x *file*	true if *file* exists and is executable.
-f *file*	true if *file* exists and is a regular file. Alternatively, if **/usr/bin/sh** users specify **/usr/ucb** before **/usr/bin** in their PATH environment variable, then *test* will return true if *file* exists and is (**not-a-directory**). This is also the default for **/usr/bin/csh** users.
-d *file*	true if *file* exists and is a directory.
-c *file*	true if *file* exists and is a character special file.
-b *file*	true if *file* exists and is a block special file.
-p *file*	true if *file* exists and is a named pipe (fifo).
-u *file*	true if *file* exists and its set-user-ID bit is set.
-g *file*	true if *file* exists and its set-group-ID bit is set.
-k *file*	true if *file* exists and its sticky bit is set.
-s *file*	true if *file* exists and has a size greater than zero.
-t [*fildes*]	true if the open file whose file descriptor number is *fildes* (1 by default) is associated with a terminal device.
-z *s1*	true if the length of string *s1* is zero.
-n *s1*	true if the length of the string *s1* is non-zero.
s1 **=** *s2*	true if strings *s1* and *s2* are identical.
s1 **!=** *s2*	true if strings *s1* and *s2* are *not* identical.
s1	true if *s1* is *not* the null string.
n1 **-eq** *n2*	true if the integers *n1* and *n2* are algebraically equal. Any of the comparisons **-ne**, **-gt**, **-ge**, **-lt**, and **-le** may be used in place of **-eq**.

-L*file* true if **file** exists and is a symbolic link. With all other primitives, the symbolic links are followed by default.

These primaries may be combined with the following operators:

! unary negation operator.

-a binary *and* operator.

-o binary *or* operator (**-a** has higher precedence than **-o**).

(*expr* **)** parentheses for grouping. Notice also that parentheses are meaningful to the shell and, therefore, must be quoted.

SEE ALSO

find(1), **sh**(1)

NOTES

The 'not–a–directory' alternative to the **-f** option is a transition aid for BSD applications and may not be supported in future releases.

The **-L** option is a migration aid for users of other shells which have similar options and may not be supported in future releases.

If you test a file you own (the *-r*, *-w*, or *-x* tests), but the permission tested does not have the *owner* bit set, a non-zero (false) exit status will be returned even though the file may have the *group* or *other* bit set for that permission. The correct exit status will be set if you are super-user.

The **=** and **!=** operators have a higher precedence than the **-r** through **-n** operators, and **=** and **!=** always expect arguments; therefore, **=** and **!=** cannot be used with the **-r** through **-n** operators.

If more than one argument follows the **-r** through **-n** operators, only the first argument is examined; the others are ignored, unless a **-a** or a **-o** is the second argument.

tfadmin (1M)

NAME

tfadmin –invoke a command, regulating privilege based on TFM database information

SYNOPSIS

tfadmin [*role***:**] *cmd* [*args*]
tfadmin -t [*role***:**] *cmd*[**:***priv*[**:***priv*. . .]]
tfadmin

DESCRIPTION

The **tfadmin** command invokes a command at the request of an administrative user. If the user is allowed to use privileges with the command, **tfadmin** places the allowed privileges in the maximum and working privilege sets of the process before invoking the command.

role is a role name defined in the administrative database for Trusted Facility Management.

cmd can be either a command defined in the TFM database or it can be the full pathname of a command. The executable file associated with *cmd* will be executed only if the user has been defined as an administrator and has access to *cmd*. If *cmd* is a full pathname, the last component of the pathname (the basename) will be searched for in the TFM database. If *cmd* or the basename does not exist in the user definition, **tfadmin** issues an error and exits with an error code. If the path associated with *cmd* in the administrative database is not equal to the full pathname specified for *cmd*, **tfadmin** issues a diagnostic message.

args are a set of command arguments to be passed to the program indicated by *cmd*.

priv is the name of a process privilege. (See **intro**(2) for a complete list of process privileges.)

In addition, if the **-t** option is used, a privilege vector, consisting of one or more privilege names separated by colons (e.g., **macread:mount**) may be appended to the role-command pair, separated from it by a colon (for example, **SSA:mount:macread:mount**). This privilege list is meaningful only when the **-t** option is used, because it is used to test whether the given command can be executed by the invoking user with the specified privileges.

The **tfadmin** command takes the following options:

-t Test whether the user can invoke the given command with the (optionally) given privileges. Do not execute the command.

No options
Execute the specified command for the invoking user taking the definition from the *role* argument (if supplied). If the *role* does not exist in that user's role list, print a message and fail.

SEE ALSO

adminuser(1M), **adminrole**(1M), **intro**(2)

DIAGNOSTICS

If the requested operation succeeds, **tfadmin** executes the command, and, therefore, does not exit. The invoked command exits with whatever value is appropriate. If the **-t** option is used and the requested privileges would have been granted to the user invoking the requested command within the requested role, **tfadmin** exits with a 0. If the operation fails, or the -t option was specified and **tfadmin** would have denied the request, **tfadmin** exits with a 1.

The following diagnostic messages are printed by **tfadmin**:

cannot execute program file: *''path''*

undefined command name *''cmd''*

user not allowed

cannot set up maximum privilege set

full path to TFM database must be specified

TFM database does not exist

improper command name: *''string''*

invalid process privilege: *''string''*

unrecognized privilege number: *''number''*

NAME

`tftp` – trivial file transfer program

SYNOPSIS

`tftp` [*host*]

DESCRIPTION

`tftp` is the user interface to the Internet TFTP (Trivial File Transfer Protocol), which allows users to transfer files to and from a remote machine. The remote *host* may be specified on the command line, in which case `tftp` uses *host* as the default host for future transfers (see the `connect` command below).

USAGE

Commands

Once `tftp` is running, it issues the prompt `tftp>` and recognizes the following commands:

`connect` *host-name* [*port*]
: Set the *host* (and optionally *port*) for transfers. The TFTP protocol, unlike the FTP protocol, does not maintain connections between transfers; thus, the `connect` command does not actually create a connection, but merely remembers what host is to be used for transfers. You do not have to use the `connect` command; the remote host can be specified as part of the `get` or `put` commands.

`mode` *transfer-mode*
: Set the mode for transfers; *transfer-mode* may be one of `ascii` or `binary`. The default is `ascii`.

`put` *filename*
`put` *localfile remotefile*
`put` *filename1 filename2 ... filenameN remote-directory*
: Transfer a file, or a set of files, to the specified remote file or directory. The destination can be in one of two forms: a filename on the remote host if the host has already been specified, or a string of the form

host`:`*filename*

to specify both a host and filename at the same time. If the latter form is used, the specified host becomes the default for future transfers. If the remote-directory form is used, the remote host is assumed to be running the UNIX system.

`get` *filename*
`get` *remotename localname*
`get` *filename1 filename2 filename3 ... filenameN*
: Get a file or set of files (three or more) from the specified remote *sources*. *source* can be in one of two forms: a filename on the remote host if the host has already been specified, or a string of the form

host`:`*filename*

to specify both a host and filename at the same time. If the latter form is used, the last host specified becomes the default for future transfers.

quit Exit **tftp**. An EOF also exits.

verbose Toggle verbose mode.

trace Toggle packet tracing.

status Show current status.

rexmt *retransmission-timeout*
Set the per-packet retransmission timeout, in seconds.

timeout *total-transmission-timeout*
Set the total transmission timeout, in seconds.

ascii Shorthand for **mode ascii**.

binary Shorthand for **mode binary**.

? [*command-name* **. . .]**
Print help information.

NOTES

Because there is no user-login or validation within the TFTP protocol, many remote sites restrict file access in various ways. Approved methods for file access are specific to each site, and therefore cannot be documented here.

When using the **get** command to transfer multiple files from a remote host, three or more files must be specified. The command returns an error message if only two files are specified.

tftpd (1M)

NAME

tftpd – DARPA Trivial File Transfer Protocol server

SYNOPSIS

in.tftpd [**-s**] [*homedir*]

DESCRIPTION

tftpd is a server that supports the DARPA Trivial File Transfer Protocol (TFTP). This server is normally started by **inetd**(1M) and operates at the port indicated in the **tftp** Internet service description in the **/etc/inetd.conf** file. By default, the entry for **tftpd** in **etc/inetd.conf** is commented out. To make **tftpd** operational, the comment character(s) must be deleted from the **tftpd** entry. See **inetd.conf**(4) for details.

Before responding to a request, the server attempts to change its current directory to *homedir*; the default value is **/tftpboot**.

OPTIONS

-s Secure. When specified, the directory change must succeed; and the daemon also changes its root directory to *homedir*.

The use of **tftp** does not require an account or password on the remote system. Due to the lack of authentication information, **tftp** will allow only publicly readable files to be accessed. Files may be written only if they already exist and are publicly writable. Note that this extends the concept of public to include all users on all hosts that can be reached through the network; this may not be appropriate on all systems, and its implications should be considered before enabling this service.

tftpd runs with the user ID and group ID set to [GU]ID_NOBODY. **-2**, under the assumption that no files exist with that owner or group. However, nothing checks this assumption or enforces this restriction.

SEE ALSO

inetd(1M), **netconfig**(4), **tftp**(1)

Sollins, K.R., *The TFTP Protocol (Revision 2)*, RFC 783, Network Information Center, SRI International, Menlo Park, Calif., June 1981

NAME

`tic` – *terminfo* compiler

SYNOPSIS

`tic` [`-v`[*n*]] [`-c`] *file*

DESCRIPTION

The command **`tic`** translates a **`terminfo`** file from the source format into the compiled format. The results are placed in the directory **`/usr/share/lib/terminfo`**. The compiled format is necessary for use with the library routines in **`curses`**(3curses).

`-v`*n* specifies that (verbose) output be written to standard error trace information showing **`tic`**'s progress. The optional integer *n* is a number from 1 to 10, inclusive, indicating the desired level of detail of information. If *n* is omitted, the default level is 1. If *n* is specified and greater than 1, the level of detail is increased.

`-c` specifies to check only *file* for errors. Errors in **`use=`** links are not detected.

file contains one or more **`terminfo`** terminal descriptions in source format [see **`terminfo`**(4)]. Each description in the file describes the capabilities of a particular terminal. When a **`use=`***entry-name* field is discovered in a terminal entry currently being compiled, **`tic`** reads in the binary from **`/usr/share/lib/terminfo`** to complete the entry. (Entries created from *file* will be used first. If the environment variable **`TERMINFO`** is set, that directory is searched instead of **`/usr/share/lib/terminfo`**.) **`tic`** duplicates the capabilities in *entry-name* for the current entry, with the exception of those capabilities that explicitly are defined in the current entry.

If the environment variable **`TERMINFO`** is set, the compiled results are placed there instead of **`/usr/share/lib/terminfo`**.

Total compiled entries cannot exceed 4096 bytes. The name field cannot exceed 128 bytes. Terminal names exceeding 14 characters will be truncated to 14 characters and a warning message will be printed.

International Functions

`tic` can translate a **`terminfo`**(4) file including variables for international functionality from the source format to the compiled format.

`tic` also recognizes the environment variable **`TERMINFO`** with a value that includes characters from the supplementary code sets as the path name for the compiled result.

Entry names in **`terminfo`**(4) files must be in single-byte characters, since the compiled result will be placed in a directory named using the first byte of the entry name.

FILES

`/usr/share/lib/terminfo/?/*` Compiled terminal description database.

SEE ALSO

`curses`(3curses), **`captoinfo`**(1M), **`infocmp`**(1M), **`terminfo`**(4)

NOTES

When an entry, for example, **entry_name_1**, contains a **use=***entry_name_2* field, any canceled capabilities in *entry_name_2* must also appear in **entry_name_1** before **use=** for these capabilities to be canceled in **entry_name_1**.

NAME

time – time a command

SYNOPSIS

time *command*

DESCRIPTION

The *command* is executed; after it is complete, **time** prints the elapsed time during the command, the time spent in the system, and the time spent in execution of the command. Times are reported in seconds.

The times are printed on standard error.

SEE ALSO

time(2), **timex**(1)

NAME

timex – time a command, report process data and system activity

SYNOPSIS

timex [*options*] *command*

DESCRIPTION

The given *command* is executed; the elapsed time, user time and system time spent in execution are reported in seconds. Optionally, process accounting data for the *command* and all its children can be listed or summarized, and total system activity during the execution interval can be reported.

The output of **timex** is written on standard error. **timex** returns an exit status of 1 if it is used incorrectly, if it is unable to fork, or if it could not exec *command*. Otherwise, **timex** returns the exit status of *command*.

The *options* are:

-p List process accounting records for *command* and all its children. This option works only if the process accounting software is installed. Suboption **f**, **h**, **k**, **m**, **r**, and **t** modify the data items reported. The options are as follows:

- **-f** Print the **fork**(2)/**exec**(2) flag and system exit status columns in the output.
- **-h** Instead of mean memory size, show the fraction of total available CPU time consumed by the process during its execution. This "hog factor" is computed as (total CPU time)/(elapsed time).
- **-k** Instead of memory size, show total kcore-minutes.
- **-m** Show mean core size (the default).
- **-r** Show CPU factor (user time/(system-time + user-time).
- **-t** Show separate system and user CPU times. The number of blocks read or written and the number of characters transferred are always reported.

-o Report the total number of blocks read or written and total characters transferred by *command* and all its children. This option works only if the process accounting software is installed.

-s Report total system activity (not just that due to *command*) that occurred during the execution interval of *command*. All the data items listed in **sar**(1M) are reported.

SEE ALSO

sar(1M), **time**(1), **times**(2)

NOTES

Process records associated with *command* are selected from the accounting file **/var/adm/pacct** by inference, since process genealogy is not available. Background processes having the same user ID, terminal ID, and execution time window will be spuriously included.

The **timex** call expects that nightly accounting will restart the **/var/adm/pacct** each day. If accounting is activated, but you do not perform nightly accounting, you should add the line **0 0 * * * > var/adm/pacct** to the adm crontab file, so **timex** can use the accounting options.

EXAMPLES

A simple example:

```
timex -ops sleep 60
```

A terminal session of arbitrary complexity can be measured by timing a sub-shell:

timex -opskmt sh

session commands

EOT

tnamed (1M)

NAME

tnamed, **in.tnamed** – DARPA trivial name server

SYNOPSIS

in.tnamed [-v]

DESCRIPTION

tnamed is a server that supports the DARPA Name Server Protocol. The name server operates at the port indicated in the name service description [see **services**(4)], and is invoked by **inetd**(1M) when a request is made to the name server.

Options

-v Invoke the daemon in verbose mode.

SEE ALSO

inetd(1M), **services**(4), **uucp**(1C)

NOTES

The protocol implemented by this program is obsolete. Its use should be phased out in favor of the Internet Domain Name Service (DNS) protocol. See **named**(1M).

NAME

touch – update access and modification times of a file

SYNOPSIS

touch [-amc] [*mmddhhmm*[*yy*]] *files*

DESCRIPTION

touch causes the access and modification times of each argument to be updated. The file name is created if it does not exist. If no time is specified [see **date**(1)] the current time is used. The **-a** and **-m** options cause touch to update only the access or modification times respectively (default is **-am**). The **-c** option silently prevents **touch** from creating the file if it did not previously exist.

The return code from **touch** is the number of files for which the times could not be successfully modified (including files that did not exist and were not created).

FILES

/usr/lib/locale/*locale***/LC_MESSAGES/uxcore.abi**
language-specific message file [See **LANG** on **environ** (5).]

SEE ALSO

date(1), **utime**(2)

NOTES

Users familiar with the BSD environment will find that the **-f** option is accepted, but ignored. The **-f** option is unnecessary since **touch** will succeed for all files owned by the user regardless of the permissions on the files.

touch assumes that an all numeric entry is a date and so will not update the times for a file when an all numeric filename is specified.

NAME

tput – initialize a terminal or query terminfo database

SYNOPSIS

tput [**-T***type*] *capname* [*parms* . . .]

tput [**-T***type*] **init**

tput [**-T***type*] **reset**

tput [**-T***type*] **longname**

tput -S <<

DESCRIPTION

tput uses the **terminfo** database to make the values of terminal-dependent capabilities and information available to the shell (see **sh**(1)), to initialize or reset the terminal, or return the long name of the requested terminal type. **tput** outputs a string if the attribute (*cap*ability *name*) is of type string, or an integer if the attribute is of type integer. If the attribute is of type boolean, **tput** simply sets the exit code (**0** for TRUE if the terminal has the capability, **1** for FALSE if it does not), and produces no output. Before using a value returned on standard output, the user should test the exit code [**$?**, see **sh**(1)] to be sure it is **0**. (See the EXIT CODES and DIAGNOSTICS sections.) For a complete list of capabilities and the *capname* associated with each, see **terminfo**(4).

-T*type* indicates the *type* of terminal. Normally this option is unnecessary, because the default is taken from the environment variable **TERM**. If **-T** is specified, then the shell variables **LINES** and **COLUMNS** and the layer size will not be referenced.

capname indicates the attribute from the **terminfo** database.

parms If the attribute is a string that takes parameters, the arguments *parms* will be instantiated into the string. An all numeric argument will be passed to the attribute as a number.

-S allows more than one capability per invocation of **tput**. The capabilities must be passed to **tput** from the standard input instead of from the command line (see example). Only one *capname* is allowed per line. The **-S** option changes the meaning of the **0** and **1** boolean and string exit codes (see the EXIT CODES section).

init If the **terminfo** database is present and an entry for the user's terminal exists (see **-T***type*, above), the following will occur: (1) if present, the terminal's initialization strings will be output (**is1**, **is2**, **is3**, **if**, **iprog**), (2) any delays (for example, newline) specified in the entry will be set in the tty driver, (3) tabs expansion will be turned on or off according to the specification in the entry, and (4) if tabs are not expanded, standard tabs will be set (every 8 spaces). If an entry does not contain the information needed for any of the four above activities, that activity will silently be skipped.

reset Instead of putting out initialization strings, the terminal's reset strings will be output if present (**rs1**, **rs2**, **rs3**, **rf**). If the reset strings are not present, but initialization strings are, the initialization strings will be output. Otherwise, **reset** acts identically to **init**.

longname If the **terminfo** database is present and an entry for the user's terminal exists (see **-T***type* above), then the long name of the terminal will be put out. The long name is the last name in the first line of the terminal's description in the **terminfo** database [see **term**(5)].

International Functions

capnames for international functionality can also be specified.

EXAMPLES

tput init Initialize the terminal according to the type of terminal in the environmental variable **TERM**. This command should be included in everyone's .profile after the environmental variable **TERM** has been exported, as illustrated on the **profile**(4) manual page.

tput -T5620 reset
Reset an AT&T 5620 terminal, overriding the type of terminal in the environmental variable **TERM**.

tput cup 0 0
Send the sequence to move the cursor to row 0, column 0 (the upper left corner of the screen, usually known as the "home" cursor position).

tput clear
Echo the clear-screen sequence for the current terminal.

tput cols Print the number of columns for the current terminal.

tput -T450 cols
Print the number of columns for the 450 terminal.

bold='tput smso'
offbold='tput rmso'
Set the shell variables **bold**, to begin stand-out mode sequence, and **offbold**, to end standout mode sequence, for the current terminal. This might be followed by a prompt:

```
echo "${bold}Please type in your name: ${offbold}\c"
```

tput hc Set exit code to indicate if the current terminal is a hardcopy terminal.

tput cup 23 4
Send the sequence to move the cursor to row 23, column 4.

tput longname
Print the long name from the **terminfo** database for the type of terminal specified in the environmental variable **TERM**.

```
tput -S <<!
> clear
> cup 10 10
> bold
> !
```

This example shows **tput** processing several capabilities in one invocation. This example clears the screen, moves the cursor to position 10, 10 and turns on bold (extra bright) mode. The list is terminated by an exclamation mark (**!**) on a line by itself.

FILES

/usr/share/lib/terminfo/?/*
compiled terminal description database

/usr/include/curses.h
curses(3curses) header file

/usr/include/term.h
terminfo header file

/usr/lib/tabset/*
tab settings for some terminals, in a format appropriate to be output to the terminal (escape sequences that set margins and tabs); for more information, see the "Tabs and Initialization" section of **terminfo**(4)

SEE ALSO

clear(1), **profile**(4), **stty**(1), **tabs**(1), **terminfo**(4)

EXIT CODES

If *capname* is of type boolean, a value of **0** is set for TRUE and **1** for FALSE unless the **-S** option is used.

If *capname* is of type string, a value of **0** is set if the *capname* is defined for this terminal *type* (the value of *capname* is returned on standard output); a value of **1** is set if *capname* is not defined for this terminal *type* (a null value is returned on standard output).

If *capname* is of type boolean or string and the **-S** option is used, a value of **0** is returned to indicate that all lines were successful. No indication of which line failed can be given so exit code **1** will never appear. Exit codes **2**, **3**, and **4** retain their usual interpretation.

If *capname* is of type integer, a value of **0** is always set, whether or not *capname* is defined for this terminal *type*. To determine if *capname* is defined for this terminal *type*, the user must test the value of standard output. A value of **-1** means that *capname* is not defined for this terminal *type*.

Any other exit code indicates an error; see the DIAGNOSTICS section.

DIAGNOSTICS

`tput` prints the following error messages and sets the corresponding exit codes.

exit code	error message
`0`	–1 (*capname* is a numeric variable that is not specified in the `terminfo`(4) database for this terminal type, for example, `tput -T450 lines` and `tput -T2621 xmc`)
`1`	no error message is printed, see the **EXIT CODES** section.
`2`	usage error
`3`	unknown terminal *type* or no `terminfo` database
`4`	unknown `terminfo` capability *capname*

NAME

tr – translate characters

SYNOPSIS

tr [**-cds**] [*string1* [*string2*]]

DESCRIPTION

tr copies the standard input to the standard output with substitution or deletion of selected characters. Input characters found in *string1* are mapped into the corresponding characters of *string2*. **tr** processes supplementary code set characters according to the locale specified in the **LC_CTYPE** environment variable [see **LANG** on **environ**(5)]. Searches and translations are performed on characters, not bytes.

Any combination of the options **-cds** may be used:

- **-c** Complements the set of characters in *string1* with respect to the universe of characters whose codes are 001 through 377 octal.
- **-d** Deletes all input characters in *string1*.
- **-s** Squeezes all strings of repeated output characters that are in *string2* to single characters.

The following abbreviation conventions may be used to introduce ranges of characters or repeated characters into the strings:

- `[a-z]` Stands for the string of characters whose ASCII codes run from character **a** to character **z**, inclusive.
- `[a*`*n*`]` Stands for *n* repetitions of **a**. If the first digit of *n* is `0`, *n* is considered octal; otherwise, *n* is taken to be decimal. A zero or missing *n* is taken to be huge; this facility is useful for padding *string2*.

The escape character \ may be used as in the shell to remove special meaning from any character in a string. In addition, \ followed by 1, 2, or 3 octal digits stands for the character whose code is given by those digits. When octal notation with the backslash (\) escape character is used, a backslash is placed before each byte of multibyte characters.

EXAMPLE

The following example creates a list of all the words in *file1* one per line in *file2*, where a word is taken to be a maximal string of alphabetics. The strings are quoted to protect the special characters from interpretation by the shell; 012 is the ASCII code for newline.

```
tr -cs "[A-Z][a-z]" "[\012*]" <file1>file2
```

FILES

/usr/lib/locale/*locale***/LC_MESSAGES/uxcore.abi**
  language-specific message file [See **LANG** on **environ** (5).]

SEE ALSO

ascii(5), **ed**(1), **sh**(1)

NOTES

`tr` will not handle ASCII **NUL** in *string1* or *string2*; it always deletes **NUL** from input.

NAME

`tr` – (BSD) translate characters

SYNOPSIS

`/usr/ucb/tr` [`-cds`] [*string1* [*string2*]]

DESCRIPTION

`tr` copies the standard input to the standard output with substitution or deletion of selected characters. The arguments *string1* and *string2* are considered sets of characters. Any input character found in *string1* is mapped into the character in the corresponding position within *string2*. When *string2* is short, it is padded to the length of *string1* by duplicating its last character.

In either string the notation:

a–b

denotes a range of characters from *a* to *b* in increasing ASCII order. The character `\`, followed by 1, 2 or 3 octal digits stands for the character whose ASCII code is given by those digits. As with the shell, the escape character `\`, followed by any other character, escapes any special meaning for that character.

OPTIONS

Any combination of the options `-c`, `-d`, or `-s` may be used:

`-c` Complement the set of characters in *string1* with respect to the universe of characters whose ASCII codes are 01 through 0377 octal.

`-d` Delete all input characters in *string1*.

`-s` Squeeze all strings of repeated output characters that are in *string2* to single characters.

EXAMPLE

The following example creates a list of all the words in *filename1* one per line in *filename2*, where a word is taken to be a maximal string of alphabetics. The second string is quoted to protect '`\`' from the shell. 012 is the ASCII code for NEWLINE.

`tr -cs A-Za-z '\012'` <*filename1*>*filename2*

SEE ALSO

`ascii`(5), `ed`(1)

NOTES

Will not handle ASCII NUL in *string1* or *string2*. `tr` always deletes NUL from input.

NAME

trchan – translate character sets

SYNOPSIS

trchan [**-ciko**] *mapfile*

DESCRIPTION

trchan performs mapping as a filter, using the same format of *mapfile* as **mapchan** [see **mapchan**(4) for *mapfile* format]. This allows a file consisting of one internal character set to be translated to another internal character set.

trchan reads standard input, maps it, and writes to standard output. A *mapfile* must be given on the command line. Errors cause **trchan** to stop processing unless **-c** is specified.

The following options can be used with **trchan**:

-c causes errors to be echoed on **stderr**, and processing is continued.

-i specifies that the input section of the *mapfile* is used when translating data.

-k specifies that the dead and compose sections of the *mapfile* are used when translating data.

-o specifies that the output section of the *mapfile* is used when translating data.

The **-i**, **-k** and **-o** options can be specified in any combination; if none are specified, **trchan** uses the entire *mapfile*, as if all three were specified together.

FILES

/usr/lib/mapchan/*

SEE ALSO

ascii(5), **mapchan**(4), **mapchan**(1M)

NOTES

trchan currently ignores the control sections of the *mapfile*.

NAME

troff – (BSD) typeset or format documents

SYNOPSIS

/usr/ucb/troff [**-afiz**] [**-F***dir*] [**-m***name*] [**-n***N*] [**-o***list*] [**-r***aN*] [**-s***N*] [**-T***dest*] [**-u***N*] [*file*] . . .

DESCRIPTION

troff formats text in the *file*s. Input to **troff** is expected to consist of text interspersed with formatting requests and macros. If no *file* argument is present, **troff** reads standard input. A **-** as a *file* argument indicates that standard input is to be read at that point in the list of input files; **troff** reads the files named ahead of the **-** in the argument list, then text from the standard input, and then text from the files named after the **-**.

The following options may appear in any order, but they all must appear before the first *file*.

-a Send a printable approximation of the formatted output to the standard output file.

-f Do not print a trailer after the final page of output or cause the postprocessor to relinquish control of the device.

-i Read the standard input after the input files are exhausted.

-z Suppress formatted output. Only diagnostic messages and messages output using the **.tm** request are output.

-F*dir* Search the directory *dir* for font width tables instead of the system-dependent default directory.

-m*name* Prepend the macro file **/usr/ucblib/doctools/tmac/***name* to the input *files*. Note: most references to macro packages include the leading **m** as part of the name; for example, the **man** macro package resides in **/usr/ucblib/doctools/tmac/an**.

-n*N* Number first generated page *N*.

-o*list* Print only pages whose page numbers appear in the comma-separated *list* of numbers and ranges. A range *N*–*M* means pages *N* through *M*; an initial -*N* means from the beginning to page *N*; and a final *N*– means from *N* to the end.

-r*aN* Set register *a* (one-character) to *N*.

-s*N* Stop the phototypesetter every *N* pages. On some devices, **troff** produces a trailer so you can change cassettes; resume by pressing the typesetter's start button.

-T*dest* Prepare output for typesetter *dest*. The following values can be supplied for *dest*:

aps Autologic APS-5. This is the default value.

-u*N* Set the emboldening factor for the font mounted in position 3 to *N*. If *N* is missing, then set the emboldening factor to 0.

FILES

`/var/tmp/trtmp`	temporary file
`/usr/ucblib/doctools/tmac/*`	standard macro files
`/usr/ucblib/doctools/font/dev*/*`	font width tables for alternate mounted **troff** fonts

SEE ALSO

checknr(1), **eqn**(1), **man**(5), **me**(5), **ms**(5), **nroff**(1), **tbl**(1)

NAME

trpt – transliterate protocol trace

SYNOPSIS

trpt [**-afjst**] [**-p** *pcb_addr*] [*system* [*core*]]

DESCRIPTION

trpt interrogates the buffer of TCP trace records created when a socket is marked for debugging [see **SO_DEBUG** in **getsockopt**(3N)], and prints a readable description of these records. When no options are supplied, **trpt** prints all the trace records found in the system grouped according to TCP connection protocol control block (PCB). The following options may be used to alter this behavior.

OPTIONS

-a In addition to the normal output, print the values of the source and destination addresses for each packet recorded.

-f Follow the trace as it occurs, waiting a short time for additional records each time the end of the log is reached.

-j Just give a list of the protocol control block addresses for which there are trace records.

-s In addition to the normal output, print a detailed description of the packet sequencing information.

-t In addition to the normal output, print the values for all timers at each point in the trace.

-p *pcb_addr*
Show only trace records associated with the protocol control block, with address: *pcb_addr*. The *pcb_addr* address can be gotten from the **PCB** field of **netstat -A** command output. See below for more information.

The recommended use of **trpt** is as follows. Isolate the problem and enable debugging on the **socket**(s) involved in the connection. Find the address of the protocol control blocks associated with the sockets using the **-A** option to **netstat**(1M). Then run **trpt** with the **-p** option, supplying the associated protocol control block addresses. The **-f** option can be used to follow the trace log once the trace is located. If there are many sockets using the debugging option, the **-j** option may be useful in checking to see if any trace records are present for the socket in question.

If debugging is being performed on a system or core file other than the default, the last two arguments may be used to supplant the defaults.

FILES

/stand/unix
/dev/kmem

SEE ALSO

getsockopt(3N), **inetd**(1M), **netstat**(1M)

DIAGNOSTICS

`no namelist`

When the system image does not contain the proper symbols to find the trace buffer;

Others which should be self explanatory.

true(1)

NAME

`true`, `false` – provide truth values

SYNOPSIS

`true`

`false`

DESCRIPTION

`true` does nothing, successfully. `false` does nothing, unsuccessfully. They are typically used in input to `sh` such as:

```
while true
do
        command
done
```

SEE ALSO

`sh`(1)

DIAGNOSTICS

`true` has exit status zero, `false` nonzero.

NAME

truss – trace system calls and signals

SYNOPSIS

truss [-p] [-f] [-c] [-a] [-e] [-i] [-[tvx] [!] *syscall* ...] [-s [!] *signal* ...] [-m [!] *fault* ...] [-[rw] [!] *fd* ...] [-o *outfile*] *command*

DESCRIPTION

truss executes the specified command and produces a trace of the system calls it performs, the signals it receives, and the machine faults it incurs. Each line of the trace output reports either the fault or signal name or the system call name with its arguments and return value(s). System call arguments are displayed symbolically when possible using defines from relevant system header files; for any pathname pointer argument, the pointed-to string is displayed. Error returns are reported using the error code names described in **intro**(2).

The following options are recognized. For those options which take a list argument, the name **all** can be used as a shorthand to specify all possible members of the list. If the list begins with a **!**, the meaning of the option is negated (for example, exclude rather than trace). Multiple occurrences of the same option may be specified. For the same name in a list, subsequent options (those to the right) override previous ones (those to the left).

-p Interpret the arguments to **truss** as a list of process-ids for existing processes (see **ps**(1)) rather than as a command to be executed. **truss** takes control of each process and begins tracing it provided that the userid and groupid of the process match those of the user or that the user is a privileged user. Processes may also be specified by their names in the **/proc** directory, for example, **/proc/1234**; this works for remotely-mounted **/proc** directories as well.

-f Follow all children created by **fork** and include their signals, faults, and system calls in the trace output. Normally, only the first-level command or process is traced. When **-f** is specified, the process-id is included with each line of trace output to show which process executed the system call or received the signal.

-c Count traced system calls, faults, and signals rather than displaying the trace line-by-line. A summary report is produced after the traced command terminates or when **truss** is interrupted. If **-f** is also specified, the counts include all traced system calls, faults, and signals for child processes.

-a Show the argument strings which are passed in each **exec** system call.

-e Show the environment strings which are passed in each **exec** system call.

-i Don't display interruptible sleeping system calls. Certain system calls, such as **open** and **read** on terminal devices or pipes can sleep for indefinite periods and are interruptible. Normally, **truss** reports such sleeping system calls if they remain asleep for more than one second. The system call is reported again a second time when it completes. The `-i` option causes such system calls to be reported only once, when they complete.

-t [**!**] *syscall,...* System calls to trace or exclude. Those system calls specified in the comma-separated list are traced. If the list begins with a '!', the specified system calls are excluded from the trace output. Default is **-tall**.

-v [**!**] *syscall,...* Verbose. Display the contents of any structures passed by address to the specified system calls (if traced). Input values as well as values returned by the operating system are shown. For any field used as both input and output, only the output value is shown. Default is **-v!all**.

-x [**!**] *syscall,...* Display the arguments to the specified system calls (if traced) in raw form, usually hexadecimal, rather than symbolically. This is for unredeemed hackers who must see the raw bits to be happy. Default is **-x!all**.

-s [**!**] *signal,...* Signals to trace or exclude. Those signals specified in the comma-separated list are traced. The trace output reports the receipt of each specified signal, even if the signal is being ignored (not blocked) by the process. (Blocked signals are not received until the process releases them.) Signals may be specified by name or number (see **sys/signal.h**). If the list begins with a '!', the specified signals are excluded from the trace output. Default is **-sall**.

-m [**!**] *fault,...* Machine faults to trace or exclude. Those machine faults specified in the comma-separated list are traced. Faults may be specified by name or number (see **sys/fault.h**). If the list begins with a '!', the specified faults are excluded from the trace output. Default is **-mall -m!fltpage**.

-r [**!**] *fd,...* Show the full contents of the I/O buffer for each **read** on any of the specified file descriptors. The output is formatted 32 bytes per line and shows each byte as an ascii character (preceded by one blank) or as a two-character C language escape sequence for control characters such as horizontal tab (\ t) and newline (\ n). If ascii interpretation is not possible, the byte is shown in two-character hexadecimal representation. (The first 16 bytes of the I/O buffer for each traced **read** are shown even in the absence of **-r**.) Default is **-r!all**.

-w [**!**] *fd,...* Show the contents of the I/O buffer for each **write** on any of the specified file descriptors (see **-r**). Default is **-w!all**.

-o *outfile* File to be used for the trace output. By default, the output goes to standard error.

See Section 2 manual pages for **syscall** names accepted by the **-t**, **-v**, and **-x** options. System call numbers are also accepted.

If **truss** is used to initiate and trace a specified command and if the **-o** option is used or if standard error is redirected to a non-terminal file, then **truss** runs with hangup, interrupt, and quit signals ignored. This facilitates tracing of interactive programs which catch interrupt and quit signals from the terminal.

If the trace output remains directed to the terminal, or if existing processes are traced (the **-p** option), then **truss** responds to hangup, interrupt, and quit signals by releasing all traced processes and exiting. This enables the user to terminate excessive trace output and to release previously-existing processes. Released processes continue normally, as though they had never been touched.

EXAMPLES

This example produces a trace of the **find**(1) command on the terminal:

```
truss find . -print >find.out
```

Or, to see only a trace of the open, close, read, and write system calls:

```
truss -t open,close,read,write find . -print >find.out
```

This produces a trace of the **spell**(1) command on the file truss.out:

```
truss -f -o truss.out spell document
```

spell is a shell script, so the **-f** flag is needed to trace not only the shell but also the processes created by the shell. (The spell script runs a pipeline of eight concurrent processes.)

A particularly boring example is:

```
truss nroff -mm document >nroff.out
```

because 97% of the output reports **lseek**, **read**, and **write** system calls. To abbreviate it:

```
truss -t !lseek,read,write nroff -mm document >nroff.out
```

This example verbosely traces the activity of process #1, **init**(1M) (provided you are a privileged user):

```
truss -p -v all 1
```

Interrupting **truss** returns **init** to normal operation.

FILES

/proc/*nnnnn*   process files

NOTES

Some of the system calls described in Section 2 manual pages differ from the actual operating system interfaces. Do not be surprised by minor deviations of the trace output from the descriptions in Section 2.

Every machine fault (except a page fault) results in the posting of a signal to the process which incurred the fault. A report of a received signal will immediately follow each report of a machine fault (except a page fault) unless that signal is being blocked by the process.

The operating system enforces certain security restrictions on the tracing of processes. In particular, any command whose object file (**a.out**) cannot be read by a user cannot be traced by that user; set-uid and set-gid commands can be traced only by a privileged user. Unless it is run by a privileged user, **truss** loses control of any process which performs an **exec**(2) of a set-id or unreadable object file; such processes continue normally, though independently of **truss**, from the point of the **exec**.

To avoid collisions with other controlling processes, **truss** will not trace a process which it detects is being controlled by another process via the **/proc** interface. This allows **truss** to be applied to *proc*(4)-based debuggers as well as to another instance of itself.

The trace output contains tab characters under the assumption that standard tab stops are set (every eight positions).

The trace output for multiple processes is not produced in strict time order. For example, a **read** on a pipe may be reported before the corresponding **write**. For any one process, the output is strictly time-ordered.

The system may run out of per-user process slots when tracing of children is requested. When tracing more than one process, **truss** runs as one controlling process for each process being traced. For the example of the **spell** command shown above, **spell** itself uses nine process slots, one for the shell and eight for the eight-member pipeline, while **truss** adds another nine processes, for a total of 18. This is perilously close to the usual system-imposed limit of 25 processes per user.

truss uses shared memory and semaphores when dealing with more than one process (**-f** option or **-p** with more than one **pid**). It issues a warning message and proceeds when these are needed but not configured in the system. However, the trace output may become garbled in this case and the output of the **-c** option reports only the top-level command or first **pid** and no children are counted.

Not all possible structures passed in all possible system calls are displayed under the **-v** option.

SEE ALSO

intro(2), **proc**(4)

NAME

`tset` – provide information to set terminal modes

SYNOPSIS

`tset` [*options*] [*type*]

DESCRIPTION

`tset` allows the user to set a terminal's ERASE and KILL characters, and define the terminal's type and capabilities by creating values for the **`TERM`** environment variable. **`tset`** initializes or resets the terminal with **`tput`** [see **`tput`**(1)]. If a *type* is given with the **`-s`** option, **`tset`** creates information for a terminal of the specified type. The type may be any type given in the **`terminfo`** database. If the *type* is not specified with the **`-s`** option, **`tset`** creates information for a terminal of the type defined by the value of the **`TERM`** environment variable, unless the **`-h`** or **`-m`** option is given. If the **`TERM`** variable is defined, **`tset`** uses the **`terminfo`** database entry. If these options are used, **`tset`** searches the **`/etc/ttytype`** file for the terminal type corresponding to the current serial port; it then creates information for a terminal based on this type. If the serial port is not found in **`/etc/ttytype`**, the terminal type is set to **`unknown`**.

`tset` displays the created information on the standard output. The information is in a form that can be used to set the current environment variables. The exact form depends on the login shell from which **`tset`** was invoked. The examples below illustrate how to use this information to change the variables.

The options are:

- **`-e`**[*c*] Sets the ERASE character to *c* on all terminals. The default setting is the BACKSPACE, or CTRL-h.
- **`-E`**[*c*] Identical to the **`-e`** command except that it only operates on terminals that can BACKSPACE.
- **`-k`**[*c*] Sets the KILL character to *c*, defaulting to CTRL-u.
- **`-`** Prints the terminal type on the standard output.
- **`-s`** Outputs the **`setenv`** commands [for **`csh`**(1)], or **`export`** and assignment commands [for **`sh`**(1)]. The type of commands are determined by the user's login shell.
- **`-h`** Forces **`tset`** to search **`/etc/ttytype`** for information and to overlook the **`TERM`** environment variable,
- **`-S`** Only outputs the strings to be placed in the environment variables, without the shell commands printed for **`-s`**.
- **`-r`** Prints the terminal type on the diagnostic output.
- **`-Q`** Suppresses the printing of the **`Erase set to`** and **`Kill set to`** messages.
- **`-I`** Suppresses printing of the terminal initialization strings, for example, spawns **`tput reset`** instead of **`tput init`**.

`-m`[*ident*][*test baudrate*]:*type*

Allows a user to specify how a given serial port is is to be mapped to an actual terminal type. The option applies to any serial port in **`/etc/ttytype`** whose type is indeterminate (for example, **`dialup`**, **`plugboard`**, and so on).

The *type* specifies the terminal type to be used, and *ident* identifies the name of the indeterminate type to be matched. If no *ident* is given, all indeterminate types are matched. The *test baudrate* defines a test to be performed on the serial port before the type is assigned. The *baudrate* must be as defined in **stty** [see **stty**(1)]. The *test* may be any combination of: >, =, <, @, and !. If the *type* begins with a question mark, the user is asked if he really wants that type. A null response means to use that type; otherwise, another type can be entered which will be used instead. The question mark must be escaped to prevent filename expansion by the shell. If more than one **-m** option is given, the first correct mapping prevails.

tset is most useful when included in the **.login** [for **csh**(1)] or **.profile** [for **sh**(1)] file executed automatically at login, with **-m** mapping used to specify the terminal type you most frequently dial in on.

EXAMPLES

```
tset gt42
```

```
tset -mdialup\>300:adm3a -mdialup:dw2 -Qr -e#
```

```
tset -m dial:ti733 -m plug:\?hp2621 -m unknown:\? -e -k^U
```

To use the information created by the **-s** option for the Bourne shell, (**sh**), repeat these commands:

```
tset -s ... > /tmp/tset$$
/tmp/tset$$
rm /tmp/tset$$
```

To use the information created for **csh**, use:

```
set noglob
set term=('tset -S ....')
setenv TERM $term[1]
unset term
unset noglob
```

FILES

`/etc/ttytype`	Port name to terminal type map database
`/usr/lib/terminfo/*`	Terminal capability database

SEE ALSO

stty(1), **terminfo**(4), **termio**(7), **tput**(1), **tty**(1)

NOTES

This utility was developed at the University of California at Berkeley and is used with permission.

NAME

tset, **reset** – (BSD) establish or restore terminal characteristics

SYNOPSIS

tset [**-InQrs**] [**-e**c] [**-k**c] [**-m** [*port* –ID [*baudrate*] : *type*] . . .] [*type*]

reset [**-**] [**-e**c] [**-I**] [**-k**c] [**-n**] [**-Q**] [**-r**] [**-s**]
[**-m** [*indent*] [*test baudrate*]: *type*] . . . [*type*]

DESCRIPTION

tset sets up your terminal, typically when you first log in. It does terminal dependent processing such as setting erase and kill characters, setting or resetting delays, sending any sequences needed to properly initialized the terminal, and the like. **tset** first determines the *type* of terminal involved, and then does necessary initializations and mode settings. If a port is not wired permanently to a specific terminal (not hardwired) it is given an appropriate generic identifier such as **dialup**.

reset clears the terminal settings by turning off CBREAK and RAW modes, output delays and parity checking, turns on NEWLINE translation, echo and TAB expansion, and restores undefined special characters to their default state. It then sets the modes as usual, based on the terminal type (which will probably override some of the above). See **stty**(1) for more information. All arguments to **tset** may be used with **reset**. **reset** also uses **rs=** and **rf=** to reset the initialization string and file. This is useful after a program dies and leaves the terminal in a funny state. Often in this situation, characters will not echo as you type them. You may have to type '<LINEFEED>**reset**<LINEFEED>' since '<RETURN>' may not work.

When no arguments are specified, **tset** reads the terminal type from the **TERM** environment variable and re-initializes the terminal, and performs initialization of mode, environment and other options at login time to determine the terminal type and set up terminal modes.

When used in a startup script (**.profile** for **sh**(1) users or **.login** for **csh**(1) users) it is desirable to give information about the type of terminal you will usually use on ports that are not hardwired. Any of the alternate generic names given in **/usr/share/lib/termcap** may be used for the identifier. Refer to the **-m** option below for more information. If no mapping applies and a final *type* option, not preceded by a **-m**, is given on the command line then that type is used.

It is usually desirable to return the terminal type, as finally determined by **tset**, and information about the terminal's capabilities, to a shell's environment. This can be done using the **-**, **-s**, or **-S** options.

For the Bourne shell, put this command in your **.profile** file:

**eval \`tset -s** *options . . .*\`

or using the C shell, put this command in your **.login** file:

**eval \`tset -s** *options . . .*\`

With the C shell, it is also convenient to make an alias in your **.cshrc** file:

```
alias tset 'eval `tset -s \!*`'
```

This also allows the command:

```
tset 2621
```

to be invoked at any time to set the terminal and environment. It is not possible to get this aliasing effect with a Bourne shell script, because shell scripts cannot set the environment of their parent. If a process could set its parent's environment, none of this nonsense would be necessary in the first place.

Once the terminal type is known, **tset** sets the terminal driver mode. This normally involves sending an initialization sequence to the terminal, setting the single character erase (and optionally the line-kill (full line erase)) characters, and setting special character delays. TAB and NEWLINE expansion are turned off during transmission of the terminal initialization sequence.

On terminals that can backspace but not overstrike (such as a CRT), and when the erase character is '**#**', the erase character is changed as if **-e** had been used.

The following options are available with **tset**:

- The name of the terminal finally decided upon is output on the standard output. This is intended to be captured by the shell and placed in the **TERM** environment variable.

-e*c* Set the erase character to be the named character *c* on all terminals. Default is the BACKSPACE key on the keyboard, usually **^H** (CTRL-H). The character *c* can either be typed directly, or entered using the circumflex-character notation used here.

-i*c* Set the interrupt character to be the named character *c* on all terminals. Default is **^C** (CTRL-C). The character *c* can either be typed directly, or entered using the circumflex-character notation used here.

-I Suppress transmitting terminal-initialization strings.

-k*c* Set the line kill character to be the named character *c* on all terminals. Default is **^U** (CTRL-U). The kill character is left alone if **-k** is not specified. Control characters can be specified by prefixing the alphabetical character with a circumflex (as in CTRL-U) instead of entering the actual control key itself. This allows you to specify control keys that are currently assigned.

-n Specify that the new tty driver modes should be initialized for this terminal. Probably useless since **stty new** is the default.

-Q Suppress printing the '**Erase set to**' and '**Kill set to**' messages.

-r In addition to other actions, reports the terminal type.

-s Output commands to set and export **TERM**. This can be used with

```
set noglob
eval `tset -s ...`
unset noglob
```

to bring the terminal information into the environment. Doing so makes programs such as **vi**(1) start up faster. If the **SHELL** environment variable ends with **csh**, C shell commands are output, otherwise Bourne shell commands are output.

-m [*port*-ID[*baudrate*]**:***type*] . . .

Specify (map) a terminal type when connected to a generic port (such as *dialup* or *plugboard*) identified by *port-ID*. The *baudrate* argument can be used to check the baudrate of the port and set the terminal type accordingly. The target rate is prefixed by any combination of the following operators to specify the conditions under which the mapping is made:

>	Greater than
@	Equals or "at"
<	Less than
!	It is not the case that (negates the above operators)
?	Prompt for the terminal type. If no response is given, then *type* is selected by default.

In the following example, the terminal type is set to **adm3a** if the port is a dialup with a speed of greater than 300 or to **dw2** if the port is a dialup at 300 baud or less. In the third case, the question mark preceding the terminal type indicates that the user is to verify the type desired. A **NULL** response indicates that the named type is correct. Otherwise, the user's response is taken to be the type desired.

```
tset -m 'dialup>300:adm3a' -m 'dialup:dw2' -m \
     'plugboard:?adm3a'
```

To prevent interpretation as metacharacters, the entire argument to **-m** should be enclosed in single quotes. When using the C shell, exclamation points should be preceded by a backslash (\).

EXAMPLES

These examples all use the '–' option. A typical use of **tset** in a **.profile** or **.login** will also use the **-e** and **-k** options, and often the **-n** or **-Q** options as well. These options have been omitted here to keep the examples short.

To select a 2621, you might put the following sequence of commands in your **.login** file (or **.profile** for Bourne shell users).

```
set noglob
eval `tset -s 2621`
unset noglob
```

If you have a switch which connects to various ports (making it impractical to identify which port you may be connected to), and use various terminals from time to time, you can select from among those terminals according to the *speed* or baud rate. In the example below, **tset** will prompt you for a terminal type if the baud rate is greater than 1200 (say, 9600 for a terminal connected by an RS-232 line), and use a Wyse® 50 by default. If the baud rate is less than or equal to 1200, it will select a 2621. Note the placement of the question mark, and the quotes to protect the **>** and **?** from interpretation by the shell.

```
set noglob
eval `tset -s -m 'switch>1200:?wy' -m 'switch<=1200:2621'`
unset noglob
```

The following entry is appropriate if you always dial up, always at the same baud rate, on many different kinds of terminals, and the terminal you use most often is an **adm3a**.

```
set noglob
eval `tset -s ?adm3a`
unset noglob
```

If you want to make the selection based only on the baud rate, you might use the following:

```
set noglob
eval `tset -s -m '>1200:wy' 2621`
unset noglob
```

The following example quietly sets the erase character to BACKSPACE, and kill to CTRL-U. If the port is switched, it selects a Concept™ 100 for speeds less than or equal to 1200, and asks for the terminal type otherwise (the default in this case is a Wyse 50). If the port is a direct dialup, it selects Concept 100 as the terminal type. If logging in over the ARPANET, the terminal type selected is a Datamedia® 2500 terminal or emulator. Note the backslash escaping the NEWLINE at the end of the first line in the example.

```
set noglob
eval `tset -e -k^U -Q -s -m 'switch<=1200:concept100' -m \
     'switch:?wy' -m dialup:concept100 -m arpanet:dm2500`
unset noglob
```

FILES

`.login`
`.profile`

SEE ALSO

csh(1), **environ**(5), **sh**(1), **stty**(1), **terminfo**(4), **vi**(1)

NOTES

The **tset** command is one of the first commands a user must master when getting started on a UNIX system. Unfortunately, it is one of the most complex, largely because of the extra effort the user must go through to get the environment of the login shell set.

This program cannot intuit personal choices for erase, interrupt and line kill characters, so it leaves these set to the local system standards.

It could well be argued that the shell should be responsible for ensuring that the terminal remains in a sane state; this would eliminate the need for the **reset** program.

NAME

tset – (XENIX) provide information for setting terminal modes

SYNOPSIS

tset [*options*] [*type*]

DESCRIPTION

tset allows the user to set a terminal's ERASE and KILL characters, and define the terminal's type and capabilities by creating values for the **TERM** and **TERMCAP** environment variables. If a *type* is given with the **-s** option, **tset** creates information for a terminal of the specified type. The type may be any type given in **/usr/share/lib/termcap**. If the *type* is not specified with the **-s** option, **tset** creates information for a terminal of the type defined by the value of the environment variable, **TERM** unless the **-h** or **-m** option is given. If the **TERM** variable is undefined, **tset** looks in **/usr/share/lib/termcap** for the appropriate information. If these options are used, **tset** searches the **/etc/ttytype** file for the terminal type corresponding to the current serial port; it then creates information for a terminal based on this type. If the serial port is not found in **/etc/ttytype**, the terminal type is set to dumb.

tset displays the created information on the standard output. The information is in a form that can be used to set the current environment variables. The exact form depends on the login shell from which **tset** was invoked. The examples below illustrate how to use this information to change the variables.

The following options are valid:

-e[*c*] Sets the ERASE character to [*c*] on all terminals. The default setting is BACKSPACE, or CTRL-**h**.

-E[*c*] Identical to the **-e** option except that it only operates on terminals that can backspace.

-k[*c*] Sets the KILL character to *c*, defaulting to CTRL-**u**.

- Prints the terminal type on the standard output.

-s Outputs the **setenv** commands for **csh**(1) or **export** and assignment commands for **sh**(1). The commands are determined by the user's login shell.

-S Only outputs the strings to be placed in the environment variables.

-r Prints the terminal type on the diagnostic output.

-Q Suppresses the printing of the "**Erase set to**" and "**Kill set to**" messages.

-I Suppresses printing of the terminal initialization strings.

-m[*ident*][*test baudrate*]:*type*
Allows a user to specify how a given serial port is is to be mapped to an actual terminal type. The option applies to any serial port in **/etc/ttytype** whose type is indeterminate (for example, **dialup**, **plugboard**, and so on). The *type* specifies the terminal type to be used, and *ident* identifies the name of the indeterminate type to be matched. If no *ident* is given, all indeterminate types are matched. The *test baudrate* defines a test to be performed on the serial port before the type is assigned. The *baudrate* must be as defined in **stty** [see **stty**(1)]. The *test* may be any

combination of: >, =, <, @, and !. If the *type* begins with a question mark, the user is asked if he really wants that type. A null response means to use that type; otherwise, another type can be entered which will be used instead. The question mark must be escaped to prevent filename expansion by the shell. If more than one **-m** option is given, the first correct mapping prevails.

tset is most useful when included in the **.login** [for **csh**(1)] or **.profile** [for **sh**(1)] file executed automatically at login, with the **-m** mapping used to specify the terminal type you most frequently dial in on.

EXAMPLES

```
tset gt42
tset - mdialup>300:adm3a-mdialup:dw2-Qr-e#
tset -mdial:ti733-mplug:?hp2621-munknown:?-e-k^U
```

To use the information created by the **-s** option for the Bourne shell, (**sh**), repeat these commands:

```
tset -s...>/tmp/tset$$
/tmp/tset$$
rm/tmp/tset$$
```

To use the information for **csh**, use:

```
set noglob
set term=('tset-S...')
setenv TERM$term[1]
setenv TERMCAP"$term[2]"
unset term
unset noglob
```

FILES

/usr/share/lib/termcap Terminal capability database.

SEE ALSO

stty(1), **terminfo**(4), **tty**(1)

NAME

`tsort` – topological sort

SYNOPSIS

`tsort` [*file*]

DESCRIPTION

The **`tsort`** command produces on the standard output a totally ordered list of items consistent with a partial ordering of items mentioned in the input *file*. If no *file* is specified, the standard input is understood.

The input consists of pairs of items (nonempty strings) separated by blanks. Pairs of different items indicate ordering. Pairs of identical items indicate presence, but not ordering.

SEE ALSO

`lorder`(1)

DIAGNOSTICS

`Odd data:` there is an odd number of fields in the input file.

NAME

`tty` – get the name of the terminal

SYNOPSIS

`tty` [`-l`] [`-s`]

DESCRIPTION

`tty` prints the pathname of the user's terminal. It accepts the following options:

`-l` Print the synchronous line number to which the user's terminal is connected, if it is on an active synchronous line.

`-s` Inhibit printing of the terminal path name, allowing one to test just the exit code.

EXIT CODES

2 invalid option

0 standard input is a terminal

1 otherwise

FILES

/usr/lib/locale/*locale***/LC_MESSAGES/uxue.abi**
language-specific message file [See **LANG** on **environ**(5).]

DIAGNOSTICS

UX:tty:ERROR:not on an active synchronous line
The standard input is not a synchronous terminal and **-l** is specified.

UX:tty:ERROR:not a tty
The standard input is not a terminal and **-s** is not specified.

SEE ALSO

ttyname(3C)

NAME

ttyadm – format and output port monitor-specific information

SYNOPSIS

/usr/sbin/ttyadm [**-b**] [**-c**] [**-r** *count*] [**-h**] [**-i** *msg*] [**-m** *modules*] [**-p** *prompt*] [**-t** *timeout*] **-d** *device* **-l** *ttylabel* **-s** *service*

/usr/sbin/ttyadm -V

DESCRIPTION

The **ttyadm** command formats data from **ttymon**(1M) and writes it to standard output, from where it can be used by the **sacadm**(1M) and **pmadm**(1M) commands to update the administrative file for **ttymon**. The Service Access Facility (SAF) requires each port monitor to provide such a command.

-b Sets the "bidirectional port" flag. When this flag is set, the line can be used in both directions. **ttymon** will allow users to connect to the service associated with the port, but if the port is free, **uucico**, **cu**, or **ct** can use it for dialing out.

-c Sets the connect-on-carrier flag for the port. If the **-c** flag is set, **ttymon** will invoke the port's associated service immediately when a connect indication is received (that is, no prompt is printed and no baud-rate searching is done).

-d *device* *device* is the full pathname of the device file for the TTY port.

-h Sets the hangup flag for the port. If the **-h** flag is not set, **ttymon** will force a hangup on the line by setting the speed to zero before setting the speed to the default or specified value.

-i *message* Specifies the inactive (disabled) response message. This message will be sent to the TTY port if the port is disabled or the **ttymon** monitoring the port is disabled.

-l *ttylabel* Specifies which *ttylabel* in the **/etc/ttydefs** file to use as the starting point when searching for the proper baud rate.

-m *modules* Specifies a list of pushable STREAMS modules. The modules will be pushed, in the order in which they are specified, before the service is invoked. *modules* must be a comma-separated list of modules, with no white space included. Any modules currently on the stream will be popped before these modules are pushed.

-r *count* When the **-r** option is invoked, **ttymon** will wait until it receives data from the port before it displays a prompt. If *count* is equal to zero, **ttymon** will wait until it receives any character. If *count* is greater than zero, **ttymon** will wait until *count* newlines have been received.

-p *prompt* Specifies the prompt message, for example, "**login:**".

-s *service* *service* is the full pathname of the service to be invoked when a connection request is received. If arguments are required, the command and its arguments must be enclosed in double quotes.

`-t` *timeout*	Specifies that **ttymon** should close a port if the open on the port succeeds and no input data is received in *timeout* seconds.
`-V`	Displays the version number of the current **/usr/lib/saf/ttymon** command.

Exit Codes

If successful, **ttyadm** will generate the requested information, write it on the standard output, and exit with a status of `0`. If **ttyadm** is invoked with an invalid number of arguments or invalid arguments, or if an incomplete option is specified, an error message will be written to the standard error and **ttymon** will exit with a non-zero status.

FILES

/etc/ttydefs

/usr/lib/locale/*locale***/LC_MESSAGES/uxcore.abi**
language-specific message file [See **LANG** on **environ** (5).]

SEE ALSO

pmadm(1M), **sacadm**(1M), **ttymon**(1M), **sttydefs**(1M)

NAME

ttymap – install and update **/var/tmp/ttymap** based on **/dev** and **/etc/ttysrch**

SYNOPSIS

ttymap

DESCRIPTION

The **ttymap** command creates and updates **/var/tmp/ttymap** with information from the **/dev** directory tree and the **/etc/ttysrch** file.

The **ttymap** command is run during system initialization to create the **/var/tmp/ttymap** file. The **/var/tmp/ttymap** file is used by the **ttyname** library function to search for terminal and terminal-related device files. The command populates **/var/tmp/ttymap** with a list of device files indexed by device ID and file system ID, and with a time-stamped map of directories within **/dev**.

The **ttyname**(3C) library function attempts to find devices by lookup based on device number and file system ID. If a candidate with matching device and file system IDs is found, **ttyname** checks its inode number. If no match is found, **ttyname** checks each directory in the map to see if it is newer than the time stamp in the **/var/tmp/ttymap** file. If a newer directory is found, **ttyname** searches the directory for device files and recursively searches any newer subdirectories.

The **/etc/ttysrch** file can be used to specify directories that should be ignored, which decreases the size of the **/var/tmp/ttymap** file, providing faster lookup, and to specify directories that contain clone devices, which allows **ttyname** to accept device files that do not match on inode number.

FILES

/etc/ttysrch
/var/tmp/ttymap
/dev/*

SEE ALSO

ttyname(3C), **ttysrch**(4)

DIAGNOSTICS

ttymap returns 0 on success or 1 if permission is denied.

NAME

`ttymon` – port monitor for terminal ports

SYNOPSIS

/usr/lib/saf/ttymon

/usr/lib/saf/ttymon -g [**-h**] [**-d** *device*] [**-l** *ttylabel*] [**-t** *timeout*]
[**-p** *prompt*] [**-m** *modules*]

DESCRIPTION

ttymon is a STREAMS-based TTY port monitor. Its function is to monitor ports, to set terminal modes, baud rates, and line disciplines for the ports, to identify and authenticate users, if required, and to connect users or applications to services associated with the ports. Normally, **ttymon** is configured to run under the Service Access Controller, **sac**, as part of the Service Access Facility (SAF). It is configured using the **sacadm**(1M) command. Each instance of **ttymon** can monitor multiple ports. The ports monitored by an instance of **ttymon** are specified in the port monitor's administrative file. The administrative file is configured using the **pmadm** and **ttyadm** commands. When an instance of **ttymon** is invoked by the **sac** command, it starts to monitor its ports. For each port, **ttymon** first initializes the line discipline, and the speed and terminal settings. The values used for initialization are taken from the appropriate entry in the TTY settings file. This file is maintained by the **sttydefs** command.

ttymon then writes the prompt and waits for user input. If the user indicates that the speed is inappropriate by pressing the BREAK key, **ttymon** hunts to the next *ttylabel* in the **/etc/ttydefs** file, adjusts **termio**(7) values, and writes the prompt again. When valid input is received, that is, one or more non-break keys followed by a newline, **ttymon** interprets the per-service configuration file for the port, if one exists, invokes the identification and authentication scheme, if one is specified, creates a **utmp** entry if required, establishes the service environment, and then invokes the service associated with the port. Valid input consists of a string of at least one non-newline character, terminated by a carriage return. After the service terminates, **ttymon** cleans up the **utmp** entry, if one exists, and returns the port to its initial state.

If *autobaud* is enabled for a port, **ttymon** will try to determine the baud rate on the port automatically. Users must enter a carriage return before **ttymon** can recognize the baud rate and print the prompt. Currently, the baud rates that can be determined by *autobaud* are **110**, **1200**, **2400**, **4800**, and **9600**.

If a port is configured as a bidirectional port, **ttymon** will allow users to connect to a service, and, if the port is free, will allow **uucico**, **cu** or **ct** to use it for dialing out. If a port is bidirectional, **ttymon** will wait to read a character before it prints a prompt.

If the *connect-on-carrier* flag is set for a port, **ttymon** will immediately invoke the port's associated service when a connection request is received. The prompt message will not be sent.

If a port is disabled, **ttymon** will not start any service on that port. If a disabled message is specified, **ttymon** will send out the disabled message when a connection request is received. If **ttymon** is disabled, all ports under that instance of **ttymon** will also be disabled.

Service Invocation

The service **ttymon** invokes for a port is specified in the **ttymon** administrative file. **ttymon** scans the character string that gives the service to be invoked, looking for one of the two-character sequences **%d** and **%%**. If **%d** is found, **ttymon** modifies the service command to be executed by replacing these two characters with the full path name of the port (the device name). If **%%** is found, **ttymon** replaces the two characters with a single **%**. When the service is invoked, file descriptors **0**, **1**, and **2** are opened to the port device for reading and writing.

If an authentication scheme is specified in the **ttymon** administrative file and there is no entry in the ID field (this is the default case), the service is invoked with the user ID, group ID, and current home directory set, through **set_id**, to the user name that is identified and authenticated by the authentication scheme. If both a user ID and an authentication scheme are specified in the **ttymon** administrative file, the authentication scheme is executed first, then the user ID is set, using the value in the administrative file, not the value given by the authentication scheme. The **login** authentication scheme is the scheme most commonly associated with **ttymon**. See **login**(1).

ttymon adds two environment variables, **HOME** and **TTYPROMPT**, to the service's environment. **HOME** is set to the **HOME** directory of the user name under which the service is invoked. **TTYPROMPT** is set to the prompt string configured for the service on the port. This is provided so that a service invoked by **ttymon** has a means of determining if a prompt was actually issued by **ttymon** and, if so, what that prompt actually was.

See **ttyadm**(1M) for options that can be set for ports monitored by **ttymon** under the Service Access Controller.

Invoking a Stand-Alone ttymon Process

A special invocation of **ttymon** is provided with the **-g** option. This form of the command should only be called by applications that need to set the correct baud rate and terminal settings on a port to invoke the **LOGIN** authentication scheme and then connect to a service, but that cannot be pre-configured under the SAC. The following combinations of options can be used with **-g**:

-d *device* — *device* is the full path name of the port to which **ttymon** is to attach. If this option is not specified, file descriptor **0** must be set up by the invoking process to a TTY port.

-h — If the –h flag is not set, **ttymon** will force a hangup on the line by setting the speed to zero before setting the speed to the default or specified speed.

-t *timeout* — Specifies that **ttymon** should exit if no one types anything in *timeout* seconds after the prompt is sent.

-l *ttylabel* — *ttylabel* is a link to a speed and TTY definition in the **ttydefs** file. This definition tells **ttymon** at what speed to run initially, what the initial TTY settings are, and what speed to try next if the user indicates that the speed is inappropriate by pressing the BREAK key. The default speed is 9600 baud.

-p *prompt* Allows the user to specify a prompt string. The default prompt is

login:

-m *modules* *modules* is a comma-separated list of pushable modules. When initializing the port, **ttymon** will pop all modules on the port and then push *modules* in the order specified. The line discipline module **ldterm** is commonly used for terminal ports.

FILES

/usr/lib/locale/*locale***/LC_MESSAGES/uxcore.abi**
language-specific message file [See **LANG** on **environ**(5).]

SEE ALSO

pmadm(1M), **sac**(1M), **sacadm**(1M), **ttyadm**(1M)

NOTES

If a port is monitored by more than one **ttymon**, it is possible for the **ttymons** to send out prompt messages in such a way that they compete for input.

NAME

tunefs – tune up an existing file system

SYNOPSIS

tunefs [**-a** *maxcontig*] [**-d** *rotdelay*] [**-e** *maxbpg*] [**-m** *minfree*]
[**-o** [**s** | **space** | **t** | **time**]] *special* | *filesystem*

DESCRIPTION

tunefs is designed to change the dynamic parameters of a file system which affect the layout policies. The file system must be unmounted before using **tunefs**. The parameters which are to be changed are indicated by the options given below:

Options

-a *maxcontig* — Specify the maximum number of contiguous blocks that will be laid out before forcing a rotational delay (see **-d** below). The default value is one, since most device drivers require an interrupt per disk transfer. Device drivers that can chain several buffers together in a single transfer should set this to the maximum chain length.

-d *rotdelay* — Specify the expected time (in milliseconds) to service a transfer completion interrupt and initiate a new transfer on the same disk. It is used to decide how much rotational spacing to place between successive blocks in a file.

-e *maxbpg* — Indicate the maximum number of blocks any single file can allocate out of a cylinder group before it is forced to begin allocating blocks from another cylinder group. Typically this value is set to approximately one quarter of the total blocks in a cylinder group. The intent is to prevent any single file from using up all the blocks in a single cylinder group, thus degrading access times for all files subsequently allocated in that cylinder group. The effect of this limit is to cause big files to do long seeks more frequently than if they were allowed to allocate all the blocks in a cylinder group before seeking elsewhere. For file systems with exclusively large files, this parameter should be set higher.

-m *minfree* — Specify the percentage of space held back from normal users; the minimum free space threshold. The default value used is 10%. This value can be set to zero, however up to a factor of three in throughput will be lost over the performance obtained at a 10% threshold. Note: if the value is raised above the current usage level, users will be unable to allocate files until enough files have been deleted to get under the higher threshold. **minfree** also determines when the file system will automatically switch between time optimization and space optimization. If there are more than **(minfree -2)** percent free fragments, the file system will switch to space optimization. If **minfree** is less than 5, then any switch to time optimization will be inhibited.

-o [s | space | t | time] — Change optimization strategy for the file system. **s** and **space** are interchangeable, **t** and **time** are interchangeable.

s or **space**	conserve space.
t or **time**	attempt to organize file layout to minimize access time.

Generally one should optimize for time unless the file system is over 90% full.

SEE ALSO

mkfs(1M), **sfs**-specific **tunefs**(1M)

NAME

tunefs (sfs) – tune up an existing file system

SYNOPSIS

tunefs [**-a** *maxcontig*] [**-d** *rotdelay*] [**-e** *maxbpg*] [**-o [s | space | t | time]**] *special* | *filesystem*

DESCRIPTION

tunefs is designed to change the dynamic parameters of a file system which affect the layout policies. The file system must be unmounted before using **tunefs**. The parameters which are to be changed are indicated by the options given below:

The options are:

-a *maxcontig* Specify the maximum number of contiguous blocks that will be laid out before forcing a rotational delay (see **-d** below). The default value is one, since most device drivers require an interrupt per disk transfer. Device drivers that can chain several buffers together in a single transfer should set this to the maximum chain length.

-d *rotdelay* Specify the expected time (in milliseconds) to service a transfer completion interrupt and initiate a new transfer on the same disk. It is used to decide how much rotational spacing to place between successive blocks in a file.

-e *maxbpg* Indicate the maximum number of blocks any single file can allocate out of a cylinder group before it is forced to begin allocating blocks from another cylinder group. Typically this value is set to approximately one quarter of the total blocks in a cylinder group. The intent is to prevent any single file from using up all the blocks in a single cylinder group, thus degrading access times for all files subsequently allocated in that cylinder group. The effect of this limit is to cause big files to do long seeks more frequently than if they were allowed to allocate all the blocks in a cylinder group before seeking elsewhere. For file systems with exclusively large files, this parameter should be set higher.

-o [s | space | t | time]
Change optimization strategy for the file system. **s** and **space** are interchangeable, and **t** and **time** are interchangeable.

s or **space** - conserve space.
t or **time** - attempt to organize file layout to minimize access time.

Generally one should optimize for time unless the file system is over 90% full.

NOTES

The tunable **minfree** is not supported on **sfs** file systems.

SEE ALSO

fork(2), **sfs**-specific **fs**(4), **mkfs**(1M), **terminfo**(4)

uadmin (1M)

NAME

uadmin – administrative control

SYNOPSIS

/sbin/uadmin *cmd fcn*

DESCRIPTION

The **uadmin** command provides control for basic administrative functions. This command is tightly coupled to low-level system administration procedures and is not intended for general use. It may be invoked only by a privileged user.

The arguments *cmd* (command) and *fcn* (function), as described on the **uadmin**(2) manual page, are converted to integers and passed to the **uadmin** system call.

SEE ALSO

uadmin(2)

NAME

ufsdump – incremental file system dump

SYNOPSIS

/usr/sbin/ufsdump [*options* [*arguments*]] *filesystem*

DESCRIPTION

ufsdump backs up all files in *filesystem*, where *filesystem* represents a special device, or files changed after a certain date, to magnetic tape; *options* is a string that specifies **ufsdump** options, as shown below. Any *arguments* supplied for specific options are given as subsequent words on the command line, in the same order as that of the *options* listed.

If no *options* are given, the default is **9u**.

Options

0–9 The dump level. All files in the *filesystem* that have been modified since the last **ufsdump** at a lower dump level are copied to the volume. For instance, if you did a level **2** dump on Monday, followed by a level **4** dump on Tuesday, a subsequent level **3** dump on Wednesday would contain all files modified or added since the level **2** (Monday) backup. A level **0** dump copies the entire filesystem to the dump volume.

b *factor* Blocking factor. Specify the blocking factor for tape writes. The default is 20 blocks per write. Note: the blocking factor is specified in terms of 512 bytes blocks, for compatibility with **tar**. The default blocking factor for tapes of density 6250BPI and greater is 64. The default blocking factor for cartridge tapes (**c** option specified) is 126. The highest blocking factor available with most tape drives is 126.

c Cartridge. Use a cartridge instead of the standard half-inch reel. This sets the density to 1000BPI and the blocking factor to 126. The length is set to 425 feet. This option is incompatible with the **d** option, unless you specify a density of 1000BPI with that option.

d *bpi* Tape density. The density of the tape, expressed in BPI, is taken from *bpi*. This is used to keep a running tab on the amount of tape used per reel. The default density is 1600 except for cartridge tape. Unless a higher density is specified explicitly, **ufsdump** uses its default density — even if the tape drive is capable of higher-density operation (for instance, 6250BPI). Note: the density specified should correspond to the density of the tape device being used, or **ufsdump** will not be able to handle end-of-tape properly.

f *dump-file* Dump file. Use *dump-file* as the file to dump to, instead of **/dev/rmt***. If *dump-file* is specified as **–**, dump to the standard output.

n Notify all operators in the operator group that **ufsdump** requires attention by sending messages to their terminals, in a manner similar to that used by the **wall** command.

s *size* Specify the *size* of the volume being dumped to. When the specified size is reached, **ufsdump** waits for you to change the volume. **ufsdump** interprets the specified size as the length in feet for tapes and cartridges, and as the number of 1024-byte blocks for diskettes. The following are defaults:

cartridge	425 feet
diskette	1422 blocks (Corresponds to a 1.44 Mb diskette, with one cylinder reserved for bad block information.)

t *tracks* Specify the number of tracks for a cartridge tape. The default is 9 tracks. The **t** option is not compatible with the **D** option.

u Update the dump record. Add an entry to the file **/etc/dumpdates,** for each filesystem successfully dumped that includes the filesystem name, date, and dump level. This file can be edited by the super-user.

w List the file systems that need backing up. This information is gleaned from the files **/etc/dumpdates** and **/etc/vfstab**. When the **w** option is used, all other options are ignored. After reporting, **ufsdump** exits immediately.

W Similar to the **w** option, except that the **W** option includes all file systems that appear in **/etc/dumpdates,** along with information about their most recent dump dates and levels. Filesystems that need backing up are highlighted.

NOTES

Fewer than 32 read errors on the filesystem are ignored.

Each reel requires a new process, so parent processes for reels already written just hang around until the entire tape is written.

It is recommended that incremental dumps also be performed with the system running in single-user mode.

FILES

/dev/rmt*	default unit to dump to
/etc/dumpdates	dump date record
/etc/group	to find group operator
/etc/hosts	

SEE ALSO

df(1M), **shutdown**(1M), **tar**(1), **ufsrestore**(1M), **wall**(1M)

NAME

ufsrestore – incremental file system restore

SYNOPSIS

/usr/sbin/ufsrestore *options* [*arguments*] [*filename* . . .]

DESCRIPTION

ufsrestore restores files from backup tapes created with the **ufsdump** command. *options* is a string of at least one of the options listed below, along with any modifiers and arguments you supply. Any *arguments* supplied for specific options are given as subsequent words on the command line, in the same order as that of the *options* listed. Remaining arguments to **ufsrestore** are the names of files (or directories whose files) are to be restored to disk. Unless the **h** modifier is in effect, a directory name refers to the files it contains, and (recursively) its subdirectories and the files they contain.

Options

`i` Interactive. After reading in the directory information from the tape, **ufsrestore** invokes an interactive interface that allows you to browse through the dump tape's directory hierarchy and select individual files to be extracted. See **Interactive Commands**, below, for a description of available commands.

`r` Restore the entire tape. Load the tape's full contents into the current directory. This option should be used only to restore a complete dump tape onto a clear filesystem, or to restore an incremental dump tape after a full level `0` restore.

`R` Resume restoring. **ufsrestore** requests a particular tape of a multivolume set from which to resume a full restore (see the **r** option above). This allows **ufsrestore** to start from a checkpoint when it is interrupted in the middle of a full restore.

`t` Table of contents. List each *filename* that appears on the tape. If no *filename* argument is given, the root directory is listed. This results in a list of all files on the tape, unless the **h** modifier is in effect.

`x` Extract the named files from the tape. If a named file matches a directory whose contents were written onto the tape, and the **h** modifier is not in effect, the directory is recursively extracted. The owner, modification time, and mode are restored (if possible). If no *filename* argument is given, the root directory is extracted. This results in the entire tape being extracted unless the **h** modifier is in effect.

Some of the following modifiers take arguments that are given as separate words on the command line. When more than one such modifier appears within *options*, the arguments must appear in the same order as the modifiers that they apply to.

`c` Convert the contents of the dump tape to the new filesystem format.

`d` Debug. Turn on debugging output.

`h` Extract the actual directory, rather than the files that it references. This prevents hierarchical restoration of complete subtrees from the tape.

`m` Extract by inode numbers rather than by filename to avoid regenerating complete pathnames. This is useful if only a few files are being extracted.

`v` Verbose. **ufsrestore** displays the name of each file it restores, preceded by its file type.

`y` Do not ask whether to abort the restore in the event of tape errors. **ufsrestore** tries to skip over the bad tape block(s) and continue as best it can.

`b` *factor*
Blocking factor. Specify the blocking factor for tape reads. By default, **ufsrestore** will attempt to figure out the block size of the tape. Note: a tape block is 512 bytes.

`f` *dump-file*
Use *dump-file* instead of **/dev/rmt?** as the file to restore from. If *dump-file* is specified as '-', **ufsrestore** reads from the standard input. This allows, **ufsdump**(1M) and **ufsrestore** to be used in a pipeline to dump and restore a file system, as shown in the example below. (The device names on your system may differ from those shown in the example.)

```
ufsdump 0f - /dev/rxy0g | (cd /mnt; ufsrestore xf -)
```

`s` *n* Skip to the *n*'th file when there are multiple dump files on the same tape, as shown in the example below. (The device names on your system may differ from those shown in the example.)

```
ufsrestore xfs /dev/nrar0 5
```

would position you at the fifth file on the tape.

ufsrestore enters interactive mode when invoked with the **i** option. Interactive commands are reminiscent of the shell. For those commands that accept an argument, the default is the current directory.

`ls` [*directory*]
List files in **directory** or the current directory, represented by a '**.**' (period). Directories are appended with a '**/**' (backslash). Entries marked for extraction are prefixed with a '*****' (asterisk). If the verbose option is in effect, inode numbers are also listed.

`cd` *directory*
Change to directory **directory** (within the dump-tape).

`pwd` Print the full pathname of the current working directory.

`add` [*filename*]
Add the current directory, or the named file or directory **directory** to the list of files to extract. If a directory is specified, add that directory and its files (recursively) to the extraction list (unless the **h** modifier is in effect).

`delete` [*filename*]
Delete the current directory, or the named file or directory from the list of files to extract. If a directory is specified, delete that directory and all its descendents from the extraction list (unless the **h** modifier is in effect). The most expedient way to extract a majority of files from a directory is to add that directory to the extraction list, and then delete specific files to omit.

extract
Extract all files on the extraction list from the dump tape. **ufsrestore** asks which volume the user wishes to mount. The fastest way to extract a small number of files is to start with the last tape volume and work toward the first.

verbose
Toggle the status of the **v** modifier. While **v** is in effect, the **ls** command lists the inode numbers of all entries, and **ufsrestore** displays information about each file as it is extracted.

help Display a summary of the available commands.

quit **ufsrestore** exits immediately, even if the extraction list is not empty.

NOTES

ufsrestore can get confused when doing incremental restores from dump tapes that were made on active file systems.

A level **0** dump must be done after a full restore. Because **ufsrestore** runs in user mode, it has no control over inode allocation; this means that **ufsrestore** repositions the files, although it does not change their contents. Thus, a full dump must be done to get a new set of directories reflecting the new file positions, so that later incremental dumps will be correct.

DIAGNOSTICS

ufsrestore complains about bad option characters.

Read errors result in complaints. If **y** has been specified, or the user responds **y**, **ufsrestore** will attempt to continue.

If the dump extends over more than one tape, **ufsrestore** asks the user to change tapes. If the **x** or **i** option has been specified, **ufsrestore** also asks which volume the user wishes to mount.

There are numerous consistency checks that can be listed by **ufsrestore**. Most checks are self-explanatory or can never happen. Common errors are given below.

Converting to new file system format.
A dump tape created from the old file system has been loaded. It is automatically converted to the new file system format.

filename: **not found on tape**
The specified file name was listed in the tape directory, but was not found on the tape. This is caused by tape read errors while looking for the file, and from using a dump tape created on an active file system.

expected next file *inumber*, **got** *inumber*
A file that was not listed in the directory showed up. This can occur when using a dump tape created on an active file system.

Incremental tape too low
When doing an incremental restore, a tape that was written before the previous incremental tape, or that has too low an incremental level has been loaded.

Incremental tape too high
When doing incremental restore, a tape that does not begin its coverage where the previous incremental tape left off, or one that has too high an incremental level has been loaded.

Tape read error while restoring *filename*
Tape read error while skipping over inode inumber
Tape read error while trying to resynchronize
A tape read error has occurred.
If a file name is specified, then its contents are probably partially wrong. If an inode is being skipped or the tape is trying to resynchronize, then no extracted files have been corrupted, though files may not be found on the tape.

resync ufsrestore, skipped *num*
After a tape read error, **ufsrestore** may have to resynchronize itself. This message lists the number of blocks that were skipped over.

FILES

/dev/rmt*	the default tape drive
/tmp/rstdir*	file containing directories on the tape
/tmp/rstmode*	owner, mode, and timestamps for directories
./restoresymtable	information passed between incremental restores

SEE ALSO

mkfs(1M), mount(1M), ufsdump(1M)

NAME

uidadmin – user-controlled ID map database administration

SYNOPSIS

uidadmin [**-S** *scheme* [**-l** *logname*]]
uidadmin -S *scheme* **-a -r** *g_name* [-l *logname*]
uidadmin -S *scheme* **-d** [**-r** *g_name*] **-l** *logname*
uidadmin -S *scheme* [**-cf**]

DESCRIPTION

The **uidadmin** command is used primarily by non-privileged users to display and update entries in the user ID mapping database.

The user ID database consists of one or more user ID map files, where each file is associated with a different authentication scheme.

Non-privileged users are limited to administering only primary attribute entries that map into their own user identities. Mapping of secondary attributes is controlled exclusively by the system administrator. The administrator of user-controlled mapping must be in group **sys**.

The options to **uidadmin** have the following meanings:

-S *scheme* Specify the name of the ID mapping scheme.

-l *logname* Specify a local name (logname) into which the remote name maps. *logname* must be a valid logname on the local machine. A non-privileged user can map a remote name only to his or her own local logname; if the **-l** option is omitted, the user's local logname is assumed. When a privileged user maps a remote name to a non-privileged user's local logname, the **-l** option is required.

-a Add a map entry. The scheme name and the remote name must be specified. A local name different from the user's logname can be specified by a privileged user.

-r *g_name* Specify the remote (global) name. The format of *g_name* is scheme-dependent; generally, it includes a login name and a machine name.

-d Delete a map entry. The scheme name and the local name must be specified. Specifying the remote name is optional. If only the local name is specified, all entries mapping to the local name are deleted. If a remote name is also specified, a particular map entry is deleted.

-c Check the consistency of a map file. The **-c** option is intended for use by a system administrator. The scheme name must be specified. Map entries containing syntax errors and unknown lognames are displayed. Lognames are unknown if they do not exist in **/etc/passwd**.

-f Fix an inconsistent map file. The **-f** option is intended for use by a system administrator. Entries that are out of order are sorted; map entries containing syntax errors and unknown lognames are displayed, and the system administrator is given the opportunity to change or delete them.

When no options are specified, **uidadmin** lists all schemes and for each scheme, indicates whether it is in **SECURE** or **USER** mode. A scheme in **USER** mode has user-controlled mapping enabled. When *scheme* is specified, **uidadmin** uses the user's real UID to determine the local *logname* and reports entries in that scheme's user map file that map into the local name. When a privileged user specifies a scheme, the entire contents of the scheme's user map file is displayed.

When *scheme* and *logname* are specified with no other options, all entries in the scheme's **uidata** file that map into the logname are reported. Only a privileged user can use this form of the command to list other users' entries.

EXAMPLES

The following line is an example of a command line that includes the **-a** option. The command adds an entry to the user map file associated with scheme **ns**. The entry maps from the remote name **our_gang:alfalfa** into the user's local logname.

```
uidadmin -S ns -a -r our_gang:alfalfa
```

The following lines are command lines that include the **-d** option. The first line deletes the entry that maps the remote name **our_gang:alfalfa** into local user **darla**. The second line deletes from the user map file all entries that map into the local name **darla**.

```
uidadmin -S ns -d -r our_gang:waldo -l darla
uidadmin -S ns -d -l darla
```

FILES

/var/adm/log/idmap.log	log file
/etc/passwd	password file

SEE ALSO

attradmin(1M), **attrmap**(3I), **idadmin**(1M), **namemap**(3I)

NOTES

All update operations are logged (whether successful or not) in the file **/var/adm/log/idmap.log**.

NAME

ul – (BSD) underline

SYNOPSIS

/usr/ucb/ul [**-i**] [**-t** *terminal*] [*file* . . .]

DESCRIPTION

The **ul** command reads the named *file*s (or the standard input if none are given) and translates occurrences of underscores to the sequence which indicates underlining for the terminal in use, as specified by the environment variable **TERM**. **ul** uses the **/usr/share/lib/termcap** file to determine the appropriate sequences for underlining. If the terminal is incapable of underlining, but is capable of a standout mode then that is used instead. If the terminal can overstrike, or handles underlining automatically, **ul** degenerates to **cat**. If the terminal cannot underline, underlining is ignored.

The following options are available:

-t *terminal* Override the terminal kind specified in the environment. If the terminal cannot underline, underlining is ignored.

-i Indicate underlining by a separate line containing appropriate dashes -; this is useful when you want to look at the underlining which is present in an **nroff** output stream on a CRT-terminal.

SEE ALSO

cat(1), **man**(1), **nroff**(1)

umask(1)

NAME

umask – set file-creation mode mask

SYNOPSIS

umask [*ooo*]

DESCRIPTION

The user file-creation mode mask is set to *ooo*. The three octal digits refer to read/write/execute permissions for *owner*, **group**, and *others*, respectively (see **chmod**(2) and **umask**(2)). The value of each specified digit is subtracted from the corresponding "digit" specified by the system for the creation of a file (see **creat**(2)). For example, **umask 022** removes **group** and *others* write permission (files normally created with mode **777** become mode **755**; files created with mode **666** become mode **644**).

If *ooo* is omitted, the current value of the mask is printed.

umask is recognized and executed by the shell.

umask can be included in the user's **.profile** (see **profile**(4)) and invoked at login to automatically set the user's permissions on files or directories created.

FILES

/usr/lib/locale/*locale***/LC_MESSAGES/uxcore.abi**
    language-specific message file [See **LANG** on **environ** (5).]

SEE ALSO

chmod(1), **chmod**(2), **creat**(2), **profile**(4), **sh**(1), **umask**(2)

NAME

uname – print name of current UNIX system

SYNOPSIS

uname [**-amnprsv**]
uname [**-S** *system_name*]

DESCRIPTION

uname prints the current system name of the UNIX system to standard output. It is mainly useful to determine which system one is using. The options cause selected information returned by **uname**(2) and/or **sysinfo**(2) to be printed. Invoking **uname** with no options is equivalent to invoking **uname -s**.

-a Print all information.

-m Print the machine hardware name.

-n Print the node name (the node name is the name by which the system is known to a communications network).

-p Print the current host's processor type.

-r Print the operating system release.

-s Print the name of this implementation of the operating system (for example, UNIX System V).

-v Print the operating system version.

-S Set both the system name and the node name to *system_name*. *system_name* is restricted to **SYS_NMLN** characters [see **limits**(4)]. Only a privileged user is allowed this capability.

This option is provided only for compatibility reasons. It is recommended that you use **setuname**(1M) instead. **setuname -s** lets you change the system name independently of the node name.

Be aware that if you change a node name, other software may break unexpectedly, so it is good practice not to change a node name once it is set. For example, networking software and application packages may save the node name of your system at the time the package is installed. Therefore, each time you change the node name, you will need to locate all the files where it has been saved and change its value. See your system administration guide for further advice.

FILES

/usr/lib/locale/*locale***/LC_MESSAGES/uxcore.abi**
language-specific message file [See **LANG** on **environ**(5).]

SEE ALSO

environ(5), **limits**(4), **setuname**(1M), **sysinfo**(2), **uname**(2)

NAME

unget – undo a previous **get** of an SCCS file

SYNOPSIS

unget [-r*SID***] [-s] [-n]** *file* . . .

DESCRIPTION

unget undoes the effect of a **get -e** done prior to creating the intended new delta. If a directory is named, **unget** behaves as though each file in the directory were specified as a named file, except that non-SCCS files and unreadable files are silently ignored. If a name of **-** is given, the standard input is read with each line being taken as the name of an SCCS file to be processed.

Keyletter arguments apply independently to each named file.

-r*SID* Uniquely identifies which delta is no longer intended. (This would have been specified by **get** as the "new delta"). The use of this keyletter is necessary only if two or more outstanding **get**s for editing on the same SCCS file were done by the same person (login name). A diagnostic results if the specified *SID* is ambiguous, or if it is necessary and omitted on the command line.

-s Suppresses the printout, on the standard output, of the intended delta's *SID*.

-n Causes the retention of the gotten file, which would normally be removed from the current directory.

unget must be performed by the same user who performed the original **get -e**.

FILES

p.*file* [see **delta**(1)]

q.*file* [see **delta**(1)]

z.*file* [see **delta**(1)]

SEE ALSO

delta(1), **get**(1), **help**(1), **sact**(1)

DIAGNOSTICS

Use **help**(1) for explanations.

NAME

unifdef – (BSD) resolve and remove **ifdef**'ed lines from **C** program source

SYNOPSIS

/usr/ucb/unifdef [**-clt**] [**-D***name*] [**-U***name*] [**-iD***name*] [**-iU***name*] . . . [*file*]

DESCRIPTION

unifdef removes **ifdef**ed lines from a file while otherwise leaving the file alone. It is smart enough to deal with the nested **ifdef**s, comments, single and double quotes of C syntax, but it does not do any including or interpretation of macros. Neither does it strip out comments, though it recognizes and ignores them. You specify which symbols you want defined with **-D** options, and which you want undefined with **-U** options. Lines within those **ifdef**s will be copied to the output, or removed, as appropriate. Any **ifdef**, **ifndef**, **else**, and **endif** lines associated with *file* will also be removed.

ifdefs involving symbols you do not specify are untouched and copied out along with their associated **ifdef**, **else**, and **endif** lines.

If an **ifdef***X* occurs nested inside another **ifdef***X*, then the inside **ifdef** is treated as if it were an unrecognized symbol. If the same symbol appears in more than one argument, only the first occurrence is significant.

unifdef copies its output to the standard output and will take its input from the standard input if no *file* argument is given.

The following options are available:

-c Complement the normal operation. Lines that would have been removed or blanked are retained, and vice versa.

-l Replace "lines removed" lines with blank lines.

-t Plain text option. **unifdef** refrains from attempting to recognize comments and single and double quotes.

-iD*name* Ignore, but print out, lines associated with the defined symbol *name*. If you use **ifdef**s to delimit non-C lines, such as comments or code which is under construction, then you must tell **unifdef** which symbols are used for that purpose so that it will not try to parse for quotes and comments within them.

-iU*name* Ignore, but print out, lines associated with the undefined symbol *name*.

SEE ALSO

cc(1), **diff**(1)

DIAGNOSTICS

Premature EOF Inappropriate **else** or **endif**.

Exit status is 0 if output is exact copy of input, 1 if not, 2 if **unifdef** encounters problems.

uniq (1)

NAME

uniq – report repeated lines in a file

SYNOPSIS

uniq [**-udc** [**+**n] [-n]] [*input* [*output*]]

DESCRIPTION

uniq reads the input file comparing adjacent lines. In the normal case, the second and succeeding copies of repeated lines are removed; the remainder is written on the output file. *Input* and *output* should always be different. Note that repeated lines must be adjacent in order to be found; see **sort**(1). If the **-u** flag is used, just the lines that are not repeated in the original file are output. The **-d** option specifies that one copy of just the repeated lines is to be written. The normal mode output is the union of the **-u** and **-d** mode outputs. The **-c** option supersedes **-u** and **-d** and generates an output report in default style but with each line preceded by a count of the number of times it occurred. **uniq** processes supplementary code set characters according to the locale specified in the **LC_CTYPE** environment variable [see **LANG** on **environ**(5)].

The *n* arguments specify skipping an initial portion of each line in the comparison:

-*n* The first *n* fields together with any blanks before each are ignored. A field is defined as a string of non-space, non-tab characters separated by tabs and spaces from its neighbors.

+*n* The first *n* characters (columns, in multibyte environments) are ignored. Fields are skipped before characters.

FILES

/usr/lib/locale/*locale***/LC_MESSAGES/uxdfm**
language-specific message file [See **LANG** on **environ**(5).]

SEE ALSO

comm(1), **sort**(1)

NAME

`units` – conversion program

SYNOPSIS

`units`

DESCRIPTION

`units` converts quantities expressed in various standard scales to their equivalents in other scales. It works interactively in this fashion:

```
You have: inch
You want: cm
                * 2.540000e+00
                / 3.937008e-01
```

A quantity is specified as a multiplicative combination of units optionally preceded by a numeric multiplier. Powers are indicated by suffixed positive integers, division by the usual sign:

```
You have: 15 lbs force/in2
You want: atm
                * 1.020689e+00
                / 9.797299e-01
```

`units` only does multiplicative scale changes; thus it can convert Kelvin to Rankine, but not Celsius to Fahrenheit. Most familiar units, abbreviations, and metric prefixes are recognized, together with a generous leavening of exotica and a few constants of nature including:

`pi`	ratio of circumference to diameter,
`c`	speed of light,
`e`	charge on an electron,
`g`	acceleration of gravity,
`force`	same as `g`,
`mole`	Avogadro's number,
`water`	pressure head per unit height of water,
`au`	astronomical unit.

`Pound` is not recognized as a unit of mass; `lb` is. Compound names are run together, (for example, `lightyear`). British units that differ from their U.S. counterparts are prefixed thus: `brgallon`. For a complete list of units, type:

```
cat /usr/share/lib/unittab
```

FILES

`/usr/share/lib/unittab`

unix2dos (1)

NAME

unix2dos – converts UNIX operating system text files to DOS format

SYNOPSIS

unix2dos [**-?hz**] [*infile* [*outfile*]]

DESCRIPTION

The **unix2dos** command allows you to view UNIX operating system text files under DOS. It accomplishes this by converting lines ending in a new-line (ASCII line-feed) to lines ending in a carriage-return and line-feed sequence. Additionally, **unix2dos** converts from the UNIX operating system code set to the DOS code page used by your personal computer.

The first file specified (*infile*) is the source file. The second file specified (*outfile*) is the target file. The source file and the target file must not have the same name. When neither file parameter is specified, **unix2dos** reads from standard input and writes to standard output. When only one file parameter is specified, that file is considered the source file, and the output is written to standard output.

If the source file is already in DOS format, **unix2dos** does not alter the format of the file, but it does translate between code page and code set by default.

Use the **-z** option if you want **unix2dos** to stop processing when it encounters the DOS end-of file (EOF) character.

If **unix2dos** doesn't convert characters as you expect, use the **-?** or **-h** option to display the options available. Refer to **charconv** in this appendix for more information.

unix2dos can be used in combination with DOS and UNIX operating system pipes and redirection.

For example, the command:

```
unix2dos phonenos | sort > phone
```

converts the host file **phonenos**, sorts the converted text, and writes it to the DOS file **phone**. Note that you cannot redirect a converted file to itself.

NAME

unshare – make local resource unavailable for mounting by remote systems

SYNOPSIS

unshare [-F *fstype*] [-o *specific_options*] {*pathname* | *resourcename*}

DESCRIPTION

The **unshare** command makes a shared local resource unavailable to file system type *fstype*. If the option **-F** *fstype* is omitted, then the first file system type listed in file **/etc/dfs/fstypes** will be used as the default. *specific_options,* as well as the semantics of *resourcename,* are specific to the particular distributed file system associated with the specified file system type.

Only a privileged user can execute this command.

FILES

/etc/dfs/fstypes
/etc/dfs/sharetab

SEE ALSO

share(1M), **shareall**(1M), **nfs**-specific **unshare**(1M), **rfs**-specific **unshare**(1M)

NOTES

If *pathname* or *resourcename* is not found in the shared information, an error message will be sent to standard error.

NAME

unshare – make local NFS resource unavailable for mounting by remote systems

SYNOPSIS

unshare {*pathname*|*resource*}

DESCRIPTION

The **unshare** command makes local resources unavailable for mounting by remote systems. The shared resource must correspond to a line with NFS as the *fstype* in the file **/etc/dfs/sharetab**.

The NFS-specific **unshare** command is called by the **/usr/sbin/unshare** command when the **-F nfs** option specified.

Only a privileged user can execute this command.

Options

The following options are available to the **unshare** command:

pathname
: The pathname of the resource to be unshared.

resource
: The name of the *resource* to be unshared.

Files

/etc/dfs/fstypes

/etc/dfs/sharetab

Exit Codes

0 Successful exit

33 Usage error

35 Could not delete from sharetab

36 Could not unshare

REFERENCES

share(1M), NFS-specific **share**(1M), NFS-specific **unshare**(1M)

NAME

unshare – make local RFS resource unavailable for mounting by remote systems

SYNOPSIS

unshare [**-F** rfs] {*pathname* | *resourcename*}

DESCRIPTION

This command is obsolete and will not be supported after this release. The **unshare** command makes a shared resource unavailable through Remote File Sharing. The shared resource must correspond to a line with rfs as the *fstype* in the file **/etc/dfs/sharetab**. The **-F** flag may be omitted if RFS is the first file system type listed in the file **/etc/dfs/fstypes**.

Only a privileged user can execute this command.

FILES

/etc/dfs/dfstab
/etc/dfs/fstypes
/etc/dfs/sharetab

SEE ALSO

unshare(1M), **share**(1M)

NAME

uptime – (BSD) show how long the system has been up

SYNOPSIS

/usr/ucb/uptime

DESCRIPTION

The **uptime** command prints the current time, the length of time the system has been up. It is the first line of a **w**(1) command.

EXAMPLE

Below is an example of the output **uptime** provides:

```
6:47am  up 6 days, 16:38,  1 user
```

SEE ALSO

w(1), **who**(1), **whodo**(1M).

NOTES

who -b gives the time the system was last booted.

Unlike other BSD versions of this command, the load averages are not computed or displayed.

NAME

urestore – request restore of files and directories

SYNOPSIS

urestore -F [**-mn**] [**-s** | **v**] [**-o** *target*] [**-d** *date*] *file* . . .

urestore -D [**-mn**] [**-s** | **v**] [**-o** *target*] [**-d** *date*] *dir* . . .

urestore -c *jobid*

DESCRIPTION

urestore posts requests for files or directories to be restored from system-maintained archives. If the appropriate archive containing the requested files or directories is on-line, the files or directories are restored immediately. If not, a request to restore the specified files or directories is posted to a restore status table, **/etc/bkup/rsstatus.tab**. A restore request that has been posted must later be resolved by an operator [see **rsoper**(1M)]. Each file or directory to be restored is assigned a **restore** job ID that can be used to monitor the progress of the restore or to cancel it.

The user must have write permission for the current directory and any subdirectories to be traversed in storing the restored files or directories. Requests for restores may be made only by the user who owned the files or directories at the time the archive containing the files or directories was made, or by a privileged user.

Options

-c *jobid* Cancels a previously issued restore request.

-d *date* Restores the filesystem or directory as of *date*. (This may or may not be the latest archive.) See **getdate**(3C) for valid date formats.

-m If the restore cannot be carried out immediately, this option notifies the invoking user (via **mail**) when the request has been completed.

-n Displays a list of all archived versions of the filesystem or directory contained in the backup history log but does not attempt to restore the filesystem or directory.

-o *target* Instead of restoring directly to the specified file or directory, this option replaces the file or directory *target* with the archive of the specified file or directory.

-s While a restore operation is occurring, displays a "." for each 100 (512-byte) blocks transferred from the destination device.

-v Displays the name of each object as it is restored. Only those archiving methods that restore named directories and files (**incfile, ffile**) support this option.

-D Initiates a restore operation for directories.

-F Initiates a restore operation for files.

DIAGNOSTICS

The exit codes for **urestore** are the following:

0 = the task completed successfully
1 = one or more parameters to **urestore** are invalid
2 = an error has occurred, causing **urestore** to fail to complete all portions of its task.

EXAMPLES

Example 1:

```
urestore -F -m bigfile
```

posts a request to restore the most current archived version of the file **bigfile**. If the restore operation cannot be carried out immediately, it notifies the invoking user when the request has been completed.

Example 2:

```
urestore -c rest-256a,rest-256b
```

cancels restore requests with job ID numbers **rest-256a** and **rest-256b**.

Example 3:

```
urestore -F -o /testfiles/myfile.b /testfiles/myfile.a
```

posts a request for the archived file **/testfiles/myfile.a** to be restored as **/testfiles/myfile.b**

Example 4:

```
urestore -D -d "december 1, 1987" /user1 -v
```

posts a request for the archived directory structure **/user1**, with all its files and subdirectories, to be restored as of December 1, 1987. If the restore is done immediately from an on-line archive, the name of each file will be displayed on standard output while the restore is underway.

Example 5:

```
urestore -D -n /pr3/reports
```

requests the system to display the backup dates and an **ls -l** listing from the backup history log of all archived versions of the directory **/pr3/reports**. The directory is not restored.

FILES

/etc/bkup/bkhist.tab	contains the labels of all volumes that have been used for backup operations
/etc/bkup/rsstatus.tab	contains status information about all restore requests from users
/etc/bkup/rsnotify.tab	contains the electronic mail address of the operator to be notified whenever restore requests require operator intervention

SEE ALSO

getdate(3C), **mail**(1), **restore**(1M)

NAME

ursstatus – report the status of posted user restore requests

SYNOPSIS

ursstatus [**-h**] [**-j** *jobids*] [**-f** *field_separator*] [**-d** *ddev*] [**-u** *users*]

DESCRIPTION

With no options, **ursstatus** reports the status of all pending user restore requests that are posted in the restore status table.

This command can request a status report for only those restore requests that the user has initiated.

Options

-h Suppresses header for the report.

-j *jobids* Restricts the report to the specified jobs. *jobids* is a list of restore job IDs (either comma-separated or blank-separated and surrounded by quotes). *jobids* must be valid for the user invoking the command.

-f *field_separator*
Suppresses field wrap and specifies an output field separator to be used. *field_separator* is the character that will appear as the field separator in the output displayed. A null *field_separator* will use a tab character as a separator.

-d *ddev* Restricts the report to pending restore jobs that could be satisfied by the specified device type or volumes. *ddev* describes the device or volumes used to select requests to be restored. *ddev* is of the form:

[*dtype*][**:** *dlabels*]

dtype is a device type (such as diskette, cartridge tape, or 9-track tape). If specified, restrict the report to posted requests that could be satisfied by volumes of the type specified.

dlabels is a list of volume names corresponding to the *volumename* displayed by the **labelit** command. *dlabels* may be either comma-separated or blank-separated and surrounded by quotes. If specified, restrict the report to posted requests that could be satisfied by an archive residing on the specified volumes.

-u *users* Restricts the report to requests submitted by the specified *users* (either comma-separated or blank-separated and surrounded by quotes). *users* must be listed in the **passwd** file.

DIAGNOSTICS

The exit codes for **ursstatus** are the following:

0 = successful completion of the task

1 = one or more parameters to **ursstatus** are invalid.

2 = an error has occurred which caused **ursstatus** to fail to complete all portions of its task.

EXAMPLE

```
ursstatus -j rest-354a,rest-429b
```

reports the status of only the two posted restore requests with the specified job IDs.

FILES

`/etc/bkup/rsstatus.tab` contains status report information for all restore requests from users

SEE ALSO

restore(1M), **rsstatus**(1M), **urestore**(1M)

NAME

useradd – administer a new user login on the system

SYNOPSIS

useradd [**-u** *uid* [**-o**] [**-i**]] [**-g** *group*] [**-G** *group*[[**,***group*] . . .]] [**-d** *dir*] [**-s** *shell*] [**-c** *comment*] [**-m** [**-k** *skel_dir*]] [**-f** *inactive*] [**-e** *expire*] [**-p** *passgen*] [**-a** *event*[**,** . . .]] *login*

DESCRIPTION

Invoking **useradd** adds a new user entry to the Identification and Authentication (I&A) data files. It also creates supplementary group memberships for the user (**-G** option) and creates the home directory (**-m** option) for the user if requested. The new login is locked until the **passwd**(1) command is executed.

As installed, defaults for the various parameters are listed in the file **/etc/default/useradd**. The defaults for the options below that offer defaults can be changed via the **defadm** command.

The system file entries created with this command have a limit of 512 characters per line. Specifying long arguments to several options may exceed this limit.

The following options are available:

-u *uid* — The user identification number (UID). This UID must be a non-negative decimal integer below **MAXUID** as defined in **sys/param.h**. The UID defaults to the next available (unique) non-aged UID greater than 99.

-o — This option allows a UID to be duplicated (non-unique). Because the security of the system in general, and the integrity of the audit trail and accounting information in particular, depends on every UID being uniquely associated with a specific individual, use of this option is discouraged (in order to maintain user accountability).

-i — Allow a UID currently being aged to be used.

-g *group* — An existing group's integer ID or character-string name. This option defines the new user's primary group membership and defaults to the default group in **/etc/default/useradd**.

-G *group* — An existing group's integer ID or character-string name. It defines the new user's supplementary group membership. Duplicates between *group* with th **-g** and **-G** are ignored. No more than **NGROUPS_MAX** groups may be specified.

-d *dir* — The home directory of the new user. This field is limited to 256 characters. It defaults to *HOMEDIR/login*, where *HOMEDIR* is the base directory for new login home directories and *login* is the new login.

-s *shell* — Full pathname of the program used as the user's shell on login. This field is limited to 256 characters. It defaults to an empty field causing the system to use **/usr/bin/sh** as the default. The value of *shell* must be a valid executable file.

-c *comment* Any text string. It is generally a short description of the login, and is currently used as the field for the user's full name. This information is stored in the user's **/etc/passwd** entry. This field is limited to 128 printable characters.

-m Create the new user's home directory if it doesn't already exist. If the directory already exists, the user being added must have access permissions to the directory.

-k *skel_dir* Copy the contents of the directory *skel_dir* into the new user's home directory, instead of the contents of the default skeleton directory, **/etc/skel**. The *skel_dir* directory must exist. The default skeleton directory contains a standard **.profile** file, and can contain other directories and files that define the user's environment. An administrator-defined *skel_dir* might contain the same types of files and directories, customized for a special purpose.

-f *inactive* The maximum number of days allowed between uses of a login before that login is declared invalid. Normal values are positive integers.

-e *expire* The date on which a login can no longer be used; after this date, no user will be able to access this login. (This option is useful for creating temporary logins.) You may type the value of the argument *expire* (which is a date) in any format you like (except a Julian date). For example, you may enter **10/6/90** or **October 6, 1990**.

-p *passgen* Indicates that the FLAG field in **/etc/shadow** is to be set to the specified value. This field is referenced by the **passwd** command to determine if a password generator is in effect for this user. The **FORCED_PASS** entry in **/etc/default/useradd** is checked if the **-p** option is not explicitly specified to determine the value for the entry in **/etc/shadow**. If **FORCED_PASS** does not exist in **/etc/default/useradd** there will be no value in the **/etc/shadow** entry. If the value of **FORCED_PASS** is **1**, then the entry in **/etc/shadow** is set to **1**. If *passgen* is neither a **NULL** string nor a printable ASCII character, a diagnostic message is printed.

-a *event* A comma-separated list of event types or classes that make up the user's audit mask. There is no default user audit mask in the system as delivered, but you can define a default in the file **/etc/default/useradd** using the **defadm** command. This option is valid only if the Auditing Utilities are installed. (To find out which packages are installed on your system, run the **pkginfo** command.)

login A string of printable characters that specifies the new login name of the user. It may not contain a colon (**:**) or a newline (**\n**). It should also not begin with a capital letter.

Note that many of the defaults for the above parameters can be changed through the **defadm** command, which administers the **/etc/default/useradd** file.

FILES

/etc/default/useradd
/etc/group
/etc/passwd
/etc/security/ia/ageduid
/etc/security/ia/audit
/etc/security/ia/index
/etc/security/ia/master
/etc/shadow
/etc/skel

SEE ALSO

defadm(1M), **groupadd**(1M), **groupdel**(1M), **groupmod**(1M), **logins**(1M), **passwd**(1), **userdel**(1M), **usermod**(1M), **users**(1)

DIAGNOSTICS

The **useradd** command exits with a return code of **0** upon successful completion. In case of errors, the following messages may be displayed:

The command line syntax was invalid.

An invalid argument was provided with an option.

The *uid* specified with the **-u** option is already in use and the **-o** option was not specified.

The *group* specified with the **-g** option does not exist.

The specified *login* is not unique.

Cannot update **/etc/group**. The login was added to the **/etc/passwd** file but not to the **/etc/group** file.

Unable to create the home directory (with the **-m** option) or unable to complete the copy of *skel_dir* to the home directory.

uid not aged sufficiently. Choose another.

An invalid option **-a** was specified; system service not installed.

An invalid audit event type or class *event* was specified.

NAME

userdel – delete a user's login from the system

SYNOPSIS

userdel [**-r**] [**-n** *months*] *login*

DESCRIPTION

The **userdel** command deletes a user's login definition from the system. It removes the definition of the specified login and makes the appropriate login-related system file and file system changes. The command also stores the user identification number (UID) being deleted in the **/etc/security/ia/ageduid** file, so the UID will not be reused until a period of time has passed. This practice of keeping a UID out of use is called UID aging.

The following options are available:

-r Remove the user's home directory from the system. This directory must exist. The files and directories under the home directory will no longer be accessible following successful execution of the command.

-n *months*
Specify a value for the number of months to age the UID. Specify **-1** to indicate the UID should never be reused. Specify **0** to indicate the UID may be reused immediately. If the **-n** option is not specified, the UID will be aged for a default number of months before it will be reused.

login A string of printable characters that specifies an existing login on the system. It may not contain a colon (**:**) or a newline (**\n**).

Warnings

Whenever you use the **userdel** command to delete a users's login, you should execute **adminuser -d** *login_name* to avoid createing any security holes; otherwise security breaches will be introduced when you remove logins for users who have been added to the TFM database. Use the desktop metaphor to remove users who have been added through the metaphor.

Not all users have privileges but desktop users usually do. If a user whose login is being removed has no privileges and you execute **adminuser -d**, you'll simply get an error message (**UX:adminuser:ERROR:Undefined user** *login_name*).

FILES

/etc/default/userdel
/etc/group
/etc/passwd
/etc/security/ia/ageduid
/etc/security/ia/audit
/etc/security/ia/index
/etc/security/ia/master
/etc/shadow

The file **/etc/security/ia/audit** is not available if the Auditing Utilities are not installed.

SEE ALSO

adminuser(1M), **dtdeluser**(1M), **groupadd**(1M), **groupdel**(1M), **groupmod**(1M), **logins**(1M), **passwd**(1), **useradd**(1M), **usermod**(1M), **users**(1)

DIAGNOSTICS

The **userdel** command exits with a return code of **0** upon successful completion. In case of errors, the following messages may be displayed:

Invalid command syntax.

The login to be removed does not exist.

The login to be removed is in use.

Cannot update the **/etc/group** file but the login is removed from the **/etc/passwd** file.

Cannot remove or otherwise modify the home directory.

NAME

usermod – modify a user's login information on the system

SYNOPSIS

usermod [**-u** *uid* [**-o**]] [**-g** *group*] [**-G** *group*[[**,** *group*] . . .]] [**-d** *dir*[**-m**]] [**-s** *shell*]
[**-c** *comment*] [**-l** *new_logname*] [**-f** *inactive*] [**-e** *expire*] [**-p** *passgen*]
[**-a** [*operator1*]*event*[**,** . . .]] *login*

DESCRIPTION

Invoking **usermod** modifies a user entry in the Identification and Authentication (I&A) data files. The system file entries created with this command have a limit of 512 characters per line. Specifying long arguments to several options may result in exceeding this limit.

NOTE: This command does not change the UID on directories and files owned by the user whose UID is being changed; the system administrator must make such changes.

The following options are available:

-u *uid* New user identification number (UID). It must be a non-negative decimal integer below **MAXUID** as defined in **sys/param.h**.

-o This option allows the specified UID to be duplicated (non-unique). Because the security of the system in general, and the integrity of the audit trail and accounting information in particular, depends on every UID being uniquely associated with a specific individual, use of this option is discouraged (in order to maintain user accountability).

-g *group* An existing group's integer ID or character-string name. It redefines the user's primary group membership.

-G *group* An existing group's integer ID or character string name. It redefines the user's supplementary group membership. Duplicates are ignored. No more than **NGROUPS_UMAX** groups may be specified as defined in **sys/param.h**.

-d *dir* The new home directory of the user. This field is limited to 256 characters.

-m Move the user's home directory to the new directory specified with the **-d** option. If the directory already exists, the specified *login* must have access to it.

-s *shell* Full pathname of the program that is used as the user's shell on login. This field is limited to 256 characters. The value of *shell* must be a valid executable file.

-c *comment*

Any text string. It is generally a short description of the login, and is currently used as the field for the user's full name. This field is limited to 128 printable characters. This information is stored in the user's **/etc/passwd** entry.

-l *new_logname*
A string of printable characters that specifies the new login name for the user. It may not contain a colon (**:**) or a newline (**\n**). Also it should not begin with a capital letter.

-f *inactive* The maximum number of days allowed between uses of a login ID before that login ID is declared invalid. Normal values are positive integers. A value of **-1** turns off inactive checking.

-e *expire* The date on which a login can no longer be used; after this date, no user will be able to access this login. (This option is useful for creating temporary logins.) You may type the value of the argument *expire* (which is a date) in any format you like (except a Julian date). For example, you may enter **10/6/90** or **October 6, 1990**. A value of **""** turns off expiration checking.

-p *passgen* Indicates that the FLAG field in **/etc/shadow** is to be set to the specified value. This field is referenced by the **passwd** command to determine if a password generator is in effect for this user. If *passgen* is neither a **NULL** string nor a printable ASCII character, a diagnostic message is printed.

-a [*operator*] *event(s)*
Set the user's audit mask based on the event(s) specified. An operator can be specified (as + to add or - to delete) or not specified (to replace). This option is valid only if the Auditing Utilities are installed. (To find out which packages are installed on your system, run the **pkginfo** command.)

login A string of printable characters that specifies the existing login name of a user. It must exist and may not contain a colon (**:**), or a newline (**\n**).

FILES

/etc/group
/etc/passwd
/etc/security/ia/audit
/etc/security/ia/index
/etc/security/ia/master
/etc/shadow

SEE ALSO

groupadd(1M), **groupdel**(1M), **groupmod**(1M), **logins**(1M), **passwd**(1), **useradd**(1M), **userdel**(1M), **users**(1)

DIAGNOSTICS

The **usermod** command exits with a return code of **0** if successful. In case of errors, the following messages may be displayed:

The command syntax was invalid.

An invalid argument was provided to an option.

The *uid* given with the **-u** option is already in use.

The login to be modified does not exist or *group* does not exist.

The login to be modified is in use.

The *new_logname* is already in use.

Cannot update the **/etc/group** file. Other update requests will be implemented.

Insufficient space to move the home directory (**-m** option). Other update requests will be implemented.

Unable to complete the move of the home directory to the new home directory.

Invalid options **-h**, **-v** system service not installed.

Invalid option **-a**, system service not installed.

Invalid audit event type or class specified.

NAME

users – (BSD) display a compact list of users logged in

SYNOPSIS

/usr/ucb/users [*file*]

DESCRIPTION

users lists the login names of the users currently on the system in a compact, one-line format.

If there are more than 200 users on the system, only the first 200 are listed, and the message:

******The number of users exceeds 200. Only the first 200 are listed.**

is displayed.

Specifying *file*, tells **users** where to find its information; by default it checks **/var/adm/utmp**.

Typing *users* is equivalent to typing **who -q**.

EXAMPLE

```
users
paul george ringo
```

FILES

/var/adm/utmp

SEE ALSO

who(1)

uucheck (1M)

NAME

uucheck – check the uucp directories and permissions file

SYNOPSIS

/usr/lib/uucp/uucheck [options]

DESCRIPTION

uucheck checks for the presence of the **uucp** system required files and directories. **uucheck** also does error checking of the *Permissions* file (**/etc/uucp/Permissions**). **uucheck** has the following options:

-v Give a detailed (verbose) explanation of how the uucp programs will interpret the **Permissions** file.

-x*debug_level*
debug_level is a number from 0 to 9. Higher numbers give more detailed debugging information.

uucheck is executed during package installation. Note that **uucheck** can only be used by a privileged user or **uucp**.

FILES

/etc/uucp/Systems
/etc/uucp/Permissions
/etc/uucp/Devices
/etc/uucp/Limits
/var/spool/uucp/*
/var/spool/locks/*
/var/spool/uucppublic/*

SEE ALSO

uucico(1M), **uusched**(1M). **uucp**(1C), **uustat**(1C), **uux**(1C)

NOTES

The program does not check file/directory modes or some errors in the *Permissions* file such as duplicate login or machine name.

NAME

uucico – file transport program for the uucp system

SYNOPSIS

/usr/lib/uucp/uucico [*options*]

DESCRIPTION

uucico is the file transport program for **uucp** work file transfers. The following options are available.

-c*type* The first field in the **Devices** file is the "Type" field. The **-c** option forces **uucico** to only use entries in the "Type" field that match the user specified *type*. The specified *type* is usually the name of a local area network.

-d*spool_directory* This option specifies the directory *spool_directory* that contains the **uucp** work files to be transferred. The default spool directory is **/var/spool/uucp**.

-f This option is used to "force execution" of **uucico** by ignoring the limit on the maximum number of uucicos defined in the **/etc/uucp/Limits** file.

-i*interface* This option defines the *interface* used with **uucico**. The interface only affects slave mode. Known interfaces are UNIX (default), TLI (basic Transport Layer Interface), and TLIS (Transport Layer Interface with Streams modules, read/write).

-r*role_number* The *role_number* 1 is used for master mode. *role_number* 0 is used for slave mode (default). When **uucico** is started by a program or **cron**, *role_number* 1 should be used for master mode.

-s*system_name* The **-s** option defines the remote system (*system_name*) that **uucico** will try to contact. It is required when the role is master; *system_name* must be defined in the **Systems** file.

-x*debug_level* Both **uux** and **uucp** queue jobs that will be transferred by **uucico**. These jobs are normally started by the **uusched** scheduler, for debugging purposes, and can be started manually. For example, the shell **Uutry** starts **uucico** with debugging turned on. The *debug_level* is a number between 0 and 9. Higher numbers give more detailed debugging information.

If you need to use this option, you must first make sure that the Connection Server (**cs**) is in debug mode. To see if **cs** is in debug mode, enter

```
ps -eaf | grep cs
```

If you don't see output similar to the following:

```
root 236 1 0 June 08 ?  0.01   /usr/sbin/cs -x
```

you must kill the current **cs** process and restart **cs** with the **-x** option by entering:

```
/usr/sbin/cs -x
```

To turn off **cs** debugging, you must kill the **cs** process that is running the debug mode, and restart **cs** normally.

FILES

/etc/uucp/Systems
/etc/uucp/Permissions
/etc/uucp/Devices
/etc/uucp/Devconfig
/etc/uucp/Sysfiles
/etc/uucp/Limits
/var/spool/uucp/*
/var/spool/locks/*
/var/spool/uucppublic/*

SEE ALSO

cron(1M), **uusched**(1M), **Uutry**(1M) **uucp**(1C), **uustat**(1C), **uux**(1C)

NAME

uucleanup – uucp spool directory clean-up

SYNOPSIS

/usr/lib/uucp/uucleanup [*options*]

DESCRIPTION

uucleanup will scan the spool directories for old files and take appropriate action to remove them in a useful way. It will

Inform the requester of send/receive requests for systems that can not be reached.

Return undeliverable mail to the sender.

Deliver **rnews** files addressed to the local system.

Remove the log files and directories in **/var/spool/.Log/uuxbf**

Remove all other files.

In addition, **uucleanup** notifies users of requests that have been waiting for a given number of days (the default is 1). Note that **uucleanup** will process as if all option **times** were specified to the default values unless *time* is specifically set. **uucleanup** does not remove the **/var/spool/uucppublic/receive** directory. **uucleanup** processes supplementary code set characters in the *string* given to the **-m** option (see below) according to the locale specified in the **LC_CTYPE** environment variable [see **LANG** on **environ**(5)].

The following options are available.

-C*days* Any **C.** files greater or equal to *days* days old will be removed with appropriate information to the requester. (default 7 days)

-D*days* Any **D.** files greater or equal to *days* days old will be removed. An attempt will be made to deliver mail messages and execute rnews when appropriate. (default 7 days)

-W*days* Any **C.** files equal to *days* days old will cause a mail message to be sent to the requester warning about the delay in contacting the remote. The message includes the *JOBID*, and in the case of mail, the mail message. The administrator may include a message line telling whom to call to check the problem (**-m** *option*). (default 1 day)

-X*days* Any **X.** files greater or equal to *days* days old will be removed. The **D.** files are probably not present (if they were, the **X.** could get executed). But if there are **D.** files, they will be taken care of by D. processing. (default 2 days)

-d Removes empty directories under the **PUBDIR** directory only if they are owned by **uucp** (UID=5).

-m*string* Include *string* in the warning message generated by the **-W** option. *string* may contain supplementary code set characters.

-o*days* Other files whose age is more than *days* days will be deleted. (default 2 days) The default line is "**See your local administrator to locate the problem**".

-**s***system* Execute for **system** spool directory only.

-**x***debug_level*
The **-x** debug level is a single digit between 0 and 9; higher numbers give more detailed debugging information. (This option may not be available on all systems.)

This program is typically started by the shell *uudemon.cleanup,* which should be started by **cron**(1M).

FILES

/usr/lib/uucp	directory with commands used by **uucleanup** internally
/var/spool/uucp	spool directory

SEE ALSO

cron(1M), **uucp**(1C), **uux**(1C)

NAME

uucollapse – remove loops in uucp mail address

SYNOPSIS

uucollapse address . . .

DESCRIPTION

/usr/lib/mail/surrcmd/uucollapse takes a mail address expressed in "bang" format, such as **sysa!sysb!user**, and removes any cycles and loops found within the address. For example,

sysa!sysb!sysa!user

can be collapsed down to

sysa!user

because **sysb** can only talk with one **sysa**. Similarly,

sysa!sysa!user

is collapsed down to to

sysa!user

This program is intended to be used from the **/etc/mail/mailsurr** file. Note: it is assumed that the address passed in contains only exclamation points and no other type of networking characters, such as "@" or "%".

SEE ALSO

mail(1), **mailsurr**(4).

uucp(1C)

NAME

uucp, **uulog**, **uuname** – UNIX-to-UNIX system copy

SYNOPSIS

uucp [*options*] *source-files destination-file*
uulog [*options*] *system*
uuname [*options*]

DESCRIPTION

uucp

uucp copies files named by the *source-file* arguments to the *destination-file* argument. A source file name may be a pathname on your machine or may have the form:

system-name!*pathname*

where *system-name* is taken from a list of system names that **uucp** knows about. The destination *system-name* may also include a list of system names such as

system-name!*system-name*!. . .!*system-name*!*pathname*

In this case, an attempt is made to send the file, via the specified route, to the destination. Care should be taken to ensure that intermediate nodes in the route are willing to forward information (see NOTES below for restrictions). The shell metacharacters **?**, ***** and **[...]** appearing in *pathname* will be expanded on the appropriate system.

These utilities process supplementary code set characters according to the locale specified in the **LC_CTYPE** environment variable [see **LANG** on **environ**(5)], except that system-dependent names (for example, user names) and the *grade* given to the **uucp -g** option (see below) must be specified in ASCII characters. When shell metacharacters are used, the target system must also be able to process supplementary code set characters.

Pathnames may be one of:

1. a full pathname;
2. a pathname preceded by ~*user* where *user* is a login name on the specified system and is replaced by that user's login directory;
3. a pathname preceded by ~/*destination* where *destination* is appended to **/var/spool/uucppublic**; (Note: This destination will be treated as a file name unless more than one file is being transferred by this request or the destination is already a directory. To ensure that it is a directory, follow the destination with a '/'. For example, ~/*dan*/ as the destination will make the directory /var/spool/uucppublic/dan if it does not exist and put the requested file(s) in that directory).
4. anything else is prefixed by the current directory.

If the result is an erroneous pathname for the remote system, the copy will fail. If the *destination-file* is a directory, the last part of the *source-file* name is used.

uucp removes execute permissions across the transmission and gives the following read, write, and ownership permissions [see **chmod**(2)]:

With **uucp** files being transferred to a user who has a valid login on the destination system, the directory created will have 0770 permissions, the file(s) will have 0660 permissions, and they will be owned by the destination user.

With **uucp** files being transferred to a non-existent user (for example, due to a typographical error) on the destination system, the directory created will have 1777 permissions (sticky bit turned on) and the file(s) will have 0666 permissions, and will be owned by **uucp**.

The **-m** option will only work sending files or receiving a single file. Receiving multiple files specified by special shell characters **? * [. . .]** will not activate the **-m** option.

The forwarding of files through other systems may not be compatible with the previous version of **uucp**. If forwarding is used, all systems in the route must have compatible versions of **uucp**.

Options — uucp

The following options are available to the **uucp** command:

-c Do not copy local file to the spool directory for transfer to the remote machine (default).

-C Force the copy of local files to the spool directory for transfer.

-d Make all necessary directories for the file copy (default).

-f Do not make intermediate directories for the file copy.

-g*grade*
grade can be either a single ASCII letter/number or a string of ASCII alphanumeric characters defining a service grade. The **uuglist** command can determine whether it is appropriate to use the single letter/number or a string of alphanumeric characters as a service grade. The output from the uuglist command will be a list of service grades that are available or a message that says to use a single letter/number as a grade of service.

-j Output the **uucp** job identification string on the standard output. This job identification can be used by **uustat** to obtain the status of a **uucp** job or to terminate a **uucp** job. It is valid as long as the job remains queued on the local system.

-m Send mail to the requester when the copy is completed.

-n*user* Notify *user* on the remote system that a file was sent.

-r Do not start the file transfer, just queue the job.

-s*file* Report status of the transfer to *file*. This option overrides the **-m** option. When the status *file* is created, it is assigned the owner (**chown**) and group (**chgrp**) attributes of the parent directory. The parent directory where the status *file* is to be written must be publically writable to allow **uucp** to create a status *file*. If the status *file* already exists, it must be be publically writable, so **uucp** can append the status information to it.

-w If a file exists in the target directory with the same name as the file being transferred, do not overwrite the existing file. Instead, try to create a new file. If the file is named *file*, create *file.N* where *N* is a two-digit number. The number appended to the file name will begin with 00 and will increase by 1 for each subsequent file of the same name to a maximum of 99. If another version of the file cannot be created, the user is notified by mail.

If the length of the file name is equal to the maximum for the system, no new version is created. If the length of the file name is less than the maximum for the system but the file name and the suffix are greater than the maximum, the suffix will be truncated. It is therefore possible for files whose names are one or two characters shorter than the maximum system file name length to be overwritten.

-x*debug_level*
Produce debugging output on standard output. *debug_level* is a number between 0 and 9; as it increases to 9, more detailed debugging information is given. This option may not be available on all systems.

uulog

uulog queries a log file of **uucp** or **uuxqt** transactions in file **/var/uucp/.Log/uucico/system or /var/uucp/.Log/uuxqt/***system*.

Options — uulog

The following options are available to the **uulog** command: **uulog** to print logging information:

-s*sys* Print information about file transfer work involving system *sys*.

-fsystem
Does a "**tail -f**" of the file transfer log for **system**. (You must hit BREAK to exit this function.)

-x Look in the **uuxqt** log file for the given system.

-number
Indicates that a "tail" command of *number* lines should be executed.

uulog with no options prints all logging information for every system that has contacted your machine.

uuname

uuname lists the names of systems known to **uucp**.

Options — uuname

The following options are available to the **uuname** command:

-c Returns the names of systems known to **cu**. (The two lists are the same, unless your machine is using different *Systems* files for **cu** and **uucp**. See the **Sysfiles** file.)

-l Return the local system name.

Files

/var/spool/uucp spool directories

`/var/spool/uucppublic/*`
public directory for receiving and sending

`/usr/lib/uucp/*` other program files

`/etc/uucp/*` other data files

Security Restrictions

For security reasons, the domain of remotely accessible files may be severely restricted. You will very likely not be able to access files by pathname; ask a responsible person on the remote system to send them to you. For the same reasons you will probably not be able to send files to arbitrary pathnames. As distributed, the remotely accessible files are those whose names begin **/var/spool/uucppublic** (equivalent to ~/).

Protected files and files that are in protected directories that are owned by the requester can be sent by **uucp**. However, if the requester is root, and the directory is not searchable by "other" or the file is not readable by "other," the request will fail.

REFERENCES

chmod(2), **mail**(1), **uuglist**(1C), **uustat**(1C), **uux**(1C), **uuxqt**(1M)

uuencode (1C)

NAME

uuencode, uudecode – encode a binary file, or decode its ASCII representation

SYNOPSIS

uuencode [*source-file*] *file-label*

uudecode [*encoded-file*]

DESCRIPTION

uuencode converts a binary file into an ASCII-encoded representation that can be sent using **mail**(1). It encodes the contents of *source-file*, or the standard input if no *source-file* argument is given. The *file-label* argument is required. It is included in the encoded file's header as the name of the file into which **uudecode** is to place the binary (decoded) data. **uuencode** also includes the ownership and permission modes of *source-file*, so that *file-label* is recreated with those same ownership and permission modes.

uudecode reads an *encoded-file*, strips off any leading and trailing lines added by mailer programs, and recreates the original binary data with the filename and the mode and owner specified in the header.

The encoded file is an ordinary ASCII text file; it can be edited by any text editor. But it is best only to change the mode or file-label in the header to avoid corrupting the decoded binary.

SEE ALSO

mail(1), **uucp**(1C), **uux**(1C), **uuencode**(4)

NOTES

The encoded file's size is expanded by 35% (3 bytes become 4, plus control information), causing it to take longer to transmit than the equivalent binary.

The user on the remote system who is invoking **uudecode** (typically **uucp**) must have write permission on the file specified in the *file-label*.

Since both **uuencode** and **uudecode** run with user ID set to **uucp**, **uudecode** can fail with permission denied when attempted in a directory that does not have write permission allowed for other.

NAME

uugetty – set terminal type, modes, speed, and line discipline

SYNOPSIS

/usr/lib/uucp/uugetty [**-t** *timeout*] [**-r**] *line* [*speed* [*type* [*linedisc*]]]
/usr/lib/uucp/uugetty -c *file*

DESCRIPTION

uugetty is identical to **getty**(1M) but changes have been made to support using the line for **uucico, cu,** and **ct**; that is, the line can be used in both directions. The **uugetty** allows users to login, but if the line is free, **uucico, cu,** or **ct** can use it for dialing out. The implementation depends on the fact that **uucico, cu,** and **ct** create lock files when devices are used. When the **open** returns (or the first character is read when **-r** option is used), the status of the lock file indicates whether the line is being used by **uucico, cu, ct,** or someone trying to login. Note that in the **-r** case, several RETURN characters may be required before the login message is output. **uucico** trying to login will have to be told by using the following login script:

```
"" \r\d\r\d\r\d\r in:--in: ...
```

where the "..." is whatever would normally be used for the login sequence.

If there is a **uugetty** on one end of a direct line, there must be a **uugetty** on the other end as well. Here is an **/etc/inittab** entry using **uugetty** on an intelligent modem or direct line:

```
30:2:respawn:/usr/lib/uucp/uugetty -r -t 60 tty12 1200
```

The meanings of the available options are

-t *timeout*
: Specifies that **uugetty** should exit if the open on the line succeeds and there is no response to the login prompt in *timeout* seconds. *timeout* is replaced by an integer.

-r
: Causes **uugetty** to wait to read a character before it puts out the login message, thus preventing two **uugetty**s from looping. An entry for an intelligent modem or direct line that has a **uugetty** on each end must use this option.

line
: Defines the name of the line to which **uugetty** will attach itself. The line name will point to an entry in the **/dev** directory. For example, **/dev/tty03**.

speed
: Defines the entry to use from the **/etc/gettydefs** file. The entry defines the line speed, the login message, the initial tty setting, and the next speed to try if the user says the speed is inappropriate (by sending a *break* character). The default *speed* is 300.

type
: Defines the type of terminal connected to the line. The default terminal is **none**, representing a normal terminal unknown to the system.

linedisc
: Sets the line discipline to use on the line. The default is **LDISC0**, which is the only one currently compiled into the operating system.

`-c` *file* Checks the speed and tty definitions in *file* and sends the results to standard output. Unrecognized modes and improperly constructed entries are reported. For correct entries, flag values are printed. *file* is replaced by **/etc/gettydefs** or a similarly structured file.

FILES

/etc/gettydefs
/etc/issue

SEE ALSO

ct(1C), **cu**(1C), **getty**(1M), **gettydefs**(4), **init**(1M), **inittab**(4), **ioctl**(2), **login**(1), **tty**(7), **uucico**(1M)

NOTES

ct does not work when **uugetty** is used with an intelligent modem such as Penril or Ventel.

NAME

uuglist – list service grades available on this UNIX system

SYNOPSIS

uuglist [**-u**] [**-x** *debug_level*]

DESCRIPTION

uuglist prints the list of service grades that are available on the system to use with the **-g** option of **uucp**(1C) and **uux**(1C). The following options are available:

-u List the names of the service grades that the user is allowed to use with the -g option of the **uucp** and **uux** commands.

-x *debug_level* Produce debugging output. **debug_level** is a single digit between 0 and 9; higher numbers give more detailed debugging information.

FILES

/usr/lib/uucp/Grades list of service grades

SEE ALSO

uucp(1C), **uux**(1C)

uusched (1M)

NAME

uusched – the scheduler for the uucp file transport program

SYNOPSIS

/usr/lib/uucp/uusched [*options*]

DESCRIPTION

uusched is the **uucp**(1C) file transport scheduler. It is usually started by the daemon *uudemon.hour* that is started by **cron**(1M) from an entry in **/var/spool/cron/crontabs/uucp**:

```
41,11 * * * * $TFADMIN /usr/lib/uucp/uudemon.hour >
/dev/null"
```

The options are for debugging purposes only. *debug_level* are numbers between 0 and 9. Higher numbers give more detailed debugging information:

-u*debug_level* The **-u** *debug_level* option is passed to **uucico**(1M) as **-x** *debug_level*.

-x*debug_level* Outputs debugging messages from **uusched**(1M).

FILES

/etc/uucp/Systems
/etc/uucp/Permissions
/etc/uucp/Devices
/var/spool/uucp/*
/var/spool/locks/*
/var/spool/uucppublic/*

SEE ALSO

cron(1M), **uucico**(1M), **uucp**(1C), **uustat**(1C), **uux**(1C)

NAME

uustat – uucp status inquiry and job control

SYNOPSIS

uustat [**-q**] or [**-m**] or [**-k***jobid* [**-n**]] or [**-r***jobid* [**-n**]] or [**-p**]
uustat [**-a [-j]]** [**-u***user*] [**-S***qric*]
uustat [**-s***system* [**-j**]] [**-u***user*] [**-S***qric*]
uustat **-t***system* [**-d***number*] [**-c**]

DESCRIPTION

uustat functions in the following three areas: displays the general status of, or cancels, previously specified **uucp** commands; provides remote system performance information, in terms of average transfer rates or average queue times; provides general remote system-specific and user-specific status of **uucp** connections to other systems.

Here are the options that obtain general status of, or cancel, previously specified **uucp** commands; **uustat** allows only one of these options to appear on each **uustat** command line execution:

-a List all jobs in queue.

-j List the total number of jobs displayed. The **-j** option can only be used in conjunction with the **-a** or the **-s** option.

-k*jobid* Kill the **uucp** request whose job identification is *jobid*. The killed **uucp** request must belong to the person issuing the **uustat** command unless one is the super-user or uucp administrator. If the job is killed by the super-user or uucp administrator, electronic mail is sent to the user.

-m Report the status of accessibility of all machines.

-n Suppress all standard out output, but not standard error. The **-n** option is used in conjunction with the **-k** and **-r** options.

-p Execute the command **ps -flp** for all the process-ids that are in the lock files.

-q List the jobs queued for each machine. If a status file exists for the machine, its date, time and status information are reported. In addition, if a number appears in parentheses next to the number of **C** or **X** files, it is the age in days of the oldest **C./X.** file for that system. The **Retry** field represents the number of hours until the next possible call. The **Count** is the number of failure attempts. NOTE: for systems with a moderate number of outstanding jobs, this could take 30 seconds or more of real-time to execute. Here is an example of the output produced by the **-q** option:

```
eagle    3C   04/07-11:07   NO DEVICES AVAILABLE
mh3bs3   2C   07/07-10:42   SUCCESSFUL
```

The above output tells how many command files are waiting for each system. Each command file may have zero or more files to be sent (zero means to call the system and see if work is to be done). The date and time refer to the previous interaction with the system followed by the status of the interaction.

-r*jobid* Rejuvenate *jobid*. The files associated with *jobid* are touched so that their modification time is set to the current time. This prevents the cleanup daemon from deleting the job until the jobs' modification time reaches the limit imposed by the daemon.

Here are the options that provide remote system performance information, in terms of average transfer rates or average queue times; the **-c** and **-d** options can only be used in conjunction with the **-t** option:

-t*system* Report the average transfer rate or average queue time for the past 60 minutes for the remote *system*. The following parameters can only be used with this option:

-d*number* *number* is specified in minutes. Used to override the 60 minute default used for calculations. These calculations are based on information contained in the optional performance log and therefore may not be available. Calculations can only be made from the time that the performance log was last cleaned up.

-c Average queue time is calculated when the **-c** parameter is specified and average transfer rate when **-c** is not specified. For example, the command

```
uustat -teagle -d50 -c
```

produces output in the following format:

```
average queue time to eagle for last 50 minutes: 5 seconds
```

The same command without the **-c** parameter produces output in the following format:

```
average transfer rate with eagle for last 50 minutes: 2000.88
bytes/sec
```

Here are the options that provide general remote system-specific and user-specific status of **uucp** connections to other systems. Either or both of the following options can be specified with *uustat.* The **-j** option can only be used in conjunction with the **-s** or **-a** option to list the total number of jobs displayed:

-s*system* Report the status of all **uucp** requests for remote system *system.*

-u*user* Report the status of all **uucp** requests issued by *user*.

Output for both the **-s** and **-u** options has the following format:

```
eagleN1bd7  4/07-11:07  S  eagle  dan  522    /home/dan/A
eagleC1bd8  4/07-11:07  S  eagle  dan   59    D.3b2al2ce4924
            4/07-11:07  S  eagle  dan  rmail  mike
```

With the above two options, the first field is the *jobid* of the job. This is followed by the date/time. The next field is an **S** if the job is sending a file or an **R** if the job is requesting a file. The next field is the machine where the file is to be transferred. This is followed by the user-id of the user who queued the job. The next field contains the size of the file, or in the case of a remote execution (**rmail** is the command used for remote mail), the name of the command. When the size appears in this field, the file name is also given. This can either be the name given by the user or an internal name (for example, **D.3b2alce4924**) that is created for data files associated with remote executions (**rmail** in this example).

-S*qric* Report the job state: **q** for queued jobs, **r** for running jobs, **i** for interrupted jobs, and **c** for completed jobs.

A job is queued if the transfer has not started. A job is running when the transfer has begun. A job is interrupted if the transfer began but was terminated before the file was completely transferred. A completed job, of course, is a job that successfully transferred. The completed state information is maintained in the accounting log, which is optional and therefore may be unavailable. The parameters can be used in any combination, but at least one parameter must be specified. The **-S** option can also be used with **-s** and **-u** options. The output for this option is exactly like the output for **-s** and **-u** except that the job states are appended as the last output word. Output for a completed job has the following format:

```
eagleC1bd3 completed
```

When no options are given, **uustat** outputs the status of all **uucp** requests issued by the current user.

FILES

/var/spool/uucp/*	spool directories
/var/uucp/.Admin/account	accounting log
/var/uucp/.Admin/perflog	performance log

SEE ALSO

uucp(1C)

DIAGNOSTICS

The **-t** option produces no message when the data needed for the calculations is not being recorded.

NOTES

After the user has issued the **uucp** request, if the file to be transferred is moved or deleted or was not copied to the spool directory with the **-C** option when the **uucp** request was made, **uustat** reports a file size of –99999. This job will eventually fail because the file(s) to be transferred can not be found.

NAME

uuto, **uupick** – public UNIX-to-UNIX system file copy

SYNOPSIS

uuto [*options*] *source-files destination*
uupick [**-s** *system*]

DESCRIPTION

uuto sends *source-files* to *destination*. **uuto** uses the **uucp**(1C) facility to send files, while it allows the local system to control the file access. A source-file name is a path name on your machine. Destination has the form:

system[!*system*] . . . !*user*

where **system** is taken from a list of system names that **uucp** knows about [see **uuname** in **uucp**(1C)]. *user* is the login name of someone on the specified system.

Two options are available:

-p Copy the source file into the spool directory before transmission.

-m Send mail to the sender when the copy is complete.

-w If a file exists in the target directory with the same name as the file being transferred, do not overwrite the existing file. Instead, try to create a new file. If the file is named *file*, create *file.N* where *N* is a one- or two-digit number. The numbers appended to the file name will begin with 00 and will increase by 1 for each subsequent file of the same name to a maximum of 99. If another version of the file cannot be created, the user is notified by mail.

If the length of the file name is equal to the maximum for the system, no new version is created. If the length of the file name is less than the maximum for the system but the file name and the suffix are greater than the maximum, the suffix will be truncated. It is still, therefore, possible for files whose names are one or two characters shorter than the system maximum to be overwritten.

The files (or subtrees, if directories are specified) are sent to *PUBDIR* on **system**, where *PUBDIR* is a public directory defined in the **uucp** source. By default, this directory is **/var/spool/uucppublic**. Specifically, the files are sent to

PUBDIR/**receive**/*user*/*mysystem*/*files*

The destined recipient is notified by **mail**(1) of the arrival of files.

uupick accepts or rejects the files transmitted to the user. Specifically, **uupick** searches *PUBDIR* for files destined for the user. For each entry (file or directory) found, the following message is printed on the standard output:

from system *sysname*: **[file** *filename*] **[dir** *dirname*]

uupick then reads a line from the standard input to determine the disposition of the file:

new-line	Go on to next entry.
d	Delete the entry.
m [*dir*]	Move the entry to named directory *dir*. If *dir* is not specified as a complete path name (in which **$HOME** is legitimate), a destination relative to the current directory is assumed. If no destination is given, the default is the current directory.
a [*dir*]	Same as **m** except moving all the files sent from **system**.
p	Print the content of the file.
q	Stop.
EOT (CTRL-d)	Same as **q**.
!*command*	Escape to the shell to do *command*.
*****	Print a command summary.

uupick invoked with the **-s** *system* option will only search the *PUBDIR* for files sent from **system**.

FILES

PUBDIR   /var/spool/uucppublic   public directory

SEE ALSO

mail(1), **uucleanup**(1M), **uucp**(1C), **uustat**(1C), **uux**(1C)

NOTES

In order to send files that begin with a dot (for example, **.profile**), the files must be qualified with a dot. For example, the following files are correct:

```
.profile  .prof*  .profil
```

The following files are incorrect:

```
*prof*  ?profile
```

Uutry(1M)

NAME

Uutry – try to contact remote system with debugging on

SYNOPSIS

/usr/lib/uucp/Uutry [*options*] *system_name*

DESCRIPTION

Uutry is a shell that is used to invoke **uucico** to call a remote site. Debugging is initially turned on and is set to the default value of 5. The debugging output is put in file **/tmp/***system_name.* Here are the options:

-c*type* The first field in the **Devices** file is the "Type" field. The **-c** option forces **uucico** to only use entries in the "Type" field that match the user specified *type.* The specified *type* is usually the name of a local area network.

-r This option overrides the retry time that is set in file **/var/uucp/.status/***system_name.*

-x*debug_level* *debug_level* is a number from 0 to 9. Higher numbers give more detailed debugging information.

FILES

/etc/uucp/Systems
/etc/uucp/Permissions
/etc/uucp/Devices
/etc/uucp/Limits
/var/spool/uucp/*
/var/spool/locks/*
/var/spool/uucppublic/*
/tmp/system_name

SEE ALSO

uucico(1M) **uucp**(1C), **uux**(1C)

NAME

uux – UNIX-to-UNIX system command execution

SYNOPSIS

uux [*options*] *command-string*

DESCRIPTION

uux gathers zero or more files from various systems, executes a command on a named system, and then sends standard output to a file on another named system. It processes supplementary code set characters according to the locale specified in the **LC_CTYPE** environment variable [see **LANG** on **environ**(5)].

For security reasons, most installations historically limited the list of commands that were executable on behalf of an incoming request from **uux**, permitting only the receipt of mail [see **mail**(1)].

An authentication mechanism has been built into **uux** that works with a key management system to authenticate requesting users and machines in a reliable way. This feature works in conjunction with the **uuxqt**(1M) command and the ID mapping feature. It allows a remote request to be executed reliably under a local identity. (Remote execution permissions are defined in **/etc/uucp/Config** and **/etc/uucp/Permissions**.)

command-string is made up of one or more arguments and looks like a shell command line, except that the command and file names may be prefixed by *system-name***!**. A null *system-name* is interpreted as the local system.

File names may be one of:

1. A full pathname.
2. A pathname preceded by ~*xxx*, where *xxx* is a login on the named system and is replaced by the login directory of user *xxx*.
3. Anything else is prefixed by the pathname of the current directory.

As an example, the command

```
uux "!diff sys1!/home/dan/file1 sys2!/a4/dan/file2 > !~/dan/file.diff"
```

will get the **file1** and **file2** files from the **sys1** and **sys2** machines, execute the **diff**(1) command on the two files and put the output in **file.diff** in the local *PUBDIR*/**dan/** directory. *PUBDIR* is a public directory defined in the **uucp** source. By default, *PUBDIR* is **/var/spool/uucppublic**.

Any special shell characters such as **<, >, ;,** | should be quoted either by quoting the entire *command-string*, or by quoting the special characters as individual arguments.

uux attempts to get all appropriate files to the system where they will be processed. For files that are output files, the file name must be escaped using parentheses. For example, the command:

```
uux "a!cut -f1 b!/usr/file > c!/usr/file"
```

gets **/usr/file** from system **b** and sends it to system **a**, executes the **cut** command on that file, and sends the output of the **cut** command to system **c**.

uux will notify you if the requested command on the remote system was disallowed. The response comes by remote mail from the remote machine. This notification can be turned off with the **-n** option.

The following options are interpreted by **uux**:

- **-** Use the standard input to **uux** as the standard input to *command-string*.
- **-a***name* Replace the initiating user id with user *name*. Notification will be returned to user *name*.
- **-b** If the exit status is non-zero, return whatever standard input was provided.
- **-c** Do not copy local files to the spool directory for transfer to the remote machine (default).
- **-C** Force the copy of local files to the spool directory for transfer.
- **-g***grade* *grade* defines a service grade. It can be a single letter, number, or a string of alphanumeric characters. The **uuglist**(1C) command determines whether it is appropriate to use the single letter, number, or string of alphanumeric characters as a service grade. The output of the **uuglist** command will be a list of the service grades available or a message that says to use a single letter or number as a grade of service.
- **-j** Output the job id string on the standard output. This job identification can be used by **uustat**(1C) to obtain the job status or terminate the job.
- **-n** Do not notify the user if the command fails.
- **-p** The same as – option. Use the standard input to **uux** as the input to *command-string*.
- **-r** Do not start the file transfer; just queue the job.
- **-s***file* Report the status of the transfer in *file*.
- **-x***debug_level* Produce debugging output on the standard output. *debug_level* is a number between 0 and 9; as it increases to 9, more detailed debugging information is given.
- **-z** Send success notification to the user.

FILES

/var/spool/uucp	spool directories
/etc/uucp/Permissions	remote execution permissions
/usr/lib/uucp/*	other programs
/etc/uucp/*	other data and programs

NOTES

Only the first command of a shell pipeline may have a *system-name***!**. All other commands are executed on the system of the first command.

The use of the shell metacharacter * will probably not do what you want it to do.

The shell tokens << and >> are not implemented.

The execution of commands on remote systems takes place in an execution directory known to the **uucp** system. All files required for the execution will be put into this directory unless they already reside on that machine. The simple file name (without path or machine reference) must therefore be unique within the **uux** request. The following command will NOT work:

```
uux "a!diff b!/home/dan/xyz c!/home/dan/xyz > !xyz.diff"
```

but the command

```
uux "a!diff a!/home/dan/xyz c!/home/dan/xyz > !xyz.diff"
```

will work (if **diff** is a permitted command).

Protected files and files that are in protected directories that are owned by the requester can be sent in commands using **uux**. However, if the requester is **root**, and the directory is not searchable by "other," the request will fail.

SEE ALSO

cryptkey(1), **cut**(1), **mail**(1), **uucp**(1C), **uuglist**(1C), **uustat**(1C)

NOTES

Any commands that a user will be allowed to execute via **uux** need to be added to the **/etc/uucp/Permissions** file, along with the actual pathname of the command. If a pathname is not specified, the default path, **/usr/bin**, is searched. If a command has a symbolic link to another command, the link will not be followed by **uux**, and the user will get back an error message stating that they do not have permission to execute the command.

NAME

uuxqt – execute remote command requests

SYNOPSIS

/usr/lib/uucp/uuxqt [*options*]

DESCRIPTION

uuxqt is the program that executes remote job requests from remote systems generated by the use of the **uux** command. (**mail** uses **uux** for remote mail requests). **uuxqt** searches the spool directories looking for execution requests. For each request, **uuxqt** checks to see if all the required data files are available, accessible, and the requested commands are permitted for the requesting system. The **Permissions** file is used to validate file accessibility and command execution permission.

There are two environment variables that are set before the **uuxqt** command is executed:

> **UU_MACHINE** is the machine that sent the job (the previous one).
> **UU_USER** is the user that sent the job.

These can be used in writing commands that remote systems can execute to provide information, auditing, or restrictions. **uuxqt** has the following options:

-s*system* Specifies the remote **system** name.

-x*debug_level* *debug_level* is a number from 0 to 9. Higher numbers give more detailed debugging information.

FILES

/etc/uucp/Permissions
/etc/uucp/Limits
/var/spool/uucp/*
/var/spool/locks/*

SEE ALSO

uucico(1M), **uucp**(1C), **uustat**(1C), **uux**(1C), **mail**(1)

NAME

vacation – automatically respond to incoming mail messages

SYNOPSIS

vacation [**-M** *canned_msg_file*] [**-l** *logfile*] [**-m** *savefile*] [**-d**] [**-f** *forward-id*] [**-F** *forward-id*]
vacation -n

DESCRIPTION

When a new mail message arrives, the **mail** command first checks the recipient's forwarding file, **/var/mail/:forward/***user*, to see if the message is to be forwarded elsewhere (to some other recipient or as the input to some command). **vacation** is used to set up forwarding via a Post-Processing Personal Surrogate so that the new message is both saved into the user's mailbox and a canned response is sent to the message's originator.

Command-line options are:

-l *logfile* File to keep track of which originators have already seen the canned response. If not specified, it defaults to **$HOME/.maillog**. The log file prevents the originator from seeing the vacation message multiple times.

-M *canned_msg_file*
File to send back as the canned response. If *canned_msg_file* is not specified, it defaults to **/usr/share/lib/mail/std_vac_msg**, which contains:

```
Subject: AUTOANSWERED!!!

I am on vacation. I will read (and answer if necessary)
your e-mail message when I return.

This message was generated automatically and you will
receive it only once, although all messages you send
me while I am away WILL be saved.
```

-m *savefile* Normally, the user's mailbox is used to store the mail. This option allows a different filename to be specified. If the file cannot be written, the user's mailbox will be used.

-f *forwarding-id*
The mail will be forwarded to this user id in addition to being stored in the user's mailbox.

-i *forwarding-id*
The mail will be forwarded to this user id *instead* of being stored in the user's mailbox. If both **-f** and **-i** are given, the mail will not be stored in the user's mailbox.

-d The day's date will be appended to the filename specified by **-m**.

-n Remove the **vacation** processing. It is equivalent to using

mail -F ""

FILES

/usr/share/lib/mail/std_vac_msg	default canned response
/var/mail/*	users' standard mailboxes
/var/mail/:forward/*	users' forwarding information
/usr/lib/mail/vacation2	program that actually sends back the canned response

SEE ALSO

mail(1), BSD-specific **vacation**(1).

NOTES

vacation uses the personal surrogate facility of **mail** to implement notifications.

If you are using **/usr/bin/vacation**, you must use **/bin/mail** as the mail delivery agent.

NAME

vacation – (BSD) reply to mail automatically

SYNOPSIS

/usr/ucb/vacation [**-I**]
/usr/ucb/vacation [**-j**] [**-a***alias*] [**-t***N*] *username*

DESCRIPTION

vacation automatically replies to incoming mail. The reply is contained in the file **.vacation.msg**, that you create in your home directory.

This file should include a header with at least a '**Subject:**' line (it should not include a '**From:**' or a '**To:**' line). For example:

```
Subject: I am on vacation
I am on vacation until July 22.  If you have something urgent,
please contact Joe Jones (jones@f40).
        --John
```

If the string **$SUBJECT** appears in the **.vacation.msg** file, it is replaced with the subject of the original message when the reply is sent; thus, a **.vacation.msg** file such as

```
Subject: I am on vacation
I am on vacation until July 22.
Your mail regarding "$SUBJECT" will be read when I return.
If you have something urgent, please contact
Joe Jones (jones@f40).
        --John
```

will include the subject of the message in the reply.

No message is sent if the '**To:**' or the '**Cc:**' line does not list the user to whom the original message was sent or one of a number of aliases for them, if the initial **From** line includes the string **-REQUEST@**, or if a '**Precedence: bulk**' or '**Precedence: junk**' line is included in the header.

The following options are available:

-I Initialize the **.vacation.pag** and **.vacation.dir** files and start **/usr/ucb/vacation**.

If the **-I** flag is not specified, and a *user* argument is given, **/usr/ucb/vacation** reads the first line from the standard input (for a '**From:**' line, no colon). If absent, it produces an error message. The following options may be specified:

-a*alias* Indicate that *alias* is one of the valid aliases for the user running **/usr/ucb/vacation**, so that mail addressed to that alias generates a reply.

-j Do not check whether the recipient appears in the '**To: ' or the 'Cc:**' line.

-t*N* Change the interval between repeat replies to the same sender. The default is 1 week. A trailing **s**, **m**, **h**, **d**, or **w** scales *N* to seconds, minutes, hours, days, or weeks respectively.

USAGE

To start **/usr/ucb/vacation**, create a **.forward** file in your home directory containing a line of the form:

username, **"|/usr/ucb/vacation** *username*"

where *username* is your login name. *username* is derived from the **USER** environment variable if it is set, otherwise, the **LOGNAME** environment variable is used.

Then type in the command:

/usr/ucb/vacation -I

To stop **/usr/ucb/vacation**, remove the **.forward** file, or move it to a new name.

If **/usr/ucb/vacation** is run with no arguments, it will permit you to interactively turn **/usr/ucb/vacation** on or off. It will create a **.vacation.msg** file for you, or edit an existing one, using the editor specified by the **VISUAL** or **EDITOR** environment variable, or **vi**(1) if neither of those environment variables are set. If a **.forward** file is present in your home directory, it will ask whether you want to remove it and turn off **/usr/ucb/vacation**. If it is not present in your home directory, it creates it for you, and automatically performs a '**/usr/ucb/vacation -I**' function, turning on **/usr/ucb/vacation**.

FILES

~/.forward
~/.vacation.mesg

A list of senders is kept in the files **.vacation.pag** and **.vacation.dir** in your home directory.

SEE ALSO

sendmail(1M), **vi**(1)

NAME

val – validate an SCCS file

SYNOPSIS

val -

val [**-s**] [**-r***SID*] [**-m***name*] [**-y***type*] *file* ...

DESCRIPTION

val determines if the specified *file* is an SCCS file meeting the characteristics specified by the optional argument list. Arguments to **val** may appear in any order. The arguments consist of keyletter arguments, which begin with a **-**, and named files.

val has a special argument, **-**, which causes reading of the standard input until an end-of-file condition is detected. Each line read is independently processed as if it were a command line argument list.

val generates diagnostic messages on the standard output for each command line and file processed, and also returns a single 8-bit code on exit as described below.

The keyletter arguments are defined as follows. The effects of any keyletter argument apply independently to each named file on the command line.

-s The presence of this argument silences the diagnostic message normally generated on the standard output for any error that is detected while processing each named file on a given command line.

-r*SID* The argument value *SID* (SCCS identification string) is an SCCS delta number. A check is made to determine if the *SID* is ambiguous (for example, **-r1** is ambiguous because it physically does not exist but implies 1.1, 1.2, and so on, which may exist) or invalid (for example, **r1.0** or **r1.1.0** are invalid because neither can exist as a valid delta number). If the *SID* is valid and not ambiguous, a check is made to determine if it actually exists.

-m*name* The argument value *name* is compared with the SCCS **%M%** keyword in *file*.

-y*type* The argument value *type* is compared with the SCCS **%Y%** keyword in *file*.

The 8-bit code returned by **val** is a disjunction of the possible errors; it can be interpreted as a bit string where (moving from left to right) set bits are interpreted as follows:

bit 0 = missing file argument
bit 1 = unknown or duplicate keyletter argument
bit 2 = corrupted SCCS file
bit 3 = cannot open file or file not SCCS
bit 4 = *SID* is invalid or ambiguous
bit 5 = *SID* does not exist
bit 6 = **%Y%**, **-y** mismatch
bit 7 = **%M%**, **-m** mismatch

val can process two or more files on a given command line and in turn can process multiple command lines (when reading the standard input). In these cases an aggregate code is returned: a logical OR of the codes generated for each command line and file processed.

SEE ALSO

admin(1), **delta**(1), **get**(1), **help**(1, **prs**(1)

DIAGNOSTICS

Use **help**(1) for explanations.

NOTES

val can process up to 50 files on a single command line.

NAME

vc – version control

SYNOPSIS

vc [**-a**] [**-t**] [**-c***char*] [**-s**] [*keyword=value* . . . *keyword=value*]

DESCRIPTION

This command is obsolete and will be removed in the next release.

The **vc** command copies lines from the standard input to the standard output under control of its arguments and of "control statements" encountered in the standard input. In the process of performing the copy operation, user-declared *keyword*s may be replaced by their string *value* when they appear in plain text and/or control statements.

The copying of lines from the standard input to the standard output is conditional, based on tests (in control statements) of keyword values specified in control statements or as **vc** command arguments.

A control statement is a single line beginning with a control character, except as modified by the **-t** keyletter (see below). The default control character is colon (**:**), except as modified by the **-c** keyletter (see below). Input lines beginning with a backslash (\) followed by a control character are not control lines and are copied to the standard output with the backslash removed. Lines beginning with a backslash followed by a non-control character are copied in their entirety.

A keyword is composed of 9 or less alphanumerics; the first must be alphabetic. A value is any ASCII string that can be created with **ed**; a numeric value is an unsigned string of digits. Keyword values may not contain blanks or tabs.

Replacement of keywords by values is done whenever a keyword surrounded by control characters is encountered on a version control statement. The **-a** keyletter (see below) forces replacement of keywords in all lines of text. An uninterpreted control character may be included in a value by preceding it with \. If a literal \ is desired, then it too must be preceded by \.

The following options are valid:

-a Forces replacement of keywords surrounded by control characters with their assigned value in all text lines and not just in **vc** statements.

-t All characters from the beginning of a line up to and including the first tab character are ignored for the purpose of detecting a control statement. If a control statement is found, all characters up to and including the tab are discarded.

-c*char* Specifies a control character to be used in place of the "**:**" default.

-s Silences warning messages (not error) that are normally printed on the diagnostic output.

vc recognizes the following version control statements:

:dcl *keyword*[**,** . . .**,** *keyword*]
Declare keywords. All keywords must be declared.

:asg *keyword=value*

Assign values to keywords. An **asg** statement overrides the assignment for the corresponding keyword on the **vc** command line and all previous **asg** statements for that keyword. Keywords that are declared but are not assigned values have null values.

:if *condition*

. . .

:end

Skip lines of the standard input. If the condition is true, all lines between the **if** statement and the matching **end** statement are copied to the standard output. If the condition is false, all intervening lines are discarded, including control statements. Note that intervening **if** statements and matching **end** statements are recognized solely for the purpose of maintaining the proper **if-end** matching.

The syntax of a condition is:

<cond>	::= ["**not**"] *<or>*
<or>	::= *<and>* | *<and>* "|" *<or>*
<and>	::= *<exp>* | *<exp>* "**&**" *<and>*
<exp>	::= "**(**" *<or>* "**)**" | *<value>* *<op>* *<value>*
<op>	::= "**=**" | "**!=**" | "**<**" | "**>**"
<value>	::= *<arbitrary ASCII string>* | *<numeric string>*

The available operators and their meanings are:

=	equal
!=	not equal
&	and
|	or
>	greater than
<	less than
( )	used for logical groupings
not	may only occur immediately after the **if**, and when present, inverts the value of the entire condition

The **>** and **<** operate only on unsigned integer values (for example, **: 012 > 12** is false). All other operators take strings as arguments (for example, **: 012 != 12** is true).

The precedence of the operators (from highest to lowest) is:

= != > < all of equal precedence
&
|

Parentheses may be used to alter the order of precedence.

Values must be separated from operators or parentheses by at least one blank or tab.

::*text*
  Replace keywords on lines that are copied to the standard output. The two leading control characters are removed, and keywords surrounded by control characters in text are replaced by their value before the line is copied to the output file. This action is independent of the **-a** keyletter.

:on
:off Turn on or off keyword replacement on all lines.

:ctl *char*
  Change the control character to *char*.

:msg *message*
  Print *message* on the diagnostic output.

:err *message*
  Print *message* followed by**:**

```
ERROR: err statement on line ... (915)
```

  on the diagnostic output. **vc** halts execution, and returns an exit code of 1.

SEE ALSO

ed(1), **help**(1)

NAME

vi – screen-oriented (visual) display editor based on ex

SYNOPSIS

vi [**-t** *tag*] [**-r** *file*] [**-l**] [**-L**] [**-w***n*] [**-R**] [**-x**] [**-C**] [**-c** *command*] *file*. . .
view [**-t** *tag*] [**-r** *file*] [**-l**] [**-L**] [**-w***n*] [**-R**] [**-x**] [**-C**] [**-c** *command*] *file*. . .
vedit [**-t** *tag*] [**-r** *file*] [**-l**] [**-L**] [**-w***n*] [**-R**] [**-x**] [**-C**] [**-c** *command*] *file*. . .

DESCRIPTION

vi (visual) is a display-oriented text editor based on an underlying line editor **ex**. It is possible to use the command mode of **ex** from within **vi** and vice-versa. The visual commands are described on this manual page; how to set options (like automatically numbering lines and automatically starting a new output line when you press RETURN) and all **ex** line editor commands are described on the **ex**(1) manual page.

When using **vi**, changes you make to the file are reflected in what you see on your terminal screen. The position of the cursor on the screen indicates the position within the file.

These utilities process and display supplementary code set characters according to the locale specified in the **LC_CTYPE** environment variable [see **LANG** on **environ**(5)], except that the character *x* given to the **r**, **f**, **F**, **m**, **t**, and **T** commands (see COMMAND SUMMARY below) must be a single-byte character. All processing, including regular expression pattern searching, is performed on characters, not columns or bytes. In command mode, the utilities recognize arguments to indicate the number of characters. Multi-column characters are split over two lines when using the full screen width. The same number of ASCII **>** characters are displayed as the split character's display width.

Invocation Options

The following invocation options are interpreted by **vi** (previously documented options are discussed in the NOTES section of this manual page):

-t *tag* — Edit the file containing the *tag* and position the editor at its definition. Note: tags in the *tag* file must be in increasing order.

-r *file* — Edit *file* after an editor or system crash. (Recovers the version of *file* that was in the buffer when the crash occurred.)

-l — Set up for editing LISP programs.

-L — List the name of all files saved as the result of an editor or system crash.

-w*n* — Set the default window size to *n*. This is useful when using the editor over a slow speed line.

-R — **Readonly** mode; the **readonly** flag is set, preventing accidental overwriting of the file.

-x — Encryption option; when used, **vi** simulates the **X** command of **ex** and prompts the user for a key. This key is used to encrypt and decrypt text using the algorithm of the **crypt** command. The **X** command makes an educated guess to determine whether text read in is encrypted or not. The temporary buffer file is encrypted also, using a transformed version of the key typed in for the **-x** option. See **crypt**(1). Also, see the NOTES section at the end of this manual page.

-C Encryption option; same as the **-x** option, except that **vi** simulates the **C** command of **ex**. The **C** command is like the **X** command of **ex**, except that all text read in is assumed to have been encrypted.

-c *command* Begin editing by executing the specified editor *command* (usually a search or positioning command).

The *file* argument indicates one or more files to be edited.

The **view** invocation is the same as **vi** except that the **readonly** flag is set.

The **vedit** invocation is intended for beginners. It is the same as **vi** except that the **report** flag is set to 1, the **showmode** and **novice** flags are set, and **magic** is turned off. These defaults make it easier to learn how to use **vi**.

vi Modes

Command	Normal and initial mode. Other modes return to command mode upon completion. **ESC** (escape) is used to cancel a partial command.
Input	Entered by setting any of the following options: **a A i I o O c C s S R .** Arbitrary text may then be entered. Input mode is normally terminated with **ESC** character, or, abnormally, with an interrupt.
Last line	Reading input for **: / ?** or **!**; terminate by pressing RETURN; an interrupt cancels termination.

COMMAND SUMMARY

In the descriptions, **CR** stands for RETURN and **ESC** stands for the escape key.

Sample commands

← ↓ ↑ →	arrow keys move the cursor
h j k l	same as arrow keys
i*text***ESC**	insert *text*
cw*new***ESC**	change word to *new*
eas**ESC**	pluralize word (end of word; append **s**; escape from input state)
x	delete a character
dw	delete a word
dd	delete a line
3dd	delete 3 lines
u	undo previous change
ZZ	exit **vi**, saving changes
:q!CR	quit, discarding changes
/*text***CR**	search for *text*
^U ^D	scroll up or down
:*cmd***CR**	any **ex** or **ed** command

Counts before vi commands

Numbers may be typed as a prefix to some commands. They are interpreted in one of these ways.

line/column number	`z G |`
scroll amount	`^D ^U`
repeat effect	most of the rest

Interrupting, canceling

ESC	end insert or incomplete cmd
DEL	(delete or rubout) interrupts

File manipulation

ZZ	if file modified, write and exit; otherwise, exit
:wCR	write back changes
:w!CR	forced write, if permission originally not valid
:qCR	quit
:q!CR	quit, discard changes
:e *name***CR**	edit file *name*
:e!CR	reedit, discard changes
:e + *name***CR**	edit, starting at end
:e +*n***CR**	edit starting at line *n*
:e #CR	edit alternate file
:e! #CR	edit alternate file, discard changes
:w *name***CR**	write file *name*
:w! *name***CR**	overwrite file *name*
:shCR	run shell, then return
:! *cmd***CR**	run *cmd*, then return
:nCR	edit next file in arglist
:n *args***CR**	specify new arglist
^G	show current file and line
:ta *tag***CR**	position cursor to *tag*

In general, any **ex** or **ed** command (such as *substitute* or *global*) may be typed, preceded by a colon and followed by a RETURN.

Positioning within file

^F	forward screen
^B	backward screen
^D	scroll down half screen
^U	scroll up half screen
*n***G**	go to the beginning of the specified line (end default), where *n* is a line number
/*pat*	next line matching *pat*
?*pat*	previous line matching *pat*
n	repeat last **/** or **?** command
N	reverse last **/** or **?** command
/*pat***/+***n*	nth line after *pat*
?*pat***?-***n*	nth line before *pat*

`]]`	next section/function
`[[`	previous section/function
`(`	beginning of sentence
`)`	end of sentence
`{`	beginning of paragraph
`}`	end of paragraph
`%`	find matching `(` `)` `{` or `}`

Adjusting the screen

`^L`	clear and redraw window
`^R`	clear and redraw window if `^L` is → key
`zCR`	redraw screen with current line at top of window
`z-`	redraw screen with current line at bottom of window
`z.`	redraw screen with current line at center of window
`/`*pat*`/z-CR`	move *pat* line to bottom of window
`z`*n*`.`	use *n*-line window
`^E`	scroll window down 1 line
`^Y`	scroll window up 1 line

Marking and returning

` `` `	move cursor to previous context
`''`	move cursor to first non-white space in line
`m`*x*	mark current position with the single-byte lower-case letter *x*
`` ` ``*x*	move cursor to mark *x*
`'`*x*	move cursor to first non-white space in line marked by *x*

Line positioning

`H`	top line on screen
`L`	last line on screen
`M`	middle line on screen
`+`	next line, at first non-white
`-`	previous line, at first non-white
`CR`	return, same as +
↓ or `j`	next line, same column
↑ or `k`	previous line, same column

Character positioning

`^`	first non white-space character
`0`	beginning of line
`$`	end of line
`l` or →	forward
`h` or ←	backward
`^H`	same as←(backspace)
space	same as→(space bar)
`f`*x*	find next single-byte character *x*
`F`*x*	find previous single-byte character **x**
`t`*x*	move to character prior to next single-byte character *x*
`T`*x*	move to character following previous single-byte character *x*

;	repeat last **f F t** or **T**
,	repeat inverse of last **f F t** or **T**
n|	move to column *n*
%	find matching ({) or }

Words, sentences, paragraphs

w	forward a word
b	back a word
e	end of word
)	to next sentence
}	to next paragraph
(	back a sentence
{	back a paragraph
W	forward a blank-delimited word
B	back a blank-delimited word
E	end of a blank-delimited word

Corrections during insert

^H	erase last character (backspace)
^W	erase last word
erase	your erase character, same as **^H** (backspace)
kill	your kill character, erase this line of input
\	quotes your erase and kill characters
ESC	ends insertion, back to command mode
DEL	interrupt, terminates insert mode
^D	backtab one character; reset left margin of *autoindent*
^^D	caret (^) followed by control-d (^D); backtab to beginning of line; do not reset left margin of *autoindent*
0^D	backtab to beginning of line; reset left margin of *autoindent*
^V	quote non-printable character

vi uses control notation for ASCII control characters, and uses octal notation for 8-bit bytes that are not printable.

Insert and replace

a	append after cursor
A	append at end of line
i	insert before cursor
I	insert before first non-blank
o	open line below
O	open above
r*x*	replace one character with the single-byte character *x*
R*text***ESC**	replace characters
~	change lower case to upper case and vice-versa

Operators

Operators are followed by a cursor motion, and affect all text that would have been moved over. For example, since **w** moves over a word, **dw** deletes the word that would be moved over. Double the operator, for example, **dd** to affect whole lines.

`d`	delete
`c`	change
`y`	yank lines to buffer
`<`	left shift
`>`	right shift
`!`	filter through command

Miscellaneous Operations

`C`	change rest of line (**c$**)
`D`	delete rest of line (**d$**)
`s`	substitute chars (**cl**)
`S`	substitute lines (**cc**)
`J`	join lines
`x`	delete characters (**dl**)
`X`	delete characters before cursor (**dh**)
`Y`	yank lines (**yy**)

Yank and Put

Put inserts the text most recently deleted or yanked; however, if a buffer is named (using the ASCII lower-case letters **a** - **z**), the text in that buffer is put instead.

`3yy`	yank 3 lines
`3yl`	yank 3 characters
`p`	put back text after cursor
`P`	put back text before cursor
"*x*p	put from buffer *x*
"*x*y	yank to buffer *x*
"*x*d	delete into buffer *x*

Undo, Redo, Retrieve

`u`	undo last change
`U`	restore current line
`.`	repeat last change
"*d*p	retrieve *d*'th last delete

AUTHOR

vi and **ex** were developed by The University of California, Berkeley California, Computer Science Division, Department of Electrical Engineering and Computer Science.

FILES

/tmp default directory where temporary work files are placed; it can be changed using the **directory** option [see the **ex**(1) **set** command]

/usr/share/lib/terminfo/?/*
compiled terminal description database

/usr/share/lib/.COREterm/?/*
subset of compiled terminal description database

/usr/lib/locale/*locale***/LC_MESSAGES/uxed.abi**
language-specific message file [See **LANG** on **environ**(5).]

SEE ALSO

ctags(1), **ed**(1), **edit**(1), **ex**(1)

NOTES

Two options, although they continue to be supported, have been replaced in the documentation by options that follow the Command Syntax Standard [see **intro**(1)]. A **-r** option that is not followed with an option-argument has been replaced by **-L** and **+***command* has been replaced by **-c** *command*.

The encryption options are provided with the Encryption Utilities package, which is available only in the United States.

Tampering with entries in **/usr/share/lib/terminfo/?/*** or **/usr/share/lib/.COREterm/?/*** (for example, changing or removing an entry) can affect programs such as **vi** that expect the entry to be present and correct. In particular, removing the "dumb" terminal may cause unexpected problems.

Software tabs using **^T** work only immediately after the *autoindent*.

Left and right shifts on intelligent terminals do not make use of insert and delete character operations in the terminal.

NAME

`vidi` – set font and video mode for console

SYNOPSIS

`vidi` [`-d`] [`-f` *fontfile*] *font*

`vidi` *mode*

DESCRIPTION

The `vidi` command loads or extracts a font or sets the video mode for the console. When `vidi` is used without arguments, it lists all valid video mode and font commands.

Font Options

Some video cards support changeable character fonts. Available fonts are `font8x8`, `font8x14`, and `font8x16`. The font options are used as follows:

`vidi` *font*	Load *font* from `/usr/lib/vidi/`*font*.
`vidi -d` *font*	Write *font* to the standard output.
`vidi -f` *fontfile font*	Load *font* from *fontfile* instead of default directory.

Mode Options

`vidi` also sets the mode of the video adapter connected to the standard input. The modes are:

`mono`	Move current screen to the monochrome adapter.
`cga`	Move current screen to the Color Graphics adapter.
`ega`	Move current screen to the Enhanced Graphics adapter.
`vga`	Move current screen to the Video Graphics adapter.

Text and Graphics Modes

The following tables list the available modes.

Text Modes

Mode	Cols	Rows	Font	Adapter
`c40x25`	40	25	8x8	CGA (EGA VGA)
`e40x25`	40	25	8x14	EGA (VGA)
`v40x25`	40	25	8x16	VGA
`m80x25`	80	25	8x14	MONO (EGA_MONO VGA_MONO)
`c80x25`	80	25	8x8	CGA (EGA VGA)
`em80x25`	80	25	8x14	EGA_MONO (VGA_MONO)
`e80x25`	80	25	8x14	EGA (VGA)
`vm80x25`	80	25	8x16	VGA_MONO
`v80x25`	80	25	8x16	VGA
`e80x43`	80	43	8x14	EGA (VGA)

Graphics Modes

Mode	Pixel Resolution	Colors
mode5	320x200	4
mode6	640x200	2
modeD	320x200	16
modeE	640x200	16
modeF	640x350	2 (mono)
mode10	640x350	16
mode11	640x480	2
mode12	640x480	16
mode13	320x200	256
att640	640x400	16
att800x600	800x600	16
att640x400	640x400	256

When using the vidi command to set modes, if the error message **Invalid argument** or **No such device or address** is displayed, either the user doesn't have permission to change the mode or the video hardware doesn't support the mode specified. For example, the mode value **vm80x25** is not valid for a system configured with an EGA video adapter.

The format of a data file for a font is an array of bytes where each byte represents one line of the pixel image for the character. The bits within the byte are "1" if the pixel should be drawn and "0" if it shouldn't be. For example, for an 8x14 font, 14 consecutive bytes are needed to represent the pixel image for the character. The bytes are ordered top to bottom.

For every font file, 256 pixel images are provided with the images ordered from 0 to 255. For example, the 8x14 font contains 14*256 bytes. The first 14 bytes are displayed for ASCII value **\0**, the next 14 bytes are for ASCII value **\001**, and so on.

SEE ALSO

stty(1)

NAME

volcopy (generic) – make literal copy of file system

SYNOPSIS

volcopy [**-F** *FSType*] [**-V**] [*current_options*] [**-o** *specific_options*] *operands*

DESCRIPTION

volcopy makes a literal copy of the file system.

current_options are options supported by the **s5**-specific module of **volcopy**. Other FSTypes do not necessarily support these options. *specific_options* indicate suboptions specified in a comma-separated list of suboptions and/or keyword-attribute pairs for interpretation by the *FSType*-specific module of the command.

operands generally include the device and volume names and are file system specific. A detailed description of the *operands* can be found on the *FSType*-specific man pages of **volcopy**.

Options

-F Specify the *FSType* on which to operate. The *FSType* should either be specified here or be determinable from **/etc/vfstab** by matching the *operands* with an entry in the table.

-V Echo the complete command line, but do not execute the command. The command line is generated by using the options and arguments provided by the user and adding to them information derived from **/etc/vfstab**. This option should be used to verify and validate the command line.

-o Specify *FSType*-specific options.

NOTE

This command may not be supported for all FSTypes.

FILES

/etc/vfstab list of default parameters for each file system

SEE ALSO

vfstab(4), **s5**-specific **volcopy**(1M), **sfs**-specific **volcopy**(1M), **ufs**-specific **volcopy**(1M), **vxfs**-specific **volcopy**(1M)

NAME

volcopy (s5) – make a literal copy of an **s5** file system

SYNOPSIS

volcopy [**-F s5**] [*generic_options*] [*current_options*] *fsname srcdevice volname1 destdevice volname2*

DESCRIPTION

generic_options are options supported by the generic **volcopy** command.

volcopy makes a literal copy of the **s5** file system using a blocksize matched to the device.

Options

-F s5 Specify the **s5**-FSType.

-a Invoke a verification sequence requiring a positive operator response instead of the standard 10-second delay before the copy is made.

-y Assume a **yes** response to all questions.

Other *options* are used with both 9-track and cartridge tapes (cartridge tapes are treated as if they were 9-track tapes.)

-bpi*density* bits per inch

-feet*size* size of reel in feet

-reel*num* beginning reel number for a restarted copy

-buf use double buffered I/O

-e process until the end of tape, then ask for the next tape in sequence.

If the **-e** option is not selected, the program requests length and density information if this is not given on the command line, or if it is not recorded on an input tape label. If the file system is too large to fit on one reel, **volcopy** prompts for additional reels. Labels of all reels are checked. Tapes may be mounted alternately on two or more drives. If **volcopy** is interrupted, it asks if the user wants to quit or escape to the command interpreter. In the latter case, the user can perform other operations (such as **labelit**) and return to **volcopy** by exiting the command interpreter. Note that the **-e** and **-feet** options are mutually exclusive.

The *fsname* argument represents the mounted name (for example, **root**, **usr**, etc.) of the file system being copied.

The *srcdevice* or *destdevice* should be the disk partition or tape. For example, **/dev/rdsk/*** or **/dev/rmt/***, where the value of * is machine specific.

The *volname* is the physical volume name. Such label names contain up to six characters. *volname* may be "**–**" to use the existing volume name.

srcdevice and *volname1* are the device and volume from which the copy of the file system is being extracted. *destdevice* and *volname2* are the target device and volume.

fsname and *volname* are recorded in the superblock.

NOTE

volcopy does not support tape-to-tape copying. Use **dd**(1M) for tape-to-tape copying.

FILES

/var/adm/log/filesave.log a record of file systems/volumes copied

SEE ALSO

cpio(1), **dd**(1M), **s5**-specific **fs**(4), **labelit**(1M), **sh**(1), generic **volcopy**(1M)

NAME

volcopy (sfs) – make a literal copy of a **sfs** file system

SYNOPSIS

volcopy [**-F sfs**] [*generic_options*] [*current_options*] *fsname srcdevice volname1 destdevice volname2*

DESCRIPTION

generic_options are options supported by the generic **volcopy** command. *current_options* are options supported by the s5-specific module of **volcopy**.

volcopy makes a literal copy of the **sfs** file system using a blocksize matched to the device.

The options are:

-F sfs Specify the **sfs**-FSType.

-a Invoke a verification sequence requiring a positive operator response instead of the standard 10-second delay before the copy is made. A positive response is always required to override warnings about mismatched system names.

Other *options* are used with both 9-track and cartridge tapes (cartridge tapes are treated as if they were 9-track tapes.)

-bpi*density* bits per inch

-feet*size* size of reel in feet

-reel*num* beginning reel number for a restarted copy

-buf use double buffered I/O

-e process until the end of tape, then ask for the next tape in sequence.

If the **-e** option is not selected, the program requests length and density information if this is not given on the command line or if it is not recorded on an input tape label. If the file system is too large to fit on one reel, **volcopy** prompts for additional reels. Labels of all reels are checked. Tapes may be mounted alternately on two or more drives. If **volcopy** is interrupted, it asks if the user wants to quit or wants to escape to the command interpreter. In the latter case, the user can perform other operations (such as **labelit**) and return to **volcopy** by exiting the command interpreter. Note that the **-e** and **-feet** options are mutually exclusive.

The *fsname* argument represents the mounted name (for example, **root**, **usr**, and so on) of the file system being copied.

The *srcdevice* or *destdevice* should be the disk partition or tape (for example, **/dev/rdsk/1s5**, **/dev/rmt/c0s0**, and so on).

The *volname* is the physical volume name. Such label names contain up to six characters. *volname* may be "–" to use the existing volume name.

srcdevice and *volname1* are the device and volume from which the copy of the file system is being extracted. *destdevice* and *volname2* are the target device and volume.

fsname and *volname* are recorded in the superblock.

NOTES

volcopy does not support tape-to-tape copying. Use **dd**(1M) for tape-to-tape copying.

FILES

/var/adm/log/filesave.log
a record of file systems/volumes copied

SEE ALSO

cpio(1), **dd**(1M), **sfs**-specific **fs**(4), **labelit**(1M), generic **volcopy**(1M)

NAME

volcopy (ufs) – make a literal copy of a **ufs** file system

SYNOPSIS

volcopy [**-F ufs**] [*generic_options*] [*current_options*] *fsname srcdevice volname1 destdevice volname2*

DESCRIPTION

generic_options are options supported by the generic **volcopy** command. *current_options* are options supported by the s5-specific module of **volcopy**.

volcopy makes a literal copy of the **ufs** file system using a blocksize matched to the device.

Options

-F ufs Specify the **ufs**-FSType.

-a Invoke a verification sequence requiring a positive operator response instead of the standard 10-second delay before the copy is made.

-y Assume a **yes** response to all questions.

Other *options* are used with both 9-track and cartridge tapes (cartridge tapes are treated as if they were 9-track tapes.)

-bpi*density* bits per inch

-feet*size* size of reel in feet

-reel*num* beginning reel number for a restarted copy

-buf use double buffered I/O

-e process until the end of tape, then ask for the next tape in sequence.

If the **-e** option is not selected, the program requests length and density information if this is not given on the command line or if it is not recorded on an input tape label. If the file system is too large to fit on one reel, **volcopy** prompts for additional reels. Labels of all reels are checked. Tapes may be mounted alternately on two or more drives. If **volcopy** is interrupted, it asks if the user wants to quit or wants to escape to the command interpreter. In the latter case, the user can perform other operations (such as **labelit**) and return to **volcopy** by exiting the command interpreter. Note that the **-e** and **-feet** options are mutually exclusive.

The *fsname* argument represents the mounted name (for example, **root**, **usr**, and so on) of the file system being copied.

The *srcdevice* or *destdevice* should be the disk partition or tape. For example, **/dev/rdsk/*** or **/dev/rmt/***, where the value of * is machine specific.

The *volname* is the physical volume name. Such label names contain up to six characters. *volname* may be "–" to use the existing volume name.

srcdevice and *volname1* are the device and volume from which the copy of the file system is being extracted. *destdevice* and *volname2* are the target device and volume.

fsname and *volname* are recorded in the superblock.

NOTE

volcopy does not support tape-to-tape copying. Use **dd**(1M) for tape-to-tape copying.

FILES

/var/adm/log/filesave.log a record of file systems/volumes copied

SEE ALSO

cpio(1), **dd**(1M), **ufs**-specific **fs**(4), **labelit**(1M), generic **volcopy**(1M)

NAME

volcopy (vxfs) – make a literal copy of a **vxfs** file system

SYNOPSIS

volcopy [**-F vxfs**] [*generic_options*] [*current_options*] *fsname srcdevice volname1 destdevice volname2*

DESCRIPTION

generic_options are options supported by the generic **volcopy** command. *current_options* are options supported by the **s5**-specific module of **volcopy**.

volcopy makes a literal copy of the **vxfs** file system using a block size matched to the device.

The options are:

-F vxfs Specify the **vxfs** FSType.

-a Invoke a verification sequence requiring a positive operator response instead of the standard 10-second delay before the copy is made.

-y Assume a **yes** response to all questions.

Other options are used with both 9-track and cartridge tapes. (Cartridge tapes are treated as if they were 9-track tapes.)

-bpi*density* Bits per inch.

-feet*size* Size, in feet, of the reel.

-reel*num* Beginning reel number for a restarted copy.

-buf Use double buffered I/O.

-e Process until the end of tape, then prompt for the next tape in the sequence.

If the **-e** option is not selected, the program requests length and density information if this information is not already provided on the command line or if this information is not recorded on an input tape label. If the file system is too large to fit on one reel, **volcopy** prompts for additional reels. Labels of all reels are checked.

Tapes may be mounted alternately on two or more drives. If **volcopy** is interrupted, the user is prompted either to quit or escape to the command interpreter. If the user chooses to escape to the command interpreter, other operations can be performed (such as **labelit**). The user can then return to **volcopy** by exiting the command interpreter. NOTE: The **-e** and **-feet** options are mutually exclusive.

The *fsname* argument represents the mounted name of the file system being copied (for example, **root** or **usr**).

The *srcdevice* or *destdevice* should be the disk partition or tape (for example, **/dev/rdsk/1s5**, **/dev/rmt/c0s0**).

volname is the physical volume name. Such label names contain up to six characters. *volname* may be "–" to indicate use of the existing volume name.

srcdevice is the device from which the copy of the file system is being extracted; *volname1* is the volume from which the copy of the file system is being extracted.

destdevice is the target device to which the file system will be written; *volname2* is the target volume to which the file system will be written.

fsname and *volname* are recorded in the super-block.

NOTES

volcopy does not support tape-to-tape copying. Use **dd**(1M) for tape-to-tape copying.

FILES

/var/adm/filesave.log a record of file systems/volumes copied

SEE ALSO

cpio(1), **dd**(1M), **labelit**(1M), generic **volcopy**(1M), **vxfs**-specific **fs**(4)

vsig (1F)

NAME

vsig – synchronize a co-process with the controlling FMLI application

SYNOPSIS

vsig

DESCRIPTION

The **vsig** executable sends a **SIGUSR2** signal to the controlling FMLI process. This signal/alarm causes FMLI to execute the FMLI built-in command **checkworld** (see Chapter 3 in the), which causes all posted objects with a **reread** descriptor evaluating to **TRUE** to be reread. **vsig** takes no arguments.

EXAMPLES

The following is a segment of a shell program:

```
echo "Sending this string to an FMLI process"
vsig
```

The **vsig** executable flushes the output buffer *before* it sends the **SIGUSR2** signal to make sure the string is actually in the pipe created by the **cocreate** function.

NOTES

Because **vsig** synchronizes with FMLI, it should be used rather than **kill** to send a **SIGUSR2** signal to FMLI.

SEE ALSO

coproc(1F), **kill**(1), **kill**(2), **signal**(2)

NAME

vtgetty – sets terminal type, modes, speed, and line discipline.

SYNOPSIS

/etc/vtgetty [**-h**] [**-t***timeout*] *line* [[*speed*[*type* [*linedisc*]]]

DESCRIPTION

The **vtgetty** command is invoked by **init**(1M). It is the second process in the series (**init-vtgetty-getty-login-shell**) that passes its arguments and executes **/etc/getty**. The **/etc/getty** process will eventually connect a user with the UNIX system. **vtgetty** can be executed only by a user with appropriate privilege (a process with the user-ID of root).

The command options are identical to those of **getty**(1M).

Initially, **vtgetty** opens the device and determines if any virtual terminals (vts) are open for that device. If there are active vts, the user will be prompted to determine if the vts should be closed automatically or manually when the user logs out. If the automatic option is selected, **vtgetty** will send the signals, **SIGHUP** and **SIGTERM**, to each open vt. It will then wait 2 seconds and send a **SIGKILL** signal to the vts to ensure that all the vts are terminated.

If the manual closure option is selected, the highest numbered vt will be activated and the user can manually close the vt. This will be repeated until all open vts are manually closed.

DIAGNOSTICS

vtgetty will fail under the following conditions:

> If there is no memory available.
> If it cannot open the device it was given.
> If it cannot convert from a file descriptor to a file pointer.
> If it cannot get the file status [**stat**(2)] of the device it was given.
> If an **ioctl**(2) call fails.

FILES

/etc/gettydefs

SEE ALSO

getty(1M), **gettydefs**(4), **init**(1M), **inittab**(4), **ioctl**(2), **kill**(1), **stat**(2), **tty**(1)

vtlmgr(1)

NAME

vtlmgr – monitors and opens virtual terminals.

SYNOPSIS

vtlmgr [**-k**]

DESCRIPTION

When you invoke the **vtlmgr** command (usually from within your **.profile**), it places itself in the background and monitors **/dev/vtmon** for signals from the keyboard/display driver to open new virtual terminals.

Option:

-k The **-k** option sends a **SIGHUP** signal to all open virtual terminals when you log off (by entering CTRL-d from your home virtual terminal). This automatically closes, if possible, existing virtual terminals. For virtual terminals that cannot be automatically closed, you are prompted about closing them manually.

After running **vtlmgr**, you open new virtual terminals and then switch between them by entering a hot-key sequence, specifically:

ALT - SYS-REQ *key*

where *key* is either a function key whose number corresponds to the number of the virtual terminal to which to switch or a letter in the table below. For example, pressing F1 switches you to /dev/vt01 (virtual terminal 01), pressing F2 switches you to /dev/vt02 (virtual terminal 02), and so on,

key	Interpretation
f	force a switch to a virtual terminal
h	home virtual terminal (/dev/vt00)
n	next virtual terminal
p	previous virtual terminal

Use the **f** key only when the current virtual terminal is locked up or stuck in graphics mode. Using the **f** key causes the virtual terminal to be reset to a sane text state and to kill all processes associated with the virtual terminal. If **X** is running in the virtual terminal, **X** and all clients will be terminated. You can use the **ALT - SYS-REQ f** (force) key sequence to recover. Typically you will be switched to the /dev/console virtual terminal where **X** may be restarted.

When the hot-key sequence is entered, the executable program pointed to by the **$SHELL** variable is executed in the new virtual terminal. If **$SHELL** is NULL or points to a program that is not executable, **/bin/sh** is executed. The newly opened virtual terminal inherits the environment in effect when the **vtlmgr** command is invoked.

You may perform setup on each new virtual terminal as it is created by **vtlmgr** through the **.vtlrc** file in your home directory. This file contains a shell script that is run by **/bin/sh** before the shell prompt is displayed. In this way, it is similar to your **.profile** file. However, you may not set and export environment variables to the shell for the virtual terminal because a different shell runs the **.vtlrc** shell script.

The system administrator can control how many virtual terminals are available by setting a parameter in the file **/etc/default/workstations**. Virtual terminals 0 through 8 are configured by default, and the default keyboard map makes up to 13 virtual terminals available (that is, an additional 4 virtual terminals can readily be defined within the default settings). The default virtual terminals are the home terminal and one corresponding to each function key. An application can make two more available to the end-user (by reprogramming the keyboard map), or can reserve the last two for programmatic use only, making 15 virtual terminals available in all.

Note that processes that are no longer visible may still be continuing. Standard output is directed to the current virtual terminal's screen. For example, you can issue a **cat** command on one virtual terminal, switch to another virtual terminal to start an application, and then switch to another to do an edit. The **cat** output will be lost if the virtual terminal scrolls the data off the screen unless you initially redirect the output to a file.

DIAGNOSTICS

The **vtlmgr** command will fail under the following conditions:

If an invalid option is specified.
If the device cannot be opened.
If the command is invoked from a remote terminal.
If **/dev/vtmon** cannot be opened.
If **$SHELL** is set and is not executable.
If **$SHELL** is not set and **/bin/sh** cannot be invoked.

SEE ALSO

keyboard(7), **newvt(1)**, **vtgetty**(1M)

NAME

vxdump – incremental file system dump

SYNOPSIS

vxdump [*options*] *filesystem*

DESCRIPTION

vxdump backs up all files in *filesystem*, or files changed after a certain date, to magnetic tape. *options* is a string that specifies **vxdump** options, as shown below.

If no *options* are given, the default is **-9u**.

The options are:

0-9 The dump level. All files in the *filesystem* that have been modified since the last **vxdump** at a lower dump level are copied to the volume. For instance, if you did a level 2 dump on Monday, followed by a level 4 dump on Tuesday, a subsequent level 3 dump on Wednesday would contain all files modified or added since the level 2 (Monday) backup. A level 0 dump copies the entire filesystem to the dump volume.

-b *factor*
: Blocking factor. Specify the blocking factor for tape writes. The default is 20 blocks per write. NOTE: The blocking factor is specified in terms of 512 byte blocks for compatibility with **tar**. The default blocking factor for tapes of density 6250BPI and greater is 64. The default blocking factor for cartridge tapes (**-c** option specified) is 126. The highest blocking factor available with most tape drives is 126.

-c Cartridge. Use a cartridge instead of the standard half-inch reel. This sets the density to 1000BPI and the blocking factor to 126. The length is set to 425 feet. This option is incompatible with the **-d** option, unless you specify a density of 1000BPI with that option.

-d *bpi* Tape density. The density of the tape, expressed in BPI, is taken from *bpi*. This is used to keep a running tab on the amount of tape used per reel. The default density is 1600 except for cartridge tape. Unless a higher density is specified explicitly, **vxdump** uses its default density — even if the tape drive is capable of higher-density operation (for instance, 6250BPI).

NOTE: The density specified should correspond to the density of the tape device being used, or **vxdump** will not be able to handle end-of-tape properly.

-f *dump-file*
: Dump file. Dump to *dump-file* instead of to **/dev/rmt8.** If *dump-file* is specified as **-**, dump to the standard output.

-n Notify all operators in the operator group that **vxdump** requires attention by sending messages to their terminals, in a manner similar to that used by the **wall** command.

-s *size*

Specify the *size* of the volume being dumped to. When the specified size is reached, **vxdump** waits for you to change the volume. **vxdump** interprets the specified size as the length in feet for tapes and cartridges, and as the number of 1024-byte blocks for diskettes. The following are defaults:

tape	2300 feet
cartridge	425 feet
diskette	1422 blocks (corresponds to a 1.44 Mb diskette, with one cylinder reserved for bad block information)

-t *tracks*

Specify the number of tracks for a cartridge tape. The default is 9 tracks. The **-t** option is not compatible with the **-f** option.

-u Update the dump record. For each filesystem successfully dumped, add an entry to the file **/etc/dumpdates** that includes the filesystem name, date, and dump level. This file can be edited by a privileged user.

-w List the file systems that need backing up. This information is gleaned from the files **/etc/dumpdates** and **/etc/vfstab**. When the **-w** option is used, all other options are ignored. After reporting, **vxdump** exits immediately.

W Similar to the **-w** option, except that the **-W** option includes all file systems that appear in **/etc/dumpdates,** along with information about their most recent dump dates and levels. Filesystems that need backing up are highlighted.

NOTES

Fewer than 32 read errors on the filesystem are ignored.

Each reel requires a new process, so parent processes for reels already written just wait until the entire tape is written.

If you have the VxFS Advanced package, it is recommended that dumps be done in multi-user mode with the online backup facility. If you do not have the VxFS Advanced package, it is recommended that incremental dumps be performed with the system running in single-user mode.

FILES

/dev/rmt8	default unit to dump to
/etc/dumpdates	dump date record
/etc/group	to find group operator
/etc/hosts	

SEE ALSO

shutdown(1M), **tar**(1), **vxrestore**(1M), **wall**(1M)

NAME

vxrestore – incremental file system restore

SYNOPSIS

vxrestore *options* [*filename*...]

DESCRIPTION

vxrestore restores files from backup tapes created with the **vxdump** command. *options* is a string of at least one of the options listed below, along with any modifiers and arguments supplied. Remaining arguments to **vxrestore** are the names of files (or directories whose files are) to be restored to disk. Unless the **h** modifier is in effect, a directory name refers to the files it contains, as well as (recursively) its subdirectories and the files they contain.

The options are:

-i Interactive. After reading in the directory information from the tape, **vxrestore** invokes an interactive interface that allows you to browse through the dump tape's directory hierarchy and select individual files to be extracted. See the section on interactive commands, below, for a description of available commands.

-r Restore the entire tape. Load the tape's full contents into the current directory. This option should be used only to restore a complete dump tape onto a clear file system, or to restore an incremental dump tape after a full level **0** restore.

-R Resume restoring. **vxrestore** requests a particular tape of a multivolume set from which to resume a full restore (see the **-r** option). This allows **vxrestore** to start from a checkpoint when it is interrupted in the middle of a full restore.

-t Table of contents. List each *filename* that appears on the tape. If no *filename* argument is given, the root directory is listed. This results in a list of all files on the tape, unless the modifier is in effect.

-x Extract the named files from the tape. If a named file matches a directory whose contents were written onto the tape, and the modifier is not in effect, the directory is recursively extracted. The owner, modification time, and mode are restored (if possible). If no *filename* argument is given, the root directory is extracted. This results in the entire tape being extracted unless the modifier is in effect.

-d Debug. Turn on debugging output.

h Extract the actual directory, rather than the files that it references. This prevents hierarchical restoration of complete subtrees from the tape.

m Extract by inode numbers rather than by filename to avoid regenerating complete pathnames. This is useful if only a few files are being extracted.

v Verbose. **vxrestore** displays the name of each file it restores, preceded by its file type.

y Do not ask whether to abort the restore in the event of tape errors. **vxrestore** tries to skip over the bad tape block(s) and continue as best it can.

b *factor*
Blocking factor. Specify the blocking factor for tape reads. By default, **vxrestore** will attempt to figure out the block size of the tape.

NOTE: A tape block is 512 bytes.

-e *extent_opt*
Specify how to handle a **vxfs** file that has extent attribute information. Extent attributes include reserved space, a fixed extent size, and extent alignment. It may not be possible to preserve the information if the destination file system does not support extent attributes, has a different block size than the source file system, or lacks free extents appropriate to satisfy the extent attribute requirements. Valid values for *extent_opt* are:

warn Issue a warning message if extent attribute information cannot be kept (the default).

force Fail the file restore if extent attribute information cannot be kept.

ignore Ignore extent attribute information entirely.

f *dump-file*
Use *dump-file* instead of **/dev/rmt?** as the file to restore from. If *dump-file* is specified as "-", **vxrestore** reads from the standard input. This allows **vxdump**(1M) and **vxrestore** to be used in a pipeline to dump and restore a file system:

```
example# vxdump  0f - /dev/rxy0g  |  (cd /mnt; vxrestore xf -)
```

s *ni* Skip to the *n*'th file when there are multiple dump files on the same tape. For example, the command:

```
example# vxrestore xfs /dev/nrar0 5
```

would position you at the fifth file on the tape.

Interactive Commands

vxrestore enters interactive mode when invoked with the **i** option. Interactive commands are reminiscent of the shell. For those commands that accept an argument, the default is the current directory.

ls[*directory*]
List files in *directory* or the current directory, represented by a "**.**" (period). Directories are appended with a "**/**" (slash). Entries marked for extraction are prefixed with an "*****" (asterisk). If the verbose option is in effect, inode numbers are also listed.

cd *directory*
Change to directory *directory* (within the dump-tape).

pwd Print the full pathname of the current working directory.

`add`[*filename*]
Add the current directory, or the named file or directory **`directory`** to the list of files to extract. If a directory is specified, add that directory and its files (recursively) to the extraction list (unless the **`h`** modifier is in effect).

`delete`[*filename*]
Delete the current directory, or the named file or directory from the list of files to extract. If a directory is specified, delete that directory and all its descendents from the extraction list (unless the **`h`** modifier is in effect). The most expedient way to extract a majority of files from a directory is to add that directory to the extraction list, and then delete specific files to omit.

`extract` Extract all files on the extraction list from the dump tape. **`vxrestore`** asks which volume the user wishes to mount. The fastest way to extract a small number of files is to start with the last tape volume and work toward the first.

`verbose` Toggle the status of the **`v`** modifier. While **`v`** is in effect, the **`ls`** command lists the inode numbers of all entries, and **`vxrestore`** displays information about each file as it is extracted.

`help` Display a summary of the available commands.

`quit` **`vxrestore`** exits immediately, even if the extraction list is not empty.

NOTES

`vxrestore` can get confused when doing incremental restores from dump tapes that were made on active file systems. Dumps should be made using the snapshot mount facilities of **`vxfs`**.

A level `0` dump must be done after a full restore. Because **`vxrestore`** runs in user mode, it has no control over inode allocation; this means that **`vxrestore`** repositions the files, although it does not change their contents. Thus, a full dump must be done to get a new set of directories reflecting the new file positions, so that later incremental dumps will be correct.

DIAGNOSTICS

`vxrestore` complains about bad option characters.

Read errors result in complaints. If **`y`** has been specified, or the user responds **`y`**, **`vxrestore`** will attempt to continue.

If the dump extends over more than one tape, **`vxrestore`** asks the user to change tapes. If the **`x`** or **`i`** option has been specified, **`vxrestore`** also asks which volume the user wishes to mount.

There are numerous consistency checks that can be listed by **`vxrestore`**. Most checks are self-explanatory or can never happen. Common errors include the following:

`Converting to new file system format.`
A dump tape created from the old file system has been loaded. It is automatically converted to the new file system format.

filename: **not found on tape**

The specified file name was listed in the tape directory, but was not found on the tape. This is caused by tape read errors while looking for the file, and from using a dump tape created on an active file system.

expected next file *inumber*, **got** *inumber*

A file that was not listed in the directory showed up. This can occur when using a dump tape created on an active file system.

Incremental tape too low

When doing an incremental restore, a tape that was written before the previous incremental tape, or that has too low an incremental level has been loaded.

Incremental tape too high

When doing an incremental restore, a tape that does not begin its coverage where the previous incremental tape left off, or one that has too high an incremental level has been loaded.

Tape read error while restoring *filename*
Tape read error while skipping over inode inumber
Tape read error while trying to resynchronize
A tape read error has occurred.

If a file name is specified, its contents are probably partially wrong. If an inode is being skipped or the tape is trying to resynchronize, no extracted files have been corrupted, though files may not be found on the tape.

resync vxrestore, skipped *num*

After a tape read error, **vxrestore** may have to resynchronize itself. This message lists the number of blocks that were skipped over.

FILES

/dev/rmt8	the default tape drive
/tmp/rstdir*	file containing directories on the tape
/tmp/rstmode*	owner, mode, and timestamps for directories
./restoresymtable	information passed between incremental restores

SEE ALSO

mkfs(1M), **mount**(1M), **vxdump**(1M)

NAME

w – (BSD) who is logged in, and what are they doing

SYNOPSIS

/usr/ucb/w [**-hls**] [*user*]

DESCRIPTION

The **w** command displays a summary of the current activity on the system, including what each user is doing. The heading line shows the current time of day, how long the system has been up, and the number of users logged into the system.

The fields displayed are: the users login name, the name of the tty the user is on, the time of day the user logged on (in *hours:minutes*), the idle time—that is, the number of minutes since the user last typed anything (in *hours:minutes*), the CPU time used by all processes and their children on that terminal (in *minutes:seconds*), the CPU time used by the currently active processes (in *minutes:seconds*), the name and arguments of the current process.

If a *user* name is included, output is restricted to that user.

The following options are available:

-h Suppress the heading.

-l Produce a long form of output, which is the default.

-s Produce a short form of output. In the short form, the tty is abbreviated, the login time and CPU times are left off, as are the arguments to commands.

EXAMPLE

Executing **w** with no options produces output similar to the following:

```
7:36am  up 6 days, 16:45,  1 user
User    tty     login@  idle    JCPU    PCPU    what
ralph   console 7:10am     1    10:05   4:31    w
```

FILES

/var/adm/utmp

SEE ALSO

ps(1), **utmp**(4), **who**(1), **whodo**(1M).

NOTES

The notion of the "current process" is muddy. The current algorithm is 'the highest numbered process on the terminal that is not ignoring interrupts, or, if there is none, the highest numbered process on the terminal'. This fails, for example, in critical sections of programs like the shell and editor, or when faulty programs running in the background fork and fail to ignore interrupts. In cases where no process can be found, **w** prints –.

The CPU time is only an estimate, in particular, if someone leaves a background process running after logging out, the person currently on that terminal is "charged" with the time.

Background processes are not shown, even though they account for much of the load on the system.

Sometimes processes, typically those in the background, are printed with null or garbaged arguments. In these cases, the name of the command is printed in parentheses.

w does not know about the conventions for detecting background jobs. It will sometimes find a background job instead of the right one.

Unlike other BSD versions of this command, the load averages are not computed or displayed.

wait (1)

NAME

wait – await completion of process

SYNOPSIS

wait [*n*]

DESCRIPTION

Wait for your background process whose process id is *n* and report its termination status. If *n* is omitted, all your shell's currently active background processes are waited for and the return code will be zero.

The shell itself executes **wait**, without creating a new process.

FILES

/usr/lib/locale/*locale***/LC_MESSAGES/uxcore.abi**
language-specific message file [See **LANG** on **environ** (5).]

SEE ALSO

sh(1)

NOTES

If you get the error message **cannot fork, too many processes**, try using the **wait** command to clean up your background processes. If this doesn't help, the system process table is probably full or you have too many active foreground processes. (There is a limit to the number of process ids associated with your login, and to the number the system can keep track of.)

Not all the processes of a 3- or more-stage pipeline are children of the shell, and thus cannot be waited for.

If *n* is not an active process id, **wait** returns immediately.

NAME

wall – write to all users

SYNOPSIS

wall [**-g** *group*] [*filename*]

DESCRIPTION

wall reads the named file, or, if no filename appears, it reads the standard input until an end-of-file. It then sends this message to all currently logged-in users preceded by:

Broadcast Message from *source*...

It is used to warn all users, typically prior to shutting down the system. If the **-g** option is given, the message is only sent to members of the specified group, instead of all users.

The sender must be a privileged user to override any protections the users may have invoked [see **mesg**(1)].

wall runs **setgid** [see **setuid**(2)] to the group ID **tty**, in order to have write permissions on other user's terminals.

wall processes supplementary code set characters according to the locale specified in the **LC_CTYPE** environment variable [see **LANG** on **environ**(5)]. It will detect non-printable characters before sending them to the user's terminal. Control characters will appear as a '^' followed by the appropriate ASCII character; characters with the high-order bit set will appear in meta notation. For example, '**\003**' is displayed as '**^C**' and '**\372**' as '**M-z**'.

FILES

/dev/term/*

/usr/lib/locale/*locale***/LC_MESSAGES/uxcore**

language-specific message file [See **LANG** on **environ**(5).]

SEE ALSO

mesg(1), **write**(1)

DIAGNOSTICS

UX:wall:ERROR:Cannot send to ...

when the open on a user's tty file fails.

NAME

wc – word count

SYNOPSIS

wc [**-lwc**] [*filename* ...]

DESCRIPTION

wc counts lines, words, and characters in the named files, or in the standard input if no *filename* appears. It also keeps a total count for all named files. A word is a maximal string of characters delimited by spaces, tabs, or new-lines.

The options **l**, **w**, and **c** may be used in any combination to specify that a subset of lines, words, and characters are to be reported. The default is **-lwc**.

When a *filename* is specified on the command line, it will be printed along with the counts.

wc processes supplementary code set characters according to the locale specified in the **LC_CTYPE** environment variable [see **LANG** on **environ**(5)]. Character counts are given in bytes; supplementary code set characters are ignored in word counts.

FILES

/usr/lib/locale/*locale***/LC_MESSAGES/uxcore**
language-specific message file [See **LANG** on **environ**(5).]

NAME

wchrtbl – generate tables for ASCII and supplementary code sets

SYNOPSIS

wchrtbl [*file*]

DESCRIPTION

wchrtbl creates tables containing information on character classification, character conversion, character set width, and numeric editing. The first table is a byte-sized array encoded such that a table lookup can be used to determine the character classification of a character, convert a character [see **ctype**(3C) and **wctype**(3W)], and find the byte and screen width of a character in one of the supplementary code sets. The size of the array is (257*2) + 7 bytes: 257 bytes are required for the 8-bit code set character classification table, 257 bytes for the upper- to lowercase and lower- to uppercase conversion table, and 7 bytes for character set width information. The second table is 2 bytes long and is encoded such that the first byte is used to specify the decimal delimiter and the second byte the thousand delimiter. If supplementary code sets are specified, additional variable sized tables are generated for multibyte character classification and conversion.

wchrtbl reads the user-defined character classification and conversion information from *file* and creates three output files in the current directory. One output file, **wctype.c** (a C language source file), contains the variable sized array generated from processing the information from *file*. You should review the content of **wctype.c** to verify that the array is set up as you had planned. The first 257 bytes of the array in **wctype.c** are used for character classification for single byte characters. The characters used for initializing these bytes of the array represent character classifications that are defined in **ctype.h**; for example, **_L** means a character is lower case and **_S**| **_B** means the character is both a spacing character and a blank. The second 257 bytes of the array are used for character conversion. These bytes of the array are initialized so that characters for which you do not provide conversion information will be converted to themselves. When you do provide conversion information, the first value of the pair is stored where the second one would be stored normally, and vice versa. For example, if you provide **<0x41 0x61>**, then **0x61** is stored where **0x41** would be stored normally, and **0x61** is stored where **0x41** would be stored normally. The last 7 bytes are used for character width information. Up to three supplementary code sets can be specified.

For supplementary code sets, there are three sets of tables. The first set is three pointer arrays which point to supplementary code set information tables. If the corresponding supplementary code set information is not specified, the contents of the pointers are zeros. The second one is a set of three supplementary code set information tables. Each table contains minimum and maximum code values to be classified and converted, and also contains pointers to character classification and conversion tables. If there is no corresponding table, the contents of the pointers are zeros. The last one is a set of character classification and conversion tables which contain the same information as the single byte table except that the codes are represented as process codes and the table size is variable. The characters used for initializing values of the character classification table represent character classifications that are defined in **ctype.h** and **wctype.h**. **_E1** through **_E8** are for international use and **_E9** through **_E24** are for language-dependent use.

The second output file (a data file) contains the same information, but is structured for efficient use by the character classification and conversion routines [see **ctype**(3C) and **wctype**(3W)]. The name of this output file is the value of the character classification **LC_CTYPE** read in from *file*. This output file must be copied to the **/usr/lib/locale/***locale***/LC_CTYPE** file by someone who is super-user or a member of group **bin**. This file must be readable by user, group, and other; no other permissions should be set. To use the character classification and conversion tables on this file, set the **LC_CTYPE** category of **setlocale** [see **setlocale**(3C)] appropriately.

The third output file (a data file) is created only if numeric editing information is specified in the input file. The name of the file is the value of the character classification **LC_NUMERIC** read from the *file*. This output file must be copied to the **/usr/lib/locale/***locale***/LC_NUMERIC** file by someone who is super-user or a member of group **bin**. This file must be readable by user, group, and other; no other permissions should be set. To use the numeric editing information on this file, set the **LC_NUMERIC** category of **setlocale** appropriately.

If no input file is given, or if the argument **-** is encountered, **wchrtbl** reads from standard input.

The syntax of *file* allows the user to define the name of the data file created by **wchrtbl**, the assignment of characters to character classifications, the relationship between conversion letters, and byte and screen widths for up to three supplementary code sets. The keywords recognized by **wchrtbl** are:

LC_CTYPE	name of the first data file to be created by **wchrtbl**
isupper	character codes to be classified as uppercase letters
islower	character codes to be classified as lowercase letters
isdigit	character codes to be classified as numeric
isspace	character codes to be classified as spacing (delimiter) characters
ispunct	character codes to be classified as punctuation characters
iscntrl	character codes to be classified as control characters
isblank	character code for the space character
isxdigit	character codes to be classified as hexadecimal digits
ul	relationship between conversion characters
cswidth	byte and screen width information
LC_NUMERIC	name of the second data file created by **wchrtbl**
decimal_point	decimal delimiters
thousands_sep	thousands delimiters
LC_CTYPE1	specify that functions for specification of supplementary code set 1 follows

LC_CTYPE2	specify that functions for specification of supplementary code set 2 follows
LC_CTYPE3	specify that functions for specification of supplementary code set 3 follows
isphonogram(iswchar1)	character codes to be classified as phonograms in supplementary code sets
isideogram(iswchar2)	character codes to be classified as ideograms in supplementary code sets
isenglish(iswchar3)	character codes to be classified as English letters in supplementary code sets
isnumber(iswchar4)	character codes to be classified as numeric in supplementary code sets
isspecial(iswchar5)	character codes to be classified as special letters in supplementary code sets
iswchar6	character codes to be classified as other printable letters in supplementary code sets
iswchar7 - **iswchar8**	reserved for international use
iswchar9 - **iswchar24**	character codes to be classified as language-dependent letters/characters
grouping^	string in which each element is taken as an integer that indicates the number of digits that comprise the current group in a formatted non-monetary numeric quantity.

The keywords **iswchar1** through **iswchar24** correspond to bit names **_E1** through **_E24** defined in **wctype.h**

Any lines with the number sign (**#**) in the first column are treated as comments and are ignored. Blank lines are also ignored.

Characters for **isupper**, **islower**, **isdigit**, **isspace**, **ispunct**, **iscntl**, **isblank**, **isxdigit**, **ul**, **isphonogram**, **isideogram**, **isenglish**, **isnumber**, **isspecial**, and **iswchar1–iswchar24** can be represented as hexadecimal or octal constants (for example, the letter **a** can be represented as **0x61** in hexadecimal or **0141** in octal) and must be up to two byte process codes. Hexadecimal and octal constants may be separated by one or more space and tab characters.

The following is the format of an input specification for **cswidth** (byte widths for supplementary code sets 2 and 3 are exclusive of the single shift characters):

```
cswidth n1[[:s1][,n2[:s2][,n3[:s3]]]]
```

where,

n1	byte width for supplementary code set 1
s1	screen width for supplementary code set 1
n2	byte width for supplementary code set 2

s2	screen width for supplementary code set 2
n3	byte width for supplementary code set 3
s3	screen width for supplementary code set 3

The dash character (**-**) may be used to indicate a range of consecutive numbers (inclusive of the characters delimiting the range). Zero or more space characters may be used for separating the dash character from the numbers.

The backslash character (****) is used for line continuation. Only a carriage return is permitted after the backslash character.

The relationship between conversion letters (**ul**) is expressed as ordered pairs of octal or hexadecimal constants: <*converting-character converted-character*>. These two constants must be up to two byte process codes and may be separated by one or more space characters. Zero or more space characters may be used for separating the angle brackets (< >) from the numbers.

EXAMPLE

The following is an example of an input file used to create the JAPAN code set definition table on a file named **LC_CTYPE** and **LC_NUMERIC**.

```
#
# locale JAPAN
#
LC_CTYPE   LC_CTYPE
#
# specification for single byte characters
#
isupper      0x41 - 0x5a
islower      0x61 - 0x7a
isdigit      0x30 - 0x39
isspace      0x20   0x9 - 0xd
ispunct      0x21 - 0x2f    0x3a - 0x40   \
             0x5b - 0x60    0x7b - 0x7e
iscntrl      0x0 - 0x1f     0x7f - 0x9f
isblank      0x20
isxdigit  0x30 - 0x39 0x61 - 0x66      0x41 - 0x46
ul         <0x41 0x61> <0x42 0x62> <0x43 0x63> \
           <0x44 0x64> <0x45 0x65> <0x46 0x66> \
           <0x47 0x67> <0x48 0x68> <0x49 0x69> \
           <0x4a 0x6a> <0x4b 0x6b> <0x4c 0x6c> \
           <0x4d 0x6d> <0x4e 0x6e> <0x4f 0x6f> \
           <0x50 0x70> <0x51 0x71> <0x52 0x72> \
           <0x53 0x73> <0x54 0x74> <0x55 0x75> \
           <0x56 0x76> <0x57 0x77> <0x58 0x78> \
           <0x59 0x79> <0x5a 0x7a>
cswidth          2:2,1:1,2:2
LC_NUMERIC LC_NUMERIC
decimal_point    .
thousands_sep
```

```
#
# specification for supplementary code set 1
#
LC_CTYPE1
isupper        0xa3c1 - 0xa3da
islower        0xa3e1 - 0xa3fa
isdigit        0xa3b0 - 0xa3b9
isspace        0xa1a1
isphonogram    0xa4a1 - 0xa4f3 0xa5a1 - 0xa5f6
isideogram 0xb0a1 - 0xb0fe 0xb1a1 - 0xb1fe 0xb2a1 - 0xb2fe \
           0xb3a1 - 0xb3fe 0xb4a1 - 0xb4fe 0xb5a1 - 0xb5fe \
           0xb6a1 - 0xb6fe 0xb7a1 - 0xb7fe 0xb8a1 - 0xb8fe \
           0xb9a1 - 0xb9fe 0xbaa1 - 0xbafe 0xbba1 - 0xbbfe \
           0xbca1 - 0xbcfe 0xbda1 - 0xbdfe 0xbea1 - 0xbefe \
           0xbfa1 - 0xbffe 0xc0a1 - 0xc0fe 0xc1a1 - 0xc1fe \
           0xc2a1 - 0xc2fe 0xc3a1 - 0xc3fe 0xc4a1 - 0xc4fe \
           0xc5a1 - 0xc5fe 0xc6a1 - 0xc6fe 0xc7a1 - 0xc7fe \
           0xcca1 - 0xccfe 0xcda1 - 0xcdfe 0xcea1 - 0xcefe \
           0xcfa1 - 0xcffe 0xd0a1 - 0xd0fe 0xd1a1 - 0xd1fe \
           0xd2a1 - 0xd2fe 0xd3a1 - 0xd3fe 0xd4a1 - 0xd4fe \
           0xd5a1 - 0xd5fe 0xd6a1 - 0xd6fe 0xd7a1 - 0xd7fe \
           0xd8a1 - 0xd8fe 0xd9a1 - 0xd9fe 0xdaa1 - 0xdafe \
           0xdba1 - 0xdbfe 0xdca1 - 0xdcfe 0xdda1 - 0xddfe \
           0xdea1 - 0xdefe 0xdfa1 - 0xdffe 0xe0a1 - 0xe0fe \
           0xe1a1 - 0xe1fe 0xe2a1 - 0xe2fe 0xe3a1 - 0xe3fe \
           0xe4a1 - 0xe4fe 0xe5a1 - 0xe5fe 0xe6a1 - 0xe6fe \
           0xe7a1 - 0xe7fe 0xe8a1 - 0xe8fe 0xe9a1 - 0xe9fe \
           0xeaa1 - 0xeafe 0xeba1 - 0xebfe 0xeca1 - 0xecfe \
           0xeda1 - 0xedfe 0xeea1 - 0xeefe 0xefa1 - 0xeffe \
           0xf0a1 - 0xf0fe 0xf1a1 - 0xf1fe 0xf2a1 - 0xf2fe \
           0xf3a1 - 0xf3fe 0xf4a1 - 0xf4fe 0xf5a1 - 0xf5fe \
           0xf6a1 - 0xf6fe 0xf7a1 - 0xf7fe 0xf8a1 - 0xf8fe \
           0xf9a1 - 0xf9fe 0xfaa1 - 0xfafe 0xfba1 - 0xfbfe \
           0xfca1 - 0xfcfe 0xfda1 - 0xfdfe 0xfea1 - 0xfefe \
 isenglish 0xa3c1 - 0xa3da 0xa3e1 - 0xa3fa
 isnumber  0xa3b0 - 0xa3b9
 isspecial 0xa1a2 - 0xa1fe 0xa2a1 - 0xa2ae 0xa2ba - 0xa2c1 \
           0xa2ca - 0xa2d0 0xa2dc - 0xa2ea 0xa2f2 - 0xa2f9 \
           0xa2fe
 iswchar6  0xa6a1 - 0xa6b8 0xa6c1 - 0xa6d8 0xa7a1 - 0xa7c1 \
           0xa7d1 - 0xa7f1
 #
 #         JIS X0208 whole code set
 #
 iswchar9  0xa1a1 - 0xa1fe 0xa2a1 - 0xa2fe 0xa3a1 - 0xa3fe \
           0xa4a1 - 0xa4fe 0xa5a1 - 0xa5fe 0xa6a1 - 0xa6fe \
           0xa7a1 - 0xa7fe 0xa8a1 - 0xa8fe 0xa9a1 - 0xa9fe \
           0xaaa1 - 0xaafe 0xaba1 - 0xabfe 0xaca1 - 0xacfe \
           0xada1 - 0xadfe 0xaea1 - 0xaefe 0xafa1 - 0xaffe \
```

```
                0xb0a1 - 0xb0fe 0xb1a1 - 0xb1fe 0xb2a1 - 0xb2fe \
                0xb3a1 - 0xb3fe 0xb4a1 - 0xb4fe 0xb5a1 - 0xb5fe \
                0xb6a1 - 0xb6fe 0xb7a1 - 0xb7fe 0xb8a1 - 0xb8fe \
                0xb9a1 - 0xb9fe 0xbaa1 - 0xbafe 0xbba1 - 0xbbfe \
                0xbca1 - 0xbcfe 0xbda1 - 0xbdfe 0xbea1 - 0xbefe \
                0xbfa1 - 0xbffe 0xc0a1 - 0xc0fe 0xc1a1 - 0xc1fe \
                0xc2a1 - 0xc2fe 0xc3a1 - 0xc3fe 0xc4a1 - 0xc4fe \
                0xc5a1 - 0xc5fe 0xc6a1 - 0xc6fe 0xc7a1 - 0xc7fe \
                0xc8a1 - 0xc8fe 0xc9a1 - 0xc9fe 0xcaa1 - 0xcafe \
                0xcba1 - 0xcbfe 0xcca1 - 0xccfe 0xcda1 - 0xcdfe \
                0xcea1 - 0xcefe 0xcfa1 - 0xcffe 0xd0a1 - 0xd0fe \
                0xd1a1 - 0xd1fe 0xd2a1 - 0xd2fe 0xd3a1 - 0xd3fe \
                0xd4a1 - 0xd4fe 0xd5a1 - 0xd5fe 0xd6a1 - 0xd6fe \
                0xd7a1 - 0xd7fe 0xd8a1 - 0xd8fe 0xd9a1 - 0xd9fe \
                0xdaa1 - 0xdafe 0xdba1 - 0xdbfe 0xdca1 - 0xdcfe \
                0xdda1 - 0xddfe 0xdea1 - 0xdefe 0xdfa1 - 0xdffe \
                0xe0a1 - 0xe0fe 0xe1a1 - 0xe1fe 0xe2a1 - 0xe2fe \
                0xe3a1 - 0xe3fe 0xe4a1 - 0xe4fe 0xe5a1 - 0xe5fe \
                0xe6a1 - 0xe6fe 0xe7a1 - 0xe7fe 0xe8a1 - 0xe8fe \
                0xe9a1 - 0xe9fe 0xeaa1 - 0xeafe 0xeba1 - 0xebfe \
                0xeca1 - 0xecfe 0xeda1 - 0xedfe 0xeea1 - 0xeefe \
                0xefa1 - 0xeffe 0xf0a1 - 0xf0fe 0xf1a1 - 0xf1fe \
                0xf2a1 - 0xf2fe 0xf3a1 - 0xf3fe 0xf4a1 - 0xf4fe \
                0xf5a1 - 0xf5fe 0xf6a1 - 0xf6fe 0xf7a1 - 0xf7fe \
                0xf8a1 - 0xf8fe 0xf9a1 - 0xf9fe 0xfaa1 - 0xfafe \
                0xfba1 - 0xfbfe 0xfca1 - 0xfcfe 0xfda1 - 0xfdfe \
                0xfea1 - 0xfefe
#
#               JIS X0208 parentheses
#
iswchar10       0xa1c6 - 0xa1db
#
#               JIS X0208 hiragana
#
iswchar11       0xa4a1 - 0xa4f3
#
#               JIS X0208 katakana
#
iswchar12       0xa5a1 - 0xa5f6
#
#               JIS X0208 other characters
#
iswchar13       0xa6a1 - 0xa6b8 0xa6c1 - 0xa6d8 0xa7a1 - 0xa7c1 \
                0xa7d1 - 0xa7f1 0xa8a1 - 0xa8bf
#
#               English letter translation table
#
ul              <0xa3c1 0xa3e1> <0xa3c2 0xa3e2> <0xa3c3 0xa3e3> \
                <0xa3c4 0xa3e4> <0xa3c5 0xa3e5> <0xa3c6 0xa3e6> \
```

```
        <0xa3c7 0xa3e7> <0xa3c8 0xa3e8> <0xa3c9 0xa3e9> \
                <0xa3ca 0xa3ea> <0xa3cb 0xa3eb> <0xa3cc 0xa3ec> \
                <0xa3cd 0xa3ed> <0xa3ce 0xa3ee> <0xa3cf 0xa3ef> \
                <0xa3d0 0xa3f0> <0xa3d1 0xa3f1> <0xa3d2 0xa3f2> \
                <0xa3d3 0xa3f3> <0xa3d4 0xa3f4> <0xa3d5 0xa3f5> \
                <0xa3d6 0xa3f6> <0xa3d7 0xa3f7> <0xa3d8 0xa3f8> \
                <0xa3d9 0xa3f9> <0xa3da 0xa3fa> \
#
#               kana translation table
#
                <0xa4a1 0xa5a1> <0xa4a2 0xa5a2> <0xa4a3 0xa5a3> \
                <0xa4a4 0xa5a4> <0xa4a5 0xa5a5> <0xa4a6 0xa5a6> \
                <0xa4a7 0xa5a7> <0xa4a8 0xa5a8> <0xa4a9 0xa5a9> \
                <0xa4aa 0xa5aa> <0xa4ab 0xa5ab> <0xa4ac 0xa5ac> \
                <0xa4ad 0xa5ad> <0xa4ae 0xa5ae> <0xa4af 0xa5af> \
                <0xa4b0 0xa5b0> <0xa4b1 0xa5b1> <0xa4b2 0xa5b2> \
                <0xa4b3 0xa5b3> <0xa4b4 0xa5b4> <0xa4b5 0xa5b5> \
                <0xa4b6 0xa5b6> <0xa4b7 0xa5b7> <0xa4b8 0xa5b8> \
                <0xa4b9 0xa5b9> <0xa4ba 0xa5ba> <0xa4bb 0xa5bb> \
                <0xa4bc 0xa5bc> <0xa4bd 0xa5bd> <0xa4be 0xa5be> \
                <0xa4bf 0xa5bf> <0xa4c0 0xa5c0> <0xa4c1 0xa5c1> \
                <0xa4c2 0xa5c2> <0xa4c3 0xa5c3> <0xa4c4 0xa5c4> \
                <0xa4c5 0xa5c5> <0xa4c6 0xa5c6> <0xa4c7 0xa5c7> \
                <0xa4c8 0xa5c8> <0xa4c9 0xa5c9> <0xa4ca 0xa5ca> \
                <0xa4cb 0xa5cb> <0xa4cc 0xa5cc> <0xa4cd 0xa5cd> \
                <0xa4ce 0xa5ce> <0xa4cf 0xa5cf> <0xa4d0 0xa5d0> \
                <0xa4d1 0xa5d1> <0xa4d2 0xa5d2> <0xa4d3 0xa5d3> \
                <0xa4d4 0xa5d4> <0xa4d5 0xa5d5> <0xa4d6 0xa5d6> \
                <0xa4d7 0xa5d7> <0xa4d8 0xa5d8> <0xa4d9 0xa5d9> \
                <0xa4da 0xa5da> <0xa4db 0xa5db> <0xa4dc 0xa5dc> \
                <0xa4dd 0xa5dd> <0xa4de 0xa5de> <0xa4df 0xa5df> \
                <0xa4e0 0xa5e0> <0xa4e1 0xa5e1> <0xa4e2 0xa5e2> \
                <0xa4e3 0xa5e3> <0xa4e4 0xa5e4> <0xa4e5 0xa5e5> \
                <0xa4e6 0xa5e6> <0xa4e7 0xa5e7> <0xa4e8 0xa5e8> \
                <0xa4e9 0xa5e9> <0xa4ea 0xa5ea> <0xa4eb 0xa5eb> \
                <0xa4ec 0xa5ec> <0xa4ed 0xa5ed> <0xa4ee 0xa5ee> \
                <0xa4ef 0xa5ef> <0xa4f0 0xa5f0> <0xa4f1 0xa5f1> \
                <0xa4f2 0xa5f2> <0xa4f3 0xa5f3>
#
# specification for supplementary code set 2
#
LC_CTYPE2
iswchar6    0xa1 - 0xdf
iswchar14   0xa1 - 0xdf
```

FILES

`/usr/lib/locale/`*locale*`/LC_CTYPE`
: data files containing character classification and conversion tables and character set width information created by **chrtbl** or **wchrtbl**.

/usr/lib/locale/*locale*/LC_NUMERIC
data files containing numeric editing information.

/usr/include/ctype.h
header file containing information used by character classification and conversion routines for single byte characters.

/usr/include/wctype.h
header file containing information used by international character classification and conversion routines for supplementary code sets.

/usr/include/xctype.h
header file containing information used by language-dependent character classification and conversion routines for supplementary code sets.

SEE ALSO

ctype(3C), **setlocale**(3C), **wctype**(3W), **environ**(5)

DIAGNOSTICS

The error messages produced by **wchrtbl** are intended to be self-explanatory. They indicate errors in the command line or syntactic errors encountered within the input file.

NAME

`what` – print identification strings

SYNOPSIS

`what [-s]` *file . . .*

DESCRIPTION

what searches the given *file*s for all occurrences of the pattern that the **get** command substitutes for `%Z%` (this is `@(#)` at this printing) and prints out what follows until the first `"`, `>`, new-line, `\`, or null character. For example, if the C program in file `f.c` contains

`#ident "@(#)`*identification information* `"`

and `f.c` is compiled to yield `f.o` and `a.out`, then the command

`what f.c f.o a.out`

prints

`f.c:`
identification information

`f.o:`
identification information

`a.out:`
identification information

what is intended to be used in conjunction with the **get** command, which automatically inserts identifying information, but it can also be used where the information is inserted manually. Only one option exists:

`-s` Quit after finding the first occurrence of pattern in each file.

SEE ALSO

get(1), **help**(1), **mcs**(1)

DIAGNOSTICS

Exit status is 0 if any matches are found, otherwise 1. See **help**(1) for explanations.

NAME

whatis – (BSD) display a one-line summary about a keyword

SYNOPSIS

/usr/ucb/whatis *command* . . .

DESCRIPTION

whatis looks up a given *command* and displays the header line from the manual section. You can then run the **man**(1) command to get more information. If the line starts "*name*(*section*) . . ." you can do "**man** *section name*" to get the documentation for it. Try "**whatis ed**" and then you should do "**man 1 ed**" to get the manual page for **ed**(1).

whatis is actually just the **-f** option to the **man** command.

FILES

/usr/share/man/whatis data base

SEE ALSO

man(1), **catman**(1M)

NAME

which – (BSD) locate a command; display its pathname or alias

SYNOPSIS

/usr/ucb/which [*filename*] . . .

DESCRIPTION

which takes a list of names and looks for the files which would be executed had these names been given as commands. Each argument is expanded if it is aliased, and searched for along the user's path. Both aliases and path are taken from the user's **.cshrc** file.

FILES

~/.cshrc source of aliases and path values

SEE ALSO

csh(1), **ksh**(1), **sh**(1)

DIAGNOSTICS

A diagnostic is given for names which are aliased to more than a single word, or if an executable file with the argument name was not found in the path.

NOTES

Only aliases and paths from **~/.cshrc** are used; importing from the current environment is not attempted.

which must be executed by **csh**(1), since only **csh** knows about aliases. If you are using **sh** instead of **csh**, **whence -v** provides similar functionality.

To compensate for **~/.cshrc** files in which aliases depend upon the **prompt** variable being set, **which** sets this variable. If the **~/.cshrc** produces output or prompts for input when **prompt** is set, **which** may produce some strange results.

NAME

who – who is on the system

SYNOPSIS

who [**-uTlHpdbrtas**] [*file*]

who -q [**-n** *x*] [*file*]

who am i

who am I

DESCRIPTION

who can list the user's name, terminal line, login time, elapsed time since activity occurred on the line, and the process ID of the command interpreter (shell) for each current UNIX system user. It examines the **/var/adm/utmp** file to obtain its information. If *file* is given, that file (which must be in **utmp**(4) format) is examined. Usually, *file* will be **/var/adm/wtmp**, which contains a history of all the logins since the file was last created.

who with the **am i** or **am I** option identifies the invoking user.

The general format for output is:

name [*state*] *line* *time* [*idle*] [*pid*] [*comment*] [*exit*]

The *name*, *line*, and *time* information is produced by all options except **-q**; the *state* information is produced only by **-T**; the *idle* and *pid* information is produced only by **-u**, **-l**, and **-T**; and the *comment* and **exit** information is produced only by **-a**. The information produced for **-p**, **-d**, and **-r** is explained during the discussion of each option, below.

With options, **who** can list logins, logoffs, reboots, and changes to the system clock, as well as other processes spawned by the **init** process. These options are:

-u This option lists only those users who are currently logged in. The *name* is the user's login name. The *line* is the name of the line as found in the directory **/dev**. The *time* is the time that the user logged in. The *idle* column contains the number of hours and minutes since activity last occurred on that particular line. A dot (**.**) indicates that the terminal has seen activity in the last minute and is therefore "current." If more than twenty-four hours have elapsed or the line has not been used since boot time, the entry is marked **old**. This field is useful when trying to determine whether a person is working at the terminal or not. The *pid* is the process ID of the user's shell. The *comment* is the comment field associated with this line as found in **/etc/inittab** [see **inittab**(4)]. This can contain information about where the terminal is located, the telephone number of the dataset, type of terminal if hard-wired, and so on.

-T This option is the same as the **-u** option, except that the *state* of the terminal line is printed. The *state* describes whether someone else can write to that terminal. A **+** appears if the terminal is writable by anyone; a **-** appears if it is not. **root** can write to all lines having a **+** or a **-** in the *state* field. If a bad line is encountered, a **?** is printed.

-l This option lists those lines on which the system is waiting for someone to login. The *name* field is **LOGIN** in such cases. Other fields are the same as for user entries except that the *state* field does not exist.

-H This option will print column headings above the regular output.

-q This is a quick **who**, displaying only the names and the number of users currently logged on. When this option is used, all other options except **-n** are ignored.

-p This option lists any other process which is currently active and has been previously spawned by **init**. The *name* field is the name of the program executed by **init** as found in **/etc/inittab**. The *state*, **line**, and *idle* fields have no meaning. The *comment* field shows the **id** field of the line from **/etc/inittab** that spawned this process. See **inittab**(4).

-d This option displays all processes that have expired and not been respawned by **init**. The **exit** field appears for dead processes and contains the termination and exit values [as returned by **wait**(2)], of the dead process. This can be useful in determining why a process terminated.

-b This option indicates the time and date of the last reboot.

-r This option indicates the current *run-level* of the **init** process. In addition, it produces the process termination status, process ID, and process exit status [see **utmp**(4)] under the *idle*, *pid*, and *comment* headings, respectively.

-t This option indicates the last change to the system clock (via the **date** command) by **root**. See **su**(1M).

-a This option processes **/var/adm/utmp** or the named *file* with the **-ulpdbrtTH** options turned on.

-s This option is the default and lists only the *name*, **line**, and *time* fields.

-n *x* This option takes a numeric argument, *x*, which specifies the number of users to display per line. *x* must be at least **1**. The **-n** option is ignored except when used with **-q**.

Note to privileged users: after a shutdown to the single-user state, **who** returns a prompt; the reason is that since **/var/adm/utmp** is updated at login time and there is no login in single-user state, **who** cannot report accurately on this state. **who am i**, however, returns the correct information.

FILES

/var/adm/wtmp
/etc/inittab
/var/adm/utmp
/usr/lib/locale/*locale***/LC_MESSAGES/uxcore.abi**
language-specific message file [See **LANG** in **environ**(5).]

SEE ALSO

date(1), **init**(1M), **inittab**(4), **login**(1), **mesg**(1), **su**(1M), **utmp**(4), **wait**(2)

whoami(1)

NAME

`whoami` – display the effective current username

SYNOPSIS

`/usr/ucb/whoami`

DESCRIPTION

whoami displays the login name corresponding to the current effective user ID. If you have used **su** to temporarily adopt another user, **whoami** will report the login name associated with that user ID. **whoami** gets its information from the **geteuid** and **getpwuid** library routines respectively. [See **getuid**(2) and **getpwent**(3C).]

FILES

`/etc/passwd` username data base

SEE ALSO

getpwent(3C), **getuid**(2), **su**(1M), **who**(1)

NAME

`whodo` – who is doing what

SYNOPSIS

`/usr/sbin/whodo` [**`-h`**] [**`-l`**] [*user*]

DESCRIPTION

`whodo` produces formatted and dated output from information in the **`/var/adm/utmp`**, **`/etc/ps_data`**, and **`/proc/pid`** files.

The display is headed by the date, time, and machine name. For each user logged in, device name, user-ID and login time is shown, followed by a list of active processes associated with the user-ID. The list includes the device name, process-ID, CPU minutes and seconds used, and process name.

If *user* is specified, output is restricted to all sessions pertaining to that user.

The following options are available:

`-h` Suppress the heading.

`-l` Produce a long form of output. The fields displayed are: the user's login name, the name of the tty the user is on, the time of day the user logged in (in *hours*:*minutes*), the idle time — that is, the time since the user last typed anything (in *hours*:*minutes*), the CPU time used by all processes and their children on that terminal (in *minutes*:*seconds*), the CPU time used by the currently active processes (in *minutes*:*seconds*), and the name and arguments of the current process.

EXAMPLE

The command:

```
whodo
```

produces a display like this:

```
Tue Mar 12 15:48:03 1985
bailey

term/09     mcn         8:51
    term/09    28158     0:29 sh

term/52     bdr        15:23
    term/52    21688     0:05 sh
    term/52    22788     0:01 whodo
    term/52    22017     0:03 vi
    term/52    22549     0:01 sh

xt/162      lee        10:20
    term/08    6748     0:01 layers
    xt/162     6751     0:01 sh
    xt/163     6761     0:05 sh
    term/08    6536     0:05 sh
```

The above is an example of what is displayed for any user.

FILES

/etc/passwd
/etc/ps_data
/var/adm/utmp
/proc/pid

DIAGNOSTICS

If the PROC driver is not installed or configured or if **/proc** is not mounted, a message to that effect is issued and **whodo** will fail.

The exit status is zero on success, non-zero on failure.

SEE ALSO

ps(1), **who**(1)

NAME

whois – Internet user name directory service

SYNOPSIS

whois [**-h** *host*] *identifier*

DESCRIPTION

whois searches for an Internet directory entry for an *identifier* which is either a name (such as "Smith") or a handle (such as "SRI-NIC"). The default is for **whois** to search the Internet directory, **sri_nic.arpa**. For users who do not have direct access to Internet, **whois** provides the **-h** option, which allows users to specify a host from which to request information.

To force a name-only search, precede the name with a period; to force a handle-only search, precede the handle with an exclamation point.

To search for a group or organization entry, precede the argument with * (an asterisk). The entire membership list of the group will be displayed with the record.

You can use an exclamation point and asterisk, or a period and asterisk together.

EXAMPLES

The command

```
whois Smith
```

looks for the name or handle SMITH.

The command

```
whois !SRI-NIC
```

looks for the handle SRI-NIC only.

The command

```
whois .Smith, John
```

looks for the name JOHN SMITH only.

Adding `. . .` to the name or handle argument will match anything from that point; that is, `ZU . . .` will match ZUL, ZUM, and so on.

wksh (1)

NAME

wksh – Windowing KornShell, graphical extensions to **ksh**

SYNOPSIS

wksh [–*mode*] [±**aefhikmnprstuvx**] [±**o** *option*] . . . [–**c** *string*] [*arg* . . .]

DESCRIPTION

wksh offers a number of extensions to the standard Korn Shell [see **ksh**(1)] in order to create and manage graphical user-interface widgets. All normal **ksh** commands and features are supported.

The following sections give some background information on concepts that are shared by a number of commands.

Widget Handles

Most commands that would return a widget in the C language MooLIT API will instead set an environment variable to a widget handle in **wksh**. A widget handle is an ASCII string used by **wksh** to access an actual widget pointer. Commands that create widget handles take as an argument an environment variable name set to the handle. For example, the **XtCreateManagedWidget** command looks like this:

```
XtCreateManagedWidget MYWIDGET widget form $TOPLEVEL height:200
```

After a command like this, **$MYWIDGET** can be used to attach children to the newly created form. Note that in the call above, **$TOPLEVEL** was also set up by another builtin (**OlInitialize**) in an analogous fashion.

This manual page uses the following conventions in defining arguments to a command:

variable name of the environment variable set as a side effect of the function to a returned widget handle

$handle or
$parent environment variable that was previously set to a widget handle by some other **wksh** command

Resources

wksh has internal tables to convert resources, all conversions are automatic.

Resources are set using the notation:

*resource***:***value*

In this notation, *resource* is the name of the resource, *value* is a string representation of the value. **wksh** uses String-to-*Type* converters on this value, as appropriate for the resource in question.

Here are some examples of resource setting notation:

```
XtSetValues $MYWIDGET x:0 y:100 label:"a string"
XtSetValues $WIDGET3 xRefWidget:"$WIDGET2"
```

When resources are retrieved using **XtGetValues**, a similar notation is used:

*resource***:***variable*

the resource is the resource name as above. The variable is the name of an environment variable that receives a string representation of the value.

Aliases

For efficiency, a standard set of aliases are predefined for all of the X Intrinsics built-ins. These aliases follow a general naming standard: they always drop the "Xt" prefix, they include just the first character of each "word" in a command. There are a few exceptions to preserve uniqueness, but in all cases the aliases were chosen to be mnemonic and require minimal input. For example, **XtCreateManagedWidget** is aliased **cmw**, **XtAddCallback** is aliased **acb**.

Each command description lists the aliases available for that command. Some commands also have aliases providing short forms for commonly used options on that command. For example, **ScrollingListOp -a** is aliased **sladd**, **CursorOp -b** is aliased **curbusy**. These aliases provide enhanced readability.

Options

The **wksh** command accepts one new option

-mode GUI mode, either **motif** or **openlook**

Other options available to **wksh** are the same as **ksh** [see **ksh**(1)].

Shell Variables

The following environment variables are used by **wksh** and its associated commands. Full details concerning each environment variable are provided under information on specific commands.

BUTTONTYPE
TOPLEVEL
CAPARGS
TFARGS
TROPTS

Sub-object Convenience Variables

Some widgets which contain sub-objects automatically store the widget handle of the sub-object in a variable when the widget is created. The variable name which holds the sub-object handle is constructed by adding a suffix to the parent's variable name.

Callback Convenience Variables

Callbacks can be any arbitrary **wksh** command line. During execution of the command line, the environment variable **CB_WIDGET** will be set to the handle of the widget on whose behalf the callback is being executed. Also if a **Flat** widget, the variable **CB_INDEX** is set to the index of the sub-object that invoked the callback.

Other callback related convenience variable are:

widget	variable
`Scrollbar`	`CALL_DATA_NEW_LOCATION`
	`CALL_DATA_NEW_PAGE`
	`CALL_DATA_OK`
	`CALL_DATA_SLIDERMIN`
	`CALL_DATA_SLIDERMAX`
	`CALL_DATA_DELTA`
	`CALL_DATA_MORE_CB_PENDING`
`ScrollingList`	`CALL_DATA_ITEMS`
`Slider`	`CALL_DATA_NEW_LOCATION`
	`CALL_DATA_MORE_CB_PENDING`
`TextField`	`CALL_DATA_REASON`
	`CALL_DATA_STRING`
	`CALL_DATA_OK`

USAGE

A distinction is made between **wksh** builtin commands and functions. Builtin commands are built into the shell, much like other standard **ksh** builtin commands, for example **echo** or **cd**. Functions are **wksh** scripts pulled into an application the first time referenced. Text for the convenience functions are contained in the directory **/usr/lib/wksh/olfuncs**. It is often convenient to take these standard functions and modify them for slightly different purposes. Most of them are short (ten to twenty lines).

Commands

addbuttons *$parent* [*label command*] **...**
addbuttons -w *$parent* [*variable label command*] **...**

Add a set of buttons to a menu or a control area. This command is useful for adding a set of buttons to a menu or control area in a concise manner.

In the first form, the parent is the first argument to the function, followed by any number of pairs or arguments specifying the label on the button and the command to be executed if the button is selected.

In the second form, with the **-w** option, **addbuttons** takes triplets of arguments after the parent is specified. Each triplet specifies the environment variable to be set to the handle of the newly created button, the label, and the associated command.

By default, **addbuttons** creates **OblongButtonGadgets**. Set the environment variable **BUTTONTYPE** to obtain a different kind of button.

addfields *$parent* [*variable label verification charsvisible*] **...**

Add a set of captioned text fields to a control area. This command is useful for adding a set of captioned text fields to a control area in a concise manner.

The parent is the first argument to the function, followed by any number of 4-tuples of arguments specifying the variable to contain the **TextField** widget handle, the caption label, the verification function called on the **TextField** widget, and the width of the **TextField** in number of characters.

On return, each variable contains the widget handle of the corresponding **TextField** widget. A variable whose name is the **TextField**'s variable with **_CAP** appended holds the handle of the caption widget that was created.

Three additional environment variables modify the initial resources on the created **Caption** and **TextField** widgets:

$CAPARGS list of resource definitions passed to the newly created **caption** widgets

$TFARGS list of resource definitions passed to the newly created **TextField** widgets

$TFOPTS the arguments used on a **TextFieldOp** call which will be performed on each **TextField** widget.

ChangeBarOp [**-sct**] *$widget*

Manipulate change bars on the children of **ControlArea** widgets. This command can make using change bars very simple. If a new kind of widget is dynamically added, **ChangeBarOp** may not know how to set up change bars for the new widget type.

Each of the options on **ChangeBarOp** corresponds to an alias normally used to access the functionality in a more readable manner. For example, **ChangeBarOp -s** is identical with **cbsetup**.

Aliases:

cbsetup *$widget*

setup change bars on the widget tree. The **cbsetup** command sets up all children recursively under *$widget* so that change bars will change when the contents of action widgets change. Only action widgets who are direct descendents of **ControlArea** widgets with the **allowChangeBars** resource set to **true** are affected. In each case, special callback functions are added to the widgets such that if their value is changed, then the **changeBar** is enabled.

cbclear *$widget*

clear all change bars on the widget tree. The **cbclear** command descends the *$widget* tree recursively and clears all change bar resources found.

cbtest *$widget*

test for any active change bars under the widget tree. The **cbtest** command descends the *$widget* tree recursively and returns 0 if at least one change bar is set and 1 otherwise. Thus, it can be used to see if any changes were made under a popup, for example:

```
if cbtest $POP_UCA
then confirm "Throw away the changes?" \
             throw_away_func save_func
fi
```

If the programmer dynamically adds a new kind of widget, these commands may not know how to set up change bars for the new widget type.

cmdload *cmdname* . . .

attach new built-in commands to the **wksh** process. Create a dynamic shared object file containing the *cmdname* definition using the **libload** command. The attach it to **wksh** by executing the command **libload** with only one argument, the path to the shared object. Note that a full path to the shared object should be used if it does not reside in **/usr/lib**. Call **cmdload** giving the arguments the names of the built-in commands as the user should type them.

For each command, a function is needed following these interfacing rules:

the name of the function must be the same as the name of the new built-in command, prepended with **b_**

the arguments to the function are **int argc** and **char *argv[]**, the same kind of arguments used for a **main** function. As usual, **argv[0]** is set to the name of the command, the rest of the arguments are the strings the user passed down on the call.

the function should return **int**, return **0** on success and nonzero on failure

in the current version of **wksh**, **stdin** of the command cannot be read, get information through the argument list

to print to the command's **stdout**, use **altprintf** instead of **printf**, use the same arguments as **printf**

some provided functions allow access to **wksh** environment variables or execute other shell command lines

int altprint(char ****format*,** *type* **arg, . . .);**
use this rather than **printf**

void env_set(char ****name=value*);**
set the *name* environment variable to *value*

void env_gbl(char ****name=value*);**
set global environmental variable *name* to *value*

void env_set_var(char ****name*, char****value***);**
same as **env_set**

char*env_get(chap ****name*);**
get the current value of *name* environment variable

char * env_get_gbl(char ****name*);**
get the current value of *name* global environment variable

Widget
return the widget identifier of a *handle*

void ksh_eval(char ****command*);**
evaluate *command*

confirm

confirm asks for a confirmation before executing a command. The **warn**, **fatal**, and **confirm** functions provide commonly needed notice shell functionality and are automatically included the first time they are referenced. Each creates a notice shell the first time it is called, and re-uses it on subsequent calls.

confirm displays *message*, and creates two buttons, YES and NO. If YES is selected, then *ycommand* is executed. If NO is selected, then **ncommand** is executed. Both *ycommand* and *ncommand* must be valid **wksh** commands.

fatal The **fatal** function is useful in non-recoverable situations. It displays *message* inside a notice shell with an OK button, and exits as soon as the OK button is selected.

warn The **warn** function is useful if a non-fatal error has occurred. It displays *message* inside a notice shell with an OK button that does nothing.

CursorOp [**-bdmpqstu**] *$widget*

change the shape of the mouse pointer cursor. For example, to change the cursor to a "busy" shape during a time consuming operation. This command automatically calls **XFlush** after changing the cursor.

The aliases, corresponding to the options **bdmpqstu** respectively, and associated standard cursor shapes are:

curbusy *$widget*	change to the "busy" cursor
curdup *$widget*	change to the "duplicate" cursor
curmove *$widget*	change to the "move" cursor
curpan *$widget*	change to the "pan" cursor
curquest *$widget*	change to the "question" cursor
curstand *$widget*	change to the "standard" cursor
curtarget *$widget*	change to the "target" cursor
curundef *$widget*	change to the "undefined" cursor

DataOp [**-prs**] *$widget*

Print and set data throughout widget trees. These commands are useful in a number of situations, for example, implementing quick databases, implementing property windows, and easing the implementation of the Reset and Reset to Factory buttons (see **CHeckBox**, **Slider**, and **TextEdit** widgets). The **DataOp** options corresponds, respectively, to the aliases:

dataprint *$widget . . .*

print data from widget trees. It recursively descends the *$widget* tree and prints to stdout a set of *name=value* lines that corresponds to the data stored in each *data* widget. The *name* printed is the name of the widget in question.

datareset *$widget*

parse and reset data to widget trees. It takes a set of pairs of widget trees and data of the same form as that printed by the **dataprint** command, and sets the values on all the widget trees to the named values. It error checks to ensure consistency with the *name* portion of the data.

data is information displayed visually by **CheckBox**, **TextField**, **RectButton**, and **Slider** widgets.

-s print data in "short" form. In short form, each piece of data is printed separated by the "|" symbol.

If any widget has the name **nodata** then the recursion does not descend that widget. Thus, a widget hierarchy can be designed to gather data from some subtrees and not others.

EventOp -d *$widget . . .*

This command provides event handling from the **wksh** command level. It has only one function: change the DEFAULT action (usually mapped to the <RETURN> key) to cause focus traversal to the next widget. This is useful when creating fill-in style forms. Thus, widgets like **sliders** and **abbrevMenuButtons** can be skipped by hitting <RETURN>. Most users find this action logical.

FocusOp [**-acsghm**] *$widget* [*args*]

test and change the current input focus widget. The options, **acsghm**, correspond respectively to the following aliases:

focacc *$widget*

call the focus accept function. The **focacc** command calls *widget*'s focus accept function. Note that the widget may not accept the focus, if, for example, is not sensitive.

foccanacc *$widget*

test if a widget can accept the focus. The **foccanacc** command tests whether *widget* is able to accept the focus and returns **0** if it can, nonzero otherwise. This command is easily used with the **wksh if** command.

focset *$widget*

set the current focus widget. The **focset** command sets the focus to a particular widget.

focget *$widget variable*

get the current focus widget. The **focget** command gets the current focus widget. The arguments to **focget** are the widget tree under which to look for the focus widget, and the name of an environment variable that will be set to the widget handle of the focus widget.

fochas *$widget*

test if a certain widget has focus. The **fochas** command returns **0** if the named widget has the focus, and nonzero otherwise.

focmv *$widget direction*

move the focus. The **focmv** command takes a widget and a direction specification and moves the focus based on the specification. Valid directions are:

immediate	move the focus to *widget*
moveright	move the focus "right"
moveleft	move the focus "left"
moveup	move the focus "up"
movedown	move the focus "down"
nextfield	move the focus to the next field that will accept it
prevfield	move the focus to the first previous field that will accept it

MnemonicOp [**-sc**] *$widget*

manipulate mnemonics throughout widget trees.

mnsetup *$widget* . . .

setup mnemonics on the widget trees The **mnsetup** command sets up all children recursively under *$widget* so that mnemonics will appear on all action widgets and captions. It first scans the entire tree of all its arguments looking for children that already have mnemonics, keeping track of them. Then it takes a second pass over the tree and finds unique single letter keys to use for the mnemonics. It uses an internal scoring system to find the "best" mnemonic for each item in turn, preferring letters closer to the front of each "word" in each string, capital letters, removing whitespace, and so on. It is possible for the command to not find a unique mnemonic, either because none exists or because finding a unique set would be too time consuming. In this case, it prints a warning to **stderr**.

mnclear *$widget* . . .

clear all mnemonics on the widget trees The **mnclear** command descends the *$widget* tree recursively and clears all mnemonics resources.

OlInitialize *variable app-name app-title* [*args* . . .]

OlInitialize must be the first graphical command executed, because it initializes the toolkit. This command's alias is **oi**.

variable the name of an environment variable that will be set up with the widget handle of the top level application, and can be used with further commands.

app-name

string that will be used as the application name.

app-title application title,

arguments

list of arguments appropriate for a call to **OlInitialize** [see **OlInitialize**(3Olit)].

OlRegisterHelp *$widget tag* [*string*]
OlRegisterHelp *$widget tag* [*-f filename*]

The **OlRegisterHelp** command registers a help string with the MooLIT help system. The alias for this command is **orh**. If the user requests help by pressing the F1 key, then MooLIT will see if any help is registered with the widget on which help was registered.

$widget is the handle of the widget that will get the help. *tag* is a help tag that MooLIT uses. A *string* may be specified directly on the command line, or, with the **-F** option, in *filename*, which contains the text.

ScrollingListOp [**-advecitnupPgG**] *$widget arguments . . .*

operate on a scrolling list. Each of the options, **advecitnupPgG**, corresponds respectively to the following aliases:

sladd *$widget* [**-U**] . . .
sladd *$widget* [*item*] . . .
sladd *$widget* [**-f** *file*] . . .
sladd *$widget* [**-I** *index*] . . .

add items to a scrolling list. The **sladd** command can be used to add new items to a scrolling list. After the *$widget* argument, further arguments can be

-U arguments are paired. The first member of the pair is displayed in the scrolling list, the second argument of the pair is an arbitrary string associated with the item. This string is called "user data" and can be used for any purpose. In conjunction with the **-f** option, this causes lines in the file to be interpreted as pairs.

item text of an item to add to the list

-f *file* file containing lines to add as items to the list. Using the *-f* option to add each line of a file to the list is a highly efficient way to maintain large lists.

-I *index* index of existing item. New items will be inserted after this index. If the **-I** option is not used, new items are added to the end of the list.

sldel *$widget index . . .*

delete items from a scrolling list. After the *$widget* argument, additional arguments are indexes of items to delete. Note that the indexes are kept constant during the life of the command, and after the items are deleted all remaining items are renumbered so the list of indexes are always consecutive and start at 1.

slview *$widget index*

bring an item into view on a scrolling list. The list will be scrolled as little as possible to bring the given item, *index*, into view.

sledit *$widget index*

start edit on item in a scrolling list. To stop editing, an application must call **slclose**.

slclose *$widget*

end edit on item in a scrolling list started by **sledit** or **slinsert**

slinsert *$widget index*

insert an item in a scrolling list. **slinsert** inserts an empty item following the named index and begins editing, allowing the user to insert a new item. **slclose** must be used to close out the edit.

sltouch *$widget index*
touch an item in a scrolling list. This forces the **ScrollingList** widget to update the given item indices.

slnoupdate *$widget*
turn off updates of a scrolling list. Stop updating the visuals on a Scrolling List. This is particularly useful when adding or deleting a large number of items on the list.

slupdate *$widget*
turn on updates of a scrolling list. Start updating the visuals on a Scrolling List. This is particularly useful when adding or deleting a large number of items on the list.

slput *$widget index item . . .*
change an existing item at an index. Name pairs of indexes and items can be used.

slputud *$widget index item . . .*
change existing user data at an index. Name pairs of indexes and user data can be used.

slget *$widget index . . .*
print out data at given index.

slgetud *$widget index item . . .*
print out user data at given index.

TextEditOp [**-ecr**] *$widget*
operate on a text edit widget.

teecho *$widget*
print the text from a **textEdit** widget to **stdout**

teclear *$widget*
clear the text from a **textEdit** widget. The cursor position and selection start and end are all set to 0.

teredraw *$widget*
redraw a **textEdit** widget

TextFieldOp [*options*] *$widget . . .*
operate on a **TextField** widget. All of these features are implemented using standard callbacks of the **TextField** widget, and can be reproduced in C code. This functionality is provided because it is commonly needed for form-driven applications.

The options are:

-r make <RETURN> go to the next field automatically.

-c blank out the input caret when the field has focus. This changes the caret color to the background color when focus is lost.

-f *color* change the text field's background color to *color* when it has the focus. This improves human factors by making it obvious which field has the focus.

-n *color* change the text field's background color to *color* when it does not have the focus.

-t traverse to the next field automatically when **maxSize** is reached. The **maxSize** resource must exist and be set.

-b blank out the field if the user types in character position 0. This is a useful feature for forms with filled in defaults, the user need not explicitly delete the old contents before typing a new value.

-w clip off leading and trailing whitespace during verification time

-u automatically upper-case all characters in the **textField** at verification time

-l automatically lower-case all characters in the **textField** at verification time

-i automatically initial-capitalize the **textField** at verification time

-v *pattern* validate each character according to *pattern*. *pattern* must be of the [] variety. For example, **-v '[0-9]'** would restrict to numeric characters, while **-v '[^a-fA-F]'** would dissallow the letters A through F in upper or lower case. The bell is rung and input is ignored, on disallowed characters.

under *$widget* [*pixels*]
rightof *$widget* [*pixels*]
floatbottom
floatright
spanwidth
spanheight

add form constraints to the children of **Form** widgets. These functions are automatically included the first time referenced.

Each echos to **stdout** a set of form constraints to perform the desired action. Thus, they are most often used inside backquotes in the resource list of the child be added to the form.

under specifies the child should be placed under another child in the form. If *pixels* is not specified, it defaults to **0**.

rightof places a new child to the right of another child a certain number of pixels.

Floatbottom and **floatright** make a child float along the bottom edge of the form, or along the right edge, respectively. They take no arguments. **floatbottom** may be used in conjunction with **under** or **spanwidth**. **floatright** may be used in conjunction with **rightof** or **spanheight**.

spanwidth and **spanheight** make the child span the entire width or height of the form, respectively. They take no arguments. **spanwidth** may be used in conjunction with **under** or **floatbottom**. **spanheight** may be used in conjunction with **rightof** or **floatright**.

widlist [**-r**] [*args* . . .]
widlist [**-R**] [*args* . . .]
widlist [**-c**] [*args* . . .]
widlist [**-h**] [*args* . . .]

list information about widgets and their resources to **stdout**. **widlist** is useful for debugging, quickly finding the exact spelling of a particular resource name, or determining what widget classes are available.

widlist, with no options, lists currently active widgets along with information about their parents, handles, name, and state. In all cases, if *args* is not specified, information for all widgets is listed.

The **-r** option lists resources for each of *args*, which may be either widget class names or widget handles. The **-R** option lists constraint resources, if any. Constraint resources are resources that a manager class widget imposes on its children. The **-c** option lists all available widget class names. The **-h** option lists all widget handles.

widload *classname* . . .

attach customized widgets to the **wksh** process. To use **widload**, first attach a dynamic shared object file to **wksh** containing the widget's definition and code using the **libload** command. Call **widload** giving as its arguments the class record symbol names of the widgets to attach. Create an instance of the new widget by specifying the widget name with an **XtCreateWidget** or **XtCreateManagedWidget** call. (or follow the normal **wksh** convention for gadgets). **wksh** searchs for a symbol with the correct name and considers it the class record constant to use.

When adding customized widgets, there should be String to Type and Type to String converters registered for any resource accessed by the **wksh XtGetValues** or **tSetValues** commands that the widget uses. **wksh** provides enough converters to handle most MooLIT widget resources. The easiest way to register additional converters is to write an attachable **wksh** command that will do all the registration, or use the **call** command to call an internal subroutine written to do such initializations. Better yet, the widget should automatically register all the converters it needs when its class initialize function is invoked, then no special action is needed.

XBell [*volume*]

ring the terminal bell. *volume* range -100 and +100, the default is 0, which rings the bell at the server default value. The alias is **bell**.

XFlush

flush the X Event queue. This command is generally not needed because the queue is flushed automatically whenever the client is awaiting user input. This command is normally explicitly invoked when the program writes a message to a widget and then performs some time consuming operation. Unless **XFlush** is explicitly invoked, the message will not appear until the operation has completed and the client again begins processing user input. For example, to write "Please Wait" to a **StaticText** widget and then perform a long operation, call **XFlush** right after setting the string resource so the user sees the message immediately.

XtAddCallback *$widget resource ksh-command*
add the named *ksh-command* to the callback list *resource* on the widget handle *$widget*. The alias for this command is **acb**. The order callbacks are executed if more than one callback is registered for the named resource is undefined. It is also possible to set a callback list resource to a **ksh**-command using **XtSetValues** but all other previously registered callbacks are lost. **XtAddCallback** simply adds a new callback to the list.

XtCallCallbacks *$widget resource*
execute all callbacks that are registered with *$widget* on *resource*. The alias for this command is **ccb**.

XtRemoveAllCallbacks *$widget resource*
remove all callbacks associated with the *widget's resource*. The alias for this command is **racb**.

XtAddInput [*device*] [*ksh-cmd* . . .]
XtAddInput [**-d** *file-descriptor*] [*ksh-cmd* . . .]
register an input source with the X Intrinsics. The alias for this command is **ain**. Whenever an input line is available on the named source, *ksh-cmd* is called one by one, and the arguments to these commands will consist of the (unquoted) line. If the *ksh-cmd* argument is not present, it defaults to the shell **eval** command. Usually a user defined function is used as the *ksh-cmd*.

The input source may be a *device*, or a fifo pipe. With the *-d* option, a numerical file descriptor may be named.

XtAddTimeOut *$TOPLEVEL milliseconds* [*ksh-cmd* . . .]
register a *ksh-cmd* to be executed *milliseconds* in the future. The alias for this command is **ato**. The *ksh-cmd* may be any arbitrary **wksh** command line. Note that the commands are executed only once, if the command should be executed again another timeout should be scheduled within the command itself. The actual resolution of the internal timer is server and operating system dependent, and a request may be rounded to the nearest time interval supported on the system.

XtAppCreateShell *variable wid-name wid-class $parent* [*res*:*value* . . .]
create a new **TopLevelShell** widget. The alias for this command is **acs** *variable* is the name of an environment variable receiving the widget's handle. This handle can be used on other **wksh** command calls to operate on the widget. *wid-name* is the name of the widget, and is used by the X Windows System for resource defaults and other purposes. *class* is one of the supported **wksh** shell widget classes such as **topLevelShell**. *$parent* is the handle of the parent widget, the toplevel widget of the entire application. After these basic arguments, there can be any number of pairs of resources and values separated by colons.

XtCreatePopupShell *variable wid-name wid-class $parent* [*res*:*value* . . .]
create a new popup shell widget. The alias for this command is **cps**. *variable* is the name of an environment variable receiving the widget's handle. This handle can be used on other **wksh** command calls to operate on the widget. *wid-name* is the name of the widget, which is used by the X Windows System for resource defaults and other purposes. *class* is one of the

supported **wksh** shell widget classes such as **popupWindowShell** or **menuShell**. *$parent* is the handle of the parent widget, the toplevel widget of the entire application. After these basic arguments, there can be any number of pairs of resources and values separated by colons.

XtCreateWidget *variable wid-name wid-class $parent* [*res*:*value* . . .]
XtCreateManagedWidget *variable wid-name wid-class $parent* [*res*:*value* . . .]

create a new widget. The alias for these commands is **cw** and **cmw** respectively. A child created using **XtCreateWidget** is not managed by the parent. If a child is not managed, it will not appear on the screen initially. Whether or not a child is managed can be changed by the **XtManageChildren** and **XtUnmanageChildren** commands.

variable is the name of an environment variable receiving the widget's handle. This handle can be used on other **wksh** command calls to operate on the widget. *wid-name* is the name of the widget, which is used by the X Windows System for resource defaults and other purposes. *class* is one of the supported **wksh** shell widget classes such as **popupWindowShell** or **menuShell**. *$parent* is the handle of the parent widget, the toplevel widget of the entire application. After these basic arguments, there can be any number of pairs of resources and values separated by colons.

XtDestroyWidget *$widget* . . .

destroy widgets and all their children. The alias for this command is **dw**. **XtDestroyWidget** takes a list of widget handles as its arguments, and destroys them in turn. Any environment variables holding handles to the widget or their children become invalid. Most widgets also have **destroyCallback** resources which will be executed immediately before the widget is destroyed.

XtGetValues *$widget resource*:*variable* . . .
XtSetValues *$widget resource*:*value* . . .

take a widget handle and get or set resource values for that widget. The alias for these commands are **gv** and **sv** respectively. The widget handle presumably comes from a previous call to **XtCreateManagedWidget**, **XtCreateWidget**, **OlInitialize**, and so on.

XtGetValues takes a list of one or more *resource*:*variable* pairs and stores an ASCII version of each *resource* value into the corresponding *variable*.

XtSetValues takes a list of one or more *resource*:*value* pairs and sets *resource* value into the corresponding *value*.

XtMainLoop

The alias for this command is **ml**. go into an infinite loop processing X events. It would typically be the final line of an **wksh** script. However, while creating widgets interactively, this command can be interrupted via the *Intr* key on the keyboard. Thus, to make widgets display on the screen, you can use the **XtMainLoop** command. If something looks incorrect, hit the *Intr* key, interactively modify the widgets, then call **XtMainLoop** again.

If **XtMainLoop** is not executing, no X events for the application are processed, and so nothing happens on the screen in response to keyboard, mouse actions, and so on, until **XtMainLoop** is executed again.

XtManageChildren *$widget . . .*
XtUnmanageChildren *$widget . . .*

manage or unmanage widget children. The alias for these commands are **mc** and **umc** respectively. These commands take any number of widget handles (presumably from a previous call to **XtCreateManagedWidget**, **XtCreateWidget**, **OlInitialize**, and so on). All the widgets named in a given call must have a common parent. When a widget is "managed" its parent will take it into account when determining screen layout. Even if the widget is managed, it will not appear on the screen unless it is also realized and mapped. Most widgets by default are mapped when they are managed, but this behavior is controlled by a boolean resource called **mappedWhen-Managed**.

XtMapWidget *$widget . . .*
XtUnmapWidget *$widget . . .*

map or unmap widgets. The alias for these commands are **mw** and **umw** respectively. These commands take any number of widget handles (presumably from a previous call to **XtCreateManagedWidget**, **XtCreateWidget**, **OlInitialize**, and so on). When a widget is "mapped" its window is displayed on the screen. In order to be mapped, a widget must also be realized and managed. If the widget has children, then are recursively mapped or unmapped as well.

XtPopup *$widget* [**GrabNone**]
XtPopup *$widget* [**GrabExclusive**]
XtPopup *$widget* [**GrabNonexclusive**]
XtPopdown *$widget*

bring up and down windows previously created using **XtCreatePopup-Shell**. The alias for these commands are **pu** and **pd** respectively. **XtPopup** takes a widget handle, and optionally a grab type, and brings up the popup window. The default is **GrabNone**.

XtPopdown takes a widget handle as its argument and pops down the widget, which then disappears from the screen.

XtRealizeWidget *$widget . . .*
XtUnrealizeWidget *$widget . . .*

realize or unrealize widgets. The alias for these commands are **rw** and **urw** respectively. These commands take any number of widget handles (presumably from a previous call to **XtCreateManagedWidget**, **XtCreateWidget**, **OlInitialize**, and so on). When a widget is "realized" its window is created on the display and final initialization of the widget is completed. If the widget has children, they are recursively realized or unrealized as well.

XtSetSensitive *$widget* [**true**]
XtSetSensitive *$widget* [**false**]

set a widget to be sensitive (**true**) or insensitive (**false**). The alias for this command is **ss**. This command takes a widget handle (presumably from a previous call to **XtCreateManagedWidget**, **XtCreateWidget**, **OlInitialize**, and so on). When a widget is insensitive, the user is unable to interact with it. Some widgets change their visual appearance if they are insensitive as well. If the widget has children, they are recursively set to be sensitive or insensitive as well.

This command must be used rather than simply setting the **sensitive** resource of a widget, since this command correctly takes care of subwidgets.

call [**-F**] [**-n**] [**-r**] *func* [*arg*] . . . [**++**] [*arg-modifier*] . . .

call calls a C function with a desired set of arguments. It puts the return value of *func*, in hex, into the environment variable **RET**. By default, *call* returns the return value of the function. However, the **-r** option reverses the notion of success for the function (0 is failure, nonzero is success), and the **-n** option returns success if the function returns a nonnegative value.

The argument *func* is either the name of a C function, to be looked up in the internal table of functions, or a hex address. Due to the danger in calling a function with a misinterpreted address, a hex address must begin with **0x**.

A maximum of 10 *args* is allowed and each argument is one of three types:

type/value descriptor
: *arg* starts with an **@**. This argument types has two parts: the type descriptor and the value descriptor. The type descriptor is the name of a 'C' data type (for example, **long**, **struct**, **strbuf**, **char** *); if the type is a structure type, the type will be considered to be a pointer to that type. The value descriptor is a legal value of this type.

number
: *arg* starts with a number. Numerical arguments are interpreted as unsigned long integers and are parsed in that form. For example, the argument **3** is equivalent to **@ulong:3**.

string
: *arg* is a string. This argument is taken directly from the command line.

Any memory allocated due to the parsing of the type/value descriptor mechanism will be freed after *func* has returned, unless the **-F** option has been given. When you need to free the structure, use **strfree**. (The memory for the string or number is not allocated using malloc and can not be freed or stored, it will be overwritten.)

The set of arguments, *arg-modifier* (often referred to as a "overrides"), are used to change certain fields of some arguments. The form of these modifiers is:

field subscript-expression operator=val

where:

field refers to a field of one of the arguments. The argument number or argument type may be used to limit the search for field. If the field is left out, this implies an override for the whole first argument.

subscript-expression
optional and of the form '[integer expression]'. The type of the field must be an array or pointer type.

operator=val
may only be used if the field is an integer type. The set of operators is +, -, &, |, *, /, %, and ^, interpreted as in C. *val* must be a valid value descriptor for the type of the field.

cmdload *command*[=address] . . .
location of designated built-in commands. Each of these functions should expect **argc, argv** style arguments and return 0 upon success and a nonzero value upon failure.

The argument *address* must be valid. For each command, if the address is not supplied, the address is the location of the symbol **b_***command*.

define [**-R**] *name value*
add a new **#define** to the list. *name* should be a valid 'C' define name; *value* must be an integer value.

If *name* has already been defined, and the **-R** option is present, the value will not be re-assigned.

deflist [[**-p**]*name*] *address*
add a new list of **#define**s to the define list. These lists are sets of name/value pairs represented by structures of type **symarray**, preferably sorted.

```
struct symarray {
    const char *str;
    unsigned long addr;
};
```

address address of an array of **symarray** structures

name tag for this set of define's

deref [**-p**] [**-l**] [*-len*] *address* [*shell-variable*]
read the contents of a pointer. **deref** will show the contents of the pointer, *address*, in hexadecimal, either byte-by-byte (where each byte is represented by a pair of hex digits) or long-by-long. By default, the output is long-by-long, with only the first long being printed. If the *–len* option (where *len* is an integer) is supplied, then the output is byte-by-byte for *len* bytes. If the **-l** option is supplied, the output will be printed long-by-long. Note that the long-by-long output can look very different based on the machine's byte ordering.

The **-p** option will cause the output to be printed on the standard output, otherwise, the output will be placed in *shell-variable*. If *shell-variable* is not supplied, **RET** will be used.

field_comp *type address* [*criterion*] . . .
compare internal data at *address* of the designated *type* against criteria supplied to the command. These criteria are of the form: field=value.

type type descriptor

address address descriptor

field a field of *type*

val a legal value for *field*'s type

field_get [**-v** *shell-variable*] *type address* [*field-name*] . . .
print internal data at *address*, of the designated *type*, selecting fields supplied to the command. *field-name* must be a valid field name or a '.' for the whole value.

If *shell-variable* is given, the output will be put in the environment; otherwise, it is printed to **stdout**.

finddef *defname* [*shell-variable*]
find the value of a **#define**, (see **deflist** and **define**). It should not be necessary to use this function frequently, since the parser will substitute the value while parsing. **finddef** places the value in *shell-variable*, or, by default, **RET**.

findsym *symbol-name* [*shell-variable*]
find the address of a symbol in the running process.

libload [[**-p**] *name*] *object-name*
libload [[**-n**] *name*] *object-name*
access a needed shared object. If the architecture does not support dynamic shared objects nothing is actually loaded.

name the object. If there is a symbol accessible by the name *name*_**libinit** or **libinit**_*name*, this function will be called.

sizeof *typename* [*shell-variable*]
find the size of a C type

struct [**-R**] *name fld*[**:***type*] . . .
declare a structure, *name*, with fields *fld*. If type is not present for a field, the type is assumed to be *long*.

If *name* has already been defined, and the *-R* option is present, the value will not be re-assigned.

symbolic -m -t *type*[**.***field*] . . . *symbolic* . . .
associate symbolic names with a designated type or a field of a structure of this type. *symbolic* must be **#define**'s declared earlier. Any type assigned symbolic values must be of an integer valued type. The *-m* option causes each value to be considered a mask and the set of values on output should be separated by | symbols.

typedef *type typename*
: declare new types. *type* must be a valid type descriptor. *typename* is the name of the type being defined; it must be a valid identifier.

dbpr *level command*
: execute command if the variable DEBUG is greater than or equal to *level*

decl *type var*
: declare an environment variable as representing a pointer to the designated C type

findxsym *symbol-name*
: use **nm** to find symbol. This is only necessary for static variables.

free *var*
: free the memory of a previously allocated and declared environment variable representing a C data structure

getaddr *symbol-or-address*
: put the address of the expression into **RET**, like **getaddr**

help [*function*]
: print out a designated shell function or all, sending the output through **pg**

iset *var val*
: set value of integer variable to new value

kload [**-f** *function-array*] [**-a** *alias-array*] [**-v** *var-array*]
: read in an array of built-in variables, aliases or functions

malloc *count var*
: allocate space using **malloc**(3C) and put the pointer in *var*

new @*type*:*value var*
: use call to allocate a data structure and put the pointer into the named variable

newfree *var*
: free a data structure allocated by new

prctl [**-v** prvar] [**-p**] [**-d** *symbol* . . .] [*type*]
: control the output of **strprint**/**field_get**. The **-v** option allows capturing the output in a variable, if there is output. The **-p** option forces the current setting to be output. The normal reset form allows the specifying of print conventions (names: field names are printed, hex: integer output is in hex, dec: integer output is in decimal). The **-d** option allows for passing the output captured with a previous *prctl* back in as input. *symbol* can be **PRSYMBOLIC**, **PRHEX**, and so on. By default, the output setting is **PRSYMBOLIC|PRMIXED|PRNAMES** (output will use symbolics when available, will print both hex and decimal for integer values and will print field names within structures).

revreturn *command*
: reverse failure return codes

`set_special` `[-f` *free-function*`]` `[-P` *print-function*`]` `[-p` *parse-function*`]` *type* `[`*type*`]` . .
designate a new parse, print or free function for a data type

`setargs` *arguments*
take out overrides from list of arguments and put them in specargs array

Examples

This example demonstrates using **addbuttons** to create **rectButton** widgets inside an **Exclusives** widget, the following code would take advantage of the shell feature whereby a variable can be set just for the execution of a single command:

```
cmw EX ex exclusives $TOPLEVEL
BUTTONTYPE=rectButton addbuttons $EX \
          "First"  do_first \
          econd" do_second
```

An example using the **addfields** function: if **$POP_UCA** is the upper control area of a **popupWindowShell**, one can add several captioned **textFields** to it as follows:

```
sv $POP_UCA alignCaptions:true
addfields $POP_UCA \
          NAME    "Name:"      :   16 \
          ADDR    "Address:"   :  20 \
          PHONE   "Telephone:" : 18
```

To put the captions above each **textField**, use the **CAPARGS** variable as follows:

```
sv $POP_UCA alignCaptions:true
CAPARGS="position:top" addfields $POP_UCA \
          NAME    "Name:"      :   16 \
          ADDR    "Address:"   :  20 \
          PHONE   "Telephone:" : 18
```

The following is an example of using **CursorOp** for a time consuming operation performed inside a callback. This example changes the cursor to the "busy" shape (a clock), performs the operation, and changes the cursor back to the standard shape.

```
bigCB() {
          curbusy $TOPLEVEL    # change to the "busy" cursor

          slowop               # a time consuming operation

          curstand $TOPLEVEL
}
```

In this example of **OlInitialize**, any arguments to the **wksh** script are passed in to **OlInitialize**, which is normally the way it should be done.

```
OlInitialize TOPLEVEL myapp Myapp "$@"
```

An example of using the **sladd** command:

```
sladd $W -a 4 "Item 1" "Item 2"
```

Will add the strings **Item 1, Item 2** after the 4th item in the list. Item indices always start at 1. Using **0** as the index will add items to the start of the list.

As an example of the **sldel** command, the following two lines perform the same function:

```
sldel $W 1 2
sldel $W 1; sldel $W 1
```

The first command deletes the first and second items in one operation, the remaining items are renumbered. The second line deletes the first item, remaining items are renumbered, then deletes the first item again (thus deleting the second item of the original list).

In this example of the **under** command, if **$FORM** is a **Form** widget and **$CHILD1** is an existing child of the form, then this will place a button 3 pixels under **$CHILD1** in the form:

```
cmw BUTTON button oblongButton $FORM 'under $CHILD1 3'
```

Using **widload**, for example, if a new widget whose class record symbol is **fancyLookingWidgetClass** is contained in a dynamic shared object named **libfancy.so**, the commands would be:

```
libload /usr/lib/libfancy.so
widload fancyLooking
```

After this, create an instance of the new widget by specifying **fancyLooking** on an **XtCreateWidget** or **XtCreateManagedWidget** call. If the widget is really a Gadget, then use normal **wksh** conventions, **fancyLookingGadget** in the above example.

An example of a newly created managed child widget using **XtCreateManagedWidget**:

```
XtCreateManagedWidget   TEXT1   text1   staticText   $PARENT
string:"hello world"
```

Examples of using **XtGetValues** and **XtSetValues**:

```
XtGetValues $TEXT string:S width:W
```

Would store the current **string** resource into the environment variable **$S** and the current width into the variable **$W**.

```
XtSetValues $TEXT string:"Hello World" background:Yellow
```

Would set the current **string** resource to the string "Hello World" and the current background color to Yellow.

callP examples:

Example 1:

```
call malloc 1024            # Allocates a buffer
BUF=$RET                    # Stores pointer in BUF
echo $BUF
```

RESPONSE: `0x4581568` `# Notice that BUF is a pointer`

```
call strcpy $BUF 'hello world' # Copies string into BUF
  call altprintf '%s
  ' $BUF                       # Print the contents of BUF
```

RESPONSE: `hello world`

```
call free $BUF                 # Frees the buffer
```

Example 2:

```
call strdup 'a:b:c'            # mallocs space for a:b:c
  BUF=$RET
  call strtok $BUF :           # breaks up string by :
  while true
  do
      P=$RET                   # set P to current segment
      call altprintf '%s
  ' $P                         # Print out current segment
      if call strtok 0 :       # see if the return is 0
      then
          break                # break if it is
      fi
  done
  call free $BUF
```

This will print out:

```
a
b
c
```

Example 3:

Suppose you have declared (see **struct**, **typedef**)

```
typedef struct hello {
        int x;
        int y;
  } hello_t;
```

you can say

```
call hellofunc @hello_t:{1,30}
```

and get a POINTER to a structure of type **hello** passed to **hellofunc**.

Example 4:

Suppose you have declared:

```
struct sub {
       int subsubx;
  };
  struct sub {
       int subx;
       struct subsub *suby;
  };
  struct top {
       int x;
```

```
        struct sub y;
    };
```

```
call strprint top '@top:{1,{2,{3}}}'
```

RESPONSE: `{ x=1, { subx=2, {subsubx=3 } }`

Using an argument modifier:

```
call strprint top '@top:{1,{2,{3}}}' ++ subsubx=4
```

RESPONSE: `{ x=1, { subx=2, {subsubx=4 } }`

Or, alternatively (they all do the same thing):

```
call strprint top '@top:{1,{2,{3}}}' ++ 2.y.suby.subsubx=4
call strprint top '@top:{1,{2,{3}}}' ++ y.suby.subsubx=4
call strprint top '@top:{1,{2,{3}}}' ++ y.subsubx=4
```

RESPONSE: `{ x=1, { subx=2, {subsubx=4 } }`

A **define** command example:

```
define X 1
define -R X 2
call strprint -p long '@long:X'
```

RESPONSE: `long=1(0x1)`

A **deflist** command example:

```
#include "my.h"
#include "exksh.h"

struct symarray Mydefines[] = {
    { "MYVAL", MYVAL },
    { "MYOTHERVAL", MYOTHERVAL },
    { NULL, 0 }
};
```

In a script, you can then say:

```
deflist Mydefines
```

A **deref** example:

```
# Output is for an intel 386 machine
    call strdup "hi there"       # Allocates a duped pointer
    BUF=$RET                     # Stores pointer in BUF
    deref -9 $BUF aaa
    echo $aaa
    deref -l -9 $BUF aaa
    echo $aaa
```

RESPONSE: `0x686920746865726500 # the hex equivalent of "hi there"`
`0x742069686572656800000000`

A **field_comp** example:

```
struct strbuf maxlen:int len:int 'buf:char *'
call malloc 4096                      # Allocate a character buffer
buf=$RET                              # Store its pointer in buf
```

```
call -F nop "@strbuf:{4096, 0, p$buf }"# Allocates a strbuf
strbuf=$RET                           # Store pointer in strbuf
call getmsg $FD $strbuf 0 0           # Call getmsg with the strbuf
field_comp strbuf $strbuf len=4       # Before going on, make sure
                                      # the len is 4
```

An example of `field_get`

```
struct strbuf maxlen:int len:int 'buf:char *'
call malloc 4096                      # Allocate a character buffer
buf=$RET                              # Store its pointer in buf
call nop "@strbuf:{4096, 0, p$buf }"# Allocates a strbuf
strbuf=$RET                           # Store pointer in strbuf
call getmsg $FD $strbuf 0 0           # Call getmsg with the strbuf
field_get strbuf $strbuf len          # See the value of len
```

At this point, the length field is printed to the stdout.

`symbolic` Examples:

Example 1:

```
struct mine a b c
define MY_VAL1 1
define MY_VAL2 2
symbolic -t mine.a -t mine.c MY_VAL1 MY_VAL2
call -F nop '@mine:{MY_VAL1, MY_VAL2, 2}'
ptr=$RET
field_get mine $ptr .
```

RESPONSE: `{ a=MY_VAL1, b=2, c=MY_VAL2 }`

Example 2:

```
struct mine a b c
define MY_VAL1 1
define MY_VAL2 2
symbolic -m -t mine.a -t mine.c MY_VAL1 MY_VAL2
call strprint mine '@mine:{3, MY_VAL2, 2}'
```

RESPONSE: `{ a=MY_VAL1|MY_VAL2, b=2, c=MY_VAL2 }`

SEE ALSO

cc(1), **Converters**(3Olit), **ksh**(1), **OlRegisterHelp**(3Olit), **ScrollingList**(3Olit)

NAME

write – write to another user

SYNOPSIS

write *user* [*line*]

DESCRIPTION

write copies lines from your terminal to that of another user. When first called, it sends the message:

> **Message from** *yourname* **(term/**??**)** [*date*]**. . .**

to the person you want to talk to. When it has successfully completed the connection, it also sends two bells to your own terminal to indicate that what you are typing is being sent.

The recipient of the message should write back at this point. Communication continues until an end of file is read from the terminal, an interrupt is sent, or the recipient has executed "**mesg** *n*." At that point **write** writes **EOT** on the other terminal and exits.

If you want to write to a user who is logged in more than once, the **line** argument may be used to indicate which line or terminal to send to (for example, **term/12**); otherwise, the first writable instance of the user found in **/var/adm/utmp** is assumed and the following message posted:

> **user is logged on more than one place.**
> **You are connected to ''***terminal***.''**
> **Other locations are:**
> *terminal*

Permission to write may be denied or granted by use of the **mesg** command. Writing to others is normally allowed by default. Certain commands, such as the **pr** command, disallow messages in order to prevent interference with their output. However, if the user has appropriate privilege, messages can be forced onto a write-inhibited terminal.

If the character **!** is found at the beginning of a line, **write** calls the shell to execute the rest of the line as a command.

write runs **setgid** [see **setuid**(2)] to the group ID **tty**, in order to have write permissions on other user's terminals.

write processes supplementary code set characters according to the locale specified in the **LC_CTYPE** environment variable [see **LANG** on **environ**(5)]. It will detect non-printable characters before sending them to the user's terminal. Control characters will appear as a '**^**' followed by the appropriate ASCII character; characters with the high-order bit set will appear in meta notation. For example, '**\003**' is displayed as '**^C**' and '**\372**' as '**M-z**'.

The following protocol is suggested for using **write**: when you first **write** to another user, wait for them to **write** back before starting to send. Each person should end a message with a distinctive signal (that is, **(o)** for "over") so that the other person knows when to reply. The signal **(oo)** (for "over and out") is suggested when conversation is to be terminated.

FILES

/var/adm/utmp to find user

/usr/bin/sh to execute **!**

/usr/lib/locale/*locale***/LC_MESSAGES/uxcore**
language-specific message file [See **LANG** on **environ**(5).]

SEE ALSO

mail(1), **mesg**(1), **pr**(1), **setuid**(2), **sh**(1), **who**(1)

DIAGNOSTICS

UX:write:ERROR:User is not logged on.
if the person you are trying to **write** to is not logged on.

UX:write:ERROR:Permission denied.
if the person you are trying to **write** to denies that permission (with **mesg**).

UX:write:Warning: cannot respond, set mesg -y.
if your terminal is set to **mesg n** and the recipient cannot respond to you.

UX:write:ERROR:Can no longer write to user.
if the recipient has denied permission (**mesg n**) after you had started writing.

X(1)

NAME

X - X Window System server

SYNOPSIS

X [**:***displaynumber*] [*–option ...*]

DESCRIPTION

X is the X Window System server. It is frequently a link or a copy of the appropriate server binary for driving the most frequently used server on a given machine.

Options

The following options can be given on the command line to the XWIN X server.

-auth *authorization-file*
: specify a file of authorization records used to authenticate access

disable certain kinds of error checking, for bug compatibility with previous releases

-bs disable backing store support on all screens

-renderer *string*
: font renderer

-fontconfig *string*
: font configuration file

-class [*mode*]
: scheduler class, can be **fixed**, **realtime**, or **timeshare**

-config *string*
: server configuration file

-cmap *string*
: colormap definition file; valid for VGA, 16 color modes

-co *filename*
: set name of RGB color database

-fc *cursorFont*
: set default cursor font

-fn *font* set the default font

-fp *fontPath*
: set the search path for fonts. This is a comma separated list of directories the sample server searches for font databases.

-logo turn on the X Window System logo display in the screen-saver. This requires that **-v** also be used since video blanking is the default. There is currently no way to change this from a client.

0logo turn off the X Window System logo display in the screen-saver. There is currently no way to change this from a client.

-xnetaccess *state*
: turn network access checking on or off, **state** can be **on** or **off**

-p *seconds*	set screen-saver pattern cycle time (seconds)
-help	print usage message
-s *seconds*	set screen-saver timeout time (seconds)
-su	disable save under support on all screens
	set video-on screen-saver preference
-v	set video-off screen-saver preference
-I	cause all remaining command line arguments to be ignored
-wm	force the default backing-store of all windows
-bp *color*	black pixel for screen
-wp *color*	white pixel for screen

USAGE

Starting the Server

The server is usually started from **desktop**. This utility starts the server and the appropriate clients, such as the window manager, desktop manager, and other miscellaneous clients. The server can be started separately in the background by running **X &**. To run X in the background, the user environment cannot be **ksh**. If the server is started by **desktop** and if for any reason **dtm** is killed, **desktop** kills the server.

When the sample server starts up, it takes over the display. If you are running on a workstation whose console is the display, you cannot log into the console while the server is running unless you switch virtual terminals or login through **xdm**. To switch virtual terminals, see EXAMPLES.

The default runtime scheduler class for the server is **FIXED**, if invoked by **desktop**. Also, the user has an option to run the server in either **realtime** or **timeshare** scheduler classes. **Fixed** class is a new category which has a priority range that is above **timeshare** and below **realtime** classes. The user has to be very careful while running the server in **realtime** class; do not run any clients that loop, the server takes all the CPU cycles and practically all the other timeshare processes will be useless (that is, will not get any CPU time).

Security

The server uses a host-based access control list for deciding whether or not to accept connections from clients on a particular machine. This list initially consists of the host on which the server is running as well as any machines listed in the file **/etc/X***n***.hosts**, where *n* is the display number of the server. Each line of the file contains a hostname with no leading or trailing spaces on any lines. For example:

```
joesworkstation
```

Users can add or remove hosts from this list and enable or disable access control using the **xhost** command from the same machine as the server. For example:

```
%  xhost +janesworkstation
janesworkstation being added to access control list
%  xhost -star
%  xhost +
all hosts being allowed (access control disabled)
```

```
% xhost -
all hosts being restricted (access control enabled)
% xhost
access control enabled (only the following hosts are allowed)
joesworkstation
janesworkstation
```

X has no notion of window operation permissions nor does it place restrictions on what a client can do; if a program can connect to a display, it has full run of the screen. Sites that have better authentication and authorization systems might wish to make use of the hooks in the libraries and the server to provide additional security models.

Fonts

Fonts are ususally stored as individual files in directories. The list of directories in which the server looks when trying to open a font is controlled by the font path. Although most sites will choose to have the server start up the appropriate font path, it can be overridden using the **xset** command.

The default font path for the sample server is set in the **Xwinfont** configuration file that is found in the **/usr/X/defaults** directory. To set or change the font path for all users, edit this file and change the line starting with **fontpath=** to the desired font path. This is a list of font path elements that the server will use in resolving font requests. It contains a comma separated list of entries. If a full pathname is not given, the server will check the **XWINHOME** environment variable for the location of the installed X tree, and will prepend that path to the location in the file. The default font path is shown below:

```
fontpath=lib/fonts/misc/,lib/fonts/Xol/,lib/fonts/75dpi/, \
    lib/fonts/type1,lib/fonts/mitType1
```

The **lib/fonts/misc** directory contains several miscellaneous fonts useful on all systems. It contains some fixed width fonts and the cursor font, and has font name aliases for the commonly used fonts fixed.

The **lib/fonts/Xol** directory contains OPEN LOOK fonts used for sliders, scroll bars and glyphs.

The **lib/fonts/75dpi** directory contains fonts for 75 dot per inch displays. It contains the OPEN LOOK and MOTIF default fonts.

The **lib/fonts/type1** contains Type1 format scalable fonts if they are installed on the system.

The **lib/fonts/mitType1** directory contains Type1 scalable fonts donated to the X community for use with X.

The **lib/fonts/folio** directory is an optional directory that is part of the font path if the optional Folio Scalable Font package is installed. These are F3 format scalable fonts.

XWINFONTPATH is an environment variable that can be used to set a user's font path and exported. It will override any setting found in the **Xwinfont** configuration file.

Both the default font path and the **XWINFONTPATH** environment variable can be overridden by using the **-fp** command line argument when starting the server.

Files

/usr/X/defaults/Xwinconfig	configuration file for the server
/usr/X/defaults/Xwincmaps	R, G, B values to be used for 16 color static colormaps
/usr/X/defaults/Xwinfont	font configuration R, G, B values to be used for 16 color static colormaps
/etc/X*.hosts	initial access control list
/usr/lib/X11/fonts/misc **/usr/lib/X11/fonts/75dpi** **/usr/lib/X11/fonts/100dpi**	font directories
/usr/lib/X11/rgb.*display_type***.txt**	color database
/usr/adm/X*msgs	error log file

Examples

To run the server with private copies of configuration and colormap files:

```
desktop -- -config /usr/foo/mycfg -cmaps /usr/foo/mycmap
X -config /usr/foo/mycfg -cmaps /usr/foo/mycmap &
```

In the example above, the server is started with a private copy of the configuration and colormap files, instead of the system default files.

To run the server in a particular scheduler class:

```
desktop -serverclass realtime
priocntl -e -c RT X &
priocntl -e -c FC X &
priocntl -e -c FC -m 25 -p 25 X &
```

In the first example, **desktop** starts the server in **realtime**. The argument **realtime** can be replaced with **timeshare** or **fixed**. The default runtime class, if the server is started from **desktop** is **fixed** class. In the second example, the server is started manually in **realtime**. In the third and fourth examples, the server is started manually in **fixed class**. **fixed** scheduler class is valid only in SVR4.1ES and later versions of the operating system.

To switch VT's:

ALT - SYS_REQ p
OR
ALT - SYS_REQ <F1|F2..F8>

Hold ALT and SYS REQ keys simultaneously, release them and then press either p or n; p for previous vt, n for next vt If you have the **vtlmgr** running, you can press any one of the keys from F1 through F8 instead of p or n.

To switch to high resolution modes (for VGA only):

run the **setvgamode** command. Only users with appropriate privileges can execute this command.

[see **setvgamode**(1M)]. To edit the configuration and colormap files (only for advanced users), see **Xwinconfig**(4) and **Xwincmaps**(4) respectively.

SEE ALSO

desktop(1), **mkfontdir**(1), **setvgamode**(1M), **xdm**(1M), **xhost**(1), **xsetroot**(1), **xterm**(1), **Xwincmaps**(4), **Xwinconfig**(4), **Xwinfont**(4)
X Window System Protocol, *Definition of the Porting Layer for the X v11 Sample Server*, and *Strategies for Porting the X v11 Sample Server*

NOTES

The X server must be killed with a **-2** and not a **-9**; this allows the server environment to reset itself to its previous state. The X server resets itself to default settings when no clients are active.

NAME

x286emul – emulate 80286 XENIX systems

SYNOPSIS

x286emul [*arg* . . .] *prog286*

DESCRIPTION

x286emul is an emulator that allows programs from XENIX System V/286 Release 2.3 or XENIX System V/286 Release 2.3.2 on the Intel 80286 to run on the Intel 80386 processor under UNIX System V.

It is not necessary to invoke **x286emul** directly; instead, just run your programs using the same command line as you would use on XENIX System V/286. When it recognizes an attempt to **exec**(2) a 286 XENIX program, UNIX System V automatically **exec**'s **x286emul** with the arguments to the 286 program, *arg* . . . (if any), followed by the 286 program name, *prog286*.

x286emul reads the 286 program's text and data into memory and maps them through the LDT [via **sysi86**(2)] as 286 text and data segments. It also fills in the jam area, which is used by XENIX programs to do system calls and signal returns. **x286emul** starts the 286 program by jumping to its entry point.

When the 286 program attempts to do a system call, **x286emul** takes control. It does any conversions needed between the 286 system call and the equivalent 386 system call and performs the 386 system call. The results are converted to the form the 286 program expects, and the 286 program is resumed.

The following are some of the differences between a program running on a 286 and a 286 program using **x286emul** on a 386:

> Attempts to unlink or write on the 286 program will fail on the 286 with **ETXTBSY**. Under **x286emul**, they will not fail.
>
> **ptrace**(2) is not supported under **x286emul**.
>
> *prog286* must be readable and executable by the invoking user (instead of just executable, like other programs), because **x286emul**, which runs as the invoking user, must be able to read *prog286*.

The emulator must have this name and be in **/bin** if it is to be automatically invoked when **exec** is used on a 286 program.

SEE ALSO

exec(2), **sysi86**(2), **ptrace**(2)

NAME

xargs – construct argument list(s) and execute command

SYNOPSIS

xargs [*flags*] [*command* [*initial-arguments*]]

DESCRIPTION

xargs combines the fixed *initial-arguments* with arguments read from standard input to execute the specified *command* one or more times. The number of arguments read for each *command* invocation and the manner in which they are combined are determined by the flags specified.

command, which may be a shell file, is searched for, using one's **$PATH**. If *command* is omitted, **/usr/bin/echo** is used.

Arguments read in from standard input are defined to be contiguous strings of characters delimited by one or more blanks, tabs, or new-lines; empty lines are always discarded. Blanks and tabs may be embedded as part of an argument if escaped or quoted. Characters enclosed in quotes (single or double) are taken literally, and the delimiting quotes are removed. Outside of quoted strings a backslash (\) escapes the next character.

Each argument list is constructed starting with the *initial-arguments*, followed by some number of arguments read from standard input (Exception: see **-i** flag). Flags **-i**, **-l**, and **-n** determine how arguments are selected for each command invocation. When none of these flags are coded, the *initial-arguments* are followed by arguments read continuously from standard input until an internal buffer is full, and then *command* is executed with the accumulated args. This process is repeated until there are no more args. When there are flag conflicts (for example, **-l** vs. **-n**), the last flag has precedence. Valid *flags* are:

-l*number* — *command* is executed for each non-empty *number* lines of arguments from standard input. The last invocation of *command* will be with fewer lines of arguments if fewer than *number* remain. A line is considered to end with the first new-line *unless* the last character of the line is a blank or a tab; a trailing blank/tab signals continuation through the next non-empty line. If *number* is omitted, 1 is assumed. Option **-x** is forced.

-i*replstr* — Insert mode: *command* is executed for each line from standard input, taking the entire line as a single arg, inserting it in *initial-arguments* for each occurrence of *replstr*. A maximum of five arguments in *initial-arguments* may each contain one or more instances of *replstr*. Blanks and tabs at the beginning of each line are thrown away. Constructed arguments may not grow larger than 255 characters, and option **-x** is also forced. **{ }** is assumed for *replstr* if not specified.

-n*number* — Execute *command* using as many standard input arguments as possible, up to *number* arguments maximum. Fewer arguments are used if their total size is greater than *size* characters, and for the last invocation if there are fewer than *number* arguments remaining. If option **-x** is also coded, each *number* arguments must fit in the *size* limitation, else **xargs** terminates execution.

-t Trace mode: The *command* and each constructed argument list are echoed to file descriptor 2 just prior to their execution.

-p Prompt mode: The user is asked whether to execute *command* each invocation. Trace mode (**-t**) is turned on to print the command instance to be executed, followed by a **?. . .** prompt. A reply of **y** (optionally followed by anything) executes the command; anything else, including just a carriage return, skips that particular invocation of *command*.

-x Causes **xargs** to terminate if any argument list would be greater than *size* characters; **-x** is forced by the options **-i** and **-l**. When neither of the options **-i**, **-l**, or **-n** are coded, the total length of all arguments must be within the *size* limit.

-s*size* The maximum total size of each argument list is set to *size* characters; *size* must be a positive integer less than or equal to 470. If **-s** is not coded, 470 is taken as the default. Note that the character count for *size* includes one extra character for each argument and the count of characters in the command name.

-e*eofstr* *eofstr* is taken as the logical end-of-file string. Underbar (_) is assumed for the logical **EOF** string if **-e** is not coded. The value **-e** with no *eofstr* coded turns off the logical **EOF** string capability (underbar is taken literally). **xargs** reads standard input until either end-of-file or the logical **EOF** string is encountered.

xargs terminates if either it receives a return code of **-1** from, or if it cannot execute, *command*. When *command* is a shell program, it should explicitly **exit** (see **sh**(1)) with an appropriate value to avoid accidentally returning with **-1**.

EXAMPLES

The following examples moves all files from directory $1 to directory $2, and echo each move command just before doing it:

```
ls $1 | xargs -i -t mv $1/{} $2/{}
```

The following example combines the output of the parenthesized commands onto one line, which is then echoed to the end of file **log**:

```
(logname; date; echo $0 $*) | xargs >>log
```

The user is asked which files in the current directory are to be archived and archives them into **arch** (1.) one at a time, or (2.) many at a time.

```
1.  ls | xargs -p -l ar r arch
2.  ls | xargs -p -l | xargs ar r arch
```

The following example executes **diff**(1) with successive pairs of arguments originally typed as shell arguments:

```
echo $* | xargs -n2 diff
```

SEE ALSO

sh(1)

NAME

xdm – X Display Manager

SYNOPSIS

xdm [**-config** *config_file*] [**-nodaemon**] [**-debug** *debug_level*] [**-error** *error_log_file*] [**-resources** *resource_file*] [**-server** *server_entry*]

DESCRIPTION

xdm manages a set of X displays, on local host or remote servers, and provides services similar to **init**, **getty** and **login** services on character terminals, that is, prompting for login name and password, authenticating the user, and running a session. After a session is terminated, *xdm* resets the X server and restarts the process.

xdm is an arbitrary session manager. In a windowing environment, a user's login shell process does not necessarily connect to a terminal-like interface. When a terminal session manager does not exist, a window manager or terminal emulator is treated as the "session manager," and *xdm* terminates the session when that process terminates.

The options are:

-config *config_file*
: *config_file* specifies resources to control the behavior of **xdm**; the default is **/usr/X/lib/xdm/xdm-config**

-nodaemon
: suppress normal behavior; that is, do not close all file descriptors, disassociate from the controlling terminal, or start up in the background. The **DisplayManager.daemonMode** resource is **false**.

-debug *debug_level*
: print debugging statements to the terminal if *debug_level* is non-zero. This option also disables the **DisplayManager.daemonMode** resource, forces *xdm* to run synchronously, and sets the value of the **DisplayManager.debugLevel** resource.

-error *error_log_file*
: write **xdm** errors and **stderr** output of scripts and programs run during the progress of the session to *error_log_file*. This option also sets the value of the **DisplayManager.errorLogFile** resource.

-server *server_entry*
: specify a display to manage constantly and set the value of the **DisplayManager.servers** resource

-xrm *resource_specification*
: specify an arbitrary resource

Resources

xdm behavior can be specified in a configuration file in the X resource format. Resources which apply to a specific display have the display name in the resource name between **DisplayManager** and the final resource name segment. All other resources apply to all displays.

Colons (`:`) are used by the resource manager to separate the name of the resource from its value and dots (`.`) to separate resource name parts, so *xdm* replaces both dots and colons with underscores (_) when generating the resource name.

`DisplayManager.DISPLAY.authComplain`
If set to **`false`**, disables the use of the **`unsecureGreeting`** in the login window. See the Authentication Widget subsection. The default is **`true`**.

`DisplayManager.authDir`
This names a directory in which **`xdm`** stores authorization files while initializing the session. The default value is **`/usr/X/lib/xdm`**.

`DisplayManager.DISPLAY.authFile`
This file is used to communicate the authorization data from **`xdm`** to the server, using the **`-auth`** server command line option. It should be kept in a directory which is not world-writable as it could easily be removed, disabling the authorization mechanism in the server.

`DisplayManager.DISPLAY.authorize`
`DisplayManager.DISPLAY.authName`
`authorize` is a boolean resource which controls whether **`xdm`** generates and uses authorization for the local server connections. If authorization is used, **`authName`** is a whitespace-separated list of authorization mechanisms to use. When **`authorize`** is set for a display and authorization is not available, the user is informed by having a different message displayed in the login widget. By default, **`authorize`** is **`true`**; **`authName`** is **`MIT-MAGIC-COOKIE-1`**.

`DisplayManager.autoRescan`
This boolean controls whether **`xdm`** rescans the configuration, servers, access control and authentication keys files after a session terminates and the files have changed. By default it is **`true`**. You can force **`xdm`** to reread these files by sending a **`SIGHUP`** to the main process.

`DisplayManager.daemonMode`
Normally, **`xdm`** attempts to make itself into a daemon process unassociated with any terminal. This is accomplished by forking and leaving the parent process to exit, then closing file descriptors and releasing the controlling terminal. In some environments this is not desired (particularly when debugging). Setting this resource to **`false`** will disable this feature.

`DisplayManager.debugLevel`
If the integer value of this resource is greater than zero, reams of debugging information will be printed. It also disables daemon mode, which would redirect the information into the bit-bucket, and allows non-root users to run **`xdm`**, which would normally not be useful.

`DisplayManager.errorLogFile`
Error output is normally directed at the system console. To redirect it, set this resource to a file name. A method to send these messages to **`syslog`** should be developed for systems which support it; however, the wide variety of interfaces precludes any system-independent implementation. This file also contains any output directed to **`stderr`** by the **`Xsetup`**, **`Xstartup`**, and **`Xreset`** files, so it will contain descriptions of problems in those scripts as well.

`DisplayManager.exportList`
A whitespace-separated list of additional environment variables to pass on to the `Xsetup`, `Xstartup`, and `Xreset` programs.

`DisplayManager.DISPLAY.failsafeClient`
If the default session fails to execute, `xdm` will fall back to this program. This program is executed with no arguments, but executes using the same environment variables as the session would have had (see the Session Program subsection). By default, `/usr/X/bin/nondesktop` is used.

`DisplayManager.DISPLAY.grabServer`
`DisplayManager.DISPLAY.grabTimeout`
To improve security, `xdm` grabs the server and keyboard while reading the login name and password. The `grabServer` resource specifies if the server should be held for the duration of the name/password reading. When `false`, the server is ungrabbed after the keyboard grab succeeds, otherwise the server is grabbed until just before the session begins. The default is `false`. The `grabTimeout` resource specifies the maximum time `xdm` will wait for the grab to succeed. The grab may fail if some other client has the server grabbed, or possibly if the network latencies are very high. This resource has a default value of 3 seconds; you should be cautious when raising it, as a user can be spoofed by a look-alike window on the display. If the grab fails, `xdm` kills and restarts the server (if possible) and the session.

`DisplayManager.lockPidFile`
This is the resource which controls whether `xdm` uses file locking to keep multiple display managers from running amok.

`DisplayManager.DISPLAY.openDelay`
`DisplayManager.DISPLAY.openRepeat`
`DisplayManager.DISPLAY.openTimeout`
`DisplayManager.DISPLAY.startAttempts`
These numeric resources control the behavior of `xdm` when attempting to open intransigent servers. `openDelay` is the length of the pause (in seconds) between successive attempts, `openRepeat` is the number of attempts to make, `openTimeout` is the amount of time to wait while actually attempting the open and `startAttempts` is the number of times this entire process is done before giving up on the server. After `openRepeat` attempts have been made, or if `openTimeout` seconds elapse in any particular attempt, `xdm` terminates and restarts the server, attempting to connect again. This process is repeated `startAttempts` times, at which point the display is declared dead and disabled. Although this behavior may seem arbitrary, it has been empirically developed and works quite well on most systems. The default values are 5 for `openDelay`, 5 for `openRepeat`, 30 for `openTimeout` and 4 for `startAttempts`.

`DisplayManager.pidFile`
The filename specified will be created to contain an ASCII representation of the process-id of the main `xdm` process. `xdm` also uses file locking on this file to attempt to eliminate multiple daemons running on the same machine, which would cause quite a bit of havoc.

DisplayManager.DISPLAY.pingInterval
DisplayManager.DISPLAY.pingTimeout

To discover when remote displays disappear, **xdm** occasionally pings them, using an X connection and **XSync** calls. **pingInterval** specifies the time (in minutes) between each ping attempt, **pingTimeout** specifies the maximum amount of time (in minutes) to wait for the terminal to respond to the request. If the terminal does not respond, the session is declared dead and terminated. By default, both are set to 5 minutes. If you frequently use X terminals which can become isolated from the managing host, you may wish to increase this value. The only worry is that sessions will continue to exist after the terminal has been accidentally disabled. **xdm** will not ping local displays. Although it would seem harmless, it is unpleasant when the workstation session is terminated as a result of the server hanging for NFS service and not responding to the ping.

DisplayManager.randomFile

A file to checksum to generate the seed of authorization keys. This should be a file that changes frequently. The default is **/dev/mem**.

DisplayManager.DISPLAY.reset

This specifies a program which is run (as root) after the session terminates. Again, by default no program is run. The conventional name is **Xreset**. See the Reset Program subsection.

DisplayManager.DISPLAY.resetForAuth

The original implementation of authorization in the sample server reread the authorization file at server reset time, instead of when checking the initial connection. As **xdm** generates the authorization information just before connecting to the display, an old server would not get up-to-date authorization information. This resource causes **xdm** to send **SIGHUP** to the server after setting up the file, causing an additional server reset to occur, during which time the new authorization information will be read. The default is **false**.

DisplayManager.DISPLAY.resetSignal

The number of the signal **xdm** sends to reset the server. See the Controlling the Server subsection. The default is 1 (**SIGHUP**).

DisplayManager.servers

This resource either specifies a file name full of server entries, one per line (if the value starts with a slash), or a single server entry. See the Server Specification subsection for the details.

DisplayManager.DISPLAY.setup

This specifies a program which is run (as root) before offering the Login window. This may be used to change the appearence of the screen around the Login window or to put up other windows (for example, you may want to run **xconsole** here). The conventional name for a file used here is **Xsetup**. See the Setup Program subsection.

DisplayManager.DISPLAY.startup

This specifies a program which is run (as root) after the authentication process succeeds. By default, no program is run. The conventional name for a file used here is **Xstartup**. See the Startup Program subsection.

DisplayManager.DISPLAY.systemPath

Xdm sets the **PATH** environment variable for the startup and reset scripts to the value of this resource. The default for this resource is specified at build time by the **DefaultSystemPath** entry in the system configuration file; **/sbin:/usr/sbin:/usr/bin:/etc:/usr/X/bin** is the default setting. Note the absence of "**.**" from this entry. This is a good practice to follow for root; it avoids many common Trojan Horse system penetration schemes.

DisplayManager.DISPLAY.systemShell

xdm sets the **SHELL** environment variable for the startup and reset scripts to the value of this resource. It is **/bin/sh** by default.

DisplayManager.DISPLAY.termSignal

The number of the signal **xdm** sends to terminate the server. See the Controlling the Server subsection. The default is 15 (**SIGTERM**).

DisplayManager.DISPLAY.terminateServer

This boolean resource specifies whether the X server should be terminated when a session terminates (instead of resetting it). This option can be used when the server tends to grow without bound over time, in order to limit the amount of time the server is run. The default value is **false**.

DisplayManager.thrashThreshold

This is the maximum time **xdm** will attempt to restart a failed server. **xdm** will attempt to restart the server **DisplayManager.trashThreshold** times during this interval, and if it does not succeed, will completely shut down, dumping an error message to **/dev/X/xdm-errors**. The default is 60 seconds.

DisplayManager.trashThreshold

This is the number of attempts **xdm** will attempt to restart a failed server during the threshold time (see **DisplayManager.Threshold**) before giving up. The default is 5 tries.

DisplayManager.DISPLAY.userAuthDir

When **xdm** is unable to write to the usual user authorization file (**$HOME/.Xauthority**), it creates a unique file name in this directory and points the environment variable **XAUTHORITY** at the created file. It uses **/tmp** by default.

DisplayManager.DISPLAY.userPath

xdm sets the **PATH** environment variable for the session to this value. It should be a colon separated list of directories [see **sh**(1) for a full description]. **:/usr/bin:/usr/X/bin** is the default setting. The default value can be specified at build time in the X system configuration file with **DefaultUserPath**.

USAGE

First, the **xdm** configuration file should be set up. Make a directory (usually **/usr/X/lib/xdm**) to contain all of the relevant files. Here is a reasonable configuration file, which could be named **xdm-config**:

```
DisplayManager.servers:       /usr/X/lib/xdm/Xservers
DisplayManager.errorLogFile: /dev/X/xdm-errors
DisplayManager*startup:       /usr/X/lib/xdm/Xstartup
DisplayManager.pidFile:       /dev/X/xdm-pid
DisplayManager._0.authorize: true
DisplayManager*authorize:     false
```

Note that this file simply contains references to other files. Note also that some of the resources are specified with "*" separating the components. These resources can be made unique for each different display, by replacing the "*" with the display-name, but normally this is not very useful. See the Resources subsection for a complete discussion.

The first file, **/usr/X/lib/xdm/Xservers**, contains the list of displays to manage. Most workstations have only one display, numbered 0, so the file will look something like this:

```
:0 Local local /usr/X/bin/X :0
```

This will keep **/usr/X/bin/X** running on this display and manage a continuous cycle of sessions.

The file **/dev/X/xdm-errors** will contain error messages from **xdm** and anything output to **stderr** by **Xsetup**, **Xstartup**, or **Xreset**. When you have trouble getting **xdm** working, check this file to see if **xdm** has any clues to the trouble.

The **Xstartup** file shown here simply prevents login while the file **/etc/nologin** exists. As there is no provision for displaying any messages here (there isn't any core X client which displays files), the user will probably be baffled by this behavior. Thus this is not a complete example, but simply a demonstration of the available functionality.

Here is a sample **Xstartup** script:

```
#!/bin/sh
#
# Xstartup
#
# This program is run as root after the user is verified
#
if [ -f /etc/nologin ]; then
      exit 1
fi
exit 0
```

Server Specification

The resource **DisplayManager.servers** gives a server specification or, if the values starts with a slash (/), the name of a file containing server specifications, one per line.

Each specification indicates a display which should constantly be managed. Each consists of at least three parts: a display name, a display class, a display type, and (for local servers) a command line to start the server. A typical entry for local display number 0 would be:

```
:0 local /usr/X/bin/X -xnetaccess on
```

The display types are:

local   local display: **xdm** must run the server

foreign   remote display: **xdm** opens an X connection to a running server

The display name must be something that can be passed in the **-display** option to an X program. This string is used to generate the display-specific resource names, so be careful to match the names (for example use **:0 local /usr/X/bin/X :0** instead of **localhost:0 local /usr/X/bin/X :0** if your other resources are specified as **DisplayManager._0.startup**). The display class portion is also used in the display-specific resources, as the class of the resource. This is useful if you have a large collection of similar displays (like a corral of X terminals) and would like to set resources for groups of them. You can run **xdm** in debug mode and look at the resource strings it generates for that device, which will include the class string.

Setup Program

The **Xsetup** file is run after the server is reset, but before the Login window is offered. The file is typically a shell script. It is run as root, so users should be careful about security. This is the place to change the root background or bring up other windows that should appear on the screen along with the Login widget.

In addition to any specified by **DisplayManager.exportList**, the following environment variables are passed:

DISPLAY	the associated display name
PATH	the value of **DisplayManager.DISPLAY.systemPath**
SHELL	the value of **DisplayManager.DISPLAY.systemShell**
XAUTHORITY	may be set to an authority file

Note that since **xdm** grabs the keyboard, any other windows will not be able to receive keyboard input. They will be able to interact with the mouse, however; beware of potential security holes here. If **DisplayManager.DISPLAY.grabServer** is set, **Xsetup** will not be able to connect to the display at all. Resources for this program can be put into the file named by **DisplayManager.DISPLAY.resources**.

Authentication Widget

The authentication widget reads a name/password pair from the keyboard. Some of the other actions taken by the widget are:

check for account expiration and inactivity

check for password expiration and prompt for a new password and make sure that password passes the rules specified by **passwd**

check for a valid shell program to execute

check for the existence of the user's home directory

Resources for this widget are stored in the file **/usr/X/lib/app-defaults/Dtlogin**. The default resources are:

```
dtlogin*background:          #aa00aa00aa00
dtlogin*foreground:          black
dtlogin*inputFocusColor:     #00000000e000
dtlogin*company_logo*string: UNIX System Laboratories
```

Users who wish to display their company name should change the **dtlogin*company_logo*string** line. For example:

```
dtlogin*company_logo*string: Univel Inc.
```

Localization of Authentication Widget

The graphical login can be localized on a system basis. Localization on a per user basis is not available. Several files need changed to localize the graphical login, they are

dtlogin.h
: update the location of message catalog files

/usr/X/lib/app-defaults/Dtlogin
: add any pertinent system locale dependent resources, for example, the following for a Japanese localization:

```
#
# Sample Japanese localization settings
#
dtlogin*xnlLanguage:          japan
dtlogin*basicLocale:          japan
dtlogin*displayLang:          japan
dtlogin*fontGroup:            mincho
dtlogin*fontGroupDef:         mincho=r14/k14/r14
dtlogin*inputLang:            japan
```

/usr/X/lib/app-defaults/Nondesktop
: add any pertinent system locale dependent resources, for example, the following for a Japanese localization:

```
#
# Sample Japanese localization settings
#
nondesktop*xnlLanguage:       japan
nondesktop*basicLocale:       japan
nondesktop*displayLang:       japan
nondesktop*fontGroup:         mincho
nondesktop*fontGroupDef:      mincho=r14/k14/r14
nondesktop*inputLang:         japan
```

/etc/rc2.d/S69xdm
: add all pertinent system locale dependent environment variables

Startup Program

The **Xstartup** file is typically a shell script. It is run as root and should be very careful about security. This is the place to put commands which mount users' home directories from file servers, display the message of the day, or abort the session if logins are not allowed.

In addition to any specified by **DisplayManager.exportList**, the following environment variables are passed:

DISPLAY	the associated display name
HOME	the initial working directory of the user
USER	the user name
PATH	the value of **DisplayManager.DISPLAY.systemPath**
SHELL	the value of **DisplayManager.DISPLAY.systemShell**
XAUTHORITY	may be set to an authority file

No arguments are passed to the script. **xdm** waits until this script exits before starting the user session. If the exit value of this script is non-zero, **xdm** discontinues the session and starts another authentication cycle.

Reset Program

Symmetrical with **Xstartup**, the **Xreset** script is run after the user session has terminated. Run as root, it should contain commands that undo the effects of commands in **Xstartup**, removing entries from **/etc/utmp** or unmounting directories from file servers. The environment variables that were passed to **Xstartup** are also passed to **Xreset**.

Controlling the Server

xdm controls local servers using POSIX signals. **SIGHUP** is expected to reset the server, closing all client connections and performing other cleanup duties. **SIGTERM** is expected to terminate the server. If these signals do not perform the expected actions, the resources **DisplayManager.DISPLAY.resetSignal** and **DisplayManager.DISPLAY.termSignal** can specify alternate signals.

To control remote terminals, **xdm** searches the window hierarchy on the display and uses the protocol request **KillClient** in an attempt to clean up the terminal for the next session. This may not actually kill all of the clients, as only those which have created windows will be noticed.

Controlling xdm

xdm responds to two signals: **SIGHUP** and **SIGTERM**. When sent a **SIGHUP**, **xdm** rereads the configuration file, the access control file, and the servers file. For the servers file, it notices if entries have been added or removed. If a new entry has been added, **xdm** starts a session on the associated display. Entries which have been removed are disabled immediately, meaning that any session in progress will be terminated without notice and no new session will be started.

When sent a **SIGTERM**, **xdm** terminates all sessions in progress and exits. This can be used when shutting down the system.

xdm attempts to mark its various sub-processes for **ps**(1) by editing the command line argument list in place. Because **xdm** can't allocate additional space for this task, it is useful to start **xdm** with a reasonably long command line (using the full path name should be enough). Each process which is servicing a display is marked *–display*.

Other Possibilities

You can use **xdm** to run a single session at a time, using the 4.3 **init** options or other suitable daemon by specifying the server on the command line:

```
xdm -server ":0 SUN-3/60CG4 local /usr/bin/X :0"
```

Or, you might have a file server and a collection of X terminals. The configuration for this is identical to the sample above, except the **Xservers** file would look like

```
extol:0 VISUAL-19 foreign
exalt:0 NCD-19 foreign
explode:0 NCR-TOWERVIEW3000 foreign
```

This directs **xdm** to manage sessions on all three of these terminals. See the Controlling xdm subsection for a description of using signals to enable and disable these terminals in a manner reminiscent of **init**(1M).

NOTES

One thing that **xdm** isn't very good at doing is coexisting with other window systems. To use multiple window systems on the same hardware, you'll probably be more interested in **xinit**.

Portions of this page are derived from material which is copyright 1988 Massachusetts Institute of Technology.

FILES

$(HOME)/.Xauthority	user authorization file
/usr/X/lib/xdm/Xaccess	access file (lists authorized displays)
/usr/X/lib/xdm/xdm-config	configuration file
/usr/X/bin/xrdb	resource database loader
/usr/X/lib/xdm/Xservers	server file (lists servers to manage)
/usr/X/bin/nondesktop	failsafe client
/usr/X/bin/X	server
/dev/X/A*host-suffix*	authorization files location

SEE ALSO

ps(1), **sh**(1), **X**(1)

xhost (1)

NAME

`xhost` - server access control for X

SYNOPSIS

`xhost` [+-] [*hostname* . . .]

DESCRIPTION

The **`xhost`** command is used to add and delete hosts to the list of machines that are allowed to make connections to the X server. This provides a rudimentary form of privacy control and security. It is only sufficient for a workstation (single user) environment, although it does limit the worst abuses. Environments which require more sophisticated measures should use the hooks in the protocol for passing authentication data to the server.

The server initially allows network connections only from programs running on the same machine or from machines listed in the file **`/etc/X*.hosts`** (where * is the display number of the server). The **`xhost`** command is usually run either from a startup file or interactively to give access to other users.

Options

`Xhost` accepts the following command line options described below. For security, the options that effect access control may only be run from the same machine as the server. `xhost` invoked with no options prints the list of hosts allowed to connect (on `stdout`) and indicates if access control is enabled.

[+] *hostname* add *hostname* to the list of machines allowed to connect to the X server

– *hostname* remove *hostname* from the list of machines allowed to connect to the server. Existing connections are not broken, but new connection attempts will be denied. Attempts to remove the local host will result in an access error.

\+ access control off. Access is granted to all, ignoring the allowed hosts list.

– access control on. Access is restricted to the allowed hosts list.

Files

`/etc/X*.hosts`

Environment

The following environment variables are used:

`DISPLAY` to get the default host and display to use

Exit Codes

The `xhost` command returns

0 success

1 failure

SEE ALSO

`X`(1)

NOTES

You can't specify a display on the command line because **`-display`** is a valid command line argument (indicating that you want to remove the machine named **`display`** from the access list).

NAME

xinstall – (XENIX) XENIX system installation shell script

SYNOPSIS

/sbin/xinstall [*device*] [*package*]

DESCRIPTION

Use **xinstall** to install XENIX system distribution (or XENIX application program) floppies. It performs the following tasks:

prompts for insertion of floppies
extracts files using **tar**(1)
executes **/once/init.*** programs on each floppy after they have been extracted
removes any **/once/init.*** programs when the installation is finished

device the device to install the software from. The default device is **/dev/rfd0**.

package the package to be installed. The default package is the XENIX base package.

NOTES

xinstall is provided for use with any existing XENIX packages that you want to install on your system. **xinstall** does not work with UNIX system applications. Use **pkgadd** to install UNIX System V packages which were created using the packaging format provided beginning with UNIX System V Release 4 [see **pkgadd**(1M) and **pkginfo**(4)]. For pre-Release 4 packages, use **installpkg**.)

FILES

/once/init.*

SEE ALSO

custom(1M), **fixperm**(1M), **fixshlib**(1M), **pkgadd**(1M), **pkginfo**(4), **tar**(1)

NAME

xpr – print an X window dump

SYNOPSIS

xpr [**-o** *output-name*] [**-a** *path-name* [**-n**]] [**-d** *name*] [**-h** *text*] [**-t** *text*] [**-W** *decimal-number*] [**-H** *decimal-number*] [**-l**] [**-p**] [**-L** *decimal-number*] [**-T** *decimal-number*] [**-s** *integer*] [**-S** *integer*] [**-r**] [*path-name*] [**-C**] [*color-list*] [*input-name*]

DESCRIPTION

The **xpr** command takes an X window dump file produced by **xwd** and formats it for output on one of several printers. If no *output-name* argument is given the standard output is used. If no *input-name* argument is given the standard input is used.

By default the **xpr** program prints the largest possible representation of the window which will fit on the output page. Options allow the user to add a header and a trailer, specify margins, adjust the scale and orientation, and append multiple window dumps to a single output file.

Options

-o *path-name*
: output to *path-name*. (If *path-name* exists, the contents are overwritten; if *path-name* does not exist, create it.)

  When printing files formatted via **xpr** with **lp**, include in the **lp** command line the option **-o stty=opost**. This should be all that's needed for printers administered via **lpadmin**. If this isn't sufficient, try adding **-T** *devicetype*, where *devicetype* is the same that was given in the **xpr** command (**-d** *devicetype*).

-a *path-name*
: append output to *path-name*. The original file should already include any necessary printer initialization sequences. On an empty or non-existent file, the created file will not have printer initialization sequences, the printer must be initialized by other means.

-n
: remove any formfeed or other page break control sequences from the end of the original content of the output file. This allows concatenating of images. The default margins, or margins specified with the **-L** and **-T** options, are still applied to the new image, use the **-T** option to force the new image to follow immediately after the old image. Do not use this option with postscript printers. The **-a** option must be used with this option.

-d *name*
: convert image to a printer-ready version for the device named in *name*

-h *text*
: place header given in *text* 1/4 inch above the image in approximately 15 point type. Any printable ASCII text plus spaces may be included in *text*.

-t *text*
: place the trailer given in *text* 1/4 inch below the image in approximately 15 point type. Any printable ASCII text plus spaces may be included in *text*.

-W *decimal-number*
scale image to be at most *decimal-number* inches wide. For some devices the width may be significantly less than *decimal-number*. This option overrides the **-S** option. Requested widths resulting in a scale less than one, default to a scale of one; thus the image may be larger than requested.

-H *decimal-number*
scale the image to be at most *decimal-number* inches high. For some devices the height may be significantly less than *decimal-number*. This option overrides the **-S** option. Requested heights resulting in a scale less than one, default to a scale of one; thus the image may be larger than requested.

-l
rotate image 90 degrees counter-clockwise, (''landscape'' mode). By default the image is printed so that its longest side parallels the longest edge of the printed page.

-p
print image upright. By default the image is printed so that its longest side parallels the longest edge of the printed page.

-L *decimal-number*
print image *decimal-number* inches right from the leftmost printable column of the paper. Due to paper alignment differences in printers, the actual margin may vary.

-T *decimal-number*
print image *decimal-number* inches down from the top-most printable row of the paper. Due to paper alignment differences in printers, the actual margin may vary.

-s *integer*
split image, including headers and trailers, onto *integer* pages. The complete image can be pasted together by hand from the separate strips printed on each page. This is typically needed for printers that cannot handle a large image on one page due to memory limitations.

-S *integer*
scale image by *integer*. This defaults to the largest scale which allows the full image to be printed on a page, and limits the size of individual pixels to less than 1/4 inch on a side.

-r
print an inverted **xwd** file dumped from a monochrome screen or to a monochrome printer. The printed image is ''intensity inverted,'' that is, where ink would be applied in the printed image without the **-r**P option, ink is not applied, and vice versa.

-C *color-list*
assume the printer has colors in *color-list*. The colors must be listed from darkest to lightest. For example, the typical ribbon used with color printers would be specified as **-C black,cyan,magenta,yellow**.

If a printer that normally has a multicolored ribbon has a single-color ribbon (for example, black), use the **-C** option to get a monochrome printout, for example, **-C black**.

Exit Codes

USAGE

The **xpr** program is installed with several Terminfo entries. These will overwrite entries currently installed on your system. Similarly, installing the Terminal Information Utilities (TIU) will overwrite the Terminfo entries supplied with **xpr**. This requires saving any entries which would be overwritten and adding them at the end of the second installation.

> *UNIX System V/386 Release 4 only:*
> The **terminfo** entries are contained only with TIU.

These will overwrite any entries currently resident on the system. If the **xpr** versions of the Terminfo entries are overwritten, you may get the message

> **xpr: Device** *<name>* **not supported.**

The **-r** option may be necessary for printing monochrome images; for example, images with no color table.

When using **xpr**, certain printers may produce a split image across pages. This can be corrected by changing margins and/or height and width.

Long text strings are truncated and a tab is not expanded but printed as a space.

The append (**-a**) and output (**-o**) options are now mutually exclusive. If both options are specified on the same command line, **xpr** will exit with an error message. If the file specified by the append option is unreadable, **xpr** will print an error message and exit.

Bitmaps (or "color" images of depth 1) are not reproduced using the **-dpostscript** option (nothing is printed). The **-dps** option can be used to print such images.

Titles are not produced well with the **-dpaintjet** option (the header and trailer appear but inside a black box).

Splitting of images across multiple pages does not work well with the **-dpostscript** option (subsequent pages show the split images but on a dark page). Similarly, the **-a** option does not work well with the **-dpostscript** option (dark page for subsequent images (without **-n**), or subsequent images missing (with **-n**).

For low resolution devices, the header and trailer text looks bad. Try using capital letters.

Appending images with the **-n** option behaves differently on various printers. In general, page printers, such as the LaserJet®, place the second image relative to the upper-left corner of the first page, while other printers place the second image relative to the last line of the first image.

Dual Syntax

A dual syntax is supported for **xpr**. The supported equivalents are as follows:

-o	**-output**
-a	**-append**

`-n`	`-noff`
`-d`	`-device`
`-h`	`-header`
`-t`	`-trailer`
`-W`	`-width`
`-H`	`-height`
`-l`	`-landscape`
`-p`	`-portrait`
`-L`	`-left`
`-T`	`-top`
`-s`	`-split`
`-S`	`-scale`
`-r`	`-rv`

Supported Printers

xpr currently supports the printers in the following table. The first column lists the device names supplied for the **xpr** command. The second column lists tested hardware that is supported by the device. The third column lists the generic type of printer that the hardware emulates. Generally, other printers of similar kinds can try using the device names shown in the table.

Device Name	Hardware	Emulation	Comments
455	AT&T 455		Daisywheel printer
457	AT&T 457		Daisy printer parallel
458	AT&T 458		Daisy printer serial
477-455	AT&T 477	455	
477-470	AT&T 477	470	
477ibmc	AT&T 477	IBM Color printer	
477ibmg	AT&T 477	IBM Graphics printer	
477qume	AT&T-477	Qume	
477-5x6	AT&T 477	Fujitsu DPL24C	5:6 aspect ratio
477	AT&T 477	Fujitsu DPL24C	1:1; low resolution
477-hi	AT&T 477	Fujitsu DPL24C	1:1; high resolution
470	AT&T 470	C.Itoh 8510	8"; parallel matrix printer
471	AT&T 471	C.Itoh 1550	14"; parallel matrix printer
475	AT&T 475	C. Itoh 8510	8"; serial matrix printer
476	AT&T 475	C.Itoh 1550	14"; serial matrix printer
473	AT&T 473	C.Itoh 8510EP	8"; IBM Graphics
474	AT&T 474	C.Itoh 1550EP	14"; IBM Graphics

Device Name	Hardware	Emulation	Comments
478	AT&T 478		8"; parallel matrix printer
479	AT&T 479		14"; IBM parallel; matrix printer
495ibm	AT&T 495	IBM Graphics	
495qume	AT&T 495	Qume	
495hp	AT&T 495	HP Laserjet I emulation	
5310	AT&T 5310		(EMUL set to ANSI)
5320	AT&T 5320		(EMUL set to ANSI)
570eps	AT&T 570	Epson	
570ibm	AT&T 570	IBM ProPrinter	
571eps	AT&T 571	Epson	
571ibm	AT&T 571	IBM ProPrinter	
572	AT&T 572		9-wire Matrix Printer
573	AT&T 573		9-wire Matrix Printer
580ibm-5x6	AT&T 580	IBM Proprinter XL	5:6 aspect ratio; low resolution
580ibm	AT&T 580	IBM Proprinter XL in AGM	1:1; low resolution
580ibm-hi	AT&T 580	IBM Proprinter XL in AGM	1:1; high resolution
581ibm-5x6	AT&T 581	IBM Proprinter XL	5:6 aspect ratio; low resolution
581ibm	AT&T 581	IBM Proprinter XL in AGM	1:1; low resolution
581ibm-hi	AT&T 581	IBM Proprinter XL in AGM	1:1; high resolution
583ibm-5x6	AT&T 583	IBM Proprinter XL	5:6 aspect ratio; low resolution
583ibm	AT&T 583	IBM Proprinter XL in AGM	1:1; low resolution
583ibm-hi	AT&T 583	IBM Proprinter XL in AGM	1:1; high resolution
583ibm-5x6-80	AT&T 583	IBM Proprinter XL	5:6 aspect ratio; low resolution;80-col
583ibm-hi-80	AT&T 583	IBM Proprinter XL in AGM	1:1; high resolution; 80-col
583ibm-80	AT&T 583	IBM Proprinter XL in AGM	1:1; low resolution; 80-col
580eps	AT&T 580	Epson LQ-2500	low resolution
580eps-hi	AT&T 580	Epson LQ-2500	high resolution
581eps	AT&T 581	Epson LQ-2500	low resolution
581eps-hi	AT&T 581	Epson LQ-2500	high resolution
583eps	AT&T 583	Epson LQ-2500	low resolution
583eps-hi	AT&T 583	Epson LQ-2500	high resolution
583eps-80	AT&T 583	Epson LQ-2500	low resolution; 80-col
583eps-hi-80	AT&T 583	Epson LQ-2500	high resolution; 80-col

Device Name	Hardware	Emulation	Comments
593eps	AT&T 593	Epson FX86e	
593ibm	AT&T 593	IBM ProPrinter XL	
593hp	AT&T 593	HP Laserjet II	
postscript	generic PostScript		
hppaintjet	HP PaintJet		90 dots per inch; 16 colors
hppaintjetT	HP PaintJet		For transparencies
hppaintjet-hi	HP PaintJet		180 dots per inch; 8 colors
hppaintjetT-hi	HP PaintJet		For transparencies

Output for the HP PaintJet printer, a color printer capable of handling 16 colors from a palette of 330, can be produced using the **-dpaintjet** option.

Output for the PostScript printer can now include grayscale rendering, when the **-dpostscript** option is used. With this option, the header and trailer are printed using regular PostScript fonts, instead of the font images internal to **xpr**. The **-dps** option will produce the dithering rendering provided before (for example, XWIN 2.0's **xpr -dpostscript** option is now XWIN 4.0's **xpr -dps** option).

Customizing the Terminfo Database for xpr

For the **xpr** program, all printers are currently supported via the Terminfo database. By adding new entries or changing the existing entries using the **infocmp** and the **tic** programs, you can customize the printer support. The **terminfo** capabilities used by the **xpr** program are listed below [see **terminfo**(4) for information about these and other capabilities].

colors number of colors in the ribbon (besides black)

initc* select color band

npins number of pins in print-head or graphics unit

porder matches software bits to print-head pins or unit bits

rblm end printing bit image graphics

sbim start printing bit image graphics

spinh spacing of dots horizontally in dots per inch

spinv spacing of dots vertically in dots per inch

u1* number of passes of print-head per image line

u2* type of image printing

u3* carriage return while in graphics mode

u4* repeat graphics unit

u5* newline while in graphics mode

u6* start image area

u7* end image area

u8* generate name of ribbon color

The capabilities marked with an asterisk are only temporary names; they will change in a future release. The **terminfo**(4) manual page does not describe their use, so a brief description is given below:

initc This is the control sequence used to select a ribbon band for printing. It has one argument in a call to **tparm**, the number of the ribbon band. The argument **0** always selects the black band. The band will stay selected until the next use of this string.

u1 For most printers, this value is 1. The AT&T 5310/5320 provide a higher level dot resolution vertically, as long as the application (**xpr** in this case) prints an image row in two passes. In general, **u1** should be the number of passes needed to print an image row. The **u5** (graphics newline) string is used after each pass – it is expected that the printer takes care of moving the correct distance before each pass.

u2 This should be 1 for dot-matrix type printers where each image row is constructed from byte packets representing a piece one dot wide and npins dots tall. It should be 2 for page printers where each image row is constructed from byte packets representing a piece npins wide and one dot tall. In either case, the porder string defines the mapping of bits in byte packets to printed dots. The position of each number in the porder list corresponds to a bit in the byte packet, most significant bits first. The numbers identify a printed dot: for printers of type 1, the dots are numbered from top to bottom; for printers of type 2, the dots are numbered from left to right. See the **terminfo**(4) manual page for more information on the border capability.

u3 This is the control sequence that moves the current print position to the left edge of the bit image on the current row. It is used with one argument in a call to **tparm**, the horizontal position of the left edge in dots.

u4 This is the control sequence used to compress runs of identical byte packets. It is used with 2 or more arguments in a call to **tparm**. The first argument is the string of bytes in the packet, and the second is the number of times to repeat the packet. Since the string may not be in a useful form for some printers, the individual bytes are available as the third through ninth arguments.

u5 This is the control sequence that moves the current print position to the left edge of the bit image on the next row. It is used with one argument in a call to **tparm**, the horizontal position of the left edge in dots.

u6 This is the control sequence used to start an image at a specific location on the page. It is used with 5 arguments in a call to **tparm**, The first two arguments give the horizontal and vertical position in dots. The control sequence should ensure that the printing of the image starts at that location. The third and fourth arguments are the width and height of the image in dots. The last is the scale factor; the **u6** capability should conditionally produce a non-null control sequence only for a scale the printer can handle. If the printer can't handle a needed scale, the application (**xpr**) must simulate the scale in software.

u7 This is the control sequence to terminate an image area started with **u6**.

u8 This is a conditional Terminfo string used to match the ribbon colors with the arguments to use with the initc string. It is used with one argument in a call to **tparm**, the number of the ribbon band. The string should produce the name of the corresponding color, or a null string for bands out of range. The colors should be numbered from darkest to lightest, that is, in the order they should be overstruck to avoid staining the ribbon. The color band 0 is reserved for black.

Example

```
xpr -dpostscript -S4 -h "Figure 1" foo.xwd
```

will read the file **foo.xwd** and format it for a PostScript® printer, with a caption at the top and a scale factor of four.

SEE ALSO

curs_terminfo(3curses), **infocmp**(1M), **terminfo**(4), **tic**(1M), **X**(1),

NOTES

Portions of the page are derived from material which is copyright Massachusetts Institute of Technology.

NAME

xrestore, xrestor – invoke XENIX incremental filesystem restorer

SYNOPSIS

xrestore *key* [*arguments*]

xrestor *key* [*arguments*]

DESCRIPTION

xrestore is used to read archive media backed up with the XENIX **backup**(C) command. The *key* specifies what is to be done. *Key* is one of the characters **xt** , optionally combined with **f**. **xrestor** is an alternate spelling for the same command.

f Uses the first *argument* as the name of the archive instead of the default.

F *num* Specifies the file number of the first volume to be restored.

k *vsize* Specifies the size of the volume to be restored.

x Each file on the archive named by an *argument* is extracted. The filename has all "mount" prefixes removed; for example, if **/usr** is a mounted filesystem, **/usr/bin/lpr** is named **/bin/lpr** on the archive. The extracted file is placed in a file with a numeric name supplied by **xrestore** (actually the inode number). In order to keep the amount of archive read to a minimum, the following procedure is recommended:

1. Mount volume 1 of the set of backup archives.
2. Type the **xrestore** command.
3. **r1restore** will announce whether or not it found the files, give the numeric name that it will assign to the file, and in the case of a tape, rewind to the start of the archive.
4. It then asks you to "mount the desired tape volume". Type the number of the volume you choose. On a multivolume backup the recommended procedure is to mount the volumes, last through first. **restore** checks to see if any of the requested files are on the mounted archive (or a later archive–thus the reverse order). If the requested files are not there, **xrestore** doesn't read through the tape. If you are working with a single-volume backup or if the number of files being restored is large, respond to the query with 1 , and **xrestore** will read the archives in sequential order.

X *files* Puts files in the directory specified by *arguments*.

t Prints the date the archive was written and the date the filesystem was backed up.

T This causes **xrestore** to behave like **dumpdir** (C) except that it doesn't list directories.

The **r** option should only be used to restore a complete backup archive onto a clear filesystem, or to restore an incremental backup archive onto a filesystem so created. Thus:

```
/etc/mkfs /dev/dsk/0s3 10000
xrestore r /dev/dsk/0s3
```

is a typical sequence to restore a complete backup. Another **xrestore** can be done to get an incremental backup in on top of this.

A **backup** followed by a **mkfs** and a **xrestore** is used to change the size of a filesystem.

FILES

rst*	Temporary files
/etc/default/xrestore	Name of default archive device

The default archive unit varies with installation.

NOTES

xrestore is for XENIX compatibility and should only be used to restore filesystems that were backed up under XENIX.

It is not possible to successfully restore an entire active **root** filesystem.

DIAGNOSTICS

There are various diagnostics involved with reading the archive and writing the disk. There are also diagnostics if the i-list or the free list of the filesystem is not large enough to hold the dump.

If the dump extends over more than one disk or tape, it may ask you to change disks or tapes. Reply with a NEWLINE when the next unit has been mounted.

NAME

xsetroot – root window parameter setting utility for X

SYNOPSIS

xsetroot [**-help**] [**-def**] [**-display** *display*] [**-cursor** *cursorfile maskfile*] [**-cursor-name** *cursorname*] [**-bitmap** *filename*] [**-xpm** *filename*] [**-pixmap** *filename*] [**-mod** *x y*] [**-gray**] [**-grey**] [**-fg** *color*] [**-bg** *color*] [**-rv**] [**-solid** *color*] [**-name** *string*]

DESCRIPTION

The **xsetroot** command allows you to tailor the appearance of the background ("**root**") window on a workstation display running X. Normally, a user experiments with **xsetroot** to find a personalized look, then puts the **xsetroot** command that produces it into their X startup file. If no options are specified, or if **-def** is specified, the window is reset to its default state. The **-def** option can be specified along with other options and only the non-specified characteristics will be reset to the default state.

Only one of the background color/tiling changing options (**-solid**, **-gray**, **-grey**, **-bitmap**, **-xpm**, **-pixmap**, and **-mod**) may be specified at a time.

Options

The various options are as follows:

-help print a usage message and exit

-def reset unspecified attributes to the default values. (Restores the background to the familiar gray mesh and the cursor to the hollow x shape.)

-cursor *cursorfile maskfile*
change the pointer cursor when the pointer cursor is outside of any window. Cursor and mask files are bitmaps (little pictures), and can be made with the **bitmap** command. You probably want the mask file to be all black until you get used to the way masks work.

-cursor_name *cursorname*
change the pointer cursor to one of the standard cursors from the cursor font. Refer to Appendix B of the X protocol for the names (except that the XC_ prefix is elided for this option).

-bitmap *filename*
set the window pattern to the bitmap specified in *filename*. The entire background will be made up of repeated "tiles" of the bitmap.

-xpm *filename* set the window pattern to the (color) pixmap specified in *filename*. The entire background will be made up of repeated "tiles" of the pixmap. The format expected for the pixmap file is the XPM convention developed by GROUPE BULL.

-pixmap *filename*
same behavior as for **-xpm**

-mod *x y* use a plaid–like grid pattern. *x* and *y* are integers ranging from 1 to 16, zero and negative numbers are treated as 1.

-gray set the entire background gray

-grey set the entire background grey

-fg *color* make *color* the foreground color. Foreground and background colors are meaningful only in combination with **-cursor**, **-bitmap**, or **-mod**.

-bg *color* make **color** the background color

-rv exchange the foreground and background colors. Normally the foreground color is **black** and the background color is **white**.

-solid *color* set the window color to *color*

-name *string* set the root window name to *string*. There is no default value. Usually a name is assigned to a window so that the window manager can use a text representation when the window is iconified. This option is unused since you can't iconify the background.

-display *display*
connect to server *display* [see **X**]

SEE ALSO

X(1)

NOTES

Portions of the page are derived from material which is copyright Massachusetts Institute of Technology.

NAME

xterm – terminal emulator for X

SYNOPSIS

xterm [–*toolkitoption* . . .] [–*option* . . .]

DESCRIPTION

xterm is a terminal emulator designed for use in the XWIN Graphical Window System. It emulates the UNIX Desktop system console. **xterm** also supports most of the DEC VT102™ escape sequences. When running on a color console, **xterm** honors the ANSI standard color escape sequences. Thus, curses-based color applications can run under **xterm**.

Each invocation of **xterm** produces a separate X window, in which terminal emulation is performed. This emulation allows non-X applications to be run from within the X environment.

Although more than one X window may be displayed concurrently, only one X window may accept keyboard input at a time. The window which is currently accepting keyboard input is known as the "active" window. The active window is selected by using the SELECT pointer button.

By invoking **xterm** with the **-ml** option, you can use mouseless operations to access the **xterm** menu and to operate the scrollbar. You can also use mnemonics for all **xterm** menu options. However, mouseless operations will not work for text selection.

Options

xterm accepts all of the following options:

-b *inner_border_width*
: specify the size of the inner border (the distance between the outer edge of the characters and the window border) in pixels. It can range between 3 and 40. The default is 3.

-cr *color*
: specify the color to use for text cursor (default is black)

-C
: This option allows console logging for System V Release 4 systems only. When **xterm** is invoked with the **-C** option, **xterm** displays all console messages written to the log driver. Messages written directly to **/dev/console** will not be picked up.

  Note that the **-C** option does not constitute a general console window facility. Only messages written to **/dev/console** will be picked up [see **syslog**(3) and **syslogd**(1M)].

-e *program* [*arguments* . . .]
: specify the program (and its command line arguments) to be run in the **xterm** window. The default is the user's shell. This must be the last option on the command line. *program* must be a character-based application or an X-based application that performs character-based output (usually **printf** style). **xterm** returns 0.

-E *program* [*arguments . . .*]
identical to the **-e** option, except **xterm** returns the exit status of *program*.

-fb *font* specify a font to be used when displaying bold text. There is no default.

It is the user's responsibility to select a bold font with the same height and width as the normal font. If only one of the normal or bold fonts is specified, it will be used as the normal font and the bold font will be produced by overstriking this font.

-j use jump scrolling (default)

+j do not use jump scrolling

-l send all terminal output to a log file as well as to the screen. This option can be enabled or disabled using the **xterm** property window. The default is no logging. This option can be turned on and off from the property window.

+l do not do logging

-lf *filename*
specify the name of the file to which the output log described above is written. If *file* begins with a pipe symbol (|), the rest of the string is assumed to be a command to be used as the endpoint of a pipe. The default filename is "**xtermLog.***nnnnn*" (where *nnnnn* is a string that makes the log filename unique) and is created in the directory from which **xterm** was started (or the user's home directory in the case of a login window).

-ls start the shell in the **xterm** window as a login shell, that is, the first character of **argv[0]** will be a dash, indicating to a shell that it should read the user's **.login** or **.profile**.

-mb ring margin bell when the user types near the right end of a line. This option can be turned on and off from the **xterm** property window. The default is **+mb**.

+mb do not ring margin bell

-ml recognize mouseless keyboard sequences to bring up the menu, request help, and scroll. Without this option, **xterm** forwards all keyboard input to the shell.

+ml forward all keyboard input to the child shell. This is the default.

-ms *color* specify the color of the mouse pointer (default is black)

-n *string* specify the icon name for **xterm**'s windows. (default is **xterm**)

-nb *positive integer*
specify the number of characters from the right end of a line at which the margin bell, if enabled, will ring. The default is 10.

-r simulate reverse video. It is equivalent to **-rv** and the default is no reverse video.

-rs user can resize an **xterm** window while a curses-based application is running (see **cursesResize** resource)

+rs user cannot resize an **xterm** window while a curses-based application is running (see **cursesResize** resource). This is the default.

-rw allow reverse-wraparound. This allows the cursor to back up from the leftmost column of one line to the rightmost column of the previous line. This option can be turned on and off from the **xterm** property window. The default is off. Wraparound must be enabled for reverse wraparound to work.

+rw do not allow reverse-wraparound

-sb bring **xterm** up with a scrollbar

+sb bring **xterm** up without a scrollbar The default is with scrollbar.

-sl *positive integer*
specify the number of scrolled off the top of the screen lines to save. The default is 64; the maximum allowed is 256.

-t *string*
-T *string* equivalent to the **title** resource (default is **xterm**)

-vb use visual bell. Instead of ringing the terminal bell whenever a CTRL-G is received, the window will be flashed. The default is audible.

+vb do not use visual bell

The following command line arguments are provided for compatibility reasons. They may not be supported in the next release as the X Toolkit provides standard options that accomplish the same task.

-w *positive integer*
specify the width in pixels of the border surrounding the window. It is equivalent to **-bw**. It can range between 1 and 40. The default width is one pixel.

The following standard X Toolkit command line arguments are commonly used with **xterm**:

-bd *color* specify the color to use for the border of the window. The default is "black."

-bg *color* specify the color to use for the background of the window. The default is "white."

-bw *positive integer*
specify the width in pixels of the border surrounding the window. It is equivalent to **-w**. The default width is one pixel.

-display *display*
specify the X server to contact; the default is **unix:0** and specify the console device [see **X**(1)]

-fg *color* specify the color to use for displaying text. The default is "black."

-fn *font* specify the font to be used for displaying normal text. The default font is lucidaTypewriter. If *font* is not available, **xterm** will search for and use, in descending priority, *font*, lucidaTypewriter, MoOLIT look and feel dependent font (helvetica in MOTIF mode, lucida in OPEN LOOK mode), **XtDefaultFont**. For each font it cannot find, a warning message will be printed. An appropriate size will be chosen at startup based on screen resolution, to give a 12-point font. In all cases where there is no corresponding bold font, the regular font is used in its place. Applications that require alternate character set (line drawing characters) should specify one of the following fonts: fixed, 6x10, 8x13, 8x13bold. Use **xlsfonts** to see what font are available on the server.

-geometry *geometry*

specify the preferred size and position of the **xterm** window in characters.

geometry is specified as **-geometry** *W***x***H*±*X*±*Y*, with *W* = width in columnar characters and *H* = number of rows. *X* and *Y* are always measured in pixels with the upper left corner X pixels to the right and Y pixels below the upper left corner of the screen (origin (0,0)).

The maximum **H** is 128 and maximum **W** is 200. The default **H** is 25 and default **W** is 80.

Note that if the window is larger than the screen, **xterm** will automatically reduce its size to the size of the screen. Also note that the window manager may modify geometry requests if the resulting window is totally off-screen.

*W***x***H* can be omitted to obtain the default application size, or **+***X***+***Y* can be omitted to obtain the default application position (which is usually then left up to the window manager or user to choose). The *X* and *Y* values may be negative to position the window off the screen. In addition, if minus signs are used instead of plus signs (for example, *W***x***H*-*X*-*Y*), then (*X*,*Y*) represents the location of the lower right hand corner of the window relative to the lower right hand corner of the screen.

-i ask the Window Manager to start it as an icon rather than as the normal window

-name *name*

specify the application name under which resources are to be obtained, rather than the default executable file name.

-rv reverse video will be affected by swapping the foreground and background colors The default is no reverse video.

-xrm *resourcestring*

specify a resource string to be used. This is especially useful for setting resources that do not have separate command line options.

Resources

xterm has the following resource names and classes as well as:

name (class **Name**)
specify the application name under which resources are to be obtained, rather than the default executable file name

title (class **Title**)
specify a string that will be displayed in the header of the window, if the window manager is running

allowSendEvents (class **AllowSendEvents**)
specify whether or not synthetic key and button events (generated using the X protocol **SendEvent** request) should be interpreted (**TRUE**) or discarded (**FALSE**). The default is discard. Note that allowing such events creates a very large security gap.

background (class **TextBackground**)
specify the color to use for the background of the window. The default is "white." The background will be the same color as the "Text Background" color specified on the desktop Color Property Sheet. If the background is not specified in the **.Xdefaults** file, different values for *Background* and *Text Background* will cause **xterm** menus and text windows to have different background colors.

boldFont (class **Font**)
specify the name of the bold font. There is no default.

borderColor (class **BorderColor**)
specify the color of the border surrounding the **xterm** text window. The default is "black."

console (class **Console**)
turn on console logging. When **xterm** is invoked with the **-C** option, **xterm** displays all console messages written to the log driver. Messages written directly to **/dev/console** will not be picked up. See the information under the **-C** option.

cursesResize (class **CursesResize**)
specify is users may resize the window while a curses-based application is running. When "true," a user may resize the window. When "false," a user may not resize the window. The default is "false."

font (class **Font**)
specify the name of the normal font. See **-fn** for other supported fonts and more information.

fontColor (class **TextFontColor**)
specify the color to use for displaying text in the window. Setting the class name instead of the instance name is an easy way to have everything that would normally appear in the "text" color change color. The default is "black."

fontGroup (class FontGroup)
specify several fonts used for drawing non-English characters. The **fontGroup** specified must match a valid name. **fontGroup** names are specified via the **fontGroupDef** application resource.

geometry (class **Geometry**)
specify the preferred size and position of the **xterm** window.

iconName (class**IconName**)
specify the icon name for **xterm** window. Default **xterm**.

inputFocusColor (class **Foreground**)
specify the color to use for the text cursor. The default is "black."

internalBorder (class **BorderWidth**)
specify the number of pixels between the characters and the window border. The default is 3.

jumpScroll (class **JumpScroll**)
specify if jump scrolling should be used. The default is "true."

logFile (class **Logfile**)
specify the name of the file to which a terminal session is logged. The default is "**xtermLog.***nnnnn*" (where *nnnnn* is sequence of characters that make the log file name unique).

logging (class **Logging**)
specify whether or not a terminal session should be logged. The default is "false." Note that logging can be done in only one window at a time.

logInhibit (class **LogInhibit**)
specify whether or not terminal session logging should be inhibited. The default is "false."

loginShell (class **LoginShell**)
specify whether or not the shell to be run in the window should be started as a login shell. The default is "false."

marginBell (class **MarginBell**)
specify whether or not the bell should be run when the user types near the right margin. The default is "false."

mouseless
recognize "mouseless" keyboard sequenced to bring up the menu, request help, and scroll. The default is "false." With the default, all keyboard input received by **xterm** is sent to the program running under **xterm**.

nMarginBell (class **Column**)
specify the number of characters from the right margin at which the margin bell should be run, when enabled. The default is 10 characters from the end of the line.

pointerColor (class **Foreground**)
specify the color of the pointer. The default is "black."

reverseVideo (class **ReverseVideo**)
specify whether or not reverse video should be affected. The default is "false."

reverseWrap (class **ReverseWrap**)
specify whether or not reverse-wraparound should be enabled. The default is "false."

saveLines (class **SaveLines**)
specify the number of lines to save beyond the top of the screen when a scrollbar is turned on. The maximum is 256. The default is 64.

scrollBar (class **ScrollBar**)
specify whether or not the scrollbar should be displayed. The default is "true."

signalInhibit (class **SignalInhibit**)
specify whether or not the entries in the "xterm" menu for sending signals to **xterm** should be disallowed. The default is "false."

ttyModes (class **TtyModes**)
specify **stty** values. Valid keywords include **dsusp**, **eof**, **eol**, **erase**, **flush**, **intr**, **kill**, **lnext quit**, **rprnt**, **start**, **stop susp**, **swtch**, and **weras**. The format of this resource, for example, is

```
xterm*ttyModes: erase ^H kill ^K intr ^C
```

visualBell (class **VisualBell**)
specify whether or not a visible bell (for example, flashing) should be used instead of an audible bell when Control-G is received. The default is "off."

Environment

The following environment variables are used or affected by **xterm**.

CONSEM setting this environment variable to any value and exporting it prevents **xterm** from using the **CONSOLE** emulation streams module. Not having this streams module results in **xterm** providing a lesser degree of console emulation, but improves the overall performance. By default, this is set to "no", but **xterm** does not look at the value, only that the environment variable is set.

DISPLAY Use this environment variable to specify the bitmap display terminal.

TERM **xterm** sets this environment variable properly for the type of display and font you are using. By default, **TERM=xterm** on color displays and **TERM=xtermm** on monochrome displays. If **xterm** uses a font which has alternate character set characters defined, **TERM=xterm-acs** on color displays and **TERM=xtermm-acs** on monochrome displays.

Modifying corresponding terminfo entries will produce undesirable and irrevocable damage to the X operating environment and require reinstallation of the X package.

WINDOWID **xterm** sets this environment variable to the X window ID number of the **xterm** window.

USAGE

Fonts

The default font for **xterm** does not support alternate character sets. To obtain a font with alternate character sets, use one of the following fonts: fixed, 6x10, 8x13, 8x13 bold, or any other font that has ACS defined.

Terminal Emulation

xterm VT102 emulation is fairly complete but does not support the blinking character attribute nor the double-wide and double-size character sets.

Scrollbar

The scrollbar represents the position and amount of text currently displayed in the window relative to the amount of text actually saved. As more text is saved (up to the maximum), the elevator moves to the bottom of the scrollbar.

Pressing the SELECT pointer button on the middle portion of the elevator and moving the mouse cursor up or down results in scrolling up or down through the scrolling region.

Clicking SELECT on the up or down arrow (at each end of the elevator) moves the visible text region up or down one line.

Pressing SELECT on the up or down arrow scrolls the visible text region one line at the time until the SELECT is released or the margin of the text buffer is reached.

Clicking SELECT in the scroll region above or below the elevator moves the visible region one page up or down.

In the OPEN LOOK look and feel, clicking SELECT on the top or bottom box of the scrollbar moves the visible region to the top or bottom of the text buffer.

In the MOTIF look and feel, clicking ADJUST in the scroll region above or below the elevator moves the visible region to the top or bottom of the buffer. Clicking PASTE in the scroll region will move the elevator directly to the position of the mouse pointer.

Menus

xterm's menu can be accessed by pressing or clicking the **MENU** button while on the **xterm** window pane. The menu contains commands which perform individual **xterm** functions. Choosing a button to select any of the entries on the menus activates the indicated functions. Notable entries in the command sections of the menus are the Interrupt, Hangup, Terminate and Kill, which send the **SIGINT**, **SIGHUP**, **SIGTERM** and **SIGKILL** signals, respectively, to the process group of the process running under **xterm** (usually the shell). The Properties entry on the **xterm** menu causes a property window to display. This property window sets various modes in the **xterm** emulation, among them auto wraparound, auto linefeed, and reverse wrap.

Applications

Some applications supply a private **terminfo** file, causing applications to exhibit unexpected behavior. Rather than keeping private **terminfo** files, overwrite the private file with the system **xterm terminfo** file [see **terminfo**(4)].

To resize **xterm** while curses applications are running, set the **cursesResize** resource.

xterm passes Help key events to the application when the Help key is depressed and the mouse pointer is over the **xterm** window. If the mouse pointer is not over the **xterm** window, the Help key is interpreted by the window manager and is not passed to the application.

Miscellaneous

Selecting "paste" on the 3-button mouse menu causes **xterm** to paste text from the PRIMARY selection, inserting it as keyboard input.

If a user invokes the UNIX System **exec** command from an **xterm** window, it is the **xterm** process which will disappear. This is correct behavior but most likely not desirable [see **sh**(1)].

Applications which close **stdin**, **stdout**, and/or **stderr** may produce unpredictable results and should be avoided.

If the display is monochrome and options in an **.Xdefaults** file or on a command line specify background and foreground colors that would produce black on black or white on white, **xterm** provides a default of black on white.

xterm responds dynamically to changes in text foreground, text background, and input focus color; these values can be changed via the Desktop Color property sheets.

If the stty settings you use are not those used by **xterm**, you may need to import your stty environment to **xterm**; for example, interrupt, erase, and kill characters. This could be done via the **ttyModes** resource.

If you **exec** an application that creates its own window (such as MS-DOS) and then try to change the input focus to the **xterm** window which exec-ed the application, the next attempt to input to that window will cause the **xterm** window and the exec-ed process to die. This is due to the nature of **exec** [see **exec**(2)]. The recommendation is not to **exec** programs like MS-DOS.

xterm may hang if you try to paste too much text at one time. It is both producer and consumer for the pty and can deadlock. Should **xterm** hang, the RETURN CTRL-Z RETURN sequence will return the prompt.

SEE ALSO

dtm(1), **exec**(2), **olwm**(1), **terminfo**(4)

NOTES

Variable-width fonts are not handled reasonably.

The **-w**, **-bd** and **-bw** options and the **borderColor** and **signalInhibit** resources are not available.

Tektronix emulation available in earlier releases is no longer supported. This affects the **-t** command line option.

xterm will not start if the **CONSEM** environment variable is not set and the system does not have the ACP package installed. Try setting **CONSEM=no; export CONSEM** and then run **xterm** again.

xterm(1)

NAME

`yacc` – yet another compiler-compiler

SYNOPSIS

`yacc [-vVdltw] [-Q[y|n]]` *file*

DESCRIPTION

The **yacc** command converts a context-free grammar into a set of tables for a simple automaton that executes an LALR(1) parsing algorithm. The grammar may be ambiguous; specified precedence rules are used to break ambiguities. **yacc** processes supplementary code set characters in program comments and strings, and single-byte supplementary code set characters in tokens, according to the locale specified in the **LC_CTYPE** environment variable [see **LANG** on **environ**(5)].

The output file, **y.tab.c**, must be compiled by the C compiler to produce a program **yyparse**. This program must be loaded with the lexical analyzer program, **yylex**, as well as **main** and **yyerror**, an error handling routine. These routines must be supplied by the user; the **lex**(1) command is useful for creating lexical analyzers usable by **yacc**.

-v Prepares the file **y.output**, which contains a description of the parsing tables and a report on conflicts generated by ambiguities in the grammar.

-d Generates the file **y.tab.h** with the **#define** statements that associate the **yacc**-assigned "token codes" with the user-declared "token names." This association allows source files other than **y.tab.c** to access the token codes.

-l Specifies that the code produced in **y.tab.c** will not contain any **#line** constructs. This option should only be used after the grammar and the associated actions are fully debugged.

-Q[**y**|**n**] The **-Qy** option puts the version stamping information in **y.tab.c**. This allows you to know what version of **yacc** built the file. The **-Qn** option (the default) writes no version information.

-t Compiles runtime debugging code by default. Runtime debugging code is always generated in **y.tab.c** under conditional compilation control. By default, this code is not included when **y.tab.c** is compiled. Whether or not the **-t** option is used, the runtime debugging code is under the control of **YYDEBUG**, a preprocessor symbol. If **YYDEBUG** has a non-zero value, then the debugging code is included. If its value is zero, then the code will not be included. The size and execution time of a program produced without the runtime debugging code will be smaller and slightly faster.

-V Prints on the standard error output the version information for **yacc**.

-w Generates writable **yacc** tables. These tables are read-only by default.

FILES

y.output	
y.tab.c	
y.tab.h	defines for token names
yacc.tmp, yacc.debug, yacc.acts	temporary files
LIBDIR/**yaccpar**	parser prototype for C programs
LIBDIR	usually **/usr/ccs/lib**
/usr/lib/locale/*locale***/LC_MESSAGES/uxcplu**	
	language-specific message file [See **LANG** on **environ**(5).]

ERRORS

The number of reduce-reduce and shift-reduce conflicts is reported on the standard error output; a more detailed report is found in the **y.output** file. Similarly, if some rules are not reachable from the start symbol, this instance is also reported.

NOTES

Because file names are fixed, at most one **yacc** process can be active in a given directory at a given time.

SEE ALSO

environ(5), **lex**(1)

NAME

yes – (XENIX) print string repeatedly

SYNOPSIS

yes [*string*]

DESCRIPTION

yes repeatedly outputs "y", or if a single string argument is given, *string* is output repeatedly. The command continues indefinitely unless aborted. **yes** is useful in pipes to commands that prompt for input and require a "y" response for a yes. In this case, **yes** terminates when the command that it pipes to terminates so that no infinite loop occurs.

ypcat(1)

NAME

ypcat – print values in a NIS data base

SYNOPSIS

ypcat [**-k**] [**-d** *ypdomain*] *mname*

DESCRIPTION

The **ypcat** command prints out values in the NIS name service map specified by *mname*, which may be either a map name or a map nickname. Since **ypcat** uses the NIS network services, no NIS server is specified.

Refer to **ypfiles**(4) and **ypserv**(1M) for an overview of the NIS name service.

The following options are available:

-d *ypdomain* Specify a domain other that the default domain.

-k Display the keys for those maps in which the values are null or the key is not part of the value. None of the maps derived from files that have an ASCII version in **/etc** fall into this class.

SEE ALSO

ypmatch(1), **ypserv**(1M), **ypfiles**(4)

NAME

ypinit – build and install NIS database

SYNOPSIS

/usr/sbin/ypinit -c
/usr/sbin/ypinit -m
/usr/sbin/ypinit -s *master-name*

DESCRIPTION

ypinit sets up a NIS name service database on a NIS server. It can be used to set up a master or a slave server, or a client system. To run **ypinit**, you must be the NIS administrator **root** with the appropriate privileges. It asks a few self-explanatory questions, and reports success or failure to the terminal.

It sets up a master server using the simple model in which that server is master to all maps in the data base. This is the way to bootstrap the NIS system; later if you want you can change the association of maps to masters.

All databases are built from scratch, either from information available to the program at runtime, or from the ASCII data base files in **/etc**. These files should be in their traditional form, rather than the abbreviated form used on client machines.

A NIS database on a slave server is set up by copying an existing database from a running server. The *master-name* argument should be the hostname of a NIS server (either the master server for all the maps, or a server on which the data base is up-to-date and stable).

To set up a client, **ypinit** prompts for a list of NIS servers to bind the client to, this list should be ordered from closest to farthest server.

Read **ypfiles**(4) and **ypserv**(1M) for an overview of the NIS name service.

The following options are available:

-c	Set up a client system.
-m	Indicate that the local host is to be the NIS master.
-s *master-name*	Set up a slave database.

SEE ALSO

makedbm(1M), **ypmake**(1M), **yppush**(1M), **ypserv**(1M), **ypxfr**(1M), **ypfiles**(4)

FILES

/var/yp/binding/*domainname***/ypservers**

NAME

ypmake, **ypalias** – rebuild NIS database

SYNOPSIS

cd /var/yp ; make [*map*]

cd /var/yp ; ./ypbuild SHELL=/sbin/sh [*map*]

DESCRIPTION

The file called **Makefile** in **/var/yp** is used by **make** to build the NIS name service database. With no arguments, **make** creates **dbm** databases for any NIS maps that are out-of-date, and then executes **yppush**(1M) to notify slave databases that there has been a change.

If *map* is supplied on the command line, **make** will update that map only.

There are three special variables used by **make** in the **Makefile**: **DIR**, which gives the directory of the source files; **NOPUSH**, which when non-null inhibits doing a **yppush** of the new database files; and **DOM**, used to construct a domain other than the master's default domain. The default for **DIR** is **/etc**, and the default for **NOPUSH** is the null string.

make also creates entries in **/var/yp/aliases**. These entries are generated by **/usr/sbin/ypalias**, which takes a string as input and returns the alias derived from that string.

Refer to **ypfiles**(4) and **ypserv**(1M) for an overview of the NIS.

FILES

/var/yp

SEE ALSO

make(1), **makedbm**(1M), **yppush**(1M), **ypserv**(1M), **ypfiles**(4)

NAME

ypmatch – print the value of one or more keys from the NIS map

SYNOPSIS

ypmatch [**-d** *ypdomain*] [**-k**] *key...* *mname*

DESCRIPTION

ypmatch prints the values associated with one or more keys from the NIS name services map specified by *mname*, which may be either a *mapname* or an map nickname.

Multiple keys can be specified; the same map will be searched for all keys. The keys must be exact values insofar as capitalization and length are concerned. No pattern matching is available. If a key is not matched, a diagnostic message is produced.

The following options are available:

-d *ypdomain* Specify a domain other than the default domain.

-k Before printing the value of a key, print the key itself, followed by a colon ("**:**"). This is useful only if the keys are not duplicated in the values, or so many keys were specified that the output could be confusing.

SEE ALSO

ypcat(1), **ypfiles**(4)

yppoll (1M)

NAME

yppoll – return current version of the map at the NIS server host

SYNOPSIS

/usr/sbin/yppoll [**-d** *ypdomain*] [**-h** *host*] *mapname*

DESCRIPTION

The **yppoll** command asks a **ypserv**(1M) process what the order number is, and which host is the master NIS server for the named map.

The following options are available:

-d *ypdomain* — Use *ypdomain* instead of the default domain.

-h *host* — Ask the **ypserv** process at *host* about the map parameters. If *host* is not specified, the NIS server for the local host is used. That is, the default host is the one returned by **ypwhich**(1).

SEE ALSO

ypserv(1M), **ypwhich**(1), **ypfiles**(4)

NAME

yppush – force propagation of a changed NIS map

SYNOPSIS

/usr/sbin/yppush [**-v**] [**-d** *ypdomain*] *mapname*

DESCRIPTION

yppush copies a new version of the NIS name service map from the master NIS server to the slave NIS servers. It is normally run only on the master NIS server by the **Makefile** in **/var/yp** after the master databases are changed. It first constructs a list of NIS server hosts by reading the NIS map **ypservers** within the *ypdomain*, or if the map is not set up, the local file is used. Keys within the map **ypservers** are the ASCII names of the machines on which the NIS servers run.

A transfer map request is sent to the NIS server at each host, along with the information needed by the transfer agent (the program that actually moves the map) to call back the **yppush**. When the attempt has completed (successfully or not), and the transfer agent has sent **yppush** a status message, the results may be printed to stdout. Messages are also printed when a transfer is not possible; for instance when the request message is undeliverable, or when the timeout period on responses has expired.

Refer to **ypfiles**(4) and **ypserv**(1M) for an overview of the NIS name service.

The following options are available:

-v Verbose. Print messages when each server is called, and for each response. If this flag is omitted, only error messages are printed.

-d *ypdomain* Specify a *ypdomain* other than the default domain.

FILES

/var/yp/*ypdomain***/ypservers.{***dir***,***pag***}** local file

/var/yp

SEE ALSO

ypserv(1M), **ypxfr**(1M), **ypfiles**(4)

NAME

ypserv, **ypbind** – NIS server and binder processes

SYNOPSIS

/usr/lib/netsvc/yp/ypserv

/usr/lib/netsvc/yp/ypbind [**-ypset** | **-ypsetme**]

DESCRIPTION

The NIS provides a simple network lookup service consisting of databases and processes. The databases are **dbm**(3) files in a directory tree rooted at **/var/yp**. These files are described in **ypfiles**(4). The processes are **/usr/lib/netsvc/yp/ypserv**, the NIS database lookup server, and **/usr/lib/netsvc/yp/ypbind**, the NIS binder. The programmatic interface to NIS is described in **ypclnt**(3N). Administrative tools are described in **yppush**(1M), **ypxfr**(1M), **yppoll**(1M), **ypwhich**(1), and **ypset**(1M). Tools to see the contents of NIS maps are described in **ypcat**(1), and **ypmatch**(1). Database generation and maintenance tools are described in **ypinit**(1M), **ypmake**(1M), and **makedbm**(1M).

Both **ypserv** and **ypbind** are daemon processes typically activated at system startup time. **ypserv** runs only on NIS server machines with a complete NIS database. **ypbind** runs on all machines using NIS services, both NIS servers and clients.

The **ypserv** daemon's primary function is to look up information in its local database of NIS maps. Communication to and from **ypserv** is by means of RPC calls. Lookup functions are described in **ypclnt**(3N), and are supplied as C-callable functions in the NIS library. There are four lookup functions, all of which are performed on a specified map within some NIS domain: *Match*, *"Get_first"*, *"Get_next"*, and *"Get_all"*. The *Match* operation takes a key, and returns the associated value. The *"Get_first"* operation returns the first key-value pair from the map, and *"Get_next"* can be used to enumerate the remainder. *"Get_all"* ships the entire map to the requester as the response to a single RPC request.

Two other functions supply information about the map, rather than map entries: *"Get_order_number"*, and *"Get_master_name"*. In fact, both order number and master name exist in the map as key-value pairs, but the server will not return either through the normal lookup functions. If you examine the map with **makedbm**(1M), however, they will be visible.

The function of **ypbind** is to remember information that lets client processes on a single node communicate with some **ypserv** process. **ypbind** must run on every machine which has NIS client processes; **ypserv** may or may not be running on the same node, but must be running somewhere on the network.

The information **ypbind** remembers is called a *binding*—the association of a domain name with a NIS server.

The process of binding is driven by client requests. As a request for an unbound domain comes in, the **ypbind** process steps through the **ypservers** list (last entry first) trying to find a **ypserv** process that serves maps within that domain. There must be a **ypserv** process on at least one of the hosts in the **ypservers** file. Once a domain is bound by a particular **ypbind**, that same binding is given to every client process on the node. The **ypbind** process on the local node or a remote node may be queried for the binding of a particular domain by using the **ypwhich**(1) command.

If **ypbind** is unable to speak to the **ypserv** process it is bound to, it marks the domain as unbound, tells the client process that the domain is unbound, and tries to bind the domain once again. Requests received for an unbound domain will wait until the domain requested is bound. In general, a bound domain is marked as unbound when the node running **ypserv** crashes or gets overloaded. In such a case, **ypbind** will try to bind to another NIS server listed in **/var/yp/binding/***domainname***/ypservers**.

ypbind also accepts requests to set its binding for a particular domain. The request is usually generated by the NIS subsystem itself. **ypset**(1M) is a command to access the *"Set_domain"* facility. Note: the *Set Domain* procedure only accepts requests from processes with appropriate privileges, and the **-ypset** or **-ypsetme** flags must have been set for **ypbind**.

The following options are available for the **ypbind** command only:

-ypset Allow any user to call **ypset**(1M). By default, no one can call **ypset**(1M).

-ypsetme Only allow **root** on local machines to call **ypset**(1M). By default, no one can call **ypset**(1M).

FILES

If the file **/var/yp/ypserv.log** exists when **ypserv** starts up, log information will be written to this file when error conditions arise.

/var/yp
/var/yp/binding/*ypdomain***/ypservers**

SEE ALSO

makedbm(1M), **ypcat**(1), **ypinit**(1M), **ypmake**(1M), **ypmatch**(1), **yppoll**(1M), **yppush**(1M), **ypset**(1M), **ypwhich**(1), **ypxfr**(1M), **dbm**(3), **ypclnt**(3N), **ypfiles**(4)

NOTES

Both **ypbind** and **ypserv** support multiple domains. The **ypserv** process determines the domains it serves by looking for directories of the same name in the directory **/var/yp**. Additionally, the **ypbind** process can maintain bindings to several domains and their servers.

NAME

ypset – point ypbind at a particular server

SYNOPSIS

/usr/sbin/ypset [**-d** *ypdomain*] [**-h** *host*] *server*

DESCRIPTION

In order to run **ypset**, **ypbind** must be initiated with the **-ypset** or **-ypsetme** options. See **ypserv**(1M). **ypset** tells **ypbind** to get NIS services for the specified *ypdomain* from the **ypserv** process running on *server*. If *server* is down, or is not running **ypserv**, this is not discovered until the NIS client process tries to get a binding for the domain. At this point, the binding set by **ypset** will be tested by **ypbind**. If the binding is invalid, **ypbind** will attempt to rebind for the same domain.

ypset is useful for binding a client node which is not on a broadcast net, or is on a broadcast net which is not running the NIS server host. It also is useful for debugging NIS client applications, for instance where the NIS map only exists at a single NIS server host.

In cases where several hosts on the local net are supplying NIS services, it is possible for **ypbind** to rebind to another host even while you attempt to find out if the **ypset** operation succeeded. For example, you can type:

```
# ypset host1
# ypwhich
host2
```

which can be confusing. This is a function of the NIS subsystem's attempt to load-balance among the available NIS servers, and occurs when *host1* does not respond to **ypbind** because it is not running **ypserv** (or is overloaded), and *host2*, running **ypserv**, gets the binding.

server indicates the NIS server to bind to, and must be specified as a name. This will work only if the node has a current valid binding for the domain in question, and **ypbind** has been set to allow use of **ypset**. In most cases, *server* should be specified as an IP address.

ypset tries to bind **ypbind** over a datagram transport first. Datagram Transports are recommended for higher performance. The NIS library calls, **yp_enum( )**, **yp_all( )**, **yp_next( )**, and **yp_first( )** use circuit transports regardless of the main transport being used.

Refer to **ypfiles**(4) and **ypserv**(1M) for an overview of the NIS name service.

The following options are available:

-h *host* — Set **ypbind**'s binding on *host*, instead of locally. *host* must be specified as a name.

-d *ypdomain* — Use *ypdomain*, instead of the default domain.

SEE ALSO

ypserv(1M), **ypwhich**(1), **ypfiles**(4)

NAME

ypupdated – server for changing NIS information

SYNOPSIS

/usr/lib/netsvc/yp/ypupdated [**-i**]

DESCRIPTION

ypupdated is a daemon that updates information in the NIS name service, normally started up by **inetd**(1M). **ypupdated** consults the file **updaters**(4) in the directory **/var/yp** to determine which NIS maps should be updated and how to change them.

By default, the daemon requires the most secure method of authentication available to it, either DES (secure) or UNIX (insecure).

The following options are available:

-i Accept RPC calls with the insecure AUTH_UNIX credentials. This allows programmatic updating of NIS maps in all networks.

FILES

/var/yp/updaters

SEE ALSO

inetd(1M), **keyserv**(1M), **updaters**(4)

ypwhich (1)

NAME

ypwhich – return name of NIS server or map master

SYNOPSIS

ypwhich [**-d** [*ypdomain*]] [*hostname*]
ypwhich [**-d** *ypdomain*] **-m** [*mname*]

DESCRIPTION

ypwhich tells which NIS server supplies the NIS name services to the NIS client, or which is the master for a map. If invoked without arguments, it gives the NIS server for the local machine. If *hostname* is specified, that machine is queried to find out which NIS master it is using.

Refer to **ypfiles**(4) and **ypserv**(1M) for an overview of the NIS name services.

The following options are available:

-d [*ypdomain*] Use *ypdomain* instead of the default domain.

-m *mname* Find the master NIS server for a map. No *hostname* can be specified with **-m**. *mname* can be a mapname, or a nickname for a map. When *mname* is omitted, produce a list available maps.

SEE ALSO

ypserv(1M), **ypset**(1M), **ypfiles**(4)

NAME

ypxfr – transfer NIS map from a NIS server to host

SYNOPSIS

/usr/sbin/ypxfr [**-c**] [**-f**] [**-d** *ypdomain*] [**-h** *host*] [**-s** *ypdomain*]
[**-C** *tid prog server*] *mapname*

DESCRIPTION

The **ypxfr** command moves a NIS map in the default domain for the local host to the local host by making use of normal NIS services. It creates a temporary map in the directory **/var/yp/***ypdomain* (this directory must already exist; *ypdomain* is the default domain for the local host), fills it by enumerating the map's entries, fetches the map parameters (master and order number), and loads them. It then deletes any old versions of the map and moves the temporary map to the real *mapname*.

If run interactively, **ypxfr** writes its output to the terminal. However, if it is started without a controlling terminal, and if the log file **/var/yp/ypxfr.log** exists, it appends all its output to that file. **ypxfr** is most often run from the **crontab** file of the NIS administrator with the appropriate privileges, or by **ypserv**, the log file can be used to retain a record of what was attempted, and what the results were.

For consistency between servers, **ypxfr** should be run periodically for every map in the NIS data base. Different maps change at different rates: a map may not change for months at a time, for instance, and may therefore be checked only once a day. Some maps may change several times per day. In such a case, you may want to check hourly for updates. A **crontab**(1) entry can be used to perform periodic updates automatically. Rather than having a separate **crontab** entry for each map, you can group commands to update several maps in a shell script. Examples (mnemonically named) are in **/usr/sbin/yp**: **ypxfr_1perday**, and **ypxfr_1perhour**. They can serve as reasonable first cuts.

Refer to **ypfiles**(4) and **ypserv**(1M) for an overview of the NIS name service.

The following options are available:

-c Do not send a Clear current map request to the local **ypserv** process. Use this flag if **ypserv** is not running locally at the time you are running **ypxfr**. Otherwise, **ypxfr** complains that it cannot talk to the local **ypserv**, and the transfer fails.

-f Force the transfer to occur even if the version at the master is not more recent than the local version.

-C *tid prog server* This option is *only* for use by **ypserv**. When **ypserv** starts **ypxfr**, it specifies that **ypxfr** should call back a **yppush** process at the host *server*, registered as program number *prog*, and waiting for a response to transaction *tid*.

-d *ypdomain* Specify a domain other than the default domain.

-h *host* Get the map from *host*, regardless of what the map says the master is. If *host* is not specified, **ypxfr** asks the NIS service for the name of the master, and try to get the map from there. *host* must be a name.

-s *ypdomain* Specify a source domain from which to transfer a map that should be the same across domains.

FILES

/var/yp/ypxfr.log	log file
/usr/sbin/yp/ypxfr_1perday	**cron**(1M) script to run one transfer per day
/usr/sbin/yp/ypxfr_1perhour	script for hourly transfers of volatile maps
/var/yp/ypdomain	NIS domain
/usr/spool/cron/crontabs/root	The **crontab** file of the –s1NIS administrator **root** with the appropriate privileges.

SEE ALSO

cron(1M), **crontab**(1), **ypserv**(1M), **yppush**(1M), **ypfiles**(4)

NAME

zdump – time zone dumper

SYNOPSIS

zdump [-v] [-c *cutoffyear*] [*zonename* . . .]

DESCRIPTION

The **zdump** command prints the current time in each *zonename* named on the command line.

The following options are available:

-v
: For each *zonename* on the command line, print the current time, the time at the lowest possible time value, the time one day after the lowest possible time value, the times both one second before and exactly at each time at which the rules for computing local time change, the time at the highest possible time value, and the time at one day less than the highest possible time value. Each line ends with **isdst=1** if the given time is Daylight Saving Time or **isdst=0** otherwise.

-c *cutoffyear*
: Cut off the verbose output near the start of the year *cutoffyear*.

FILES

/usr/lib/locale/TZ — standard zone information directory

SEE ALSO

ctime(3C), **zic**(1M)

NAME

`zic` – time zone compiler

SYNOPSIS

`zic` [`-v`] [`-d` **directory**] [`-l` **localtime**] [*filename* . . .]

DESCRIPTION

`zic` reads text from the file(s) named on the command line and creates the time conversion information files specified in this input. If a *filename* is '`-`', the standard input is read.

Input lines are made up of fields. Fields are separated by any number of white space characters. Leading and trailing white space on input lines is ignored. A pound sign (`#`) in the input introduces a comment which extends to the end of the line the pound sign appears on. White space characters and pound signs may be enclosed in double quotes (`"`) if they're to be used as part of a field. Any line that is blank (after comment stripping) is ignored. Non-blank lines are expected to be of one of three types: rule lines, zone lines, and link lines.

A rule line has the form

`Rule` *NAME FROM TO TYPE IN ON AT SAVE LETTER/S*

For example:

```
Rule   USA   1969   1973   -   Apr  lastSun  2:00  1:00    D
```

The fields that make up a rule line are:

NAME Gives the (arbitrary) name of the set of rules this rule is part of.

FROM Gives the first year in which the rule applies. The word **minimum** (or an abbreviation) means the minimum year with a representable time value. The word **maximum** (or an abbreviation) means the maximum year with a representable time value.

TO Gives the final year in which the rule applies. In addition to **minimum** and **maximum** (as above), the word **only** (or an abbreviation) may be used to repeat the value of the **FROM** field.

TYPE Gives the type of year in which the rule applies. If **TYPE** is '`-`' then the rule applies in all years between **FROM** and **TO** inclusive; if **TYPE** is **uspres**, the rule applies in U.S. Presidential election years; if **TYPE** is **nonpres**, the rule applies in years other than U.S. Presidential election years. If **TYPE** is something else, then **zic** executes the command

yearistype *year type*

to check the type of a year: an exit status of zero is taken to mean that the year is of the given type; an exit status of one is taken to mean that the year is not of the given type.

IN Names the month in which the rule takes effect. Month names may be abbreviated.

ON Gives the day on which the rule takes effect. Recognized forms include:

`5`	the fifth of the month
`lastSun`	the last Sunday in the month
`lastMon`	the last Monday in the month
`Sun>=8`	first Sunday on or after the eighth
`Sun<=25`	last Sunday on or before the 25th

Names of days of the week may be abbreviated or spelled out in full. Note: there must be no spaces within the **ON** field.

AT Gives the time of day at which the rule takes effect. Recognized forms include:

`2`	time in hours
`2:00`	time in hours and minutes
`15:00`	24-hour format time (for times after noon)
`1:28:14`	time in hours, minutes, and seconds

Any of these forms may be followed by the letter **w** if the given time is local "wall clock" time or **s** if the given time is local "standard" time; in the absence of **w** or **s**, wall clock time is assumed.

SAVE Gives the amount of time to be added to local standard time when the rule is in effect. This field has the same format as the **AT** field (although, of course, the **w** and **s** suffixes are not used).

LETTER/S
Gives the "variable part" (for example, the "S" or "D" in "EST" or "EDT") of time zone abbreviations to be used when this rule is in effect. If this field is '–', the variable part is null.

A zone line has the form

Zone *NAME GMTOFF RULES/SAVE FORMAT [UNTIL]*

For example:

```
Zone   PRC   8:00      PRC       C%sT
```

The fields that make up a zone line are:

NAME The name of the time zone. This is the name used in creating the time conversion information file for the zone.

GMTOFF The amount of time to add to GMT to get standard time in this zone. This field has the same format as the **AT** and **SAVE** fields of rule lines; begin the field with a minus sign if time must be subtracted from GMT.

RULES/SAVE
The name of the rule(s) that apply in the time zone or, alternately, an amount of time to add to local standard time. If this field is '–' then standard time always applies in the time zone.

FORMAT The format for time zone abbreviations in this time zone. The pair of characters **%s** is used to show where the "variable part" of the time zone abbreviation goes.

UNTIL The time at which the GMT offset or the rule(s) change for a location. It is specified as a year, a month, a day, and a time of day. If this is specified, the time zone information is generated from the given GMT offset and rule change until the time specified.

The next line must be a "continuation" line; this has the same form as a zone line except that the string "Zone" and the name are omitted, as the continuation line will place information starting at the time specified as the **UNTIL** field in the previous line in the file used by the previous line. Continuation lines may contain an **UNTIL** field, just as zone lines do, indicating that the next line is a further continuation.

A link line has the form

Link *LINK-FROM* *LINK-TO*

For example:

```
Link    US/Eastern      EST5EDT
```

The **LINK-FROM** field should appear as the **NAME** field in some zone line; the **LINK-TO** field is used as an alternate name for that zone.

Except for continuation lines, lines may appear in any order in the input.

OPTIONS

-v Complain if a year that appears in a data file is outside the range of years representable by system time values (0:00:00 AM GMT, January 1, 1970, to 3:14:07 AM GMT, January 19, 2038).

-d directory
Create time conversion information files in the directory **directory** rather than in the standard directory **/usr/lib/locale/TZ**.

-l timezone
Use the time zone **timezone** as local time. **zic** will act as if the file contained a link line of the form

Link *timezone* localtime

FILES

/usr/lib/locale/TZ standard directory used for created files

NOTES

For areas with more than two types of local time, you may need to use local standard time in the **AT** field of the earliest transition time's rule to ensure that the earliest transition time recorded in the compiled file is correct.

SEE ALSO

ctime(3C), **time**(1)

Reference Manual Index

The Permuted Index that follows is a list of keywords, alphabetized in the second of three columns, together with the context in which each keyword is found. The manual page that produced an entry is listed in the right column.

Entries are identified with their section numbers shown in parentheses. This is important because there is considerable duplication of names among the sections, arising principally from commands and functions that exist only to exercise a particular system call.

The index is produced by rotating the NAME section of each manual page to alphabetize each keyword in it. Words that cannot fit in the middle column are rotated into the left column. If the entry is still too long, some words are omitted, and their omission is indicated with a slash ("/").

How the Permuted Index Is Created

Many users find that understanding a few things about how the permuted index is created helps them to read it more effectively and clarifies what kind of information can and cannot be obtained from it.

The basic building block for the index is the one-line description given in the NAME line on the top of each manual page. For example, this is what the top of the `mountall`(1M) manual page looks like:

---

mountall(1M) **mountall(1M)**

NAME

`mountall, umountall` – mount, unmount multiple file systems

Each NAME line includes:

- the command, file format, system call or other utility for which the manual page is named (this is the primary utility; `mountall` is the primary utility in the example)
- secondary utilities, which are also described on that manual page and do not have a separate manual page of their own (`umountall` is a secondary utility in the example)

■ a brief description of the utility function(s)

For each manual page NAME line, the indexing software generates several index entries, generally one entry for each keyword in the phrase. The middle column of the index is alphabetized on these keywords.

For:

NAME

`mountall, umountall` – mount, unmount multiple file systems

This is generated:

mount, unmount multiple	file systems. /umountall:	mountall(1M)
systems. mountall, umountall:	mount, unmount multiple file	mountall(1M)
unmount multiple file systems.	mountall, umountall: mount, ...	mountall(1M)
/umountall: mount, unmount	multiple file systems.	mountall(1M)
mount, unmount multiple file	systems. mountall, umountall:	mountall(1M)
multiple file/ mountall,	umountall: mount, unmount	mountall(1M)
mountall, umountall: mount,	unmount multiple file systems.	mountall(1M)

How to Use the Index

Look in the middle column of the index for the word of interest. Then read the complete phrase by starting with the utility name, which may appear in the left or middle column. Utility names are followed by a colon.

The NAME line phrase is contained in the two columns, with long phrases wrapping around to the beginning of the left column. The right column of the index provides the manual page name and section number.

A slash (/) sometimes appears in the index entry to indicate that space limitations were exceeded and one or more words from the phrase were deleted.

Permuted Index